OPERA IN THEORY AND PRACTICE,
IMAGE AND MYTH

THE HISTORY *of* ITALIAN OPERA

Edited by LORENZO BIANCONI *and* GIORGIO PESTELLI

Part II / Systems

VOLUME 6

OPERA IN
THEORY AND PRACTICE,
IMAGE AND MYTH

Edited by

Lorenzo Bianconi *and* Giorgio Pestelli

TRANSLATIONS FROM THE ITALIAN BY KENNETH CHALMERS
AND FROM THE GERMAN BY MARY WHITTALL

The University of Chicago Press

CHICAGO & LONDON

LORENZO BIANCONI is professor of musical dramaturgy at the University of Bologna. He is the author of *Music in the Seventeenth Century*. GIORGIO PESTELLI is professor of music history at the University of Turin and music critic for *La Stampa*. He is author of *The Age of Mozart and Beethoven*.

The University of Chicago Press, Chicago 60637
The University of Chicago Press, Ltd., London
© 2003 by The University of Chicago
All rights reserved. Published 2003
Printed in the United States of America
12 11 10 09 08 07 06 05 04 03   5 4 3 2 1

ISBN (cloth): 0-226-04592-7

Originally published as *Storia dell'opera Italiana*, vol. 6, *Teorie e tecniche, immagini e fantasmi*, © 1988 E.D.T. Edizioni di Torino.

Library of Congress Cataloging-in-Publication Data

Teorie e tecniche, immagini e fantasmi. English
    Opera in theory and practice, image and myth / edited by Lorenzo Bianconi and Giorgio Pestelli ; translations from the Italian by Kenneth Chalmers and from the German by Mary Whittall.
        p.   cm. — (The history of Italian opera ; v. 6. Part II, Systems.)
    Translation of: Teorie e tecniche immagini e fantasmi.
    Includes bibliographical references and indexes.
    ISBN 0-226-04592-7
    1. Opera—Italy.   2. Opera—Italy—Dramaturgy.   3. Opera—Social aspects—Italy.   I. Bianconi, Lorenzo.   II. Pestelli, Giorgio.   III. Title. IV. Storia dell'opera italiana. English ; v. 6.   V. Storia dell'opera italiana. Parte II, Sistemi. English.
    ML1733 .S7513   1998 vol. 6
    782.1'0945—dc21

                                                      2003009361

This book is printed on acid-free paper.

Contents

3   Metrical and Formal Organization

PAOLO FABBRI

6 Opera in Italian National Culture 377

GIOVANNI MORELLI

Illustrations

Following page 146

1. Title page of the vocal score of *Rigoletto* (Milan: Ricordi, 1852). (Lithograph by Roberto Focosi)
2. Victor Hugo, *Le roi s'amuse* (Brussels: Louis Hauman, 1834). Extracts from pages 139 and 143. (Turin, Biblioteca Civica)
3. Victor Hugo, *Le roi s'amuse* (Brussels: Louis Hauman, 1834). Extracts from pages 144, 145, and 149. (Turin, Biblioteca Civica)
4. *Il duca di Vendôme*, p. 23. (Venice, Archivio Storico del Teatro la Fenice)
5. *Rigoletto* (Venice: Tipografia Gaspari, 1851), 28.
6. *Il duca di Vendôme*, p. 26. (Venice, Archivio Storico del Teatro la Fenice)
7. *Rigoletto* (Venice: Tipografia Gaspari, 1851), 31.
8. *Viscardello* (Rome: Gio. Olivieri, 1851), 22. (Venice, Fondazione Cini, Raccolta Rolandi)
9. *Viscardello* (Rome: Gio. Olivieri, 1851), 23. (Venice, Fondazione Cini, Raccolta Rolandi)
10. Sketch for *Rigoletto*, fol. 21. (Busseto, Carrara-Verdi Collection)
11. Sketch for *Rigoletto*, fol. 21, verso. (Busseto, Carrara-Verdi Collection)
12. Sketch for *Rigoletto*, fol. 22. (Busseto, Carrara-Verdi Collection)
13. Sketch for *Rigoletto*, fol. 22, verso. (Busseto, Carrara-Verdi Collection)
14. Autograph score of *Rigoletto*, fol. 223. (Milan, Archivio Ricordi)
15. Autograph score, fol. 225. (Milan, Archivio Ricordi)
16. Ricordi vocal score of *Rigoletto*, 1852, p. 192. (Milan, Archivio Ricordi)
17. Ricordi vocal score, 1852, p. 193. (Milan, Archivio Ricordi)
18. Handwritten production notes by Léonce for the staging of *Rigoletto* in 1863 at the Théâtre Lyrique. French vocal score, pp. 232–33. Paris, Bibliothèque de l'Association de la Régie Théatrale, R 12 (II). (Reproduced courtesy of H. Robert Cohen and Marie-Odile Gigou)
19. Handwritten production notes for the 1863 staging, pp. 234–35.

Following page 306

Note on Italian Prosody

For the English-speaking reader, the topic of Professor Fabbri's chapter requires a few words on the terminology used in Italian prosody. The two principal defining elements in a line of Italian verse are the number of syllables in the line and the position of the final accent. The lines are known as *quinario* (five syllables), *senario* (six), *settenario* (seven), *ottonario* (eight), *novenario* (nine), *decasillabo* (ten), and *endecasillabo* (eleven). A *piano* (plain) line, in which the final stress is on the penultimate syllable ("Bella figlia dell'a<u>mo</u>re"), is by far the most common. When the stress falls on the final syllable ("Le mie pene a consol<u>ar</u>"), the line is described as *tronco* (truncated), and when the antepenultimate syllable is stressed ("La donna è <u>mo</u>bile"), the line is known as *sdrucciolo* (slipping).

For scansion purposes, adjacent vowels in the same word are counted as one ("mie" in the *tronco* example above). The same holds for an elision, that is, when a word ending in a vowel is followed by one beginning with a vowel in the same line ("donna è").

There are also the "double" meters *quinario doppio* and *senario doppio*. Although the *quinario doppio* has the same number of syllables (ten) as a *decasillabo*, it differs in the pattern of stresses. In a *decasillabo* these are distributed throughout the line ("Va pensi<u>e</u>ro sull'<u>a</u>li do<u>ra</u>te"), but in a *quinario doppio* (commonly found in nineteenth-century operatic poetry) there are two stresses, a principal one on the ninth syllable and a secondary one on the fourth ("Stride la <u>va</u>mpa!—la folla in<u>do</u>mita"). The two *quinari* in this example are *piano* and *sdrucciolo* respectively. If the text were in plain *quinari*, then the fourth syllable of each line would receive equal stress.

Recitative is typically in alternating unrhymed lines of *settenari* and *endecasillabi*, with a rhyming couplet to close. Familiar examples of these attributes are provided by Piave's libretto for *La traviata*. At the beginning of act 2, Alfredo's opening recitative is, as normal, in *settenari* and *endecasillabi*:

> Lunge da lei per me non v'ha diletto! . . .
> Volaron già tre lune

    Dacché la mia Violetta
    Agi per me lasciò, dovizie, amori . . .

It closes with the customary couplet:

    E dal soffio d'amor rigenerato
    Scordo ne' gaudii suoi tutto il passato.

The subsequent aria is in *settenari,* and the first stanza closes with a *tronco* line, as is almost always the case in a rhymed aria text.

    Dei miei bollenti spiriti
    Il giovanile ardore
    Ella temprò col placido
    Sorriso dell'amor!

Poetics and Polemics

RENATO DI BENEDETTO

1. "TO IMITATE SPEECH IN SONG"

In Battista Guarini's 1588 treatise *Il Verrato,* amid the barrage of arguments against Dr. Iason De Nores of the Padua studio, refuting the charges of "monstrosity" and "disproportion" that had been laid at the door of the new genres of tragicomedy and pastoral, we read:

> And when we come to our own day, what need have we to exorcise terror and commiseration with tragic representations, having the most holy precepts of our religion, taught to us by the words of the Apostles? And so those hideous and threatening sights are redundant, nor does it seem to me that today one should introduce tragic action with any other goal than to entertain.[1]

Twelve years later, on the evening of 6 October 1600, Tragedy herself, playing the prologue in the performance of that "tender and most delicate tale by Signor Ottavio Rinuccini"[2] which was to become the fountainhead of opera,

---

1. Battista Guarini, *Il Verrato, ovvero Difesa di quanto ha scritto M. Giason Denores contra le tragicomedie e le pastorali in un suo discorso di poesia* (1588), in his *Opere,* ed. Marziano Guglielminetti (Turin: UTET, 1971), 729–821, quotation on 778. See also Guarini's *Compendio della poesia tragicomica tratto dai duo Verati . . . colla giunta di molte cose spettanti all'arte* (1601) in the edition of *Il pastor fido e il compendio della poesia tragicomica,* ed. Gioachino Brognoligo (Bari: Laterza, 1914), 219–88, quotation on 245.

2. Michelangelo Buonarroti, *Descrizione delle felicissime nozze dela cristianissima maestà di Madama Maria Medici regina di Francia e di Navarra* (1600), reproduced in part in Angelo Solerti, *Gli albori del melodramma* (Milan, Palermo, and Naples: Sandron, 1904; reprint, Bologna: Forni, 1976), 2:113.

raised the banner of a new, modern poetic, thus illustrating the "changed forms" and the "new path" that the followers of Apollo—or, in this case, dramatic poets—would now have to follow:

> Io, che d'alti sospir vaga e di pianti,
> spars'or di doglia, or di minacce il volto,
> fei negli ampi teatri al popol folto
> scolorir di pietà volti e sembianti,
>
>   non sangue sparso d'innocenti vene,
> non ciglia spente di tiranno insano,
> spettacolo infelice al guardo umano,
> canto su meste e lagrimose scene.
>
>   Lungi via, lungi pur da' regi tetti
> simolacri funesti, ombre d'affanni!
> Ecco i mesti coturni e i foschi panni
> cangio, e desto nei cor più dolci affetti.[3]
>
>   [I, who, desiring deep sighs and tears,
> my face spread now with grief, now with menace,
> once made the faces of those who crowded into the great theaters
> turn pale with pity,
>
>   it is not of blood shed from innocent veins,
> nor of eyes closed by crazed tyrants,
> an unhappy sight to the human gaze
> that I sing on sad and tearful stages.
>
>   Hence, hence from even royal palaces,
> gloomy images, shades of distress!
> Behold, I change my tragic garb and my dark guise,
> and waken gentler emotions in human hearts.]

Of course, we cannot know if, and to what extent, Rinuccini was here deliberately echoing Guarini's thesis, presenting it not in the context of a learned treatise but, as it were, on the field of battle, as his own personal contribution to the polemics on *Il pastor fido* which so concerned Italian literary circles at the turn of the century. In any case, whether conscious or not, the echo is there, and it confirms the natural connections between opera and pastoral tale, indeed opera's derivation from pastoral. Neither is it insignificant that this is taking place on the territory of literary theory, the very territory from which, when discussion of Aristotle's *Poetics* was at its height, in the sixteenth century, pastoral itself had drawn lifeblood for its genesis and development.

3. Ottavio Rinuccini, *L'Euridice rappresentata nello sponsalizio della cristianissima regina di Francia e di Navarra* (1600), in Solerti, *Gli albori del melodramma*, 2:107–42, quotation on 115.

Given that it is part of opera's genetic code, so to speak, a literary spirit seems suited to opera. The endless flow of theoretical writings, declarations, and illustrations or (more often) deprecations, satires, and polemics that have accompanied opera's history from its very beginnings—becoming, to a certain extent, a kind of antihistory—certainly has to be related to opera's uniquely public nature and to the potential for provocation and scandal embedded in a genre that can also, and more honestly, be charged with "monstrosity" and "disproportion." Such writings paint a picture of this weighty, multiform, and contradictory phenomenon we know as opera, either filtered through some abstract concept or other, or else conforming to some need or circumstance; but the picture is only ever partial, and frequently distorted and off-center. And yet it would be wrong to ignore or exclude these writings as if they were a parasitical growth. However hidden or diluted, the connection with that far-off source of the form is always there, and it makes the "literary" strain an essential constituent factor of opera, in its multicolored, vital, contradictory nature. And so we have to take due account of it, to be able to form an accurate and articulate judgment.

In the prologue to *Euridice,* and in the prefaces and dedications in the published editions of both the story itself and the musical setting, it is already possible to clarify some problematic areas present here in opera's embryonic state and in future discussions on opera (these arise intermittently during the seventeenth century but come thick and fast in the following century). They will become so many inescapable points to be revived and debated with obsessive insistence on every new occasion: the comparison with the tragedy of the ancients, and consequently with the ever-looming phantom of Greek music; affinities with pastoral drama; the need for a happy ending; the admissibility of acting in song—in other words, the possibility of presenting action entirely in music without offending the principle of verisimilitude, a basic criterion in a concept of art as the imitation of the natural world; and finally polemics against counterpoint.

Can, or even should, opera aspire to assume the role of legitimate heir to ancient tragedy and restorer of the mythical, lost unity of text, music, and action? This is the fundamental question, the starting point for all the arguments for and against opera. A positive or negative response will motivate not only acceptance or rejection but above all those plans for reform or regeneration which literary figures have continually proposed as the remedy for its permanently lamentable condition of decline and crisis (and which can be taken, instead, as sure evidence for just the opposite—its excellent state of health).

The same polemicists did not hesitate to credit the librettist and composer of *Euridice* with the intention of reviving ancient tragedy on the modern stage, even if there is nothing in the printed declarations by either one to support such a statement. It is true that Rinuccini, in dedicating his work to Maria de'

Medici, the new queen of France, had opened with an explicit reference to sixteenth-century polemics on the question of whether Greek tragedy was or was not entirely sung;[4] Jacopo Peri had also taken the same starting point to explain to readers what the source of his ideas was for establishing the new style of singing.[5] And it is true that a few months before *Euridice* was performed Emilio de' Cavalieri, too, in publishing his sacred oratorio *Rappresentazione di anima e corpo,* had conveyed to his publisher Alessandro Guidotti that "his singular and new musical compositions" were "made in imitation of that style with which it is said the ancient Greeks and Romans were accustomed to move spectators to different emotions on their stages and in their theaters."[6] But their words reveal no restorative purpose or any antiquarian disposition; what we find instead is the will to bring to life a new and "modern" type of theatrical representation, in relation to which ancient tragedy was an ideal model, certainly always to be kept in mind but, owing to the absence of direct evidence, something that could not actually be imitated or recovered. Cavalieri puts eloquent words into the mouth of Guidotti; Rinuccini, too, declares that his involvement in the project was due to a desire "to make a simple test of what song was capable of in our age"; while Peri, after having illustrated the principles of what (to use an expression taken from the title page of *La rappresentazione di anima e di corpo*) would be generally called *recitar cantando,* admits that he cannot declare it to be "the song used in Greek and Roman fables," but simply "that which alone can be offered by our music, to suit our discourse."

If, despite the echoes of the sixteenth-century debates, the question of the comparison with ancient theater lingers in the background, like a theory based entirely on conjecture, the pressing, manifest aims of the writers who came to the fore at the time of the first operatic performances are of quite a different nature. First of all, the entertainment itself functions as advertising and propaganda: the performance celebrates some memorable dynastic or political event, and as such it is described in minute detail to magnify the splendor or, rather, emphasize the unique, unrepeatable nature of the event. These writings form part of the dozens of accounts and descriptions of celebrations held in honor of this or that birth, wedding, victory, conquest, and so on. Second,

---

4. Rinuccini's dedication can be read in ibid., 107; and also in Angelo Solerti, *Le origini del melodramma* (Turin: Bocca, 1903; reprint, Bologna: Forni, 1969), 40–42; and in Heinz Becker, ed., *Quellentexte zur Konzeption der europäischen Oper im 17. Jahrhundert* (Kassel: Bärenreiter, 1981), 16ff.

5. The preface to Jacopo Peri's *Euridice* (1601) can be read in Solerti, *Le origini,* 45–49, and in Becker, *Quellentexte,* 20–22. In English it appears in Oliver Strunk, *Source Readings in Music History,* rev. ed., ed. Leo Treitler (New York: W. W. Norton, 1998), 659–62.

6. Guidotti's dedication and preface to Cavalieri's *Rappresentazione* of 1600 (from which these words are taken) can be read in Solerti, *Le origini,* 1–12; the preface alone is in Becker, *Quellentexte,* 13–16.

and this is, by contrast, a specific element, there is a lively, if concealed, polemic between writers as to who can rightly claim to be the inventor both of the idea of staging a theatrical performance entirely to music and of a new style of singing that will finally liberate modern music from the fetters of counterpoint and free all its infinite expressive (or, rather, "representative") potential. Last, connected to the preceding, there is an explanatory, in some ways prescriptive and didactic, function: illustrations of the theoretical foundations and the modes of performance of the "new music," including instructions on stage production and mise-en-scène—in other words, a whole body of information closely tied to musical and theatrical practice—fill out the ideological premises stated at the outset. It is worth noting, and not without an element of paradox, that it is precisely in the highly literary phase of its "origins" that literature on opera is so richly embellished with the concrete reality of the musical-theatrical event, much more so than it ever would be again. Similarly, it is worth noting that it is only in this phase that composers are so extraordinarily eloquent; later they would become increasingly quiet, to the point of total silence, objects and no longer the subjects of operatic debate.

Too complex is the confusion of polemics on the paternity of this "marvelous invention" which, in Peri's words, had "made our music heard onstage" and too dense and full of behind-the-scenes intrigues are the battles between factions that were at times—or even at one and the same time—intellectual, courtly, or political to allow more than superficial reference to them here. It is, however, interesting to note how each writer, in claiming for himself preeminence in the fundamental and definitive creation of the new style, illustrates its characteristics according to his distinct point of view, in line with his own basic objectives.

Of all of them, Peri—perhaps because he was the most directly inspired and aided by Rinuccini—is the one who shows himself to be the most sensitive to theoretical problems, going straight to the central issue of verisimilitude. His awareness of how setting a dramatic poem to music necessitates tackling the new and awkward problem of "imitar col canto chi parla" (imitating speech in song) leads him to speculate on how the ancients dealt with this problem and to come up with a theory on a middle course between the movement of the voice that they called "diastemic" (by distinctly intoned intervals) and what was called "continuous," the fluid, tonally indeterminate movement of "ordinary speech." By analogy, it led him to analyze the inflections of spoken Italian in order to distinguish between those more steadily intoned and those that move more rapidly, and to measure the relationships of movement and duration in both types in relation to the expression of emotions: it led him, in short, to the "invention" of recitative, which came into being as a leavening agent of poetic declamation.

Although Giulio Caccini was Peri's direct rival, he did not pursue specifically dramatic objectives. The problems of musical dramaturgy linked to the theatrical purpose of "music for a solo voice" remained outside his orbit, and indeed, if one were looking for his "manifesto," it would be found, not in the preface to his score of *Euridice* (where propaganda prevails, to claim rights of precedence over Peri), but in the note to readers at the beginning of the published collection *Le nuove musiche,* which was intended for chamber music performance rather than the theater. Here the composer's principal preoccupation seems to be not so much to provide reasons, or theoretical justifications, as to illustrate, at length and in detail, the attributes of the new style of song and to give singers all the necessary information for them to make best use of the new style and thus achieve the goal of the musician, "that is, to delight and move the *affetti* of the soul." [7]

It is precisely because of this eminently practical approach that Caccini's preface is ultimately more than a source of information on performance practice, however valuable it may be on that account. In fact, it gives us clear evidence of how the new style of singing was entirely bound up with the new style of composition for those composers who were in the process of forging it. Even more, it shows how the new style of composition—conceived as a stimulus of immense power to move the affections through their varied representation—came to life in a new style of singing. It is clear that *affetto* was used to mean not only the response of the spirit to the singing but also the technical procedure put into practice to achieve that response.

For this reason, the preface to *Le nuove musiche* (a piece of writing that, strictly speaking, is outside the boundaries of the history of opera) clearly records a characteristic of opera from its very beginnings, something that would remain tied to it as a constant element, whatever changes, however radical, would later affect the genre: the central role of the singer, his presence not as a passive instrument—let alone competitor or usurper—but as the natural complement to the composer, his prolongation, so to speak, his active collaborator and the person the music is first intended for (as is the case with Caccini's preface). The central position of the singer did not escape attention in subsequent writing on opera; but commentators changed its significance and cited it, particularly in the eighteenth century, as proof of a profound distortion of opera, a wicked deviation of the genre from its origins. For this reason, it is all the more significant and enlightening to find it proclaimed unequivocally in the earliest literature as intrinsic to the nature of the recitative, or representative, style, which is the indispensable requirement of opera.

If we look principally at singing, it is striking that, in the case of Caccini, who was both composer and singer, there is no document, in this first phase

---

7. The preface to Giulio Caccini's *Le nuove musiche* (1602) can be read in Solerti, *Le origini,* 55–71, quotation on 63. In English it appears in Strunk, *Source Readings,* 608–17, quotation on 611.

of the history of opera, where description of the effects of music is not associated with praise of the singers' art, which produced those effects. As evidence of "how this sort of music renewed by him moves the listener to various emotions," Cavalieri invokes the "excellence in music" of Vittoria Archilei and her magnificent performance in a pastoral that was already ten years old, *La disperazione di Fileno*. Jacopo Peri, once past the expected homage to the royal dedicatee, attributes the "greater success" of *Euridice* compared with *Dafne*—which he himself considered an experimental prototype—to the fact that the opera had been "sung by the greatest musicians of our day" (and he also emphasizes, in defending himself against the intrusions of Caccini, the close relationship between the composer's and the singer's roles: Caccini had been able to insist on collaborating in the composition of the music because the performers included "his dependents," for whom he "made the arias").

While Peri gives the names of some of his greatest interpreters, another composer, Filippo Vitali, names all those in his opera *Aretusa*, praising each one's specific skills in the preface to the published work. Indeed he dedicates his publication ideally to the "performers . . . each one of whom had desired it, as a piece in which they had exercised their skills."[8] Similarly, Marco da Gagliano, wishing to draw attention to the "highly important" part of the Messenger in his *Dafne* (highly important because "the words need to receive the greatest expression"), can think of nothing better than to regret that he cannot "recapture the way it was sung by Sig. Antonio Brandi . . . since he sang it in such a manner that I do not believe he left anything to be desired."[9] And Claudio Monteverdi, when illustrating the difficulties the protagonist of *La finta pazza Licori* will encounter, should the project of setting the tale to music be realized, also makes a point of giving the name of the designated interpreter, almost as if those difficulties had been, in a sense, measured against her skill.[10]

But the two roles, so closely connected as to be sometimes superimposed, also need to be distinguished. And it was Monteverdi himself who did this (with the sort of grasp of concepts embedded in pragmatic reality that is characteristic of his prose when he considers questions bound up with his art) in what is possibly his most famous letter, the one where he outlines his artistic and theatrical principles with remarkable concision, in the form of a protest

8. Preface to *Aretusa* by Filippo Vitali (1620), in Solerti, *Le origini*, 90–97, quotation on 97.

9. Preface to *Dafne* by Marco da Gagliano (1608), in Solerti, *Le origini*, 78–89, quotation on 87; and in Becker, *Quellentexte*, 23–26, quotation on 25.

10. See the letter to Alessandro Striggio of 7 May 1627 in Claudio Monteverdi, *Lettere*, ed. Éva Lax (Florence: Olschki, 1994), 152–54; and in Becker, *Quellentexte*, 33–35. The passage in question can also be read in a carefully edited version in *Letteratura italiana*, under the direction of Alberto Asor Rosa, vol. 4, *Teatro, musica, tradizione dei classici* (Turin: Einaudi, 1986), 354. The letter appears in English in *The Letters of Claudio Monteverdi*, translated and with introduction by Denis Stevens, rev. ed. (Oxford: Clarendon Press, 1995), 318–21.

against the incongruity of the subject suggested to him.[11] His basic objection
is noteworthy: the characters in the tale he is supposed to set to music are not
humans but divinities of the sea and air who "do not speak" and therefore do
not have emotions whose imitation can move the listener ("Ariadne was moving because she was a woman, and similarly Orpheus moved because he was
a man and not a wind"). Monteverdi continues: for such characters, who tend
more to "singing in speech" (cantar parlando) than "speaking in song" (parlar cantando), and whose goal is therefore more the seductive power of song
than the imitation of the emotion contained in the words, a composer is not
needed: the singers can easily provide the music themselves, each one for his
or her part, since each will know best how to exploit his or her own abilities.
In contrast, subjects of the other kind need the direction of "a single hand"
which can guide everything "to a single end," that is, to the representation of
emotions.

It would be an anachronism, however appealing, to interpret Monteverdi's
distinction as a claim for the status of the author, something composers would
not achieve for another couple of centuries. It is possibly more accurate to interpret it, in its historic context, as confirmation of an awareness that music
could not by itself produce the desired effects. "In such cases music is not all,"
Marco da Gagliano had already warned, identifying the new dramatic genre's
principal attraction in its very composite nature:

> truly an entertainment for princes, and more than any other most pleasing, one in
> which every most noble pleasure is united, such as invention and presentation of a
> tale, meaning, style, sweetness of rhyme, art of music, the concert of voices and in-
> struments, exquisite singing, charming dance and gesture, and it could also be said
> that no small part is played by perspective painting and the costumes; in such a way
> that together with the intellect, every most noble emotion is flattered by the most
> delightful arts that human ingenuity has ever contrived.[12]

2. "ONE OF THE MOST HONORED PLEASURES IN DRAMA"

Aimed at coordinating and ordering such a variety of means, the prefaces introducing the first published favole in musica abound, as we have seen, with
instructions, which are not limited to musical performance practice pure and
simple but extend to the placing of the singers onstage, the rhythm of gestures
and movements in time with the music, the use and positioning of the instruments, and so on. Later on, as performances grew more numerous (although
in the limited context of courts and academies), the need must have been felt

---

11. See the letter to Alessandro Striggio of 9 Dec. 1616 in Monteverdi, Lettere, 48–50; and
in Becker, Quellentexte, 30–33. It appears in English in Letters of Claudio Monteverdi, 106–11,
and can also be read in English in Strunk, Source Readings, 662–65.

12. The preface to Dafne, in Solerti, Le origini, 78 and 82; and in Becker, Quellentexte, 23.

to create a broader, organic ordering of this mixture of material, which would otherwise be lost in the multiplication of observations and directions. It is probably to such a requirement that we owe the creation, in the 1630s, of two treatises which bring together and summarize that multiplicity of experience: one has come down to us anonymously and is entitled *Il corago;* the other is by the illustrious hand of Giovanni Battista Doni and is entitled *Trattato della musica scenica:* both, however, remained in manuscript form (the first until our own day, the other for almost a century and a half).[13]

However, the two treatises differ fundamentally in their assumptions and purposes: as a result their documentary value for a modern historian of opera is vastly different. The point of view of *Il corago* is eminently pragmatic; the title itself refers to "that faculty through which men can prescribe all the ways and means necessary for a dramatic action composed by the poet to be put onstage with the perfection required to produce for admiration and pleasure that benefit and also moral fruit which the poetry will demand."[14] So at least in its declared intentions, *Il corago* is like a manual of staging, not limited to musical performances but covering all sorts of theatrical presentations. Musical performances take the lion's share in it, however, because of the three forms of performance which the author lists: one "purely in speech," one that makes use of "musica recitativa," and mime. The second is considered superior to the others as "one of the most honored pleasures in drama which have either been newly discovered or derived from ancient usage and custom in our day and age."[15] In practice, it is recognized as the most vital phenomenon in contemporary theater, and the one with the greatest potential. Nor is the author content to provide practical directives on staging, but he goes so far as to make suggestions to the poet as to the plot of the story, the qualities of the characters, the distribution of roles, meter, and rhyme, and to the composer on the appropriate use of recitative and arioso, the reasons for the prevalence of one over the other or of a judicious mixture of the two.

In short, while *Il corago* does not give the impression of wishing to dictate artistic principles, it is clear that it possesses a clear idea of the principles that must govern the creation of an opera, well in advance of its presentation onstage. Its conceptual clarity, based on the concrete observation of reality and not on abstract, theoretical assumptions, allows it to frame in clear, precise

---

13. *Il corago, o vero Alcune osservazioni per metter bene in scena le composizioni drammatiche,* ed. Paolo Fabbri and Angelo Pompilio (Florence: Olschki, 1983); excerpts in English appear in Strunk, *Source Readings,* 629–34. Giovanni Battista Doni, *Trattato della musica scenica,* in his *Lyra barberina: De' trattati di musica . . . tomo secondo,* ed. Anton Francesco Gori (Florence: Stamperia Imperiale, 1763; reprint, Bolgna: Forni, 1974), 1–144 (excerpts can be read in Solerti, *Le origini,* 195–221; and in Becker, *Quellentexte,* 41–51).

14. *Il corago,* 21.

15. Ibid., 40ff.

terms, with no burden of erudition, the basic problem of the new theatrical genre: the virtual opposition of music and acting. There is, indeed, no doubt that the true object of the art of music is "harmony, which lies in the relation between many voices and not in the progress of one alone;" [16] on the contrary, the essence of *stile recitativo* lies in the "modulated imitation of perfect delivery," [17] which can properly and only be achieved with that "progression" of a "single voice," or rather what *Il corago* defines as "modulation" as distinct from harmony.[18] "Musica recitativa" is therefore certainly a pleasant and enjoyable mode of delivery, but it is also, the conclusion seems to be, a contradiction in terms. And the problems do not stop there.

Running parallel but subordinate to the basic contradiction we find another, between the two alternatives which the composer has at his disposal to set dramatic action to music: aria and recitative (*Il corago* makes a reference to a third alternative, melodrama, as a purely theoretical possibility and on this account excludes it). We read the peremptory declaration that "the perfection of *stile recitativo* results not from the charm, eccentricity, or majesty of the aria . . . but from the variety and arrangement of modulation which is closest to our normal way of speaking." [19] On the other hand, charm, eccentricity, and majesty are qualities that belong to the way voices behave, or to that "harmony" in which, as we know, the "perfection of music" lies, and that, as is declared with equally sententious clarity, must "occur as much as possible in dramatic action," [20] to discourage the emergence of the greatly feared "tedium of recitative."

From this apparent impasse, in which a good part of future literature would find itself mired, our writer—whose point of view is from the stage— manages to grasp the effective flexibility, the richness of articulation, and the multitude of possible solutions: in a word, he is aware of the potential for creative energy which can be activated by the contradiction. He takes account of things as they are and with empirical wisdom suggests clever solutions for distribution and balancing, both in the composition of the music and in the plotting of the fable. Selected locations for aria seem to be the choruses, which he wishes to be as frequent as possible, to break the "boredom" of "musical soliloquy" with the variety and fullness of harmony,[21] the prologue, and those parts where we see characters who "do not act" but sing, and so allow the singer to abandon himself to those "charms" in which "current *stile recitativo* is lacking." [22]

Boredom can also be avoided through an astute choice of subject: miraculous and fantastic subjects allow for the use of stage diversions (machines, attractive or horrid locations, dances) which will undoubtedly achieve the de-

16. Ibid., 65.
17. Ibid., 61.   19. Ibid., 45.   21. Ibid., 65.
18. Ibid., 41, 65.   20. Ibid., 67 and passim.   22. Ibid., 67.

sired effect. But the preference for fantastic subjects—mythological or sa-cred—was motivated principally by fidelity to the principles of verisimilitude and decorum defined by the sixteenth-century tradition of treatises in the wake of Aristotle's *Poetics,* the same ones that suggested assigning the arias to the truly "singing" characters. The possibility that high-ranking characters might conduct their public affairs in song was prejudicial to both principles: for this reason, in "serious actions" only "supernatural characters" were to be intro-duced, even better if they were those whom tradition had consecrated as great "musicians"; "human" characters would be able to appear in comic parts, where "speaking in music" would not appear unseemly, because of their low social rank and the private nature of their actions. But *Il corago* appears ready to compromise even on these basic principles because, in the name of an empiricism not based on the present but projected into the immediate fu-ture, he allows the possibility that "some person near to our time" might also act and display his emotions in music without causing outrage; he allows, in short, that musical-dramatic actions might be constructed around historical subjects as well, once, thanks to greater familiarity with "rappresentazioni armoniche," usage would have transformed the original transgression into convention.[23]

The fact that this sort of development is seen purely and simply in theo-retical terms has led to the choice of 1637 as the latest date when *Il corago* could have been written. And indeed the many suggestions contained within its pages look forward to a type of spectacle that, strictly speaking, is not yet "opera," because it continues to belong to the context of courtly celebrations or the academies and, as such, is an expression of environments where the chain linking the customer, producer, and audience together had not yet been broken. This is possibly the basic reason why the author of *Il corago* (who must definitely have belonged to such a circle, if he is indeed, as is supposed, Ottavio Rinuccini's son Pierfrancesco)[24] accepts the status quo and does not propose any corrections or modifications. Indeed, he states that there is noth-ing to be improved in *musica rappresentativa:* all that is needed is some oc-casional adjustment to vary the "composition" of its constituent elements, which, viewed in isolation, can be said already to have reached their perfect state.

But this is also the reason Doni's *Trattato* is completely opposite in ap-proach to *Il corago:* not a man of the theater but a "pure" man of letters, full of antiquarian erudition, Doni judged things not for what they were but for how he wished them to be, measured against the unchanging, timeless model that is the theater music of antiquity. For him there is no question that mod-ern dramatic music came into being as the restoration or revival of ancient

23. Ibid., 63ff.
24. See the introduction, ibid., 9.

music, but for this very reason it is a long way from being perfect, because it is manifestly unable to produce those magnificent effects that, according to every source, ancient music was capable of making. Certainly at least one serious obstacle on the route to improvement will have been removed once the conviction has been eradicated that contrapuntal (or, as Doni defines it, "madrigalesque") music is "the best and most perfect type of music . . . for too great is the imperfection which causes the distortion of the poetry, the confusion of its meaning, the excess of repetition, and the disturbance of the rhythm." [25] Even what Doni calls "monody" [26] (using a term which would go on to have enduring success) is seriously lacking; in fact, dramatic music cannot be said to have progressed very far from the forms in which its first "inventors or restorers" [27] shaped it. Its serious defect is its lack of variety, which produces tedium. But the remedy he suggests is not, as in *Il corago*, frequent (although not indiscriminate) recourse to aria; instead, he recommends here a very sparing use of aria and song, for both the soloists and the chorus, as "inessential parts of the story" and so incompatible with the spirit of "representative or imitative melody." [28] The variety which is appropriate to such a melody, and which alone can guarantee it sufficient power to arouse emotions, is that of the infinite subtleties and expressive gradations which were already to be found in the modes and genres of the music of ancient Greece. It would come only to whoever managed to recover that lost richness. For this reason, Doni considers that the responsibility for the defects in modern music lies, not principally with composers, but with theorists, who have not been able to point practitioners in the right direction; thus, page after page of his *Trattato* indicates how that richness can be rediscovered and reattained.[29]

On another fundamental point Doni disagrees not only with *Il corago* but also with the entire literature on opera in its first decades: he does not share the opinion that ancient Greek drama was entirely sung but claims that only the choruses and canticles (the lyrical monologues) were. Consequently, he recommends that the same practice should be adopted in modern *azioni*: principally in tragedy, which in any case seems to contain the type of *rappresentazioni* "most capable" of melody, but also in comedy. Pastorals are a different matter: as a modern creation, built mostly on amorous subjects, they can be allowed to "have melody in all parts." [30] He does not underestimate,

25. Doni, *Trattato*, 98.

26. Giovanni Battista Doni, *Discorso sopra la perfezione delle melodie*, in his *Compendio del trattato de' generi e de' modi della musica . . . con un discorso sopra la perfezione de' concenti* (Rome: Fei, 1635), 95–125, see 103.

27. Doni, *Trattato*, 127 (in Becker, *Quellentexte*, 48).

28. Doni, *Trattato*, 14, 84.

29. See ibid., 36–63 and 127–29 (this latter passage is also in Becker, *Quellentexte*, 48–50).

30. Doni, *Trattato*, 14ff. (in Solerti, *Le origini*, 201–4).

for all this, the abruptness of the switch between song and recitation but once again invokes the authority of the ancients, interpreting literary and figurative evidence to demonstrate that they were accustomed to accompanying with instruments not only the sung passages but also those that were simply recited (conversations and quarrels). Naturally, he declares himself convinced that the same can be done in modern theater: for this reason, melodrama, which *Il corago* had dismissed as the least successful and practicable way of representing action in music, is here rehabilitated as the best remedy for the glaring basic contradiction of musical theater.[31]

I have referred above to the different significance of the different approaches taken by the two treatises. Reading them in parallel gives rise to unusual but instructive observations. *Il corago* is for us today a reliable witness and a valuable source of information on the state of musical theater in the period between 1620 and 1630; however, it has remained a dead letter for subsequent operatic historiography. On this point Doni's *Trattato* has been much more effective, although reality for him is principally the screen against which he projects his theories, to a large extent the product of abstract speculation and destined to remain so. But some of his ideas—the legend of Giovanni Bardi's *camerata* as the experimental source of modern dramatic music, the birth of opera as the restoration of ancient Greek theater, the consequent virtual equation of tragedy with opera—would remain fundamental in eighteenth-century literature, both that of the Arcadian Academy and that marked by the spirit of the Enlightenment. It is possibly no coincidence that the *Trattato* saw the light of day, in a monumental edition, at a time when the wind of reform was blowing strongest through Italian opera, and in Florence, to whose prince the most concise and essential manifesto of "reform," the dedicatory preface to Christoph Willibald Gluck and Ranieri de' Calzabigi's *Alceste,* would soon be addressed.

3. "THE MIND NOT BEING ABLE TO CONCEIVE A HERO THAT SINGS"
The institutional change which had been announced at the end of the 1630s and which rapidly became established—the decline of theatrical celebrations at court and the proliferation of operas organized by an impresario—produced, among other things, the sudden death of the debate on opera, only just after it had begun. The fact that neither *Il corago* nor Doni's *Trattato* appeared in print seems to be an eloquent indication of how, now that it had exchanged its "princely" nature for a "mercenary" one—and had thus become a consumer item—opera had ceased to be an object of scholarly attention.

It would be wrong, however, to interpret this silence—which was to go on for a good half century—as a sign of a sudden drying up of that theoretical

---

31. See Doni, *Trattato,* 117–20 and passim.

and literary root which had proved so nourishing to opera at the outset. It might be said instead that the change reinvigorated a provocative and transgressive strain, which, up to this point, had been merely latent and now found the proper place to blossom and expand. It is well known that the new mechanisms of production were determined for a while by literary academies: and it is in this context, at least where the new acerbic ideas which the freethinking current had put into circulation were most lively, that the new, unconventional theatrical genre was identified as an effective platform on which to stage the celebration (and unmasking) of deception, exposing the vacuity of the principles and laws that govern social order, and the falseness of history in its fabrication of false examples to uphold the false authority of laws and principles. It was able to do this under the protection of a poetic directed exclusively toward pleasure and in the context of a celebration that was in itself transgressive, like that of Carnival.

The connection between freethinking and the fate of opera was never made explicit in any manifesto or poetic profession, and on a practical level, the opening of the Teatro Novissimo in Venice by—as seems to be the case—the accademici Incogniti was a brief and limited episode. Certain ideas must, however, have been enduring, if we think simply of how that context produced the event that music historians have ever since indicated as the point of no return, the turning point that led opera on to tracks that it would never leave: I am referring, of course, to the adoption of a historical subject in *L'incoronazione di Poppea* by Giovanni Francesco Busenello. The choice of this subject did not signify taking up a classicist position, nor did it mean that opera was again to be considered synonymous with tragedy: on the contrary, it expressed a radical skepticism toward history, whose falsehoods and flaws were pitilessly laid bare. There were few qualms on the subject of verisimilitude or decorum: if history itself was an accumulation of more or less fabulous inventions, what was to stop anyone inventing other similar fabulous events, according to caprice and pleasure?

Here we find Busenello advising the reader not to "wince" if "some tale" is found mixed in with history as passed down to us by Plutarch and Lucan, because "in some parts current taste must be accommodated" but particularly because "the writer does not believe he has erred in writing in his own way" (*La prosperità infelice di Giulio Cesare dittatore*, 1656). Giacomo Castoreo expresses himself even more explicitly in presenting his *Pericle effeminato* (1653):

> If you find therein something historic, be aware that the rest is mere invention. . . . For I do not mean to offer you a history but to represent a fable which is historic in name only. It is indeed true that the main action is drawn from Plutarch, who

writes of the loves of Pericles and Aspasia, for which he acquired the description unmanly; but yet in putting them into the drama I have followed my own fancy.

Skepticism attacks the supposedly inviolate nature of the rules handed down by the ancients, together with the authority of history. The comparison between the ancients and the moderns, which underlies all seventeenth-century culture and is a mandatory element in polemics on opera, is naturally resolved in favor of the latter. "Unhappy age," wrote Giacomo Badoaro in the dedication of his *Ulisse errante* (1644), "if the traces of those who have passed before us made our feet follow an unalterable path; this could rightly be called the century of the blind, for we could do nothing but be led." And he continues preaching the variability of precepts in step with "the changing ages," which "bring into existence the different ways of composing," and their dependence on poetic usage, so that Aristotle himself would have formulated them differently if Homer and Sophocles had written differently; he comes to the terse conclusion: "do not burden me with rules, for the true rule is to satisfy the listener." [32] So there is no limit to the changes in time and place. And there is certainly no curb to the multiplication of arias: in the preface to *Alessandro vincitor di se stesso* (1651) the librettist Francesco Sbarra is ready to admit that "sung by Alexander and Aristotle" arias are "contrary to the propriety of such grand personages," but he is equally determined to adapt to a defect not only "tolerated by our age but applauded," convinced that "if *stile recitativo* were not interspersed with such entertainments, it might bring more irritation than pleasure."

In a different cultural context, however, it will be the skeptical, acute rationalism of free thought that will provide the ammunition for a first decisive attack on opera: decisive, it should be understood, not for opera itself, but for debate on opera, now promoted to the rank of a genuine "problem" organically implanted in European literary circles for a century and more. It is no coincidence that this occurred in France, or at least in the context of that part of French culture that had at first rejected the importation of opera from Italy and had then allowed it to be acclimatized only at the cost of radical change. And it matters little if the attack came from a writer—Charles de Marguetel de Saint-Denis, lord of Saint-Évremond—who held an eccentric, outsider position in relation to that culture. In his judgment on opera, he only had to take French literary tragedy of his day as his term of comparison for him to find himself aligned with the most intransigent classicists, to the point where he comes down firmly (at least as far as this topic is concerned) on the side of the ancients, as is clear from the following judgment, which has become notori-

32. The dedicatory preface to *Ulisse errante* can be found in Becker, *Quellentexte*, 58–63.

ous in the history of opera: "The Grecians made admirable Tragedies where they had some singing; the Italians and the French make bad ones, where they sing all."[33]

The basic accusation is that opera has subverted the fundamental principle of classical drama itself and of its so-called closed form, which would have the author completely divorced from the action and the characters completely independent onstage, as if operating in a self-sufficient world and "closed off" from any external influence. The intrusion of music shatters this complete coherence, destroys realism, and expels what Saint-Évremond calls "l'esprit de la représentation." In making the characters sing, the composer lends them his own voice, and it is toward this, not to the thoughts of the hero, that the attention of the listener is directed, the listener seeing in the characters the figure of the author, as the only person truly onstage:

> Nevertheless, our thoughts run more upon the Musician than the Hero in the Opera: LUIGI, CAVALLO, and CESTI, are still present to our imagination. The mind not being able to conceive a Hero that sings, thinks of the Composer that set the song; and I don't question but that in the Opera's at the Palace-Royal, LULLI is a hundred times more thought of than THESEUS or CADMUS.[34]

Nor is the loss of interest in the representation compensated by the sensual call of music, for when the mind is obliged to be idle, the senses quickly tire, and when the first pleasant impression has faded, pleasure turns to boredom. "A spectacle of the senses" is therefore what opera is, in the words of d'Alembert many years later, returning to the tradition of "negative" thought which actually derives from this source,[35] and to which very few will decline to pay fairly ritual homage in years to come. Even an enthusiast like Charles de Brosses felt obliged to state his own preference for tragedy and comedy rather than opera because "the pleasures of the soul are more vivid than those of the eye and ear";[36] opera is a bizarre compound of music and poetry, which harm each other reciprocally in their unhappy cohabitation. It is not that music should be completely excluded from the theater: Saint-Évremond appreciated ancient tragedy, where some things were sung. So places can be identified where music can enter without offending decorum ("la bienséance") and veri-

---

33. Saint-Évremond's essay *Sur les opéras* first appeared in 1684 but was compiled during the preceding decade and achieved widespread circulation in numerous reprintings of his *Oeuvres mêlées*. It appears in English in *The Works of Monsieur de St. Évremond Made English from the French Original,* 2d ed. (n.p.: J. J. Knapton, etc., 1728), 2:175.

34. Ibid., 174.

35. See Jean-Baptiste Le Rond d'Alembert, "De la liberté de la musique" (1759), in *La querelle des bouffons,* ed. Denise Launay (Geneva: Minkoff, 1973), 3:2203–82, quotation on 2225.

36. Charles de Brosses, *Lettres familières écrites d'Italie en 1739 et 1740* (Paris: Didier, 1856).

similitude ("la raison"): everything pertaining to prayer, sacrifices, and religious rites in general or else the excitement of nascent love or the surges felt by a heart divided between two emotions, situations that require the use of lyric verses, which are ideally suited to song (all in all, those places that Doni had classified as "choruses" and "canticles"). These apart, the effect of music was ridiculous.

In the very first years of the eighteenth century, when Saint-Évremond's writings started to circulate in Europe, Italian literary figures had already returned to opera and interested themselves in it with a previously unknown intensity and fervor. The reasons for this interest are well known. Spurred by the new currents in thought which were coming from across the Alps, goaded by the criticism also from beyond the Alps (particularly from France) of Italian literature—on its excesses, its arbitrary and unruly nature, the outrages against truth and good taste which it had committed during the seventeenth century—they set about tackling for the first time the enormous task of a critical rethinking of the entire national literature. Indeed, they set about tackling the very concept of a national literature, whose canon needed to be drawn up, its forms set in order, and its goals directed in harmony with those of a reborn, or nascent, civic conscience.

Occupied with this beneficial and edifying project, they found themselves faced by a blank space in the very place where there should have been a literary genre on a higher plane for the nobility of its style and the effectiveness of its moral teaching: tragedy. It was blank because, as they reasoned, its place had been usurped by opera, which based its very raison d'être on disorder, arbitrariness, and moral detachment. The Arcadian Academy—the institution which represented Italian literature for the first time in its history as an official and unified entity—thus took the position, in the words of its "guardian," Giovanni Mario Crescimbeni, the first to formulate the accusation, that opera had caused good and true dramatic poetry, both tragic and comic, to disappear from the stage:

[I]n order to charm with novelty the jaded taste of audiences, sickened equally by the baseness of comedies and the gravity of tragedies, the creator of operas put the two together, monstrously combining kings, heroes, and other illustrious characters with jesters, servants, and men of the lowest rank. This confusion of characters was the reason for the complete breakdown of the rules of poetry, which so fell into disuse that no regard was paid to expression, which lost its purity, being required to serve the music, and became filled with modern idioms. Regulated use of the rhetorical figures which ennoble oration was neglected, and the style was restricted to normal, familiar speech for the most part, which is more suitable to music; and finally the sequences of short meters, called ariettas in the vernacular, which are generously spread throughout the scenes, and the overwhelming impropriety of making people speak in song utterly robbed the works of the power of emotions and the means to move them in listeners.[37]

The charge continued to be current, with the tenacity of received ideas, throughout the entire eighteenth century not only among Italian literary figures, where it may to a certain extent have been legitimate, for the reasons given above (we need only think of Scipione Maffei's preface to his *Il teatro italiano,* the anthology which he intended would pick up the threads of an interrupted tradition and inspire the creation of a new repertoire),[38] but also among more detached and neutral judges, like observers from abroad. "This kind of spectacle has been so long neglected in Italy, that it seems to have been wholly lost. . . . The passion for dramas in music has ruined true tragedy, as well as comedy in this country." This was the dry comment of Charles Burney after having attended—not without his declared surprise—the performance of an "Italian *tragedy*" in a theater in Bologna during his tour of 1770: basically, a highly concentrated summary of Crescimbeni's long censure.[39]

A more acid polemic came from those who judged that opera, not satisfied with having expelled true tragedy, actually aspired to take over its function through the music which adorned the text. "I, too, must confess," admitted Ludovico Antonio Muratori reluctantly, "that modern operas are generally merely tragedies dressed with music. But it seems to me that the true face of tragedy has been altered beyond measure, that I would hardly dare to call such works tragedies, since music, such as is used in our day, does not suit them; indeed, it shrinks from them."[40]

This is the basis for discussion on the legitimacy of the comparison between opera and ancient tragedy. Preoccupied that "modern dramas," so harmful not only to good poetry but also to the customs of "well-ordered cities," could invoke the authority of the ancients in their defense, Muratori, while he was working on his *Della perfetta poesia italiana,* studied in depth the role of music in ancient tragedy, even writing a dissertation on the subject which he left unpublished, either because it was too long to go into the book or because his arguments (aimed at demonstrating that tragedies were not sung entirely with "real music," but only in the choruses) had not convinced the learned scholars of antiquity to whom he had submitted his text for comment. In any case, the terms of this question remained the same: there could be no comparison

37. Giovanni Mario Crescimbeni, *La bellezza della volgar poesia* (Rome: Buagni, 1700), 140.

38. See the preface by Scipione Maffei to *Il teatro italiano o sia Scelta di tragedie per uso della scena . . . Premessa un'istoria del teatro, e difeso di esso* (Verona: Vallarsi, 1723) 1:I–XLIV.

39. Charles Burney, *The Present State of Music in France and Italy* (London: Becket, 1771), 199 (ed. Percy Scholes under the title *Dr. Burney's Musical Tours in Europe,* vol. 1 [London: Oxford University Press, 1959]).

40. Ludovico Antonio Muratori, *Della perfetta poesia italiana* (1706), ed. Ada Ruschioni (Milan: Marzorati, 1972), 2:572.

between ancient music, "all serious and scientific," and modern music, all soft and effeminate—one able to move humanity's most noble affections and temper its most impetuous ones, the other capable only of delighting the senses.

Muratori hurls an avalanche of charges at opera. Let's start with the "defects" of modern music: the excessive artifice of contrapuntal elaboration, the spineless, enveloping flexibility of a vocal line interwoven with "the tiniest notes," the feminine timbre—real or created—of the singers' voices, and the profusion of ariettas, which dispense "immoderate pleasure." Together with these, already enough to sap the audiences' moral strength, were the defects of the poetry, unavoidable given the sway that music held over the words. Apart from the impossibility, for the poet, of spinning verses full of "strong and clever sentiments"—verses that did not have the sole function of providing a resonant and harmonious support for the music—the expansion of time imposed by singing ariettas reduced the space available for recitative, although this contained the "plot, direction, and essence of the tale." The natural development of the action was therefore compressed, suffocated, and distorted, and another unrealistic element was added to the inherent one of a drama that developed in song.[41] On this crucial point—intimately connected to the attention of the audience or, rather, the type of means that a dramatic composition can employ to maintain an audience's interest—Muratori's arguments follow those of Saint-Évremond exactly, whether or not he knew the Frenchman's letter on opera:

> Now when were men ever seen to sing as they go about their business and deal with weighty affairs? Could it ever be realistic that a person in a rage, in grief and anguish, or seriously and truly speaking of his affairs might sing? . . . And who ever saw someone in normal speech go on repeating and singing the same word, the same sentiment several times, as happens in ariettas? . . . So we shall not be surprised if modern tales, however well put together, do not rouse the various passions in the souls of listeners; for not only do such unrealities, with which custom is corrupted, take away the authority and the likelihood of the emotions represented, but the length and the lack of propriety in the singing of ariettas enfeeble the passions or diminish the little that happened to be aroused in the listeners shortly before. Whoever sings with such calm and such studied melodiousness of his affairs, his misfortunes, his contempt, can never seem to us to be speaking honestly: and so he cannot move us deeply or touch our hearts.[42]

So it might be said that where seventeenth-century literature had repeatedly cautioned composers and poets against the "tedium of recitative," now the perspective was completely the reverse, and the theory was of the "tedium of

41. See ibid., 575–79.   42. Ibid., 580–82.

aria": the laconic speech that the poet was obliged to use, far from reducing the duration of the drama, was increasing it out of proportion, all to the advantage of the music, which "however much a thing of utmost sweetness . . . nevertheless shares the same disadvantage as other sweet things, created to delight the senses, which quickly generate surfeit." Confirmation of this is the intermittent attention which listeners pay to the music itself and the varied occupations to which they devote themselves to fill the excess of empty moments. "Now what diversion," Muratori triumphantly concludes, "what pleasure is there in our famous dramas if in the middle of them they make the listener find amusement and seek other delights?"[43]

While for Muratori it is the very presence of music which discourages a comparison between modern opera and ancient tragedy, for Gian Vincenzo Gravina, a spirit at least as austere and equally aware of the urgency of restoring to Italian society an instrument of educational power as superior as that of the tragic theater, the music remains a valuable integrating element in modern opera, which must, in fact, count among the most serious causes of its decadence the separation into different "crafts" of philosophy, poetry, and music once embodied in the same person:

> [B]ecause the philosopher without the organ of poetry and the poet without the organ of music cannot offer their benefits to general and popular service. The philosopher thus remains within his restricted schools, the poet within the academies, and for the people the pure voice has remained within the opera house, stripped of all poetic eloquence and all philosophical sentiment.[44]

Without prejudice to the condemnation of modern music, Gravina poses the question in terms that are entirely the opposite of those of Muratori: if contemporary dramatic poetry is "the harmful minister of more harmful music," one cannot accuse the music of the corruption of poetry; the opposite is actually the case. Indeed, having suggested in his *Della ragion poetica* that the imitative arts (among which he includes music) are the result of a single central "shared idea,"[45] Gravina claimed that the falsification of one inevitably provokes the falsification of all interconnected arts, and particularly music, which depends on poetry "like the shadow on the body. Since poetry had

43. Ibid., 582ff.

44. Gian Vincenzo Gravina, *Della tragedia* (1715), in his *Scritti critici e teorici,* ed. Amedeo Quondam (Bari: Laterza, 1973), 504–89, quotation on 507. A translation appears in Enrico Fubini, *Music and Culture in Eighteenth-Century Europe: A Source Book,* translated from the original sources by Wolfgang Freis, Lisa Gasbarrone, and Michael Louis Leone; translation edited by Bonnie J. Blackburn (Chicago: University of Chicago Press, 1994), 37.

45. Gian Vincenzo Gravina, *Della ragion poetica* (1706), in his *Scritti critici e teorici,* 195–327, quotation on 199.

been corrupted by the excess of ornaments, it has passed its germ on into music as well, now so elaborated that it has almost lost its natural expression."[46] Even if Gravina does not carry his reasoning through to its conclusion, it would seem implicit, in this preface, that the assumed basis of the operatic reform so energetically invoked by the Arcadian writers lay, not in the expulsion of music nor in its being drastically limited to only the choruses nor even its reduction to more sober and restrained custom, but in the regeneration of poetry, no less, the element which, like the shadow to the body, the music cannot fail to follow; music would thus become once more the instrument, not of mere sensual pleasure, but of the "delight belonging to dramatic music . . . which arises from imitation."[47]

This leads to another inference. By one of those paradoxical reversals, which are not exactly rare in history, it was precisely this rigorous approach on the part of probably the most censorious commentator on modern theater, and the most radical in asserting the ethical and civic function of Arcadia, that made a "literary" justification of opera, based on the comparison with ancient tragedy, possible in the future. This was something with which Gravina had never occupied himself directly, but he had certainly condemned implicitly in disowning its forebears, tragicomedy and the pastoral. It would take only the appearance of a poet of genius, able to restore stylistic purity, to give order to the dramatic structures and to imbue them with noble, moral content, in a word, able to return theatrical poetry to the heights of its educational duties, so that it would re-create the conditions for appropriate musical expression as well. This poet—must we say it?—would be Gravina's pupil, Metastasio (and it matters little if he would very probably not have met with the approval of his overaustere teacher): the poet who, following on from Gravina, would continue to claim that ancient tragedy was all sung and would reclaim for his own dramas the description of "true tragedies."

"True, perfect, and precious tragedies" was how Metastasio's dramas were defined by Ranieri de' Calzabigi (naturally in his earlier incarnation, before he had set out on the path of reform), and not only for their "unity," "morality," "interest," and "sublime language" but also for having made their musical settings at once more dignified and functional.[48] Voltaire, too, had recognized opera's close family relationship with ancient tragedy, for the same

---

46. Gravina, *Della tragedia*, in his *Scritti critici e teorici*, 556; Fubini, *Music and Culture*, 38.

47. Ibid.

48. Ranieri de' Calzabigi, *Dissertazione . . . su le poesie drammatiche del sig. abate Pietro Metastasio*, in Pietro Metastasio, *Poesie*, vol. 1 (Paris: Quillau, 1775); now in Ranieri Calzabigi, *Scritti letterari e teatrali*, ed. Anna Laura Bellina (Rome: Salerno Editrice, 1994), 1:22–146, quotations on 24 and passim. My quotations are from Metastasio, *Poesie* (Turin: Stamperia reale, 1775), 1:vii and passim.

reason; he had, however, deplored the fact that, abandoning themselves to the pleasures of music in the overfrequent interruptions of arias, the Italians had, with one hand, destroyed that "véritable tragédie grecque" which they had reconstructed with the other.[49] But Calzabigi also redeems the aria, opera's eternal accused, and restores it to the logic of tragedy, comparing its function to that of the chorus and actually claiming that the "ingenious alteration" in having redistributed among the frequent arias the lyric poetry which in ancient tragedy was the exclusive prerogative of the chorus had "considerably advanced the perfection of tragedy." Indeed,

> the chorus, being no more than a simple spectator, as a consequence could feel only mildly moved by the passions experienced by the characters. . . . But now that these choruses have been intelligently divided by us and placed, as what we call arias, in the mouths of the actors of the tale, they not only do not delay its progress but run together with the tragedy, having become part of it, and take on the passions which pertain to the characters . . . and so offer vast space to music to display emotions and poetic images with the sweet brushstrokes of harmony, and by virtue of this and effective sounds they suggest to our very hearts the tenderness, the grandeur, the affection, fury, or delicacy of the words.[50]

Nor can there be any doubt that only the most organized structures and most noble style of dramatic poetry can permit music to display its full efficacy, mixing perfectly with the text:

> It is my belief that the power, variety, and beauty of our music depend on the majesty, energy, and brilliant imagery of the poetry of signor Metastasio. The harmony which one discovers from a mere reading of his verses quickly takes hold in the spirit of our composers and dispenses to them all the wealth of music which must command admiration and respect from the most prejudiced souls. I believe that it cannot be denied that the poetry best suited to music is the most beautiful poetry, and that the music best suited to poetry is the most beautiful music. . . . A composer would labor in vain to waken tenderness, pity, and terror when supplying music for inadequate, hard, mannered, bombastic, and insignificant words. It is not enough for the composer to portray in harmony the fear or love that the poet has made Pluto or Cupid speak. . . . If first he has not felt in his heart the different impressions of these two different sentiments, if first he has not been struck by fear or tenderness . . . the composer will not find harmony to match the subject, and feeling no agitation while he composes, because neither did the poet when he wrote, he will produce a jumble of disordered and ineffective sounds: just like an engraver, obliged

---

49. Voltaire, *Dissertation sur la tragédie ancienne et moderne* (1749), in his *Théâtre complet* (Amsterdam: Librairies associés, 1777), 4:1–28, quotation on 7.

50. Calzabigi, *Dissertazione*, in Calzabigi, *Scritti letterari e teatrali*, 31–32.

to turn the tools of his trade to a poor design, however much he labors, his copper-plate will always reveal the defects of the designer.[51]

4. "A COMPOSITION THAT MUST BE DISORDERED IF IT IS TO PLEASE"

During the eighteenth century, the idea of tragedy as a necessary term of reference and the principle—closely bound up with that idea—of music's necessary dependence on poetry remained two assumptions that theoretical literature found unavoidable: they were either accepted as the basis of argument and judgment or rejected and refuted. From this point onward, indeed, a useful distinction can be drawn between those who, unhappy with what they hear and see, generally judge opera for what it is not, and so think in terms of something that must be measured against a utopian ideal, and their counterparts, who take it for what it is, as an aspect of contemporary life, to be accepted whole-heartedly or else with a certain skeptical resignation. The latter attitude prevails among scholars, who enjoy representing themselves as obliged to tolerate the existence of a type of theater in which literature must cede to music.

Carlo Goldoni is a perfect example of this, when he recounts, in a much-quoted passage in his memoirs, having learned to his cost that a text conceived as a successful tragedy can only end up as a dreadful opera, and vice versa, for the rules of opera are "contrary . . . to those of Aristotle, Horace, and all those who have written poetry, but necessary to serve the music, the actors, and the composers," so that "what would seem a defect in a well-written tragedy becomes a thing of beauty in an opera." These were the rules to which even illustrious poets such as Apostolo Zeno and Metastasio had had to conform, and which his occasional mentor—a Milanese aristocrat, "a connoisseur of the theater, and a lover of music and theatrical poetry," who had taken the duty of consoling him for his bitter disillusionment after a first attempt at being a librettist of opera seria (*Amalasunta* in Milan in 1733)—summarized thus:

> The primo soprano, prima donna, and the tenore, the three principal actors in the drama, must sing five arias each, one *pathetic,* one *bravura,* one *parlante,* one *mezzo carattere,* and one *brillante.* The secondo uomo and seconda donna have to have four each, and the last performer three, with the same number for a *seventh* character, if the opera requires one; since (incidentally) there must be no more than six or seven characters, and your libretto has nine. . . . The leading characters' fifteen arias must be distributed in such a way that there are not two consecutive arias in the *same mood,* and the other characters' arias serve to create an effect of chiaroscuro. You let a character sing and then remain onstage, which is against the *rules.* When

51. Ibid., 136–37.

two principal characters meet you make one of them leave the stage without an
aria, after a *scena di forza,* and this again is against the *rules.* In your libretto you
have only three *scene changes,* and six or seven are required. The third act of your
libretto is the best part of the opera, but this is again against the *rules.*[52]

This exclusively practical poetics in miniature, which Goldoni claims to
have learned on the field of battle, in the form of simple instructions, could
nevertheless boast of an illustrious theoretical precedent in the precepts which
Pier Jacopo Martello had put in the mouth of the pseudo-Aristotle, his imaginary interlocutor in the dialogue *Della tragedia antica e moderna.* Published
in 1714, when scholarly minds seemed completely closed to opera, this treatise must surely win the admiration of the modern reader for the clear and, let
it be said, courageous originality with which those principles are accepted,
understood, and explained.[53] As for Goldoni's aristocratic amateur, so too for
Martello's imagined philosopher, the primary condition for the success of a
drama (in fact, what he calls a *melodramma,* for it was he who legitimized the
literary use of what was still a barely tolerated neologism) is that its author
should be clear in his mind that this particular literary genre (for such it remained for Martello, too, who is addressing his lessons to poets) has nothing
in common with tragedy. Indeed, the poet must take every care to avoid
choices which might confuse one genre with another, beginning with the number of acts into which the work is to be divided (three rather than five) and
ending with the poetic style, which must be "moderate and lovely" rather than
"serious and magnificent." [54] The distinction with tragedy actually means that
the hierarchical relationship between music and poetry, as it was generally
understood, is reversed: the poetry has to depend on the music, and the poet
has to adapt his own ideas to those of the composer. Martello is not afraid to
draw the boldest conclusion from this proposition: that in opera it is the poetry which takes its sense from the music, and not vice versa. This is, indeed,
in the final analysis, the meaning of the declaration that the "musical composition" is "the essence of opera" and the poetry is only one of many acces-
sories, an accident, just as light, depending on the consistency and form of
the object on which it falls, "is variously reflected, so does it take on various
colors." [55]

52. Carlo Goldoni: preface to vol. 11 of the Pasquali edition of Goldoni's plays (1773), in
Complete Works, ed. Giuseppe Ortolani, 5th ed. (Milan: Mondadori, 1973), 1:687–89. The
events are also recounted, with few variations, in Goldoni's *Mémoires* (1787), in *Complete Works,*
1:127–29.
53. Pier Jacopo Martello, *Della tragedia antica e moderna. Dialogo* (1714; 2d, rev. ed., 1715),
in his *Scritti critici e satirici,* ed. Hannibal S. Noce (Bari: Laterza, 1963), 187–316. An extract appears in English in Fubini, *Music and Culture,* 48–60.
54. Martello, *Della tragedia,* 289; Fubini, *Music and Culture,* 56.
55. Martello, *Della tragedia,* 294; Fubini, *Music and Culture,* 58.

Martello's complete opposition to the exclusively literary ideas that characterize the rest of eighteenth-century writing on opera is unique. To convince ourselves of this, we need only remember that the parallel with the relationship of color and form would later be one of the favorite arguments against the poisonous vices, deviations, and misuses of which opera would continue to be accused; but for this reason the terms of the relationship would be inverted, and the role of poetry assimilated to the classically dominant one of line, shape, and form: "I have striven to restrict music to its true office of serving poetry . . . and I believed that I should do this in the same way as telling colors affect a correct and well-ordered drawing, by a well-assorted contrast of light and shade, which serves to animate the figures without altering their contours." This is one of the most famous passages in the celebrated preface to Gluck's *Alceste,* which repeats almost word for word a concept expressed before by Francesco Algarotti in his *Saggio sopra l'opera in musica.*[56]

However, to give music back its primary role does not mean seeing it as the single, true raison d'être of opera, of whose composite nature Martello is always well aware, together with its being first and foremost a spectacle which—as such—finds its ultimate justification in the effect it manages to make on an audience. This is the reason for the enormous attention he pays to the here and now and to incidental elements of realization: taste, orientation, the mood of the audience, the type of theater, the form of the scenic apparatus, the quality of the voices available. One of these incidental elements of course is the music itself. It is not so much the "musical composition" itself that matters (not, that is, the music as conceived and set down on paper by the composer) as its physical resonance in the mouth of the interpreter. Or rather, the "composer's intention," which the poet has to serve, goes hand in hand with presenting the "virtues" with which the singers are uniquely endowed. The poet's job is above all to create a web of situations that can allow each of those virtues to be displayed to the best effect: this is his criterion in "cutting the cloth of the acts into scenes," or rather in establishing the greater or lesser importance of the singers as they take turns onstage (and so naturally in planning how the action unfolds).[57] This reversed perspective reveals the deep structural basis to Italian opera that had, it will be remembered, already emerged

56. Christoph Willibald Gluck, preface to *Alceste* (Vienna: Trattner, 1769). See a facsimile reproduced in *The New Grove Dictionary of Music and Musicians,* 6th ed., ed. Stanley Sadie (London: Macmillan, 1980), 7:466. Quoted ibid., 467. See also Francesco Algarotti, *Saggio sopra l'opera in musica* (1755; new ed. with additions, 1763), in his *Saggi,* ed. Giovanni Da Pozzo (Bari: Laterza, 1963), 145–92, quotation on 152. Translated anonymously into English as *An Essay on the Opera written in Italian by Count Algarotti* (London: printed for L. Davis and C. Reymers, 1767). Extracts appear in Strunk, *Source Readings,* 909–22, and Fubini, *Music and Culture,* 233–40.

57. See Martello, *Della tragedia,* 281–85; Fubini, *Music and Culture,* 52ff.

in Italian opera's original manifestation and that would be reconfirmed every time opera was later discussed in terms of "actual reality," as Machiavelli would say, rather than in moralizing sermons or pure theoretical projection. We have seen the lesson which the Milanese amateur taught Goldoni (but before him the same message had, not surprisingly, been conveyed by the composers to whom Goldoni had attempted to read his failed libretto); but even in the early nineteenth century, after a flood of literature on operatic reform, the situation was little changed, as is revealed in the most eloquent manner by the "rules" which Carlo Porta, in his unaccustomed guise of theatrical organizer, conveyed to his friend Vincenzo Lancetti on behalf of the management of La Scala when sending him a commission to write an opera libretto.[58]

It was undoubtedly a stroke of genius on Martello's part to have thought up an "impostor" to whom to assign the defense of modern culture and, by extension, opera in his *Dialogo*. The figure of the impostor-lawmaker is one of the cornerstones around which free thought revolves; and what else but an impostor-lawmaker is the pseudo-Aristotle, who sets down his laws "for a kind of composition, which, in order to please, should be entirely without rules"?[59] Amid the furious moralistic rigor of the early years of the Arcadian Academy, a spark of freethinking irreverence was needed to understand that the vices and misuses whose repression was called for were in fact the very substance of opera; to be more precise, they were the immanent prior conditions which alone could guarantee opera its unique goal: to take humanity to that state of material and moral "beatitude" not found anywhere else, a state which philosophy and poetry could not provide; only the seductive power of music could bring an ecstatic suspension of reality, after which a listener could return, with renewed vigor, to his civic duties.[60] Opera was therefore "useful to the republic" no less than tragedy and comedy. It was useful despite or rather precisely because of its dodging of the rules, its indifference to the laws of decorum and realism—almost, it would be added, a necessary and beneficial fraud. In the transgressive seventeenth century there was no lack of sharp-eyed observers who had seen in the invention of opera a fruit of the Venetian art of good government. In a completely changed climate, Martello, however orthodox, seems with genial ambiguity to want to remind his Arcadian colleagues that only by permitting an outlet for the human spirit's irrepressible

---

58. See Dante Isella, ed., *Le lettere di Carlo Porta e degli amici della cameretta* (Milan and Naples: Ricciardi, 1967), 214–21. The rules established by the composer Carlo Soliva can be read in Fabrizio Della Seta, "The Librettist," in *History of Italian Opera*, vol. 4, *Opera Production and Its Resources*, ed. Lorenzo Bianconi and Giorgio Pestelli (Chicago: University of Chicago Press, 1998), 263.

59. Martello, *Della tragedia*, 281; Fubini, *Music and Culture*, 52.

60. See Martello, *Della tragedia*, 275, 295ff.; Fubini, *Music and Culture*, 48, 59.

drive toward the unreal, irrational, and fantastical—in a word, toward an infringement of the rules—is it possible to maintain the delicate social mechanism of the "well-ordered city" in balance.

5. "RENVOYER CETTE FORME DE CHANT À LA MUSIQUE DE CONCERT?"

One of the reproaches that Goldoni had to endure in connection with his luckless *Amalasunta* was that he had misjudged his audience: his drama would have gone well if he had directed it to the French public, who were accustomed to find in opera the sense, continuity, and coherence which the notorious "rules" of opera banned from Italian opera. It is true that this detail is found only his *Mémoires,* and we can reasonably assume that Goldoni inserted it in homage to the culture of the nation of which he was by then almost a naturalized citizen. Whether true or invented, however, the episode touches on a commonplace of the period when the events took place (1733) that in the second half of the century would become even more popular: the comparison between Italian and French opera.

It has already been pointed out how the entire question of opera had its impetus in the context of arguments over one or other culture's superiority which had flared up at the end of the seventeenth and beginning of the eighteenth centuries (and it is significant, for example, that Martello's *Dialogo* is supposed to take place partly during a journey from Italy to France and partly on French soil, where the "session" dedicated to opera was, in fact, held): it was logical, therefore, that such a comparison would become a dominant idea. However, it was more a product of French culture than of Italian, and the explanation for this might simply be that French opera—unexportable because of its highly individual characteristics, in both its musical-dramatic makeup and its system of production—remained a phenomenon entirely outside the experience of the Italian scholar, who thus had no opportunity to make a comparison. (A more malicious interpretation is possible, however: that such indifference might be due to the fact that, by Italian standards, French opera seemed inherently starved of music, and this might suggest to us an ambivalent attitude on the part of our scholars, who castigated and condemned the exuberance of music in Italian opera precisely because they were irresistibly attracted to it, without, however, being able to control their fascination rationally. Another famous passage in Goldoni's memoirs seems to confirm this: the passage where the playwright tells of his surprise when, having recently arrived in the French capital and gone to the opera, he had vented his disappointment to his neighbor at not having heard a single aria for the whole length of an act, only to be told that the act had contained six arias.) [61]

61. Goldoni, *Complete Works,* 1:460.

The comparison was stimulated from the other direction first by the curiosity of travelers and then by the polemics within French culture, where Italian opera was taken up like a cudgel to beat the opposition, and its musical luxuriance and vocal enchantment from time to time praised at the expense of the rigid, ceremonial pomp or else denigrated in favor of the restraint, sobriety, and sense of French opera. In any case, whatever partisan positions were taken up, curiosity and polemical zeal often led French observers—although the same can be said of foreigners in general—to reach a more vivid perception of the specifically dramatic and musical reasoning behind Italian opera, which Italian scholars were much less able or willing to hear, concentrating, as they did, almost exclusively on the question of the literary dignity of the opera.

At the beginning of the century François Raguenet had set the comparison in terms which would remain fundamentally unchanged for the best part of the century (the tendency to repetition is a commonplace of this as in other strains of the literature on opera).[62] Apart from his observations on the most evident differences in theatrical custom (the audience's intermittent attention and generally noisy behavior), performance habits and auditory sensitivity (the greater volume and brighter, more brilliant sound of the instruments, the different relationship between them and the voices when accompanying, the predominance of high voices and the related grotesque yet fascinating phenomenon of castratos), he stops to look at more substantial dramatic and musical questions, which can be summarized in the final analysis as the age-old but eternally fresh question of the mutual compatibility of music and dramatic action and, thus, the problem of verisimilitude.

It was generally thought that French opera took the honors in this respect for its greater balance of music and poetry and for all that generally concerned the dramatic scheme, organized to accommodate the opposing and complementary needs of visual variety and the coherent and unified progress of the action. However, he recognized the incontestable musical superiority of Italian opera and looked forward to the union of tastes which François Couperin had already achieved in instrumental music being applied to opera as well. This was an inherently contradictory hope, however, as is clear from the project, drafted—it is said—by Josse de Villeneuve (or more probably by Count Giacomo Durazzo), to graft Italian music on to a text conceived according to the criteria of French opera;[63] for "music" in eighteenth-century

62. François Raguenet, *Parallèle des italiens et des français en ce qui regarde la musique et les opéras* (Paris: Moreau, 1702); translated by Johann Ernst Galliard as *A Comparison between the French and Italian Musick and Operas; Translated from the French with Some Remarks, to Which Is Added a Critical Discourse upon Operas in England and a Means Proposed for Their Improvement,* reprint ed., with introduction by Charles Cudworth (Farnborough: Gregg, 1968).

63. The *Lettre sur le méchanisme de l'opéra italien* (Naples [actually Paris]: Duchesne et Lambert, 1756), traditionally attributed to Villeneuve, has been reattributed to Durazzo, the probable

Italian opera was synonymous with "aria"—the tripartite da capo form which Villeneuve (or Durazzo) still praised for its structural balance and presented to French composers as a model to be followed to amend the monotony of their melodic invention, at precisely the same time as Francesco Algarotti was heralding its decline, condemning it as "contrary to the natural flow of discourse and passion,"[64] and the aria was unquestionably incompatible with that conception of drama.

When Villeneuve's (or Durazzo's) *Lettre* appeared in Paris, echoes could still be heard of the *querelle des bouffons,* which between 1752 and 1754 had turned the age-old controversy up to full volume. The desired compromise between French drama and Italian music was to refute the idea of French's music's "nonexistence," implacably and rigorously defended in the most scandalous pamphlet in that paper battle, Jean-Jacques Rousseau's *Lettre sur la musique française.*[65] But on close inspection, that provocative and paradoxical text might be based on the logically more tacit assumption of that incompatibility in fact than in the lucidly outlined but abstract theory of the French language's congenital unmusicality (a theory, as everyone knows, disproved in practice by Rousseau the composer himself).

In this context, too, the aria was the most thorny problem area, a tangle of glaring contradictions. Its generous dimensions, its location at the end of a scene (with the obligatory exit of the character singing it), and its effect of time being suspended pointed the way toward the charge that it was the main obstacle to the development of the plot; whatever its inherently musical merits, it remained virtually unconnected to the dramatic context (as seemed to be confirmed by the widespread practice of putting together pasticcios or— looking at it the opposite way—the proudly proclaimed example of Metastasio's librettos being, if performed without the arias, "true tragedies"). One of Rousseau's many anonymous opponents argued that while Italian music in itself was of the best quality, it sank to the worst when considered in relation to its theatrical function, because it was "presque toujours destructive des pensées et des sentiments raisonnables auxquels elle est unie" (nearly always destructive of the very fabric of the drama). This opponent countered the proclaimed inexistence of French *music* with the inexistence, by fault of the music, of Italian *opera,* which appeared to the writer to be nothing more than a

---

author, by Gabriella Gentili Verona, "Le collezioni Foà e Giordano della Biblioteca Nazionale di Torino," *Accademie e biblioteche d'Italia* 32 (1964): 405–30, see esp. 420–22.

64. Algarotti, *Saggio,* 163.

65. Jean-Jacques Rousseau, *Lettre sur la musique française* (1753), in *La querelle des bouffons,* 1:669–764. Reproduced in Jean-Jacques Rousseau, *Oeuvres complètes,* vol. 5, *Ecrits sur la musique, la langue et le théâtre,* édition publiée sous la direction de Bernard Gagnebin et Marcel Raymond (Paris: Gallimard, Bibliothèque de la Pléiade, 1994), 287–328. An abridged English translation can be found in Strunk, *Source Readings.*

pretext for creating a varied sequence of scenes crowned by the inevitable aria.[66] The question suddenly arose as to whether the concert hall was not a more suitable home for the aria than the theater, or whether opera should be judged, in substance, actually as a concert of arias (in fact, it was Rousseau himself who pointed out that opera was in danger of becoming "un véritable concert,"[67] when its music wished to claim autonomy with respect to the poetic text).

In the perspective of these polemics there is thus the notion of the so-called opera-concert, which subsequent musical historiography—growing up in the shadow of Wagnerian dramaturgy—developed in an attempt to mask opera's incurable dilemma: here was a phenomenon whose historical legitimacy was recognized thanks to the consistency of its musical qualities but at the same time denied for the inconsistency of its dramatic core. It seemed to have escaped attention that by imposing a concept of "drama" that was completely alien to it, and so disregarding its organic nature, it was not possible to make a proper evaluation of those "absolute" musical values that were to be vindicated. It is no coincidence that Rousseau's points emerge with particular clarity during the second phase of the *querelle des bouffons*—the *querelle* between the supporters of Gluck and those of Piccinni: "La question," wrote Jean-François Marmontel, "se réduit donc aujourd'hui à savoir s'il faut renvoyer cette forme de chant [meaning the aria] à la musique de concert, et l'exclure de la scène lyrique, comme les partisans de M. Gluck nous le conseillent, ou si, à l'exemple des Italiens, nous devons l'admettre sur le théâtre."[68] Obviously, this was a rhetorical question, given the position taken by Marmontel. Invoking the authority of all those, ancient and modern, who had written on the relationship between words and music onstage, his antagonist Abbé Leblond replied that Italian music had to be content to "présider aux concerts" and "régler les pas d'un ballet sans jamais se mêler des affaires de cothurne."[69] The question, however, was not a new one, and was being considered by Italian scholars. Abbé Gianmaria Ortes, for example, had already touched upon it, when he had accused the music of "modern opera seria" of being "artificial" and as such appropriate not for the theater but for "academies and ante-

66. See *Réflexions d'un patriote sur l'opéra françois et sur l'opéra italien, qui présentent le parallèle du goût des deux nations dans les beaux arts* (1754), in *La querelle des bouffons*, 3:2025–2174, quotations on 2077 and passim.

67. Rousseau, the entry "Opéra" in his *Dictionnaire de musique*; see *Oeuvres complètes*, 948–52, quotation on 955.

68. Jean-François Marmontel, *Essai sur les révolutions de la musique en France* (1777), in Gaspard-Michel Leblond, *Mémoires pour servir à l'histoire de la révolution opérée dans la musique par M. le chevalier Gluck* (Paris: Bailly, 1781), reprinted in François Lesure, ed., *Querelle des Gluckistes et des Piccinnistes: Textes des pamphlets* (Geneva: Minkoff, 1984), 1:153–93, quotation on 170.

69. Ibid.

chamers, where spirits are to be cheered," and he had in any case declared himself convinced that outside Italy such operas could please only in the guise "of a display of mime or of a concert of music mixed with dance and acting." [70]

However, a comment had already been provided by way of clarification on this point by the "dilettante" Charles de Brosses, a disinterested observer of great acuity of the situation in Italian opera in the period leading up to the 1740s. He, too, poses the question in the context of a comparison between French and Italian opera, and it has to be said that his position is far from being free of obvious contradictions, similar to those already seen in Villeneuve's comments: the difference is that, in their very clarity, such contradictions ultimately produce far fewer ambiguities than the rigid one-sided statements by partisan pamphleteers or the concealed ambiguity which we have seen emerging in the attitude of so many of our own scholars. At first de Brosses seems to harbor no doubts: better "the fable, the enchantment, the magic" on which the stories of French opera are based than the historical plots of Italian opera. In the former the problem of realism is solved at the outset, because the very subject matter lacks realism, while in the latter singing—a few moments of intense emotion aside—makes it unnatural and ridiculous. And while the endless divertissements of French opera break the listener's attention and cool the emotions, in Italian opera the arias "sewn into the end of every scene" without the necessary connection to the subject (so that they could be "cut from the opera without harming the sense") produce the same distracting effect: so one may as well choose French variety rather than Italian uniformity. [71]

Yet these opinions do not prevent him from making the partisan claim that the theater is the aria's natural habitat and from considering the aria "unsuited to chamber concerts," because "the value of these pieces extracted from the body of a tragedy lies in their expressive accuracy, which can only be understood within the flow of what has happened up to that point and in relation to the actor's actual situation." [72] It is true that in this passage de Brosses is referring specifically to the third of the categories into which, in the course of his letter, he classifies arias according to character: those "impassioned, tender, moving, true in expression, whether strong or pathetic in sentiment," [73] which in theatrical jargon were defined as *parlanti* (speaking) as opposed to *cantabili* (singing) because the emphasis was not on the singing

70. Gianmaria Ortes, *Riflessioni sopra i drammi per musica* (1757), in his *Calcolo sopra la verità dell'istoria e altri scritti*, ed. Bartolo Anglani (Genoa: Costa and Nolan, 1984), 149–64, quotations on 160 and 154.

71. See Charles de Brosses, *Lettres familières écrites d'Italie en 1739 et 1740* (Paris: Didier, 1856), 522–24.

72. Ibid., 512ff.

73. Ibid., 524.

but on the impassioned expression of given sentiments (and therefore with a closer connection between the melodic line and the poetic text). These arias, de Brosses continues, were thus particularly "suited to dramatic action and emphasizing the actor's performance." [74] But it is equally true that arias in the first category, too—those "full of noise, of music and harmony"—were rehabilitated as having a representational logic, no matter that a good many of them fall within the notorious category of "simile arias," those which were most accused of being arbitrary and unreal, which could, strictly speaking, be said to have been "sewn into the end of the scene" and which could be cut out of an opera without any harm to the continuity of the action. Indeed, de Brosses implicitly (or perhaps unconsciously) counters the abstract principle of verisimilitude with the much more concrete factor of truthful expression, certainly something inherent in the emotive power of music, but which would also be activated during the here and now of the performance onstage, where truth and a powerful sense of involvement actually seem to be heightened by the presumed unreality of the situation: "music is so beautiful, so extraordinary, it portrays objects with such artistry and truth, that it is willingly forgiven even the greatest defects, such as asking a character to remain onstage to sing an aria of immense length at the very moment when danger should force him to flee." [75]

6. "They are not arias, they are magic spells"

De Brosses has another thing clearly in mind when he carries on with his classification of arias: that the distinct characters of each of the three categories correspond to the qualities—not only vocal—of the singers for whom they are intended. Noisy arias, "full of . . . music and harmony," are suited to ringing voices; delicate, pleasant ones to gentle, flexible voices; and lastly, impassioned arias allow the performer to bring all the resources of his stagecraft into play. The problem of the aria necessarily brings in that of the singer; but in the vast majority of eighteenth-century literature the statement of this simple fact is converted into an implacable, obsessive, and incessant indictment. The singer—together with his or her greed and vanity, whims, and abuses—stands charged with the greatest responsibility for the distortion, malfunction, and offense to dramatic logic in the misuse of the aria. The centrality of the singer's role is pointed out as the clearest and most shocking proof of things being the wrong way round—"prima la musica e poi le parole" as Giovanni Battista Casti's famous satire has it—and this continues to be denounced as the ultimate origin of all opera's ills.

Everyone remembers the sarcastic instructions given by Benedetto Marcello in his *Il teatro alla moda:* to the composer, to observe duly respectful be-

74. Ibid.
75. Ibid.

havior in the company of the "virtuoso," to stand by holding his hat, humbly give him precedence, and walk one step behind him and, in the work, to pay proper homage to the prima donna's role in number and quality of arias but at the same time to appease surreptitiously the seconda donna's impatience and eagerness to compete with the prima donna; to the singer, on the contrary, to deal condescendingly not only with the composer but also with the writer (as befits the difference in rank between one who, in popular opinion, is considered a "virtuoso" and one who is "an ordinary man"), to take all liberties he pleases onstage (mangle and change the words, alter every note in the da capo, add trills, ornaments, and cadenzas where he sees fit), and then, when it is not his turn to perform, to show the greatest contempt for the action, so that it will be clear to all that "he is the singer Signor Alipio Forconi and not the Prince Zoroastro he is representing." [76]

It is not by chance that to illustrate this chapter on operatic polemics two examples have been drawn from satirical literature, because it was this that contributed most to the formation of certain stereotypes. It is no surprise that such a multifaceted, compound, abnormal, and eccentric phenomenon as musical theater should be the favored butt of satire, nor that, within the phenomenon itself, the easiest target should have been the most apparent element, the singer. However, not enough attention was paid to the fact that, at least in this case, satire is not—or is not only—censure and condemnation of a chronic state of decadence but in fact insistent and innate evidence of irrepressible vitality, which indeed draws its nourishment from that disordered, seething mass of nonsense and oddity, contradictions and transgressions, like a balancing act between illusion and reality: so much so that a theater that was hygienically cleansed of all this would be not decadent but actually dead. Indeed, the strain of satire on opera is something that is part and parcel of opera itself; it belongs to the species of the play within a play: self-mockery, an amused display of its own defects, but at the same time an awareness of not so much those individual defects as the condition of the "defect" itself (which includes opera's instability, uncertainty, impermanence, its readiness to compromise according to changing, day-to-day conditions, as well as the malicious dialectic of "virtues" and "vices") are the nature of the theater— and that theater in particular—and constituent elements of its fascination.

In one way, Marcello's pamphlet might also be considered a play within a play: think of the short, vivid scenes contained in it, and the wit and realism of the jokes put into the mouths of the characters who feature in it. Once elevated to the position of the founding father of this strain of satire, however, he contributed much to setting the course of the distorted and incomplete type

---

76. Benedetto Marcello, *Il teatro alla moda* (Venice, 1720; reprint, Milan: Bottega di poesia, 1927), 53 and passim. A complete English translation by Reinhard G. Pauly appears in *Musical Quarterly* 34 1948): 371–403, and 35 (1949): 85–105.

of reception which has been discussed. It is very revealing to reread Francesco D'Arcais's review of it at the time of the new edition brought out by Ricordi in 1883. For this nineteenth-century critic, *Il teatro alla moda* was not merely "a lively, satirical portrait" of opera in the previous century but no less than a "valuable document for the history of Italian opera because it faithfully reflects the theatrical art of Marcello's day." So Marcello, the sharp-tongued critic of theatrical custom of his day, is, we take it, no different from the composer of the *Salmi,* which is "the undying monument of inspiration, musical doctrine, and religious feeling" and as such therefore "undoubtedly the most pure and splendid of the glories of Italian music after Pier Luigi da Palestrina." Why should one not take at face value a lesson handed down from such heights? And how could its author—a contemporary of Zeno and of Vivaldi—fail to be seen in the role of solitary and, for the time, unheeded prophet of "music drama," whose advent, between Meyerbeer, Verdi, and Wagner, was being preached at the time (naturally, to the accompaniment of passionate polemics)? To be honest, it did not escape D'Arcais's notice that, for all the change in time and conditions, "the theater has not altered so much, and humankind in particular has not changed so much, that opera's strange habits and risible foibles are not still to be found in different guise," that, in short, apart from music drama, the "defects" of opera are still alive and thriving (and chief among these is "the conceit of artists"). It was only that he—like the majority of operatic historians and critics before and after—was unable to pause and consider that, for all those inextricable defects, opera had continued to exist and thrive for a century and a half. The conclusion he draws instead is, once again, the need for a reform to finish off something that has been proceeding by fits and starts.[77]

The complement to the mirage of the future reform of opera was the legend of an unaffected past of simplicity and truth of expression, in styles both of musical composition and of singing: it is clear that both that future and that past are metahistoric categories, standing in for qualitative judgments. The idea of the past, in particular, is merely a projection of the "ancient/modern" dichotomy and of the unique inversion found in our scholars' interpretation of the two terms, at least as far as their judgments on opera are concerned: those who are currently modern, the reformers, identify the "ancient" with a simple, smooth singing style, concerned only with discreetly coloring the emotion contained in the words, and "modern" with bel canto dishonesty, something which corrupts the sense of the poetry and is itself lacking in any musical sense.

This is how an Enlightenment figure like Algarotti, possibly unaware of the prodigious feats of male and female virtuosos that fill seventeenth-

---

77. Francesco D'Arcais, "Rassegna musicale," *Nuova antologia* 18, vol. 71 (1883): 337–45, quotations on 338 and passim.

century chronicles, and certainly oblivious of the accusations made against seventeenth-century opera by the founding fathers of the Arcadian Academy, finds himself denouncing a paradoxical exchange of roles, as far as the relationship between poetry and music is concerned, between the seventeenth and eighteenth centuries: the latter seems to him a century of "extravagant composers" who have corrupted poetry from the "right path" of nature and truth; and the former, a century when music "was far from exhibiting the affectations and long-windedness of today . . . it was, in a word, tender and simple at a time when poetry, far from being true, was hyperbolic, full of conceits, and fantastic."[78] And it also happened—even more significantly—that one and the same person at one time filled the role of open-minded innovator (and virtual corrupter of taste) while at another played the part of champion of a lost simplicity and purity of style. Vincenzio Martinelli, the lively exponent of the group of "London Italians," in listing the names of those singers who, over the century, progressively strayed from the "pillars of Hercules . . . of correct and moderated singing," ascribed the greatest responsibility for that "musical revolution" to Farinelli and, while recognizing him as a "miracle of nature and art," does not hesitate to add that his appearance "cost the republic of music dearly, because since then every singer, composer, and instrumentalist has wanted to 'farinellate' to the point that naturalness and all other propriety is now practically extinct."[79] But some decades later, Matteo Borsa, in the course of his polemic against opera seria, gives a lurid picture of the virtuoso in the grip of bel canto fervor ("he stops, mouth open, with his hand motionless on his breast for three or four bars while he sings a single note almost until he has lost his breath and then, the orchestra having dutifully fallen silent, entertains himself with a trill followed by a crazed vocal passage without design, known as a 'cadenza,' then hardly has he come back to his senses and uttered a few words on his situation than he stumbles fatally into an A or an O which sends his epiglottis into a convulsion") and concludes his tirade by contrasting this with a nostalgic invocation of Farinelli ("Ah, certainly Leo and Pergolesi never wrote like this, and neither did Farinelli ever sing thus").[80]

It is really not hard to find our scholars, on this subject as well, blatantly contradicting themselves. Martinelli himself, who deplores the tyranny that

---

78. Algarotti, *Saggio*, 164ff.

79. Vincenzio Martinelli, *Al sig. conte di Buckinghamshire: Sulla origine delle opere in musica*, in his *Lettere familiari e critiche* (London: Nourse, 1758), 353–63, quotations on 361ff. The letter can also be read in Sergio Durante, "Alcune considerazioni sui cantanti di teatro del primo Settecento e la loro formazione," in *Antonio Vivaldi: Teatro musicale, cultura e società*, 2 vols., ed. Lorenzo Bianconi and Giovanni Morelli (Florence: Olschki, 1982), 2:427–81, quotations on 462–65.

80. Matteo Borsa, *Saggio filosofico sopra la musica imitativa teatrale*, in *Opuscoli scelti sulle scienze e sulle arti* (Milan: Marelli, 1781), 195–234, quotation on 212ff., then in his *Opere* (Verona: Giuliani, 1800), 1:3–82.

singers exercise over composers, "obliged to adapt to that singular natural
beauty of the voice," implies that he, too, considers the main attraction of an
operatic performance to be the singer. Here he is, using the following little
panegyric to the soprano Regina Mingotti as the magnet to entice an aristocratic lady away from her country leisure up to London to hear the latest opera:

> Last night I went to the opera, and they are giving *Siroe* at present. Signora Min-
> gotti changed her skirt for a tunic, and in that masculine costume she conquered
> the air and breeze for grace and delicacy. . . . I find that there are two persons in
> her: the perfect imitation of a man, with the addition of all the grace that Signora
> Mingotti possesses as a woman. . . . And then, the arias which this new muse sings
> in this opera are not arias, they are magic spells, draughts to make one forget one's
> ills completely from the first bar. May Your Ladyship leave her embroidery frame
> and her beloved paints as soon as she can, and . . . come to hear this lovely opera,
> certain that Jove never had such elegant entertainment on Olympus.[81]

This is an indirect but eloquent piece of evidence of the singer's essentially creative role, in whom the spellbinding power of music takes human form and
is, so to speak, identified. It is clear that those arias, so enthusiastically evoked,
are "draughts" and "magic spells" to the extent that they are distilled and
cast by that voice, by that person. But there is even more convincing evidence,
also indirect, from someone just as austere as Martinelli, Saverio Mattei, who
would have liked audiences to go to the theater "with the same prayerful modesty as one goes to a sacred rite." [82]

    In singing the praises of Niccolò Jommelli (to whom he attributes, among
other things, credit for having placed firm limits on singers' free rein), Mattei
does not neglect to inveigh against a musical taste that is "utterly corrupt, principally because of the singers," [83] and to list the "abuses" as a result of which
Jommelli, on his return from Germany, had found Italian opera on its knees
("Continual dissipation, irritating chatter, a liking for flabby, enervated music, an aversion to everything that requires effort, the freedom to sing at pleasure, an ill-judged and ill-timed display of skill").[84] But in the middle of this
dissolution, an extraordinary opera like *Armida abbandonata* of 1770 could
still appear. Mattei describes the circumstances that gave rise to its creation:

---

    81. Vincenzio Martinelli, *A Milady Newdigate a Arbury: Invitandola a venire a Londra per
veder l'opera del Siroe,* in his *Lettere familiari,* 135ff. The opera was *Siroe, re di Persia,* music by
Lampugnani, given in London in 1755 and 1756, with Mingotti in the part of Emira, the heroine
(disguised as a man).

    82. Saverio Mattei, *Elogio del Jommelli o sia Il progresso della poesia e musica teatrale,* in his
Memorie per servire alla vita del Metastasio (Colle: Martini, 1785; reprint, Bologna: Forni, 1987),
59–136, quotation on 69.

    83. Ibid., 110.

    84. Ibid., 90ff.

Happier than I [that is, in establishing a collaboration with Jommelli] was a pupil of mine, Francesco Saverio de' Rogati. . . . I suggested him to Jommelli, so that at his pleasure he could write with him a new opera for the Royal Theater of San Carlo, choosing the characters that would best suit Signora De Amicis and Signor Aprile, who fortunately had then been chosen for that company. While there was nothing that these two great singers were not capable of expressing . . . nevertheless the young poet . . . fitted the part of Rinaldo so well to the man's abilities, and that of Armida to the woman's, that neither could fail to be pleased. . . .

Jommelli was rather reluctant to conform to the general requirements of the court, the impresarios, and the entire audience. . . . He thought only of the abilities of the two singers and wrote that matchless music which surprised and moved all and attracted the imitation of both the ignorant and the learned.[85]

The relationship of mutual collaboration and understanding between the virtuoso singer and the composer ("who leaves up to the intelligence of the singer," as Rousseau himself puts it, "those implied notes" which in Italian melody "are no less essential to the melody as the written ones")[86] could be grasped with greater clarity by minds which lacked the professional, as it were, humanistic prejudice that music was exclusively the "minister" (or "servant," as Metastasio scornfully suggested)[87] of the poetry. I have already referred to the clear insight of de Brosses. Even more explicit is John Brown—a Scottish painter long resident in Italy, so once again a "lay" observer—when he exposes the circular relationship between the art of the singer, the compositional style, and the expressive intention where scholars were determined to see a hierarchy turned on its head, one that had to be returned to its proper order.[88] In what he writes we have confirmation of how, still in the late eighteenth century, an opera's identity was perceived as the sum of the arias of which it consisted. His description of Italian opera is therefore a description of the various possible types of aria ("cantabile," "di portamento," "di mezzo carattere," "parlante," "di bravura," and "airs of imitation," etc.), and the distinction between these—as he himself recognizes—if based on empirical and heterogeneous criteria, since they are intended to emphasize now one aspect of current compositional and performance practice and now another, is tangible and real in that each refers to various human affections, all of which can find appropriate expression in one or other of those types.[89] But here again the description of the arias is first and foremost a description of the

---

85. Ibid., 89–91.

86. Jean-Jacques Rousseau, *Lettre sur la musique française,* in *Oeuvres complètes,* 300.

87. Letter of 15 July 1765 to François-Jean de Chastellux, in Pietro Metastasio, *Tutte le opere,* ed. Bruno Brunelli, 5 vols. (Milan: Mondadori, 1943–54), 4:397–99, quotation on 399.

88. John Brown, *Letters upon the Poetry and Music of the Italian Opera* (before 1787) (Edinburgh and London: Bell and Bradfute, Elliot and Kay, 1789).

89. See ibid., 36–42, 113ff.

qualities of the singer who is to interpret them. And this is not, it should be pointed out, because singers exhibit defining features that bring out the specific character of each type of aria; on the contrary, it is the aria—understood as the composer's creation—that must be conceived in such a way as to let the specific qualities of the singer shine.

So musical composition and the art of singing are each other's reciprocal means and end. This is most apparent in the description of the cantabile aria, "emphatically so called, as being the highest species of Song." Its melody must be made up of fairly long notes, and it must proceed with the utmost simplicity, to allow the singer the fullest opportunity to demonstrate his or her skill and bring out the qualities he or she ought to have: a lovely voice, so that the ear can be charmed by those long-held notes; great sensitivity, so that the sentiment is expressed in such a way as to move the listener; taste and imagination, to give the melody elaborate ornamentation; judgment, so as not to let the imagination exceed proper limits; perfect grasp of counterpoint, so that the improvisation matches the harmonic movement of the other parts.[90]

What this shows is that the conduct which customarily attracted the most scornful condemnation of the singer was precisely that in which the singer's art was called upon to provide the principal determining feature. Far from the cliché that reduced the cantabile aria to "little else than a string of flourishes, originating almost entirely in the caprice of the performer,"[91] Brown vindicates the essential function of ornamentation and variation, both of which give the melody the touch of elegance which is indispensable for sweetening its pathetic intensity and arousing the pleasure of being moved, which is the very substance of artistic enjoyment.

7. "A UNIFIED, COMPLETE, AND MUSICAL WHOLE"

During the nineteenth century Benedetto Marcello was elevated to the status of champion and defender of the "purity" of Italian music; this was a century that had made "purity in music" one of its favorite cults. But it could be claimed that the process had already got under way in the middle of the eighteenth century, with the first steps on an imaginary path later to link— according to a certain type of learned reception, if not actually in musical historiography—Marcello's satire with Gluck's "reform" and on to the post-Wagnerian conception of "music drama." A fundamental stage on this journey is Francesco Algarotti's *Saggio sopra l'opera in musica,* over which the Venetian patrician Marcello certainly casts a shadow: not only does he merit a mention as being, among musicians, "possibly second to none among the ancients, and certainly first among the moderns," [92] but the very structure of the *Saggio* can be said to a certain extent to follow (with the negative quality of sarcasm changed to a positive one of recommendation and advice) that of *Il teatro alla*

---

90. See ibid., 43–47.   91. Ibid., 52.   92. Algarotti, *Saggio,* 167.

moda, being divided into chapters on the separate elements of that delicate "composite" of opera. And there is also a clear allusion to Marcello's carica-tures in the censure of singers who do their utmost to destroy the audience's illusion by reminding them that when they are onstage, instead of "Achilles or Cyrus . . . they are in reality Signor Petriccino, Signor Stoppanino, and Signor Zolfanello [Mr. Stubborn, Mr. Tousled, and Mr. Quick-Temper]." [93]

Algarotti's *Saggio* appeared in 1755 and brilliantly took stock, not so much of the condition of opera which it proposes to reform, as of the state of the "question of opera," which had by then been under discussion for half a century. The "failings" that it denounces are the same as ever. What is differ-ent, in the altered cultural context, is the perspective from which they are ex-amined. The first and most radical change is the scholarly acceptance of opera, in place of the unthinking hostility of the early decades of the century: a truce, to be honest, and a cautious one, but peace of a kind nevertheless, fa-vored by the perfect marriage of rationality and sensitivity, impeccable style and dramaturgical balance, which Metastasio had created in his librettos. In-deed, it is Metastasio's poetry Algarotti means when he talks of poetry once again taking the "right path" (after the disgraceful excesses of "compositori secentisti," composers, that is, as overblown in their way as seventeenth-century poets had been), and it is also Metastasio's librettos that he judges to be "very close to the projected model" [94] of an opera that, starting with the very choice of subject, can perfectly achieve its goal, "which is to move the heart and delight the eyes and ears without going against reason." [95] But de-spite the praise, the remedies put forward depart considerably from the model invoked; indeed, they end up rejecting some of the essential given elements, including the choice of subject.

The old question of which type of subject, historical or mythological, is best suited to opera reappears: a question linked, as we know, to the problem of verisimilitude. Even if Saint-Évremond's supremely rational arguments against *parlar cantando* had already been refuted at the beginning of the eighteenth century by the German librettist Barthold Feind, who recognized that the im-itation of nature is by necessity governed by convention, in opera no less than in any other form of artistic representation, [96] the issue had never been entirely settled. It reared up again in the years after 1750, undoubtedly because the polemic on Italian opera versus French opera had been stoked up again, and also in the more general context of discussion of theater, affected by a power-ful impulse toward innovation in European culture coming out of Paris in the work of the philosophes. Diderot had declared that the miraculous was "hors de la nature" in his poetic of bourgeois tragedy and that it should be banned

93. Ibid., 169.   94. Ibid., 156.   95. Ibid., 155.
96. See Barthold Feind, *Gedancken von der Opera,* in his *Deutsche Gedichte* (Stade: Brum-mer, 1708), 74–114.

not only from dramatic but also from lyric theater, that is, opera; he hoped
for a genius to appear and "bring it down from the regions of enchantment
to the world which we inhabit." [97]

Diderot had French opera in mind and invited poets to take their subjects
from classical tragedy, even imagining a sort of musical script of a passage from
Racine's *Iphigénie*. For Rousseau, an intransigent supporter of Italian opera,
the genius had already appeared in the person of Metastasio, who, completing
what his predecessor Apostolo Zeno had initiated, had successfully brought
characters like Cato and Caesar on to the stage and managed to make audiences not so much accept as forget that they were singing.[98] Rousseau thus
completely revolutionizes the concept of "verisimilitude" as it had been applied to opera up until that time: music having taken full possession of its imitative faculties and learned to speak the language that, more than any other,
is capable of expressing "the force of all emotions, the violence of all passions," [99] the problem is no longer that of distancing the action from the observer to justify to him or her the unnatural phenomenon of singing but, on
the contrary, that of bringing the observer as close as possible, to the point
where he or she becomes totally involved. The distance, if any, is to be between
ordinary, everyday feelings and extraordinary ones—extraordinary because
raised to the highest degree of intensity—which are portrayed on the stage:
"It is easily to be imagined that sentiments so different from our own must
thus be expressed in a different tone." [100] Music's masterstroke, therefore,
having drawn the spectator into its magic circle, will be to make itself disappear: ultimately the very expedient that had been most frequently used in order to give the involvement of music in the action the impression of realism—
having a character sing a song—is condemned as the one that most bluntly
destroys this profound, genuine verisimilitude. The gods were expelled, and
men and women began to appear. But what characters can express sentiments
and passions most intensely if not the great heroes of ancient history, idealized
models of humanity not yet corrupted by progress? (For this reason, the reader
will recall, it is ancient history and not modern that Saint-Preux includes in his
plan of studies drawn up for Julie in *La nouvelle Héloïse*, the novel in which
comment—the epiphonema, as Stefano Arteaga would have said—on the passions gripping the characters is often made by quoting from Metastasio librettos such as *Attilio Regolo*, *Demofoonte*, *Ciro riconosciuto*, and *Antigono*.)

Historical subject matter had thus become completely legitimate. Rousseau

---

97. Denis Diderot, *Entretiens sur "Le Fils naturel"* (1757), in his *Oeuvres complètes*, vol. 10,
Le drame bourgeois, ed. Jacques Chouillet and Anne-Marie Chouillet (Paris: Hermann, 1980),
83–162, quotations on 150ff., and passim.

98. See Rousseau, the entry "Opéra," in his *Dictionnaire de musique*, 954–55.

99. Ibid.

100. Ibid.

was followed by writers such as Antonio Eximeno, although he argued from an opposite point of view (music lends historical characters a "certain air of divinity . . . as a result of which, if opera shows me characters as divine beings, I shall not find it strange to hear them speak the divine language of music"),[101] and Arteaga again, who, having invoked "the unspoken convention that exists between the listener and the composer"[102] to support the verisimilitude of sung action, explains how "having to represent human events, which the composer has seen so often," can be "of enormous assistance" to him "the more to interiorize the passions and penetrate further into the soul of the listener."[103]

Algarotti takes the opposite view and considers historical subjects to be contrary to the aims of opera: he brings up the old arguments of propriety and verisimilitude ("it does not seem that the trills of some arietta sit so well in the mouth of Julius Caesar or Cato as they would in the mouths of Apollo or Venus"); he further accuses historical subjects of "severity" and "monotony," precisely because the poet has no opportunity to introduce any marvels into the action that will allow him to "weave in dances and choruses and introduce various types of decoration."[104] This is why he suggests a compromise between "the merits of subjects of our time" (in other words, action "of the utmost simplicity and familiarity," which, as such, would attract the listener's interest) and "the merits of the fabled subjects of days gone by" (in other words, distancing the action to "remote and alien" times and locations, which would simultaneously meet the needs of verisimilitude and of entertaining variety).[105] This is the reason behind the choice of the Metastasio librettos that he gives as examples, *Didone abbandonata* and *Achille in Sciro;* but these are pieces that belong to a minor strain in the poet's work (as is known, Metastasio's declared preference was, instead, for his more properly historic works, such as *Catone in Utica* and, particularly, *Attilio Regolo*).

In this fondness for what we might call "a human marvel," Algarotti's *Saggio* certainly concurs with the conclusions of Ranieri de' Calzabigi's contemporary *Dissertazione . . . su le poesie drammatiche del sig. abate Pietro Metastasio;* in veiled contradiction of his opening apologia, it reveals Calzabigi's preference for a model of opera that—in line with Diderot's reforming proposals of the very same period—retains the rich spectacular accoutrements of French opera (the "ballet," the "large chorus," the "scenery united with the

---

101. Antonio Eximeno y Pujades, *Dell'origine e delle regole della musica colla storia del suo progresso, decadenza e rinnovazione* (Rome: Barbellini, 1774), 441.

102. Esteban de Arteaga, *Le rivoluzioni del teatro musical italiano dalla sua origine fino al presente*, 2d ed. (Venice: Palese, 1785; reprint, Bologna: Forni, 1969), 1:4.

103. Ibid., 50.

104. Algarotti, *Saggio*, 154ff.

105. Ibid., 155ff.

poetry and music in masterly fashion") but that is freed from the burden of the supernatural and put instead in the service of "purely human actions." [106]

Another departure from Metastasian opera, in the *Saggio,* lies in the criticism of the abrupt break between recitative and aria: the former too "bland" and the latter "worked with all the refinements of the art," so that the passage from one to the other is compared to the behavior of someone who, "walking along, suddenly took to leaping and jumping." [107] Here the observation is directed at the composer, not the poet, but ultimately it rebounds on the latter, because the basic polarity of recitative and aria (which Martello had already declared: that recitative had "all that is narrated, or unagitated expression," while the aria had all that "has the impulse of passion") [108] was in fact the outcome of Metastasio's skill, as a literary man and dramatist, in defining and exalting the opposing and complementary functions of each, so that there was only the very minimum space in his librettos for procedures of the aria cavata type, still fairly frequent in early-eighteenth-century opera. Besides, the remedy suggested by Algarotti, an increase in obbligato recitative, was not one to meet with the approval of a poet who, on at least one occasion, had shown that he was fully aware of how "making this ornament too familiar" inevitably upset the balance of his own highly astute dramatic scheme. [109]

Similar observations can be made in connection with the disapproval expressed of the music in the arias. The longing for the da capo to be abolished had to contend with the fact that the architecture of the Metastasian double strophe was intimately tied up with that musical structure and set out in such a way as to allow the greatest expansion (indeed, when the librettos were reworked in the second half of the century once the new, two-movement aria form had been adopted, the prevailing tendency was to replace the original aria text with other, specially written lines). Approval of only the single category of arias "called *parlanti*" [110] implies disapproval of those moralizing or simile arias which were just as important to Metastasio and no less essential to his own dramaturgical scheme.

It thus came about that the Metastasian libretto, at the same time as it was being honorably welcomed into the literary citadel, was implicitly, if not deliberately, being attacked for the very basic features that had assured its triumph. And this (even more than the attention paid to problems neglected or

---

106. Calzabigi, *Dissertazione,* 143.

107. Algarotti, *Saggio,* 161.

108. Martello, *Della tragedia,* 285.

109. Letter of 20 Oct. 1749 to Johann Adolf Hasse, in Metastasio, *Tutte le opere,* vol. 3 (1951), 427–36, quotation on 434. See also his letter of 30 Jan. 1751 to Farinelli (ibid., 619ff.), in which he explains the quite exceptional reasons why he has inserted "two short lines . . . in the guise of a *cavata* of the utmost brevity" in a recitative for Iarba in the revision of *Didone abbandonata.*

110. Algarotti, *Saggio,* 164.

only touched upon by scholars who had written on opera before Algarotti: attention to acting, to mise-en-scène, costumes, the suitability of the architecture of the theater) seems to me the most important aspect of the *Saggio* in that it signals a sea change in the taste of the most cultivated and active section of the audience: a change that was to go hand in hand with equally significant alterations in the form and dramaturgy of opera. (However, the system of production, theatrical custom, and social consumption did not undergo significant change.) As a result, decades of the customary litany of accusations of the usual "abuses" followed. There was less than ever change in the relationship between music and text, as the scales tipped increasingly in favor of the former. This gave rise to repeated protests against pointless display of learned counterpoint, against vocal tessituras that were too taxing, instrumental textures that were too elaborate, overlong ritornellos, concertante scoring for the arias, repetitions and the arbitrary reordering of words and verses, and so on.)

In the second half of the eighteenth century, discussion of opera seria, at least in Italy, turned essentially on the validity of the Metastasian model. Even among his apologists there was a belief that the model was in decline, if only as a natural, almost inevitable effect of its having reached a point of perfection; "the same things which brought music and poetry to perfection have ruined it,"[111] was the judgment of Saverio Mattei, who fixed the period of Italian music's "virility" as being between 1733 (the year of *Olimpiade,* immortalized in 1735 in Pergolesi's music) and 1760 (Hasse's setting of *Alcide al bivio*).[112] The arts have a beginning, a development, and an unalterable and sure decline, like the rotations of the stars,"[113] advised Arteaga, who considered the "golden age" of music to be that of the period of Metastasio.

According to Mattei, Metastasio's genius had so exhausted the field he had cultivated that it was not possible for anyone to shine by following in his footsteps. The lack of novelty was thus the principal reason for the current state of decline in opera: a lack that artists were trying to conceal by adding ever more extravagances and gilding merely to flatter the ear, or by fighting back with remedies that left things worse than ever. Such indeed was the solution proposed by Calzabigi and Gluck, who were severely castigated for such grave errors as suppressing secondary roles, excluding simile arias, and using only accompanied recitative. This was a scheme, argued Mattei, suitable for "one or two cantatas"—he had *Orfeo ed Euridice* in mind when he made this judgment—but which would produce "endless monotony if fifty or sixty operas were to be written in this manner"[114] (an argument that demonstrates,

---

111. Saverio Mattei, *La filosofia della musica o sia La riforma del teatro,* in Pietro Metastasio, *Opere* (Naples: De Bonis, 1781), 3:iii–xlv, quotation on xxviii.

112. Mattei, *Elogio del Jommelli,* 74, 109.

113. Arteaga, *Le rivoluzioni,* 2:177.

114. Mattei, *Elogio del Jommelli,* 106–8 and passim.

among other things, how Mattei's way of thinking was entirely bound up with
the system of production by season, organized by impresarios, which he and
others condemned as the main reason for the iniquities perpetrated on the operatic stage).

Arteaga's position was ambivalent: he accused Metastasio of various
"faults"—of having given too much space, and often in a contrived manner,
to love in his librettos, for a start, thereby diminishing not only their moral in-
tegrity but also their purely theatrical effectiveness—but he also crowns him
the "greatest lyric-dramatic poet in the universe." [115] It is in fact the simile
arias that he singles out for praise and, with some reservations, the moralizing
ones.[116] What is to be regretted, however, is that those very "lyric beauties"
have led "unphilosophical" composers to abuse their art and smother the
sense of the poetry, and therefore the genuine expression of an emotion, with
too rich an orchestral accompaniment.[117] As for the current decline of opera,
which has to be demonstrated as being consistent with the above thesis, the
causes and effects are described with copious reference to the preceding literature, whose arguments are developed out of all proportion; certainly, some
individual exceptions to this rule are signaled,[118] but they are too few to reverse the overall negative trend.

It is worth remembering that Arteaga's attack on opera after Metastasio
not only attracted the polemical response of Calzabigi, irritated by criticism
of his own works, but also sparked a reaction from one of the very few musicians who, in Italy, raised his voice in this debate entirely dominated by literary scholars. Defending music, Vincenzo Manfredini made sound observations in opposition to Arteaga. First of all, "among the most difficult of fine
arts . . . the majority cannot be the best," and it is in any case "a highly mistaken opinion . . . that the condition of an art in a century, and in a nation,
should be measured according to the majority." [119] Then, the accusation that
the primary cause of the supposed current decadence is the wish of "unphilosophical" composers to be original at all costs, together with the knee-
jerk repetition of all the criticisms of opera over the decades, puts Arteaga in
the paradoxical situation of accusing the opera of the day of things that belonged to the music "of thirty and forty years ago," that is, of his golden age,
things that the much criticized quest for the new had actually annulled: the
abundance of decorations in cantabile arias, "that repetition of the words of
the first part of an aria four times, and only one appearance of the words of

115. Arteaga, *Le rivoluzioni,* 2:176 (and passim, esp. 140–76).
116. See ibid., 1:30–38.
117. See ibid., 2:263 and passim.
118. See ibid., 326–30.
119. Vincenzo Manfredini, *Difesa della musica moderna e de' suoi celebri esecutori* (Bologna:
Trenti, 1788; reprint, Bologna: Forni, 1972), 177ff.

the second section," "those two, sometimes four cadenzas," as well as the much decried da capo, had all disappeared, together with many other "irritants," with the advent of the slimmed-down, more balanced, expressive, and energetic aria with two themes and two movements, the (inaccurately named) *rondò*, which is instead "a grand aria, and a truly heroic one." [120]

On the opposite front, the most radical counterattack came, naturally, from Calzabigi, whose poetics could be summed up in the motto *rem, et non sermones,* which he proudly affirmed in the face of Arteaga, who had accused him of being an aberration.[121] This motto contains the idea of a theater, not as a web of "gallant chit-chat," clever aphorisms, and artificial similes, but as strong actions able to rouse hot, intense passions—strong because "simple and single" according to Horace's precept, resolutely aiming toward their ending because they have finally been stripped of the parasitic web of secondary plots which had been woven in order to provide food for those vacuous speeches. Now the music would arise naturally from the true accent which the poet had been able to give to those passions and which would thus furnish a sure guide for the composer's invention. In the earlier case, all the music could do was to spread itself, like a pleasant but futile ornamentation, over a text that was itself insubstantial.

Without reaching the virulent tone of Calzabigi's polemic, Antonio Planelli is equally firm in asking that maxims and aphorisms be kept to the minimum in opera, and limited to the recitative in any case; they should be excluded from the arias because they are digressions, they freeze the action, spoil the drama, and embarrass the composer, who, left to his own devices, is obliged to cling to unsteady and senseless music.[122] In this regard he resurrects, only to refute it, Martello's old assertion that "in the ariettas, the more generalized the subjects, the more appealing they are to the audience, since finding the ideas expressed likely, or true, they hoard them up to sing at home." (To digress, this is an assertion that Planelli attributes to Quadrio, although the latter had in fact copied it entirely from Martello:[123] a mere oversight, but one that can nevertheless be taken as evidence of the fact that the deviant position of Martello's text in relation to the constantly negative line

120. Ibid., 195ff. For the introduction of the *rondò* aria type, see Mattei, *La filosofia,* xxxv; and Arteaga, *Le rivoluzioni,* 2:298.

121. See Arteaga, *Le rivoluzioni,* 3:121; Ranieri de' Calzabigi, *Risposta che ritrovò casualmente nella gran città di Napoli il licenziato Don Santigliano di Gilblas . . . alla critica ragionatissima della poesie drammatiche del C. de' Calsabigi fatta dal baccelliere D. Stefano Arteaga suo illustre compatriotto,* in Calzabigi, *Scritti letterari e teatrali,* 2:423.

122. See Antonio Planelli, *Dell'opera in musica* (1772), ed. Francesco Degrada (Fiesole: Discanto, 1981), 48–54.

123. Ibid., 50; see Francesco Saverio Quadrio, *Della storia e della ragione d'ogni poesia* (Milan: Francesco Agnelli, 1744), vol. 3, pt. 2:447; Martello, *Della tragedia,* 290.

taken by Italian literature on opera had led to his being marginalized and neglected. But in the late nineteenth century a journalist could still claim to be
disappointed by a new opera because "you don't go home singing a single
theme," [124] which is proof, if any were needed, of how much the idea of "taking home"—here "themes" instead of "aphorisms," but the faculty of memory associates the two elements indissolubly—was profoundly rooted in the
mentality of the Italian spectator.) Logically, therefore, Planelli sides with
Calzabigi, to whom he assigns the credit for having avoided "in all his arias
those faults which are under discussion here" and of having thus favored the
"lovely effect" made by *Alceste* on the Vienna stage.

Matteo Borsa also looks to Calzabigi: his *Orfeo,* which he "read and saw
with such great pleasure" (seen, however, not in Gluck's setting but in that by
Ferdinando Bertoni), seems to Borsa the "best model" for opera as "a unified,
complete, and musical whole." [125] Unreservedly, Borsa considers it "impossible" to achieve such an effect in traditional opera seria. When he speaks of
an opera that is wholly "musical," he is referring to what he calls the "imitative melody," which can vie with poetry and rhetoric in moving the human
heart, as opposed to "pure, natural melody," which is good only for "flatter-
ing the sense without tending at all to move the affections." [126] And in his
opinion, there are very few places in opera seria where imitative melody can
be applied. Excluded are past events, narrations, arguments, conversations,
and also those places in the text that are more lyrical than dramatic ("meditations" and "comparisons"). The virtuoso characters are resistant to imitation, given the monotony that necessarily informs their serious and poised
discourse. However, some passions are also immune: those that are "ugly and
cowardly" and noble ones when they rise to the heights of the sublime, for in
both cases, although for opposite reasons, the voice cannot sing out but tends
instead to break and choke. That leaves love and those "free, open passions
which love to be eloquently expressed." To be able to achieve "musical completeness," a libretto would thus have to be organized "without narrations,
deliberations, plots, expedients, . . . without confidantes and counselors, without persons of probity, prudence, and virtue, and without any envious traitor
whose evil intent is concealed." [127] This is impossible, of course, in the way
opera seria is conceived, where real dramatic music is restricted, in the best
examples, to a few marvelous passages; the rest should not really be sung,
and if it is, it is because it turns to natural melody, as lacking in meaning and
foundation as instrumental music. (And yet instrumental music is warmly applauded in the context of accompanied recitative or, rather, those passages in
which the performer, in the grip of some sublime passion, is not able to utter

124. See the review of the first performance in Naples of Filippo Marchetti's *Ruy Blas,* in
L'omnibus 39, no. 49, 25 Apr. 1871.

125. Borsa, *Saggio filosofico,* 216.

126. Ibid., 201.   127. Ibid., 207.

a word. Then "the action of music" preserves "the reticence, one might say the overpowering of the actor, while the orchestra, in his silence, displays the feelings in his soul." [128] This praise certainly shows an influence from Rousseau but is expressed in terms that seem to look forward to—the thought is inescapable—the "sonorous silence" of Wagner.)

Nevertheless, the same reasons for there being so little space for music in opera seria are the ones that offer huge space for it in comic opera, where the fact of the action taking place in private situations means that the characters lose the gravity, uniformity, and official poise which make the characters in opera seria almost impervious to imitative melody. The characters in comic opera fear no contradictions, are versatile, and are easily gripped, not by extreme passions, but by "straightforward, lively, and innocent ones"; they "speak up and give vent to their passions" in the popular way, or at least as they would at home. They are thus naturally "perfectly modulated," where in opera seria they are almost "voiceless." [129] The structure of familiar speech, made up of short spans and brief vocal inflections, led composers to create equally short-winded musical periods, in an almost syllabic singing style: so there is no place in comic opera for all the hindrances of ornaments that burden opera seria. As a rule, one can read between the lines of their polemics the scholars' sympathy for comic opera (except for Arteaga, who is most severe in his condemnation,[130] and Calzabigi, too, who thought that transplanting the act finales of comic opera would harm the dignity of opera seria).[131] And yet only Borsa tackled this by no means marginal topic and attempted to construct a theory on it: this is certainly his claim to fame even if we can see underneath his theorizing the old, seventeenth-century idea of verisimilitude, in which singing by public and high-ranking figures was condemned, but singing by characters of more humble station was acceptable—with a comic connotation no less. (Borsa lets slip a rather spiteful touch against musicians when he concedes that although "not very cultivated and by no means given to study," they have no difficulties in imitating the characters in opera buffa through the "closeness and familiarity" between themselves and "the originals.") [132]

Mattei also devotes a certain amount of space to comic opera, and while on the one hand he contemplates the utopia of a "sacred theater" on the model of Metastasio's sacred dramas as a way of moving opera seria out of the impasse in which he finds it, on the other he suggests, more realistically, using the example of the music heard in the "teatrini" (small theaters) to bring some

---

128. Ibid., 226.   129. Ibid., 220ff.

130. See Arteaga, *Le rivoluzioni*, 3:135–51.

131. See Ranieri de' Calzabigi, *La Lulliade* (compiled between 1753–54 and 1789), annotations to canto 4, strophe 39, in Gabriele Muresu, *La ragione dei "buffoni"* (Rome: Bulzoni, 1977), 261.

132. Borsa, *Saggio filosofico*, 223.

flexibility and variety to structures that have become too uniform and monotonous and, in addition, naturally, to rescue singing from the vanity of an excess of virtuoso gilding. (Like Algarotti before him, Mattei saw the different
systems of production, which prevented singers from exercising their tyranny
over comic opera, as a fundamental factor in the greater level of "truth" in
comic opera than in opera seria.)[133] But the most acute observation is possibly that made in passing by Gianmaria Ortes, who contrasts the generally
"artificial" music in opera seria (that is, easily adapted to this word or that,
this subject or that) with the "expressive" music (tied to the words and characters for whom it was written) of "certain modern comedies, especially at
the ends of the acts," intuitively grasping the peculiar and original character
of comic opera and the basic reason for its extraordinary effectiveness, which
lay in its unity of music and action.[134]

There is one point, though, on which all seem to be in agreement—Metas-
tasians and anti-Metastasians, traditionalists and reformers—and that is the
unqualified condemnation of the impresario (rather as happens in theatrical
satires, where he is the most abused character). For Algarotti the primary condition for operatic reform is the removal of theater management from the ve-
nal hands of the impresario and its transferal to those of a director endowed
with the authority of an enlightened prince.[135] Planelli describes in detail how
such a director should exercise his power to keep a check on the unruly crowd
of those involved in the performance, but even more how he can thwart the
interests of the impresario, who, if left uncontrolled, dominates and unsettles
the theater.[136] Mattei invokes government involvement to make the sacred
theater he dreams of a reality.[137] While Manfredini refutes Arteaga's sermonizing, he does admit that the blameworthy custom of abandoning direction
of performances "to the judgment of the most foolish people in society has
proved a failure."[138] And yet, despite this chorus of agreement, the attack on
the impresario system is probably the most abstract of all those made against
the world of opera, if we take account of the actual situation—amply described in another part of this *History*[139]—in which the impresarios operated; far from being despots or judges, they were actually dependents and, in
a sense, agents of the will and taste of the highest levels in society, those who
held the power that was invoked to suppress or rein them in. At the turn of

133. See Mattei, *La filosofia,* xviii–xx; Mattei, *Elogio del Jommelli,* 111; Algarotti, *Saggio,*
165.
134. See Ortes, *Riflessioni,* 157.
135. Algarotti, *Saggio,* 151.
136. Planelli, *Dell'opera in musica,* 127–29.
137. Mattei, *La filosofia,* xliii–xlv.
138. Manfredini, *Difesa,* 178 n.
139. See John Rosselli, "Opera Production, 1780–1880," in *The History of Italian Opera,*
vol. 4, *Opera Production and Its Resources,* ed. Lorenzo Bianconi and Giorgio Pestelli (Chicago:
University of Chicago Press, 1998), 81–164.

the century, a representative of those ranks, a member of the association of proprietors of La Fenice, presented to his friends a plan for reorganizing the financial management of the theater, a plan that, among other things, involved strict control of the impresario's work, for this reason:

> In the fine days of antiquity, when one looked to the stage as a school of virtue or morals, a Choragus or Aedile presided with public authority over the good order of what was represented. Now that politics sees performance as no more than a means to keep the people entertained for the peace of the State, and now that the populace sees the theater as no more than a place where one can relieve the boredom of leisure, the theater is at the disposal of Impresarios who try to turn the curiosity of a few into profit, without knowing in most cases what needs to be done for this, or without being able to carry this out, given the thousand considerations they must first resolve. It would not therefore be inappropriate to come to the aid either of their inexperience or their inefficiency and in some measure help with the good progress and agreed execution of the performances. To this end I propose the appointment of an Inspector, who will add to his discernment vigilance and determination to maintain discipline among a band of persons involved in the theater whose actions have most often quite another goal than working together for the successful creation of the spectacle.[140]

I have included this long quotation, not because it contains something original, but on the contrary because it repeats, almost word for word, the same line of thought which half a century before Algarotti had laid out in the introduction to his *Saggio:* undoubtedly a sign of the persistence of the impulse to reform but also of the great distance between that ideal and the reality of a form of theater that in every aspect, beginning with the way it was organized, worked perfectly well for the society whose faithful expression it was.

8. "PRECIOUS STONES HELD TOGETHER WITH MUD"

It was clear to early-nineteenth-century scholars that the changes effected in the structure of Italian opera of the last decades of the eighteenth century had allowed the decline of the Metastasian model without as a result approaching in the slightest the ideals laid out in reforming literature. Nor had any of the "abuses" which the literature had obsessively condemned been cleaned up; indeed, the debate on opera was still in good health, although, to be honest, pursued with far less clamor and devotion than in the past. At the very beginning of the century Giuseppe Carpani declared the futility of the "erudite complaints of the Algarottis, Arteagas, Napoli-Signorellis, and Planellis, etc."[141]

---

140. Giuseppe Giacomo Albrizzi, *Piano economico proposto alla società de' proprietari del Teatro di S. Fantino* (Venice: Palese, 1800), 34ff.

141. Giuseppe Carpani, *Le rossiniane ossia Letter musico-teatrali* (Padua: Tipografia della Minerva, 1824; reprint, Bologna: Forni, 1969), 17. The passage quoted is taken from the letter dated 12 Dec. 1804.

and saw opera increasingly reduced to the status of a "concert of music and song," and thus ever further removed from the drama. Abandoning the Metastasian path, instead of producing a renewed balance between recitative and aria, had in fact led to the almost complete eclipse of the former and transformed opera into an unmotivated sequence of self-sufficient musical numbers: "a mass of unannounced consequences; a succession of effects without apparent causes,"[142] Carpani continues, using an expression which, taken out of context, sounds surprisingly prophetic.

And this was not all: the lack of balance between the two principal structures of operatic dramaturgy had a negative effect on the aria: without the proper preparation of recitative it lost its sense of range of expression. For this reason,

> now that the simple beauty of Italian melody is gone . . . it has to be replaced by harmony and by more parts, that is, the so-called ensembles, as a way of regaining with art the pleasure that was formerly the fruit of well-observed and respected nature. Listeners have thus become accustomed to preferring to a fine solo piece, unless it displays the utmost perfection and mastery, the pieces for several voices. Now . . . there is no sign [in Metastasio's librettos] of those studied and dramatized miracles of music which we know today as finales, and which, to be honest, do not end an act badly and are an invention to be preserved.[143]

The glaring contradiction in his final observation compared with what precedes is no surprise at this point on our journey. It was, besides, destined to recur in Carpani's pro-Rossini stance, that is, in his passionate apologia for the *musical* genius who was making his own mark on the framework of the very style of opera whose formal and dramaturgical principles Carpani censured so severely.

At the end of this period, the age of Rossini that Carpani had proclaimed at its opening, we find similar considerations and a similar dichotomy—the first developed at greater length, the other consciously adopted as the basis for argument—in the essay that is certainly the broadest and richest consideration of early-nineteenth-century Italian music, and which at the same time provides possibly the last attempt to put together a systematic "poetics of opera": Carlo Ritorni's *Ammaestramenti alla composizione d'ogni poema e d'ogni opera appartenente alla musica* (1841).

Ritorni defines the third age of opera as "Rossinian par excellence" and "completely musical," preceded, in order, by the "mythological" and the "historic" eras; his epithets "Rossinian" and "completely musical" derive from the fact that there could be no better name for the era than that "of the name of the great composer, in whose time the poetry needed to be, and was, noth-

142. Ibid., 113.
143. Ibid., 24.

ing." [144] It is the perfect antithesis of Metastasian opera. Jokingly pretending for a moment to assume "the masterly authority of modern composers," Ritorni makes this paradoxical pronouncement:

> Metastasio is not, could not become, and possibly never could have been an author of librettos that can be set to music. How could they [modern composers] ever apply their system of scientific music to those long dialogues or action and recitative, with no cavatinas or rondos, no grand scenas and no choruses? And where could an introduction and finale in several real parts be added? . . . It would be the same for them as having any tragedy, whatever the length of the scenes, to set to music. Nor would the fact that their tragedy's scenes end without two lyrical strophes make a difference: it would not be difficult to turn the last lines of every scene with music into an aria with music. Then, too, the long recitatives have nothing to do with modern scientific music, nor do those uniform monologue arias that are inserted without adequate reason into the tragedies of the former musical poet Metastasio. [145]

The "materials" and "parts" of modern opera are already enumerated in his ironic statement of his position, and Ritorni goes on to describe them in detail and illustrate their internal structure and function,[146] only ultimately to denounce their inherently antidramatic nature. The introduction consisting of a showy "preliminary ceremony" that does not get the action under way but holds it back is against the rule of a "modest opening" and then a slow, progressive "increase." The cavatina that a character sings on entering, without any action to provide preparation or motivation, represents an absurdity equivalent in a tragedy to "the interlocutors . . . entering reciting a sonnet referring to their situation." And again "the vast disparity and disruption between song and recitative" transform the ensemble pieces (of which the acts are principally made up) into something like "eclogues" which "interrupt and create a pause in the natural flow of the action"—indeed, when one considers the inflexible metrical regularity governing their harmonic structure, into nothing less than "sung pas de deux." And to top it all, there is "a finale that is no finale, because it is placed in the middle of the action, crowning the first act to introduce a huge division at the center of the opera, removing every pretext for a good start to the second." [147] In a word, opera is altogether reduced to "a grand symphony with characters, composed of regular components and forms, performed by two large orchestras, one of singers and one of instruments, one following the other, and possibly both battling in turn or simultaneously." [148]

Behind his statements we can sense purely classicist principles at work: the

---

144. Carlo Ritorni, *Ammaestramenti alla composizione d'ogni poema e d'ogni opera appartenente alla musica* (Milan: Pirola, 1841), 33ff.

145. Ibid., 30ff.   147. Ibid., 51–55.

146. Ibid., 40–50.   148. Ibid., 73.

distinction between genres, which "completely musical" opera casually mixes
and even swaps, adopting—both in the poetry and in the music—meters,
forms, and styles that belong to the lyric, rather than the dramatic, genre. (In
the former the author "appears in the first person" and "expresses himself as
a composer and as a poet." As a result the poetry can display "certain difficult
and arcane meters," and equally the music can be "worked out in elaborate
meters and studied chords." In the latter—the dramatic genre—both composer and poet "make characters speak who it is pretended are alive," and
the poetry must be "simple in delicate forms" and the music must also be the
"simple stuff of the passions, and of mutual dialogue.")[149]

While Ritorni's classicism is clearly in sympathy with that of other early-
nineteenth-century scholars—with whom he agrees that the music of Rossini
and his followers is "romantic," meaning "all that which is luxuriant without drama, and which departs from the rules that the reasoning of the tragic
art prescribes"[150]—it does not translate into nostalgia for a past golden age,
nor does it long for restoration. Instead, it is ready to concede—somewhat
softening the irony of the paradox concerning Metastasio mentioned above—
that while "monstrously far from the virtues of Metastasian opera," for having cast out the rigid alternation between recitatives and "uniform ariettas,
uniformly situated," modern opera does possess the potential for flexibility
which poets, because of their "inexperience," and composers, because of their
"lack of restraint," have not been able or willing to exploit; put to the service
of proper dramatic thought, this could at last produce a "lyric tale, in which
the situations of the action matched the forms of singing, in such a way that
the moments of pathos of one would define the beginning, the growth, the
plot, and development of the other."[151]

In any case, Bellini—whom Ritorni welcomed, in antithesis to Rossini, as
the composer of "scores" which were "*melodrammi*, not pieces of music"[152]
—had shown the way to return opera from the lyrical to the dramatic, not
only restoring to singing the simplicity and expressive force of tragic declamation but also turning the very forms of modern opera to "considered" use.
Norma was a perfect example: the heroine's cavatina is justified by the dramatic situation, because it really is sung, "being a hymn and a sacred prayer
in the rite"; the finale is placed in the correct position ("an opera in which the
finale is final, not coming after the first part"); the arias and duets are not "a
jumble of disconnected pieces" but a linear succession of "sung scenes, flowing from one into the next," giving the impression that the opera was "made
in a single span."[153]

An opera that, if I might suggest so compromising a term, could be de-

---

149. Ibid., 93–95.   151. Ibid., 151.   153. Ibid., 159–66.
150. Ibid., 67.   152. Ibid., 61.

scribed as *durchkomponiert,* an opera that is "entirely sung" (but, evidently, not "lyrically" sung), accorded exactly with Ritorni's leanings, and he states the rules that can "make the music a considered servant of dramatic exposition." [154] These rules can be summed up in one basic principle: avoidance of "disconnectedness," the segmentation which in turn is the basic architectural principle of the nineteenth-century number opera. The total rejection of the latter principle is expressed with his customary irony:

> This score, one commonly says, is made up of so many pieces. Instead of opera being a work made up of harmonically contrasting sections, so that the chiaroscuro of the relationship between them shows more clearly the unity, identity, and solidity of a single corpus, its so-called numbers are set out as delicacies to lure greedy palates, being presented at random in a bit of tasteless broth to keep them moist and separate, not a dry dish, but with the intention that others can pluck them out from their liquid at will.
>
> Thus the writer of the music, when he sets to making a score from a libretto, looks first at how many pieces have been prepared for him, and he begins to work on them with varying diligence, one by one, but with no need to preserve their natural order. Sometimes the poet provides them piece by piece, also without following the dramatic order. Then when the composer has finished setting them to music, and put them together to create his dramatic concert, he remembers the recitatives, putting notes to which is a crude and monotonous job. . . . Just imagine what an impression can be made by precious stones held together with mud in creating an edifice of Roman sumptuousness! [155]

A simple and radical remedy is suggested: a ban on "a hard meter of lyric strophes" and a ban on "disconnected music for sonorous songs" (and consequently a ban on the tyranny of "four-square" rhythms and symmetrical musical periods, which instead have to be shaded off and subdivided "into phrases of differing appearances"). [156] And since the poet is still the initial creator of an opera, it will be his duty to avoid the artificial fixed nature of the strophes and arrange instead continual series of free verse, varying according to the ideas being expressed: a "suite of verses," [157] on whose pattern the composer can extend the diagram of the passions in their contrived rising and falling trajectories and thus satisfy the long-standing desire to fuse the recitative into song and song into recitative, and finally make the ideal mutual correspondence of *recitar cantando* and *cantar recitando* a reality.

In the same period as Ritorni was assembling the materials for his *Ammaestramenti,* Giuseppe Mazzini wrote and published in Paris his *Filosofia della musica:* in it, emancipation from Rossini and the era he represents is also

154. Ibid., 167.
155. Ibid., 53.
156. Ibid., 130ff.
157. Ibid., 136.

proclaimed as the most urgent requirement facing Italian music. Mazzini's assumptions and predictions are, of course, quite different from Ritorni's. Rossini's "romanticism" does indeed lie in his negation of the classical rules of drama, but Mazzini sees this negation as something positive, of having set free the genius from the bonds of imitation and of having thus established a basis for the regeneration of music. However, this is still to be fostered and will only be achieved by abandoning the merely hedonistic conception of contemporary opera and opening it up to a social and, indirectly, political dimension. But when attention turns to opera per se, reforming critiques and proposals turn out to be substantially similar: no to segmentation, a desire for continuity which can represent the emotional dynamic, not the lyrical contemplation of emotions embodied in the static closed number. Mazzini is certainly more simplistic than Carpani in hoping that this continuity can be realized by extending accompanied recitative to the entire length of an opera:

> [W]hy might accompanied recitative, formerly the principal part of an opera and now so rare . . . , not take on greater importance and all the effectiveness of which it is capable in future compositions? Why should a manner of musical development capable . . . of the greatest dramatic effects ever achieved—a manner which can lead the listener through countless gradations, of which arias are incapable, to the furthest point of an emotion; which can develop the slightest, most imperceptible movement of the heart and uncover, not snatch, their secrets; which exposes not just the dominant element but all the elements of a passion one by one—a manner which dissects the conflict when arias can only, without the gravest difficulty, produce the results and, since it does not distract the attention from the music to the mechanics of the performance, as in arias, leaves its power over the spirit intact— have to remain relegated to one corner of the drama, instead of expanding, improved, at the expense of the often uninteresting cavatinas and the inevitable da capos? [158]

It might come as a surprise to find this convergence, however accidental and superficial, between the imaginative classicism of the Reggio Emilian patrician Ritorni and the revolutionary zeal of the prophet of the "Third Italy." However, to the extent that the flow of poetics and polemics on opera can appear—at least from the early eighteenth century to this point on our journey—as a type of self-contained small literary genre, with its conventions, its formulas, its ritual paths, running parallel with the conventions, formulas, and paths taken by its object, such a convergence can reveal a deep structural truth. On the one hand, the object of the criticism—opera—functions as a

---

158. Giuseppe Mazzini, *Filosofia della musica* (1836), ed. Marcello De Angelis (Florence: Guaraldi, 1977), 67. This edition includes an anthology of writing on musical aesthetics by Andrea Majer, Marco Santucci, Lorenzo Neri, Abramo Basevi, and Giovanni Battista Rinuccini. Contained in Strunk, *Source Readings*, 1085–94.

reaction to the utopian tendencies of those who see in what it is mainly the opposite of what it should be, according to their particular ideals; on the other, such utopias, within the inexorable cyclical return of the most overworked clichés, which always look the same, whatever the point from which they are viewed, confirm the certain identity of the very object, the depth of its roots in historical reality.

9. "THE LIGHTEST OF TRANSPARENT VEILS, OBSCURING NOTHING OF THE DRAMA"

It is certainly a coincidence, although there is a symbolic element there, too, that the year after the *Ammaestramenti* appeared in print, the *Gazzetta musicale di Milano*, a famous organ of the Ricordi company, began publication. I have written above that the *Ammaestramenti* represents possibly the last attempt to construct a systematic poetics of opera; what I should now add is that it was also the last study on opera written predominantly from a literary point of view, although graced by sophisticated and serious musical knowledge. In this it was therefore the product of a mind-set still operating from an eighteenth-century viewpoint, although an extremely wide-ranging one. From that time onward, the number of specialist publications would grow, and observations, judgments, and polemics on opera would become increasingly the preserve of militant music criticism or of nascent historic research or possibly—although in quite exceptional cases, to be honest—of philosophical reflection, as a set of aesthetic questions. In any case, it was no longer a pastime for literary figures (noble or "amateur") but a specific professional activity.

The terms of the questions under discussion did not change much as a result of the shift in frame of reference; as we have discovered, they changed in perspective and point of view, within the context of a radical transformation of the world of Italian opera—in means of production and, of course, in the product itself.

A clear signal was given by the establishment of the *Gazzetta musicale*, which indicated the growing presence of publishing in Italian musical life and announced its imminent takeover of the opera market. Another signal, also accidentally but significantly contemporary with the publication of the *Ammaestramenti,* was the first performance in Italy of a Meyerbeer grand opéra, *Robert le diable*, in Florence in 1840. This opened the floodgates to a surge of imports into a country which until then had been completely self-sufficient in opera. Over the next twenty years, a theatrical model that was utterly incompatible with the craft and "journalistic" rhythms of the old, impresario system in Italy was imposed. And last, to complete the chain of coincidences, we should not forget the "real," white-hot beginning of Verdi's career in 1842; here was an artist who not only belonged completely to this process of transformation but dominated it, irreversibly endorsing the central position of the composer in the process of opera production and also solving once and for all the question—one almost as old as opera itself—of the primacy of composer or librettist.

In the eyes of the critics of his day Verdi was undoubtedly a champion of "dramatic music." In his commentary on *Ernani* Abramo Basevi cites Donizetti's *Lucrezia Borgia* as the first attempt to introduce into Italian music a quality of "realism" for which there was no precedent. Having pointed out that the revolutionary dramaturgy of Victor Hugo calls for this, he outlines what the new relationship should be between music and a drama conceived in this way: "Since dramatic music takes its power from the drama to which it is fitted, it should be like the lightest of transparent veils, obscuring nothing of the drama over which it is spread and wound." [159]

A few lines further down, however, it becomes clear that it is the composer who is to decide how that veil should be spread and wound: in so-called dramatic music he, not the librettist who provides the verses, is the real dramaturge. Analyzing the first-act finale, Basevi observes that Verdi has followed the text only at arm's length, taking account "only of the words which suit him"; far from being shocked at this, Basevi recognizes the composer's right to do so, in terms that leave no doubts as to the functional and subordinate role of the poetry:

> It has been said that Verdi frequently writes his music before the words. Such a procedure cannot be condemned out of hand. . . . The composer would be worthy of derision if he proved indifferent to the poet's words; but not when touched by a given situation, and having already invented suitable music, he asks the writer to give poetic form to those ideas which have come into the said composer's mind. . . . If the poet expresses the situation well, the composer has only to provide a proper clothing of notes for the poetry; but when the poet has failed in his task, the composer can think up music to match a situation without bothering with the poetry he has been given, having it changed later to suit the music.[160]

The purely functional role of the poetry is confirmed in even clearer terms in yet another redefinition of the relationship between recitative and aria. Basevi broadly defines recitative as "the musical expression which timidly and slavishly follows the words and phrases which make up the poetry, step by step"; it is the "first step in the musical-dramatic art." Aria—understood even in the broad sense, as a large-scale piece of ensemble music—is a later achievement, and in its "greater breadth and perfection" lies "the future of music." In the aria, music "has achieved a certain independence and acquired greater dignity, creating musical pictures which exist in their own right, even

---

159. Abramo Basevi, *Studio sulle opera di Giuseppe Verdi* (Florence: Tofani, 1859), 41.
160. Ibid., 48ff.

without the poetry," whose task is simply to "interpret" such pictures. Basevi uses the fourth-act finale of Meyerbeer's *Le prophète* to clarify his ideas:

> This piece, a clear example of musical painting, cannot help but move the listener, although in an undefined manner. When the poetry is added, the listener will then understand the cause of his emotion. Now the poetry does not make the piece more effective simply because it is poetry, that is, through its own artistic virtue, but as the interpretation of the music.
>
> For this reason, it is understood why the composer does not ask the poet for work which is perfect in itself, but rather a skeleton which, covered and concealed by flesh, does not lose but instead communicates its form to that covering.[161]

The section quoted is taken from Basevi's highly critical commentary on a passage in *Simon Boccanegra*, the duet between the Doge and Fiesco which, according to Basevi, Wagner could easily subscribe to, so little melody has it, and so much is it dominated by recitative. If Verdi wished to follow Wagner "and other innovators" on the path of the music of the future, he has taken the wrong direction, because, as we have seen, the future lies in perfecting and expanding the aria, while a return to recitative would mean wishing to go backward in history.

This is one of the first hints of the storm of polemics that was soon to be unleashed on, first, the theories and, then, the music of Wagner. It is no coincidence that the starting point is the contrast between recitative and aria, between musically formed song and pitched textual declamation. (At the beginning of the century Carpani had already formulated the opposition of Italian and German music in very much the same terms, rejecting a Berlin critic's attacks on Rossini's *Tancredi* and describing German music as "not allied to the words but a slave to them . . . singing which is not singing but a frustrated de-

---

161. Ibid., 271ff. It is surprising to observe how here and in the preceding passage Basevi seems to want to fit to his "Hugoesque" concept of dramatic music the ideas on music expressed by Rossini—who we must assume would have had no time for such a concept—in his famous interview with Antonio Zanolini. The echo is clear: as Zanolini notes it down, Rossini defines music accompanying dramatic action as "the moral atmosphere which fills the setting in which the characters of the drama are representing the action." And further on, "A composer's mastery lies in laying out the scenes or, one should say, the principal situations of his opera for the minds of the audience. . . . He will pause on the words only to make the vocal line accord with them, but without altering the overall character of the music, which he will have chosen so that the words serve the music rather than the music the words. . . . If the composer follows the meaning of the text word by word, then he will compose music that is not in itself expressive but is poor, vulgar, made, I should say, like a mosaic, inappropriate or ridiculous." See Antonio Zanolini, *Una passeggiata in compagnia di Rossini* (1836), reproduced in Luigi Rognoni, *Gioacchino Rossini* (Turin: EDT, 1968), 375–81.

It is clear, in any case, that Basevi subscribes to the dramaturgical approach of Meyerbeer, which sees the tableau as the basic formal element in opera.

sire to sing . . . and so accompanied declamation, with occasional flashes of
beauty but never opera, for music must mean song.")[162] While Basevi was
writing his *Studio,* and in the years immediately following, the Wagnerian
question was still only a vaguely threatening cloud on the horizon. Much
more current was the comparison between Italy and Germany, sparked by the
growing popularity of Meyerbeer's operas—an essentially "German" composer to Italian ears—and by the dramaturgical developments in Verdi's
work. The point of dispute, the future of music as "dramatic music," meant
that it was not felt as unreconcilable opposition but as a preparatory stage for
a synthesis of the two nations' characters, out of which the perfect form of
musical drama would be born.

The philosopher-general Nicola Marselli sums up the question, presenting
it as the development of a genuine triadic process. On the one hand, there is
Germany, with music that is "highly thought out and essentially deterministic" and that has produced a school that is "profoundly reflective and harmonic" and consequently able to discern "principally the way in which to
render the drama just as it is, with its many recitatives, with little emphasis
on singing and melodic pieces." However, in such deterministic concentration
it is pedantic and too caught up with its harmonies. On the other, we have the
Italian school, which, enriched by the divine spark of melody but content
with this natural treasure alone, "thinks only of seeing through the piece" and
so remains the prisoner of a "servile, shackled" type of opera, stuck to predetermined formulas.[163] In their very opposition, however, the two schools
share a mutual attraction, as the careers of their two respective champions,
Verdi and Meyerbeer, demonstrate:

> They stretch out a hand to one another, for in one dramatic Music has risen to the
> greatest heights ever in Italy, and in the other there is more melody than is custom-
> ary in the German school. The man who can shake both these hands will be the
> Artist of the Future. The position lies vacant, and more than ever Music awaits the
> great composer who, with richer means, will be a new Mozart and produce that
> perfect fusion of the Schools that will satisfy Art for all time. However hard he tries,
> Verdi can never break free entirely from independent song, just as Meyerbeer lacks
> melody, in which the essence of Music still lies. The knowledge of how to discover
> and realize that midpoint in which the Music follows the Poetry and is dramatic yet
> does not lose the life, spontaneity, warmth, and fluidity of melody will be the work
> of the future Artist.[164]

162. Carpani, *Le rossiniane,* 78.

163. Nicola Marselli, *La ragione della musica moderna* (Naples: Detken, 1859), 60–62.

164. Ibid., 101ff. Similar declarations can be found in Abramo Basevi, "Se Meyerbeer scri-
vesse oggi un'opera italiana," *L'armonia* 1, no. 6 (4 Feb. 1856); and in Francesco D'Arcais, "Giuseppe Verdi e la musica italiana," *Nuova antologia* 3, vol. 7 (1868): 566–75. Besides, Mazzini had
already referred to the fusion of Italian melody (an expression of individuality that could not be

However, the appearance of Wagner transformed the comparison into a dispute, with the result that German music changed from being the opposite pole with which to create a synthesis into an enemy to be repulsed—or else, much more rarely, an alternative. Even writers and critics with no revolutionary credentials had started to question the traditional characteristics of Italian melody, its "entirely musical" euphony, regular periodicity, and soaring phrases.[165] Now those characteristics come into their own again, as has already been glimpsed in the early anti-Wagnerian skirmishes of Basevi himself.

Francesco D'Arcais demonstrates his perceptiveness when he points out that the poetics of Wagnerian music-drama is quite different from the integration of music with drama understood as a literary text: far from being a novelty, the latter has been a tendency of Italian opera from the time of Monteverdi. Consequently, if young Italian composers wish to create music-drama, rather than imitating Wagner they should keep faith with that tendency, possibly developing it to that level of perfection at which "both music and poetry should spring from the same mind," but without consequently "displacing the foundations of our musical edifice, turning their backs on simple, clear and rhythmic melody, or falling into the Wagnerian melos."[166]

And that's not all: it is also the case that, conversely and complementarily, techniques that had once been invoked as cure-alls for Italian opera's "faults" are now blamed for having corrupted it. Take for example the (once) famous question of "singing one note per word," which, transformed into "singing one note per syllable," now sounded to Girolamo Alessandro Biaggi like another way of saying "dramatic singing" in the accepted meaning of "the aesthetic theories of the French and Germans," which "do not wish melody to contain, in a vast synthesis, the expression and feeling of a practical concept [sic], but instead that, pedestrian and subdued, it should stumble along disjointedly under the words and follow them one by one."[167] It should be noted that the passage quoted is taken from an apologia for comic opera, whose

---

transcended) and German harmony (a social expression with tendencies toward abstraction and mysticism), going beyond national schools to create "a European musical school" (see his *Filosofia della musica*, 53–61). It is worth remembering that while it was only toward the end of the century that Mazzini's pamphlet was known in its entirety in Italy, parts of it—including the passage quoted—were published in the *Rivista musicale di Firenze* in 1840, the year when *Robert le diable* was performed (see De Angelis's introduction to *Filosofia della musica*, 22).

165. Basevi, *Studio sulle opere di Giuseppe Verdi*, 108–9: "the rhythm constitutes such a large part of the melody that it would not be just to describe as *original* a writer who uses ancient rhythms and changes the notes to create new themes. The much vaunted *facility* of many Italian *arias* derives in large measure from the great age of the rhythms."

166. Francesco D'Arcais, "Il teatro musicale in Italia," *Nuova antologia* 1, vol. 1 (1866): 114–30, quotations on 115–17.

167. Girolamo Alessandro Biaggi, "Rassegna musicale," *Nuova antologia* 9, vol. 25 (1874): 997–1007, quotations on 1001ff.

neglect is bemoaned as one of the most eloquent signs of Italian art's surrender to foreign imports. This association of comic opera with the vanished
splendors of Italian bel canto, involves another 180-degree turn from the
eighteenth-century literary outlook (comic opera was then appreciated as a
"poor man's" art, with no opportunities for displays of bel canto). Francesco
D'Arcais confirms this opinion when he observes that only "distinguished
singers" would be able to do justice to comic opera roles "as intended and
composed by Paisiello, Cimarosa, Guglielmi, Rossini, and Donizetti," and
consequently that reviving them "would require, apart from perseverance, a
wad of cash." [168]

With Antonio Tari, we move finally from the area of militant criticism to
philosophical thought. Italian music had in Tari an energetic defender against
the charge of sensuality and superficiality; rather, he sees in it an art that refused to let the imagination be contaminated by logic and reflection, and so,
the more music is raised above the other arts, the more it is to be blamed when
it allows itself to participate in illicit commerce (*Cogitat, ergo non est!!* is the
joking motto that Tari adopts to condemn "abnormal music making" [169] as
non-art). On this basis, the traditional opposition (with its consequent scale
of values) of Italian lightheartedness and German thoughtfulness has no place:

> For all the reasons indicated above I find myself very far from those who harp on
> about the superficiality of certain schools and the profundity of others, the lightness
> of certain composers and the seriousness of others, and other such commonplaces
> of the critical indictments of Italian music's degeneracy. The momentary iridescence
> of a soap bubble is no less a miracle than the sparkle of an age-old diamond,
> wrapped in the dross of the mine and hidden from profane gaze. The opaline-
> winged butterfly, in its ephemeral Sylph-like existence, is no less a marvel than
> mother-of-pearl, which waits for centuries at the bottom of the ocean for the in-
> trepid diver and the art of the stonecutter. What intransigent preference for content
> over form would dare to condemn the Greeks' predilection for pure beauty, which
> became almost their sole obsession? What practicing Pharisee would cast the first
> stone at the adulterous woman in the form of Anacreontic raving, Catullus's *Nu-
> gae,* or a Rossini *Cabaletta,* most beautiful of them all? [170]

10. "THE SINGLE UNIVERSAL FORM OF MUSICAL EXPRESSION AND CONTENT"

I have mentioned above how, around the middle of the century, the predominantly literary nature of writing on opera tended to turn professional and

---

168. Francesco D'Arcais, "Rassegna musicale," *Nuova antologia* 13, vol. 38 (1878): 156–71,
quotation on 162.

169. Antonio Tari, *Avvenire e avveniristi* (1884), in his *Saggi di estetica e metafisica,* ed. Benedetto Croce (Bari: Laterza, 1911), 81–128, quotation on 91.

170. Antonio Tari, *Sull'essenza della musica secondo Schopenhauer e i Wagneriani,* in his
Saggi, 65–80, quotation on 77ff.

provided the first attempts at historical research, among other things, or at least amassed, in the daily exercise of criticism, the materials that would then help to establish some of the fundamental lines of later operatic historiography. Sifting through the flow of periodicals, specialized and general, in the second half of the nineteenth century, we can see at least two such tendencies[171] in sufficiently clear outlines.

The first is the establishment of an "Italian teleology" that is the exact counterpart to the German one, and although it is destined to come out the loser by comparison, it has a similar reductive and false view of the complex reality of historical phenomena. This direction sees in Gluck's "reforms" the essential crossroads in eighteenth-century operatic trends: a crossroads and also a purifying and regenerating filter from which stemmed the line leading opera finally toward "music-drama." The aim of this line seems at first to be a new Italo-German synthesis, with Gluck as its first incarnation. "Bellini is the direct descendant of Gluck, who was the founder of that eclectic Italian-Germanic school which we now intend to revive in Italy,"[172] wrote Abramo Basevi, arguing with Giuseppe Rovani, who, in an article published in *Italia musicale,* had claimed Bellini to be a champion of the pure Italian school, in contrast with Meyerbeer, the champion of the Franco-German one. D'Arcais echoes Basevi almost word for word:

> If one takes account of the difference in period and conditions, one comes to the conclusion that in the last century Gluck initiated that fusion of the Germanic and Italian schools which was then . . . brought almost to perfection by Meyerbeer and Verdi. Certainly Gluck does not belong to the German school . . . he is, strictly speaking, neither German nor Italian, and modern music criticism would describe him as an eclectic. Nevertheless, he made a powerful contribution to setting musical drama on the proper course, and the signs of his influence remain in the art.[173]

Once the myth of that synthesis had faded, the goal of such a line of descent had to be seen in the context of Italian music. Reviewing a performance in Rome of *Orfeo ed Euridice,* D'Arcais forcefully denies the commonly held view, credited to Wagner himself, "that the composer of *Lohengrin* is a successor to the composer of *Orfeo,*"[174] the latter having two qualities which the former absolutely lacks: simplicity and clarity. And in order to rebut the accusations of Wagnerian lapses leveled against Verdi after the appearance of

171. A broad summary of them can be found in the preface to the fourth volume of this *History of Italian Opera.*

172. Abramo Basevi, "Rassegna di giornali musicali," *L'armonia* 1, no. 15 (8 Apr. 1856): 59.

173. Francesco D'Arcais, "I maestri italiani di musica a Parigi," *Nuova antologia* 3, vol. 8 (1868): 603–17, quotation on 611.

174. Francesco D'Arcais, "L'*Orfeo* del Gluck," *Nuova antologia* 23, vol. 102 (1888): 111–23, quotation on 114.

Aida, he extended the line with which Basevi had linked Gluck to Bellini to reach Verdi's opera:

> Verdi takes us back to Gluck. . . . From Gluck he borrows not only the general idea of what opera is, a true, just idea such as that which places the strict correspondence between notes and words at its root; from Gluck he likewise adopts the breadth of the recitatives, the declamatory melodic style, and the importance of the chorus; and at last we see again that independence of form which was the principal merit of the masters of the past. I further say that even the splendor of the stage spectacle and the frequency of dances recall the composer of *Orfeo,* . . . who understood perfectly how to make mime and dance serve the development of the dramatic action.[175]

The other tendency that can be made out is the one that reduces the history of opera to a mere branch of the history of music, conceived exclusively as a history of texts, forms, and musical styles. My feeling is that this is a consequence of the absolute authority the composer acquired in comparison with his collaborators, despite their being indispensable (a phenomenon which, while it belongs to the transformation in modes of production referred to above, is naturally linked to the new intellectual prestige gained by the composer in the nineteenth century, as opposed to the old "craft" of composition): it was only a short step from the conviction that the composer was the sole, true author of an opera to equating the opera with his score. The reinforcement of this attitude and the addition of a theoretical awareness of it was undoubtedly aided by the diffusion of the aesthetic of Eduard Hanslick, whose study on the beautiful in music (*Vom musicalisch-Schönen,* 1854), translated into Italian by Luigi Torchi, had a considerable influence on us at the end of the nineteenth century.[176]

So when the *Gazzetta musicale di Milano* opened a discussion on verismo —sparked by a polemical response by Alfredo Untersteiner to German criticism of the coarseness and "crass realism" of recent Italian operas[177]—the defense of verismo opera was conducted on the basis of the assumption that a judgment on an opera was a judgment on its "absolute" musical values, with arguments clearly inspired by Hanslick's ideas. A contribution by Arnaldo Bonaventura is illuminating in this respect:

175. Francesco D'Arcais, "Appendice," *L'opinione* (18 Feb. 1872).

176. See the review of it by Enrico Panzacchi, "Del bello nella musica: A proposito d'una recente pubblicazione," *Nuova antologia* 18, vol. 72 (1883): 685–99. This review also appeared under the title *Alcune idee sul bello nella musica,* in his *Nel mondo della musica: Impressioni e ricordi* (Florence: Sansoni, 1895), 3–37.

177. Alfredo Untersteiner, "Un'accusa ingiusta: Lettera aperta a certi critici musicali tedeschi," *Gazzetta musicale di Milano* 51 (1896): 556–58.

However, certain *goals* . . . elude music just as they elude architecture. The *Beautiful* which these arts depict is *inherent within them;* and it derives, in architecture, from the harmony of the lines, in music from the harmony and the succession of sounds: so the idea of *verismo* is outside them and cannot inform them in any way. . . . No language is less able than music to describe and reproduce reality exactly, since in itself it has no precise significance. . . . If music cannot mean anything, it is even less able to be realistic; and to be realistic it would have to cease to be music. . . . If we speak of verismo operas, it is because of an illusion, even, to express it better, a misunderstanding . . . in confusing the form of dramatic action with the music, which, whether it deals with demigods and heroines or villains and knaves, continues to be music pure and simple . . . nice or nasty, good or bad.[178]

And yet the same principle of absolute music can lead to the total condemnation of verismo opera, indeed of Italian opera *tout court,* of which verismo opera would represent its complete degeneration. On this principle, Fausto Torrefranca, in his famous attack on Puccini, sees a double teleology in the history of Italian opera: the first, positive line leads from Palestrina, where "the longing of the words to become divine . . . is expanded and lost in the music," and the second, negative one comes from Monteverdi, where, instead, music "looks to the words to give it a precise sense of what it is, to attempt to recognize itself, take possession of itself, give itself a face and become human." And while one therefore brings the progressive emancipation of music from words and leads to the classical-romantic sonata and symphony (whose "Italian origins" Torrefranca was famously reclaiming), the other, in its anxiety to humanize itself, falls ever lower, until it "confuses humanity with brutality, reality with realism, sincerity with verismo, from Monteverdi or Cavalli to Giuseppe Verdi or Giacomo Puccini."[179]

Torrefranca's ideas are too well known to stop to consider them here. What is worth observing is that, setting out from a supposition of the incontestable greater "exemplary dignity" of the symphony compared with opera (and generally of "pure music" compared with any kind of vocal music), the terms in which Torrefranca ultimately condemns opera are not dissimilar, in substance, to those of the most severe eighteenth-century scholars:

The history of Italian opera, from the end of the seventeenth century down to the present day, has two dominant characteristics: its fragmentary nature with regard to the music and its superficiality with regard to the poetry . . . opera can be said to be the attempt to create with the brief lyric of the aria and its derivatives—duet or finale—the vast framework of the drama, the theatrical tale or the epic represented.

178. Arnaldo Bonaventura, "Il realismo nella musica," *Gazzetta musicale di Milano* 51 (1896): 604ff.

179. Fausto Torrefranca, *Giacomo Puccini e l'opera internazionale* (Turin: Bocca, 1912), 13–15.

Now, drama, storytelling, and the epic are the very artistic styles least found in our literature, and opera, which aims at replacing them, has all the air of a substitute. . . . But just as myriads of moons with their aureoles would not succeed in bringing daylight to the night sky, so no series of lyrics is capable of giving us drama as it truly is.[180]

And again:

And yet it is even natural for third-rate writers, incapable of creating something alone . . . to turn to the commercial production of that type of poetry which, to be completed, requires music. So, in the operas of today, even more than at the time of Saint-Évremond, two incomplete elements merge, two impotent powers collaborate, two weaknesses prop one another up.[181]

But if the result is the same, the principles are opposing: some in the eighteenth century condemned opera in the name of the primacy of poetry and would have liked to expel the contamination of music from it; Torrefranca was against it in the name of the primacy of pure music, which he was indignant to see serving poetry. This paradoxical coincidence of opposites seems to wish to bring a cyclical end to the age-old story, and we can thus take it as the end of our journey.

The tale of operatic poetics and polemics has, however, another point of departure in the twentieth century, not disastrously closed but cheerfully open. Still in the name of absolute music—but an absolute quality that has nothing to do with Hanslick's formalism but instead means total freedom from form, understood as a material limitation placed on an art that had "the divine privilege to soar"[182]—Ferruccio Busoni prophesied that opera would rise to the level of "the highest form, specifically . . . the single universal form of musical expression and content." Indeed, it can contain both the visible (the exterior events) and the audible (the interior ones), and the artificial division into genres and categories that contradicts the fundamental unity of all musical manifestations will finally be overcome. Faithful to the abstract nature of music, it must not imitate but dissociate itself from life and must ally itself once more with the ancient Mystery, whose ritual and religious atmosphere it will re-create; it will reassume its didactic function but restore its playful character as well. In its formal structure, however, it can benefit from observing the models of the old Italian masters, especially Mozart for the condensing of

180. Ibid., 20ff.
181. Ibid., 9.
182. Ferruccio Busoni, "Abbozzo di una nuova estetica della musica" (1907), in the collection of his writings *Lo sguardo lieto*, ed. Fedele D'Amico (Milan: Il Saggiatore, 1977), 39–72, quotation on 43.

the poetic text, and the vast space which this provides for the music to expand in. But such an opera can be only a one-time feat in the life of a composer, who "would have to bring to a single opera everything that moves him, everything he imagines, everything he knows; a *Dante* of music, a musical *Divine Comedy!*"[183]

In its massive effort—retrieving the past to project it toward the future—this final poetics, unlike everything that we have read up until now, has no polemical objectives; it thus has no concrete reality to oppose. At the end of its span, the history of opera leaves the torch of utopia lit symbolically in the literature that has always accompanied it, never having forgotten, evidently, the intellectual impulse that had assisted at its birth.

183. Ferruccio Busoni, "Abbozzo di un'introduzione alla partitura del *Dottor Faust* con alcune considerazioni sulle possibilità dell'opera" (1921), in *Lo sguardo lieto*, 116–30, quotation on 121.

BIBLIOGRAPHIC NOTE

There is no single study on the poetics of opera, but a historical outline can nevertheless be drawn from Andrea Della Corte, *La critica musicale e i critici* (Turin: UTET, 1961). However, a rich anthology of sources on "polemics" can be found in *Satire e grotteschi di musiche e di musicisti d'ogni tempo* (Turin: UTET, 1946) by the same author. In Alberto Asor Rosa, ed., *Letteratura italiana*, vol. 6, *Teatro, musica, tradizione dei classici* (Turin: Einaudi, 1986), the section on the relationship between literature and music contains many references to the subject of this chapter where it touches on the history of opera: Lorenzo Bianconi, "Il Cinquecento e il Seicento," 319–63; Renato Di Benedetto, "Il Settecento e l'Ottocento," 365–410; Sergio Sablich, "Il Novecento: Dalla 'generazione dell'80' a oggi," 411–37. Finally, given the strong similarity or, in many cases, the incidence of the very same problems in musical dramaturgy examined here, the reader is advised to complement this chapter with the detailed introduction to the miscellany edited by Lorenzo Bianconi: *La drammaturgia musicale* (Bologna: Il Mulino, 1986), 7–49.

The declarations, apologias, and documents related to the very earliest phase in the history of Italian opera can be found in two anthologies by Angelo Solerti, *Le origini del melodramma* (Turin: Bocca, 1903; reprint, Bologna: Forni, 1969) and *Gli albori del melodramma* (Milan, Palermo, and Naples: Sandron, 1904; Bologna: Forni, 1976); as well as the more recent Heinz Becker, ed., *Quellentexte zur Konzeption der europäischen Oper im 17. Jahrhundert* (Kassel: Bärenreiter, 1981). The humanist circles in Florence and their research into Greek tragedy and music and the connections between these and contemporary musical practice have been covered by Claude V. Palisca: see his "The *Alterati* of Florence, Pioneers in the Theory of Dramatic Music," in *New Looks at Italian Opera: Essays in Honor of Donald J. Grout*, ed. William W. Austin (Ithaca, N.Y.: Cornell University Press, 1968), 9–38; "The 'Camerata Fiorentina': A Reappraisal," *Studi musicali* 1 (1972): 203–36; "A Discourse on the Performance of Tragedy by Giovanni de Bardi(?)," *Musica Disciplina* 37 (1983): 327–43; *Humanism in Italian Renaissance Musical Thought* (New Haven: Yale University Press, 1985), esp. chap. 14, 408–33, on Francesco Patrizi, Girolamo Mei, and Jacopo Peri. The myth that the Camerata Bardi was where the idealistic plan to revive ancient tragedy was hatched, only to give birth to opera, has been brilliantly analyzed and exploded by Nino Pirrotta, "Temperamenti e tendenze nella Camerata fiorentina" (1953), in his *Scelte poetiche di musicisti* (Venice: Marsilio, 1987), 173–95 (in English in *Musical Quarterly* 40 [1954]: 169–89). The same author's essay "Early Opera and Aria," in *New Looks at Italian Opera,* 39–107, which later appeared as the final chapter of his *Li due Orfei: Da Puliziano a Monteverdi,* 2d ed. (Turin: Einaudi, 1975), reconstructs musicians' conflicting claims of precedence in creating the new "invention" and allows a reading of their poetic declarations in the light of their compositional practice.

Regarding *Il corago,* see the introductory pages to the edition by Paolo Fabbri and Angelo Pompilio, *Il corago o vero Alcune osservazioni per metter bene in scena le composizoni drammatiche* (Florence: Olschki, 1983). On Doni, see the essay by Claudio Gallico, "Discorso di G. B. Doni sul recitare in scena," *Rivista italiana di musicologia* 3 (1968): 286–302; and Margaret Rosso Grossman's dissertation, "Giovan Battista Doni and Theatrical Music" (Ph.D. diss., University of Illinois, Urbana, 1977). On Doni's intellectual approach, see Claude V. Palisca, "G. B. Doni, Musicological Activist, and His *Lyra Barberina,*" in *Modern Musical Scholarship,* ed. Edward Olleson (Stocksfield, Northumberland, and Boston: Oriel Press, 1980), 180–205.

Piero Weiss has plotted a differentiated map of how pseudo-Aristotelian doctrines were applied in opera in his "Opera and Neoclassical Dramatic Criticism in the Seventeenth Century," in *Studies in the History of Music,* vol. 2, *Music and Drama* (New York: Broude, 1988), 1–30. The "libertine" tendencies of seventeenth-century Venetian opera have been examined by Ellen Rosand in her two essays "In Defense of the Venetian Libretto," *Studi musicali* 9 (1980): 271–85, and "Seneca and the Interpretation of *L'incoronazione di Poppea,*" *Journal of the American Musicological Society* 38 (1985): 34–71. On the normalizing cultural function of Arcadia, see the enlightening essay by Amedeo Quondam, "L'istituzione Arcadia: Sociologia e ideologia di un'accademia," *Quaderni storici* 8 (1973): 389–438. The essays by Nathaniel Burt, "Opera in Arcadia," *Musical Quarterly* 41 (1955): 145–70, and Robert S. Freeman, "Apostolo Zeno's Reform of the Libretto," *Journal of the American Musicological Society* 21 (1968): 321–41, cover the influence of Arcadian ideology on the evolution of opera, as does Freeman's *Opera without Drama: Currents of Change in Italian Opera, 1675–1725* (Ann Arbor, Mich.: UMI Research Press, 1981). Piero Weiss explores the reception in Italy of French classicist theories in "Teorie drammatiche e 'infranciosamento': Motivi della 'riforma' melodrammatica nel primo Settecento," in *Antonio Vivaldi: Teatro musicale, cultura e società,* 2 vols., ed. Lorenzo Bianconi and Giovanni Morelli (Florence: Olschki, 1982), 2:273–96.

Elvidio Surian's *A Checklist of Writings on 18th-Century French and Italian Opera* (Hackensack, N.J.: Boonin, 1970) serves as a guide through the thick forest of eighteenth-century writings on opera, while for an overall view of the "question of opera" the reader can still turn to the treatise by Hugo Goldschmidt, *Die Oper des 18. Jahrhunderts in der Beurteilung der Zeitgenossen und der Aesthetitker insbesondere,* which forms the second part of his *Die Musikästhetik des 18. Jahrhunderts und ihre Beziehungen zu seinem Kunstschaffen* (Zurich and Leipzig: Rascher, 1915): a classic of early-twentieth-century musicology. Also dating from the early twentieth century is the single overall attempt to examine the testimonies of visitors to Italy from abroad:

Giuseppe Roberti, "La musica in Italia nel secolo XVIII secondo le impressioni di vi-
aggiatori stranieri," *Rivista musicale italiana* 7 (1900): 698–729, and 8 (1901): 515–
59. Remo Giazzotto's book *Poesia melodrammatica e pensiero critico nel Settecento*
(Milan: Bocca, 1952) gives an exclusively Italian overview. For information on the
many echoes created by the French and Italian disputes of the seventeenth and eighteenth centuries north of the Alps, see Gloria Flaherty, *Opera in the Development of
German Critical Thought* (Princeton, N.J.: Princeton University Press, 1978). Questions concerning the poetics of opera are covered, directly or indirectly, in the essays
by Francesco Degrada, collected in his *Il palazzo incantato: Studi sulla tradizione del
melodramma dal barocco al romanticismo*, 2 vols. in 1 (Fiesole: Discanto, 1979); those
from volume 1 that should be mentioned here are "Una minuscola poetica del melodramma tra Barocco e Arcadia," 27–39 (on Giuseppe Riva's "Avviso ai compositori
ed ai cantanti"; Degrada's essay first appeared in *Analecta Musicologica* 4 [1967]); *Il
palazzo incantato: Voltaire, la musica, l'opera*, 99–113 (originally in *Quaderni della
Rassegna musicale*, vol. 3 [Turin: Einaudi, 1965]); *Due volte di "Ifegenia,"* with the
appendix "Le due Ifigenie e la Querelle Gluck-Piccinni," 155–208 (originally in *Chigiana* 32 [1975]).

   There are various studies on individual writers of the Arcadian period. For Muratori, see Alfredo Cottignoli, *Muratori teorico: La revisione della "Perfetta poesia" e la
questione del teatro* (Bologna: Clueb, 1987), a collection of essays, with an appendix
that includes an unpublished dissertation by Muratori on music in ancient theater, superseded by the definitive version of his *Perfetta poesia italiana*. Martello's individual
position and his ironic ambiguity are efficiently covered in Claudio Gallico, "P. I. Martello e 'La poetica di Aristotile sul melodramma,'" in *Scritti in onore di Luigi Ronga*
(Milan: Ricciardi, 1973), 225–32; theoretical questions are placed in the wider context
of Arcadian dramatic activity in Bologna by Maria Grazia Accorsi, "Pastori e teatro:
Dal melodramma al dramma ebraico," in *La Colonia Renia: Profilo documentario e
critico dell'Arcadia bolognese*, 2 vols., ed. Mario Saccenti (Modena: Mucchi, 1988),
2:267–359. On Scipione Maffei, see Gianfranco Folena, "'Prima le parole, poi la musica': Scipione Maffei poeta per musica e *La Fida ninfa*," in *Vivaldi veneziano europeo*,
ed. Francesco Degrada (Florence: Olschki, 1980), 205–33 (now also to be found in his
L'italiano in Europa: Esperienze linguistiche del Settecento [Turin: Einaudi, 1983],
235–61); and Laura Sannia Nowé, "Una voce sul melodramma nelle discussioni del
prima Settecento (S. Maffei)," in *Metastasio e il melodramma*, ed. Elena Sala Di Felice
and Laura Sannia Nowé (Padua: Liviana, 1985), 247–70. Eleanor Selfridge-Field spec-
ulates on the circumstances that might have prompted Benedetto Marcello to write his
celebrated satire in "Marcello, Sant'Angelo, and 'Il teatro alla moda,'" in *Antonio Vivaldi: Teatro musicale, cultura e società*, 2 vols., ed. Lorenzo Bianconi and Giovanni
Morelli (Florence: Olschki, 1982), 2:533–46; to essays from the volume *Benedetto
Marcello, la sua opera e il suo tempo*, ed. Claudio Mandricardo and Franco Rossi
(Florence: Olschki, 1988), are particularly relevant to the themes covered here: Sergio
Durante, "Vizi privati e virtù pubbliche del polemista teatrale da Muratori a Mar-
cello," 415–24; and Luca Zoppelli, "Le Pindare, le Phidias, le Michel-Ange des musi-
ciens: Note sulla fortuna critica dei 'Salmi' nel '700," 403–14.

   The texts of the two main episodes in the age-old *querelle* between Italian music
and French music—also covered from another point of view by Michel Noiray in a

forthcoming volume of this *History of Italian Opera*—are collected in Denise Launay, ed., *La querelle des bouffons*, vol. 3 (Geneva: Minkoff, 1973); and in François Lesure, ed., *Querelle des Gluckistes et des Piccinnistes: Textes des pamphlets*, vol. 1 (Geneva: Minkoff, 1984). The history of this topic, from its origins to the period prior to the *querelle des bouffons*, has been reconstructed by Georgia Cowart, *The Origins of Modern Criticism: French and Italian Music, 1600–1750* (Ann Arbor, Mich.: UMI Research Press, 1981). From the wealth of writing on the *encyclopédistes* and music, mention should be made of Enrico Fubini, *Gli enciclopedisti e la musica* (Turin: Einaudi, 1971); and Beatrice Didier, *La musique des lumières: Diderot, l'Encyclopédie, Rousseau* (Paris: PUF, 1985).

For the influence of Diderot's thinking on the development of Italian opera, see Daniel Heartz, "From Garrick to Gluck: The Reform of Theatre and Opera in the Mid-eighteenth Century," *Proceedings of the Royal Musical Association* 94 (1967–68): 111–27; the same writer returns to the theme in "Les Lumières: Voltaire and Metastasio, Goldoni, Favart and Diderot," in *International Musicological Society: Report of the Twelfth Congress, Berkeley 1977*, ed. Daniel Heartz and Bonnie Wade (Kassel: Bärenreiter, 1981), 233–38 (but see also the report of the entire conference "Opera and Enlightenment," ibid., 212–55, with contributions also from Walter E. Rex, Denise Launay, Michael F. Robinson, Thomas Bauman, Gernot Gruber, and comments by Ludwig Finscher and Pierluigi Petrobelli). The influence of Italian opera (and particularly that of Metastasio) on Rousseau's thinking is the subject of two essays by Giovanni Morelli: " 'Éloges rendus à un singulier mélange de philosophie, d'orgueil, de chimie, d'opéra, etc.' Sulle ascendenze melodrammatiche della antropologia di Jean-Jacques Rousseau," *Rivista italiana di musicologia* 9 (1974): 175–228, and " 'Prend ton Métastase et travaille': Per una indagine melodrammaturgica di 'Julie, ou La nouvelle Héloïse,' " in *Musica e filologia: Contributi in occasione del festival Musica e filologia, Verona, 30 settembre–18 ottobre 1982*, ed. Marco Di Pasquale with the collaboration of Richard Pierce (Verona: Società Letteraria, 1983), 201–12.

Metastasio's single theoretical work, the *Estratto dell'arte poetica d'Aristotile e considerazioni su la medesima*, is examined in Piero Weiss's "Metastasio e Aristotele," in *Metastasio e il mondo musicale*, ed. Maria Teresa Muraro (Florence: Olschki, 1986), 1–12 (an English translation appears in *Journal of Musicology* 1 [1982]: 385–94). Elena Sala Di Felice reconstructs Metastasio's essential conception of opera through a rereading of his letters and the texts themselves, as well as of the *Estratto*, in *Metastasio: Ideologia, drammaturgia, spettacolo* (Milan: Angeli, 1983). References to these problems can, however, be found in the rich harvest of studies that appeared around the time of the bicentenary of the poet's death (1982) and are analyzed by Giovanna Gronda in "Metastasiana," *Rivista italiana di musicologia* 19 (1984): 314–32.

For the poetics of Calzabigi, his connections to Metastasio and the theme of reform, see (in addition to Heartz's "From Garrick to Gluck," mentioned above) Gabriele Muresu, "Ranieri de' Calzabigi e la 'querelle des bouffons,' " in his *La parola cantata: Studi sul melodramma italiano del Settecento* (Rome: Bulzoni, 1982), 55–77 (which first appeared in *Analecta Musicologica* 19 [1979]); and the two-part essay by Paolo Gallarati, "L'estetica musicale di Ranieri de' Calzabigi: *La Lulliade*," *Nuova rivista musicale italiana* 13 (1979): 531–63, and "L'estetica musicale di Ranieri de' Calzabigi: Il caso Metastasio," *Nuova rivista musicale italiana* 14 (1980): 497–538, as well as the many ideas found in his *Musica e maschera: Il libretto italiano del Settecento* (Turin: EDT/Musica, 1984). Discussions of Metastasian opera in the second half of the eighteenth century are the subject of a well-documented investigation by Giorgio Mangini, "Le passioni, la virtù, la morale nella concezione tardo-settecentesca dell'opera metastasiana," *Rivista italiana di musicologia* 22 (1987): 114–44. The relationship between opera and tragedy in the writings of Algarotti, Planelli (see also the introduction to Antonio Planelli, *Dell'opera in musica* [1772], ed. Francesco Degrada [Fiesole: Discanto, 1981]), and Arteaga is covered by Maria Teresa Marcialis in "Il melodramma o le trasgressioni della tragedia," in *Metastasio e il melodramma,* ed. Elena Sala Di Felice and Laura Sannia Nowé (Padua: Liviana, 1985), 225–46. On the theory of opera buffa according to Matteo Borsa, see F. Alberto Gallo, "L'estetica dell'opera buffa nel saggio sulla 'Musica imitativa teatrale' di Matteo Borsa," *La rassegna musicale* 32 (1962): 56–65.

Giorgio Pestelli's essay on the aesthetic conceptions of Abbé Carpani, "Giuseppe Carpani e il neoclassicismo musicale della vecchia Italia," in *Quaderni della Rassegna musicale* (Turin: Einaudi, 1968), 4:105–21, remains a key text; on Carpani's personality, see Helmut C. Jacobs, *Literatur, Musik und Gesellschaft in Italien und Österreich in der Epoche Napoleons und der Restauration: Studien zu Giuseppe Carpani (1751–1825)* (Frankfurt am Main: Lang, 1988). Ritorni's classicism and the correspondence between his and Stendhal's musical taste are illustrated in detail by Paolo Fabbri, "Le memorie teatrali di Carlo Ritorni, 'Rossiniste de 1815,'" *Bollettino del Centro rossiniano di studi,* 1981, 85–128 (some excerpts from his *Ammaestramenti* are included in the appendix). Scott L. Balthazar, "Ritorni's *Ammaestramenti* and the Conventions of Rossinian Melodramma," *Journal of Musicological Research* 8 (1988): 281–311, shows how Ritorni's critique of the mechanism of the "wholly musical" opera can become a keen analytical tool precisely because of its relevance (and this is articulately outlined by Daniele Seragnoli, *L'industria del teatro: Carlo Ritorni e lo spettacolo a Reggio Emilia nell'Ottocento* [Bologna: Il Mulino, 1987]). For the prevailing drift of musical aesthetics in the early nineteenth century, see Agostino Ziino, "Luigi Romanelli ed il mito del classicismo nell'opera italiana del primo Ottocento," *Chigiana* 36 (1979): 173–215; and the introduction and comments on the texts collected by Marcello De Angelis in Giuseppe Mazzini, *La filosofia della musica* (Florence: Guaraldi, 1977). Gary Tomlinson, "Italian Romanticism and Italian Opera: An Essay on Their Affinities," *19th Century Music* 10 (1986–87): 43–60, is an attempt, although summary, to bring together the history of ideas with the history of opera composition.

Italian music criticism in the second half of the nineteenth century has not been the subject of systematic investigation. Research is still at the stage of registering the materials and of examining the vast number of sources, promoted by the Répertoire International de la Presse Musicale (see the account given by H. Robert Cohen and Marcello Conati, *Acta Musicologica* 59 [1987]: 308–24). A first exploration of how Meyerbeer was received in Italy and how familiarity with his works changed Italian operatic thinking has been made by Fabrizio Della Seta, "L'immagine di Meyerbeer nella critica Italiana dell'Ottocento e l'idea di dramma musicale," in *L'opera tra Venezia e Parigi,* ed. Maria Teresa Muraro (Florence: Olschki, 1988), 147–76. Research is more advanced on the fortunes of Wagner, and the vast volume by Ute Jung, *Die Rezeption der Kunst Richard Wagners in Italien* (Regensburg: Bosse, 1974), provides a huge amount of information. The first part *(Ort- und zeitgebundene Wagner-Rezeption in Italien)* appears in Italian translation in the miscellany *Wagner in Italia,* ed. Giancarlo Rostirolla (Turin: ERI, 1982), 55–225. This volume also contains the essay by Agostino Ziino, "Aspetti della critica wagneriana in Italia," 315–407: this is the second, expanded version of the previous "Rassegna della letteratura wagneriana in Italia," in *Colloquium Verdi-Wagner Rom 1969,* ed. Friedrich Lippmann (Cologne and Vienna: Böhlau, 1972), 14–139, which, with a broad selection of critical texts attached, the same author had published as *Antologia della critica wagneriana in Italia* (Messina: Peloritana, 1970). For the aesthetics of Marselli and Tari, see Alfredo Parente, "La fine della musica" (1929) and "La musica e il riscatto dell'autonomia dell'arte in Antonio Tari" (1932), in his *Castità della musica* (Turin: Einaudi, 1961), 182–97 and 198–221.

From the late nineteenth century onward, opera once again aroused the interest of the literati, now far less as the object of critical reflection than as a source of imagery. The study by Adriana Guarnieri Corazzol, *Richard Wagner nella letteratura italiana* (Bologna: Il Mulino, 1988), highlights the attitude toward Italian opera from D'Annunzio on, by way of the Wagnerian "reaction" (D'Annunzio in particular is the subject of another important study by the same writer, *Sensualità senza carne: La musica nella vita e nell'opera di D'Annunzio* [Bologna: Il Mulino, 1990]). Halfway between literary invention and musical criticism stands "writing on music" (Bastianelli, Barilli, Benco, Bontempelli, Savinio, Vigolo, Dal Fabbro, Gavazzeni), and this has been examined with equal perspicacity by Marzio Pieri in "Le scritture della meraviglia: Sullo scriver di musica nel Novecento," *Paragone letteratura* 33, no. 388 (June 1982): 30–53, and "Le meraviglie della storia: Ancora sullo scrivere di musica," *Paragone letteratura* 33, no. 390 (Aug. 1982): 43–65.

On Busoni, see the chapter on his aesthetic thinking in Sergio Sablich, *Busoni* (Turin: EDT/Musica, 1982), 111–39. The judgments made on verismo opera outside Italy, and their effects on Italian music criticism, are covered in Fiamma Nicolodi, "Parigi e l'opera verista: Dibattiti, riflessioni, polemiche," *Nuova rivista musicale italiana* 15 (1981): 577–623 (later also in her *Gusti e tendenze del Novecento musicale in Italia* [Florence: Sansoni, 1982], 1–66). On the dichotomy of absolute music versus opera, see Marcello De Angelis, "Note sul melodramma, la musica pura e l'Europa in Giannotto Bastianelli," in *Musica italiana del primo Novecento: "La generazione dell'80,"* ed. Fiamma Nicolodi (Florence: Olschki, 1981), 261–77. The poetics of the antiverismo movement and the plans for the renewal of opera declared and acted on by that generation are clearly focused on by Virgilio Bernardoni, *La maschera e la favola nell'opera italiana del primo Novecento* (Venice: Fondazione Levi, 1986). Finally, mention should be made of a fine anthology of writings on opera collected by a musician rather than a literary figure: Gian Francesco Malipiero, *I profeti di Babilonia* (Milan: Bottega di poesia, 1924). It reads like a paradoxically reversed image of the myth of Italian music that so energetically promoted musical renewal in Italy in the early twentieth century and that is lucidly analyzed in Francesco Degrada's "La 'generazione dell'80' e il mito della musica italiana," in *Musica italiana del primo Novecento,* 83–96.

The Dramaturgy of Italian Opera

CARL DAHLHAUS

Categories and Concepts

1. WHAT IS MUSICAL DRAMATURGY?

The term "musical dramaturgy" is not simply descriptive but expresses the far from self-evident proposition that the primary constituent of an opera *as a drama* is the music.

It may be best to establish first and foremost what this fundamental proposition means by reference to a problem in the discussion of nineteenth-century opera: what is to be understood by the "action" of works like *Il pirata* or *Ernani*? Part of the "story line"—the narratable action—is a complex prehistory of no direct importance to the action realized in the music. Musical realization in Italian opera—unlike Wagnerian music-drama—is closely associated with what is visibly represented on the stage; it is thus different in principle from verbal realization in spoken plays, which enables things to be part of the drama even when they are not visibly represented on the stage. (In French classical tragedy, indeed, the greater part of the action is represented in speech alone and not visibly on the stage.) In other words, because a prehistory is less accessible to music than to speech, it is a less important constituent of the "drama" in an opera than in a play.

But if we regard the affects, the emotions, and the emotional conflicts expressed musically onstage in the form of arias, duets, and ensembles as the "true" musical drama, dramaturgical analysis of an opera should not start with the way a narratable action is reflected in music. Rather, quite the reverse, it should try to show how an action constituted as a drama of affects, primarily by musical means, comes to be based on a story line (or *fabula,* see §7 below) in order to take shape on a stage.

The literal meaning of the word "dramaturgy" is the origination and performance of drama, but the use of two words, unavoidable in modern languages, separates creation from realization, with the awkward result of suggesting that the text (whether words alone or words and music) already constitutes a "drama," which is then realized on the stage as "theater," whereas the original meaning was that only as theater did the text become a drama rather than merely a draft for one. (The term "theater" emphasizes the visual element: *theatron* was the Greek auditorium.)

But in addition to the "production" (origination and realization) of dramas, "dramaturgy" also covers the principles or rules underlying the production (or postulated as doing so). And insofar as the emphasis falls on the establishment of principles, rather than on application, a dramaturgy is a theory of drama (as in the case of Lessing's *Hamburgische Dramaturgie*). Thus—broadly speaking—the word referred initially to *poiesis* as the making of a work, then to poetics as the theory of *poiesis,* and finally to theories justifying the principles of poetics.

In the age of historicism, however, theory tended to be absorbed into analysis or interpretation of individual works or groups of works. The rules laid down in the poetics of the seventeenth and eighteenth centuries were concerned with establishing aesthetic norms; dramatic form seemed fixed, and the dramatist's first task, as Goethe and Schiller agreed still in their correspondence at the end of the eighteenth century, was to find subject matter to satisfy the rules of the genre. But the theorists of the age of historicism discovered not only that there were profound differences between fundamental structures of historical types of drama but also, and above all, that mutually exclusive types were aesthetically equal. Furthermore the categories of poetics—now a poetics of specific epochal, national, or even individual types of dramas— were no longer regarded as norms but as conceptual aids toward the understanding of single works in their individuality. "Explicit" dramaturgy, formulated as a theory or part of a theory, no longer created a book of rules to which works had to conform, but a kind of categorial scaffolding allowing them to be rearranged, and as soon as its purpose of reconstructing the "implicit" poetics of individual works had been fulfilled, the scaffolding could be dismantled.

The degree of abstraction chosen when outlining a dramaturgy depends, for one thing, on the end in view and, for another, on the level of scholarship assumed as starting point. Too often, elaborate investigation of detail is partnered by a minimal consideration of basic concepts, with the result that the accumulated facts and observations remain almost useless because the interpretive categories are inadequate. It may be appropriate, therefore, to give priority to remarks of a general character. The belief that one knows perfectly well what a drama is may be an illusion; the purpose of reflection about this confusingly complex concept is not, however, to construct a theory of "the" drama—a circular and self-serving aesthetic procedure—but to develop criteria which enable us to determine the specific elements that make, for example, Rossini's or Verdi's *Otello* "a" drama. The particular does not serve as material for the theory; the theory serves as premise for interpretation of the particular. The more systematic the premise, however, the more usable it is (contrary to what some historians believe), so long as systematization is not an end in itself but a procedure helping concepts to be differentiated by means of the reciprocal relationships created between them. The attempt to outline a dramaturgy of opera is therefore a matter of systematic probing with a historiographical purpose.

2. THE DRAMA OF THE MODERN ERA AND OPERA

If we start with the premise that opera came into existence at the same time as the drama of the modern era—the drama of Shakespeare and Racine—and shares the context of that drama so far as concerns the history of forms and ideas, we can orientate ourselves, in this attempt to outline a dramaturgy of opera, by the spoken theater of the period from the seventeenth to the twentieth centuries, rather than by classical tragedy or medieval mystery plays: in other words, we can base discussion of analogies and differences between the spoken play and opera on the relationships between Metastasio and Racine, or Verdi and Shakespeare.

We cannot presume a fixed concept of drama as something established and beyond question. Tentatively, however, and allowing for revision or retraction if necessary, we might define the drama of the modern era as action (1) represented on a stage, (2) involving dealings between people, (3) manifested primarily in the medium of speech, while its parts (4) compose a cohesive context of meaning and motivation directed toward a particular end. A comparison of opera with drama in the light of such a definition reveals some characteristics peculiar to the musical theater (although the divergences are not necessarily the essential traits).

1. Insofar as the term "drama of the modern era" is understood to mean the spoken play of the period from the Renaissance through classicism to realism, even a fleeting comparison shows that opera has a special tendency toward stage spectacle going beyond the usual conventions of the spoken play, and that it shares this with the baroque theater. The origins of this tendency

lie in the (to some extent) "natural" affinity between music on the one hand and religious or profane rituals, processions, and festivities on the other. Just as rituals in real life use music as a support, so ritual has a place in musical drama that it does not find in spoken drama, unless onstage music is required.

2. It is a striking characteristic of early opera that the essential action consists less in confrontations between human beings than in human dealings with the classical gods or the Christian powers of heaven and hell. (This is true of baroque theater generally, but it lasts much longer in the history of opera.) The explanation lies, first, in music's ability to suggest and make credible the "marvelous" or supernatural and, second, in the difficulty of representing confrontations between human beings by musical means. ("Representing" in this context means that music is essential rather than an incidental embellishment of speech, as in recitative.) Dialogue, as a verbal confrontation producing a decisive outcome, and monologue, as "interior dialogue" leading to a decision, are as awkward in opera as they are natural in the spoken play. (Recitative, at least when secco, is a form of utterance governed by speech rather than music and is therefore of minor importance in a dramaturgy of opera starting from the concept of a drama constituted by musical means.)

3. The premise that drama of the modern era—except for baroque theater—is enacted primarily in the medium of language and not in events shown onstage is questionable with respect to opera, because music can be both an illustration of verbal language and a language in its own right. Moreover, its independent—or partly independent—linguistic character does not always mean the same thing in different epochs, genres, or forms. The extent to which music is either a visual language of stage action or a language of lyrical contemplation varies as much as the dramatic functions it fulfills in those two roles. (The musical process in an exit aria or a *pezzo concertato* should not be dismissed a priori as "undramatic": when musically expressed, the contemplative is not the antipole of the dramatic but one of the means used in a specifically musical constitution of drama.)

4. The individual moment in drama of the modern era is filled with backward and forward references, so that it functions primarily as the consequence of past events and the precondition of future ones, instead of containing its main significance within itself. An operatic scene, by contrast, usually seems to take place purely in the present time, isolated from either past or future. Music imposes present time inasmuch as it holds the dramatic situation fast in a "timelessness" in which, in an extreme case, memory of earlier time and expectation of future time are equally tenuous. ("Purely present time" is more a negation of time than one of its modes.) It is true that in opera and in spoken drama alike the tension in a situation is founded in the conflicts that drive events forward out of the past and into the future: but the musical represen-

tation serves to foreground the emotional substance of the onstage events, not the dialectics of the dramatic process.

The hypothesis that it is above all the music that constitutes an opera as musical drama (this hypothesis amounts to more than the truism that the music dominates) presents a discussion of the dramaturgy of opera with the task of determining the music's relationship to the other components from which the eventual work is constructed, in a hierarchy in which degrees of sub- and superordination can vary. We can accept as given, without losing our way in the detail of particular cases, that the relationship (the remoteness or closeness) of the music to the *fabula,* to the conceptual structure, to the configuration of characters, to the onstage events, to the language (whether that of action or of expressive contemplation), to the "interior action," and to the stage setting will prove to be extremely varied both in individual cases (individual works or types of work) and in general (in opera as a whole or in its genres). A primary affinity to a setting—a "local color" depicted in the music as well as on the stage and relevant to the course of the dramatic action (Cherubini's *Elisa,* Weber's *Freischütz,* Puccini's *Bohème*)—or to stage action (Mozart's *Figaro,* Verdi's *Falstaff*) is just as possible, and as reasonable, as an affinity to an "interior" action almost detached from stage events (Wagner's *Tristan*), to the configuration of characters (Verdi's *Trovatore*), or to the conceptual structure (Wagner's *Parsifal*). And it would be mistaken to call any one of these tendencies "undramatic" for no better reason than that it departs from the conventions of spoken drama. The trite observation that all the components constantly work together should not blind us to the fact that it is precisely the apparently insignificant shifts in the scheme of the work constructed from them which denote the specific character of an opera conceived as a musical drama. A *fabula* is undoubtedly essential (except in some works of modern music theater which do not belong in the opera category at all); but whether the story is the center around which the other components group themselves (Weill's *Aufstieg und Fall der Stadt Mahagonny*) or serves merely as the raison d'être of a configuration of characters, whose emotions and emotional conflicts, expressed in music, represent the true drama (Verdi's *Ernani*), can be discerned from the function of the music: the function of the music determines finally what type of musical drama an opera represents. But if the focal point in the scheme of the components constituting an opera varies from one group of works to another, and if it is on the music first and foremost that this variable emphasis depends, it means that there is no fixed definition of the term "musical drama"; it can only be defined by first lining up the heterogeneous characteristics and then recognizing the hierarchy that develops among them as founded in the musical structure. The determining factor is not music's "dominance" but the function its dominance lets it perform in the constitution of musical drama.

3. THE MEANS OF MUSICAL DRAMA

The musical-dramatic means available to composers of opera, and the principles from which they can proceed, are uncommonly heterogeneous by comparison with those in other musical or theatrical genres. This has less to do with differences in the stylistic traditions converging in one work than with the divergences between the forms in which music fulfills dramaturgical functions. No inner connection exists, for example, between onstage music supporting and illustrating a scene and the emotional expressiveness that makes music a language in its own right, often almost independent of the text.

The most influential and enduring of the principles underlying the aesthetics of opera from the seventeenth century to the twentieth have been the theory of affects and the idea of the marvelous. Despite the changes undergone by the concept of affect or emotion over the four centuries, and notwithstanding the fluctuations in the number of phenomena regarded as marvelous at different times, it must be true to say that these are fundamental categories which have influenced the theory of opera as much as they have dominated it in practice. The popular aesthetics of opera consists almost exclusively of paraphrases of the concept of emotion, and theorists from Charles Batteux through E. T. A. Hoffmann to Ferruccio Busoni have repeatedly placed the category of the marvelous in the foreground, regardless of changing circumstances in the history of ideas and composition.

Admittedly, where the principal substance of a work consists of the musical expression of affects, or feelings, the marvelous is not dominant, and vice versa. The principle of confrontation between human beings—the release of emotions—and that of supernatural intervention are diametrically opposed.

This is not to deny that there are operas in which (as in ancient Greek tragedy) human beings are tormented by emotions and inner conflicts caused by gods, so that, as Richard Alewyn put it, the action seems to have been transferred from a horizontal stage to a vertical one. Yet the distinction between the primacy of affect and that of the marvelous is an important one, and its impact on dramaturgy can even be illustrated by comparing operas such as Gluck's *Orfeo ed Euridice* and *Alceste,* which appear at first sight to be similar in conception. In *Orfeo,* despite the duet and aria in the third act in which the "true" drama (concerning the relationship between the human beings, Orfeo and Euridice) is concentrated, the greater part of the action (from Amore's intervention after the funeral rites, through the scenes in Hades and Elysium, to the appearance of the deus ex machina) is a tragedy worked out between human beings and supernatural powers: powers, moreover, who appear on the stage. The affects arise from the fates the gods impose on the humans, who react rather than act. By contrast, although it is Apollo who "stages" the starting point of the action of *Alceste* and at the end dissolves the knot that has gone beyond human power to untie, the opera is essentially a tragedy between Alceste and Admeto, one from which there is no more escape than from a tragedy by Racine, despite the happy ending.

The awkward relationship between some musical-dramatic means and principles makes mediation difficult for a composer, while an inner affinity reigns in other cases. The characteristic connection in Wagnerian music-drama between the gestural molding of the music, which has precursors in *recitativo accompagnato,* and leitmotivic technique, which Wagner claimed was an assimilation of symphonic tradition, is immediately comprehensible, despite the heterogeneous historical premises: the visual, gestural clarity of the onstage exposition of a leitmotiv is one of the conditions of its ability later to fulfill its dramaturgical function of recalling past events.

But if leitmotivic technique and gestural music are compatible, for all their disparate origins, the association between musical local color and the representation of the marvelous is less clear-cut, because local color admits a romantic interpretation as well as a realistic one. (Under the influence of Walter Scott's novels, local color became a dominant element not only in libretto writing but also in operatic composition in the nineteenth century.) The local color that determines the "tone," or what Verdi called the *tinta musicale,* of romantic operas such as Weber's *Freischütz,* Meyerbeer's *Robert le diable,* and Verdi's *Macbeth* is so closely interwoven with the supernatural as to become an element in the opera's action, instead of merely a background. In the seventeenth and eighteenth centuries, however, an aesthetics of the marvelous was obviously possible without any musical local color (except in *ombra* scenes), and, vice versa, in the late nineteenth and twentieth centuries (in Verdi's *Aida* or Puccini's *Bohème*) musical local color has been possible without the slightest admixture of the marvelous. The linking or separation of the two is historically variable.

There would appear to be no connection between dramaturgical justification of the marvelous by musical means and the use of onstage music or incidental music for realistic, "quotational" purposes, as in the spoken theater, without any foundation in the specific musical language of the opera. Yet both are indispensable to spoken plays and to opera. The representation of elves and fairies without music is unthinkable, either in Shakespeare or in Ferdinand Raimund, and so is the idea of staging marches, processions, or dances without musical accompaniment. But if it is rare in the spoken theater to encounter both romantically and realistically motivated stage music in one and the same play, the conjunction is common in opera. (In the case of "heroic-romantic" subject matter, derived directly or indirectly from Ariosto, chivalresque rhythms are in general as indispensable as the harmonies weaving the spell to which the hero succumbs.)

The ease with which songs can be integrated into scenes in opera is not affected by stylistic differences as a rule, being no greater and no less in baroque opera than it is in romantic or realistic opera. (Classical era opera is the exception here, as the aesthetic precept of a uniform stylistic level was unfavorable to the inclusion of songs.) The dramaturgical basis for interpolating songs varies, however. If a song in a baroque opera represents an intermezzo in the "low" style (an interpolation of commedia per musica in a dramma per musica), by the romantic period it stands for the sphere of everyday life, in all its difference from the marvelous. (The clash between the marvelous and the everyday is the source of the tragic dialectic of the underlying dramaturgical pattern in works such as *Undine, Der fliegende Holländer,* and *Rusalka.*) In realistic opera, finally, a song contributes to the depiction of a milieu and comes aesthetically very close to instrumental local color, though far removed from it in terms of compositional technique. The change of function is thus a matter of dramaturgy rather than musical style: it is not the fundamental musical character of the song that changes but its theatrical raison d'être.

Music's ability to express simultaneously the different emotions of several people singing together in an ensemble is one of the essential ways in which opera differs from the spoken play, where to have everyone talking simultaneously creates chaos; but relationships between this ability and other musical-dramatic means are complex and not always immediately convincing. It can scarcely be combined with leitmotivic technique at all, as Wagner recognized. Its awkward relationship to local color is stranger but also not incomprehensible. In the third act of *La Bohème,* a paradigm of musical scene painting, the possibilities of presenting heterogeneous material simultaneously in music, for which the libretto offers abundant scope, are scarcely exploited, except in the quartet at the end of the scene. It would be absurd, however, to doubt Puccini's dramaturgical intuition. His restraint in the use of ensemble or montage acknowledges that atmospheric uniformity, resulting from musical and scenic local color, and the emotional divergence that gives an ensemble passage its inner tension are difficult to reconcile without aesthetic discord.

If we do not flinch from the crude simplifications necessary at this early stage in the process of trying to find our bearings in a confusing abundance of material, we can say that the central importance of affects and emotional conflicts in Italian opera has placed other musical-dramatic means either in the foreground or at the periphery.

First, by comparison with French opera, stage music in support of spectacular tableaux is relatively rare in postbaroque Italian opera. Where that is not so, as in Rossini's and Verdi's late operas, the French influence is unmistakable; indeed, such works were often originally French and only later Italianized (Rossini's *Guglielmo Tell,* Verdi's *Don Carlo*), by the composers themselves or in accordance with general practice. Second, the onstage song remained peripheral, despite its role in Rossini's and Verdi's *Otello,* because it was almost unknown in opera buffa (unlike opéra-comique and singspiel), and the dramaturgy of the comic genre influenced that of the serious. Third, the Nile scene in *Aida* and the street scenes in *La Bohème* notwithstanding, the trend toward local color typical of the nineteenth century as a whole was weaker in Italian opera than in French, German, Czech, or Russian. Fourth, operatic composers did not adopt leitmotivic technique to any great extent (Puccini less than Massenet), because the principle of constantly recalling something earlier or anticipating something yet to come is inimical to the spontaneous expression of emotions, which relies on what is present on the stage and contributes to the fullness of the moment.

Instead, gesture and the simultaneous utterance of heterogeneous emotions in ensemble singing are among the essential characteristics of Italian opera because they relate directly and evidently to its main principle, the expression of affects rooted in the interaction of human beings. It would be wrong to be dogmatic about fixed and unvarying relationships of dependency and exclusion between musical and dramatic means and principles, but it is nevertheless obvious that certain configurations dominate in different national or regional operatic traditions.

4. METHODOLOGICAL CONSIDERATIONS

The musical means at an opera composer's command are so heterogeneous that we can scarcely speak of "operatic" style as we speak of "symphonic" or "chamber-music" style. There is no connection in either musical substance or dramatic function between a song interrupting the dialogue in a singspiel, an ensemble allowing characters to express their differing emotions simultaneously, and a leitmotivic web joining the present to reminiscences of the past and anticipations of the future. At the same time it is undeniable that a prose libretto causes a breakdown of musical periodic structure, and that leitmotivic technique is one of the means of compensating for the loss of the form-building function of regular meters—in Mussorgsky, Massenet, and Puccini, as much as in Wagner. In other words, the structural characteristics of musical drama display divergent traits as well as affinities, and describing and explaining them are among the central tasks of a musical dramaturgy. The methodological premises to be adopted are at first uncertain, however.

1. Typologies such as the distinction between what Volker Klotz termed "closed" and "open" forms of drama—between the unity, continuity, regularity, and homogeneity of a tragedy by Racine and the multiplicity, discontinuity, irregularity, and stylistic mixture of one by Shakespeare—are usually dichotomous in construction. They also entail assertions about intrinsic relationships between musical, verbal, and scenic elements. The basis for the penchant toward dichotomy, rather than three- or four-part classification, appears to lie less in the nature of the issue itself, however, than in a long-

established, traditional way of thought: yet the archaic origin, far from vali-
dating the tradition, should prompt skepticism. The argument that these are
intrinsic relationships (rather than connections arising from special historical
circumstances and individual conceptions) is only partly sustainable. It is immediately obvious that the unities of place and time are two facets of the same
thing, but it is difficult to demonstrate an intrinsic, "natural" relationship between unity of action, a disproportionate emphasis on prehistory, the muting
of affects, and a tendency toward aphorism: the structure of French classical
tragedy is not a "natural form" in drama.

2. The construction of an "ideal type," as defined by Max Weber, differs
from the dichotomous typologies fashionable among academics around 1910,
first in its disavowal of systematic completeness and second in the logical status it claims and the methodological function it fulfills. The number of ideal
types with which a historian of opera operates is not so much prescribed in
the nature of his work as dependent on the goal he aims to reach. If it is
accepted that a "romantic opera" may be an opéra-comique (Boieldieu, *La
Dame blanche*) or a singspiel (Weber, *Der Freischütz*) or an opera seria
(Donizetti, *Lucia di Lammermoor*) or a grand opéra (Meyerbeer, *Robert le
diable*), then *Robert le diable* may be considered in the context of romantic
opera alongside *Der Freischütz,* or in that of grand opéra alongside *Les Huguenots,* without it being necessary to regard either the one or the other of
those ideal types as the "intrinsic form" of *Robert.* Ideal types are not the substance of operatic history but aids to conceptualizing this work or that, while
an opera's standing as a work of art rests on its individuality. There is a connection, to be sure, between the various elements from which ideal types are
constructed, but almost always in historical reality some drop out while others are added. This is not a defect in the construction, as such, but one of the
conditions under which the ideal type fulfills its purpose, which is to demonstrate that the particularities of historical phenomena are modifications of a
general type and, as such, accessible to conceptual definition.

3. To be effective, an ideal type requires a certain minimum number of affinities between musical-dramatic structural traits. It is admittedly impossible
to draw a line, saying "the concept is useful thus far and no further"; and it
is debatable whether the fact that the text of a *Literaturoper* (an opera setting
the text of a play word for word, even if abridged) is usually prose is already
enough to justify calling it an ideal type. (A prose libretto creates problems of
musical syntax, which in turn necessitate cohesive structuring of the orchestral writing.)

4. The idea that in principle any and all musical-dramatic structural traits
can be combined, making it possible to describe, case by case and unburdened
by theory, what particular combination characterizes one particular work,

has its attractions for rigorous empiricists, because it completely avoids the speculative elements (evident or latent) in assertions about affinities and intrinsic relationships. But this extreme postulate is scarcely practical. For example, there is a compelling connection between the form (cantabile followed by cabaletta) of the duet for Rodolfo and Federica in Verdi's *Luisa Miller* and the changes made to the prehistory of the characters' relationship in the process of adaptation from Schiller's play *Kabale und Liebe*. The recognition that here the musical form dictates the content, while the contrary may happen in other operas, is simple and unproblematical in itself but amounts to little without a theory of the dialectics of form and content, which is one of the central themes of a musical dramaturgy.

It is clear from the foregoing that methodological extremes lead to restrictions, either of vision or of conceptual penetration of reality. A strictly dichotomous typology which casts (Italo-French) opera as the complete opposite of (Wagnerian) music-drama—as if *Götterdämmerung* were not partly a grand opéra—is as questionable historiographically as the kind of empiricism where rejection of theory is only a smokescreen concealing a rudimentary, undeveloped, and prejudiced theory. At the same time, the extent to which either the construction of an ideal type or the mere acknowledgment of affinities between structural elements seems an appropriate basis for interpretation is both controversial and liable to vary historically. As said, it is debatable whether *Literaturoper* is an ideal type or not. And the element of historical variability means that the combination of musical-dramatic elements constituting an ideal type was generally more firmly fixed in the eighteenth century than in the New Music of the twentieth, from which, once again, different consequences can be drawn: either we abandon all conception of an ideal type with respect to modern opera, or we relax the conditions it must fulfill.

5. MUSIC THEATER, OPERA, MUSICAL DRAMA

As use of the term "music theater" spread, its meaning grew ever more diffuse. It is not a synonym for "opera," although it is often used as such, for even a cursory analysis reveals that it entails sometimes more and sometimes less.

1. The need for an overarching term to cover not only opera, operetta, the musical, and the *melodramma* but also ballet, pantomime, and "instrumental theater" (à la Maurizio Kagel) prompted the recourse to "music theater," but the very fact that the term embraces every kind of stage work with music, except plays with incidental music, means that it loses in substance what it gains in scope.

2. In the late 1920s the practice arose of using "music theater" as an alternative to "opera" to classify all stage works with music that, for one reason or another, people did not want to call operas, although no similarities exist be-

tween a montage of spoken narrative, dialogue, and pantomime (Stravinsky's *L'histoire du soldat*), an opera-oratorio (Stravinsky's *Oedipus Rex*), a "Song-spiel" (Weill's *Mahagonny*), and an "antiopera" (Ligeti's *Aventures et Nouvelles aventures*). Defined by nothing except not being opera, the expression "music theater," like every other term arising out of pure negation, runs the risk of gathering an arbitrary agglomeration of heterogeneous phenomena into a concept or pseudoconcept which remains insubstantial for the lack of anything in common.

3. It is misleading to distinguish between "musical drama" and "music theater" by understanding "drama" as the musical and verbal text and "theater" as the realization on the stage, inasmuch as it is absolutely fundamental to a workable theory of drama that one holds fast to the inseparability of "origination" and "performance," following the example of ancient Greek theater. The habit of detaching the scenic element, thus truncating the concept of drama, results from the literary bias of nineteenth-century aesthetics. As a premise it reduces analysis of opera, all too often, to investigation of the "word-tone relationship."

4. An emphasis on the theatrical element distinguishes the *intermedi* of the fifteenth, sixteenth, and seventeenth centuries, and the serenatas of the eighteenth, from later stage works with music classified, for various reasons, as music theater rather than opera. This theatricality (no pejorative sense intended) is as remote from opera qua musical drama as it is effective in demonstrating music's striking affinity to nondramatic stage spectacle. Religious, mythological, or dynastic allegories, tableaux employing ingenious stage technology, ballets in which symbolic implications are just as important as the demonstration of aristocratic attitudes—in short, the forms that we feel to be specifically courtly—are a long way from drama as an action involving the dealings between human beings and developing along logical lines, but they are all the closer to music for that reason. That the combination of music and theater tends toward musical drama at all is therefore anything but self-explanatory.

In view of the close relations between music and theatricality, it would be aesthetically blinkered to dismiss the tableaux, rituals, processions, and dances which often predominate over the dramatic content (in the narrower sense) of eighteenth-century tragédie lyrique and nineteenth-century grand opéra as "external" elements smothering opera, which ought "really" to be a musical drama. Rather, the theatrical and the dramatic have equal rights in opera: rights bestowed on them by the music, which enables each to make its specific effect on a stage.

The kind of stage spectacle that cannot exist without musical support and, vice versa, gives music better opportunities to unfold than almost any other stage form is even, fundamentally, closer to music than drama itself. Linking drama with music has always been a dubious undertaking because a play does not need music, other than some interpolated forms, and music is not, of itself, "melody shaped as dialogue" (*dialogisierte Melodie*, in Wagner's phrase).

Any theory that attempted, contrary to practice, to exclude theatricality from opera would be dogmatically restricted; but it is necessary to isolate musical drama from the larger categories of opera and music theater in order to clarify the central concern of a musical dramaturgy. As musical drama, and without necessarily banning theatricality, opera is founded on the idea that conflicts and confrontations between human beings can be represented on a stage in forms that are musical in substance.

That the historical origins of opera lie in the baroque era is not fortuitous, however. Music's close relationship to theatricality and spectacle—closer than to drama, insofar as drama is expressed primarily in words, the medium of interaction between human beings—constituted an intrinsic affinity to the theater of the baroque age, the century into which opera was born. But in opera the spirit of baroque theater outlasted its age in the aesthetics of the marvelous, which was tolerated in operatic theory even in the ages of classicism and realism by theorists who despised opera and those who adored it alike. The marvelous is the opposite of the probable, the fundamental category of the poetics of the spoken play. The marvelous showed the gods descending to earth from Mount Olympus in order to intervene in the action of an opera, thus transforming the classical "horizontal stage" into the baroque "vertical stage" (in Richard Alewyn's terminology). The marvelous also embraced the supernatural events in the "romantic" singspiel, which provided the opportunity for technological wizardry, amazed contemporary audiences, and were mocked by posterity, and finally it sanctioned both subject matter from fairy tales and legends, hailed by E. T. A. Hoffmann and other romantic aesthetic theorists of the early nineteenth century as the only fit subjects for opera, and the mythology of Wagnerian music-drama, in which, to be sure, gods and human beings meet on the "horizontal stage" and are stirred by similar inward motives.

The Libretto and Its Functions

6. THE LIBRETTIST'S MÉTIER

It is not skill at writing verse that determines the librettist's métier but a talent for producing a scenario as true to the musical-formal conventions or emerging trends of its time as to the maxim that music creates its own specific kind of dramatic art, which is not the same as that of the spoken play. A good libretto provides musical drama with the condition of possibility. (In the twentieth century, incidentally, the librettist's métier threatens to dissipate toward the extremes of either the literary or the amateur.)

The characteristics of a successful libretto are the subject's amenability to the structure and sense of the musical forms of the time; presentation of the essential elements of the action onstage, in the drama's present time, thus avoiding complicated prehistory and concealed strands of plot; attention to contemporary ideas about what can and what cannot be set to music; and finally responsiveness to dominant contemporary literary genres (Walter Scott's novels and Victor Hugo's plays in the early nineteenth century, for example). All these are subject to major or minor historical changes, affecting different elements to differing degrees. For example, the requirement for the main part of the action to take place onstage, in "present" time, is more enduring than attachment to the concept of the marvelous as an aesthetic criterion of what can be represented in music, while the literary genres plundered by librettists change about as rapidly as the musical forms imposed upon them.

Recognizing the differences in pace at which historical change overtakes various components of a libretto is easier than reaching agreement about how far librettists, if they are to rise above mere theatrical jobbery, can or should go in the effort to do justice to an operatic subject's conceptual structure—which does not necessarily coincide with the conceptual structure of a literary model.

The central conflict in drama of the modern era is between love and politics (or honor). In more complex dramaturgical constructions this well-worn but almost inexhaustible theme does not consist merely in the inner anguish of people who are lost whatever the decisions they make, but becomes truly tragic when a decision that at first seemed a moral triumph turns out to be moral corruption. The accident of being forced to part from a person one loves for political reasons is less tragic than the necessity, arising from intricately interlocking complications, to abuse love, deeply rooted though it may be, as a political tactic, with the result that the other person, the victim, not only believes that he or she is the prey of fate but also feels betrayed and destroyed in the emotion that had seemed to be the core of his or her existence. Although a conflict of this nature seems to be the specific manifestation of tragedy in a drama of affects, it is doubtful whether opera—either in general or at any specific period in its history—is capable of representing it at all. If we compare two such very different operas as Bononcini's *Camilla* and Bellini's *I Puritani,* separated by almost 150 years and extreme changes in musical form, the tragic motive outlined above proves to remain equally latent in both; the conceptual structure is implicit in the subject matter but is suppressed by the form of musical drama, albeit for different reasons.

"Beautiful confusion"—Boileau's *beau irrégulier*—sums up what audiences of the baroque era expected from an opera plot. They cannot have been disappointed by what Silvio Stampiglia served up in the libretto for Giovanni Bononcini's most famous opera, *Il trionfo di Camilla, regina de' Volsci* (1696). The opaque plot, filled with disguises, simulated madness, attempted poisonings, wars and the rumors of wars, can be followed only because its underlying dramaturgical structure is the simple, even stereotypical one of conflict between two hostile nations, with a cast consisting of three pairs of lovers (one comic), a tyrant, and a confidant.

"Beautiful confusion" was an aesthetic concept of the seventeenth century, swelling to grotesque proportions in the European novel and invading opera as it did other genres, but it was also the correlative of the principle of constructing an opera from a large number of relatively small arias expressing contrasting affects. The dramaturgy is determined by the combination of three things: the stage reached in the development of aria form, the aesthetics of representing affects, and the tendency toward labyrinthine plots. A complicated *fabula* is necessary to motivate a sufficient variety of situations to give rise to the affects that can be expressed in short and therefore numerous arias. Although it cannot be said, strictly, that there is any compelling inner connection between the aesthetic concept of "beautiful confusion" and the historical development of aria form, nevertheless the external correlation, for reasons of dramatic technique, is obvious.

The mutual love of Camilla, queen of the Volscians, who are oppressed by the Latini, and Prenesto, a prince of the Latini, drives them into a tragic dialectics from which there is apparently no way out. Camilla believes, with the legitimate patriotic rigor of the oppressed, that she must take advantage of Prenesto's love to serve a political end; Prenesto is forced to think that the love which seemed the mainspring of his existence was mere deception, and he falls into profound despair. But there is no question of Stampiglia's developing this tragic motive into an action played out between Camilla and Prenesto. Instead, the same situation keeps on recurring in varying colorations but always showing Camilla torn between patriotism and love, while Prenesto, who knows her only in her disguise as Dorinda, innocently parades his love and interprets politically motivated problems as personal in origin. Things change abruptly when Camilla reveals her true identity and has Prenesto cast into prison, which kindles violent hatred in him. In the end, having condemned Prenesto to death, Camilla pardons him, and the lovers' private reconciliation is simultaneously celebrated as a political settlement between the Volscians and the Latini.

There is nothing here of a tragic dialectics, of the irresistible corruption of divided and confused emotions, never entirely to be healed even by a happy ending. The only trace of it is in the plot, the purpose of which is to create rapidly shifting situations, occasions for outpourings of feeling expressed in short arias. The inner action implicit in the subject matter is almost indiscernible behind the façade of the outer.

Bellini's *Puritani,* composed nearly 150 years later on a libretto by Carlo Pepoli, has an analogous tragic intrigue as its foundation, but again it remains latent for musical reasons, if completely different ones. The opera is set in the seventeenth century, during the English Civil War, when the King's party was opposed by the Puritans led by Cromwell. The fact that Arturo is an adherent of the King, and Elvira, whom he loves and who loves him, is from a Puritan family, leads to a situation in which Elvira cannot but believe her innermost feelings have been betrayed. Minutes before their wedding, Arturo leaves her without a word, in order to help the Queen escape her enemies. Yet even though the conflict that should be resolved between Arturo and Elvira can be regarded as the true tragic subject, it does not determine the actual layout of the work as musically constituted in arias, duets, and ensembles. (It would be a grave mistake to interpret the tragic element as the concealed essence of the musical phenomenal form: as Hegel states in the *Enzyklopädie der Wissenschaften* [§131], the essence must be apparent in the phenomenon and not vanish behind it into the unknowable; an essence that does not show itself is not an essence.) The tragedy implicit in the subject matter is reduced to a mere misunderstanding, and for Arturo and Elvira love is the only unconditional emotion. They are, after all, the principal characters of a romantic opera, despite the school of opinion which regards *I Puritani* as the musical-dramatic expression of the spirit of the Risorgimento. Arturo is able to clear up the misunderstanding in a few words in part 3, and the action that is the musically realized subject of the dramaturgy is totally different from the tragedy outlined above. Elvira, on discovering what she believes is Arturo's treachery, goes mad (part 1); Riccardo, who cherishes a hopeless passion for Elvira, is persuaded to look for Arturo, in the hope that his sudden reappearance will shock Elvira back to sanity (part 2); Elvira, briefly appeased by Arturo, goes mad again when she hears the drums of approaching Puritan soldiers (the sound she associates with the interruption of her wedding, which caused her insanity) but recovers her wits when Arturo is threatened with death; an amnesty declared by Cromwell then leads to a *lieto fine,* but it could equally well have been a *tragico fine* without offending dramaturgical logic (part 3). The drama brought into being by what is seen taking place on the stage and heard in the musical expression is thus not the story of emotions tragically alienated by politics but a tale of madness brought on by the alienation.

The first mad scene is a cantabile ("Oh vieni al tempio"), a simple declaration of love with an intimacy that acquires a distancing aspect only from the uncomfortably public nature of the scene: in terms of musical form, from the *pertichini* and chorus added to the solo. In part 3 the moving aspect of Elvira's madness is expressed by a romanza colored by reminiscences. Finally, the reconciliation scene (duet and finale) is conventional in itself, and the appearance of unusualness comes from "outside": from the fact that one and the same music, the drums of the Puritan soldiery, both unleashes Elvira's hallucinations and threatens Arturo with imminent death. Recognition of his danger gives Elvira back her sanity; and for the second time a duet ("Credeasi, misera"; formally a quartet with chorus) gains inner tension from being perceived against the dark foil of cured madness and rising at the same time above a danger from which there is no escape, as its melody seems to soar above the abyss. So it is not the "classical" dialectics of a tragic, and simultaneously moral, conflict of emotions but the representation of "romantic" madness that forms the underlying pattern of the dramaturgy which is the source of the musical process.

There is a dialectics in drama between form and content—in opera between musical form and the content represented onstage. In its specific manifestations it is historically determined, because both forms and contents change structurally and substantially in the course of historical processes. Hegel expressed this in the lapidary formula "content is nothing but form inverted into content, and form nothing but content inverted into form" (*Enzyklopädie*, §133). The aesthetics of an era, the musical structures at its disposal, and the underlying dramaturgical pattern on which it relies can be said to generate each other. In both *Camilla* and *I Puritani* they affect each other reciprocally in a way that makes distinguishing between premises and results—deciding, that is, whether the major role is played by "beautiful confusion" or by the brevity and number of arias—less important than bearing in mind that the one element "inverts" into the other.

The concept of the dialectics of form and content entails recognition that not only the content but also the form in which it appears and on which it is partly dependent convey something essential. It is possible to imagine a central dialogue in *Camilla* in which the tragic dialectics would develop between two people face-to-face, but no such scene takes place. The fragmentation of the dialogue in arias representing different affects, motivated by the far-fetched situations of an action reduced to an intrigue, is the expression of a dramaturgy based on the anthropological notion that human beings, rather than have things out in verbal exchanges, are swept from one emotion to another by chance events and betrayals.

When the source of a libretto is a play, the musical form obviously alters the meaning of the play as much as it does the structure that partly constitutes the meaning; this is so whether or not it is agreed that the adaptation is legitimate and justified or has gone awry. Salvadore Cammarano displayed positive virtuosity in quarrying Schiller's *Kabale und Liebe* for the libretto of Verdi's opera *Luisa Miller*, and the fact that the libretto is as "well made" as any play is the corollary of his uninhibited treatment of the original play, discarding and exchanging the motives behind its action without scruple. The musical schema prescribing the paths Cammarano had to take, sacrificing Schiller's dramaturgy as he went, consists of the obligatory two-part aria (slow cantabile and fast cabaletta), which can alternatively be broken down, for purposes of both musical and dramaturgical analysis, into five parts (scena, *tempo d'attacco,* cantabile, *tempo di mezzo,* cabaletta). At the start of the opera, Luisa's love for Rodolfo (Schiller's Ferdinand) is still unclouded because she does not know that he is the son of Count Walter (President Walter in Schiller's play, that is, chief minister of the small principality) but believes he belongs to the same social class as herself. Hopeful longing (cantabile) and joy when he arrives (cabaletta) provide the affective content of the arioso sections, marked by changes of tempo, which function as the framework of the introduction. In the second scene, Miller refuses Wurm's demand that Luisa be forced to marry him, on the grounds that although he is her father, he will not be a tyrant (cantabile); Wurm then vengefully reveals Rodolfo's true identity, and Miller is appalled (cabaletta). The woman Walter wants his son to marry is Federica, a childhood friend of Rodolfo, not the Prince's mistress, as in Schiller. (Though he does not appear, the Prince is omnipresent in the play as a force corrupting the judgments of everyone involved.) And whenRodolfo and Federica meet again, in line with the conventions of Cammarano's dramaturgy the scene falls easily into sentimental reminiscences (cantabile) followed by vehement argument after Rodolfo admits that he loves Luisa (cabaletta).

The play turns to tragedy as the consequence of differences in rank, creating a net in which the characters are ensnared in spite of wishing to behave with unprejudiced humanity. In the libretto the number of strands in the plot in which Rodolfo and Luisa become entangled has to be much larger because otherwise it would be hard to fulfill the dramaturgical demand for situations (approximately as many as there are numbers in the opera) to motivate not just the expression of affects but also rapid changes of affects in order to produce the cantabile-cabaletta schema. It does not matter whether the *tempo di mezzo* is short or long, musically thin or rich; it must be there, coming between, and linking, the slow and fast sections, to mark the dramatic event which justifies the sudden switch from one emotion to another: the arrival of another character, the discovery of a deception, the confession of a previously hidden emotion, an unforeseen decision, and so on.

That one and the same action can appear in different types of drama does not mean, however, that the type with the more profound conceptual structure is superior and satisfying and the other inferior and unsatisfying. The dialectics of form and content urges, rather, that in principle—without prejudging the aesthetic merits of individual cases—the differing forms in which the same subject matter may be dressed are dramaturgically equal.

7. FABULA AND INTRIGUE

The term *fabula,* a cardinal category in the theory of narrative elaborated by Russian formalists, denotes the story of an action, with incidents arranged according to their logical sense and temporal sequence. Brecht's theory of "epic theater" (*Little Organon for the Theater,* §§65 ff.) placed it at the center of dramaturgy, including the operatic dramaturgy he developed with Weill in connection with *Aufstieg und Fall der Stadt Mahagonny,* as it evolved from "Songspiel" to opera. The anomaly that in this usage *fabula* both denoted an indispensable component of the drama and also provided a key term for an out-of-the-ordinary interpretation of the "narratable story" as the substance of an opera was glossed over because the debatable theory seemed to be borne out by the elementary fact.

The statement that a narratable story—*mythos* in Aristotle's *Poetics*—is one of the components of a drama is at once indisputable and banal. Interpreting it as the essence of the drama, however—with the implication that dramaturgy is a matter of disposing of means in order to realize a narratable story in words, music, and spectacle—is only partly valid and cannot be sustained as a general principle. And it would be wrong to assume that the issue of what is part of a *fabula* and what is not is something immutably established.

First, the banal fact that "one and the same" *fabula* can be compressed or expanded is by no means unimportant or superficial. (Brecht wrote a sonnet in the fourteen lines of which he retold the *fabula* of Shakespeare's *Hamlet*— or so he thought.) If we start from the premise that the narration of what is "in" an opera should give priority to explaining the dramatic substance and function of the arias, duets, and ensembles, the outcome, with respect to what is musically realized, is a ratio between prehistory and onstage action considerably different from what is usual in the synopses in opera guides or program books. (A sketch of Don Ottavio's dramatic function in *Don Giovanni* would need to be detailed enough to prevent his arias from seeming merely abstractly beautiful and his character merely naively, almost comically honorable.)

Second, the difference between the drama as musically realized in arias, duets, and ensembles and the story as narrated in the usual synopses should enable us to draw conclusions, some aesthetic and some with practical theatrical applications. The bourgeois birth and prehistory of the Countess in *Le nozze di Figaro* may be part of the narratable story, and as familiar to operagoers in the eighteenth century from Paisiello's *Barbiere di Siviglia* as to later audiences from Rossini's opera; but it is not a component of the drama as musically realized, and therefore it is also not part of the *fabula* in any sense relevant to the musical realization. So attempts, in the name of realism, to depict on the stage more and other things from the prehistory and narratable history than are present in the music and the action outlined by the music must be judged inappropriate.

Third, the *fabula*'s position in the hierarchy of components constituting an opera as musical drama is not fixed but varies according to the type of opera, and even from opera to opera. It seems to me worthwhile to undertake a few cursory analyses in order to shed some light on the issue, not primarily to serve as interpretations of the works in question.

The dramatic substance of Bellini's *Norma* consists of a configuration of characters—Pollione, Norma, and Adalgisa—who are moved by contradictory, rather than simple, affects and compulsions, and whose relationships to one another are equally complex. Each stands to each of the others in a relationship that can reasonably be called dialectical; the same word also describes their relationship with the religious and national duties by which each feels bound. And the arias, duets, and one trio are simply the expression of the conflicts between and within them—whether the conflict forms the musically explicit content of a cantabile ("Meco all'altar di Venere") or has a double meaning, conveyed by the action and needing to be read into an aria's musical semantics by the listener ("Casta diva, che inargenti"). The interior and interpersonal conflicts, all the elements of which have been presented before the first act is over (by the trio in the act finale), do not motivate an action which, as *fabula*, forms the substance of the drama; quite the reverse: the action is a vehicle for displaying the characters' relationships and introducing scenes that make it possible for the conflicts to be expressed in music. Felice Romani's libretto is as ingenious in assisting this as the *fabula* is abstruse. The chief emphasis of *Norma* as a musical drama falls, not on the action and the logic and connectivity of its motivation, but on the emotional dialectics of the principal characters, for which the sequence of events onstage merely provides a framework. The *fabula* is a function of the configuration of characters, not the other way round.

But if the action in *Norma* is scarcely more than a vehicle for the emotions, in the prologue of *Simon Boccanegra*—an opera within the opera—the affects of love, hatred, and political ambition that drive the characters are the motives of a *fabula* that is the "real" drama. The conflicts between Boccanegra and Fiesco and the ambivalent relationship of Boccanegra and Paolo (each using, or thinking he uses, the other for his own ends) form the dramatic substance in that they are the motivating elements of the *fabula* in themselves, not on account of their affective content. The meeting between Paolo and Boccanegra is witnessed in the light of the preceding scene between Paolo and Pietro, and the story of Maria and "Amelia"—part of the prehistory and action not seen on the stage—is an essential component of the dialogue in the duet for Boccanegra and Fiesco, not just an excuse for realizing the emotional clash of the two men with the supreme musical force of which Verdi was the unrivaled exponent.

The *fabula* can become the substance of a drama only to the degree to which it expresses the underlying idea. Brecht's placing it at the center of drama—both musical and spoken—and treating the verbal, musical, and scenic structures as means toward the concrete representation of the *fabula* have to be interpreted anthropologically, in a way that in turn casts light back on to anthropological implications of earlier opera. The premise of Brecht's theory of drama is that a human being's essence is revealed in his social behavior: in brief, that the "external" is the essential. Only where sociological categories dominate, rather than psychological ones, is it possible to group words, music, and stage setting around the *fabula* as that which gives them sense, instead of using the *fabula* (as Bellini and Romani did) as a vehicle for creating situations that permit, even demand, the musical expression of emotional conflicts—the psychological substance that makes human beings what they really are. All dramaturgies, consciously or not, are also anthropologies.

The habit of associating the term *fabula* primarily with tragedy and the term "intrigue" with comedy is understandable but should be questioned. *Don Carlo* is in fact a paradigmatic drama of intrigue (*Un ballo in maschera* is another): the action is determined by intrigues which intersect and counter one another, and thereby produce an outcome that no one intended. (To that extent, the drama of intrigue is a basic model of political drama, which owes its authenticity not to the historical facts it uses but to its underlying idea that catastrophe is chance.)

Le nozze di Figaro, similarly, is structured from many intersecting intrigues—producing a happy ending instead of a catastrophe, but still by chance (whereas the fact that the single intrigue of *Così fan tutte* is pursued to its end gives this dramma giocoso some of the traits of a dramaturgical machinery that carry it away in the direction of a *farsa*). In *Figaro*, it is not the intrigues as such but the confusion as they become entwined, their lack of success, and the perverse situations that result that are decisive for their dramaturgical function. The way the different intrigues become entangled is more important than the logic of each one individually. If, generally, intrigue is a means of laying traps for characters and causing them to drop their masks, the greater complication of one element is the correlative of greater differentiation in another. The schematic characters of a type of opera buffa that still feeds on the commedia dell'arte tradition are the dramaturgical complement of a simple intrigue; conversely, the complex of intrigues in *Figaro*—which audiences can just about manage to follow, and which could in theory be pursued indefinitely—corresponds to the greater psychological differentiation.

Without the confusing multiplicity of changing situations that subtler differentiation could not be realized in a work of musical theater.

For the spectator (not necessarily for the participants) the primary goal of a comic intrigue is to see characters unmasked, although no lasting change is likely to come of it, in either Molière or Plautus; Count Almaviva's plea "Contessa, perdono" moves us for the very reason that the emotion expressed in the music is as sincere as it is transient.

8. *PAROLA SCENICA* AND SOUNDING SILENCE

Plato's injunction that, of the constituent elements of music, *logos* (the word) must take precedence over *harmonia* (mode, signifying proportion in relations between tones) and *rhythmos* (including dance meters) had immeasurable historical influence, resounding down the centuries. It was reiterated when opera began as a genre strongly associated with the classical past ("l'orazione sia padrona de l'armonia e non serva" [let speech be the mistress of harmony, not its servant]) and was invoked later to justify every new round of operatic reform—meaning a restitution of the origins in order to recover the essence. The most famous instance is Gluck's preface to *Alceste:* "Pensai di ristringer la Musica al suo vero ufficio di servire alla Poesia" (I have striven to restrict music to its true office of serving poetry). The thesis has its antithesis, everyone's favorite version of which is Mozart's formulation: "In an opera the poetry simply must be the music's obedient daughter." The debate around these two postulates has raged endlessly—and fruitlessly, because it starts from a questionable premise, namely that the "word-tone relationship," as it has come to be known, is the fundamental issue in opera. Both sides in the debate share this basic belief, it is the common ground over which they fight, but it distorts the view of some essential facts.

The persistence of the debate, even forming the subject matter of Strauss's opera *Capriccio,* is all the more surprising in that both Verdi, with his idea of *la parola scenica,* and Wagner, with his thesis that the music and words of an opera were functions and means of the drama, brought to the fore an element which made the argument about "word and tone" relatively unimportant, and that is the action presented on the stage.

It is difficult to see why the controversy plagued discussion of operatic aesthetics for centuries unless we understand the extent to which the theory of opera depended on that of the spoken play: because language is the medium of the play, there seemed to be no escaping the conclusion that language must be the vehicle of the drama in opera too—either the language of words, common to operas and plays, or a specific language of music. Yet not even Wagner's theory of opera, contrary to a deeply rooted belief, supports the analysis of opera in terms of the relationship between music and words—the advancement of either over the other. When Wagner postulated in *Oper und Drama*

(1851) that music must be a means serving the purpose of the drama, what he meant by "drama" was not the words but the action constituted by the combination or commingling of music, words, and what happens on the stage. The emphasis in Wagner's writings usually falls on the action. The long-running argument about the hegemony of words or music might abate if we regarded both as functions of the action, so that it depends on the individual situation on the stage at any given moment whether the music (carried by the words) or the text (illustrated or interpreted by the music) is dominant (each yielding to the other after a time). In other words, whether the situation onstage, where analysis of opera must start, is illuminated primarily by the words or by the music must be decided from one scene to the next: it is not predetermined by some doctrine of operatic aesthetics puffed up into one of the rules of the genre.

A brief comparison of extreme examples should suffice to suggest what forms the relationship between words and music can take when it is dramaturgically based.

When Wagner wrote of "sounding silence" *(tönendes Schweigen)* in his treatise *Zukunftsmusik* (1860), he meant an orchestral melody expressing emotions characters feel even while they remain silent. Emotions that seem impossible to speak aloud are, for that very reason, especially accessible to music, according to nineteenth-century romantic aesthetics. Moreover, as Wagner added, opera is able to extend a moment of fraught silence to a duration commensurate with its significance in the drama, while it might be no more than a passing instant in a play. Wagner himself seems not to have appreciated fully the implications of his own concept, for it applies to more than orchestral passages such as Siegfried's Funeral Music in *Götterdämmerung*: a vocal ensemble such as the one at the end of act 2 of *Lohengrin* can also be interpreted as sounding silence. The text here is not "real" speech, as might be uttered in a play, but "unreal," its function solely to provide the opportunity for music in which the expressive content of the sounding silence can be heard. The concept of sounding silence proves, no doubt against the will and without the knowledge of its originator, to be a theory of the *pezzo concertato*.

The finale of act 1 of Rossini's *Otello* includes a trio for three characters— Desdemona, Elmiro, and Rodrigo—who are moved by very different emotions yet express themselves in the same melody, slightly modified only by coloratura (larghetto: "Ti parli l'amore"). The term *pezzo concertato* should not divert attention from the fact that the piece is also thoroughly dramatic in form, not just motivated by the action but constituting the drama as musical drama. When a moment of general, highly charged feelings, in which time seems to stand still, is extended long enough for the emotional confusion to sink in fully, it is as much a dramatic element—one denied the spoken play— as the rapid tempo in a scene of frenetic activity, which is what is commonly meant by "dramatic." And the expression of heterogeneous affects in the same or similar melodic terms signifies, in the examples from both *Otello* and *Lohengrin,* that behind the differences and contradictions of the characters' reactions there lies concealed a common feeling of being trapped in a situation they cannot unravel, from which there is no escape.

Where words in a *pezzo concertato* are merely the means to sustain a cantabile medium in order to express emotions that would have to remain unspoken in a play, Verdi's *parola scenica* presents an extreme contrast, yet both techniques can be used in one and the same work. The term *parola scenica* has been blunted by excessive and imprecise use: Verdi meant by it a form of words that encapsulates a situation precisely and drastically. Busoni regarded it as an indispensable tool in a libretto and called it by the German word *Schlagwort.*[1] Verdi wrote to the librettist of *Aida:*

> Non so s'io mi spiego dicendo *parola scenica;* ma intendo dire la parola che scolpisce e rende netta ed evidente la situazione. Per esempio i versi: "In volto gli occhi affisami / E mente ancor se l'osi: Radames vive . . ."; Ciò è meno teatrale delle parole (brutte, se vuole): "con una parola / strapperò il tuo segreto, / Guardami, t'ho ingannata: / Radames vive." (Letter to Ghislanzoni, 17 August 1870)

> [I don't know if I make myself clear, saying *la parola scenica;* but I mean the expression which sculpts the situation, making it stand out cleanly and plainly. For example, the lines "Turn your eyes upon me / And lie again if you dare: / Radames is alive . . ." are less theatrically effective than these words (vile as you may think them): "With one word / I will root out your secret, / Look at me, I tricked you: / Radames is alive."]

The essential characteristics of Verdi's example are rhythmic irregularity; concentration on the important point and avoidance of the verbal embellishment taken for granted as "poetic" in his time; gestural or arresting vocabulary ("strapperò," "guardami"); and a crescendo of excitement within the few lines.

The "theatrical" or "dramatic" language that strikes home to make a situation clear is, conversely, a language that needs the situation to give it the clarity and almost physical intensity that make it a language for the theater. Illuminating the situation through the words is the corollary of intensifying the words through the situation. Often only fragmentary phrases stand out from a sung text, the sole function of which otherwise is as a vehicle for the music; they come as a surprise, mediating between the drama of affects expressed by the music and the visible action that gives the affects their stage presence.

---

1. "Head word," "catchword"; but a primary meaning of *Schlag* is a blow, so in this context *Schlagwort* might be translated as "the word that strikes home."—Trans.

9. TEXT AND "WORK"

A theory of opera that aims to be undogmatic must be flexible about categories, especially fundamental ones such as "theater," "drama," "work," "text," and "interpretation," instead of squeezing them into definitions that satisfy a scholarly requirement for order but fall short of reality as judged by the history of ideas.

If we understand an operatic score to comprise a text of both music and words (as well as the explicit stage directions, supplemented by the implicit directions of the verbal and musical text), then analysis, which must serve the discipline of theater studies as well as that of musicology, is faced with the alternatives of emphasizing either the text or the events on the stage. The problem is a real one and will not be dismissed by the truism that these elements are complementary. It is seldom articulated explicitly but is contained, unspoken, in the wavering use of the concept of the "work," which, in discussions of operatic aesthetics, sometimes means the verbal and musical text but sometimes the performance through which the text is realized in the theater.

If we speak of "work and reproduction" as Hans Pfitzner did in his polemical treatise on the aesthetic theory and practice of opera in his day (*Werk und Wiedergabe,* 1929), "work" is clearly understood to be the verbal and musical text; performance is a matter of interpretation and presentation before an audience but does not constitute the work. (In the terminology of idealist aesthetics, the theater is the "phenomenal form" of the "essential form" contained in the text.) Pfitzner regards stagecraft as reproductive, not productive: a means allowing the work to be manifested, not an end served by the verbal and musical text, which may be subject to locally variable conditions of performance.

Yet Wagnerian music-drama, the foundation for Pfitzner's theories, is marked by a paradox. On the one hand, it subscribes to the tendency to fix the verbal and musical text as a "work"—*opus perfectum et absolutum,* to use a term formulated in the sixteenth century: a finished artifact in which, as in a symphony, no note or letter may be changed, and to which performance stands in a reproductive relationship, not a productive one. On the other hand, Wagner—and he was of one mind with Verdi on this—understood the onstage realization by singing, acting performers as the "real" work: the "drama," which is the end served by the means of words and music.

The problem is the more complex because, in the case of Wagner, the verbal and musical text (the score) contains or prescribes a quite unusual proportion of gestural and other visible elements. The first consequence is that a producer is forced to choose between overruling the stage business integrated in Wagner's texts or adhering to an old-fashioned style of production. And second, the difficulty mentioned above—that Wagner insisted both on the in-

violability of the text of words and music (that which is "perfect and absolute") and on the primacy of the theater as a productive, not merely a reproductive, art form—is made more acute by the integration of visual and
gestural matter in the score, because the integration has weakened with time,
inasmuch as style changes faster and more radically in stage production than
it does in the interpretation of words and music.

In principle, the question whether a score is a work in itself, demanding
nothing more than suitable reproduction, or merely a prototype not realized
as a "perfect and absolute work" until production (performance) takes place
is as relevant to the symphony as it is to opera. But in the case of instrumental music the issue was resolved earlier and more emphatically through the establishment of the score as a work in itself. The distinction between a text (inviolable) and its interpretation (assimilative and liable to change) goes back
to theology, jurisprudence, and the humanist reception of classical texts and
arises from the need to interpret a text from the past in such a way as to make
it applicable in the conditions of the present. Even in the disciplines where the
principle originated, the distinction creates some almost insoluble problems
and is sometimes hard to maintain in the case of instrumental music. Yet it is
possible to assert, without venturing into more speculative areas, that, in instrumental music, at the latest Beethoven's symphonies, quartets, and sonatas
and, in opera—posthumously—some of the works of Gluck and Mozart, followed by Wagner's music-dramas, were accepted as texts in the emphatic
sense, comparable to the Scriptures in biblical exegesis and the classics in humanist interpretation. (The idea of an inviolable text, as distinct from the con-
tingencies of notation, is fundamental to the concept of musical classicism.)

Until about the middle of the nineteenth century, however, an opera score
was only a prototype or a ground plan for the work to be realized in performance. The degree of elaboration required was an index of the difference between text and prototype, but the essence of the difference was more a matter
of aesthetic understanding. (Opera scores were not printed in eighteenth-
century Italy, unlike in France, and this can perhaps be taken as a sign that
they did not count as works in themselves, whereas the dramas of Metastasio
claimed the standing of poetic drama, readable in their own right—not just
as drammi per musica—and accordingly were often published and reprinted
in literary editions.) As a prototype, however, a score could be changed, and
in almost unlimited ways, dependent on conditions that varied from place
to place. Adapting it to the singers and players available, as well as to the
audience's expectations, was the normal and aesthetically legitimate practice.
Eventually, later in the nineteenth century, such treatment of scores came to
be regarded as an offence against an inviolable text—accepted, indeed, but
only under compulsion and unwillingly. Until that happened, however, the
sole purpose of a score was to provide the substratum for a performance—

and just the specific, imminent performance at that. (In terms of the history of ideas, a crucial element in this practice is not only the manner but also the frame of mind in which it is done: even *Tristan und Isolde* and *Parsifal* are quite often performed cut, just like *Lucia di Lammermoor,* but the perpetrators have an uneasy aesthetic conscience; and even if cuts were sometimes made in Beethoven's symphonies, they were always deemed indefensible.)

The process of establishing the concept of a "perfect and absolute work" in the opera house was a general trend in the nineteenth century, exemplified by the careers of Meyerbeer and Verdi as much as Wagner's. Verdi, admittedly, did not evolve an aesthetic theory granting the superiority of the verbal and musical text over realization or interpretation—he always thought of himself as a "man of the theater." In his case, after his triumphs of 1853 and in an environment where the relationship between composer, librettist, impresario, producer, and singers was always volatile, inviolability of the text was his reward for fighting his way up to the position of an unchallenged dictator. He no longer needed to adapt himself to external conditions of any kind but could compel others to accept the idea of the work as he saw it.

But the premises that originated with Verdi and Wagner created a paradoxical situation in twentienth-century opera. On the one hand, the establishment of the verbal and musical text as a "work" in the emphatic sense has been adhered to: a score by Puccini (the product of five years' toil, not five weeks') is available in an authentic version, as a printed text (regardless of the countless mistakes and corrections observable from one edition to another); the idea of adapting it to suit the abilities of a particular singer is contrary to aesthetic norms. On the other hand, in theory and practice alike, it has become increasingly common to place the character singing and acting on the stage at the heart of the opera phenomenon, not the score. To be more precise: while Italian practice adopted the concept of a "text" from German aesthetic theory, conversely German aesthetic theory came to be guided by the concept of theater stemming from Italian practice. (Musicologists now regard analysis of an opera solely from the viewpoint of the "word-tone relationship," while the staged reality is neglected, as obsolete.)

The Theatrical Dynamic

10. THE SCORE AS PRODUCTION BOOK

The thesis that an opera score is the production book which must serve as the basis for any staging is well enough established to be a commonplace and would appear to be unassailable as an aesthetic premise, yet it turns out to be so questionable in its technical applications that the aesthetic principle itself loses some of its authority. No one denies, at any rate in theory, that a pro-

duction fails if it sacrifices the meaning and character of the music to a production concept imposed from outside, however effective and intellectually
substantial that concept may be. But the notion that it is enough to be guided
by the music is only a half-truth. The problems lie, first, in the fact that the
music only ever partly expresses the interior and exterior actions; second, in
the historical conditionality of musical "meaning"; and third, in the many-
layered nature of music—the overlapping of musical structures, wherein the
dominance of one or the other is not always obvious, so that deciding between them is a matter for argument.

Given the popularity of the oversimplifying dictum that the "whole" mise-
en-scène is contained in a score, openly or latently, for those who have eyes
to read it, it is worthwhile repeating the truism that a score never expresses
more than part of the interior and exterior dramatic events. It is necessary to
ask constantly which elements are placed in the foreground and which in the
margins, and for what dramaturgical or formal-musical reasons. In the fifth
scene of the introduction of *Rigoletto,* festive music underpins a dialogue between the Duke and Rigoletto, giving their discourse the freedom to alternate
instantly between cantabile phrases ("La cara sua sposa è un angiol per me!")
and scraps of recitative ("Rapitela"). But the festive music is abruptly interrupted for eight bars by a chromatic unison progression in which Rigoletto's
scheming malevolence is the only feature ("È ben naturale! . . ."). The orchestral music can be said to alter the dramatic perspective: instead of continuing to paint the festive ambience, against which the dialogue forms a distinct, second musical layer, for a moment it aligns itself with the voice and
focuses on a segment of dialogue which sheds a harsh light on Rigoletto's
equivocal character. Thus, the macabre thrust of the whole scene is expressed
indirectly at first, in the contrast between the speakers' easy, conversational
tone and their criminal intent, and then directly and undisguised, by means of
a threatening musical gesture duplicated in the orchestra. What is a *direttore
di scena* to do? Must the direction of the scene mirror first the predominance
of well-mannered social behavior in the music, while danger is latent, and then
the musical unsheathing of the threat and the sudden interruption of the festive music? Or can the music be trusted to depict the difference unaided?

Furthermore, the "meaning" of the music, invoked by proponents of the
idea of the score as production book, permits different—sometimes extremely
different—interpretations, and hence divergent stagings. The Countess's cavatina at the beginning of act 2 of *Le nozze di Figaro* ("Porgi amor, qualche
ristoro") expresses a despairing plea, without for a moment losing sight of the
nobility that is both characteristic of the Countess's personality and appropriate to her rank. The spectrum of possible ways to stage this scene ranges from
the bad old tradition of showing only the aristocratic bearing, wrapped in
the aura of beautiful music, to the equally questionable opposite extreme of

revealing only the wretchedness of a deserted wife, so that the cantilena no longer expresses anything of the composure the Countess maintains but is only a memory or an illusion of a happier past. The reason for the problem lies, as it almost always does in matters of production, in the opera's reception history, which has generated readings that a producer need not accept but cannot cancel at a stroke. As soon as the expressiveness of the cavatina is neutralized and it becomes merely a beautiful cantabile, a producer is left with virtually no alternatives but either to bow to the tradition rooted in the audience's consciousness—that is, let the nobility drive out the expression of despair—or willfully to defy the tradition and show the Countess's unhappiness by means of drastic realism, so that the cantilena becomes a contrast to what is actually visible on the stage, an intuition of a utopia hovering somewhere above the reality. Overruling tradition, it seems, is as impossible as not overruling it.

It is scarcely necessary to say that not every instance of overlapping but divergent musical structures causes production headaches: the theater is as rich as music itself in potential for displaying the simultaneity of heterogeneous elements. Yet there are situations where music and theater are jointly involved in which a producer is forced to make decisions for which cogent grounds are hard to find. In act 1 of *La traviata*, the waltz played by a *banda sul palco* in the adjoining room at the beginning of the duet for Alfredo and Violetta is not merely background but part of the blatant depiction of the contrast between the glamour and the misery of a courtesan's life ("splendeur et misère des courtesanes," in Balzac's phrase). The suggestion of musical-semantic mediation between the *banda* music and the dialogue lies in a chromatic motive ($E\flat$–D–$D\flat$–C) that is not at all ill-suited to a waltz, but in the context of the scene, and in association with its other features, it has an expressivity that makes it stand out from the dance music. The waltz also has a musical-structural function equal to its symbolic and dramaturgical significance. Like the scene from *Rigoletto* referred to above, the dialogue here alternates rapidly and abruptly between cantabile and parlando, and syntactically speaking, the more regular the periodic structure of the waltz underpinning it, the more rhapsodic (that is, "realistic") the dialogue can be. The producer has a choice of ways to interpret the scene's dependence on the syntax of the waltz (without which the dialogue would be, musically, a ragbag of disjointed particles): he can try to make the regular periodicity of the musical background perceptible in the mise-en-scène, or he can ignore it as just a device removing syntactical constraints from the musical dialogue and allowing it to be staged realistically. (In the dialogue between the Duke and Borsa in the opening scene of *Rigoletto*, it would be a mistake to take the latter course and separate the mise-en-scène from the syntax of the background music, because here the dialogue follows the 4/4 rhythm of the *banda*.)

11. THE PRIMACY OF THE PRESENT

The report of the death of Eurydice, casting the shadow of tragedy across the pastoral, stands at the very beginning of the history of opera. Yet the theatrical conventions of the messenger's report, teichoscopy (the view from the wall), and narrated prehistory are techniques of spoken drama that are generally less effective in opera because musical expression, unlike verbal, is more inclined to make its point in a purely present time and place. It is difficult for music to gain access to what is spatially or temporally distant, unless it calls on Wagnerian leitmotivic technique, and so it is difficult to make a prehistory or an unseen action strike home in opera. ("Unseen action" refers to events that take place during the drama's present time—unlike the prehistory—but offstage, and are conveyed to the audience by means of teichoscopy, a messenger's account or dialogue.)

The incontrovertible assertion that musical expression in opera, when it comes into its own, strives to be "purely present," and so make the action and even time stand still, appears confusingly to contradict the aesthetic commonplace that it is in music's nature to articulate and make perceptible the passage of time. We tend to expect, rather, that a theory of opera will begin with an attempt to discover an inner connection between the processes of music and drama. But the fact that Beethoven, whose symphonies embody with special clarity the idea of urgently goal-directed, forward-speeding musical evolution, was guided in *Fidelio* by formal and structural ideas owing relatively little to principles of symphonic development is enough to cast doubt on the simple correlation of musical and dramatic teleologies. If we want to get beyond the paradox that Beethoven's symphonies are dramatic and his only opera undramatic, we must bear in mind that the principle of inexorably forward-moving logic, which provides the foundation for the time structures of both the symphony and the play (or at least the play in a "closed" form, observing the classical three unities), cannot take effect in opera, or not to the same extent, and does not need to. (The quartet in *Fidelio* [no. 3], a contemplative ensemble, is no less constitutive for the opera as a musical drama than are the dungeon scenes.)

References to the dominance of "the present" on the operatic stage call for some clarification of the term's dual sense: there is present time, which is self-sufficient in that its inner tension does not come from being perceived as a consequence of the past and a precondition of the future; and there is scenic presence in the sense that elements of the action in an opera must be presented to the eye and not to the ear alone if they are to strike home. In Wagner's *Ring* cycle the identifying characteristics entailed in the concept of scenic presence make their mark in conjunction with one another. What is present on the stage is always connected to the past and the future by leitmotivs, the dramaturgical function of which Wagner defined as "memory" *(Erinnerung)* and "premonition" *(Ahnung)*, so that the time structure corresponds to that of a play. However, in order for leitmotivs to fulfill their dramaturgical function, they must be accompanied when first introduced not only by a verbal association but also, if at all possible, by something visible onstage. So if what is "present" onstage intersects with leitmotivic technique, it is also, as the visible manifestation of musical expression, one of the preconditions of dramaturgically effective leitmotivic technique.

If, in a play, emphasis lies less on what is happening at the present moment than on the relations to past and future that generate the dialectics of the moment, it is because of the primacy of speech over scenic elements (the principle does not remain valid when the scenic element dominates). In opera, conversely, the focus on the present moment has to do with music's affinity to the scenic, which is manifested both in ritual's need for music and vice versa in opera's penchant for ritual (see §5). The dramatic effect of language unfolds in the purposeful connecting of events—in the interpenetration of memory and premonition, to use Wagner's terms—but the dramatic effects of music and scenic elements unfold in the immediate present. (Of course, as soon as theory turns to interpretation, the necessary limitations of the all too-crude-antithesis of language as "active," "present" speech and leitmotivic technique as a web of musical references reaching forward and backward can no longer be ignored.)

In spoken plays, especially classical or classical-style ones, only a small part of the action takes place onstage or in the play's present time (or both). The more "closed" the form (that is, the more strictly it observes the unities), the more restricted the range of events seen onstage. The requirement for the action to start in medias res, while a sometimes extremely complex prehistory is revealed only gradually, is founded in the wish to begin with an already exciting situation instead of an involved explanation of circumstances. Furthermore, recounting the prehistory provides material for dialogue in which internal and external conflicts are revealed: recapitulation of earlier events, in the expositions required by the formal convention of beginning in medias res, both lends tension to the present situation and urges the action forward.

Thus, the spoken words in a play always reach out beyond what is shown visually and, through the narration of prehistory and unseen action, constitute an invisible drama behind the visible one. This invisible drama is often the essential one, but opera focuses instead on the present time and place. The reason for this dramaturgical difference is not as obvious as might appear. That sung text is only partly understood is undoubtedly an important factor (the banality of the observation should not be a reason for underrating it), but as a purely negative feature it is not enough to explain the primacy of the onstage here and now in opera. Opera is not a deficient species of play, in which drastic pictorialism must compensate for a lack of verbal clarity. Rather, an important difference exists between play and opera that is exemplified by spoken dialogue as a verbal duel and the duet as a conflict of emotions. A verbal duel, insofar as it develops in the form of argument and counterargument, constantly refers to the prehistory or unseen action, and conversely it provides the opportunity to bring the prehistory and unseen action "into play." Emotional conflict, the basis of the type of duet predominant in Verdi, also arises out of events but is not conducted by means of arguments that make it necessary to cite anything remote in time or place; it centers instead on the momentary dissension which unfolds musically, without developing discursively. (Of course, the text often contains arguments, but they are not the substance realized musically, and hence they do not constitute the opera as a musical drama.)

The ideal type of operatic action is one without a prehistory, in which everything needed for comprehension is presented visually onstage and not merely verbally (Scribe's libretto for Meyerbeer's *Le prophète* is a good example). On the other hand, the relationship between narrated prehistory, onstage action, and underlying musical-dramatic structure is especially revelatory for the dramaturgy in the case of operas with librettos decried as hackwork that are nonetheless effective despite this (alleged) deficiency.

The prehistory of *Il trovatore*, which the audience has to reconstruct from Ferrando's racconto (no. 1) and the scene for Azucena and Manfredo consisting of the Scena e Racconto (no. 5) and Scena e Duetto (no. 6), is not only confused but also of little importance to the central configuration of Count De Luna, Manrico, Leonora, and Azucena. The persecution of the gypsy woman and Manrico's death-defying love for his mother would both be immediately understandable without the complicated "background." The arias, duets, and ensembles that together constitute the musical drama—the "real" action manifested in musical forms, as distinct from the "narratable action"— form a dramaturgical ground plan on which the story of the kidnapped babies has no bearing. The one scene in which the tale is the precondition for a musically realized affect is the one for Azucena and Manfredo (nos. 5 and 6), yet this scene remains peripheral to the action because Azucena retracts her words (although it is indispensable to the musical disposition because it provides a duet for these two characters). The prehistory therefore fulfills a dramaturgically rare function of motivating only an enclave in the action—although the enclave is necessary for equal representation of the voices.

In a play in which only part of the action is presented onstage, the prehistory or unseen action is integrated into the drama when its recapitulation simultaneously impels the action forward (as Hagen's report of Brünnhilde does in act 1 of *Götterdämmerung,* for the dramaturgy of that opera uses the expository techniques of a play). In an opera, however, the decisive factor is whether or not the narration of a prehistory has any effect on the configuration of the characters and thus on the emotional conflict essential to the musical-dramatic structure as a whole. Again, examples can be found in *Il trovatore:* Ferrando's racconto is weakly integrated, and Ferrando is a dramaturgical lay-figure, whereas Azucena's narrative and its retraction belong at least partly to the real substance of the musical drama (and not just to the disposition of vocal numbers) because, without contributing to the central action, they motivate a musically represented conflict of affects and an essential component of the configuration of characters.

12. STAGE MUSIC AS QUOTATION AND REALITY

"Stage music" exists as a pragmatic, aesthetic, and dramaturgical category, yet clear-cut distinctions are never possible between the different elements it embraces. It cannot be said with certainty whether it is a sample of "actual" reality intruding from outside into the theatrical reality or a fiction within the fiction.

The pragmatic criterion, the placing of musicians onstage, before or behind the scenery, can be aesthetically essential or nonessential. It is important when a spatial effect is intended in order to make a dramaturgical point; for example, the transition at the beginning of act 2 of *Tristan und Isolde,* from the ever-more-distant sound of the offstage horns, embodying the departure of the hunt (and, with it, the dramatic presence of Marke), to the woodland idyll to which Isolde summons Tristan, expresses the fundamental dichotomy that shapes the whole work: the stage music is the external world, the orchestral music the inner.

On the other hand, the positioning of the harp for the minstrels' contest in act 2 of *Tannhäuser* has no essential dramaturgical importance. Aesthetically, the harp chords and arpeggios are also stage music, although technically the instrument on the stage is a fake and the playing mimed, while the sound comes out of the orchestra pit. That the real instrument is in the pit and not the wings is due to the compositional need to augment the harp with other instruments during a scene more than 400 bars long. The coloristic variation provided by the other instruments prevents placing the harp in the wings because the spatial separation would be contrary to sense, as it is not at the start of act 2 of *Tristan:* the low strings in the accompaniment to Wolfram's song are distinguished from the harp by the fact that the latter has an onstage presence, but not for any musical or dramaturgical reason.

Emblematic stage music is one of the oldest traditions in theatrical history: trumpets proclaim the entry of princes or the start of a battle, muffled drums accompany a funeral cortège, horns denote hunting, trombones the underworld, a harp or a lute the declamation of an epic or the singing of a song. These musical conventions have a long tradition and are understood by everyone, but for that very reason they present a problem in opera: they stick out like quotations—intrusions from another world outside, it seems—in a context where music is the language of the drama's entire world, presenting itself as natural and spontaneous, artificial and conventional though it be. (It is significant that Italian opera, the original opera and still the paradigm, does not have a counterpart to singspiel or opéra-comique.) Stage music is interpolated music, and integrating it into a form of drama that has its own autonomous musical language is not easy.

Moreover, we are not sure, at first hearing, whether the primary source of a quotation in stage-music form is reality or a theatrical convention. Our initial reaction may be to interpret stage music as a montage of fragments of reality in opera, but at the same time we cannot deny what we know from experience: there is not the slightest aesthetic difference between unreal, mythological trombones from the underworld and real, emblematic trumpets emanating from the historical reality of feudal society. Equally, the high string sounds with which the world of fairy tales and folktales is conjured up in both operas and plays are stage music in the same sense as marches and dances transposed to the theater from the everyday real world: there is no aesthetic or dramaturgical difference. The quotational character of stage music that does not differentiate between real and unreal obviously owes more to its origin in the conventions of spoken drama than to any association with reality.

The music that emerges from the orchestra pit also has a specific kind of onstage presence: its aesthetic place is on the stage, even if its acoustic place is elsewhere. As parts of a musical whole focused on the people singing and acting onstage, the vocal and instrumental components belong together. Verdi and Wagner were of one mind on this. The Valhalla motive in the orchestra is as inseparable from Wotan as any phrase he sings, while the instance from *La traviata* cited earlier—the aesthetic separation of vocal and instrumental material in the act 1 duet—is not the norm but an exception and needs a special dramaturgical rationale. However, when instrumental music is split between the stage and the pit, as a rule the two layers make themselves felt not only acoustically but also aesthetically. The stage music is, as said, a quotation; and the quotational character owes less to the reference to reality (which passes seamlessly into the unreality of a music invoking the realm of faerie in the romantic singspiel) than to the connection with the tradition of music in plays.

Recognition of the quotational character of stage music is essential to an analysis appropriate to its ambivalent dramaturgical functions. The minuet in the introduction to *Rigoletto* is a fragment of reality by virtue of being a quotation of "early music" (that the local color for an action set in the sixteenth century is provided by a musical style from the eighteenth is not important). Conversely, the *traurige Weise* in act 3 of *Tristan und Isolde* is a reminiscence, and so part of the "interior action" to which Wagner's designation of his work as "action" *(Handlung)* refers (the shepherd's song might also be heard by Tristan inwardly, not in reality). It reminds Tristan of his parents, with whose deaths he associates it in his imagination, and thus it is an expression of his yearning for death and of his being already marked for death: the basis of the unresolvable dialectics of his love for Isolde.

Stage music is dramaturgical in a specific sense set apart from other compositional practice in that its aesthetic and technical significance can be reduced or increased when its stage function justifies divagations from the norm that either represent "regression" or anticipate "future music." The stage music with which Verdi experiments so ingeniously in the *Rigoletto* introduction enables not only quotation of a past style, like the minuet, but also uninhibited recourse to musical means that Verdi would avoid elsewhere; here, however, with a vividness he could scarcely have achieved by other means, they fulfill the dramaturgical function of bringing out the strand of cruelty in the amusements of the ducal court. Conversely, the spatial separation of the horns (not only from the rest of the orchestra but also from each other) at the start of act 2 of *Tristan* is the necessary condition of a movement away from the norm in the opposite direction: the legitimation of a chordal structure of layered fifths or fourths. In spite of its similarity to, and historical associations with, the beginning of the finale of Beethoven's *Pastoral* Symphony, Arnold Schoenberg had good reason to cite this passage in the appendix to his *Theory of Harmony*, praising it for its anticipation of modernism, as preparation for the fourths-based harmonies of the early twentieth century.

13. TIME STRUCTURES

The perception that the time structures of operas and spoken plays are fundamentally different is one of the commonplaces of dramatic aesthetics that seem so self-evident as to render closer analysis unnecessary. ("Opera," here, must be understood to exclude Wagnerian music-drama, where the time structure is that of plays.) Stating the obvious fact that the tempo of sung text is slower than that of spoken seems no more necessary than mentioning the difference between recitatives, which are closer to the speed of real speech and sometimes exceed it, and closed numbers, in which time expands or even stands still in order to give sufficient space to an expression of feeling removed from time.

But the impression that the question of time structures in opera is an open-and-shut case, and no effort need be spent on considering it, is deceptive. The briefest analysis of an opera seria or a nineteenth-century grand opéra shows that the distinction between real and expanded time manifested in the difference between recitative and aria is by no means sufficient to take account of the infinite gradations in the musical-dramatic reality. There is little to be learned from recitative, in which musical-formal time usually is approximately commensurate with real time, but the passage of time in closed numbers is problematical and requires interpretation because it is almost always irregular and in some sense rhapsodic. This is not the case in spoken drama, where time proceeds continuously, by contrast with the discontinuity in opera.

Saying that the passage of time is irregular is not the same as remarking that dialogue can be spoken at faster or slower speeds—something spoken plays share with reality outside the theater. "Discontinuity" refers rather to a rarely mentioned attribute of opera, namely that the measure of real time represented can vary from one extreme to another within one and the same scene.

For example, in part 1 of *Il trovatore,* in the group of numbers comprising the Scena, Romanza e Terzetto number 3, we can observe at least three different relations between the musical-formal passage of time and the represented time.

1. In both the Count's scena and Manrico's romanza the real time represented (which can be accepted as a matter of general, everyday perception, not needing to be measured exactly) is approximately the same as the time in which it is presented. The time structure is not affected by the fact that the scena is an interior monologue and the romanza is stage music. The troubadour's song is real in its time structure as a complete entity because it is stage music and thus a quotation from the real world outside the theater.

2. The first part of the trio (allegro agitato: "Qual voce!")—a parlante (as Basevi calls it) that fulfills the function of a *tempo di mezzo* and refers back to the Count's scena—consists of dialogue without repetition of either text or music. (There is one exception, the repetition of four bars of the Count's music—"Il tuo fatale / Al mio sdegno vittima"; the reason for this is that although the words are not the same, their meaning is.) The dialogue structure, at this rapid speed, almost but not quite results in agreement between represented time and performance time (the norm in spoken drama). It is possible here because the orchestra's motivic material ensures unbroken musical continuity, thereby freeing the vocal material from the obligation to provide it. The rhythmic ostinato is developed motivically by repetition of groups of bars $(8 + 8$ and $2 + 2)$, separation and sequential treatment of individual segments $(1 + 1 + 1)$, rhythmic contractions (4), variations of a model $(4 + 4)$, and sequential processes $(4 + 4 + 4)$: altogether a dense weave, which conceals the melodic disjointedness of the vocal material.

3. The cabaletta of the trio (allegro assai moderato: "Di geloso amor sprezzato") exhibits a marked contrast between the time represented and the time in which it is musically presented, for the very reason that the vocal material is self-sustaining. The text structure can afford to be diffuse, because it is not at issue. The Count alternates between interior monologue and real speech directed at the others; Leonora and Manrico sing the same music, but their

words are not only different but actually divergent. The layering of their different texts into the three-part texture with which the trio ends, together with the frequent repetition and the fact that the characters do not so much speak with each other as express the emotional substance of one particular moment in musically expansive—and expanding—formulas, means that the trio moves out of real time to some extent. (The fact that Manrico sings the same phrase over and over again, alternately confronting the Count angrily and swearing fidelity to Leonora, is an absurdity illustrating a certain indifference to the implications of the text.)

The alternation between flowing and halting action and speech in opera leads to the dissociation of time into a formal passage of time manifested by the duration of the performance and a passage of time within the action, which the members of the audience must deduce from the progress of events on the basis of everyday experience. This dual perception of time, in which the public involuntarily engages even if unconsciously, says something about opera's relation to other genres, inasmuch as it is commonplace in epic poetry but uncommon in drama. At least with respect to analysis of time structures, opera is closer to the novel and other narrative forms than to the play. Differentiation between the time a narrative takes and the time narrated, that is, the expansion or contraction of different stages in the story, is one of the everyday artistic devices indispensable to every storyteller (admittedly, Joyce comes close to agreement of the two modes of time in *Ulysses*). But the opposite obtains in the play, or at least within an individual scene, where the time represented and the time taken to represent it characteristically agree: the duration of the event and that of its performance are identical. (Jumps in time between scenes and acts are permissible and almost unavoidable.)

The agreement in a play between performance time and represented time is, however, the complement of another temporal separation, which is more apparent in spoken drama than in the novel, namely the dissociation of a present time that is shown and an imaginary time that is only evoked. To put it another way, there is a separation of the present time of the events and dialogue on the stage from a nonpresent time, the events of which are only talked about in the dialogues. In the play, at least in plays observing the unities, almost every moment is laden with forward- and backward-directed references bringing the prehistory to bear, so that the goal-directed, teleological structure of the genre is made palpable by the sense of past events pressing forward to the future.

It is different in opera, which is, in its ideal-typical state, a drama absolutely of the present, so that a prehistory features as a tiresome explanation of onstage events that must be got through quickly rather than as a means of propelling the action forward. But if even the prehistory is a scarcely avoidable evil in opera rather than a mainstay of the real dramaturgical construction (that is, that which is presented to the eyes and ears of the audience), the techniques constructing a secondary, imaginary action alongside or beyond the visible events of spoken plays (teichoscopy, the messenger's narration and the unseen action: see above, §11) are entirely alien to opera in principle, even if sometimes they seem unavoidable.

Thus, in the play (as also in Wagnerian music-drama, with its playlike time structure) a second sequence of events, composed of prehistory and unseen action, often claims equal status with the dialogue and onstage events: the abstract imagination of what is narrated forms a counterpart to the concrete presence of what is represented and can even become the more important of the two. Imagined events and passing time evoked through words alone are sometimes no less essential to the meaning of a play than events and dialogue watched and heard onstage in the present tense. In opera, by contrast, an action that is only imagined, insofar as the librettist cannot avoid it altogether, is almost always colorless or hard to understand, and the present tense is the only one that counts in musical drama.

The first number in part 1 of *Il trovatore* is essentially a genre picture in the dark colors of a novel by Walter Scott, and the librettist's determination to make it dramaturgically functional had a problematical outcome. Ferrando's statement that the Count wanders about at night (unseen action) is unnecessary because the Count is seen doing so onstage only a little later, and the narration of part of the prehistory in the racconto (a cantabile, alternating twice between andante mosso and allegretto), together with the chorus's stretta, highlights ghost stories and acts of witchcraft which obfuscate the real matter of the exposition: the old Count's burning of Azucena's mother at the stake, and Azucena's burning of one of his sons in revenge. The substance of this exposition becomes incidental; what is seen onstage and represented musically—the eerie feeling induced by darkness and ghost stories—dominates over the prehistory and unseen action. The functionalization is too weak to assert itself against the musical scene setting.

The simplification which seems to lie in the concentration on the onstage present time complements the differentiation created by the discrepancy between performance time and represented time, the novel-like expansion or contraction of stages in the action. (The difference between the musical reasons for time to slow down in opera and the causes of contraction and expansion in the novel to suit the pace of events or the narrator's role as commentator is of no importance in this context.)

That there is no necessity for the musical tempo of an operatic scene to coincide with the speed of dialogue or events is another precondition of something that has scarcely ever been analyzed, since it is so trivial: the simple fact that a slowing or even a standstill of the action in an opera is entirely compatible with a vehement access of emotion expressed in the music. However fast the tempo that the emotion implies psychologically, its musical representation may extend almost indefinitely. No one has ever objected to an expanse of time between the anger expressed musically and the deed it triggers.

The several interlayered tempos forming the time structure of an operatic scene (the musical tempo, the speed at which the characters speak and act, the tempo of their emotions) and the measure of real time represented (which can differ immensely from the time taken to present it) relate to one another in ways ranging from unobtrusive convergence to blatant divergence; the latter is the only thing that forces consciousness of the time structure upon the spectator. If we regard straightforward agreement of tempos as the unproblematic ideal, deviations make us look for an explanation in the dramatic situation. If the tempo of verbal utterance in a scene contradicts the musical pulse, if the time represented comes to a halt in spite of a torrential outpouring of emotion—if, that is, the time structure of a scene is fissured—it needs to be justified and not simply accepted as one of the peculiarities of opera, an instance of the genre's notorious artificiality.

In its two sections—parlante and cabaletta—the trio of number 3 in *Il trovatore* first presents itself as an ensemble of action and dialogue, moving for the most part in a way similar to a play. There are no lacunae in the sequence of events: Leonora's mistaking the Count for Manrico in the dark motivates her admission to Manrico that she loves him, which in turn provokes the Count's anger and his threat to kill Manrico in a duel. At the words "M'odi . . ." (Leonora) and "No!" (Count), the flow of words and answers comes to a halt, in exactly the same way that the logical linking of verbal particles is replaced by little more than gabbling. The dramatic advance freezes into a tableau vivant (the cabaletta). That the Count repeatedly bursts out jealously (sixteen bars) and threatens Manrico (twenty-four bars), that Leonora tries to pacify him (thirty-two bars) and Manrico feels compelled to issue counterthreats (thirty-two bars, in unison with Leonora), not only prolongs a situation that would last a minute in reality or in a play but also allows time as a process to recede so far into the background, faced with this musically prolonged moment, that it is almost irrelevant. Moreover, nothing is said that was not already said in the first part. The subject of a verbal duel with vehement visible action in the parlante petrifies in the cabaletta to emotional attitudes, expressed and augmented musically. What happens in the cabaletta—a fleeting moment in real time—assumes in the unreal time of the tableau a form in which duration is indefinite and text merely the vehicle of melody expressing the inner turmoil of the characters, somewhere beyond spoken speech.

Thus, the musical tempo is a speech tempo in the parlante and a tempo of emotion in the cabaletta. The actual dialogue, in which the performance time more or less coincides with the time represented, breaks off abruptly at the end of the parlante, which we can think of as a semimelodicized scena. The formal time in which the cabaletta expands is unreal with respect to its content, and the words, which in reality would be exclamations of strong emotion, are extended by poeticism, paraphrase, and repetition into a pseudo-language, which functions only as a substratum of the music and cannot be taken literally as poetry or dramatic text: precisely because it has so little substance and says all but nothing, it makes room for music to transform the situation into sound.

It would be wrong to say that this "musicalization" lacks a dramaturgical function because of the abrupt switch from musical drama (the parlante of the first part of the scene) to "lyric" opera (the cabaletta for three voices); it is perfectly possible to interpret the divergence of the formal passage of time from its dramatic context by means of dramaturgical categories, although underlying everything is a musical-formal stereotype to which the librettist strove to conform. The unreal prolongation of a moment depicting the three central characters of the drama with the concentration of a tableau vivant is not realistic, but it is dramaturgically justified. It is precisely in deviating from the realistic passage of time that the musical form does justice to the dramatic significance of the situation: the situation demands a special marker because it demonstrates that the substance of the drama is a configuration of characters rather than an intrigue. In other words, the basis for the divergence between represented time and performance time in this scene is not an abstract musical matter but one of musical theater. As well as fulfilling musical expectations, it is also an artistic device, an undoubtedly legitimate theatrical means even though almost unknown in spoken drama, and it should not be misunderstood as a diversion into the concert hall.

If the difference between represented time and the time taken to present it seems in general a trait that opera shares with the novel, and that distinguishes opera from the play, operatic dramaturgy's affinity with narrative becomes especially obvious in the genre scenes and depictions of communal and social settings found in almost every nineteenth-century opera. With the sanction of the aesthetics of description, a counterpart to the aesthetics of beauty, the era as a whole had a penchant for *couleur locale*.

A playwright is forced, as a rule, to blend explanations of circumstances and background into the action in the form of dialogue, resulting, in Ibsen and Chekhov, in those conversations that seem to go round in circles. In epic poetry, on the other hand, the firsthand depiction of recurrent events or long-standing circumstances is one of the simplest and commonest artistic devices. With reference to the epic procedure of including what is permanent in the time structure of a scene in the narrative's present, it would be only a slight exaggeration to speak of time spent in presentation, as it were, without any time being represented: the formal passage of time required by the act of narration mirrors a depiction of circumstances and background that, as a matter of long-standing duration or as the continual recurrence of something that is always the same, is untouched by time as a perceptible process.

The narrative technique of describing successively things that happen in different places simultaneously (that is, the method of painting a panorama which builds up into simultaneity in the reader's imagination) has left traces in musical drama, although aesthetic theories of opera, taking their lead from the dramaturgy of the spoken play, have scarcely acknowledged them. The introduction (act 1, no. 1) of Rossini's *Guillaume Tell* is a genre picture assembled from heterogeneous components: the actors—peasants, shepherds, a fisherman, Tell himself, brooding as he digs his garden—are scattered across the stage like figures in a landscape painting, essentially unrelated to each other and held together dramaturgically only because they add up to a phantasmagoria of an ideal Switzerland. What is meant to be simultaneous, and is presented as such on the stage, has to be presented successively in the music, because the different melodic characters of the parts of the scene are too strongly contrasted to fit together in an ensemble with a contrapuntal structure compatible with Rossini's notion of musical unity. The peasants' chorus, the young fisherman's romance, and Tell's lament at the political oppression of his homeland are expounded one after another, as if they were stages in an action, not parts of a depiction of circumstances. While the scenic panorama remains constant, the musical technique that paints the same scene with the means of musical *couleur locale* is like the method of a narrator describing one place after another but suggesting an overall picture to the reader by allowing it to come into view gradually.

Forms and Contents

14. NUMBER OPERA AS A DRAMATIC FORM

Number opera is a stumbling block for historians who, consciously or unconsciously, take Wagnerian music-drama and a concept of the "dramatic" derived from it as the norm—although the fact that a phenomenon has survived for centuries should of itself prevent its being unceremoniously dismissed as an aesthetic error.

While some have condemned opera seria for a lack of connection between individual numbers, historians attempting to do justice to Metastasian opera on aesthetic grounds, or at least put it in its historical context, have denied that there is any such lack, have found dramaturgical reasons to justify it, or have treated it as the early stage of a musical-dramatic form that discovered its "true" but previously latent expression from the mid–eighteenth century onward in those "reform operas" in which arias, duets, and ensembles grew together into complex scenes.

1. Writing history teleologically, treating one type of opera as merely the precursor of another, is obsolete in theory but proves almost ineradicable in historiographic practice. Faced with the reform operas of Jommelli, Traetta, and Gluck, composed under the influence of literati as modifications of the Metastasian type, it is difficult for historians *not* to interpret them as solutions to problems unsolved in the older dramma per musica or as attempts to compensate for its deficiencies. This interpretation rests, however, on a one-sided concept of the "dramatic" derived from the reform operas themselves. The only appropriate procedure, methodologically, would be to reconstruct the specific idea of the dramatic that really underlay earlier opera seria.

2. The attempts to refute the charge of a lack of connectedness by appeals to formal analysis do not seem any more convincing. The hypothesis that an internal connectedness between numbers was intended in the scheme of the tonalities of individual arias has proved hard to verify (in the example of operas by Handel) and is also questionable insofar as it is rarely possible to detect a dramaturgical purpose in the construction of a network of tonal relationships: the principle of tonal integration has been borrowed, unwittingly, from symphonic form.

As a purely theoretical experiment, it is actually not difficult to design an operatic structure in which the scheme of key relationships would be dramaturgically integrated, but the resulting construct would correspond to little or nothing in historical reality. No one denies that the alternation of affects determining the order of arias in an opera seria was calculated in order to achieve a balance of contrasts, degrees, and complementarities; in other words, that care was taken in designing a dramatic *fabula* to ensure that the emotions displayed during the course of the action would form an intelligible pattern. Moreover, if affects are associated with certain keys—as they may be, within limits—the attempt to impose a systematic order on the resulting sequence of tonalities appears possible and sensible in principle: mediation between dramatic action, calculated variation of affects, association of keys with characters, and tonal integration of the whole would then be complete. But it would obviously be almost impossible to realize; and it is also impossible to argue convincingly that such an operatic structure was the ideal hovering before composers—or aesthetic theorists—as the "true" idea of opera.

In practice, moreover, the decisive factor was the conception of a stage production, on which singers had as great an influence as composers and librettists—and not merely by reason of their performances. As Reinhard Strohm has pointed out, it is precisely the variability of all the factors, not their immutable relationship in an intact work of art, that is the condition of a unity which was always new and differently realized on each occasion. Neither the libretto nor the score was inviolable, and it was accepted as aesthetically legitimate that the work—as a prototype—was adapted to suit the singers, and not that singers adjusted their performances to suit the work. (Librettists who objected got as short shrift in the eighteenth-century opera house as writers in the film industry today.) Singers were changed, the text of an aria was provided with new music, or the music with a new text, with the result that aesthetic unity, so far as it existed at all, resided nowhere except in specific productions in individual theaters.

3. The premise from which both accusation and defense proceed—the idea that there must be something beyond the course of events to connect the numbers if an opera is to have any claim to be a musical drama—is not self-evident. It was argued earlier that opera differs from the teleological, goal-directed construction of the spoken play by its concentration, or containment, in the present time and place represented in the music and on the stage; if we accept that, then it is doubtful what kind of connection there might be from one moment to the next, apart from the course of events. We cannot expect to find in opera the kind of connection that exists in a play, where each scene and each part of a scene not only are the consequence of earlier events and the precondition of events yet to come but also build inner tension by anticipating future events. At the same time, it would be overdoing things to claim the alleged lack of connection between numbers as a positive virtue, or assert that only each situation in isolation is relevant to the specific dramatic concept that opera embodies and that the course of the action as a whole is irrelevant. Undoubtedly, the single scene or situation is less a function of the whole in an opera than it is in a play; quite the reverse: the action serves as a vehicle for motivating and illuminating the dramatically charged situations that provoke emotional outpourings. The present time and place represented musically and onstage are important in their own right, and not just for the past events they interpret or the consequences they allow us to predict. And to the extent that this applies to opera in general, number opera is the paradigm of the genre and not a degenerate form: the idea of the "moment seized and held," containing its dramatic substance in itself, provides the closed number's aesthetic right to existence.

But although this explanation seems cogent, it does not go far enough. The element of process may be less important, but it cannot be banished altogether from musical drama: that is, from drama constituted by music, not just by the extramusical elements of *fabula* and text. The attempt to take this into account dominates operatic theory and starts from the difference between recitative and aria, perceived as a matter of their different dramaturgical roles. There can be no question about the descriptive accuracy of an interpretational scheme that sees a contrast between the dramatic action and forward movement of time in recitative and the contemplative reaction and temporal stasis in an aria, yet this scheme is wide of the mark categorially insofar as it claims the realm of the "dramatic" on behalf of recitative and excludes the aria—the actual substance of an opera seria—as if aria were a "nondramatic" enclave.

Metastasio wrote in the *argomento* of *L'Olimpiade* that "the ending, or principal event, of the drama" is the discovery that Licida is the son, previously believed dead, of King Clistene, and that the truth is gradually brought to light by "the passionate love of Aristea, the heroic friendship of Megacle, the inconstancy and hotheadedness of Licida, the noble compassion of faithful Argene." The emphasis of the *argomento,* a theory of opera in a nutshell, is that the dramatic knot is untied by an action resulting from the interplay of the contradictory emotions of the members of the cast as they act with and against each other. In other words, the configuration of the affects—the thing represented by the music—forms the mechanism of the dramatic events.

Affects and their conflicts also provide the basis of dialogue in a play, but there they may be open or hidden. That they are open in opera, dominating the arias, only accentuates a motivational structure which is also present in plays without being allowed to occupy the foreground in isolation. Conversely, the rational (or pseudorational) argumentation forming the manifest content of the dialogue in a play is consigned in an opera to recitative, that is, to the periphery of the drama as constituted by the music. These two elements—affects as a motivational structure and rational argument as the surface feature of the dialogue—are inseparable, however, in the concept of what is dramatic, in opera and in play alike; in principle, having them divided between recitative and aria in opera is no less dramatic than the simultaneity of manifest argument and latent emotional motivation in the dialogue of a play. At the beginning of act 2 of Mozart's *La clemenza di Tito,* the dramatically essential element of the recitative dialogue between Sesto and Annio is less the news that Tito is alive than the contrast in their different views of the consequences to be drawn from that news. And this contrast, which is one of emotions, then determines the dramatic function of the aria that follows ("Torna di Tito a lato"), even though it is sung by Annio alone. What he expresses arises from and is explained by the recitative, and at the same time the aria casts light back onto the emotional substance of the motives stirring the participants in the recitative.

15. THE CONFIGURATION OF CHARACTERS AND THE ACTION

The basis of every opera is a given configuration of characters, and the action is the outcome of that configuration. That the configuration of characters, the action, and the repertory of musical forms available at the time of composition appear in an individual work as different aspects of one thing is so self-evident that it scarcely warrants mention. Nevertheless, its banality should not be allowed to disguise the fact that the historical changes to which the constituent elements of musical dramaturgy are subject can lead to varying degrees of awkwardness or difficulty in their relationships.

Handel's *Giulio Cesare in Egitto* was composed in 1724 using a revised version of a Venetian libretto dating back to 1677. Between a chorus at the start and a duet at the end, act 1 contains no fewer than fourteen arias (if a monologue designated "recitativo accompagnato" and an arioso are included), which introduce and establish the conventional six principals of an eighteenth-century opera seria. These are three Romans and three Egyptians: Julius Caesar (Giulio Cesare, alto castrato); Cornelia (contralto), widow of Pompey (Pompeo); Sextus (Sesto, soprano), son of Pompey and Cornelia; Queen Cleopatra (soprano); King Ptolemy (Tolomeo, alto castrato), Cleopatra's brother; and Achillas (Achilla, bass), Ptolemy's general.

The repertory of forms available to the composer at that point in musical history is the reason for the necessity, first, to motivate a large number of arias by a complicated action (also prompted by the general trend of baroque tradition), second, to differentiate the arias by a nicely calculated variety of affects and vocal characters, and, third, to demonstrate the hierarchy of the characters by the number of arias they sing. This necessity, in turn, produces a musical dramaturgy in which the variability of the musical consequences drawn from a situation is quite as important as the compulsion not only to multiply strands in the plot but also to move from one to another with some degree of arbitrariness.

The configuration of the characters—the relationships created by their intentions and hopes—is like a piece of machinery, set in motion by an event (Pompeo's murder, ordered by Tolomeo) that also explains the logic of its structure. Cesare's revulsion at the murder (contrary to Tolomeo's expectation, as Pompeo was Cesare's enemy) sets off a chain reaction: Cleopatra sees her chance to win Cesare over to her ambition to force Tolomeo from the throne he shares with her; Tolomeo therefore plots Cesare's death; Achilla is ready to kill Cesare in return for Tolomeo's giving him Cornelia (later he learns that Tolomeo also desires her).

To begin with, the characters are independently motivated: Cornelia, Sesto, and Cesare by the desire to avenge Pompeo's death; Cleopatra by ambition; Achilla by his desire for Pompeo's widow. Strictly speaking, there is no straightforward story that can be narrated, with each event the consequence of an earlier one and the precondition of a later one; rather, there is a complicated dramaturgical apparatus comprising the characters' intentions, the configurations in which events place the characters, the resulting intrigues, and the devices necessary to make this "beautiful confusion" seem a coherent whole. Conditions govern the start and rules determine the working of this machinery, whose purpose is to present a large number of arias (in accordance with the stylistic premises of the age), disposed in a well-contrasted order.

Giulio Cesare is a drama without a main character. ("Officially" it is Cesare, and accordingly he has the largest share of the arias, but there is no overwhelming dramaturgical justification for this.) Insofar as there is one person at the center of the action or web of intrigues it is Tolomeo, who arouses the enmity of every other character. Sesto and Cesare want to kill him in revenge for Pompeo's murder, while Tolomeo is just as eager to see Cesare killed; Achilla deems himself cheated over Cornelia; and these hostilities put into the hands of his sister Cleopatra the means to use against him in her ambition to win the throne of Egypt for herself alone. All the plot lines, which would otherwise be hard to connect, converge on the villain. The happy ending in this drama comes in the form of successful revenge.

The unity of action postulated by the aesthetics of French classical tragedy is replaced by a unity of one central figure around whom all the events cluster ever more densely; and the diversity that is the other side of the coin of the unities in eighteenth-century poetics consists of an accumulation of subplots, which fulfills the musical conditions of an opera seria: the immense number of arias, the contrasting affects they express, and their assignment according to a hierarchy of characters.

One of the devices facilitating the relationship between a complicated dramaturgy and the expectations embedded in the distribution of the arias is a certain interchangeability of the musical consequences that can be drawn from a situation—whether the order of the arias, their content, or who sings them. After the scene in which Achilla produces Pompeo's severed head (act 1, scene 3) the distribution of the arias expressing reactions to this horrifying event is quite arbitrary: Cesare's shrill outpouring of disgust (no. 3: "Empio, dirò, tu sei"), Cornelia's lament (no. 4: "Priva son d'ogni conforto"), and Sesto's vow of vengeance (no. 5: "Svegliatevi nel core") could be interchanged without causing any dramaturgical damage. The given disposition almost seems to take account of their social rank.

Another example of interchangeability is the scene in which Cleopatra and Tolomeo face each other in open conflict (act 1, scene 5), the musical consequence of which could be an outbreak of anger on Tolomeo's part rather than Cleopatra's ironic response (no. 6: "Non disperar, chi sa?"). (Instead, Tolomeo's anger motivates an aria in the next scene—no. 7: "L'empio sleale indegno"—but there it is directed against Cesare.) And the scene that shows Tolomeo and Cesare filled with mutual but concealed mistrust (act 1, scene 9) is followed by an aria (no. 14: "Va tacito e nascoso, / quand'avido è di preda, / l'astuto cacciator"), the sentiment of which would suit Tolomeo just as well as it does Cesare, who actually sings it.

Thus, there is not always a compelling connection between a situation and the emotion expressed in the aria it occasions, or the character who sings it. On the other hand, the postulate of musical variety can at times only be met by mixing various strands of the plot together. The principle of contrast is taken to such an extreme in the great scene at Pompeo's tomb (act 1, scenes 7–8) that it comes very close to the grotesque. Cesare's philosophizing in his lament for Pompeo (no. 8, monologue: "Alma del gran Pompeo"); the arcadian tone he adopts to express his enchantment at the sight of Cleopatra, who is seeking help in adversity (no. 9: "Non è si vago e bello / il fior sul prato"); Cleopatra's self-confidently sententious aria on the power of beauty (no. 10: "Tutto può donna vezzosa"), which provides her with an independent exit; Cornelia's elegy (no. 11: "Nel tuo seno, amico sasso"); Sesto's hope for a peace of mind he will obtain only by avenging himself on Tolomeo (no. 12: "Cara speme, questo core"); and Cleopatra's doubt as to how far Cesare's love, which she wanted only to exploit as a weapon against Tolomeo, will affect herself (no. 13: "Tu la mia stella sei")—all these combine to create a pattern whose rationale seems to be pure confusion. Subplots come under the spotlight or disappear into the shadows and run concurrently or replace each other without any linking thread but the very thin one of Cleopatra, who enters in search of Cesare and remains onstage for no reason but to declare her readiness to help the vengeful Sesto obtain access to Tolomeo. The relationship between the dramaturgical and the musical structures remains largely formal: the musical and dramaturgical elements are joined together by external ties rather than because either justifies the other from any internal necessity.

16. INTERIOR AND EXTERIOR DIALOGUE

Just as dialogue is the essential medium of spoken drama, the aria can claim to be the characteristic form in opera, although it must be combined with recitative if it is to play its full dramaturgical role. The claim is undeniable in the eighteenth century, if a little weaker in the nineteenth. But even though the duet decisively developed greater significance in the nineteenth century— hardly less in Italian opera than in French and German—it would nevertheless be wide of the mark to construct a dramatic theory of opera primarily according to the principle of dialogue dominant in the spoken play. That the aria, in which a person is alone with his or her own thoughts (or with a confidant who is only a second self), should rank as the paradigmatic form in a drama that relies for its basic structure on the dealings between human beings may sound somewhat paradoxical, yet it is an inescapable consequence of the premise that opera must be understood as drama constituted by means of musical forms, and not as the alternation of recitatives (dramatic but not very musical) and arias (musical but not very dramatic).

To resolve the paradox we need to recall that, as with opera, in the classical play—whether in seventeenth-century France (Corneille's *Polyeucte*, Racine's *Phèdre*) or in late-eighteenth-century Germany (Goethe's *Iphigenie,* Schiller's *Maria Stuart*)—the principal character is accompanied as a rule by a confidant, who does not so much speak or act on his own behalf as express some of what moves the principal actor or reveal motives that the principal would prefer to conceal from himself. Dialogues with a confidant are thus essentially monologues, in which the principal actor's divided self is manifested in the exterior distribution of the arguments between two people. Conversely, when the principal actor is alone, monologue is cast in the form of interior dialogue. The underlying forms of dialogue with a confidant and monologue as the expression of a consciousness divided against itself are one and the same.

In dramaturgical terms, therefore, both the monologue and the dialogue with confidant are manifestations of the classical or classicizing tendency to transpose a drama's center of gravity away from exterior action to the interior; in this, French classical tragedy was in agreement with opera seria. As well as events that result in dialectically tense situations and dialogue that manifests confrontation in verbal forms, an important part of the substance of a drama is formed by the emotions of the leading characters, the reflections with which they seek to reassure themselves, and the inner contradictions they weigh in monologues or in dialogues constructed on the lines of monologue; the epithet "dramatic" cannot be denied to this interiorized part of the action. Reflection on an event, leading in turn to a decision to act, and the emotion, single or divided, that underlies the reflection are no less "dramatic" than the actions with which we primarily associate the word. So although the accent in opera falls on the aria instead of on dialogue, yet, given the role of interior dialogue in French classical tragedy, the difference between the two genres is one of degree, not principle: a difference within essentially similar structures, in which it is not only important to have the exterior action spring from the interior but also to have the substance of the exterior drama revealed above all in the interior drama. The dichotomy of essence and appearance (phenomenon), a fundamental distinction of classical philosophy, thus also underlies classical drama. And to the extent that the action of a drama is regarded as appearance, the purpose of which is to reveal the essence—the interior drama as a configuration of states of mind—so the essence can be manifested in musical forms exactly as in verbal ones.

It is true that nothing in opera, not even in the form of the large-scale monologue that replaced the traditional aria in a few outstanding examples in the nineteenth century, measures up in every respect to the complexity of a monologue such as that of Rodrigue, the hero of Corneille's *Le Cid,* in its stringent development from the feeling that he is nothing but a passive tool of fate to a clearer understanding of the conflict at the heart of which he finds himself, to a tragic mood in which death seems to offer his only means of escape, and finally to the conviction, which takes him as inner exaltation, that he must sacrifice personal inclination to the political whole. The scene between Wotan and Brünnhilde in act 3 of *Die Walküre,* in which Brünnhilde alternates between the roles of confidant and antagonist, resembles the monologue of a classical play to the extent that reflection leads to decision: finally Wotan truly wills the "end" that he has earlier identified as essential.

King Filippo's monologue in Verdi's *Don Carlo* ("Ella giammai m'amò") is not the expression of an interior debate leading to a decision but depicts emotions circling round and round without finding escape, so that it makes dramaturgical sense, as well as meeting the demands of musical form, that the opening section returns as the last and the cantabile ("Dormirò sol nel manto mio regal") as the penultimate. Eboli's "aria" ("O don fatale") differs from Filippo's "scena" in that, while more conventional in form, its interior structure seems closer to that of a monologue in a play. As in a monologue of the classical type, Eboli's recognition of the issues in a situation drives her to seek a resolution. The contrast between the cantabile ("O mia Regina, io t'immolai") and the cabaletta ("Oh ciel! E Carlo? a morte domani . . .") is still recognizable, at least partly, as the formal framework corresponding to a contrast of emotions: remorse for her betrayal and enthusiasm for the idea of rescue. But the first relates to Queen Elisabetta, the second to Carlo: Eboli is indeed torn by contrary aims but, instead of stringently elaborating a conflict, the aria presents an abrupt alternation between two subjects for arioso outpourings. Essentially, the exterior jolt that usually motivates a cabaletta is replaced by a change in the direction of the confused emotions. This is not to say that the confusion is less "realistic" psychologically than the logic of a classical monologue, but it illustrates that the principle of development—which Wagner contrasted with that of alternation in his open letter *Über Franz Liszts symphonische Dichtungen* (1857), laying claim to it for his type of musical drama—creates difficulties when it is realized in opera.

17. INTERIOR ACTION

The classical aesthetic postulate that an opera must depict well-differentiated characters who develop during the course of the action unmistakably originates in theories of the dramaturgy of the spoken play. It was ignored during the eighteenth century, for a variety of reasons. Opera buffa's depiction of characters as types militated against any tendency toward finer differentiation or development, while the representation of character was excluded from opera seria, as a drama of affects, because any form of fixity is incompatible with a storm of affects, continually changing direction as it breaks over the dramatis personae.

Of course, the word "character" also covers the concept of established idiosyncrasy stamped by one prominent character trait, making it possible to call Molière's *L'avare* and *Le malade imaginaire* comedies of character as well as comedies about comic types. But if the term embraces both the single aspect and the rounded personality, it cannot be used in an essential historical differentiation mapping the transition from type to character.

Whatever the term "character" is understood to mean, the difference between spoken play and dramma per musica remains the same, because every definition presumes something fixed or established, and in opera seria that is precisely what is missing, in the principal actors at least. On the contrary, they are prey to affects that change from one scene to the next, without having the inner means to resist the changes, as well-founded characters should. Thus, the essential dramaturgical category of a dramma per musica is situation, which releases affects, not character, which motivates or provokes intrigue.

As a drama of affects, opera seria is confronted with a type of problem whose resolution—or nonresolution—has no small influence on the standing of a work. The aria, the almost exclusively dominant form of the eighteenth century, may appear to be merely a reaction to a situation of conflict, occasioned by events in the action, to be sure, but having little influence on dramatic developments, so that the musical expression has a peripheral, explanatory role but almost no dramaturgical function. Alternatively, the composer, and after him the performers, may succeed in presenting the configuration of arias, and the people expressing themselves in them, as the true drama: that which forms the infrastructure, to some extent, of the events enacted on the stage and creates an interior action distinct from the exterior one. The premise underlying the latter alternative is that the action consists in the presentation and development of a configuration of characters rather than that the configuration of characters provides the impetus for an action. The rationale may seem odd, but it was, nevertheless, a feature common to opera seria and French classical tragedy. In Racine's *Andromaque,* for example, how the machinery of the complicated relationships between Pyrrhus, Andromaque, Hermione, and Oreste functions as the action proceeds is less important than the structure itself, which is gradually brought to light by the events.

The idea that an aria, as a moment of lyrical contemplation or an outpouring of emotion, is merely the reaction to events taking place in the recitatives provided the aesthetic premise behind the procedure which dominated opera interpretation for many decades: a musical connection between the (musically central but dramaturgically peripheral) arias was reconstructed by interpreting the sequence of tonalities as "large-scale form," by analogy with symphonic instrumental music. Thus, the arias were deemed to be linked in terms of musical form, to some extent independently of their place in the action—although it is almost impossible to choose a key that is both characteristic of an affect and fits into any tonal system linking the arias together, however liberal one's definitions of "characteristic" key and tonal system (see §14).

The concept of the aria as occasioned by the exterior action but then left to its own devices, isolated unless linked musically to other arias by the all-too-vague and hypothetical device of a scheme of tonalities, is obviously unsatisfactory. If the concept is to be revised, or at least augmented, however, an interior action, the outcome of the configuration of affects and characters, must be distinguished from the exterior action.

In the five arias that, in addition to choruses, make up the first act of Mozart's *Idomeneo*, the four principal characters give verbal expression to the conflicts of the situations in which they find themselves. This process provides the exposition of two initially separate strands of action. In one, Idomeneo despairs at the vow he made in fear of death to sacrifice the first human being he meets on reaching land safely (no. 6), and Idamante bewails the horror with which his father dismissed him (no. 7). In the other, Ilia vacillates between her love for Idamante and her grief at the fall of Troy, which makes it impossible for her, a Trojan and a prisoner, to love a Greek (no. 1); Idamante suffers at being forced to sacrifice his love for Ilia because of political events that were none of his doing (no. 2); and Elettra gives vent to hatred because she feels humiliated by Idamante, who rejects her, and by Ilia, a mere slave, who nevertheless thwarts the desires of a princess of the house of Atreus (no. 4).

Idamante is a passive hero, who has not hitherto suffered at the hands of fate, yet he is the focal point of the interior action outlined above—the drama of affects, all of which center on him, without his knowledge. Ilia loves him, Elettra feels spurned by him, and to Idomeneo he is the victim who must be sacrificed to Neptune. This is not to say that Idamante is the protagonist, however; it is generally the case that a distinction needs to be made between figures on whom the emotions of others center and those in whom the underlying tragic structure of a drama is manifested: if *Idomeneo* is understood as a tragedy with some ancient Greek elements in the plot, it is Idomeneo who—like Agamemnon in Euripides' *Iphigeneia in Aulis* or Pentheus in *The Bacchae*—dares to take up the hopeless challenge of defying the god whose victim he is.

The only essential thing in the order of the arias in act 1 is that the fourth (Idomeneo, no. 6) must precede the fifth (Idamante, no. 7). Otherwise, Mozart and his librettist had a free choice, in principle, because what the characters expound in them is less the action than themselves, and specifically the configuration of their relationships, which is, for the time being, static. Every one of the arias expounding, variously, Ilia's divided emotions, Idomeneo's despair, Elettra's jealousy, and Idamante's indignation at the intrusion of politics into his private feelings could come at the beginning of the work, underlining the point that the primary subject matter of the early scenes is a configuration of characters (as in Racine's *Andromaque*) who, except for Idamante, are already burdened by their individual fates.

In the drama of affects the arias are allowed to be musically closed numbers.

The formal scheme Mozart usually adopts in *Idomeneo* is that known as "sonata without development": a misnomer, since sonata form itself has no first, let alone exclusive, claim on it. The scheme goes as follows: first subject (tonic)—second subject (dominant or relative)—first subject (tonic)—second subject (tonic). It is by no means a limbless torso, or formally defective, for having no development. Contrast between the two themes can represent interior conflict (Ilia) or divergent forms of expression given to one and the same affect (Idamante's complaint to the gods and his overtures to Ilia, Elettra's conjuration of demons and outpouring of hatred for Ilia and Idamante, Idamante's perplexity at Idomeneo's repulsion of him and his return to reflection on his own emotional state). The decisive thing is, however, that these are not themes in the sense the term has in instrumental music but are groups of motives, the nature and extent of which are based on the textual particles and emotions they express. (The sonata form of Mozart's instrumental works, often perceived as an assemblage of musical ideas failing to measure up to the rule of strict sonata form, is an opera composer's sonata form: a variant of aria form, not the model for it.) Mozart demonstrates his unrivaled mastery of the art of modulation, not in development sections, but in the differences between the first and second versions of the motivic complexes: in Elettra's aria (A B A′ B′), the F major of the B segment (the relative of the tonic D minor) is modified slightly to F minor, so creating the impression that the C minor in A′, which also effects a contrast of key within the recapitulation (C minor in the A′ segment, D minor in the B′), has been prepared and therefore justified.

In order to understand the fine distinctions of affects and the emotional dilemmas manifested by the arias as the elements of an interior action revealed primarily in musical forms and not by onstage events, it is necessary to step back from the "appearances" of the stage action and enter the "essence" of the music. The affects of the five arias in act 1 of *Idomeneo* reveal the integrated configuration of characters constituting the interior action in immediately perceptible terms. The revelation neither rests on the exterior course of events (as already mentioned, some changes to the order of scenes and numbers would be feasible) nor tolerates narrow musical-symbolic interpretation as a large-scale form shaped by a scheme of tonalities. The crucial thing is that the audience recognizes, in the configuration of affects and characters, a system of associations partly independent of the course of events and unperceived or only fragmentarily perceived by the actors, which therefore cannot find its dramatic expression in dialogue, the paradigmatic form of the spoken play, but must be experienced by the audience as an integrated musical and dramatic form.

18. "PATHOS" AND "ETHOS"

The "pathos" rejected as stilted by the standards of nineteenth-century bourgeois realism was the verbal or musical form in the drama of the modern era that expressed the suffering and passion that the Greek word unites. It was distinct as much from the prose of everyday speech as from the regularity of simple verse structures. Pathos, as a style, was neither realistic nor formalistic. It rested on the assumption that unbearable suffering is expressed in speech that bursts all bounds, fragmented and irregular—that is, in the abrupt (and highly artificial) alternation between long and short lines, and between iambs, trochees, and dactyls. The musical forms regarded as appropriately equivalent were the *recitar cantando* and *cantar recitando* of early opera, the *récit*, or large-scale monologue, of tragédie lyrique, and the *recitativo accompagnato* of the eighteenth century, used to overwhelming effect in some scenes by Handel.

One of the Latin words equivalent to Greek *pathos* (but not the only one) is *affectus,* and for centuries, almost independently of changes in style, the concept of "affect" was the fundamental category of opera as musical drama: arias expressed affects such as love, jealousy, sorrow, pain, and anger, evoked in the course of the action and propelling it further. But the affect providing the substance of an aria in the eighteenth century, the single nature of which was a premise of thematically closed, large-scale form, did not express itself in the "pathetic" style, fragmented by the force of the inner motion, but in a musical structure described as *style d'une teneur* (consistent, homogeneous style) by a writer of the time (*Mercure de France,* April 1772) and as *Einheitsablauf* (uniform process) by Heinrich Besseler in his paper "Characterthema und Erlebnisform" (*Kongreßbericht Lüneburg 1950* [Kassel, n.d.], 7–32). The reason was that the eighteenth-century stylistic ideal was melodic and motivic continuity, not expressive, rhapsodic discontinuity. Unity of affect was the correlative of the large-scale, thematically integrated musical form, and large-scale form was the musical manifestation of unity of affect.

Thus, though they are synonymous linguistically, pathos and affect were divided as categories of musical dramaturgy between *recitativo accompagnato* or *recitar cantando,* on the one hand, and the aria, on the other—especially the da capo aria in five sections. The division was only partial, and it would be as wrong to exaggerate it as to ignore it altogether. Cicero first considered using *morbus* to translate *pathos* but settled on *perturbatio.* If the former highlights the element of infection—the idea that an affect attacks a person like an illness, having an external origin—the latter denotes straying from the path of *ethos* and represents *pathos* as an exceptional psychological state. Both characteristics—disorder and aberrance—contribute to the pathetic style of *recitativo accompagnato* and to the affect that gives an aria internal unity. In the earlier psychology, which survived in opera after it had disappeared in science, both were understood as powers that took possession of human beings from outside them, at the behest of gods or demons. The soul is more the showplace of affects than their place of origin. Accordingly, various passions frequently shake one and the same person in an abrupt succession, without any stringent relationship or mediation between them founded in the character's consistency or direction of development. It is not at all unusual or aesthetically objectionable in an opera seria—by Handel, for example—if, at the sight of a *locus amoenus*, a tyrant whose predominant affects are anger and fear falls into a pastoral tone better fitted to an arcadian shepherd.

From the standpoint of classical, idealistic aesthetics, the propensity of dramatis personae to let themselves be tossed to and fro by extreme affects without summoning the consistency and fixity of character to resist them (because a loosely constructed cluster of potentially interchangeable arias was the correlative of strict, closed aria form) was a defect of baroque drama, the dramaturgy of which persisted in opera longer than in the spoken play. Condemnation was all the harsher partly because it embraced certain sociopolitical assumptions (consistency of character was seen as an essential trait of the middle-class merchant, along with reliability and predictability) and partly because its foundations were weak, trusting more to utopian anthropology than to any adequate understanding of reality.

The proposition that human beings exhibit complete consistency of character and are not exposed to changes of emotion generated by the situations in which they find themselves is a postulate of bourgeois humanism bearing little relationship to psychological reality. The notion that a character develops along a continuous line, with inner aptitude and exterior circumstances combining to assist the process, in order to confirm an ethos or (as in Stravinsky's *Rake's Progress*) see it disintegrate, is also a poetic notion; though it underlies the entwicklungsroman (the genre includes examples of downward, as well as upward, progress), it again has little to do with real life. Baroque dramaturgy is therefore more realistic than bourgeois-idealist aesthetics was prepared to acknowledge, although the proportion of anthropological truth in an aesthetic judgment cannot really be cited as a demonstration of its authority: critiques of baroque art and countercritiques of classicism mean nothing more than that two incommensurable premises have equal aesthetic rights to stand side by side.

"Representation of character in music," postulated by Christian Körner in 1795 (in his essay "Charakterdarstellung in der Musik"), is extremely rare in both eighteenth-century opera seria and nineteenth-century musical drama, in the sense either of a fixed, permanent ethos or of a stringent, continuous development. But there are reasons for this rarity, both in musical dramaturgy's need for frequent, abrupt, and musically well-contrasted changes of affect and in human psychology. It can be said, without exaggeration, of the typical heroes of nineteenth-century opera—Max in *Der Freischütz*, Jean in *Le prophète*, Alfredo in *La traviata*, even Siegfried in *Götterdämmerung*— that they are not characters at all in the strict sense in which classical aesthetics understood the term. By the standards of bourgeois ethics they have neither "good" nor "bad" characters, for they have none at all. This exposes them, virtually powerless to resist, to the passions which, in their diversity and cumulative complexity, create the substance of the operas. If fate and character are mutually exclusive, as Walter Benjamin thought, it is fate which rules in opera, driving human beings from one affect to the next with all the more power because the "characters" in the cast are not "characters" in the ethical sense.

19. DIALOGUE AND DUET

The form with which opera makes its strongest claim to be musical drama is undoubtedly the duet. The Verdian type of opera—if "type" can be singular in the context—can be defined, at the cost of some simplification, by the dominance in it of the duet, not the aria or the ensemble, as the form providing the backbone of the overall musical-dramatic structure. A change in the hierarchy of forms may seem a purely exterior factor, but it is one of the tangible features distinguishing Italian opera in the nineteenth century from both Metastasian dramma per musica and Wagnerian music-drama. The dramaturgy of the opera-of-duets is fundamentally different from that of the earlier opera-of-arias, as much as it is from that of the contemporary opera-of-dialogue.

Bellini and Donizetti still sought unmistakably to balance both the number and the succession of arias, duets, and ensembles, and the overriding importance they gave to the principle of formal balance means that the degree of dramatic justification for the different musical forms changes constantly, without any perceptible unambiguous tendency in one direction or another.

In the cantabile of the first duet in Bellini's *I Capuleti e i Montecchi* (allegro moderato: "Si, fuggire! a noi non resta"), Romeo's and Giulietta's parts (both thirty-eight bars) are melodically the same, although they express opposing affects and intentions; however, the subsections (thirteen and twenty-five bars) are melodically contrasted, although the difference is not justified by the text, the content of which remains the same. It is thus reasonable to say that the musical form overrides the text for the sake of regularity and simplicity.

While in that duet the abstract musical structure takes a priority it should not really have according to the dramaturgical principles of Italian romanticism, in another instance, the duet for Romeo and Tebaldo in act 2 ("Stolto, a un sol mi grido"), it does not matter at all that, trading insults like Homeric heroes before they start fighting, the two sing the same melodic phrases, whether at some distance apart, in rapid alternation, or in parallel thirds: the same affect—blind rage—has hold of both throughout the exchange, and the formal simplicity corresponds exactly to the dramaturgical situation.

In the allegro of the duet for Romeo and Giulietta with which the opera ends ("Ah! crudel, che mai facesti?"), musical coherence rests on the strictly regular ("quadratic") syntax observed by both voices and orchestra (and on the cadential harmony which is its correlative), so that the dialogue—fragmented phrases, expressing the catastrophe—can develop freely without melodic correspondence. The andante ("Vivi, ah vivi, e vien talora") modulates from D major to C minor as if it were recitative. Although at first the musical expression seems rhapsodic here, inner unity reveals itself retrospectively to some extent: when alternation gives way to overlapping utterance ("Un solo accento ancor"), much of the melodic material alludes to earlier material, giving the texture a density that it seemed to lack at the start, where the emphasis was on expressiveness. In strong contrast to the first duet, therefore, the musical form is not forcibly imposed on the text but either makes a second layer alongside the verbal-melodic expression (allegro) or constitutes itself secondarily as a web of motivic associations between melodic phrases that at first seemed musically scarcely coherent and justified solely by the text.

Of the three duets in Donizetti's *Lucrezia Borgia,* the second, Lucrezia's confrontation with Don Alfonso, is dramatic in the specific sense that the dialogue draws close to that of a play: in this it illustrates one of the several possible ways of making a duet a distinctly dramatic form, able to constitute opera as musical drama. The short recitative raises the tension in the situation to an intolerable degree, and the cantabile (larghetto: "Soli noi siamo. Che chiedete?") reveals the discrepancies between what is said and what left silent, bringing a latent conflict out into the open. The larghetto begins as a rapid exchange of dialogue, sustained musically by recurring orchestral motives which join up to make regular, closed periods: the form is what Eduard Hanslick termed *Rhythmus im Großen* (rhythm over a large span). It continues with a series of cantabile periods for Lucrezia (with interjections from Alfonso), on a simple, conventional formal plan. The *tempo di mezzo* ("Chi? . . . tu!") drops the bombshell that changes the entire situation and motivates the cabaletta. In the cabaletta (allegro mosso), which is constructed on a regular plan (A B A' C; C is the stretta), the open conflict that broke out in the *tempo di mezzo* spreads itself in extended melodic periods, in which the two characters confront each other as in a tableau vivant representing their affects. The B segment is partly a contrast, as the situation demands, but Donizetti seeks nevertheless to mediate in the interests of musical unity, balancing opposition in the ways the A and B segments start against agreement in the ways they end, and using Alfonso's interpolations as a means of modifying the reprise (A'). The dialogue is almost a verbal duel, like a quarrel in a play: argumentation is the dominant style of utterance, although the substance of the scene is made up of complicated conflicts of affect—in Lucrezia's case the conflict between aristocratic arrogance and a guilt she has not yet incurred but anticipates emotionally. And the possibility of developing a closed musical form from a verbal duel is realized by the following means: first, the antagonist's part is reduced to mere interjections, which demonstrate opposition without disrupting the melodic continuity; second, the composer exploits the common experience that opposing positions in an argument involve some of the same affects (A and B segments in the cabaletta); third, he makes dramatic use of cantabile counterpoint, a compositional technique in which extreme rhythmic contrasts are sustained by a simple harmonic framework (this technique is characteristic of nineteenth-century music in general, not opera alone, but still awaits theoretical exposition and aesthetic interpretation).

A musical sense of form is demonstrated, at least in the nineteenth century, less by the talent to fill given, fixed schemata with meaningful content and thereby justify them from within yet again but rather by the skill to develop variants that, insofar as they allow the fundamental model on which they rely to be perceptible beneath the variant, demand from the listener the discrimination to perceive norm and variant simultaneously. Dramaturgically the difference between tradition (bestowing legitimacy) and progress (developing while preserving tradition) means that either the librettist must adapt the content to the canon of musical forms or the composer, conversely, must adapt the modified formal canon to the content, in such a way that the form does not dissolve or disintegrate but fulfills a dramaturgical function by the very juxtaposing of norm and variant.

There are innumerable ways to vary the norm, without losing sight of it, in order to perform a dramaturgical function, and it is not easy to select a few examples that would typify the full range. But since Verdi's operas are preeminent examples of operas-of-duets (operas in which duets form the musical-dramaturgical framework) and since, furthermore, they provide an especially clear picture of the transition from merely filling in a given schema to calculatedly breaking it open, it may be sufficient to illustrate the main principles of the process by means of the three duets for Carlo and Elisabetta in *Don Carlo*.

Only the five-act version of the opera (Paris, 1867, and Modena, 1886) will serve for this purpose. Don Carlo's romance in the monastery scene of the four-act version, salvaged from the original first act (set in Fontainebleau) and turned into a lament for what he lost there, narrates the prehistory instead of showing it; it is therefore dramaturgically a weak substitute for the great duet during which the love between Elisabetta and the prince flowers only to be trampled underfoot immediately, onstage, in the dramatic present. This duet is conventionally laid out, insofar as the startling news that Elisabetta is to marry King Filippo of Spain, and not his son Carlo *(tempo di mezzo)* represents the shock that, in accordance with the rules of both Parisian grand opéra and Italian *melodramma,* motivates the switch from cantabile to cabaletta. The cantabile, however, lying between the scena and the *tempo di mezzo,* is disproportionately prolonged and also unusual in that its internal subdivisions are governed by the categories of the multisectional duet (cantabile: "Terror arcano invade questo core"; *tempo di mezzo:* "Perchè mi balza il cor?"; cabaletta: "Di qual amor"; *tempo di mezzo:* "Qual rumor!"; cantabile: "Spari l'orror della foresta"; reprise of cabaletta: "Se tremo ancor"). Verdi uses the traditional form but composes not so much "within" it as "with" it.

The subdivision according to onstage events, which are presented in the semirecitative *tempo di mezzo* sections (the surprise of the picture from which Elisabetta recognizes Carlo; the cannon shots signaling the start of festivities, for reasons which the couple misinterpret; the news that Elisabetta is to marry Filippo), is a stern reminder of the formal tradition, which was too deeply embedded in the memory to be erased by any variants. Because the first cabaletta ("Di qual amor") uses the same music as the second ("Se tremo ancor"), and moreover both differ little in tempo from the first cantabile (metronome 108 instead of 69), the second cabaletta (metronome 120) is a suitable end to the whole, counterbalancing the first despite its relative brevity. (Another possible interpretation is that the one cabaletta is recapitulated after two different cantabile sections, which would make the conclusion only a stretta, appropriately in view of its brevity; this would not make any difference to the musical-dramaturgical argument.)

The complicated musical form—complicated by the simultaneity of the norm remembered and the variant presented—expresses an interior action entailing so many changes, succeeding each other at such a pace, that it is unimaginable as the substance of a conventional duet, and Verdi, who was quite as much a formalist as a dramatist, wanted to avoid simply following the ups and downs of the text, now rhapsodically, now amorphously. A single duet scarcely seems to have room for the transition from secret attraction (Carlo pretends to talk of a third person while really meaning himself) to recognition when Elisabetta sees Carlo's portrait, and from spontaneous falling in love (over which a shadow of apprehension falls, although the love is as yet legitimate) to the harsh intervention of the outside world and the resolution to withstand misfortune. The overlapping and contraction of the forms constituting the duet in musical terms are thus shown, both in the overall length and in the abrupt changes of situation, to have sound dramaturgical foundations.

The duet for Elisabetta and Carlo in act 2 of the five-act version ("Io vengo a domandar") has the simple title "Duetto," instead of the more usual "Scena e duetto." This does not mean that it lacks the recitative-like sections normally implied by the term "scena," nor that they are somewhat longer than usual, as might appear to be suggested in some editions, which call it "Gran scena e duetto." Rather, it reflects the fact that the boundary between scena and duetto is unclear, because motivic working in the scena and passages of recitative in the duet bridge the stylistic contrast. The immediate repetition

("Perduto ben," "Clemente Iddio") or later recapitulation of a cantabile period ("Bontà celeste") may be regarded as providing a formal framework, the more so because the melodic phrase will recur as a reminiscence in their last duet. The essential musical-dramatic process consists, however, of the stages by which Carlo works himself into a paroxysm—at first under the sway of his emotions and eventually rapt in a visionary trance. In terms of musical form, nothing whatever links his periods ("Ciel! non un sol, un sol detto," "Perduto ben," "O prodigio! Il mio cor," "Qual voce a me dal ciel"), neither motivic relationships nor the rudiments of any traditional formal design. The musical form can be understood only as a musical-dramaturgical one—not, let it be said, a purely dramaturgical one. In Elisabetta's case, the rhythmic similarity of the first and second periods and melodic identity of the third and fourth observe the tradition of closed form, and it is precisely the contrast between the formal openness or fragmentation of the tenor's part and the regularity or composure of the soprano's that is dramaturgically essential, for the raving Carlo confronts an Elisabetta who has herself under control and prays to heaven. Strictly speaking, this is neither dialogue, in which people present each other with alternating arguments, nor a duet expressing shared or disparate emotions but rather two monologues, delivered side by side: Carlo does not speak *with* Elisabetta but *about* the image of her in his memory; she does not turn to him but to God. The musical consistency resides partly in the dramatic justification for the double monologue and also in the way that the open form of Carlo's rising paroxysm is supported, and thus saved from amorphousness, by the closed form with which Elisabetta retains her composure. The relationship between closed and open form is dramaturgical, because it needs the contrast between the two characters, but it is also musical inasmuch as it expresses the dramatic configuration Carlo–Elisabetta. (The cabaletta shows two people addressing each other in a conflict of affects: anything but uncommon in a nineteenth-century opera.)

The "Duetto d'addio" for Carlo and Elisabetta, as rewritten for the four-act version of 1883 and retained in the definitive, five-act version of 1886, begins (or perhaps the scena ends), as mentioned earlier, with a reminiscence ("Vago sogno m'arrise") of their second duet, not their first. That a moment when they appeared estranged should be recalled, rather than one when happiness appeared to be within their grasp, makes sense inasmuch as the elements of opposition, not simply those of mutual devotion, are fixed in the memory as the substance of this love story. For the rest, it is based unmistakably on the conventional formal schema (cantabile and cabaletta), but with the two sections transposed, for an equally obvious reason: a tone of transfiguration resolving all the problems fated not to be solved on earth transcends a warlike intention, which fails. The reversal of the usual order of cabaletta (marziale: "Si, l'eroismo è questo") and cantabile (assai sostenuto: "Ma lassù

ci vedremo") is one of the simplest ways to make a formal stereotype eloquent by means of a dramaturgically motivated variation—one that relies on
awareness of the norm from which it departs to make its dramaturgical function effective.

20. SIMULTANEITY

When people speak simultaneously in a play, each on his own account and
not as dialogue, it is an effect from the theater of the absurd, by means of
which speech is reduced to acoustic-rhythmic structures and the expression
of affects. (György Ligeti demonstrated vividly in *Aventures et Nouvelles
aventures* that emotions can be made comprehensible by speech morphemes
alone without any help from semantics.) In opera, however, the simultaneous
utterance of heterogeneous material is a characteristic and frequently used
form of composition for ensemble, concentrating the drama of affects by musical means. There is even a tendency among some music historians to treat it
as the epitome of the specifically operatic phenomenon, although the ensemble
did not come into existence as a type of operatic movement earlier than the
mid–eighteenth century. Moreover, in the commedia per musica, where it
originated (works such as Paisiello's *Il barbiere di Siviglia*), techniques were
at first restricted to the simplest structures: rapid alternation between the
persons speaking above an orchestral ostinato base, homorhythmic chordal
writing (whether the voices sing the same or different words), or a parlando
commentary by one character providing a counterpoint to a cantabile or declamatory top line sung by another.

Historically, the adoption and development of ensemble techniques in
opera seria were at least as significant as their origins in opera buffa, so it is
not inappropriate to illustrate the dramaturgical uses of the musical structures in ensemble movements with an example from Rossini's *Otello* as well
as others from Verdi's *Rigoletto* and *Don Carlo*.

The finale of act 1 of *Otello* meets Lorenzo da Ponte's recommendation of
a "picciol dramma" within the drama, containing "un novello intreccio ed un
interesse straordinario." It is assembled from a succession of abruptly changing situations, and the changes are the consequences, not of confrontations
conducted in dialogue, as they would be in a play, but of unexpected turns of
events. When Desdemona's father, the patrician Elmiro Barberigo, presents
his daughter and Rodrigo, the Doge's son, to the chorus as a betrothed couple
(on the basis of a letter his daughter wrote to Otello, which he believes to have
been addressed to Rodrigo), it creates a situation of general astonishment, in
which everyone is alone with his or her own thoughts: Desdemona is deeply
distressed, Rodrigo is tormented by doubt, and Elmiro—for the present—
senses nothing of the confusion he has caused. Time stands still to some ex-

tent in the trio in which these contradictory emotions confront each other (it has different "antecedent" sections but a "consequent" that recurs to ensure musical integration); the situation is prolonged musically but lasts only a moment of "real" time. The second part, a cantabile in a slow tempo (larghetto), accentuates the astonishment, common to all the divergent emotional reactions, that is the basis for the impression that time has been suspended. The fact that, as in the quartet in *Fidelio* (no. 3), the characters' heterogeneous feelings are expressed musically by means of one melody circling in a quasi-canonic fashion should be interpreted, not as a *pezzo concertato* in which Rossini makes a musical effect but ignores the dramatic-psychological elements, but rather as a musical sign of a sense of unconscious alliance in a situation so complicated as to be almost beyond hope of untangling. Otello's entrance in the background—unnoticed at first by the others—brings about an ambivalent situation in musical-dramaturgical terms: the sung dialogue still consists essentially of the confrontation of Elmiro, Desdemona, and Rodrigo, but the orchestral music—martial and aggressive—is unmistakably an aural emblem of Otello. Yet by the criteria of musical form, it is part of the trio, forming its concluding allegro. Or, to put it another way, the change of tempo within the trio is motivated from outside—by Otello's entrance and the music depicting it—instead of resulting from the inner process of the trio itself. In the allegro section of the quintet, among the rapid exchanges of dialogue above ostinato repetitions of an orchestral motive, certain fragments of text illuminating the situation stand out clearly—*parole sceniche* in Verdi's sense: Otello's claim ("Il suo core . . . / amore mel diede") and Desdemona's admission ("È ver: giurai . . ."). The slow section of the quintet (andante maestoso) is again, like that of the trio, an ensemble in which time seems to stand still in the shock delivered by Elmiro's curse, as the characters subside, each individually, into inner contemplation of the new situation. It would be wrong to speak of a "purely musical" form, forced on the composer by a banal text leveling the differences between the emotional reactions, for the commonplace words ("Incerta l'anima / vacilla e geme") express the distress felt by all the characters, even if for different reasons. That the dramatic impetus is suspended at the exact moment when an irreconcilable conflict is revealed to general view does not by any means signify a recourse to music without regard to the drama, but rather a pause marking a decisive moment, the prolongation of which in the music emphasizes its dramaturgical weight. (Wagner cites the silence of Joan of Arc when accused of witchcraft in Schiller's play *Die Jungfrau von Orleans* in order to explain the idea of "sounding silence," but it would need to last longer than a silence can be allowed to last in a play; in an opera the prolongation takes the form of either an orchestral melody or a vocal ensemble, singing words that mean little in themselves but allow a cantabile to unfold and express the emotion underlying the astonished silence, so that the ensemble scarcely differs from Wagnerian orchestral melody in terms of dramaturgical significance.)

In the quartet in *Rigoletto,* the first section (allegro) consists of two separate dialogues, between the Duke and Maddalena and between Rigoletto and Gilda. They are supported by an orchestral melody which is the principal voice and ensures musical cohesion while allowing the singers' parts to alternate rapidly between parlando and cantabile without any risk of a break in continuity. Not until the second section (andante) does the musical connection result from the relationship between the vocal parts, which articulate a kind of counterpoint typical of the nineteenth century (and discussed earlier): a simple, solid harmonic foundation supports a vocal texture in which the rhythmic divergence is sometimes so great as to let the impression arise that there is no relatedness within the simultaneity—it is an extreme example of independence in voice leading. Apart from that, principal and subsidiary parts are clearly distinguished, with the lead passing from one voice to another. The traits by which romantic counterpoint differs noticeably from that of the late baroque era—the simple, fixed harmonic foundation, the extreme rhythmic contrast that it makes possible, and the development of a frequently changing hierarchy of independent parts—are the very things that predestine it to be a dramatic counterpoint. And in fact the essential vocal phrases in the *Rigoletto* quartet—the Duke's seductive cantabile and the parlando of Maddalena's teasing resistance—are at first expounded separately and then (from bar 26 of the andante) shown in the simultaneous relationship that is their proper one. Gilda's melody, a sighing motive which is only an interpolation to begin with, dominates in the second part of the andante (beginning at bar 33 and repeated after eight bars), while the motivic or melodic substance of Maddalena's parlando and the Duke's cantabile is reduced. (Whether or not a psychological-dramaturgical interpretation can be given to the fact that the chromatic descent in the Duke's part, modified, crosses over into Gilda's sigh is an open question.) The dramatic situation does not change at all during the quartet: the scene holds it fast. The transition from the allegro to the andante is not motivated dramatically, by an event, and there are no textual changes to support the internal binary division of the andante. Yet it would be restrictive to speak of a structure governed by merely musical-formal considerations, imposed on the dramatic situation from outside; rather, the fact that in the middle of the andante the lead passes from the Duke to Gilda can be understood as a musically founded dramaturgical stroke. The music allows Gilda's reaction to replace the Duke's action in the foreground; her suffering dominates over the deed that causes it. And insofar as precisely this kind of change of focus is one of the simplest and oldest means known for structuring dialogue, it may be said that the schema underlying the quartet is that of a latent dialogue between the Duke, who is unaware of it, and Gilda, who is painfully only too aware of it. Thus, on the one hand, the simultaneous utterance of heterogeneous material is justified by a situation in the stage action to which external circumstances have led the characters in a fateful meeting, while inwardly they are at a great distance from each other; on the other hand, the latent dialogue—behind the one of which the Duke is aware—is the psychological-dramaturgical correlative of the musical form that ensures cohesion but signifies more. Rather, by its very plausibility in terms of musical form, unsupported by the onstage situation or the text, the structure fulfills a dramaturgical function within the "interior action." In the quartet in *Don Carlo* (in act 4 of the five-act version), each of the characters is alone with his or her own thoughts, as in some parts of the finale of act 1 of Rossini's *Otello*. Filippo is ashamed of his wrongful supicion, Eboli feels remorse and despair at her betrayal of Elisabetta, Rodrigo interprets the situation as a chance to realize a great political act, which obsesses him beyond every other consideration, and Elisabetta's awareness of her own isolation weighs more heavily upon her than ever. Musical cohesion is created in part by melodic forms and in part by motivic variation and development, and the use of both techniques is not only dramaturgically justified but even generated by the dramaturgical significance of the moment. The opening phrase, sung by Filippo (largo, bars 1–3), recurs at the end (bars 38–40) and again in the orchestral postlude, and the main melody of the quartet is stated first by the orchestra and taken up twice by Filippo (bars 6–9, 14–17, 26–29), making it the framework of the musical form. This structure not only is the consequence of the situation in the plot, held fast in this tableau of a moment suspended in time, but also focuses on Filippo as the protagonist, to whom the unhappiness and hopes of the other three characters relate. It is harder to interpret the network of motivic relationships. Eboli's motives, a mournfully repeated semitone figure (bar 5: F–G♭–F) and descending chromatic motion (traveling a fourth in bars 7–8 and 26–28, and a sixth in bars 14–16), are taken up, in slightly modified form, by Elisabetta, so that when the two women share a chromatic descent an octave apart (bars 29–33), it seems to be the consequence and audible representation of the references gradually forming to link the two parts. Furthermore, a contrapuntal connection evolves between the melodic form in Filippo's part and the process of motivic development, in that Eboli's chromatic figure provides a contrast and counterpoint to Filippo's main melody (bars 6–9, 14–17, and 26–29). As in the quartet in *Rigoletto,* neither the dramatic situation nor the text undergoes change during the entire length of the quartet in *Don Carlo.* But if the static form of the main melody can be seen as equivalent to the situation held fast here, and to Filippo's central position in it, the developing variation of motives, whereby Elisabetta and Eboli are drawn closer together (not in the manifest dramatic situation, in which they are at odds, but musically), is justified by the latent psychological configuration: both are the King's victims and therefore must suffer humiliations. That the proximity in which they are placed is vague and uncertain, an inner association of which the audience becomes aware only gradually, makes the technique of developing variation especially appropriate.

Questions of Genre

21. THE OPERA AS NOVEL

"Confusion," or "beautiful confusion," was a term of praise in the vocabulary of baroque poetics and only became pejorative under classicism. People wanted to be entertained in the theater by the illusions and labyrinthine plotting that they feared in reality and suspected everywhere. And the theatrical effectiveness of the librettos set by Cavalli and Cesti is not in the least diminished if the audience—pardonably—loses the thread of the plot from time to time; unlike other dramaturgical concepts, confusion tolerates less-than-perfect understanding.

In *L'Erismena,* an opera by Cavalli with a libretto by Aurelio Aureli (1655), King Erimante of Media is the only principal character whose identity is certain from the first. The list of characters already gives an impression of the labyrinth the action has in store: Erismena, unacknowledged daughter of Erimante, disguised as a knight; Idraspe, prince of Iberia, known as Erineo, Erimante's cupbearer; Aldimira, unacknowledged sister of Idraspe, disguised as a slave. It would take all the details of the plot to demonstrate the full extent of the beautiful confusion, which was as indispensable in works for the theater as in novels, but the mere outline of the action of act 1 will have to serve as illustration here: King Erimante dreams of a stranger knight who takes his crown (scene 1); Erismena, seeking her faithless lover, Idraspe, disguises herself as an Armenian soldier (scene 2) and is wounded and captured by the Medians (scene 17); Erimante recognizes in her the knight in his dream and orders her death (scene 18). (Of course, the oracular dream is realized at the end, with Erismena inheriting her father's throne.)

The historical background of the poetic theory from which such a libretto springs lies primarily in Hellenistic fiction and its rebirth in the early novel in the baroque era, although there are also unmistakably connections with the spoken play of the same period. As "ideal types," both the musical and the spoken forms of baroque drama are derivatives of the novel, for it was only in that genre's almost unlimited space that the interplay of deceptions, calumnies, misunderstandings, and mistaken identities could achieve the essential degree of complication.

Theater is always a matter of masks. But the baroque era surpassed every other in theatrical history in the degree to which the illusory nature of the appearances of both people and things dominated not only the form but also the very content of dramas. The "playacting" we call theater was duplicated in the deceptiveness of everything the theater presented as reality, and not just in comedy, which continued with the play of disguises and mistaken identities in later centuries, but also—indeed, above all—in tragedy and the dramma per musica.

The elements of the novel into which the ancient myth of Semiramis is transformed in *La Semirami* by Antonio Cesti and Giovanni Andrea Monuglia (1667) can already be perceived in the exposition, in which the queen of the Assyrians, Semirami, changes clothes with her son, Nino, in order to take his place leading a war against Babylon, while Elvida, a Babylonian princess, is living in Assur as a slave, under the name of Iside, because she loves Nino. As a general rule, if a slave is not introduced as a comic character in baroque opera, we may be sure that he or she will turn out to be of royal blood, especially if he is a he and a queen loves him—as in *Orontea*, a libretto by Giacinto Andrea Cicognini (Venice, 1649), which Cesti also set (Innsbruck, 1656)—so that the indispensable happy ending is not prevented by a difference of rank too great to be overlooked, even in the theaters of republican Venice.

Seventeenth-century audiences must always have expected that another reality would be revealed behind the reality shown them onstage and narrated as prehistory. Yet it would be problematical to call this further reality the "actual" one. It is "more real" in the abstract, but only in the abstract, not in the theater, where only what is apparent to the eyes and ears has meaning and substance. The philosophy implicit in baroque theater asserts, not that the reality hidden at the beginning and gradually brought to light behind the reality shown first is the "true" one, but that all reality represents a world of illusion. The happy ending, allowing the second reality to appear to be the true one, is a less accurate reflection of the theater's image of the world than the whole course of the action, which amounts to aimless wandering in illusion.

The tale told in a first prehistory as part of the drama's exposition is proved unreal in a second prehistory, which is revealed only step-by-step until the last revelation brings the opera to its conclusion. But the technique of a twofold prehistory, originating in the novel, presents dramaturgical problems. One prehistory, of indubitably factual content, has already been shown to be at a disadvantage in musical drama with respect to the greater immediacy of what the audience witnesses onstage (see above, §11); and it would seem almost impossible to reconcile the existence of two with the requirements of a libretto amenable to realization in music. Yet resolving the problem may be possible, if we bear in mind the abstruse dialectics of illusion and truth in musical expression and in the visible reality onstage.

The world in which human beings live, and to which their affects are the reactions, is terra non firma in baroque theater. So frequently are characters mistaken about themselves and about each other that it might almost be called a rule of the genre; they deceive each other and are deceived, the instigators of one intrigue becoming the victims of another—in tragedy just as much as in comedy. The fundamental dramaturgical category of deception is problematical in opera, however, inasmuch as music, as almost every aesthetic theorist would agree, always makes the emotion it expresses seem truthful, that is, to possess a truth of which the musical expression is to some extent the guarantee.

At the same time, affects are expressed in musical language—which is itself a fiction. (The seventeenth century was still a long way from the view of music as a primeval, Adamic language of feeling.) But this aesthetic fiction is ambivalent: it may be the precondition, accepted without reflection, of the self-contained world that opera purports to be; or the attention paid to the musical language and the world of feeling it constitutes may include consciousness of its fictional character. In the latter case, the consciousness of illusion (unlike the view of music as a linguistic convention) contributes aesthetically to the dramaturgical structure of the opera, the heart of the matter.

The logic of differentiation between the illusoriness of musical language when it is accepted without reflection and when it is present to the consciousness becomes clearer if we distinguish between fiction (or illusion) as a means of representation and as the thing represented. We can then see that, quite apart from the illusory nature of the representation (the theater is the play of masks and disguises; the music is not a natural language but a conventional expression of affects), it is characteristic of baroque opera that what is represented is also fiction or illusion, both in the interior world of feelings and in the exterior world of people and things. If genuine emotions arise out of illusory preconceptions, in a play by Heinrich von Kleist it is a catastrophe, bringing a world down; but in a baroque opera the characters—like the audiences, who recognize their own sense of the world in them—are always well aware that they live in a world of illusion.

Affects make up the substance of the arias or aria-like structures through which the characters express their reactions in a situation that touches them immediately. But if affect represents the essence of musically constituted drama, it does not mean that emotion is an ultimate touchstone of inner truth and reality. The "erring conscience," a fundamental category of Catholic theology, finds a counterpart in the "erring emotion" that is a fundamental concept of the dramaturgy of opera, an art form on which Catholicism leaves its imprint.

22. TRAGEDY AND THE *LIETO FINE*

The *lieto fine*—happy ending—was a norm of eighteenth-century dramma per musica. It tolerated exceptions, but they did not detract from its general validity. A new school of operatic aesthetics, objecting to conventions in the name of dramatic truth and, openly or latently, representing bourgeois opposition to court culture, rejected it with polemical emphasis. The happy ending was condemned as an offense against the rules of tragedy and a survival from an outdated, baroque aesthetics of the marvelous, of which the dramaturgical expedient of the deus ex machina was the foremost manifestation. It was alleged, further, to underestimate the public, who could take "pleasure in tragic subjects" (as Schiller said) in opera as well as in other genres, without detriment to opera's particular festive character. Finally, it was said to mistake the nature of music, which was well able to express or depict a tragic catastrophe. While it is not for the historian to adopt a historically conditioned position—be it of the eighteenth or the nineteenth century—he must make some attempt to see aesthetic and historical justice done on behalf of a principle that survived for a century before it was suppressed, by interpreting it from within.

1. The charge that a happy ending breaks one of the rules of tragedy is based on the almost ineradicable belief that the ending reveals the essence of a dramatic work more clearly than any other part. (This opinion is strangely inept, ignoring the character of a work of art as something complete and present in all its parts.) Yet the process shown in a drama is tragic in all the situations it traverses, and not solely in the ending to which it is directed. Often it is possible to turn the ending in a different direction without making any difference to the substance of the tragic course of events leading to it. The inner devastation suffered by Agamemnon, Clitemnestre, and Iphigénie, the victims of the tragic entanglement of Gluck's *Iphigénie en Aulide,* is hardly affected at all by the intervention of Artemis, who carries Iphigénie away to Tauris. No one can be in any doubt as to the tragic nature of the opera, regardless of how it ends. And the objection that the logic of events demands that a catastrophe should ensue misses the point, inasmuch as the true catastrophe takes place inside the characters. Agamemnon's attempts to evade the goddess's command by schemes and stratagems are the twists and turns of a victim and are doomed to fail. At the end he is both inwardly and outwardly a ruin of his former self, beaten and humiliated. And since the goddess is arbitrary in the exercise of her power, it scarcely matters whether she demonstrates it by an act of magnanimity or annihilation, in a happy ending or a tragic one. When human beings are caught in the gods' toils, any resistance, whether heroic or underhand, is futile and hopeless, and the tragic process remains the same.

2. Taking a broad, schematic view, it seems obvious that the aesthetics of

the marvelous, which in tragedy has as much to do with a surprising turn of fortune as with the intervention of a god, originated in the baroque, was wholly alien to the nature of classicism, and was then restored under romanticism. In eighteenth-century opera seria, admittedly, the determinism of the history of ideas was overlaid by the determinism of social history, or social psychology, which demanded an apotheosis of higher powers in opera performed at court, as well as by an aesthetic determinism, which made audiences believe that where there was singing, the tragic entanglement could not be as bad as it appeared: if the Furies let their implacability be known by means of singing, as they do in Gluck's *Orfeo ed Euridice,* they can be expected to soften. The association between musical performance and a tragic ending has always been an awkward one, at every period in operatic history. It is an intractable problem, and the opposite consequences drawn from it in the eighteenth and the nineteenth centuries were equally "unnatural," if viewed open-mindedly; the criterion of naturalness is inappropriate for opera. If a god halts the infernal machinery of tragedy (Cocteau's *machine infernale*), it is as fantastic, from the standpoint of a realist aesthetics, as the dramaturgical idea of letting people who have been condemned to death and entombed alive express their feelings in a cantabile. To common sense (which really has no business in opera) a tragic ending, transfigured by music, is no more "true" than a happy one. Basically, nothing more happened historically than that one improbability was replaced by another: that was all, and it produced no "development" capable of interpretation as either progress or decline.

3. Schiller's assumption, in *Über den Grund des Vergnügens an tragischen Gegenständen* (1792), that people can take "pleasure in tragic subjects" rests on the inner distance audience members keep between themselves and events onstage, even while their involvement in the action and the characters allows them to forget themselves. And insofar as music is one means of increasing the distance, it ought to be the case that a more ruthless accumulation of horrors can be stomached in an opera than in a play. Yet Verdi's plan to write an opera about Lear, cherished over many years, came to nothing, probably not least because the inner distance at which music can set an event is different from the distance created by awareness that the event is only acted. Distancing through music rests on a transformation of the tragic event into an emotion at a remove from reality, which goes beyond the elementary distancing worked by the art of theater. In *Über den Grund des Vergnügens an tragischen Gegenständen,* Schiller proposed that the reason people enjoy tragedy lies in the tragic hero's moral superiority in the face of an overwhelming fate; even in acknowledging his guilt he preserves this superiority, insofar as consciousness of guilt proves the validity of the moral law. But in opera it is less a moral sense than an emotion that holds firm in the face of catastrophe or is restored by it. Whether Sesto in *La clemenza di Tito* is executed or magnani-

mously pardoned is less important than the fact that his emotional confusion gives way to clarity, an inner regeneration that could be manifested just as well in a tragic ending as a happy one.

4. The eighteenth century was well aware of music's ability to depict catastrophe when it is an interior event, as in the many operas about Dido abandoned by Aeneas (while the musical means to represent exterior disasters remained weak, up until Jean-François Lesueur's *La caverne* of 1793). The immeasurable depth of the emotion sustaining Dido has an unfortunate consequence for musical dramaturgy, however, because the natural form of expression for a person whose inner existence—the certainty of her emotion—has been destroyed is not lamentation but silence. Orpheus, from whom Eurydice is snatched by a higher power, can express his unhappiness in song because the emotion that inspires him has not been touched; but Dido is the victim of an inner voice heard by Aeneas, a voice of divine origin that makes him forsake human ties, and she can only fall silent or seek refuge in a death rite that does not give her silence a voice but renders self-expression superfluous.

But if the tragic ending as internal collapse has the drawback that the theater does not permit silence as a conclusion, the tragic ending as interior regeneration in the midst of exterior catastrophe, when both the regeneration and catastrophe are to be represented onstage, requires the musical ensemble to have evolved technically to a level that it did not reach until the nineteenth century. Rossini depicts the massacre of the Corinthians by the Turks in the last scene of *Le siège de Corinthe* (1826) with all the musical means of savagery at his command, but he cannot simultaneously bring to the despair and suicide of Pamyra the degree of immediacy that they merit as the conclusion of the tragic dialectics of the interior action, the drama of affects. Little more than two decades later, however, in Meyerbeer's *Le prophète* (1849), the music is successful in realizing the simultaneous occurrence of an exterior disaster—the collapse of the roof of the Great Hall in the palace in Münster, killing all the Anabaptists—and the resolution of the tragic dialectics underlying the interior action in the reconciliation of Jean and Fidès, with an astonishing balance between the representation of the explosion and the cantilena rising dithyrambically above it. It is true that this particular tragic ending entails neither the annihilation of the emotion that has sustained a person's existence nor inner regeneration in the face of exterior disaster, but an exterior catastrophe that enables an interior one to be represented visibly onstage (the exterior catastrophe might also be said to be the fulfillment of the interior one). Nevertheless, music discovers its limits in this scene: almost silent emotion and noisy horrors are mutually exclusive. The true ending of *Cavalleria rusticana*—to be precise, the true ending of the opera—is Turiddu's farewell to Lucia: the outcome of the duel is preordained by the con-

ventions of tragedy. The "realistic" ending, dispatched in a few bars of melodrama, is strictly speaking superfluous under the premises of operatic dramaturgy—of drama constituted by music, that is—and actually consists not so
much of a representation of catastrophe in music as rather a suspension of
music for the sake of a catastrophic effect; the catastrophe, however, is not
founded in the work's structure but in an external stylistic trend, the verismo
current around 1890.

23. COMEDY WITH MUSIC AND COMIC OPERA

In a comedy that obeys the rules of the genre rather than satisfying the audience's need to identify, it is even less permissible to take sides than it is in tragedy. A perfect equilibrium between ideas is the only appropriate state for the
theater, as it is for the essay (as distinct from the tract). And the structure of
a not entirely resolvable paradox, which underlies all drama except works
written in support of a thesis, is clearest of all in comedy. The least important
aspect, therefore, is the ending: although it is what classifies a work as comedy, the ending does not so much represent an outcome as break off a dialectical argument that continues beyond the play in some respects. An ending to
a comedy must leave something open or it is not an ending to a comedy.

Tracing the descent of comic opera from the play with inserted songs is
wrong, in both aesthetic and historical terms. (The singspiel, which existed
long before opera, was drawn into operatic history only after the event.)
Rather, a poetics of opera buffa should begin with an explanation of the preconditions and limits of creating comedy by musical means, instead of merely
interpolating music in a comedy.

Nineteenth-century aesthetic theory responded to the challenge of the elusive phenomenon of comedy with a strange pedantry, constantly making new
attempts to define and classify. As a rule, the theorists defined the comical in
comedy as the contrast between lofty aspirations, which prove untenable, and
base reality, to which the aspirations are incessantly dragged down. It was
easy to transfer this schematic explanation to comic opera, because parody of
the high style of opera seria is an elementary and almost indestructible requi-
site of opera buffa: by various musical means—confrontation with analogous
affects in a debased musical idiom, exaggeration of the sublime till it topples
into bathos, skeptical interjections in a brusquely contrasting parlando, or
sideslips into banality—pathos is brought down to earth as effectively as by
an inappropriate dramatic context.

The "contrast" theory of the comical, albeit restricted, undeniably accounts for some examples of the phenomenon. We need look no further than
Verdi's Falstaff or Strauss's Baron Ochs von Lerchenau, however, to recognize
that it is only partly true that the comic effect is created by the way their relapses into baser concerns and earthier urges constantly undermine their aris-

tocratic airs: there is more to it than that. Even when unmasked, Falstaff and, to a lesser degree, Ochs retain a certain superiority over their milieu, and we feel for them a vague, half-unconscious sympathy such as impulsive hauteur attracts willy-nilly when it comes into conflict with reason and moderation.

In order to be able to sketch at least a general outline of the possibilities open to a "comedy for music" (Hugo von Hofmannsthal, *Komödie für Musik;* commedia per musica), we need to refine the concept of the "height of fall," the starting point for all theories of comedy, by being as attentive to the level from which the fall begins as to that at which it ends, and moreover being aware of the sometimes quite different moral-cum-social levels at which judgment is made, in the work (implicitly) and by the audience (explicitly). The fact that Falstaff—unmasked by an intrigue, in conformity with the schema of most comedies—is brought low in a way that lays bare the base truth behind the dignified appearance assumes that sentence is passed according to the standards of moderate, bourgeois reason, in whose sight something higher is transformed to something lower. But the viewpoint of bourgeois rationality is at odds with the dramaturgical possibilities of music, and it is not Verdi's viewpoint.

In music, the "last word" cannot be that of reason and moderation. Falstaff is the paradigmatic protagonist of a comic opera because even as antihero he remains a hero, always rising up out of defeat, regenerated and sovereign, whenever he appears to be merely a butt for comedy. Music extends its sympathy not to the average or moderate but, on the one hand, to sublimity—to the parody as much as to the genuine article—and, on the other, to the baseness the composer permits himself in opera buffa, sanctioned by dramaturgical priorities. (Strauss made no secret of his delight in the triviality in which he could indulge himself in comic opera, where the aesthetic risk is less, in order to create a comical or ironically nuanced sentimental effect.)

What is implicit in the very nature of music—alternation between extremes while avoiding or suppressing whatever lies midway—says something important about some general psychological or anthropological implications of comedy, which are clearer in comedy for music than anywhere else. In comedy, the audience's sympathy is not only for egalitarian justice, which is how it regards the fall from apparent height to corresponding depth, but also, simultaneously if perhaps also secretly, for baseness itself—a state of affairs Bertolt Brecht, a genius at malignity if ever there was one, summed up in the most extreme way when he had his antihero in the opera *Mahagonny* speak of a yen to throw off the burden of humanity once and for all ("Ich will doch gar kein Mensch sein" [I don't *want* to be a human being]).

In comedy, then, the height of fall is from the sublime to the base, not merely to the reasonable and moderate, and the base and the ridiculous can both, moreover, arouse a delight in triviality and preserve a touch of sovereign superiority. This ambivalent and paradoxical dramatic genre is drawn to musical form, to comic opera, for the simple, banal reason that music is not really a suitable champion for bourgeois rationality. It is no accident that, as a rule, opera composers have avoided setting the comedies of Molière, in which a hypochondriac, a misanthropist, or a miser learns the benefits of bourgeois rationality at least for a moment, the last or last but one of the play. The reality principle—the principle of destroying illusions in order to allow reality, as it appears to bourgeois reason, to claim its proper dramatic place— is not a fundamental rule of comic opera.

Reconstructing the values and presuppositions behind the reception of a commedia per musica in the later eighteenth and early nineteenth centuries is difficult, perhaps impossible. But undoubtedly the pleasure it gave did not derive primarily from any sense of superiority that an audience convinced of its own reasonableness might feel toward the shortcomings of the characters on the stage. The moralizing theory of comedy—testament of an age when pedagogic philanthropy loomed large—is questionable, and it is more probable, as already stated, that members of the audience, even while they felt that, as rational beings, they were above the relapses into the low style, secretly and simultaneously identified with them—musically as well as dramaturgically— in order to enjoy a moment's relief from social pressures.

But if at least at the end of a work (although that is not the conclusive and sole place where any judgment is pronounced), comedy declares itself in favor of a reasonable life, neither reaching too high nor sinking too low, it is not surprising that the Age of Reason was also the age of commedia per musica. (In the seventeenth century, comedy in music consisted essentially of inserted episodes in a contrasting, low style, and after Rossini's *Barbiere*, the historical culmination of the genre, it survived into an age of serious opera only in occasional exceptions such as *Don Pasquale* and *Falstaff*.)

One problem, admittedly, is that it is characteristic of comic opera, unlike spoken comedy, for high style and low style to confront each other directly while the voice of moderation is passed over, even if it gets to pronounce the final sentence. In looking for an explanation we come upon a fundamental dramaturgical difference between play and opera: in a spoken comedy— Molière's *Tartuffe* or Lessing's *Minna von Barnhelm*—the voice of bourgeois reason is represented on the stage by one of the characters, but in a comic opera, with its inclination toward stylistic extremes for musical reasons, it exists only as the perspective of the audience, keeping at an approximately equal distance from all the characters. The laughter unleashed by a comic opera is aimed as much at sentimentality, self-absorbed and blind to reality, as at aristocratic or snobbish arrogance breaking down under the pressure of an intrigue or at impulsive behavior unrestrained by social norms. Unlike spoken comedy, the rationality of opera buffa, without which it would not have become the characteristic genre of the Age of Enlightenment, comes into force only in its reception by an audience: it is a latent center amid the turbulence onstage. (Mozart's Susanna—as rapid and accurate in her reasoning as the maid Franziska in *Minna von Barnhelm*—is an exception to the rule of indirect, unspoken rationality, almost beyond the ability of music to express, but she is a character in a work that is an exception to almost all the other norms as well.)

The hypothesis that rationality in commedia per musica is transposed from the stage to the audience's perspective needs elaboration if it is to be plausible. The role of the intrigant involuntarily moves close—musically and therefore also dramaturgically—to the reasonable, moderate style which, if such a musical language existed, would be that of common sense. It is no coincidence that the intrigant in *Così fan tutte* is also the *raisonneur*: Don Alfonso shows one side of himself in number 5 ("Vorrei dir, e cor non ho"), an extremely short piece that, as an aria d'azione, could just as well be recitative, and the other side in number 30 ("Tutti accusan le donne, ed io le scuso"), an arioso in the form of a stanza after the pattern of Ariosto, which leads to the comedy's moral—or amoral—final judgment. Reasoning is part of the intrigue—a psychological masterstroke; in Despina's arias, number 12 ("In uomini, in soldati") and number 19 ("Una donna a quindici anni"), the comedic tone (which is genuine, not parodistic, arising from the mixture of song-style and parlando) gives her fatal advice an appearance of harmlessness that is created by the music.

If the *raisonneur*, the representative of bourgeois rationality, is close to the intrigant in comic opera, the distance from which the dramaturgical positions appear to be in suspension expresses different meanings for the history of ideas, although the dramaturgical function does not change. *Don Pasquale* and *Falstaff*, the two mid- and late-nineteenth-century exceptions, differ from opera buffa of the eighteenth and early nineteenth centuries, which had developed within an established generic tradition, and it is not an overstatement to claim that they do so because they are no longer sustained by trust in rationality and its power to restore balance but by a mood of serene resignation. It is characteristic of the nineteenth century that the same mood dominates both where it is integral to the work, embodied in a character with whom the audience identifies (Hans Sachs in *Die Meistersinger von Nürnberg*), and where it is only an exterior perspective emanating from the audience *(Don Pasquale)*: works with diametrically opposite dramaturgical structures are linked by their proximity in the history of ideas.

The first act of *Don Pasquale* consists, apart from Norina's cavatina, of three large-scale duets (Malatesta / Don Pasquale, Ernesto / Don Pasquale, Norina / Malatesta), all conforming to the cantabile-cabaletta model: the disposition of the numbers is as conventional as the form. The schema, lifted directly from opera seria, is parodied: Malatesta's cantabile ("Bella siccome un angelo") is not an authentic paean of praise but invented in support of the intrigue, Ernesto's outpouring of emotion ("Sogno soave e casto") is intercut maliciously by Don Pasquale's parlando, and Norina's maestoso ("Pronto io son, pur ch'io non manchi") is pure humbug; but that makes no difference to the schema's stabilizing function in the musical form. And the music's "insincerity" means that, as a constituent part of the musical drama, it does not identify itself with any of the positions represented in the piece: not (it goes without saying) with Don Pasquale's blind vanity, not with Ernesto's sentimentality, not even with the intriguing of Malatesta. This impassive quality— Flaubert's *impassibilité*—is therefore the outcome of the balanced serenity of a comedy that has long ceased to take a social-critical stance: a serenity with an undertone of resignation.

1.   Inside the tavern, the amorous dandy does battle with the less-than-impregnable virtue of a gypsy girl; on the other side of the wall, unobserved, another couple looks on with horror. This famous lithograph appears on the frontispiece of the original vocal score of *Rigoletto* (Milan: Ricordi, 1852) and depicts the climactic scene of the opera, the "quartet in one movement"—that is, without the customary cabaletta—which simultaneously "expresses opposing ideas: on the one hand, flirting and seduction; on the other, the anguish of love betrayed, anger planning vengeance." Much praised by critics of the time ("out of the contrast between these four emotions, which alternate, come together, and intertwine, comes a melodic grouping of sublime beauty and painful complexity") and considered highly by Verdi himself ("in terms of effect, the quartet scene will always be one of the best our opera tradition has to boast of"), the quartet in *Rigoletto* gave a wholly new musical and theatrical immediacy to the development of the drama: Gilda's appalling disappointment in love, deliberately achieved by Rigoletto, is transformed into a heroic rapture that will lead her to turn the "just vengeance" plotted against the seductive monarch toward herself and her father. At the same time, the quartet tackles a poetic problem that much concerned Verdi: in the wake of Victor Hugo, and following the example of Shakespeare, how to bring together on stage—as in life—tragedy and comedy, sarcasm and grief.

ACTE IV.

*La grève déserte voisine de la Tournelle (ancienne porte
de Paris). — A droite, une masure misérablement
meublée de grosses poteries et d'escabeaux de chéne,
avec un premier étage en grenier où l'on distingue un
grabat par la fenêtre. La devanture de cette masure,
tournée vers le spectateur, est tellement à jour qu'on
en voit tout l'intérieur. Il y a une table, une cheminée, et au fond un raide escalier qui mène au grenier.
Celle des faces de cette masure, qui est à la gauche de
l'acteur, est percée d'une porte qui s'ouvre en dedans.
Le mur est mal joint, troué de crevasses et de fentes,
et il est facile de voir au travers ce qui se passe dans
la maison. Il y a un judas grillé à la porte, qui est re-
couverte au dehors d'un auvent et surmontée d'une enseigne d'auberge. — Le reste du théâtre représente la
grève. A gauche, il y a un vieux parapet en ruine, au
bas duquel coule la Seine, et dans lequel est scellé le
support de la cloche du bac. — Au fond, au-delà de la
rivière, le vieux Paris.*

TRIBOULET.

Eh bien! regarde donc, et vois si tu peux voir!

Il désigne à Blanche une des crevasses du mur de la maison;
elle regarde.

BLANCHE, *bas.*

Je ne vois rien qu'un homme.

TRIBOULET, *baissant aussi la voix.*

Attends un peu.

Le Roi, vêtu en simple officier, paraît dans la salle basse de
l'hôtellerie. Il entre par une petite porte qui communique avec
quelque chambre voisine.

BLANCHE, *tressaillant.*

Mon père!

Pendant toute la scène qui suit, elle demeure collée à la cre-
vasse du mur, regardant, écoutant tout ce qui se passe dans l'intérieur de la salle, inattentive à tout le reste, agitée par momens
d'un tremblement convulsif.

2

2–3. As early as 1849, Verdi was entertaining the idea of basing an opera on *Le roi s'amuse,* "a
fine drama with wonderful situations." The spark was literary rather than theatrical: in fact,
Hugo's play had had a single, turbulent performance in 1832. But even from simply reading the
text, the sonorous elegance of the dialogue seems brought to life by the copious stage directions.
It was precisely those stage directions—in particular, the one at the beginning of act 4 and then
after the king's words "Quelle fille d'amour délicieuse et folle"—that provided the inspiration for
the wholly Verdian concept of the quartet. The simultaneous expression of different emotions is
indeed a resource peculiar to operatic dramaturgy, not possible in straight theater.

LES MÊMES, LE ROI, MAGUELONNE.

Le Roi frappe sur l'épaule de Saltabadil, qui se retourne, dérangé brusquement dans son opération.

LE ROI.

Deux choses, sur-le-champ.

SALTABADIL.

Quoi ?

LE ROI.

Ta sœur et mon verre.

TRIBOULET, *dehors.*

Voilà ses mœurs. Ce Roi par la grâce de Dieu
Se risque souvent seul dans plus d'un méchant lieu,
Et le vin qui le mieux le grise et le gouverne
Est celui que lui verse une Hébé de taverne !

LE ROI, *dans le cabaret, chantant.*

Souvent femme varie,
Bien fol est qui s'y fie !
Une femme souvent
N'est qu'une plume au vent !

Saltabadil est allé silencieusement chercher dans la pièce voisine une bouteille et un verre qu'il apporte sur la table. Puis il frappe deux coups au plafond avec le pommeau de sa longue épée. A ce signal, une belle jeune fille, vêtue en bohémienne, leste et riante, descend l'escalier en sautant. Dès qu'elle entre, le Roi cherche à l'embrasser, mais elle lui échappe.

LE ROI.

Quelle fille d'amour délicieuse et folle !

Il la prend sur ses genoux et se met à lui parler tout bas. Elle rit et minaude. Blanche n'en peut supporter davantage. Elle se retourne, pâle et tremblante, vers Triboulet.

TRIBOULET, *après l'avoir regardée un instant en silence.*

Hé bien! que penses-tu de la vengeance, enfant?

BLANCHE, *pouvant à peine parler.*

O trahison ! — L'ingrat ! —Grand Dieu ! mon cœur se fend !
Oh! comme il me trompait !—Mais c'est qu'il n'a point d'âme,
Mais c'est abominable, il dit à cette femme
Des choses qu'il m'avait déjà dites à moi !

Cachant sa tête dans la poitrine de son père.

— Et cette femme, est-elle effrontée! — oh!...

TRIBOULET, *à voix basse.*

Tais-toi.

Pas de pleurs. Laisse-moi te venger!

3

Atto Terzo

Una deserta sponda della Senna. A sinistra è una casa mezzo diroccata indue piani; ~~la fa~~ quello superiore rappresenta una osteria ~~con botti~~; il superiore, a cui si ascende per una scala, mostra un granaio con un letteruccio. Ciò si vedrà dalla fronte ~~volta~~ ~~alla spettatore~~ che sarà aperta allo spettatore. Nella facciata che dà sulla strada è una porta che s'apre per di dentro; di piano alla ~~pos~~ detta porta il muro è sì sbarciato che dalle fessura si può facilmente scorgere quanto accade nell'interno. *(Na ~~passa~~)* Dietro alla casa scorre la Senna. ~~Dietro un prospetto necessario~~

Scena I

Rigoletto seguito da Gilda nella via; Maddalena nell'osteria fra lavorando.

Ri:	(So ch'egli è là... tentiam l'ultima prova.) *(Da sé indicando l'osteria)* E l'ami?
Gi:	Sempre.
Ri:	Pure tempo a guarirne t'ho lasciato.
Gi:	Io l'amo.
Ri:	Povero cor di donna!... E t'ha tradita... Ad altra ei pensa... ma ne avrò vendetta.
Gi:	Padre, nol credo.
Ri:	E se tu certa fossi ch'ei ti tradisse, l'ameresti ancora?
Gi:	Nol so,... ma pur m'adora.
Ri:	Egli?
Gi:	Sì.
Ri:	Ebben, osserva dunque... *(La conduce presso la fessura del muro, ed ella vi guarda.)* Nulla.
Gi:	Vedo.
Ri:	Per poco attendi. *(tuona.)*

ATTO TERZO.

Deserta sponda del Mincio. A sinistra è una casa in due piani,
mezza diroccata, la cui fronte, volta allo spettatore, lascia
vedere per una grande arcata l'interno d'una rustica osteria
al piano terreno, ed una rozza scala che mette al granaio, entro
cui, da un balcone, senza imposte, si vede un lettuccio. Nella
facciata che guarda la strada è una porta che s'apre per di
dentro; il muro poi n'è sì pien di fessure, che dal di fuori si
può facilmente scorgere quanto avviene nell'interno. Il resto
del teatro rappresenta la deserta parte del Mincio, che nel fondo
scorre dietro un parapetto in mezza ruina; al di là del fiume è
Mantova. È notte.

SCENA I.

GILDA e RIGOLETTO *inquieto, sono sulla strada,* SPARAFUCILE
*nell' interno della osteria, seduto presso a una tavola, sta
ripulendo il suo cinturone, senza nulla intendere di
quanto accade al di fuori.*

RI.   E l'ami?
GI.   Sempre.
RI.   Pure
Tempo a guarirne t'ho lasciato.
GI.   Io l'amo.
RI.   Povero cor di donna!.. Ah il vile infame!..
Ma avrai vendetta, o Gilda ...
GI.   Pietà, mio padre ...
RI.   E se tu certa fossi
Ch'ei ti tradisse, l'ameresti ancora?
GI.   Nol so, ma pur m'adora.
RI.   Egli!..
GI.   Sì.
RI.   Ebbene, osserva dunque. (*la conduce presso
una delle fessure
del muro, ed ella
vi guarda.*)
GI.   Un uomo
· Vedo.
RI.   Per poco attendi.

5

4-5. The libretto for *Rigoletto* had an extremely tortuous genesis, because of the censor: the
subject matter was considered to be indecent, immoral, and subversive filth. In the course of the
laborious negotiations with the director of La Fenice and the police, Verdi was concerned above
all that Piave should not alter "the scene where Francesco [the Duke] goes to the house of Saltabadil [Sparafucile]: without this, the drama is dead." A comparison between *Il duca di Vendôme*
(the earliest version known, turned down by Verdi) and the 1851 libretto, apart from the few important revisions, reveals how the ordering of the scenes, based step for step on Hugo, was already
broadly in place.

Gi.
Ah l'infame!... Le parla d'amore
Come un giorno a parlarmi l'ho udito!
Infelice mio core tradito
Per l'angoscia ti sento popiar.
Perchè mai, troppo creduto core,
Quell'ingrato dovevi tu amar!

Ri.
Taci, taci, il tuo pianto non vale,
Sai del suo tradimento or pensa...
Di punirlo a me lascia la cura
Lascia a me la vendetta affrettar.
Noi l'avrem pronta pronta portare
So dovunque il saprò fulminar.

Va.
Di' che m'ami, mi rendi' beato...
Trova un loco per me nel tuo core...
Ah se bella tu sei come un fiore,
N'a vo il dolce qual ape libar.
Più di tutti farò fortunato,
Se per me ti vedrò palpitar.

Ma
Ah ah rider mi fanno di core
Tai follie che vi costan sì poco...
Non son pazza nè credo a tal gioco,
Che mi piace burlar.
Che han appressar.
Sono avvezza garbato signore,
A vedermi d'intorno scherzar.

Ri
M'odi... in mia casa torna... nella frassa   (a Gilda)
Di tua madre un viril abito avrai...
Oro prendi e un destriero...
E alla volta d'Ewer parti all'istante..
Domani il padre ti raggiungerà!... ti
Or venite...
        Impossibile!...
                Avremo!...
                        Va. ( )
(Durante questa luna e la seguente Vendome e Maddalena
sanno fra loro parlando, ridendo, bevendo. Partita Gilda Rigo-
letto va dietro la casa, e ne ritorna parlando con Sparafucile.)

6

Du. Bella figlia dell' amore
   Schiavo son de' vezzi tuoi;
   Con un detto sol tu puoi
   Le mie pene consolar.
   Vieni, e senti del mio core
   Il frequente palpitar.

Mad. Ah! ah! rido ben di core,
   Chè tai baie costan poco;
   Quanto valga il vostro giuoco,
   Mel credete, so apprezzar.
   Sono avvezza, bel signore,
   Ad un simile scherzar.

Gi. Ah così parlar d' amore
   A me pur l' infame ho udito!
   Infelice cor tradito,
   Per angoscia non scoppiar.
   Perchè, o credulo mio core,
   Un tal uom dovevi amar!

Ri. Taci, il piangere non vale; (a Gilda)
   Ch' ei mentiva or sei secura ...
   Taci e mia sarà la cura
   La vendetta d' affrettar.
   Pronta fia, sarà fatale,
   Io saprollo fulminar.

Ri. M' odi, ritorna a casa ...
   Oro prendi, un destriero,
   Una veste viril che t' apprestai,
   E per Verona parti ...
   Sarovvi io pur domani ...

Gi. Ora venite ...

Ri.   Impossibil.

Gi.   Tremo.

Ri.   Va. (Gilda parte)
   (durante questa scena e la seguente il Duca e Maddalena stanno fra loro parlando, ridendo, bevendo.
   Partita Gilda Rigoletto va dietro la casa, e ritorna
   parlando con Sparafucile, e contando delle monete.)

6–7. The text of the finished quartet, in *ottonari* in *Rigoletto,* is still in anapestic *decasillabi* in *Il duca di Vendôme.* According to Verdi, this was an "easy" meter for Piave. But with its percussive and rousing rhythm, *decasillabi* would undoubtedly have thwarted the controlled synergy of the four different speeds that Verdi gave his characters (Maddalena takes half a bar to sing her *ottonari;* Gilda, one; the Duke, two; and Rigoletto, sometimes as many as four).

Vis.　　Ebbene, osserva dunque. (*la conduce presso l' inferriata ed ella ascesa sur una pietra guarda nell' interno*)

Gil.　　　　　　　　　　　　　Un uomo

Vedo.

Vis　　Per poco attendi.

SCENA II.

Detti, ed il *Duca* in costume di scudiere, entra nella
　　sala terrena per una porta a sinistra.

Gil. (*trasalendo*)　　　　Ah padre mio !

Due. Due cose e presto.　　　　　(*a Sparafucile*)

Spa.　　　　　　Quali ?

Duc. De sedere e del vino .. (*1*)

Vis. È questo il suo costume !

Spa.　　　　　　Ehi ! già del vino !

(*battendo col pomo della sua lunga spada al sof-
fitto ; dopo aver ceduto il suo posto al Duca: entra quindi a sinistra*)

Duc.　　La donna è mobile
　　　　　Qual piuma al vento ,
　　　　　Muta d' accento - e di pensier.

　(*2*)Spesso un amabile
　　　　　Leggiadro viso
　　　　In pianto o in riso - è menzogner.

　(*3*) E' spesso misero
　　　　Chi a lei s' affidà ,
　　　　Chi le confida - mal cauto il cor.

　(*4*)Pure di vivere
　　　　Lieto sol crede
　　　　Chi da lei chiede - fede ed amor.

Spa. E' là il vostr' uomo... viver dee o morire ?

　(*5*)(*uscendo sulla strada, mentre una giovane scende
　　la scala con una bottiglia di vino e un bicchiere*)

Vis. Più tardi tornerò l' opra a compire. (*Si allontana*)

SCENA III.

Gilda e *Viscardello* sulla via, il *Duca* e *Maddalena*
　　nel piano terreno.

Duc.　　Un dì, se ben rammentami,
　　　　　O bella, t' incontrai...
　　(*6*) E a te da presso un giovane

8

8.　During the early period of *Rigoletto*'s success in the theater, censors inflicted some grotesque
distortions on the text. In this copy of *Viscardello* (the title of the censored version, Rome, 1851),
a nineteenth-century hand has listed on page 22 the points where the text differs from the official
one. The reader can make his or her own comparison.

(*)Snello e genial mirai...
Oh vidi ben allora
Che te quel vago adora...

Mad. No, no... La è questa istoria
Inganno di memoria.
Non esco dell' ostello
Che sol con mio fratello...

Duc. Sì?... dunque errai?...

Mad. (*altera*) Credetelo,
Signore.

Duc. Ih sei ben fiera !

Mad. Son tale.

Duc. Or via, sii docile,
Non farmi sì l' altera...
Forse a gentile vergine
E' colpa un puro amore?...
Tu vago sposo meriti !...

Mad. Scherzate voi signore.

Duc. No, no.

Mad. Son brutta.

Duc. (*scherzando*) Io palpito...

Mad. Per me? (*Ironica*)

Duc. D' ardente affetto. (*c. s.*)

Mad. Davver non ho sospetto, (*c. s.*)
Che voglia canzonar !

Duc. No, no, ti vo' sposar. (*ridendo*)

Mad. Non sperda la parola... (*c. s.*)

Duc. Amabile figliuola ! (*ironico*)

Vis. Ebben ?... ti basta ancor?... (*a Gilda che
avrà tutto osservato ed inteso*)

Gil. Iniquo traditor !

Duc. Puoi tu, figlia dell' amore, (*con caricatura*)
Schiavo farmi ai vezzi tuoi ;
Con un detto sol tu puoi
Le mie pene consolar
Sento, ah sento che il mio core
Per te s' apre, a palpitar.

Mad Ah ! ah ! rido ben di core,
Chè tai baie costan poco ;
Quanto valga questo giuoco,
Mel credete, so apprezzar.
Or vi prego, bel signore,
Basta simile scherzar.

Gil. Ah così parlar d' amore

9

9.   On page 23 of the same libretto, the dialogue between the Duke and Maddalena, along with their respective stage directions, has been completely rewritten. The mindless attempt to cast a veil of modesty over the scene has so altered the sense and the mechanism of seduction as to make the indignation of the two watching characters—Gilda and Viscardello—more or less incomprehensible.

10–11. In August 1850, as the first objections from the censor were appearing, Verdi declared that by that time, "the idea, the musical *tinta* were all in place: . . . the main and most effortful work was done." More concretely, the compositional process is documented in the sketch for *Rigoletto*, which was nothing less than a melodic "screenplay" for the entire opera and was made between November 1850 and January 1851.

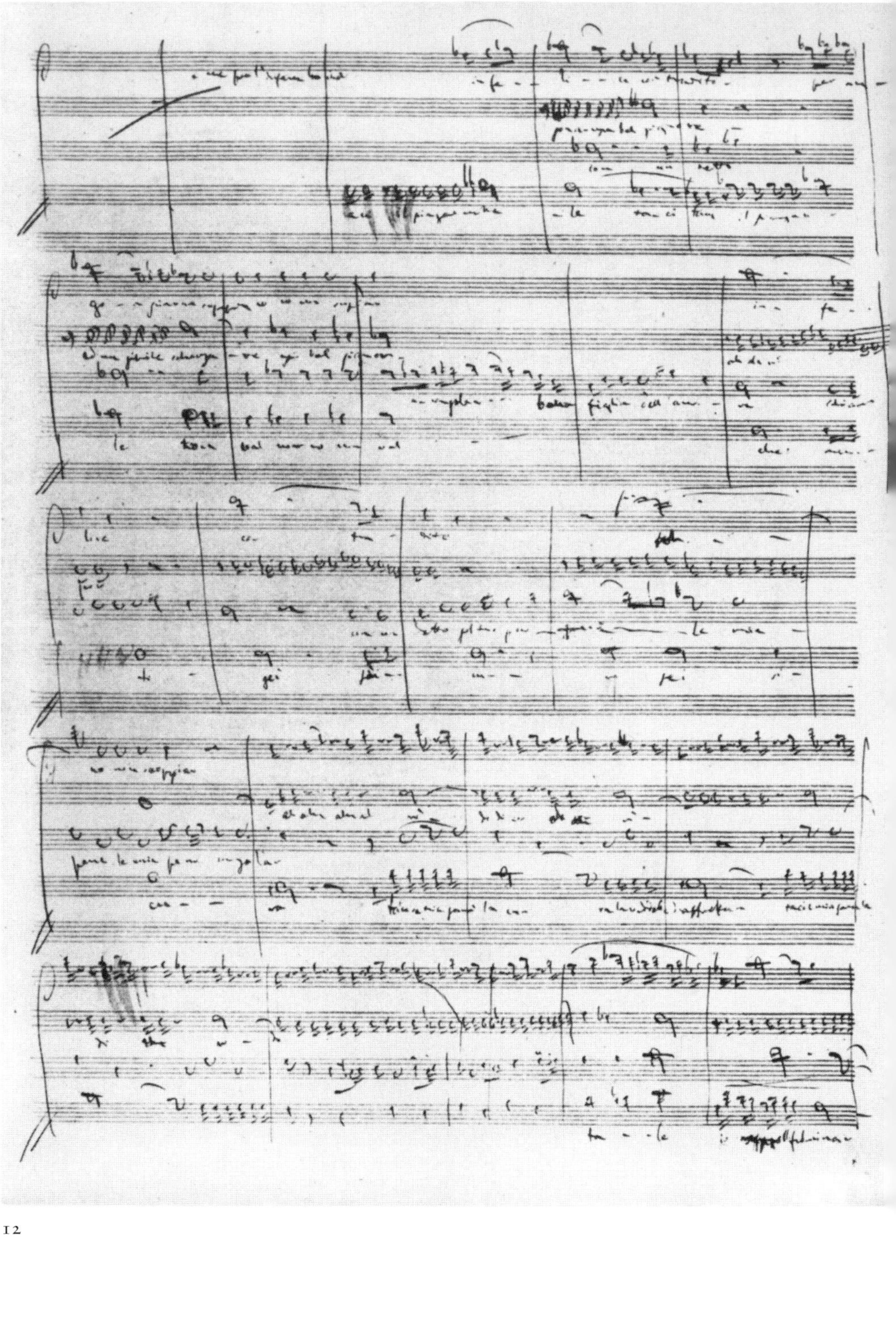

12–13. Of all the numbers in the opera, the only one that shows no divergences between the sketch and the finished score is the quartet. It is almost as if the sound-picture of the amorous rendezvous in Sparafucile's tavern, and its dramatic imagery, were already present in the composer's mind before he took up his pen. In the initial "parlante" section ("Un dì, se ben rammentomi," an allegro in E major), Verdi notes both the syllabic declamation of the voices and the continuous violin melody on which they hang: the bass line is blank for long stretches, but not for the central modulation from A to B major. In the ensemble ("Bella figlia dell'amore," an andante in D-flat major), the way the voices work together defines the melodic counterpoint and the harmonic framework. Verdi takes a linear approach to distributing the four speakers' comments, which dramatically as well as musically make up a simultaneous double duet: he positions Maddalena's and Rigoletto's syllabic semiquavers, and Gilda's and the Duke's legato lines, filled with bars and rests, to create the minimum reciprocal crowding. At one key point, he has also fixed a dynamic indication: the pianissimo and crescendo on Gilda's high B-flat. Immediately afterward, in contrast, he has left the text blank under Gilda's sobbing melody (fourth system in plate 12); the passage in Piave's libretto that should correspond to the last two lines of Gilda's sextet is completely absent from the score, whether intentionally or by accident cannot be said.

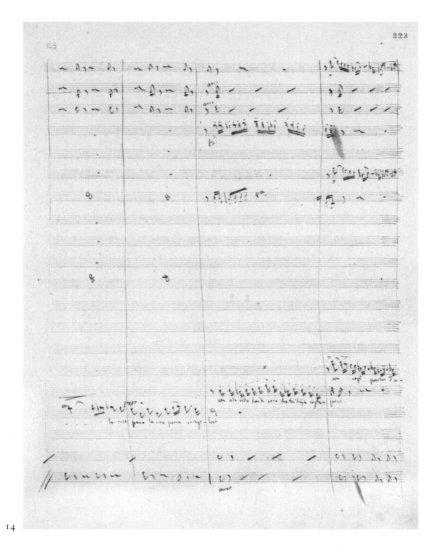

14. In the sketch for the andante, the rhythmic character of the four voices is perfectly defined. What is missing is any kind of indication of the metrical pulse which runs through the whole of the finished piece and which, given to the orchestral accompaniment, creates equilibrium and unity but also serves as a powerful engine of emotional expression. Félix Clément pointed this out: "It is the rhythm in particular that gives this ensemble its exceptional impetus."

15. In Verdi's autograph orchestral score, not only the instrumentation but the metrical pulse as well is made explicit. The systole and diastole of the accompaniment—the bass on the downbeats and the rest of the strings on the offbeats—accelerate twice in succession. On page 223, at the end of the Duke's solo and the entry of the other voices, the pulsation changes from quarter notes (played pizzicato) to eighth notes (arco). In the second half of the piece—where Gilda's melodic sobbing dominates (page 225)—the music changes to a pulsation of sixteenth notes.

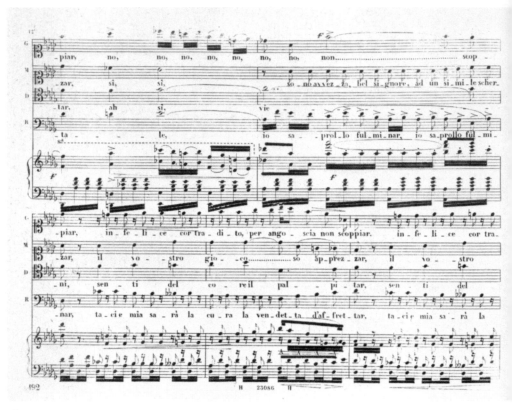

16. The only notable variant in the passage from sketch to finished version appears in the coda to the quartet. A comparison between the original Ricordi vocal score (1852) and plate 13 illustrates the difference. In the sketch, Maddalena's chromatic chattering, when exposed, twice lands on a third inversion of a dominant seventh on the flattened leading note (C-flat): a juicy interrupted cadence, placed immediately before the dominant of the home key (A-flat—D-flat). Why did Verdi leave it out of the final version, anchoring the harmony on a tonic pedal? Was it perhaps to avoid again touching, however fleetingly, on a sound he had already "used up" in the first part of the andante, at the place where the music does temporarily modulate to F-flat (that is, enharmonically, E major, which is also the key of the first section)? In other words, was it to avoid suggesting falling back to a previous tonality at the very point where, instead, the music needs to move toward the basic key of the following scene (D major)?

17. The chromatic sequence of repeated paired notes, given to Maddalena in the sketch, are given instead to Gilda and Rigoletto in the finished version: one line ascends while the other descends, each answering the other antiphonally. So it is not the gypsy girl's compulsive laughter but the diverging voices of the two observers in the dark that seal the dramatic musical scene. The musical discourse is like a moving target, as the focus shifts from one part of the stage to another: during the quartet, this focus definitely moves from inside the tavern to outside, from a scene of dissolution to one of desperation. If the Duke and Maddalena are unaware they are part of a quartet and behave, dramatically and musically, accordingly, then Rigoletto and Gilda are all too aware of the fact but react in the opposite way. The audience in the theater thus observes the seduction in two ways: with their own eyes and at the same time through the eyes of Gilda and Rigoletto (in musical dramaturgy, "spectator" always stands for "listener" as well, "see" for "hear" and "eye" for "ear").

18

18. Nineteenth-century Italian operatic stage production practice, an eminently oral tradition, was not set down in writing until, following Parisian practice, Verdi and Ricordi introduced the production book *(disposizione scenica)*. For *Rigoletto,* an idea of mid-nineteenth-century productions, according to those very same French practices, is provided by the manuscript notes of the producers who staged the opera at the Théâtre Lyrique in 1863. Written in a conversational style, or noted down on the vocal score and libretto, these notes expand and determine the stage movement already set out abundantly by the original stage directions, which in turn are based on Hugo's script. Often they simply spell out implied stage directions, understood from the dialogue, or the gestures suggested by particular melodic and rhythmic movements.

19. Not surprisingly, the producer Léonce created a lively mime for the conversation between the Duke and Maddalena—that is, for a scene that is already conceived as an episode from a comic opera. As well as those visible in the plates reproduced here, the notes on page 233 (on the back of the page stuck into the vocal score), state: "*A*—Le Duc va à Madeleine et l'attire vers la table. *B*—Gilda, avec horreur, s'éloigne de la fenêtre et, cachant son visage avec ses mains, elle passe devant Rigoletto à l'extrême [du] jardin" (The Duke approaches Maddalena and draws her toward the table. Gilda, horrified, moves away from the window and, hiding her face in her hands, passes in front of Rigoletto at the end of the garden).

(La lutinant.)

Allons, sois donc plus docile. ①

MADELAINE, résistant.

Votre cœur est bien fragile.

LE DUC ② ~~la prenant dans ses bras.~~

Viens !

MADELAINE.

Laissez-moi.

LE DUC.

Je t'aime tant !

GILDA.

Horreur !

MADELAINE, se défendant.

Laissez !

LE DUC.

Viens, bel' enfant.

(Il lui prend la main.)

MADELAINE.

Voyons, laissez ma main ; elle est laide et vulgaire

LE DUC.

Non, je la veux garder.

MADELAINE.

Seigneur, et pourquoi fair

LE DUC. ③

Acceptes-tu la mienne ?

RIGOLETTO, à sa fille.

En croiras-tu tes yeux ?

GILDA.

Mon malheur est certain.

MADELAINE, riant.

Sa main ! c'est sérieux !

LE DUC, lui tendant la main.

A toi, si tu la veux.

① Le Duc l'attire vers la table

② Il s'est assis sur l'escabeau devant la table et veut la placer sur ses genoux, elle ne veut pas s'asseoir mais elle lui laisse sa main qu'elle feint de retirer.

③ Il se lève et le quatuor se chante ainsi.

R　　G　　|　　M　　D

20. In the Parisian producers' notes for *Rigoletto*, the stage movement comes to a halt as if by magic when the quartet gets properly under way (the andante). Again at the Théâtre Lyrique, the only notes in the margin of the libretto are as follows: "The quartet is sung thus:

Rigoletto	Gilda		Maddalena	The Duke
·	·		·	·

The ensemble is thus understood as a moment frozen in time: a motionless but sonorous tableau vivant. (But at the Opéra in 1885 a more naturalistic idea of gesture made its way even into the quartet: "Pendant la ritournelle le Duc a donné un verre à Madeleine et lui verse à boire; il ne cesse de la tourmenter. Elle se défend à peine et en riant. Gilda de temps à autre regarde ce qui se passe dans la maison et revient, de temps en temps, près de son père, qui la reçoit dans ses bras" (During the ritornello the Duke has given Maddalena a glass and he fills it for her; he never ceases pursuing her. She barely manages to fend him off with laughter. Gilda alternately watches the events inside the house and returns to her father's arms).

21. In the eyes of the caricaturist Henriot (Henri Maigrot) of the journal *Illustration*, the quartet in *Rigoletto* also appeared to be a paradoxical, grotesque tableau vivant. The four, with the Duke at their head, pedal together toward catastrophe, singing at the tops of their voices, astride a double tandem of truly "exceptional impetus."

22

22. Giuseppe Bertoja's set designs for the world premiere of *Rigoletto* were seen and approved by Verdi, to whom Piave wrote on 21 January 1851 that he had "given all the orders" for work to start on "the decorations, which will be magnificent." It is possible that Bertoja's sets were not so much "magnificent" as coherent and extremely functional, and in fact, they became the prototype for an enduringly effective model. For the "deserted bank of the Mincio" in act 3, the stage direction in the libretto (based on Hugo's for the fourth act of *Le roi s'amuse*) presented the designer with a number of difficulties. In the action, tragedy and comedy had to intermingle, and visually the stage had to represent at the same time the rustic image of the "half-dilapidated house" *(masure)* and the monumental image of the city, seat of sovereign power (Mantua standing for Paris). In addition, the rustic picture was divided into exterior *(devanture/façade)* and interior ("on en voit tout l'intérieur"/"si può facilmente scorgere quanto avviene nell'interno" [what takes place inside can easily be seen]): and this contravened all the traditions of set design (typological unity of settings, distinction between outside and inside). For this scene, Bertoja made an initial sketch (plate 22), which he then went on to elaborate in a more finished design (plate 24).

RIGOLETTO

del Maestro Verdi.

Composte da

AUGUSTO GIAMBONI

23. The illustration on the title page of Augusto Giamboni's Variations on themes from *Rigoletto* derives from the structure of Bertoja's set for the Venetian premiere (plates 22 and 24). However, some details (like the arched windows) are taken from the initial sketch, plate 22, while others (the tavern sign, the draining board) are linked to the sketch in plate 24. There is one notable variation: to further spotlight the characters, the artist has made the background simpler and more cursory. In Bertoja's designs, beyond the bridge over the Mincio there appears a towered building that can be identified as the Castello di San Giorgio, although it has not been reproduced exactly. There is thus a significant link between the two geographical (but also dramatic) extremes of the plot, from the opening in the magnificent hall of that ducal palace, which Bertoja evokes much like a memory of past events. In the illustrator's version, this link is somewhat looser.

24

25

26

24–25. The setting of the fourth act of *Le roi s'amuse* was established by Hugo with a wealth of details; many of these were deleted from the stage directions for the third act of *Rigoletto* but preserved in the work of set designers, who evidently were familiar with the French text. Both Bertoja's sketch (plate 24) and that by Romolo Liverani (plate 25), made not long afterward, include the *grosses poteries*, the *table, cheminée,* and *enseigne* asked for by Hugo. What is not seen, in contrast, is the *grabat*, which does appear in the libretto stage direction ("lettuccio," broken-down old bed); possibly the censor would have considered it sinful. Like Bertoja, Liverani also shows the Castello di San Giorgio in the background; he also puts in Filippo Iuvarra's cupola for the church of Sant'Andrea—an anachronism that reflects the convention of identifying dramatic locations by referring to famous buildings not yet in existence.

26. In Italian sets, the "dilapidated house" is always stage left, while in French sets, by contrast, the *auberge en ruines* is sometimes stage right (like the *masure* in *Le roi s'amuse*), as it is in this design by Philippe Chaperon. The design also diverges from the Italian model with the inclusion of the bed and by the look of the background, where the Mincio runs through a hilly landscape which an Italian audience would have found surprising in Mantua, but which a Parisian one was not in a position to contest.

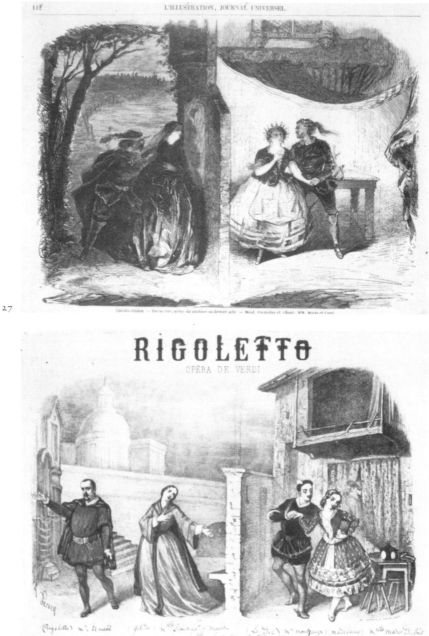

27

Théâtre-Italien. — RIGOLETTO, scène du quatuor au dernier acte. — Mesd. Frezzolini et Alboni. MM. Mario et Corsi.

28

27–29. The stages in the success of *Rigoletto* in Paris are marked by these images, all of them—significantly—showing the quartet scene. The picture from *L'illustration* (plate 27) reflects the production at the Théâtre Italien in 1857 (in the background one can make out a delicate riverside landscape). Lecoq's illustration (plate 28) includes a reference at the bottom to the French version of 1863 at the Théâtre Lyrique, and the cupola of Sant'Andrea looms down on the characters. The caricature by Stop (Louis Morel-Retz, plate 29) is connected with the revival at the Opéra in 1885. The *auberge en ruines* has almost become a suburban house, surrounded by a "mur de la vie privée" watched over by the bandit and lit by the sun while in the background (which shows Paris, not Mantua) threatening, zoomorphic clouds gather around a raging Monterone: a "caprice" that perhaps alludes to the success of the "musique si claire, si chaude" of *Rigoletto*, compared with the "dissonances brutales" of other, unnamed composers.

30

30. Carlo Songa's sketch for a production at the Teatro alla Scala, from the turn of the twentieth century, demonstrates the exemplary effectiveness (after half a century) of Bertoja's model
(plate 24). Here the greenery is more abundant, the view of Mantua wider and almost photo-
graphic in style (the Castello di San Giorgio is immediately recognizable), but the structure is essentially the same. We can even see the bridge linking the banks of the Mincio, which is not ex-
pressly asked for in the stage direction in the libretto; indeed, its absence was implicit in the
scenario of Le roi s'amuse, which mentions a bac, that is, a ferry. This is not an unimportant element: in stage-picture terms, the presence of a bridge between two banks indicates continuity, an
affinity between the locations (and the characters) the river separates; its absence indicates opposition between different worlds, civilizations, and standards of behavior. Since the quartet finds all
the protagonists brought together for the first time in the opera, it is justification enough to have,
if not insist on, the presence of the bridge.

31. To avoid falling into the presumed "tautology" of showing onstage what is already stated in a works' verbal and musical text, and is, in any case, extremely familiar to the audience, opera production often draws back from reproducing the action as the authors have prescribed it. The decision can be legitimate or not: it depends on the relevance of the rereading to the particular dramaturgical structure of the opera. The idea of a Rigoletto without his hump, which Verdi himself found unacceptable, is and always will be nonsense. But to transfer the action to the slums of a port city—where the Duke is a small-time Mafia boss and Sparafucile a barman leading a double life—in its own way gives tangible life to the sort of dissolute brutality that, like the code of honor, belongs equally to the courts of the Renaissance and contemporary urban criminal life.

32

32.   Opera and cinema are intricately linked in terms of production and shared expressive parentage. The score of an opera can be read like a precisely measured screenplay, in terms of shots, sequences, and gestures. The expressions in the eyes of Gilda and Rigoletto (actors doubled by
singers) give a good example of the expressive intensification that film and opera together seek, although by different means — in this case, by focusing all the attention on the horrified reactions of
the spectators rather than on the shocking action itself. The still is taken from *Rigoletto e la sua
tragedia*, a "parallel opera" by Flavio Calzavara (1954). In the 1950s the genre of a mixture of
spoken dialogue and famous musical numbers — almost a musical based on a given opera — successfully replaced the highly successful opera films of the immediate postwar period; these were
film versions of (more or less) complete operas that exploited low production costs, the fame of
the singers involved, an extensive distribution circuit, and emotional impact to bring even to the
most remote provinces a form of theater — opera — in tune with the collective imagination and yet
perfectly suited to cinema. (Carmine Gallone's 1947 *Rigoletto*, sung by Tito Gobbi and Lina Pagli-
ughi and conducted by Tullio Serafin, made the equivalent of two billion lire at the box office in
the space of five years.)

33

34

33–34. In the 1970s and 1980s, the opera-film returned to favor, helped in part by the ease of programming opera on television, but this time with total respect for the "script" (the score), in the hands of such directors as Bergman, Losey, and Rosi. Paradoxically, the elements specific to film became heightened rather than debased. Take, for example, the quartet in *Rigoletto*, filmed by the opera producer Jean-Pierre Ponnelle "on location" (the accidental Mantuan setting of the opera, an expedient to satisfy the censor, is fundamental to operatic imagination in Italy): film's intrinsic propensity for movement assists the music, alternating the interior and exterior scenes. What is missing—to use cinema jargon—is the long shot, the fixed framework that only the proscenium stage can offer the dramatic and musical simultaneity of the quartet.

35

35. The third act of Ponnelle's opera-film is set in an old mill at Acquanegra sul Chiese, in the province of Mantua. Rigoletto and Gilda have little more than twenty bars—about ninety seconds—to cross the river and go up to one of the lit windows. The camera, with its mobility, here demonstrates a widespread tendency in opera production no less than in the aesthetic perception of audiences: in cinema and opera house alike, long stretches of the music are reduced to a mere soundtrack for an evocative view or an attractive shot.

BIBLIOGRAPHIC NOTE

For an orientation on the themes covered in this chapter, the reader with a knowledge of Italian can take advantage of the critical anthology Lorenzo Bianconi, ed., *La drammaturgia musicale* (Bologna: Il Mulino, 1986). It contains eighteen essays by fifteen authors taking different methodological approaches, with a general introduction and an appendix with bibliographical references. Consequently, one need only mention here a few sources and updated references most pertinent to the questions covered in the chapter.

Two decades' worth of reexaminations of the theory and practice of Wagnerian dramaturgy preceded the present chapter, all of which was brought together in two monographs: Carl Dahlhaus, *Wagners Konzeption des musikalischen Dramas* (Regensburg: Bosse, 1971); and Carl Dahlhaus, *Richard Wagners Musikdramen* (Velber: Friedrich, 1971), translated into English by Mary Whittall as *Richard Wagner's Music Dramas* (Cambridge: Cambridge University Press, 1979). Carl Dahlhaus's long series of essays on Wagner and on modern and contemporary opera are collected in his *Vom Musikdrama zur Literaturoper: Aufsätze zur neueren Operngeschichte* (Munich and Salzburg: Katzbichler, 1983). See also his chapter "Wagner's Conception of Musical Drama," in *Nineteenth-Century Music,* trans. J. Bradford Robinson (Berkeley and Los Angeles: University of California Press, 1989), 195–206. Other of his essays that deal with themes touched on here: "Ethos und Pathos in Glucks *Iphigenie auf Tauris,*" *Musikforschung* 27 (1974): 289–300 (with the consequent discussion in *Musikforschung* 28 [1975]: 305–11; 29 [1976]: 72 ff.); and "Zum Affektbegriff der frühdeutschen Oper," *Hamburger Jahrbuch für Musikwissenschaft* 5 (1981): 107–11.

The considerations and analysis of dramaturgy in the present chapter were stimulated by such German literary dramatology as Robert Petsch, *Wesen und Formen des Dramas: Allgemeine Dramaturgie* (Halle an der Saale: Niemeyer, 1945); Emil Staiger, *Grundbegriffe der Poetik* (Zurich: Atlantis, 1946), translated into English by Janette C. Hudson and Luanne T. Frank as *Basic Concepts of Poetics* (University Park: Pennsylvania State University Press, 1991); Peter Szondi, *Theorie des modernen Dramas, 1880–1950,* rev. ed. (Frankfurt am Main: Suhrkamp, 1959), translated into English as *Theory of the Modern Drama: A Critical Edition,* ed. and trans. Michael Hays (Minneapolis: University of Minnesota Press, 1987); Richard Alewyn and Karl Sälzle, *Das große Welttheater: Die Epoche der höfischen Feste* (Hamburg: Rowohlt, 1959); Volker Klotz, *Geschlossene und offene Form im Drama*, 4th rev. ed. (Munich: Hanser, 1969); and Walter Benjamin, *Ursprung des deutschen Trauerspiels* (1928; reprint, Frankfurt am Main: Suhrkamp, 1963), translated into English by John Osborne as *The Origin of German Tragic Drama* (London: NLB, 1977). In turn, the critical categories that have been developed are now more widely disseminated in *Pipers Enzyklopädie des Musiktheaters: Oper, Operette, Musical, Ballett*, ed. Carl Dahlhaus and the Forschungs-Institut für Musiktheater der Universität Bayreuth under the direction of Sieghart Döhring (Munich and Zurich: Piper, 1986–). The encyclopedia is subdivided into a "works" section ordered by author—composer or choreographer—and a "subject" section for terms and concepts.

Musical dramaturgy is an ambiguous area, and one of its determining factors is its intermingling of the disciplines connected with opera: musicology, literary philology and exegesis, and theatrical studies. It thus lends itself to comparative examination, and it is no surprise that the key contributions have come from those areas—Germany and the United States—where comparative studies have become a particular academic tradition. Some of the many writings that have an important application for Italian opera should be mentioned: Joseph Kerman, *Opera as Drama* (New York: Knopf, 1956); Leo Karl Gerhartz, *Die Auseinandersetzungen des jungen Giuseppe Verdi mit dem literarischen Drama: Ein Beitrag zur szenischen Strukturbestimmung der Oper* (Berlin: Merseburger, 1968); Jerome Mitchell, *The Walter Scott Operas: An Analysis of Operas Based on the Works of Sir Walter Scott* (Birmingham: University of Alabama Press, 1977); Gary Schmidgall, *Literature as Opera* (New York: Oxford University Press, 1977); and Herbert Lindenberger, *Opera: The Extravagant Art* (Ithaca, N.Y.: Cornell University Press, 1984).

Study of librettos has recently become a popular area with linguists, philologists, and literary scholars in Italy, Germany, France, and English-speaking countries, although there has been little exchange of methodological information until now. Musical dramaturgy is involved to the extent that the investigation, rather than dealing with the text itself, is focused on its relationship with the music and the musical-dramatic nature of opera. From this viewpoint, studies of the librettist's craft have come mostly from musicologists. A few, highly selective references will suffice: Harold S. Powers, "Il Serse trasformato," *Musical Quarterly* 47 (1961): 481–92, and *Musical Quarterly* 48 (1962): 73–92; Reinhard Strohm, *Die italienische Oper im 18. Jahrhundert* (Wilhelmshaven: Heinrichshofen 1979), with an extensive bibliography; Reinhard Strohm, *Dramma per Musica: Italian Opera Seria of the Eighteenth Century* (New Haven: Yale University Press, 1997); Sabine Henze-Döhring, "*Combinammo l'ossatura* ... : Voltaire und die Librettistik des frühen Ottocento," *Musikforschung* 36 (1983): 113–27; Friedrich Lippmann, *Vincenzo Bellini und die italienische Opera Seria seiner Zeit: Studien über Libretto, Arienform und Melodik* (Cologne and Vienna: Böhlau, 1969); John Black, *The Italian Romantic Libretto: A Study of Salvadore Cammarano* (Edinburgh: Edinburgh University Press, 1984); and Peter Ross, *Studien zum Verhältnis von Libretto und Komposition in den Opern Verdis* (Bern: Gnägi, 1980). For the case of a projected opera that foundered on the difficult relationship between the structure of the libretto, the musical forms at the composer's disposition, and the identification of the dramatic model, see Gary Schmidgall, "Verdi's *King Lear* Project," *19th Century Music* 9 (1985/86): 83–101.

On the morphological resources available to the librettist and composer, and their dramaturgical application in serious and comic opera practice at different periods, see, as well as the books by Strohm and Lippmann mentioned above, Rudolf Bossard, *Giovanni Legrenzi: "Il Giustino": Eine monographische Studie* (Baden-Baden: Koerner, 1988); Reinhold Kubik, *Händels "Rinaldo": Geschichte, Werk, Wirkung* (Neuhausen and Stuttgart: Hänssler, 1982); Reinhard Strohm, *Italienische Opernarien des frühen Settecento (1720–1730)*, 2 vols. (Cologne: Volk, 1976); Wolfgang Osthoff, "Die Opera buffa," in *Gattungen der Musik in Einzeldarstellungen: Gedenkschrift Leo Schrade*, ed. Wulf Ant et al. (Bern and Munich: Francke, 1973), 678–743; Daniel Heartz, "Mozart and His Italian Contemporaries: *La clemenza di Tito*," in *Mozart-Jahrbuch 1978/79* (Kassel: Bärenreiter, 1979), 275–93; Sabine Henze-Döhring, *Opera seria, Opera buffa und Mozarts "Don Giovanni": Zur Gattungskonvergenz in der italienischen Oper des 18. Jahrhunderts* (Laaber: Laaber, 1986); Scott L. Balthazar, "Ritorni's *Ammaestramenti* and the Conventions of Rossinian Opera," *Journal of Musicological Research* 8 (1988): 281–311; and Harold S. Powers, " 'La solita forma' and 'the Uses of Convention,' " in *Nuove prospettive nella ricerca verdiana* (Parma and Milan: Istituto di Studi Verdiani and Ricordi, 1987), 74–109 (also in *Acta Musicologica* 59 [1987]: 65–90).

The notions of (operatic) "text," "opera" (in the sense of an inviolable "opus"), and "author" are crucial in any discussion of the dramaturg of Italian opera: however inconstant and variable throughout history, they are nevertheless fundamental to the critical assumptions that music has the primary role in the dramatic definition of opera and that the composer is responsible for the ultimate artistic result. Nevertheless, in the wake of the current enthusiasm for so-called critical editions, ideas on these categories are not very far advanced in the area of opera. The most interesting contributions for musical dramaturgy tend to have come not so much from scholars intent on restoring an authentic version, a fixed model of an opera (if such a rare bird could be found), as from those who have investigated the tortuous creative process behind a given opera first and the checkered performance practice afterward. For the inside story of Mozart's operatic "texts," see, for example, Daniel Heartz, "The Genesis of Mozart's *Idomeneo*," *Musical Quarterly* 45 (1969): 1–19; Daniel Heartz, "Constructing *Le nozze di Figaro*," *Journal of the Royal Musical Association* 112 (1986/87): 77–98; and Alan Tyson, "Some Problems in the Text of *Le nozze di Figaro*: Did Mozart Have a Hand in Them?" *Journal of the Royal Musical Association* 112 (1986/87): 99–131 (with references to the existing bibliography). For Verdi, there has been a flurry of writing on the most troubled scores; see, in particular, three important essays on *Boccanegra*: Wolfgang Osthoff, "Die beiden *Boccanegra*-Fassungen und der Beginn von Verdis Spätwerk," *Analecta Musicologica* 1 (1963): 70–89; Frits Noske, "*Simon Boccanegra*: One Plot, Two Dramas," in his *The Signifier and the Signified: Studies in the Operas of Mozart and Verdi* (The Hague: Nijhoff, 1977), 215–40; and Harold S. Powers, "*Simon Boccanegra* 1. 10–12: A Generic-Genetic Analysis of the Council Chamber Scene," *19th Century Music* 13 (1989): 101–28 (also published in *Atti del XIV con-*

gresso della Società Internazionale di Musicologia [Turin: EDT/Musica, 1991]). See also the long series of preparatory studies that resulted in the synoptic edition of the various versions of *Don Carlos,* edited by Ursula Günther and Luciano Petazzoni (Milan: Ricordi, 1980); see the important review by Andrew Porter in *Journal of the American Musicological Society* 35 (1982): 360–70. For Puccini, research has only just got under way: see Jürgen Maehder, "Studien zum Fragmentcharakter von Giacomo Puccinis *Turandot,*" *Analecta Musicologica* 22 (1984): 297–379; and Jürgen Maehder, "Paris-Bilder: Zur Transformation von Henry Murgers Roman in den *Bohème*-Opern Puccinis und Leoncavallos," in *Jahrbuch für Opernforschung 1986* (Frankfurt am Main: Lang, 1987), 109–76. On the vicissitudes of the reception of eighteenth-century opera, which have an important bearing on its dramaturgical definition, see two different examples: Helga Lühning, *"Titus"-Vertonungen im 18. Jahrhundert: Untersuchungen zur Tradition der Opera Seria von Hasse bis Mozart* (Laaber: Volk and Laaber, 1983); and the synoptic edition of Cimarosa's *Gli Orazi e i Curiazi,* vol. 2, ed. Giovanni Morelli and Elvidio Surian (Milan: Suvini Zerboni, 1985). The introductory essays to facsimiles of seventeenth- and eighteenth-century scores reproduced in *Drammaturgia musicale veneta* (Milan: Ricordi, 1983–) give a great deal of coverage to dramaturgical questions connected with their fortunes in the theater.

The papers from the conference *Werk and Wiedergabe: Musiktheater exemplarisch interpretiert,* ed. Sigrid Wiesmann (Bayreuth: Fehr, 1980), deal with the ambiguous relationship between the "text" of an opera and its theatrical "realization," where it is still undecided where the "opus" stands. In this volume, two more or less opposing positions (equally revealing of and determined by the respective subject of study) are taken in the essays by Wolfgang Osthoff, "Werk und Wiedergabe als aktuelles Problem," 13–44, and Reinhard Strohm, "Zum Verständnis der Opera Seria," 51–70 (the latter translated into English as "Towards an Understanding of the Opera Seria," in Strohm's *Essays on Handel and Italian Opera* [New York: Cambridge University Press, 1985], 93–105).

The following essays deal in different ways with the implicit gestural qualities in the musical structures of Mozart, Verdi, and, in contrast, Wagner: Thrasybulos Georgiades, "Aus der Musiksprache des Mozart-Theaters," in *Mozart-Jahrbuch 1950* (Salzburg: Internationale Stiftung Mozarteum, 1951), 76–98; Marco Beghielli, "Per un nuovo approccio al teatro musicale: L'atto performativo come luogo dell'imitazione gestuale nella drammaturgia verdiana," *Italica* 64 (1987): 632–53; and Carl Dahlhaus's lecture published as *Die Bedeutung des Gestischen in Wagners Musikdramen* (Munich: Oldenbourg, 1970), now also to be found in Dahlhaus, *Vom Musikdrama zur Literaturoper,* 74–85.

The perspective of the observer-listener—or of the opera audience—is also a "function," and a vital one, in the overall dramaturgical structure of an opera. The best portrayal, in terms of Italian opera, can be found in two essays by Fedele D'Amico: "Note sulla drammaturgia verdiana," *Analecta Musicologica* 11 (1972): 272–87, and "A proposito d'un *Tancredi*: Dioniso in Apollo," *Analecta Musicologica* 21 (1982): 61–71.

Metrical and Formal Organization

PAOLO FABBRI

I. METER AND RHYTHM

Around the end of the 1780s, one of the arguments in the dispute that broke out between Vincenzo Manfredini and Stefano Arteaga, author of *Le rivoluzioni del teatro musicale italiano dalla sua origine fino al presente,*[1] which had only just appeared, concerned the mismatch, or not, of the mensural system peculiar to music with the metrics of modern poetry. Accepting unreservedly Padre Sacchi's distinction between the "metrical" verse of classical Greek and Roman poetry ("in which only the quantity of time is measured) and the "harmonic" verse of modern languages (which takes "only the number of syllables and the order of accents" into consideration),[2] Arteaga declared that as far as rhythm was concerned, music and poetry were put together arbitrarily. In the eternal *querelle des anciens et des modernes,* the unarguable superiority of the ancients had to be recognized.

[I]n terms of exactness of duration, given that each syllable of poetry was assigned its intrinsic value, short or long, and the long took twice the amount of time to pronounce as the short, the consequence was that musical time was completely regulated by the prosody, so that the composer, to keep perfect time, needed do no more than follow the poet blindly. We do not observe this practice, since in our poetry

1. Esteban de Arteaga, *Le rivoluzioni del teatro musicale italiano dalla sua origine fino al presente,* 3 vols. (Bologna: Trenti, 1783, 1785, 1788; reprint, Bologna: Forni, 1969).
2. Giovenale Sacchi, *Della divisione del tempo nella musica, nel ballo e nella poesia* (Milan: Mazzucchelli, 1770; reprint, Bologna: Forni, 1969), 120.

we ignore the syllabic quantity and in the formation of a line attend only to the number of syllables; musical meter is thus left to itself and rarely is in agreement with the poetry. . . . Do they [that is, the creators of modern music] not notice that where a language has no regular, stable prosody, musical meter must also share such irregularity? That it is difficult to accord notes a value when the syllables have no fixed quantity? That the movement and tempo will lack their due precision if they wish to keep up with the words? That at most it can be achieved in purely instrumental music, that is, in the least perfect musical genre, since it is the one that lacks the principal source of energy, which resides in the expression of some individual state of mind? That because of such uncertainty the composer is often obliged to change meter, principally in the recitative, where, the intervals in the vocal line being less wide and the pronunciation consequently more rapid, the notes cannot follow the order of syllables? And that in the arias themselves, where the voice rests longer on the respective vowels, and the notes can more easily be accommodated, the composer is too uncertain as to the number of notes that ought to correspond to each syllable and the time that must be used in setting them? Thus, the lack of exact prosody is a real failing in our languages, and the influence this has in music gives a clear representation of their difference from classical languages.[3]

Manfredini was of the opposite opinion, for he felt that modern Italian had both stresses and "quantity." In fact, the latter quality was, for him, much more important for the needs of music than the former, for in his opinion,

the different stresses serve to speak with force and expressivity in prose and to declaim in verse; and let me say further that their greater frequency and variety make a language more musical, because it is more sonorous and melodic, as indeed is our language. The stresses are not, however, the most fundamental thing for music, since the composer can alter their nature, that is, he can actually set a high stress with a low note, or a low stress with a high note; but he cannot thus decide the quantity of the syllables without prejudicing the true expression of the words. . . . I declare myself increasingly convinced that in our language the quantity of the syllable is one thing, and the stress quite another, if we consider that a speaker may declaim a given piece of poetry without expression or emphasis and in a low monotone, but if the person is educated, they will not fail to express the length of the syllables, accelerating the duration of the short ones and prolonging that of the long ones; but if at the same time, if the speaker does not allow the diversity of stresses to be heard through different sounds and by modulating the voice, how dull the recitation will be and how little pleasure it will impart to the soul of the listener.[4]

Opposing positions these may be, but they both demonstrate that the relationship between poetry and music is a difficult one also in its rhythmic as-

3. Arteaga, *Le rivoluzioni*, 2:31 and 34ff.

4. Vincenzo Manfredini, *Difesa della music moderna e de' suoi celebri esecutori* (Bologna: Trenti, 1788; reprint, Bologna: Forni, 1972), 94ff. Arteaga's opinion is given on 91ff.

pect, an aspect that cannot help but reveal the incompatibility of the two systems, a source of frequent internal tensions, sometimes painless compromises, and sometimes the victory of one over the other. This is possibly made clearer in the passage from the sequence of stresses of poetry to musical rhythm measured in bars, with its periodic scansion into strong and weak beats, into which literary stresses are often uncomfortably squeezed. There is no question, for example, that Verdi was frequently brutal in the way he forced lines, such as "La dònna è mòbile / qual piùma al vènto" or "Di quélla pìra / l'orrèndo fòco" to become "Là donna e mòbile / quàl piuma al vènto" and "Dì quella pìra / l'òrrendo fòco." Elsewhere, spacing out causes many of the syllables in a verse to be placed in a strong position, cramming it with extra accents: to stay with famous examples, we can think of "Stride la vampa!—la folla indomita," which, by extending each *quinario* for four bars, stresses almost every syllable.

In any case, by being set to music and taking on music's mensural character, the poetic text comes to assume—or to reveal more clearly, if we embrace Manfredini's thesis—clear metrical features, fixing the discretionary and vague qualities of each of its syllabic durations and restricting the freedom of their articulation overall by specifying it with notation. All the possible rhythmic combinations take on a concrete form, which we can summarize in broad categories: syllabic or melismatic writing, using the same number of syllables per note or differing numbers of syllables, and if the same, with or without diminutions (for example, in a series of quarter notes for each syllable, the variant of little vocalizations of two eighth notes or four sixteenth notes). And yet it should not be forgotten that even when the setting is syllabic, the music can change the type of meter by choosing to avoid an elision, for example, lengthening a commonplace *ottonario piano* into a *novenario* ("La calunnia è un venticello"). Possibly it is the metrical elasticity which verse can acquire through its union with music that helps to explain the mixed meter of much early Romance poetry. Where leveling possibilities were absent, this poetry came increasingly to follow the path of greater regularity: is it any surprise that the principle of metrical homogeneity was established first in Provençal poetry and then in Sicilian, that is, in the two literary schools that show the move toward detachment from and a complete break with music respectively? Let us not overlook repetitions, even only of words, which composers are generally accustomed to use in abundance, and which the language of sounds not only tolerates but often actually begs for and imposes, something unthinkable in a text that is not sung. Such reiterations can, in addition, deal the fatal blow in the process of disruption that a composer can effect on verse: in any case, they represent an additional element that further complicates the coexistence of music and poetry.

2. OPEN FORM: THE PROSODY OF BLANK VERSE

Italian opera certainly has a major role to play in this field, given that it has always and almost exclusively used verse and its various formalizations. When prose does appear, it is very rare for it to be unmetered: examples are the dialogues in the original *Nina* by Carpani and Lorenzi and Paisiello (1789); *I solitari di Scozia* by Tottola and Vaccai (1815), through the influence of opéra-comique; or the letter that Figaro reads in act 1, scene 4, of *Il barbiere di Siviglia* by Sterbini and Rossini (1816).

From the outset, the type of verse generally adopted for opera was the prevailing one of sixteenth-century pastoral (above all, Tasso's *Aminta* and Guarini's *Il pastor fido*), to which opera was so closely related: that is the *endecasillabo,* preferably *piano,* that is, with the stress on the penultimate syllable, either "complete" or "broken." In modern terms, this is the free combination of eleven and seven syllable lines *(endecasillabo* and *settenario)* which had stood the test of time in song and, on a simpler level, in the recently introduced madrigal. The coupling is the result of their homogeneity and the possibility of the shorter being absorbed by the longer: an *endecasillabo* actually is perceived as the sum of a *settenario* and a *quinario* (what is known as the *a maiore* type) or the other way round *(a minore),* the *settenario* being merely the larger ingredient. The combination, which clinched the success of the *endecasillabo* in Italian poetry, had various advantages: the necessary "prosaic" quality for its conversational use onstage; length (the longest of compound verses); a flexibility resulting from the internal articulation referred to above and a lack of any rigid scheme of stresses. If we think of the first three lines of the *Divine Comedy* (Nel mezzo del cammin di nostra vita / mi ritrovai per una selva oscura / che la diritta via era smarrita), we can see for ourselves how, while the overall length of each line remains constant, the distribution of tonic and unstressed accents is always changing, without that mechanically rhythmic effect inherent in the much more fixed plan of stresses of the *decasillabo* and *ottonario* (the *novenario,* the only compound verse not yet considered, is already found set aside in Dante's *De vulgari eloquentia* as a regional usage, possibly an unconscious archaism). For its part, the *settenario* enjoyed similar advantages: like all simple verse forms, of which it is the longest, it has only one fixed stress—the principal one, on the sixth syllable—and a secondary, movable one that can fall on any of the syllables between the first and the fourth inclusive. (It is probably worth remembering at this point that Italian verse meters are defined in terms of the most important fixed stress, which in a *piano* line falls on the penultimate metrical syllable: thus, for example, a fixed stress on the fifth syllable of a *senario* and on the tenth of an *endecasillabo.*)

The modern reinventors of the *stile rappresentativo* aimed to realize onstage the ideal of "almost speaking in harmony," [5] that is, lines "of seven and eleven syllables, which are more than others close to prose," in Andrea Perrucci's later definition. [6]

In parallel with this, just as the poetic language of the stage, in eleven-syllable blank verse, aspired to the casualness of prose, its musical adornment was content to seem little more than an amplification of spoken language and its phonic qualities. The singing voice, which Mei defined as "diastemic and, so to speak, intervallic," [7] was asked to moderate its numerous possibilities by employing melodic and rhythmic self-restraint. Galilei is even more explicit in referring to spoken intonation, determinedly advising composers to pay close attention to the vocal diagrams used by professional public speakers, especially orators and actors. [8]

Such research was to leave due theoretical and practical traces in the prefaces to the works which advertised the new style in print: Peri's *L'Euridice* and Caccini's *Le nuove musiche* and his *L'Euridice*. [9] In fact, Peri and Caccini, when faced with the blank-verse parts of Rinuccini's text, tacitly observed some general rules, which might be summarized thus:

- A predominance of syllabic writing in the relationship between text and music, based on the harmonies held in the basso continuo: in Peri the few melismas—usually on accented syllables—mostly belong to the category of expressive embellishments *(accenti,* charming *gruppetti,* short *passaggi),* while in Caccini they are more frequent and are usually found at the end of a phrase.
- Irregular, not periodic, rhythmic scansion, wholly influenced by the changing, flexible stresses of *endecasillabi* and *settenari*. To obtain this, imperfect time (C)

5. This definition comes from Giulio Caccini's preface to *Le nuove musiche* (Florence: Marescotti, 1601), Florentine style (1602): a modern edition of Caccini's preface can be found in Angelo Solerti, *Le origini del melodramma* (Turin: Bocca, 1903; reprint, Bologna: Forni, 1969), 55–71; quotation on 57. A translation of excerpts in English appears in Oliver Strunk, *Source Readings in Music History,* ed. Leo Treitler (New York: W. W. Norton, 1998), 608–17.

6. Andrea Perrucci, *Dall'arte rappresentativa premeditata ed all'improvviso* (1699), ed. Anton Giulio Bragaglia (Florence: Sansoni, 1961), 101.

7. Girolamo Mei, *Discorso sopra la musica antica e moderna* (Venice: Ciotti, 1602; reprint, Bologna, Forni, 1968), 3; see also 4, 8, and 11.

8. Vincenzo Galilei, *Dialogo . . . della musica antica et della moderna* (Florence: Marescotti, 1581; reprint, New York: Broude Brothers), 89. Extracts in English appear in Strunk, *Source Readings,* 463–67. Around 1640 he was echoed in two treatises that remained in manuscript form for a long time: the *Trattato della musica scenica* by Giovan Battista Doni (included in his *Lyra barberina: De' trattati di musica . . . tomo secondo,* ed. Anton Francesco Gori [Florence: Stamperia Imperiale, 1763; reprint, Bologna: Forni, 1974], 1–144, esp. 11, 18, 32–33, 34, and 122) and *Il corago, o vero Alcune osservazioni per metter bene in scena le composizioni drammatiche,* ed. Paolo Fabbri and Angelo Pompilio (Florence: Olschki, 1983), 42–43, 45, 61, and 82.

9. All have been reprinted in modern times in Solerti, *Le origini,* see esp. 45–49, 51, 56–57, 59–60, and 75.

is constantly used: with its range of note lengths from the whole note to the six-teenth note, invariably binary, it allowed the greatest variety of combinations, all the more obvious if we compare it with the rigidity of the iambs, trochees, and dactyls in the only two tiny passages in triple time which Peri introduces signifi-cantly at two joyful moments: in the opening scene (Ninfa: "Dite liete e festose") and the penultimate one (Aminta: "tutto lieto e giocondo").

- An almost total absence of verbal repetitions; the few there are, because of their very rarity, carry greater emotional weight.
- In the melodic outlines, a preference for stepwise movement (as in speech): here again, departures from this tendency serve to emphasize tonic syllables, some-times approached and/or quitted by a leap, or to signify psychological excitement (observe the greater use of nonstepwise movement in both Peri and Caccini at the point where Euridice's death is announced and in the latter's setting where Arce-tro describes Orfeo's despair: "Et egli, o fere, o piante, o fronde, or fiori"). In each case the leaps used are mostly of a third, fourth, and fifth: only in exceptional cases is there a leap of a sixth (particularly in Caccini).
- Emphasizing of stressed syllables: through the use of greater durations than those of the immediately preceding unstressed syllables (if the vowel is truncated, then it is followed by a rest); making them coincide with the strong beat in the bar and be in harmony with the bass; in secondary ones, mostly approaching them from below and sometimes marking this motion with a sudden fall in the voice imme-diately before, as if to give an impulse (if, however, the first syllable is to be stressed, then the melodic shape will be descending or at most level); with a vocalization, particularly using an *accento*. The simultaneous use of more than one of these is clearly intended to reinforce a point.
- Even the most complex syntactic unit is on a small scale and consists of the phrase line: it ends with the completion of the melodic arch, which is almost always in-dicated by a cadence in the basso continuo. Rarely does the vocal range of any phrase in Peri go beyond a fifth, and in Caccini a sixth: further extensions—up to an octave—come either in moments of particular dramatic tension or else also at a cadence, to make an expansive, sonorous gesture.

The result is a musical idiom that is strongly paratactic, consisting of seg-ments whose numerousness is a consequence of the brevity of their melodic span, and that achieves the stylistic simplicity and linearity recommended for texts intended to be sung. The cadences operate as musical punctuation marks, creating a sequence of periods that are more complex than the phrase line (usually two by two, as suggested by the frequent rhyming couplets). Weak or medium-to-strong cadential formulas (a comma or colon) are character-ized by the following: a simple inflection of the vocal line with the principal stress emphasized, on a static bass; imperfect cadence; feminine cadence, with the unstressed syllable following the principal stressed one at the same pitch (sometimes with the same duration). Their greatest effectiveness (the equiva-lent to a semicolon or period) is achieved by the use of perfect, masculine cadences, animating an otherwise sluggish basso continuo and giving the voice a broader gesture both in terms of range and in the use of vocalization, as described above, but also by extending the phrasing beyond the customary coupling of connected verses. Then, often as a cadence approaches for which a definite sense of closing is desired, we meet clear breaches of the "regular" approach to the system of stresses: tonic syllables on weak beats and, vice versa, unstressed ones on strong beats, syncopation, descending lines—rather than ascending—on the principal stressed syllable. All things considered, masculine cadences are themselves a blatant distortion, since the almost total absence of truncated lines in the literary text excludes their "natural" use. The need to create them leads to metrically inaccurate stresses (see example 1, at the point marked o). His goal being the avoidance of such obvious inversions of role between stressed and unstressed syllables, Peri initiated the practice—which became widely used over the next hundred years—of placing on the upbeat the last (unstressed) syllable and making it a brief appoggiatura which resolves on the next beat with a tiny vocalization (see example 1, at the point marked *). Each of these departures from more purely declamatory customs is a source of propulsion (rhythmic, melodic, and harmonic) intended to speed up the discourse and intensify the braking effect of the cadence. In designing the phrase, the composer tends to expand some of the phonetic properties of the textual content, as has been described, but in order to make clear the articulation he must use cadences whose effectiveness is the greater the more they use purely musical mechanisms.

Something of these practices also found a place in the theoretical writings of the 1630s and 1640s, which reflect to a greater or lesser extent the customs and rules implicit in those early decades of opera. Emphasizing the greater rhythmic freedom that the system of stresses gave modern composers compared with the rigidity of the old quantitative meters with their fixed connections between long and short (from 1 to 1, 2 to 1, 3 to 2), the author of *Il corago* also referred to the greater values usually given to the syllable carrying the principal stress and to the following, concluding one:

> Composers of our day are free from these limitations and requirements because they are not obliged to shorten or lengthen any syllable except the penultimate one of words that are made up of more than two syllables, not even the fewer final syllables of the verse, which want to be held long. In addition, the composer is not normally obliged to observe between adjacent notes only the equal or duple or two to three proportions, as he can use whatever other mixture he pleases.[10]

Doni suggests that this sense of repose must, however, be avoided in interrogative phrases, precisely because they end with a suspension, not a conclu-

10. *Il corago*, 51–52.

Ex. 1.   Rinuccini–Peri, *L'Euridice* (1600).

sion: "in questions . . . the last note should not be white but rather black and
rapid," and they "are beautifully expressed by making the final note higher
than the penultimate." [11] For him, ascending motion has a psychologically
positive connotation ("certain modulations in ascending steps and imitative
in movement are good for expressing happy ideas"),[12] while more generally
the following maxim can be established: "movement by steps or small intervals makes the melody soft and gentle, expressing meek and feminine habits,
but modulating by leaps or distant intervals makes the vocal line virile and
elevated and expresses such characteristics." [13] With great clarity Doni judges
cadences to be as "necessary in melody as punctuation in oration": for that

11. Doni, *Trattato,* 82 and 81.
12. Ibid., 81.   13. Ibid., 79.

reason, "they appear in every vocal line like periods in oration," and "in those with a sense of full close the cadence must end with the principal chords" so as to make clear the logical completion.[14]

The predominantly declamatory vocal style which Peri and Caccini applied to most of the sung text appears in a slightly modified version in sections that are also in blank verse but differentiated from what is around them by their specific dramatic function. Usually these are fairly lengthy contributions from a single character, narrative monologues like that of Dafne on the death of Euridice ("Per quel vago boschetto"), Arcetro's description of the appearance of Venus to the despairing Orfeo ("Con frettoloso passo"), and Aminta's narration of the return of the hero ("Quand'al tempio n'andaste"), or else passages of oration or prayer (Orfeo: "Funeste piagge, ombrosi orridi campi"). In addition to the more frequent abandonment of stepwise movement, the greater range, and chromatic alterations, there are occasional textual repetitions, decorations, and, above all, a remarkably static approach to both melody—often with the repeated use of some key note—and bass, giving a feeling of sorrow and solemnity: at the beginning of Orfeo's prayer referred to above, Caccini freezes the continuo for five consecutive lines. And again in this monologue the presence of a poetic and musical refrain ("Lagrimate al mio pianto, ombre d'Inferno") divides the text into three unequal sections, introducing a structural principle into the free flow of the blank verse.

In the sung recitations of blank verse, Doni later identified at least three melodic levels: "That simple style which we may call narrative, since it is used in the narrations of messengers, descriptions, and similar calm discourse," "which in the opinion of some is true recitative and which astute composers use only in narrations and unemotional discourse, which lingers greatly on the same chords and offers little melodic diversity";[15] that which "is formed by accurate observation of the stresses and dips of the natural voice that can be heard in speech";[16] and lastly "where there is fully-developed song, almost in the style of madrigals" for the sections most rich in emotion.[17]

3. CLOSED FORM: THE ARIA

If such stylistic traits were sufficiently able to highlight certain dramatic situations in music, those parts of the dramatic text that stood out clearly from the monologues and dialogue in blank verse, because of the different meters in use and/or an almost constant recourse to strophic form, assumed particular sig-

---

14. Ibid., p. 51 of the appendix for the first quotation, and p. 64 for the rest.

15. Ibid., 33, 27.   16. Ibid., 34; see also 27.

17. Ibid., 27; see also 32 and 36. John Walter Hill also deals with this tripartite division in "Le 'Arie' di Frescobaldi e la cerchia musicale del cardinal Montalto," in *Girolamo Frescobaldi nel IV centenario della nascita*, ed. Sergio Durante and Dinko Fabris (Florence: Olschki, 1986), 215–32, quotation on 216–17.

nificance: prologues, choruses, morals, expressions of joy, condemnations. As for the way they were set, if the stanzas in the prologue have a declamatory style that differs from that of blank verse only in its repetitive quality (which the presence of an instrumental ritornello between the strophes makes clear), other poetic forms correspond to a musical style that is also generally divided into verses and is characterized as follows: by being predominantly strophic, whether totally or partially (bass alone); by using polyphonic writing for the chorus; greater movement in the continuo, which clings to the vocal line and closely follows its rhythmic and harmonic contours; by the use of a smaller range of note values, in which the predominant ones are usually combinations of adjacent durations (for example, whole note–half note, or half note–quarter note, and so on, keeping the greater lengths for the stressed syllables); a resultant tendency to rhythmic rigidity, even more obvious where triple time is used; some repetitions of parts of the text, especially closing lines; less attention to respecting the correct verbal stress, which is often sacrificed to rhythmic and musical demands; a vocal line not modeled on declamation of the literary text.

In these combinations (described as "arias" or "canzones" and also by the diminutive forms of the words) the relationship between text and music was in every way much more generic, for the rights of music overcame the demands of the text, aided by poetic rhythms quite different from the proselike tendencies of blank verse. In opposition to the analytical word setting of recitative was the closed and compact form of the aria, "lacking perfect imitation of the emotions and of common discourse, for while a cheerful aria signifies cheerfulness, it does not, however, express in particular each verse and word in the way that it should." The recitative "expresses more particularly each word and embodies the emotion and sense of the poetry, whereas the [aria] does it more coarsely and generically." [18]

In the area of metrical organization, Italian literary tradition offered poets writing for music tried and tested models based on the *endecasillabo:* tercets, quatrains, sextets, octaves. Groupings of *endecasillabi* and *settenari* then gave rise to stanzas similar to those of canzones (or rather of canzonets, because of the constant use of rhyme). But apart from these forms based on a single type of verse or, at most, including an abbreviated variant of it, poetry for music from the very beginning capitalized on the enormous potential of Anacreontic poetry. Gabriello Chiabrera introduced it into Italian literature, and it offered a wide sample of meters other than the *endecasillabo* that could be used in mixed combinations and in stanzas of very different kinds. Precisely because of these characteristics, this type of poetry was unpopular with theo-

18. *Il corago,* 60ff.

rists of Lodovico Zuccolo's type, for he felt that only a highly selective number of verse types (in practice, only the *endecasillabo* and *settenario* plus, at
the most, the *quinario,* the ones, that is, of the most elevated tradition) were
valid and considered lines with even numbers of syllables to lack genuine rhythmic properties. For example, the *quadrisillabo* used by Chiabrera in "Dami-
gella / tutta bella" "is more skipping than rhythmic" in Zuccolo's opinion.[19]
Similar, related "versetti,"

> which we reject, will be judged better than the others, for musicians vary their notes
> to the greater pleasure of listeners and with less effort to themselves on short verses
> rather than long ones: and the more uneven are the numbers and times, the more this
> is the case. Chiabrera, as he himself confessed through the words of Lorenzo Fabri,
> divided his canzonet into short verses for no other reason than to accommodate soft
> and delicate material to fitting verses and so allow musicians to adapt their notes
> with ease. . . . The reason so many short Italian verses, formerly used by the most an-
> cient poets and then abandoned by Petrarch and other writers of perfect judgment
> as invalid or unsuitable to bear their ideas, have swarmed into the light again must
> be entirely attributed to the change in music, which some years ago entered Italy
> from France, softer and more delicate and wanton than we are used to. Thus, our po-
> ets, not content with the sweeter, softer madrigal of years gone by, have also turned
> their hands to many tender, effeminate canzonets, which we currently read and
> which are so to the liking of composers. So, because it is not music that is adapted to
> verses, but verses, against all right, adapted to music, poetry has lost all modesty, all
> decorum, and has almost changed from a modest young girl to a wanton strumpet.[20]

Short, isometric strophes of *quinari* and *ottonari* can indeed be found in
the earliest operas, which also tried out some combinations—although these
were really quite restrained because of the similarities of the two meters—such
as the *ottonario* and *quadrisillabo,* as in the chorus "Bella ninfa fuggitiva" in
Rinuccini's *Dafne,* or the *settenario* and *quinario* of Salvadori and Gagliano's
Flora (act 1, Napee: "Dive de' monti"). But soon meters that were not so similar were brought together, with the very intention of creating clashing patterns of stresses that were mutually inflexible. Each quatrain of *settenari* and
endecasillabi that the jubilant Orfeo sings when he returns from Hades in the
Striggio and Monteverdi setting opens with an *ottonario* (act 4: "Quale onor
di te fia degno"), and again in *Flora,* a bizarre infernal chorus sings in *trisillabi* and *quinari,* equally *sdruccioli* and *tronchi* (act 3: "Diléguati"). Later, in
Rospigliosi and Landi's *Sant'Alessio,* a similar demonic group sings *quadrisil-*

---

19. Lodovico Zuccolo, *Discorso delle ragioni del numero del verso italiano* (Venice: Ginami,
1623), 49.
20. Ibid., 56 and 65.

labi, quinari, and *endecasillabi* in lines that are both *sdrucciolo* and *piano* (act 1, scene 4:[21] "Si disserrino").

These customs are more or less recorded in detail and approved in the works of theorists in the 1630s and 1640s. Once it had been established that a large part of the text had to proceed in blank verse, Doni also accepted that metric verse could, when necessary, be varied in canzonets of *settenari, ottonari, quinari,* and *quadrisillabi.*[22] A much broader illustration is offered in *Il corago,* with metrical schemes and strophic forms of the greatest variety: stanzas that bring together between four and ten lines, and verse types that range from the *settenario* to the *endecasillabo,* and down to the *quadrisillabo* and *quinario* as well, in *piano, tronco,* and *sdrucciolo* variants, with a preference for polymetrical combinations.[23] As well as verses that are rarely found in Italian poetry, such as the *novenario,* there are even Gallicisms such as the line of thirteen syllables,[24] which Doni himself, with his love of long, majestic lines, had looked forward to: "Since not only do lines of eleven syllables not seem to me to be too long, I would in fact like our language to be capable of longer ones, like French with its thirteen syllables, although these are really two short lines, one of six and the other of seven syllables rather than whole lines, as we know because they are always divided."[25] In addition, this openness of poetry for music to metrical traditions unknown in Italy is documented by Ottaviano Castelli, who, in his *Dialogo sopra la poesia drammatica,*[26] declares that he has used "verses of eight and nine syllables without the Italian rests" (that is, without pauses, stases, or caesuras), on the model of "the Spanish romanza and *ridondiglia*" and the "French feminine line of 13 syllables." A taste for metrical experimentation seems to have been particularly intense in Rome, where more than in other places in the early seventeenth century opera achieved a certain stability: it is no coincidence that it was from this milieu that the theoretical meditations of Castelli, Doni, and the anonymous author of *Il corago* derive. The author of *La morte d'Orfeo,* set to music by Landi, gives evidence of this interest when in act 1 he gives to the character of Eurus a stanza of *endecasillabi, quinari, senari,* and *settenari* ("Già puro in ogni parte il ciel si mostra"), and in act 5 to Charon a canzonet in which each strophe has a quatrain of *novenari* followed by a refrain that begins with a *quadrisillabo,* broadens to a *quinario,* and ends with a *settenario.*

---

21. In the notes and in parenthetical references in the text, act and scene numbers will be given in the following format: 1.4 (for act 1, scene 4).

22. See Doni, *Trattato,* 18ff.   24. See ibid., 75, ex. 23.

23. See *Il corago,* 70–79.   25. Doni, *Trattato,* 18.

26. Ottaviano Castelli's *Dialogo* is attached to his sylvan fable *La sincerità trionfante overo L'erculeo ardire* (Rome: Mascardi, 1640); it has been reprinted in part in Heinz Becker, ed., *Quellentexte zur Konzeption der europäischen Oper im 17. Jahrhundert* (Kassel: Bärenreiter, 1981), 51–57.

Beva, beva securo l'onda	[Drink, drink without fear the water
che da Lete tranquillo innonda:	which calmly flows from Lethe:
beva, beva chiunque ha sete	drink, drink, whoever thirsts,
il sereno liquor di Lete.	the calm liquid of Lethe.
Non più affanni,	No more anguish,
non più morte,	no more death,
non più sorte:	no more fate:
privo di doglia,	free from grief,
pien di piacere,	full of pleasure,
venga chi ha sete a bere.	come, those who thirst, and drink.]

At the end of the preceding act there is a chorus of shepherds ("O tutti, rac-colti") entirely made up of a long chain of *senari,* a meter that seems to appear in this text for the first time, and that not even *Il corago,* otherwise so open and disposed to all metrical inventiveness, contemplates. Some years later this unfamiliar verse scheme is revealed to be completely acclimatized in the works of Giulio Rospigliosi, the official theatrical poet for the performances in the Barberini palace.

Such a metrically stimulating, even variable, poetic basis called more than ever in this period for arias, mostly set syllabically in triple time, that used almost no verbal repetitions from beginning to end; the text was thus adhered to without too many jolts or pauses: one either took advantage of the flexibility of such verses as *settenari* and *endecasillabi,* possibly anchoring them to the stability of an ostinato bass (as in many of Cavalli's lamenting arias),[27] or let the pattern of stresses be influenced by a conveniently varied text.

> As for meter, while in other forms of poetry it is permissible or fitting to employ variety and eccentricity, in this it seems praiseworthy and permitted with greater reason to offer the composer an opportunity to abandon uniformity: in this way each emotion will have its appropriate and particular meter, and this has been especially noteworthy in the choruses, which admit canzonets of various types and inspire the composer of the music to produce harmonic oddities.[28]

Similarly, in his *Venere gelosa* (Venice, 1643) Niccolò Enea Bartolini declared: "I have maintained the style and have endeavored, through a diversity of meter and the choice of the words, to provoke the imagination of the person who will set them to music." Despite the fact that the music could now be in either duple or triple time, and a tendency to flights of bel canto was be-

---

27. In this connection see three works by Ellen Rosand: *Aria in the Early Operas of Francesco Cavalli* (Ann Arbor, Mich.: UMI, 1984), 83ff.; "Comic Contrast and Dramatic Continuity: Observations on the Form and Function of Aria in the Operas of Francesco Cavalli, *Music Review* 37 (1976): 92–105; "Aria as Drama in the Early Operas of Francesco Cavalli, in *Venezia e il melodramma nel Seicento,* ed. Maria Teresa Muraro (Florence: Olschki, 1976), 75–96.

28. *Il corago,* 70.

ginning, even in subsequent operas canzonets still remained irregular; they were syllabic, even isosyllabic, or else—particularly with more lively meters—they played with closely related durations, such as *longa/brevis,* with a few internal repetitions of isolated syntagmas or portions of text, although the preference was for repetitions of concluding sections. The range of meters was now as broad as possible and covered everything from the *trisillabo* to the *endecasillabo,* including the *decasillabo* and even the *novenario,* which Aureli in particular had started to use regularly from the end of the 1660s onward.[29] In turn, Salvadori would mark out as particularly suited to music the "tripping" *ottonario* and *senario,* followed by the *decasillabo, settenario,* and *quinario,* with special praise for the mixtures of "these very different meters," unfamiliar to traditional poets: "They are known to those who have worked in the theater and are accustomed to composing dramas for music and are musicians, because attention is drawn to such verses in music and not elsewhere." [30] For example, in *L'Adelaide* by Dolfin and Sartorio (1672), out of a total of fifty-five arias, thirty-five are in mixed meters, while the following example, from *Totila* by Noris and Legrenzi (1677; 1.3), with its metrical lurches between almost every line, displays the end result of such a taste:

> Arda Roma e Roma esangue
> tra sangue
> e cenere
> mi cada al piè.
>   Ma se vinta e fulminata,
> spopolata,
> terra o sito più non ha,
> questo braccio formidabile,
> insuperabile,
> qual impero abbatterà?
>   Forma novelli mondi, o dio tonante,
> o farò guerra al vasto ciel stellante.

> [Let Rome burn and let a lifeless Rome
> amid blood
> and ash
> fall at my feet.
>   But if conquered and overwhelmed,
> devoid of people,
> it no longer has a place on earth,
> what empire will this powerful,

29. See Paolo Fabbri, "Riflessioni teoriche sul teatro per musica nel Seicento: *La poetica toscana all'uso* di Giuseppe Gaetano Salvadori," in *Opera e libretto* (Florence: Olschki, 1990), 1:1–31.

30. Ibid.

unconquered arm
overthrow?
    God of thunder, make new worlds
or I shall wage war against the vast starry heavens.]

At the end of the seventeenth century this demand for perpetual irregularity can be seen as one of the oddest contrivances in music drama. Perrucci perceived in the opera of his day "such variety of arias, with diverse meters and verses," "composed with such variety of rhythms, meters, and rhymes that there are none left to be desired, nor invented."[31] In the following century, Padre Sacchi referred to the "writers of operas" as among those "who in seeking new meters knew no laws or bounds."[32]

Amid all this it should not be forgotten that apart from the meter itself and its strophic organization, the way the lines ended played an important part in the arias. This was never made theoretically explicit, but we can see that in practice that *sdrucciolo* endings were used to identify pastoral characters (following a convention that possibly makes a classical analogy with dactylic closes and had been sanctioned by Sannazaro's *Arcadia*) or else to characterize satyrs, demons, magical or monstrous beings, and even grotesque and comic ones. In some cases (*Sant'Alessio* by Rospigliosi and Landi, 1.2: "Se l'ore volano") they were also used "where haste, speed, and urgency are to be denoted," as Minturno had said, or for those characters "who suddenly act with haste or in anger," according to what can be read in Ruscelli.[33] For his part, the author of *Le nozze d'Enea in Lavinia*, set by Monteverdi, in an introductory *Lettera* to its relevant *Argomento e scenario* (Venice, 1640), declared: "And so to suit the characters and the emotions which they must express, I have used several verse meters, that is to say, I have given the *sdrucciolo* ones to low-born characters and short, *tronco* ones to those in anger."

More or less personal intentions apart, a *tronco* ending in poetry for music has nevertheless been of fundamental importance and has a long successful history in providing masculine cadences that efficiently bring periods or entire sections to a decisive conclusion. Awareness of this runs right through

31. Perrucci, *Dell'arte rappresentativa,* 92 and 101.

32. Sacchi, *Della divisione del tempo,* 180.

33. Cf. Silke Leopold, "'Quelle bazzicature poetiche, appellate arie': Dichtungsformen in der frühen italienischen Oper (1600–1640)," *Hamburger Jahrbuch für Musikwissenschaft* 3 (1978): 113–21. On the use of *sdrucciolo* lines, see also Wolfgang Osthoff, "Musica e versificazione: Funzioni del verso poetico nell'opera italiana," in *La drammaturgia musicale,* ed. Lorenzo Bianconi (Bologna: Il Mulino, 1986), 125–41; Wolfgang Osthoff, "Händels 'Largo' als Musik der goldenen Zeitalters," *Archiv für Musikwissenschaft* 30 (1973): 175–89; Silke Leopold, "Madrigali sulle egloghe sdrucciole di Iacopo Sannazaro: Struttura poetica e forma musicale," *Rivista italiana di musicologia* 14 (1979): 75–127; Lorenzo Bianconi, *Music in the Seventeenth Century,* trans. David Bryant (Cambridge: Cambridge University Press, 1987).

the history of the opera libretto from its very beginning. As early as the time of *Il corago* it was suggested that it was much better to seal an arietta "with a natural monosyllable or with a polysyllable in which the last syllable is stressed" (such as "pietà") rather than "using abbreviated or *tronco* words" (such as "ardor").[34] Castelli is even more explicit when he writes that he has formulated his verse with a preference for a *tronco* ending, "that is, 'la fenice del bello, la sincerità' in place of 'sinceritate' so that the final syllable 'tà' can be heard, which works very well in music, as do 'fa, fu, fo, sì, no, dà, do,' etc., the ends of which are found in all modern arias, approved by use and custom."[35] In the eighteenth century this custom became a norm, first for Martello (it is "very lovely to hear the line itself cut short, especially where the cadence should be")[36] and then for Quadrio:

[T]he ariettas better accommodate *tronco* rather than *piano* rhymes, whenever they are used judiciously, and utterly abhor *sdrucciolo* endings. The reason is because the voice rests on a stressed syllable more majestically and more harmonically than on a syllable that does not have a strong stress: ariettas should in consequence end mostly with a *tronco* line, so that the song concludes in a dignified manner.[37]

Padre Sacchi too later confirmed that "the perfect ending of music is always a strong beat, for when the vocal line ends on an upbeat, the listeners are left in suspense."[38]

4. RECITATIVE AND CAVATA

The strophic element (or, in any case, organization into stanzas), metric peculiarity, the rhyme, and even the endings of final lines—in sum, the whole literary basis of arias—encouraged composers to widen the distance that separated them from the free flow of blank verse, irregularly punctuated here and there by rhyming couplets whose principal value was as a literary cadence, which the concomitant harmonic cadence served to underline. In addition— from the early seventeenth century onward—the way the blank verse was delivered became much more rapid and simplified, with less rhythmic and melodic variety: rhythmically, one could have whatever resulted from the prevalent use of two types of adjacent durations (especially quarter note–

34. *Il corago,* 78.

35. Castelli, *La sincerità trionfante,* 53.

36. Pier Jacopo Martello, *Della tragedia antica e moderno: Dialogo* (Rome: Gonzaga, 1715), reprinted in modern times in his *Scritti critici e satirici,* ed. Hannibal S. Noce (Bari: Laterza, 1963), 189–316, quotation on 287.

37. Francesco Saverio Quadrio, *Della storia e della ragione d'ogni poesia* (Milan: Francesco Agnelli, 1742), vol. 2, pt. 2:337.

38. Sacchi, *Della divisione del tempo,* 156.

eighth note, eighth note–sixteenth note), with occasional rare prolongations. Melodically, a reduction in inflections and the range of intervals led toward patterns of repeated notes.

At the same time, opera librettos became increasingly verbose. The plots became more complicated and could not easily be developed with the modest eloquence of the original pastorals (with their abundance of rhyme and the division into periods generally contained within a distich). Instead, the new operas required more leisurely, broader dialogues, which consequently had now to be set with a more rapid hand. Doni himself in his day maintained that *stile recitativo* (or simply *recitativo*) "lingers very much on the same chords and has little melodic diversity," "in fact varying very little the pace of utterance heard in everyday speech." [39] With the obstacle removed of having to cadence too frequently, thanks to less clear-cut and short-breathed harmonic sequences, the composer could proceed with a less rigidly paratactic discourse. Articulated more broadly, even using parenthetic, secondary enjambments, the text was now able to sound more conversational, compared with the greater rigidity of previous patterns. For *Il corago* too, in recitative "the composer should not follow only the meter of the verse, but the sense, in such a way that he will be able to split verses deliberately if the sense of the work demands it and distribute the poet's words as if they were in prose." [40]

The move made by composers toward setting blank verse in this way was accompanied by much protesting about the tedium this sort of "recitative" generated (Vincenzo Giustiniani and Pietro Della Valle speak about it in their musical *Discorsi* of 1628 and 1640 respectively) [41] and by various proposals to mitigate this effect: by inserting arias and "half-arias" (Mazzocchi, in his *Catena d'Adone*, 1626) [42] and by using "diverse intervals, frequent ornamentation, changes where they are required, and such like," [43] to enhance the "variety and musical animation and charm" prompted by the "imagination, mood, figures, and meters" discovered by the poet. [44] Nevertheless, the recitative in Monteverdi's surviving Venetian operas is completely sui generis. Instead of trusting to rapid, pedantic declamation of all the blank-verse sections, Monteverdi often intervenes in the text, isolating important features (from a single element, such as a noun, an adjective, or a verb, to a more elaborate phrase) and lingering over them with descriptive figurations, repetitions, and progres-

---

39. Doni, *Lyra barberina: De' trattati di musica . . . tomo secondo*, pp. 27 and 26 of the appendix.

40. *Il corago*, 82.

41. See Solerti, *Le origini*, 122 and 155.

42. See Stuart Reiner, "'Vi sono molt'altre mezz'Arie . . . ,'" in *Studies in Music History: Essays for Oliver Strunk*, ed. Harold S. Powers (Princeton: Princeton University Press, 1968), 241–58.

43. Doni, *Trattato*, 27.   44. *Il corago*, 62.

sions which create little entities with their own musical sense and vivid representational imagery.[45] This constituted a negative feature for those who were
against any sort of analytical setting of the text (it was Doni's idea that "the
imitation of particular words has too much of the comic, indeed mimicry");[46]
but Monteverdi was drawing on his long and continuing work in madrigal
writing, which he again brilliantly reinvented for expressive purposes.

But this was certainly not the approach to a dramatic idiom in blank verse
that the Venetian composers disseminated and established together with their
model of production and spectacle. Let us look at the example given below
from *Gli amori d'Apollo e di Dafne* by Busenello and Cavalli (1640; ex. 2).
The predominant uniformity of the setting, which runs through the text without lingering on anything in particular and reduces any illustration of individual words to the minimum with the single goal of emphasizing the text in
declamation, is dominated by the ideal of rational, conversational musical eloquence, as mentioned above: it is the articulation of the syntax that dictates the
greater or lesser breadth of the phrase, makes the accentual impulses closer
together or further apart, together with the harmonic rhythm contained in the
basso continuo, and motivates the more or less decisive cadential choices, according to the demands of punctuation. Within this homogeneous texture,
closed episodes can blossom (in triple time but also in common time) and are
well defined with musical characteristics similar to some of those punctuating
the recitative style of so many scenes in Monteverdi. Although in some cases
these episodes were positioned with the intention of highlighting certain more
emotional points in the text, more often they served to emphasize a decisive
concluding line in a speech and thus had a more rhetorical than expressive
function.

This momentary departure from declamation in the course of blank verse
to give it, temporarily, the features of melody, harmony, and rhythmic periods more similar to those of the aria became a fairly widespread habit from
the middle of the seventeenth century onward. The example mentioned above
by Cavalli—a composer who made particular use of this feature in his operas
on texts by Faustini, that is between 1642 and 1652[47]—is one such. In operatic jargon these episodes were called cavate (arie cavate, to be precise), from
cavare, "to extract," in that they were almost extracted, or isolated, from the
more properly recitative context to highlight a certain passage in the text. The
term appears for the first time in the score of Boretti's *L'Ercole in Tebe* (1671,
2.3) during a recitative for Megara: some pages before, a similar passage, al-

45. See Paolo Fabbri, *Monteverdi,* trans. Tim Carter (Cambridge: Cambridge University
Press, 1994).

46. Doni, *Trattato,* 74.

47. See Thomas Walker, the "Cavalli" entry in *The New Grove Dictionary of Music and Musicians,* 6th ed., ed. Stanley Sadie (London: Macmillan, 1980), 4:24–34, esp. 29.

Ex. 2. Busenello–Cavalli, *Gli amori d'Apollo e di Dafne* (1640).

though much more limited, had been accompanied only by a tempo indication ("adagio"), to signify a request for a broader singing quality and a rhythmic sense distinct from the surrounding recitative.[48] Writing from Venice on 26 June 1673 to Giovanni Maria Pagliardi, who was to set to music his *Lisimaco*, Cristoforo Ivanovich made the suggestion that "if there be some emotion in the recitative that can be adapted into a cavata, do not neglect to do so, for some sudden prominence is pleasing."[49] Later, theoretical approval for these two possible treatments of blank verse can be read in the very first

48. A facsimile score of this work is published in Howard M. Brown and Eric Weimer, eds., *Italian Opera, 1640–1770: Major Unpublished Works in a Central Baroque and Early Classical Tradition* (New York: Garland, 1977–84), vol. 6.

49. The letter, later published in Cristoforo Ivanovich, *Poesie* (Venice: Ciotti, 1675), 372–74, can be read in Becker, *Quellentexte*.

treatise on Italian versification to allow space for the literary problems of dramatic texts for music, Giuseppe Gaetano Salvadori's *Poetica toscana all'uso:*

> In musical poetry the term recitative is used for everything made up of *piano* verses of seven or eleven syllables, because in such verse the sense is expressed in speech or recitation, but they always move forward in one manner in music, words are not repeated, and the music does not make much effort to set them. . . . Arie cavate are those that are extracted by the composer, the poet does not write them for this purpose. These consist of one complete line of eleven syllables, or two at most, when such a verse is at the end of some period . . . and words can be repeated, and elaborations made on them.[50]

One of the first eighteenth-century lexicographers, Johann Gottfried Walther, records this etymological, accepted meaning:

> Cavata (Ital.) is an *adjective,* which is used as a *noun,* with the omission of the same, and means 1) when the entire content of a long *recitative* is, as it were, concentrated into a very few words and *exposed* in such a way that (to make a distinction) it is necessary to place such *sententious* words after the bar and set them as an arioso.[51]

As these words confirm, apart from the adjective (cavata), at the end of the seventeenth century there was already increasing recourse to terms that used the noun (aria): Pasquini wrote the instruction "in aria," that is, "in the manner of an aria," in his *Idalma* (1680, 1.4), and "arioso" was also subsequently increasingly used.

However, it was not always particular lyrical outpourings or satisfyingly epigrammatic, firm cadences that suggested the possibility of creating a cavata to composers. Often it was the poet himself who clearly indicated it by inserting into the flow of blank verse some metrical eccentricities: a few *quinario* lines (Busenello does this in *Gli amori d'Apollo e di Dafne,* 1640, 2.4, and in *L'incoronazione di Poppea,* 1642, 1.1), *senari* (Minato's *Scipione Africano,* 1664, 1.12), an *ottonario* (Moniglia's *Ercole in Tebe,* 1661, 2.9). And it was not rare for the same cavata to appear several times in the course of the recitative, as a refrain or else at the beginning and end, like a ritornello. But these organizational principles of recitative, just like the spontaneous crystalliza-

50. Giuseppe Gaetano Salvadori, *Poetica toscana all'uso* (Naples: Gramignani, 1691), 72 and 75 (reprinted in Paolo Fabbri, "Riflessioni teoriche").

51. Johann Gottfried Walther, *Musicalisches Lexicon* (Leipzig: Deer, 1732; reprint, Kassel: Bärenreiter Verlag, 1953), 150. For the history of the terms "cavatina" and *cavata,* see Nino Pirrotta, "Falsirena e la più antica delle cavatine," in *Collectanea Historiae Musicae* (Florence: Olschki, 1956), 2:355–66; Wolfgang Osthoff, "Mozarts Cavatinen und ihre Tradition," in *Helmuth Osthoff zu seinem siebzigsten Geburtstag,* ed. Wilhelm Stauder, Ursula Aarburg, and Peter Cahn (Tutzing: Schneider, 1969), 139–77.

tion into arioso patterns for expressive or rhetorical purposes in the cavate, were still exceptions in a musical style that was generally fluid and unstructured or else dominated by a syntactic and morphological articulation of the poetic discourse. In any case, it should be noted that as early as the 1680s few cavate are to be found in opera scores, and in subsequent years they became rarer until finally they disappeared altogether.

5. FROM INTERPOLATIONS TO THE DA CAPO

This was happening just when the aria was undergoing the opposite process of growth in both dimensions and frequency. The most prevalent aria form in the seventeenth century, which could be called an aria with ballata strophes, was particularly affected, in that it ended with a refrain repeating the opening phrase, and its rhyme scheme links the last lines of the strophe with those— or the single one—of the refrain (in *L'Adelaide,* referred to above, thirty-one canzonets out of fifty-five take this form). Let us look at an example taken from *Gli equivoci nel sembiante* by Contini and Scarlatti (1679, 1.8):

Lasciami sola a piangere,	[Leave me alone to weep,
non v'è pietà per me:	there is no mercy for me;
o se vuoi dare aita	or if you want to assist
all'alma mia tradita,	my betrayed heart,
preparati a compiangere	then sympathize
la mia delusa fè.	with my betrayed trust.
Lasciami sola a piangere	Leave me alone to weep,
non v'è pietà per me.	there is no mercy for me.]

This sort of poetic and musical refrain is mostly found described as an *intercalare,* or recurring phrase,[52] but the term "ritornello" is also used, according to the description given at the end of the seventeenth century by Loreto Mattei:

Of the *intercalare,* or ritornello.

We have already put the finishing touches to the picture; it remains only to adorn it with the frame, as we may describe that lovely refinement which it is customary to call by the Latin term *intercalare,* and which we in the vernacular call ritornello. This is indeed like an all-embracing frame that crowns the strophe, link-

52. See Reinhard Strohm, *Italienische Opernarien des frühen Settecento* (1720–1730) (Cologne; Volk, 1976), 1:192ff. The use of the term is also documented in Pierfrancesco Tosi, *Opinioni de' cantori antichi e moderni* (Bologna: Dalla Volpe, 1723)—a modern edition is *La scuola di canto nell'epoca d'oro: Opinioni de' cantori antichi e moderni di Pier Francesco Tosi* (Bologna: Forni, 1968)—and in Quadrio, *Della storia e della ragione d'ogni poesia* (1744), vol. 3, pt. 2:444. A contemporary translation of Tosi is *Observations on the Florid Song; or, Sentiments on the Ancient and Modern Singers: Written in Italian by Pier. Francesco Tosi . . . translated into English by Mr. Galliard* (London: J. Wilcox, 1742).

ing the opening with the end by repeating the first verse at the close. And it is better when it contains some lovely phrase worthy of being repeated several times, so
that it imprints itself more easily on the mind. This figure of *intercalare* repetition
was practiced by the Romans, as in Virgil's eclogue "Ducite ad urbe domum, mea
carmina ducite Daphnim," and then by the early Tuscans, as in Boccaccio's ballate.
But the modern authors have given it such repute that in truth nothing more attractive and graceful can be desired in drama. It is achieved by repeating one or
two, and sometimes even three, of the first lines, on occasion even left unrhymed
and whose endings are then matched with the final rhymes of the strophe at its
close.[53]

Crescimbeni too (1698) was explicit in finding the model in the traditional
scheme of the ballata:

> The use of the ritornello in these arias is by no means a modern invention, in that
> the ritornello comes from the ballate sung in days gone by, which ended with a rep-
> etition from the beginning up to the first break, or part of the ballata, so that the
> last line rhymed with the one at which the above-mentioned break was made.[54]

It was the *intercalare* repeated cyclically "da capo" that underwent the
process of expansion mentioned above to the greatest extent and gradually
acquired its own melodic and harmonic individuality, thereby becoming an
increasingly independent section of the formal structure. Rather than figuring
as the necessary extension and completion of the poetic and musical discourse, as it had been up until that point, it started to stand out from the rest
of the strophe, breaking away from it to take a dominant, emblematic position that further increased the prominence given to the incipits of the arias,
due to the later seventeenth-century custom of setting them apart at the head
of the piece (almost like a motto, or a "Devise," as Hugo Riemann described
it at the beginning of the twentieth century). Such developments eventually
had visible repercussions both on the score and on the libretto, influencing
the overall layout of the verses of the arias. Strophic forms were now disappearing, and most arias came to be split up into two sections, generally asymmetric, but with the respective final lines rhyming, and conceptually independent, as recommended in Quadrio's example.[55] The need for unambiguous
cadences led to the extension of *tronco* endings to each of the two sections,
whose effectiveness for similar situations had been demonstrated according to
Planelli, among others: "The *tronco* line has particular force at the end of

53. Loreto Mattei, *Teorica del verso volgare e prattica di retta pronunzia* (Venice: Albrizzi,
1695), 78ff.
54. Giovanni Mario Crescimbeni, *L'istoria della volgar poesia*, 3d ed. (Venice: Basegio, 1731),
1:69.
55. See Quadrio, *Della storia e della ragione d'ogni poesia*, vol. 3, pt. 2:44.

each part of the arias, since its accent on the final syllable supports that part which would fall away languidly if it ended with a *piano* line." [56] In splitting the text of an aria in two (which the typesetter assisted when the libretto was printed, making the division immediately visible), the poet also observed quantitative criteria, determining the number of lines needed for the *intercalare* according to their length.[57]

> Every aria consists usually of two parts, although it can also have more. The customary lines of which it is made up are either complete or truncated or mixed, as best suits. . . . The number of lines that make up the first part of an arietta is open to choice and may be two, three, four, and even more, according to their dimensions, long or short. The second part may either match the first or be different. If it matches, it is often the case that the length and number of lines that make up the first part are repeated exactly in the second. It can otherwise be different, because the second part can have more verses than the first and can also have some of different lengths.[58]

At the same time, as the music became less subject to the text, the way was opened up for less restricted manipulations: apart from the proleptic isolation of the "Devise," mentioned above, echoes and sequential repetitions or else simple repetitions of words and more frequent (especially from around 1690) and expansive passages of vocalizing, sometimes in progressive sequences, tended to attenuate the metric and accent pattern of the musical setting. Textual redundancy, until then generally restricted to the final sections of ariettas repeated as a block, spread out to cover their entirety and entered the spiral of reiterations on different harmonic levels.

> It is a perpetual jig, sparkling and leaping without respite; the voice begins alone, then the instrument echoes the voice. This pattern, often on a bizarre melody, continues not only on all the chords of the key but also on all the alien ones, whether they match well or not, so that their pieces cover all the notes and change key continually and so that by the end one could not say to which one it belonged. After this long procedure, during which the same melody is repeated twenty times by both the voice and the instrument, they have to return da capo.[59]

56. Antonio Planelli, *Dell'opera in musica* (1772), ed. Francesco Degrada (Fiesole: Discanto, 1981), 35.

57. See Martello, *Scritti*, 287.

58. Quadrio, *Della storia e della ragione d'ogni poesia*, vol. 2, pt. 2:335. "Simple" arias, ones of a single strophe and as such suitable for inconclusive situations, were now known as *cavate*: "If it is wished to compose a simple canzonet, the wise and inventive composer can make it undemanding or without returning da capo, in the manner of an aria *cavata*." (ibid., vol. 3, pt. 2:442).

59. L. T., "Dissertation," *Mercure*, Nov. 1713, 14–16; quoted in Paul-Marie Masson, "Musique italienne et musique française: La première querelle," *Rivista musicale italiana* 19 (1912): 541.

For the vocalized "passaggi" the favorite location was the end of the *inter-calare,* where the chain of melismas was followed by a final repetition of the last verse, this time set syllabically: "On the final syllable of the last word, which often makes no sense, but where there will be some *a* or *o* which suits their merry passaggi, they set a 5- or 6-bar roulade, after which they repeat over again the last line 3 or 4 times, and on it goes for another quarter of an hour." [60] For those who asserted the primacy of poetry, this was just the latest of many musical abuses of the text: "And who ever saw someone in the course of normal conversation going on repeating and singing several times the same word, the same sentiment, as happens in ariettas?" lamented Muratori,[61] while even Marcello waxed ironical on the modern fashion for repetitions and the proliferation of vocalizing. Marcello recommended the poet to

> visit the maestro di cappella . . . and then give him in the arias very short *ritornelli* and *passaggi* (but preferably many repetitions of entire words), to render the poetry more enjoyable. . . . If proper names are included in the arias, such as *padre, impero, amore, arena, regno, beltà, lena, core,* etc., etc., *no, senza, già,* and other adverbs, the *modern* composer must set them to a long *passaggio:* for example, *paaaa . . . impeeee . . . amoooo . . . areeee . . . reeee . . . beltàaaa . . . lenaaaa . . . coooo . . .* etc., *noooo . . . seeeen . . . giàaaa . . .* etc. And this will avoid the *antico stile,* which did not employ *passaggi* on proper names or adverbs, but rather only on significant words such as *passione o moto, tormento, affanno, canto, volar, cader,* etc. etc. etc. . . . All the canzonettas must consist of the same things, that is extremely long *passaggi,* syncope, semitones, alterations of syllables, repetitions of meaningless words, such as *amore amore, impero impero, Europa, Europa, furori furori, orgoglio orgoglio,* etc. etc. etc.[62]

At the same time as its formal design was expanding, the aria was also establishing its definitive location at the end of a scene, immediately before the departure of each character: that is, at the climax of every dramatic segment, a strategic position for the performer's goal of achieving a personal success, in line with the phenomenon of the star singer.

These characteristics of the modern aria, founded on a simple harmonic syntax with openly functional relationships, had led to the creation of clear-cut formal schemes, already developed in the operas of the 1690s. First, there was the exposition of the *intercalare* in a fairly flowing, rapid manner, leading either to the dominant or the relative major and often ending with a vocalization on some accented syllable in the final line—a principal one, but it

60. The observation is by Lecerf (1705) and is quoted in Masson, "Musique italienne," 541.

61. Ludovico Antonio Muratori, *Della perfetta poesia italiana* (Modena: Soliani, 1706), ed. Ada Ruschioni, 2 vols. (Milan: Marzorati, 1971–72), 1:48.

62. Benedetto Marcello, *Il teatro alla moda* (Venice, 1720; reprint, Milan: Rizzoli, 1959), 29, 32–34. A complete English translation by Reinhard G. Pauly appears in *Musical Quarterly* 34 (1948): 371–403, and 35 (1949): 85–105.

could also be a secondary one. Then came a fairly extended reexposition of fragments already heard, with every greater manipulation of musical elements often inferred or derived from the initial material, or even merely related to and prompted by it. Instrumental "ritornellos" punctuated the separate sections of the aria, constituting a framework which made its division into parts based on distinct but not unrelated harmonic levels even more obvious. The more animated setting of the second stanza of the aria ended up making it a simple wandering harmonic diversion before returning to the desired repeat of the *intercalare*. The result of this was that of the two more or less equivalent sections into which the text was divided, that of the *intercalare* was heard at least four times in its entirety, with the addition of an unspecified number of greater and lesser repetitions which reached their climax in its second section, in which composers liked to "parade, so to speak, their idea through all levels of counterpoint and modulation." [63] According to Saverio Mattei, this was rhetorical bombast, the equivalent of the arguments with which a fine orator backs up his thoughts and persuades his listeners.[64] To gain an idea of the casualness with which the composer treated his literary basis and bent it to the needs of a now fully emancipated musical language, see Mattei's description of an aria by Metastasio (from *Alessandro nell'Indie*, 1.2) as set by an unspecified composer.

Let us open a volume of music at random: we read the words of an aria, let it be that of Poro to Alessandro:

> Vedrai con tuo periglio
> di questo acciaro il lampo,
> come baleni in campo
> sul ciglio al donator.

Now let's look at what the maestro di cappella has done with it: "Vedrai, vedrai, vedrai con tuo periglio, Di questo acciaro, acciaro il lampo" (ten bars of gurgling on this "lampo") "Come, come baleni in campo Sul ciglio, sul ciglio al donator. Vedrai con tuo periglio Di questo acciaro il lampo Come baleni" (ten more bars of passaggi on that "baleni") "Sul ciglio al donator Come baleni in campo Di questo acciaro il lampo Sul ciglio, sul ciglio al donator." Did we perhaps think that it had finished? With this vehicle we have come from the key of F to the key of C; now we have to take a return carriage to come back once again by the same route to C.

---

63. [Giuseppe Riva], *Avviso ai compositori ed ai cantanti* (London: Edlin, 1728); edition with commentary in Francesco Degrada, "Una minuscola poetica del melodramma tra Barocco e Arcadia" (1967), in his *Il palazzo incantato: Studi sulla tradizione del melodramma dal Barocco al Romanticismo* (Fiesole: Discanto, 1979), 1:27–39, quotation on 33.

64. Saverio Mattei, "La filosofia della musica, o sia La musica de' salmi: Dissertazione," in his *I libri poetici della Bibbia tradotti dall'ebraico originale, ed adattati al gusto della poesia italiana*, (Naples: Porcelli, 1779), 5:300.

Here is how it resumes: "Vedrai, vedrai con tuo periglio, vedrai di questo acciaro il lampo, Vedrai, Come baleni" (here we break into a gallop with hundreds of sixteenth-note arpeggios) "Sul ciglio al donator, con tuo periglio, vedrai il lampo" (here we do not run but fly on the wings of other gurgling notes) "come baleni, baleni in campo, sul ciglio, Sul ciglio al donator." And then? And then the horses, exhausted by their long gallop, throw themselves down on the ground, and in general silence we have the cadenza, wasting a quarter of an hour on the *a* of "donator" to satisfy the inane singer. But at last we get on our way again, and will the singer stay down? Not at all. The singer rises up again like Antaeus, sings a few notes of a second section (which errs in the opposite direction in its excessive brevity), which serves as a breather, and then returns valorously to the race, not to go forward but to turn back again twice more with that "Vedrai, vedrai," since the first part must be repeated. And while Poro is enjoying himself in this way, Alessandro, with the patience of Job, stands onstage to listen and see where this highly impertinent coming and going is to end. Is this music? Is it for this that people go to the theater? Did all those Greek philosophers provide the laws of music to create these trifles?

It is not that I am saying that nothing should be repeated, because that would be impossible in music, but since the customary number of repetitions in poetry and oratory is two, let us allow music four, but not a hundred, not everywhere, and not where it is unrealistic.[65]

In becoming song, the text underwent such manipulation and shuffling as to render it metrically unrecognizable in practice.

For some time now composers have invented an art that in terms of extravagance yields nothing to those mentioned above. This is to turn poetry into prose, transposing the words at a whim, breaking and confusing the meter and ruining the sense, and, when they cannot do further injury to the arias, they slap in a *sì* or a *no*, equally harmful to the sense and the meter as those impertinent transpositions.[66]

"And then those repetitions and jumbling of the words done purely for the sake of the music and which make no sense whatsoever, there are no words to convey how intolerable they are to the listener," wrote Algarotti,[67] while

---

65. Ibid., 306ff.

66. Vincenzio Martinelli, *Lettere familiari e critiche* (London: Nourse, 1758), 372.

67. Francesco Algarotti, *Saggio sopra l'opera in musica* (Livorno: Coltellini, 1763), 35. Extracts in English appear in Strunk, *Source Readings*, 909–22. In a letter of 1769 Jommelli lamented, in the opposite sense but in the same general direction, the narrow confines into which current literary conventions squeezed the composer, warning the librettist Gaetano Martinelli (who was to prepare for him a "new *serio-buffo* libretto") to avoid "the usual dry, arid rubric, or measure of the ariettas. Those eternal 4 verses per part, in every aria, and always at most 7 or 8 feet each; and what is worse, that repetition, in such a small number of verses, of the same words, as if the poet had to buy them at the market and pay a high price: as, for example, the lovely arietta, or cavatina, by Metastasio himself in *Nitteti* 'Povero cor, tu palpiti, / né a torto in questo dì / tu

Mattei deplored "the surpassingly meek and enfeebled cantabile, too full of passaggi, which loses sight of the meter." [68] And Planelli, complaining of "our composers who with a disordered repetition of the same words make the briefest of arias into an immensely long rigmarole," [69] added: "The composer must take care to retain the number of syllables and rhythm of the verse. There are composers who destroy every trace of the verse in the poetry so completely that it becomes pure and simple prose: and so their music destroys, instead of making the most of, the poetic line." [70]

As if this were not enough, as Martinelli had pointed out, those convenient, intrusive (generally) monosyllables (*sì, no,* interjections, and the like) that composers slipped in arbitrarily for their own musical needs also contributed to blurring the original metrical plan. "The composer should, much more, avoid adding from his own head insignificant little words. The audience does not care to hear the maestro di cappella play the poet. Such additions destroy the measure of the verses," noted Planelli.[71] The mannerism, which Mozart was to exploit wittily in a short duet in *Le nozze di Figaro* (3.2), was satirized in Calzabigi's *Opera seria* (2.6), together with the unscrupulous manner in which composers had become accustomed to moving the text around for their own pleasure.

RITORNELLO

　E viva il sior maestro!

DELIRIO

　　　　　　Ella mi scusi:
　qui fa a' calci la musica
　colle parole. Dica: perché replica
　que' sì, que' no? Perché a rovescio alloga
　l'una e l'altra particola?

SOSPIRO

　Non rispondo a una critica ridicola.

[RITORNELLO

　Hurrah for the composer!

---

palpiti così, / povero core.' See the economy of words. The 3rd and 4th lines are made up entirely of the words of the first. Certainly it is lovely, very lovely to read, but not so suitable for setting to music. If the poet is so keen to sing, very little indeed is left to the poor composer." The passage is quoted in Marita McClymonds, *Niccolò Jommelli: The Last Years, 1769–1774* (Ann Arbor, Mich.: UMI Research Press, 1980), 488ff.

68. Letter from Saverio Mattei to Metastasio, sent from Naples on 10 June 1770, printed in his *Libri poetici della Bibbia* (Naples: Stamperia Simoniana, 1773), 2:220.

69. Planelli, *Dell'opera in musica,* 77.

70. Ibid., 75ff.　　　　　　　　　　71. Ibid., 77.

DELIRIUM
                                        With your permission:
here the music clashes
with the words. Tell me, why repeat
these yeses and nos? Why
swap them round?

SIGH
I do not answer ridiculous criticism.]

6. OPERA IN ITS CLASSICAL PHASE: METASTASIO

Such a high level of verbal repetition, aggravated by the intrusion of extrane-
ous elements and above all by the progressive transformation in the relationship between text and music that became fully clear at the end of the seventeenth century (departure from syllabic setting, use of more varied and flexible
rhythms, increasing vocalization), deprived the old polymetric aria especially,
with its continually shifting accents, which had formerly been so important
in inspiring the composer's rhythmic and melodic invention, of significance.
This coincided with the propensity to regularization of certain librettists who
were more attuned to the classical poets: among all the illogical conventions
of opera, they must have found particularly intolerable those accumulations
of the most varied patterns of stress in a single short strophe. In Apostolo
Zeno's *Lucio Vero* (1700) and *Alessandro Severo* (1716), for example, most
of the arias are isometric: many of the others are only apparently in a mixture of meters, given that it is possible to rewrite them in much more regular
form. To take the *intercalare* in one of Giulia's arias in this last opera (1.3:
"Sdegno, / ingegno, / affetti, / inganni, / tutti a' danni / io vi voglio / di una
perfida beltà") as an example, the seven mostly different lines can easily be
turned into a periodic series of three *ottonari*, the final one of which is *tronco*.
In similar cases it almost seems as if the poet wished to pay superficial homage to long-standing habits while actually revealing between the lines—or,
rather, with their realignment—the tendency toward a more "tragic" and dis-
ciplined style of theater which was starting to be forcefully advocated at the
end of the seventeenth and beginning of the eighteenth centuries in the literary surroundings of the Arcadian Academy. But where the poetic combinations are resolutely polymetric, there is a preference for mixtures of the least
mutually unrelated verse types as possible (as Loreto Mattei had recommended in his *Teorica del verso volgare* of 1695) using principally the main
ingredients of the *endecasillabo (settenario* and *quinario),* which, dislocated
into vertical sequences when placed in line, make up the greater line length
(*Alessandro Severo,* 1.9: "Dirò . . . la madre . . . il foglio, / dal talamo . . . dal
soglio . . . / ah, dirti non poss'io, / se non che sei 'l cor mio, / dolce mia sposa.
/ Madre crudel, / perché volermi tôr / moglie tanto fedel, / tanto amorosa?"

with three examples in verses 4–5, 8–9, and 6–7, the last with, unusually, the *quinario* first).

In the 1720s this was the point of departure for Metastasio too, an ever more resolute advocate of the aria in a single meter, with the single exception of the combination of a *settenario* and *quinario* (*ottonario* and *quadrisillabo* are found only in his early *Giustino* of 1712 and in what is, however, a doubtful case, *Didone abbandonata*, 1724, 3.8).[72] Of the twenty-five arias, more or less, in a Metastasio opera, generally two or three mix the two meters. It is usual for a *quinario piano* to close a strophe of only *settenari*, thus breaking the rule of a *tronco* close (which can, however, be restored by the composer by using appoggiaturas in *tronco settenari* and by shifting the accent in *piano* ones; see, for example, Aristea's aria "Caro, son tua così" in Caldara's *L'Olimpiade*, 1733, 3.2): two *tronco* lines, generally a couplet, precede the *quinario*, and at the opening there is more often one *piano* or possibly *tronco*, or very rarely *sdrucciolo* (*Ezio*, 2.10; *Antigono*, 1.11; *La Nitteti*, 2.1, see n. 67). It is very rare, however, for there to be metrical schemes where the *quinario* does not in practice join a *settenario tronco*. The *intercalare* in Demetrio's aria in *Antigono* (3.6) has three *piano settenari*, the last of which, however, can make an elision with the following *quinario*, while in Eurinome's aria in *Issipile* (2.1) the *quinario* is in the opening position, which I have described as exceptional, but does not flow into the *settenario piano* that follows it, and so there is no resulting *endecasillabo*.

Although he was Metastasio's necessary forerunner, Zeno was generally thought to lack "a certain natural quality, beauty and, in the end, that ear for harmony and music so necessary, especially for the lyric theater and for selection and combination of meters," while in contrast, in Metastasio works, "the choice of meters, their layout, and harmony enchants and enthralls:"[73]

> Zeno himself, . . . who brought a regular form to opera, was harsh and irregular in his arias, often coupling verses of different structures, unequal meters, and with the stresses placed so variously that the music could find no fluid, continuous theme to fit to them. For example, what regular melody could the composer find for Ambleto's aria "Teneri sguardi, / vezzi bugiardi, / già mi preparo a fingere, / anima mia, per te?" where the first and second lines have nothing in common with the meter of the following two . . . ?[74]

72. For an account of Metastasio's metrics, the reader is referred to Bruno Brizi, "Metrica e musica verbale nella poesia teatrale di P. Metastasio," *Atti dell'Istituto Veneto di Scienze, Lettere ed Arti* 131 (1972–73): 679–740, and the review of Brizi's article by Franco Gavazzeni in *Metrica* 1 (1978): 320–23.

73. Saverio Mattei, *Saggio di poesie latine ed italiane, colla Dissertazione del nuovo sistema d'interpretare i tragici greci* (Naples: Porcelli, 1780), 198ff.

74. Saverio Mattei, *Memorie per servire alla vita del Metastasio* (1785; reprint, Bologna: Forni, 1987), quoted in Elvidio Surian, "Metastasio, i nuovi cantanti, il nuovo stile: verso il clas-

Calzabigi too, taking his cue from the following aria in Zeno's *Sisara:*

Non amo una vita	[I do not love a life
dolente e romita,	of sorrow and loneliness,
costretto a piangere	forced to weep
de' patrii altari,	over the destruction
de' miei più cari	of the altars of my homeland
l'ultima sorte.	and of those I hold most dear.
In sì gravi angosce e pene,	In such terrible anguish and torment
quella che viene	the worst,
più lenta e tarda	most cruel death
è la più barbara,	is the one
la peggior morte.	which comes most slowly.]

made a comparison between the regular quality of Metastasio's writing and some of his predecessor's uneven strophes:

> Music was not yet tied to a continuous flow of melody before Metastasio imposed a regularity on the poetic text which showed composers melodic continuity. There was little difference between the recitative and the music of the madrigals, which used to be so highly regarded. The first two lines of this aria have nothing in common with those following, and the first line of the second part is more irregular. The supreme regularity of Metastasio has caused a different defect in composers today, that is, monotony, but it is not necessary to place a fish's tail on a human head to avoid this.[75]

Similarly, in an aria from *Il Daniello* "the first line, 'Più di leon feroce,' has two syllables more than all the rest," and so "how can the composer's theme for the *settenario* verse fit the *quinari* verses? There can be no theme: the result will be a gradual, not an aria."[76]

After Metastasio the isometric aria became more or less stable. The "use of verses in a single meter" by "modern opera composers"[77] became a rule, according to which, for example, Goldoni in 1735 rewrote for Vivaldi one of the arias from Zeno's *Griselda* (1701):[78]

---

sicismo: Osservazioni sull'*Artaserse* (Venezia 1730) di Hasse," in *Venezia e il melodramma nel Settecento*, ed. Maria Teresa Muraro (Florence: Olschki, 1978), 344ff.

75. Quoted in Remo Giazotti, *Poesia melodrammatica e pensiero critico nel Settecento* (Turin: Bocca, 1952), 91.

76. Ibid.

77. Sacchi, *Della divisione del tempo,* 161.

78. See Franco Fido, "Le tre 'Griselde': Appunti su Goldoni librettista di Vivaldi," in *Antonio Vivaldi: Teatro musicale, cultura e società,* ed. Lorenzo Bianconi and Giovanni Morelli (Florence: Olschki, 1982), 2:345–63; quotation on 354. The reader is referred to this essay for a more detailed comparison of the rewriting of Zeno's text and for the relevant bibliography.

ZENO (2.13)

  Vorresti col tuo pianto
in me destar pietà,
ma nasce il mio piacer dal tuo dolore.
  Il fato
spietato
con la sua crudeltà
serve il mio core.

GOLDONI (2.11)

  Tu vorresti col tuo pianto,
co' sospiri aver il vanto
di svegliare in me pietà.
  L'alma tua mentre sospira,
emendar del fato l'ira
col suo duolo ancor non sa.

Quite apart from being overwhelmingly isometric or at most a homogeneous combination of a *settenario* and a *quinario*, all the while maintaining a mostly asymmetric rhyme scheme, the two strophes of the Metastasio aria tended to level out over time, each one gradually containing the same number of lines as the other. In the operas of his Italian period (from *Didone abbandonata* to *Artaserse*, 1724–30), arias with two unequal stanzas number between a third and less than half of those with equal ones. Subsequently, the proportion of equal to unequal stanzas saw a rapid increase in the operas between *Issipile* (1732) and *Achille in Sciro* (1736), ranging between 7 to 1 and 12 to 1. Finally, the works of the period from *Temistocle* (1736) to *Ruggiero* (1771) contain one or two examples of the unequal type at most, or none at all.

    The meters that appear in them are, in order of frequency, the *settenario* followed by the *ottonario* and, further down the scale, *senario, quinario,* and *decasillbo;* they are laid out as two stanzas, generally of four lines (sometimes three in the case of the *decasillabo* because of its greater length), but initially also with irregular schemes such as, for example, 3 + 4 or 5 + 4 or vice versa for a *settenario* and 3 + 4 or vice versa for the *decasillabo;* for the (shorter) *quinario* and *senario* there is also the possibility of a six-line stanza.[79] But as has been pointed out, in this as well a perfect balance tends to prevail, with a general preference for a double tetrastich or at most a double tristich. Martello had already set out these meters and recommended their use in arias, but he gave considerable preference to the *ottonario* (a meter he favored for its "greater resonance") and then the *settenario, senario, quinario,* and *decasillbo.*[80]

    As for Padre Sacchi, he referred to the favor "principally among dramatic poets who write for music" enjoyed by "three-foot anapestic lines," of the *decasillabo* type in the aria "Quel destrier, che all'albergo è vicino," because of the resonance of the "triple rhythm" of an anapest and dactyl, "to which the ear is very sensitive and yet in some way . . . skips along."[81] This led the com-

79. See B. Brizi, *Metrica e musica verbale,* 689–700, which also examines Metastasio's nonoperatic work, but only up to 1740.

80. See Martello, *Scritti,* 287–89. These aspects are all covered in Quadrio, *Della storia e della ragione d'ogni poesia,* vol. 3, pt. 2:444.

81. Sacchi, *Della divisione del tempo,* 146 and 155ff.

poser often to model his phrases as repeated figures with this characteristic, as can be seen in the aria for Arsace in Sarro's opera of the same name (1718, 2.11), Leone's aria in Gasparini's *Bajazet* (1719, 3.2), and Argene's aria in Caldara's *L'Olimpiade* (1733, 3.4). The *settenario* made a contrast with this because of the flexible way its shifting accent could be manipulated, although it was "very noble and easily adaptable to different subjects: if the rule of stress is observed exactly, it should be harmonious and very pleasant to hear; so the ariettas of the famous Metastasio are of the utmost sweetness." [82]

What Padre Sacchi has to say also reflects an expressive poetics that, although unspecified, associated certain meters with certain emotions. As early as 1695 Loreto Mattei found that an anapestic *decasillabo* was, "because of its fluidity, very suitable for expressing cheerful themes," and he similarly considered the dactylic *senario* "suitable for cheerful themes"; in contrast, a trochaic *senario* "is for pathetic subjects." [83] "Anger is better, in fact almost solely expressed in its greatest fearfulness, in a line of ten syllables, especially if you make it *sdrucciolo*," wrote Martello, who further considered the *quinario sdrucciolo* perfect for "the languor of love" and the "feeble state of a soul abandoning itself to it," while the remainder could be used for "every kind of passion less strong than anger." [84] Apart from making Martello's words his own, Quadrio adds:

> For example, if the sentiment is joyful, lively, cheerful, the *decasillabo* will be ideally suited for fashioning [an arietta].
>
> Similarly, frightening and ruinous things come across marvelously in this sort of verse. A line of six syllables lends itself wonderfully to ideas that are all delicacy, modesty, sweetness, and tenderness. ... A *quinario sdrucciolo* is also perfectly suited to the same effects and depicts the feeble state of a soul abandoned to the languor of love especially well. ... The other meters are less specific than those mentioned above and can, with care, be used for every sort of passion less strong than anger.[85]

Arteaga too aligns himself, although more generally, with these dictates, advising that the "singular dexterity" of Metastasio be taken as a model in adapting "the various meters to the various passions, making use of short lines in affections that express languor, when the soul is prostrate, so to speak, and lacks the strength to escape the emotion. ... Full, rapid, and fluid lines where courage is expressed 'Fiamma ignota nell'alma mi scende' ... and so on." [86] For Planelli, on the other hand, a distinction must be made between

82. Ibid., 135.
83. L. Mattei, *Teorica del verso volgare,* 41 and 46ff.
84. See n. 80.
85. Quadrio, *Della storia e della ragione d'ogni poesia,* vol. 2, pt. 2:335, and vol. 3, pt. 2:445ff.
86. Arteaga, *Le rivoluzioni del teatro,* 1:337ff.

"fast" and "slow lines," depending on whether or not they have "two short syllables together," as in lines made up predominantly of dactyls (but also ana-pests, it is inferred). Planelli makes much of the type of accents in a line, more than their length (like the resonance of Sacchi's "triple rhythm"), judging the "fast" ones to be effective for "expressing impulsive, clamorous emotions," and "slow" ones to be ideal for those that "depress and lower the spirit, these being sadness, tenderness, and the like." [87]

What can be deduced from Metastasio as far as choice of meter is con-cerned is a tendency to uniformity and at the same time to balancing the two strophes of an aria. While they are always in the majority, arias in *settenari* or—fewer—in *ottonari* are noticeably predominant in the period between 1724 and 1740: there are between a half and a third as many arias in all the other meters combined as in *settenari* and *ottonari*, although there are more evenly balanced examples between 1726 and 1728 *(Siroe, Catone in Utica, Ezio)* and again between 1733 and 1736 *(L'Olimpiade, Demofoonte, Achille in Sciro)*. But from 1744 onward, the supremacy of the dominant meters is no longer opposed, and the proportions go from a minimum of 3 to 1 to as high as 9 to 1.

All together, there is a marked tendency to reduce the number of metrical types: apart from the *settenario* and *ottonario*, and not forgetting the pairing of *settenario* and *quinario*, there are on average three or four other metrical schemes in use in every opera before 1744, but later these are reduced to two or three, and the predominance of those that were already in the majority is further accentuated.

Finally, the total supremacy of the two-strophe aria in Metastasio's operas should be borne in mind: as has been described, the first of these is repeated "da capo" and is almost always positioned immediately before the character leaves the stage. The exceptions to this are a couple of entrance arias *(Issip-ile, 2.9; Il trionfo di Clelia, 2.2)* and an intermediate one *(Demofoonte, 1.5)* where the singer is prevented from departing, as he would wish, only by events. The occasional ariettas that are incomplete because of some incident onstage *(Ciro riconosciuto, 1.8; Ipermestra, 3.8; Antigono, 3.7; L'eroe ci-nese, 3.1)* are no more than a variant on the prevailing scheme. There are only rare cases of ariettas with a single strophe—now known as cavate, as we have already seen from Quadro (see n. 58)—whether opening or closing *(Didone abbandonata, 1.2 and 3.8; Alessandro nelle Indie, 1.6; Artaserse, 3.1; Achille in Sciro, 1.8; Il re pastore, 1.1)*. Multistrophic arias are extremely rare: they are actually to be found only in *Didone abbandonata* (1.17: four tercets of *settenari*), *Artaserse* (1.14: three quatrains of *settenari*), and *L'Olimpiade* (2.10: three quatrains of *senari*). In tribute to the spread of the standard two-strophe form, the first of which is to be repeated, Vinci, in his *Didone abban-*

87. Planelli, *Dell'opera in musica,* 35–37.

donata (1726), made the aria in act 1, scene 17, a normal da capo one, using the first two strophes as the *intercalare* and the others as the middle section. Megacle's aria in *L'Olimpiade* ("Se cerca, se dice") was given the customary shape by both Leo (1737) and Traetta (1767), but with an *intercalare* of two strophes, which the latter composer shortened in the repeat. On the other hand, Galuppi (1747) for once omitted the da capo, while both Pergolesi (1735) and, especially, Caldara (1733) had previously made versions more freely inspired by the prevailing scheme: the former by using an *intercalare* of two strophes plus a coda with a reexposition of the third; the latter (who worked directly with Metastasio in Vienna, it should be remembered) actually tended decidedly toward through-composition.

Ensembles are equally rare and are mostly limited to a short final chorus of praise or judgment, frequently in two strophes of *ottonari* (if others appear during the course of the opera, as happens particularly between 1733 and 1736, they have more strophes and also a refrain), or to a duet usually placed at the end of act 2 or—more rarely—act 1, divided into chains of strophes of a varied number of lines but metrically homogeneous; single lines or hemistiches passed between the two characters, or sung together, are also possible. Such duets could also use the da capo scheme, as Caldara does with "Ne' giorni tuoi felici" at the end of act 1 of *L'Olimpiade,* where the central section is the last strophe of Metastasio's text, all set for both voices and followed by a repeat of the first part. From *Antigono* onward (1743–44) a further ensemble was added to these: a second duet (*Il re pastore:* one at the end of each of the first two acts), a trio (*Nitteti,* 2.12), and an ensemble scene as a finale *(Antigono, Il trionfo di Clelia, Romolo ed Ersilia).*

7. THE ANTI-METASTASIO OPPOSITION AND COMIC OPERA

The great development of the aria between the seventeenth and eighteenth centuries had jeopardized even more any chance of patching over the break between aria and recitative, now much more noticeable because of the simultaneous deterioration of some of recitative's own tendencies, which became increasingly evident in the new century: a more limited bass with more schematic harmonies and increasing rigidity of cadential formulas, as the tonal system and its functional supports fell into place; the "prosody" of blank-verse text reproduced concisely in a casual, "speaking" vocal style; the disappearance of the cavata (the new accompanied recitative was something different; even if accompanied by the orchestra, it was still recitative); and stereotyped melodic shapes, particularly apparent in certain rhetorical situations (in questions, for example, the fall and then rise of the voice, and in cadences a descending fourth leap, or the more pathos-laden descent by step with an appoggiatura, marked in example 3 with *).[88]

88. See Edward O. D. Downes, "Secco Recitative in Early Classical *Opera Seria* (1720–80),"

Ex. 3. Metastasio–Piccinni, *Artaserse* (1768).

At the beginning of the new century, in 1702, Raguenet had already noticed this contemporary Italian psalmodic approach to recitative, "which is
too simple and unvaried; it's the same throughout and can't properly be called
singing. Their recitative is little better than downright speaking, with hardly
any inflection or modulation of the voice." Nevertheless he appreciated the
effectiveness of its accompaniment.[89] Later in the eighteenth century, the schematic, functional quality of its punctuation was to come out even more, as
demonstrated by the delay of the cadence in the bass, with respect to the voice,

Journal of the American Musicological Society 14 (1961): 50–69; Frederick Neumann, "The Appoggiatura in Mozart's Recitative," *Journal of the American Musicological Society* 35 (1982):
115–37.

89. François Raguenet, *A Comparison between the French and Italian Music and Opera*,
trans. Oliver Strunk, in *Musical Quarterly* 32 (1946): 411–36, quotation on 425.

Ex. 4.   Metastasio–Hasse, *Artaserse* (1730 and 1762).

almost like an echo. It can be seen in a fragment from *Artaserse,* set by Hasse
in 1730 for Venice and then in 1762 for Naples (see example 4).[90]

The gulf thus created between recitative and aria made the passage from
the musical dominance of blank verse to that of closed strophes for individual display and the few ensemble pieces feel even more uncomfortable: the
same effect as if "in the middle of walking, one suddenly started leaping and
prancing." [91] The remedy would have been to rethink from scratch the whole
question of dramatic writing for music, something that not even the most convinced reformers of Italian opera did, restricting themselves to lessening the
difference with more frequent (sometimes exclusive) use of the obbligato, or
accompanied recitative variant. It was more the two-strophe da capo aria
that was involved in their reforming plans, as it was coupled with or largely
replaced by more varied structures: single-strophe cavate, arias with several
strophes, and stanzas with more lines, sometimes set out in rondo pattern.
(Only Mozart, in *Don Giovanni,* to enliven Donna Elvira's entrance aria, "Ah
chi mi dice mai," 1.5, did not hesitate to insert fragments of the subsequent
dialogue between Don Giovanni and Leporello in the gaps in the aria, dialogue originally intended as recitative but here transformed almost into interjections for subsidiary characters.) In the Calzabigi and Gluck *Orfeo ed
Euridice,* which marks a departure from Metastasian opera in the choices of
meter also, one can see a representative collection of such alternatives, both
in individual pieces and as a whole, the result of variety and multiplicity being pursued with an energy equal to and in contrast with the formal mono-

90. See Sven H. Hansell, "The Cadence in 18th-Century Recitative," *Musical Quarterly* 54
(1968): 228–48; Winton Dean, "The Performance of Recitative in Late Baroque Opera," *Music
and Letters* 58 (1977): 389–402.

91. E. Arteaga, *Le rivoluzioni del teatro,* 2:107–9 and 112ff. See also ibid., 1:48–50.

chrome nature Metastasio's works. A summary of points of nonrecitative can confirm this.

Act 1

- Chorus, "Ah! se intorno a quest'urna funesta": two quatrains *(abba)* of austere *decasillabi* punctuated by the metrically extravagant invocations of Orfeo, the first of which is repeated da capo further on, but with a different conclusion.
- Strophic aria for Orfeo, "Chiamo il mio ben così": in three fragments separated from his recitatives, each of which is made up of a sort of cavatina which uses two tercets and a pair of *tronco settenari*, ending with a *quinario piano*.
- Aria for Amore, "Gli sguardi trattieni": two strophes of five *senari (ababc' dedec',* where the apostrophe marks a *tronco* ending), in two parts (it could be said) almost like a double cavatina.

Act 2

- Chorus of demons, "Chi mai dell'Erebo": in strophes of five *sdrucciolo quinari* with the final one *tronco,* interrupted by three quatrains *(abbc)* of Orfeo's *tronco* and *piano ottonari* ("Deh placatevi con me") treated unstrophically; the metrical count of the first includes a comment from the chorus.
- Elysian chorus, "Vieni a' regni del riposo": tercets of *ottonari aab'-ccb'* and *dxy'-dxy',* strophic in pairs and separated by recitative for Orfeo.

Act 3

- Duet for Orfeo and Euridice, "Vieni, appaga il tuo consorte": in *ottonari.*
- Aria for Euridice, "Che fiero momento!" with a truncated da capo, in two quatrains of *senari abbc'-axyc',* but with the central section also involving Orfeo in duet, for which two similar strophes are used.
- Aria for Orfeo, "Che farò senza Euridice": one quatrain plus one tercet of *ottonari* treated in rondeau fashion, with the first distich transformed into a refrain framing the remainder.
- Final celebratory chorus in double *quinari.*

Even for Saverio Mattei, Metastasio's metrical regularity, which had initially made such a positive contribution to the theater and music, had, in the long run, the negative effect of imposing such uniformity that all capacity for dramatic communication was lost. To avoid this, he hoped again for greater metrical variety but did not put his trust in such structures as the cavatina, with its small number of lines equally prey to the same vice of interminable verbal repetitions. In *Ifigenia in Tauride* (1763), for the "development" of Oreste's cavatina "Oh Dio, dov'è la morte" (1.6), Traetta even found it necessary to use some lines from the preceding recitative. Mattei thought instead of the possibility that poets could write more expansive strophes for composers, with a

greater variety of lines to be used for those repetitions of figures, parts of
phrases, or entire musical periods essential to musical discourse, or even strophic structures in which a musical repetition such as a da capo would not necessarily involve repeating a section already heard.

> Composers ought not to be so pitifully stilted and should explore new paths; and
> poets ought to help them in this by introducing new meters or at least different
> combinations; and while Metastasio may have chosen the best, and the ones he
> avoided are the less pleasant, that should not stand in the way of some occasional
> cautious variation or at least the lengthening of the strophes of seven or eight lines
> in the arias or making the arias with more strophes, in such a way that composers
> would not be constricted. There are examples in Metastasio himself, such as "Se
> cerca, se dice," "Tradita, sprezzata," "Dimmi che un empio sei." In his first operas
> he was more liberal, as can be seen in *Semiramide* especially; then he became more
> sparing, and has almost restricted himself to a more regular metrical style. . . . Be-
> sides, since we desire more music in our arias than did our forefathers, this prob-
> lem can be cured rather by expanding the poetry and giving the arias more stro-
> phes. This is why the music in the popular theater [*teatrini*] is generally more lifelike,
> because the arias are long and there are so many finales, which are sorts of duets,
> trios, and quartets with many strophes, and the composers are not obliged to re-
> peat the same words so often. So this system should be introduced gradually into
> the superior theater [*gran teatro*] too.[92]

So the area where Mattei suggested new poetic and musical models could
be found was that of comic opera. This occupied a lower position in the aesthetic hierarchy of the day but was a genre that had seen several decades'
worth of interesting experiments, some of the results of which had been imported into opera seria: action arias, ensemble pieces, musical numbers divided into several movements.

Apart from the use of *sdrucciolo* lines in some arias, which has been mentioned, there were not many specifically comic mannerisms in eighteenth-
century opera: in recitative there was an intermittent use of the more char-
acterful variants of the *settenario* and *endecasillabo,* that is, the *tronco* and
sdrucciolo ones (which appear in brief sequences in *Idalma,* 2.14, and previously in *Ercole in Tebe* by Moniglia and Melani, 2.10), and of the hyperme-
ters generated by the effects of laughter, yawning, and particularly stammer-
ing, which had been so widespread in early Venetian opera of the 1640s (see,
for example, Orcone's stuttering in *Il Tigrane* by Lalli and Scarlatti, 1715;
Flacco's yawning in *La caduta de' decemviri* by Stampiglia and Scarlatti, 1697;

---

92. S. Mattei, "La filosofia," 306ff. and 310. On the need to give the strophes more and more
varied lines, see also Vincenzo Manfredini, *Regole armoniche* (Venezia: Zerletti, 1775), 22ff.; and
Matteo Borsa, "Saggio filosofico sopra la musica imitativa teatrale," in *Opuscoli scelti sulle
scienze e sulle arti* (Milan: Marelli, 1781), 195–234, esp. 216.

and Svegliato's yawning and Giovinetto's sneezing in *Il barbiere di Siviglia* by Petrosellini and Paisiello, 1782, 1.12). In any case, comic scenes were defined more by their musical style than by versification: an excessively analytical and deliberately musical illustration of individual words (a mannerism that Doni had already signaled; see n. 46), mannered expressivity, sudden verbal repetitions, almost neurotic tics, and violent syllabications that swell the text into an endless whirl of obsessive, rapid repetitions, often on reiterated notes. Many of these characteristics, already to be found in the comic sections of Monteverdi's *Il ritorno d'Ulisse in patria* (Iro, and especially his ridiculous "lament" in 3.1) and *L'incoronazione di Poppea* (Valletto), would later become typical features of the comic musical idiom and, firmly established, would last for centuries.

One just has to look at the arias and duets in such a well-known piece as *La serva padrona* (1733) for it to become clear how the comic vocal style of the early eighteenth century had picked up and institutionalized those stylistic features: concise, springy phrasing created by the abundance of *tronco* endings, which could "dicter à l'acteur le geste qu'il doit faire" (Diderot),[93] detached syllabication, hammered notes, rising motorized excitement, spinning repetitions, an insistence on melodic and rhythmic tics, chains of (sometimes onomatopoeic) monosyllables that would themselves create—in contact with the music—dizzying whirlpools in the metrical body of the text. In any case, Pergolesi's intermezzos use no meters other than the *ottonario,* the *settenario,* and, on one occasion only, the *quinario* (principally *tronco,* during "Sempre in contrasti"). Bernardo Saddumene had anticipated Pergolesi's librettist Gennarantonio Federico in the musical numbers of his *Zite 'ngalera,* set by Vinci, in 1722 when he used predominantly the same meters, occasionally touching on the *decasillabo* as well, and also employing the now less fashionable multiple meters (and often this is mainly just a graphic convention in accordance with what we have observed in Zeno: see the arias for Meneca in 1.8 and 2.7). The proportion is the same in *La finta cameriera* by Barlocci and Latilla (1738), *Il governadore* by Canicà and Logroscino (1747), and *La diavolessa* by Goldoni and Galuppi (1755). In the first two the *decasillabo* appears only to imitate the style of opera seria in pieces that use marine metaphors or that are explicit parodies (1.6, Giocondo: "Agitato il mio cor si confonde"; 2.9, Don Ciccio: "Pupilline del fosco mio sole"), and in the third it is found only in two cases, as an example of extended speech in sententious arias for Ghiandina (1.4: "Una donna che apprezza il decoro") and Dorina (1.7: "Si distingue dal noble il vile"). With the addition of the *senario,* the meters referred to are generally also those adopted in Goldoni's comic librettos

---

93. Quoted in Gianfranco Folena, *L'italiano in Europa: Esperienze linguistiche del Settecento* (Turin: Einaudi, 1983), 227.

in the mid–eighteenth century (*La contessina,* 1743; *La scuola moderna,* 1748; *Bertoldo, Bertoldino e Cacasenno,* 1749), in which the tangled poly-metrical nature of some of the arias in his early intermezzos has given way to greater concern for metrical consistency.[94]

The higher ambitions of comic opera—compared with the more knock-about nature of the intermezzo—and a more contained style, together with the contemporary customs of Metastasian opera seria, had an equal influence on this development. It is no coincidence that the classic dimensions for an aria of two quatrains with all the lines either *settenari* or *ottonari* appear pre-cisely where there is a wish to emphasize the moral contained in the strophes or when the aria is associated with the lovers or (as in *Il mercato di Mal-mantile,* 1758) for characters of an elevated social status. Nonetheless, there are several points of versification that distinguish the comic genre from the se-rious one. Although less inclined to the sort of irregular segmentation of "tragic" speech and more disposed toward the phonic appeal of rhyme, comic recitative—almost exclusively secco—also obviously makes use of blank verse, but not only of *piano endecasillabi* and *settenari:* where possible, other endings are welcomed, occurring even in such recitative monologues as Lui-gino's "Mi sta ben, me lo merito" in Goldoni's *La bella verità* (1762, 2.9), where every line is *sdrucciolo.*

There is greater variety for the musical numbers: not only are more types of lines used than in Metastasian opera, generally the *ottonario, settenario, quinario, decasillabo,* and *senario* (plus a few other meters at times), as well as mixed combinations, but also they are presented in different proportions, overturning the primary position of the *settenario* and focusing on the more springy *ottonario* and the rushing *quinario.* Equally, there are plenty of ex-amples of conscious popular allusion, achieved with the *novenario* or a par-ticular use of the *endecasillabo.* The first appears mixed in with other meters (*decasillabi, ottonari, quadrisillabi*) in Rosina's account of her childhood ("Una piccola bambinella") in *I bagni d'Abano* (1753, 2.8), in the second part of a "canzone" for the servant Berto in *La cascina* (1756, 3.1; the first part is a quatrain of *endecasillabi*), and in the comments of the sailor's daugh-ter, Giacinta ("Se ne trovano tanti e tanti"), in *L'isola disabitata* (1757, 2.12), all by Goldoni. In his operas, wherever the *endecasillabo* is not used deliber-ately for parody (the sonnet sung by Melibea and Pegasino in *Le virtuose ridi-cole,* 1752, 1.8; the sestet recited by Artimisia in *De gustibus non est dis-putandum,* 1754, 1.1), it is inserted into quatrains and, more frequently,

94. For example, the arias of the heroine of *La pelarina* (1730, 3.1: "Veduto ho talvolta") and of Rosalba in *La pupilla* (1734, 2.3: "Signor tuttore") juxtapose *senari, settenari,* and *quinari.* In *La pupilla,* an aria for Giacinto ("A una donna che patisca") brings together *ottonari, quinari,* and *decasillabi,* while *senari* and *quadrisillabi* are both used in Ranocchio's aria in *L'ippocondriaco* (1735, 1.3: "La gambe mi tremano").

octaves for serenades, folklike rispettos, and songs for working girls. Included in the last category are the stornello-like octave for Menghina ("Ciascun mi dice ch'io son tanto bella") from *Bertoldo, Bertoldino e Cacasenno* (1.8) and those sung by the "women spooling the silk" (as Goldoni's stage direction has it) in *La mascherata* (1751, 1.1), while Madama Garbata and Sordidone bring their extemporized songs in a scene from *Arcifanfano re dei matti* to an end with an octave of annoyance ("Se non volete amarmi, non importa"). The "canzonetta in lingua napolitana" which Beltrame sings, again in *La mascherata* (2.6), has a rhyme scheme typical of a southern Italian octave. The "carcioffola," a typically Neapolitan serenade that Don Fabio and Sandrino perform in *La conversazione* (1758, 3.4),[95] as is the one that the hero of Agasippo Mercotellis's *Patrò Tonno d'Isca* (1714, 1.1) had sung "with a *colascione* [a kind of lute] . . . under Carmenella's window," and Ciccariello at the beginning of *Li zite 'ngalera,* are in quatrains. Eighteenth-century comic opera went on to maintain these metrical practices in the case of the *endecasillabo*. The hero's "canzone" ("La moglie quando è buona è sempre bella") in *Giannina e Bernardone* by Livigni and Cimarosa (1781, 1.10) has the same scheme, in imitation of the Venetian villota, and similar folklike forms are found in Donina's song "Che bella cosa egl'è far all'amore" in the first-act finale of *Fra i due litiganti il terzo gode* by Sarti (1782; a version of Goldoni's *Nozze*), while the five couplets of Susanna's serenade "Deh vieni, non tardar, o gioia bella" in *Le nozze di Figaro* (Da Ponte and Mozart, 1786, 4.10) have similar origins in the villota, as does the serenade "Deh vieni alla finestra, o mio tesoro" Don Giovanni sings in Da Ponte and Mozart's opera of 1787 (2.3), laid out as two quatrains.[96] The *sdrucciolo* tercet and the octave that Don Alfonso uses in Da Ponte and Mozart's *Così fan tutte* (1791, 1.7 and 2.13 respectively) are a perfect setting for the character's detached moralizing, giving it a serious, solemn tone which, in the case of the former, is increased by the quotation from Sannazaro.[97] In *Li zite 'ngalera,* Belluccia's recitation of an octave from *Gerusalemme liberata* (7.2, taken from the flight of Erminia) is quite a different matter; it is a fragment of a piece of romantic, epic literature that was widely known, even among lower social strata.

It was in the context of comic opera that librettists' and composers' interest in polymeters revived, both in the customary combinations of related types, not unknown in opera seria (*ottonario* and *quadrisillabo, settenario* and *quinario;* one example each of both of these can be found in *L'Arcadia in Brenta* by Goldoni, 1749: respectively the arias for Fabrizio in 1.10 and Rosanna in

95. See Wolfgang Osthoff, "Gli endecasillabi villotistici in *Don Giovanni* e *Nozze di Figaro,*" in *Venezia e il melodramma nel Settecento,* ed. Maria Teresa Muraro (Florence: Olschki, 1978), 2:293–311, esp. 311.

96. See ibid. for discussion of these Mozartian questions.

97. Ibid., 293ff.

2.4), and in mixed combinations of unrelated meters: to stay with Goldoni, *senari, quadrisillabi, ottonari,* and *quinari* in *Bertoldo, Bertoldino e Cacasenno* (2.14), *settenari* and *senari* in *La calamita de' cuori* (1753, 2.8), *novenari* and *decasillabi,* then *ottonari,* and then *quadrisillabi* plus two final *decasillabi* in Rosina's narration from *I bagni d'Abano* (2.8), mentioned above, and *decasillabi* and *ottonari,* double *quadrisillabi* and *quinari* in *Il talismano* (1779, 2.5).

Another typical feature of comic opera is the systematic mixing of *srducciolo* and *tronco* versions of the same meter (*La mascherata,* 3.3; *Lo speziale,* 1755, 1.6; *Il mercato di Malmantile,* 3.1; *Il viaggiatore ridicolo,* 1761, 2.1), as the beginning of Ferramonte's aria in *Il mondo alla roversa* demonstrates (1750, 2.6; similar cases can be found in 1.5 and 2.9):

Quando le donne parlano	[When women speak
io lor non credo affé.	I don't trust a word they say.
Se piangono, se ridono,	Their weeping and laughter
lo stesso è ognor per me.	are all the same to me.
Io so che sempre fingono,	I know it's all a pretense
che fede in lor non v'è.	and they're not to be trusted.]

The widespread use of two-part lines corresponds to the similar habit of distributing text—often also to be seen in the layout—in shorter segments: it is very common to find double *quinari* that produce false *decasillabi* (a single example will serve: Tagliaferro's aria "Ah, come tutto—je consolar" in *La buona figliola,* 1757, 3.7) or pseudo-*endecasillabi* (*L'Arcadia in Brenta,* 2.1: "Corpo del diavolo!—parmi un po' troppo"), but it is also quite common to find *settenari* divided into two *trisillabi* (*Il mondo alla roversa,* 3.3) and *senari* placed together to create a rare sighting of a *dodecasillabo* (*La bella verità,* 2.10: "La testa! La posta!—La bile! Cospetto!").

Comic singing, predominantly syllabic in nature, built on these deviations and this fragmented distribution into minute particles to establish its prerogatives of lively rhythms, light, fluid movement, and the springy quality of short phrases. At the same time, the fact that arias were no longer necessarily structured in two strophes suggested musical constructions no longer modeled solely on tripartite designs with a da capo, whether complete or truncated. For example, some of the arias in *La buona figliola* are in three stanzas (1.5: "È pur bella la Cecchina!" 2.10; 3.1), as are a number in *Il talismano* (1.12; 2.3, 6, 9, and 14; 3.6), which also includes arias in four stanzas (1.8 and 2.15), such as had already been seen in *La bella verità* (2.5) and *Il mondo della luna* (1750, 3.2). Even more frequently found is a vast expansion in the number of lines in arias in a single block: looking only at *L'Arcadia in Brenta,* Fabrizio's aria (1.2) has twelve *ottonari,* and Laura's arias in act 1, scene 3, and act 2, scene 10, have 18 *quinari* and 19 *ottonari* respectively. It is true that if the composer wished, such hefty chunks of text could also be adapted to the prevailing da capo structure, but in any case their existence reveals a search for more varied textual shapes which clearly could not result solely from the dissatisfaction of librettists. Some textual material already organized according to the customary form appeared with special characteristics such as, for example, the avoidance of the repeat of the *intercalare* (*La diavolessa* by Goldoni and Galuppi, 1.10) or particular richness of vocabulary, which made the word repetitions typical of such cases seem less insistent. For example, there are twelve *quinari* in the *intercalare* of Col'Agnolo's aria "N'ommo attempato" in *Li zite 'ngalera* (1.7) and nine for Ciccariello further on ("Si masto mio," 2.4), followed by eight in the second section. In *La finta cameriera* we find examples of *intercalare* of eight and twelve *senari* (3.8 and 1.9), eight *quinari* (1.4), and ten *settenari* (2.10). Other groupings could produce settings inspired by the single-strophe arietta of opera seria (the cavata). In fact the block of eight *quinari* that Leonora sings in *Il governadore* (3.11: "Come in ziel tremola") is defined as a "cavatina," whose text is heard only once, as was the case in the first sections of *intercalari;* there is no returning to the beginning to repeat it completely or in part, with a conclusion in the home key, in a subsequent "development."

In contrast, more lively articulations were favored for arias in several strophes or distinct sections, particularly polymetric ones, with changes of meter from one part to another. Staying with Goldoni, in *Il mondo alla roversa,* opening stanzas in *ottonari* or *settenari* are followed by *quinari* and double *quinari* (1.4 and 5). Some of the pieces in *Il filosofo di campagna* (1754) are also in several sections: *tronco decasillabi, tronco senari,* an *endecasillabo,* and another *tronco decasillabo* in act 1, scene 10; a series of *tronco settenari* and then a concluding *quinario* in act 2, scene 12. Goldoni also uses metrical accelerations in passing from a stanza in *settenari* (at first alternately *sdrucciolo* and *tronco,* then in *tronco* and *piano* couplets) to one in *senari* (2.14). Similarly, in *La buona figliola* he leaps from an *ottonario* to a *senario tronco* (1.10) but also inserts a quatrain in this same meter in the middle of two strophes in *decasillabi* (2.10). In *Il mercato di Malmantile* the quack-doctor Rubicone's prattling (1.1: "Noi sottoscritti—facciamo fede") opens with a preamble in false *decasillabi;* he rattles off his merits, slipping in a series of *settenari* and continues to repeat them in *quinari,* which finally make up a *decasillabo* couplet.

But it was in the ensemble pieces, more than anywhere else, that division into various meters was exploited to the full, and these were among the most appealing features of comic opera. The pieces by Goldoni and Galuppi from midcentury were already apportioned according to the following scheme: a fairly rapid opening and conclusion, complex finales at the end of the first and, more so, second acts (when the plot had to seem at its most tangled), some duets or trios (later a quartet as well) scattered here and there, especially in the final two acts, and one in particular positioned just before the definitive unraveling of the plot. A summary of the plan used in each of the three finales in Goldoni's *La finta semplice* (1764) provides an example of the format of similar ensemble pieces in multiple sections.[98]

Characters	*Situation*	*Versification*
Finale 1 (108 lines)		
ROSINA; her brother FRACASSO; POLIDORO; NINETTA	The first two confront Polidoro with writing a love letter intended for Rosina: Polidoro is obliged to ask for pardon.	*Piano* and *tronco ottonari* in *aab* tercets, then in couplets and in single lines.
The same and CASSANDRO	Cassandro also starts to berate his brother Polidoro, but Rosina leads Cassandro to believe that she wrote the letter for him.	Quatrains of *piano* and *tronco quinari*, then couplets and single lines.
	Polidoro tries to have Rosina accept a present, but she gets Cassandro to give her a ring.	Various groupings of *piano* and *tronco settenari*, from one to four lines (the tercets are *aab*), sometimes divided between two speakers.
The same and SIMONE	Rosina is called away; Cassandro would like his ring back.	Various groupings of *piano, tronco*, and *sdrucciolo quinari* (from one to six lines).
	General rejoicing for the coming celebration.	Five-line strophes of *piano* and *tronco* (the last one) *ottonari*.
Finale 2 (108 lines)		
CASSANDRO, POLIDORO, NINETTA	Cassandro is jealous and quarrels with his brother and tries to beat him.	*Piano* and *tronco senari*, initially in a quatrain, then separately or in couplets.
The same and ROSINA	Seeing this, Rosina feels faint, then comes round, and tries to leave.	*Piano* and *tronco ottonari*, later also *sdrucciolo*, first in a quatrain, then generally in single lines (sometimes split between two speakers).

98. See also Daniel Heartz, "The Creation of the Buffo Finale in Italian Opera," in *Proceedings of the Royal Musical Association* 104 (1977–78): 67–78; Francesco Blanchetti, "Tipologia musicale dei concertati nell'opera buffa di Giovanni Paisiello," *Rivista italiana di musicologia* 19

The same and FRACASSO	Fracasso stops her and asks her to account for her behavior, announcing that the sister of Polidoro and Cassandro has run off with a huge sum of money.	*Piano* and *tronco quinari* (sometimes also *sdrucciolo*) organized into strophes of between two and five lines.
The same and SIMONE	Simone announces that Rosina's maid Ninetta has also run off with some money.	*Piano* and *tronco ottonari*, first in *abbc* quatrains, then in couplets and *aab* tercets.
	General expressions of hope.	Two uneven strophes (four and five lines) in *sdrucciolo*, *piano*, and *tronco quinari*.

Finale 3 (4 lines: the preceding scene contains a long duet in multiple sections of 54 lines: *settenari, ottonari, quinari, ottonari*)

	Tutti moral	Quatrain of alternate *sdrucciolo* and *tronco ottonari*.

8. THE ENERGY OF COMEDY IN OPERA SERIA

Of all that opera seria in the second half of the eighteenth century took over from comic opera, it was alternatives to the two-strophe da capo aria and multisectional ensembles that received most attention in terms of versification. These were precisely the intrusions which the high-minded Calzabigi lamented in the annotations to his *Lulliade* (1754–89): "There is worse in our age: finales, formerly limited to comic opera, have been introduced to opera seria; composers have wretched poets write them in various meters to allow space for changing tempos and keys and make the simple-minded believe that they are doing something new." [99]

One practical gauge of the changes under way at the end of the eighteenth century and the beginning of the nineteenth is provided by the amendments made to an antiquated Metastasio text, *La clemenza di Tito* (1734), by Caterino Mazzolà for Mozart (1791), Gaetano Rossi for Antonio Del Fante (1803), and an anonymous librettist for Marcos Antonio Portugal (1807): two-strophe arias generate others of several strophes; recitatives and arias are recast as ensembles; and there is greater chorus involvement. [100] If composers of this period

---

(1984): 234–60; Paolo Gallarati, *Musica e maschera: Il libretto italiano del Settecento* (Turin: EDT/Musica, 1984), 145ff.

99. Calzabigi's *Lulliade,* with his *Annotazioni,* can be read in Gabriele Muresu, *La ragione dei "buffoni"* (Rome: Bulzoni, 1977). The passage quoted can also be found in Gabriele Muresu, *La parola cantata: Studi sul melodramma italiano del Settecento* (Rome: Bulzoni, 1982), 76.

100. For all this, see Helga Lühning, *"Titus"—Vertonungen im 18. Jahrhundert: Untersuchungen zur Tradition der Opera Seria von Hasse bis Mozart* (Laaber: Volk-Laaber, 1983).

were already moving away from the da capo plan for the customary two stanzas of the tripartite aria, it is easy to imagine how a greater number of lines
laid out in more sections increased this tendency. In Mozart's *La clemenza di
Tito,* Sesto's aria "Parto, ma tu ben mio" (1.9), with an extra couplet added,
gives rise to a musical organism in three sections of increasing tempo, adagio–
allegro–allegro assai, each of which is essentially based on the corresponding
three-part scheme of the text (first quatrain, second quatrain, additional couplet, respectively) before returning to the textual material already heard (the
allegro on the whole first quatrain, the allegro assai on the first two lines of
the second). The character's other aria, "Deh, per questo istante solo" (2.10),
with its *ottonari* set out as three quatrains and a couplet, replaces Metastasio's "Vo disperato a morte (3.6: two tercets of *settenari*). With its first two
quatrains, the later text makes for a traditional, if brief, da capo aria, with no
"development" following the exposition, but then it uses the other tercet as a
transition to a rondo where the finale couplet serves as a refrain, while the
second and third strophes are used for the intermediate episodes. Similarly,
Augusto's aria "A' dolci affetti tuoi" in *La morte di Cleopatra* by Sografi and
Guglielmi (1796) builds a complex piece in six sections out of its two quatrains and a couplet of *settenari,* in which the quatrains reappear in different
musical guises.[101]

Composers were further prompted to construct such shapes when the librettist had already chosen to write arias in metrically distinct blocks, in the
manner of comic opera. *Settenari, dodecasillabi* (double *senari*), *senari,* and
again *piano* and *tronco dodecasillabi* all come together in the four sections of
Boleslao's aria "Ma pria ch'io vada al campo" in *Lodoiska* by Gonella and
Mayr (1796, 1.3), and in exactly the same way *settenari, decasillabi* (double
quinari), *quinari,* and *piano, tronco, piano,* and also *sdrucciolo decasillabi*
are found in the heroine's aria "Perdei quel ben che solo" (2.7). An extremely
irregular example is found in Orazio's aria "Nacqui, è ver, tra grandi eroi" in
Gli Orazi e i Curiazi by Sografi and Cimarosa (1797, 1.10). The aria consists
of one quatrain of *piano* and *tronco ottonari,* one quatrain of *sdrucciolo,
piano,* and *tronco quinari,* a pair of *sdrucciolo* and *tronco settenari,* then again
a quatrain of *quinari* and a couplet as before, and, last, a return to the opening quatrain. An equally complex scheme is found in Gusmano's aria "Fra le
palme, gli allori, le rose" (2.15) and Idalide's "Che barbaro affanno" (2.8) in
Gli americani by Rossi and Mayr (1806). These consist of three and five different sections respectively: the first has a quatrain of *piano* and *tronco decasillabi,* the same of *ottonari,* and a sestet of *sdrucciolo* and *tronco quinari;* this
is followed by *senari, ottonari, settenari, senari,* and *ottonari,* mostly *piano*

---

101. See Friedrich Lippmann, *Vincenzo Bellini und die italienische Opera Seria seiner Zeit:
Studien über Libretto, Arienform und Melodik* (Cologne and Vienna: Böhlau, 1969), 59ff.

and *tronco*. Zamoro's aria "Sorgerà serena e bella" (2.18) is a particularly significant one: it opens with ten *ottonari*, followed by a contribution from the chorus ("Deh calma, o misero": a sestet of *quinari*), which inspires a transitional quatrain from the soloist ("Felicità! . . . per me?" a mixture of *settenari* and *ottonari*, preparing the ground for five *ottonari* of resolution ("Va', tiranno, omai comprendi"). This is basically nothing more than a more monumental version of the bipartite cantabile-cabaletta scheme that would later triumph with Rossini, but it had had considerable success before then, in that Rossi, again in his *Gli sciti* (1800) for Mayr, wrote Indatiro's aria "Più soave e dolce istante" (2.5) as a quatrain of *ottonari* followed by a sestet of *decasillabi*. Large-scale arias for the principal characters close to the last-act finale, with a wealth of metrical changes, can also be seen in Luigi Romanelli's librettos—again written for Mayr—such as *Adelasia e Aleramo* (1807, 2.14, Adelasia: "Di tua man mi squarcia il seno") and *Raul di Crequì* (1810, 2.13). In the latter opera it is once again a choral episode in *settenari* that separates the opening *senari* ("Sull'orme di Adele) from the aggressive determination of the close in *quinari* ("Alfin l'acciaro"); this was the model that would be so widely and successfully used in mid-nineteenth-century opera.

However, it is not uncommon to find similar designs—apart from the predominantly isometric ones—in ensemble pieces, which were larger in scale and more frequently used by the new composers than their predecessors. For example, Rossi and Mayr's *I cherusci* (1808) opens with a choral introduction first in *quinari*, then in *senari*;[102] in act 2, the duet in the second scene moves from *ottonari* to *quinari* and back again, and the duet with chorus in scene 5 alternates *settenari* and *senari*. The same author and composer provide a fine example of polymeters in *Gli sciti*, in the chorus "Della Scizia gloria e amore" (2.5), where there are tercets and quatrains respectively of *ottonari* plus *decasillabi*, and *senari*. Whole scenes can go by without the traditional blank verse for recitative scenes that are set to music in blocks, respecting the new dramatic trend: in the one-act *L'amor coniugale* (1805) by Rossi and Mayr, scenes 16 *(ottonari* and *settenari)* and 18–19 *(senari* and *settenari; ottonari)*; in *Gli Americani*, in act 1, scenes 16–17 *(ottonari; ottonari, settenari, ottonari)* and in act 2, scene 12 *(settenari, ottonari, settenari)*. In *I cherusci* the whole first-act block of scenes 14–18 alternates *settenari* and *ottonari* from one scene to the next.

The expansion of the musical numbers in opera seria and the loss of their almost exclusively monologue, static character produced a demand for met-

102. At the beginning of the nineteenth century, both Ritorni and Mayr comment on the expansion of introductions with some irony; see, respectively, Paolo Fabbri, "Le memorie teatrali di Carlo Ritorni, 'Rossiniste de 1815,'" *Bollettino del Centro Rossiniano di Studi* (1981), 87–128, esp. 95; and Guido Zavadini, *Donizetti: Vita, musiche, epistolario* (Bergamo: Istituto Italiano d'Arti Grafiche, 1948), 884.

rical variety such as that already found in the introductory, intermediary, and final ensembles in comic opera. The following table shows clearly how operas between the end of the eighteenth and beginning of the nineteenth centuries saw an increase in numbers divided into blocks of different meters compared with those in a single meter.

| Composer and Librettist | Title and year | Total nos. | In a single meter | | | | | poly-metric |
			qui-nario	se-nario	sette-nario	otto-nario	deca-sillabo	
Gonella and Mayr	Lodoiska, 1796	23	3	1	11	3	1	4
Sografi and Cimarosa	Gli Orazi e i Curiazi, 1797	22	2	2	4	6	2	4
Rossi and Mayr	Gli sciti, 1800	21	1	3	8	6	—	3
Colloredo and Cimarosa	Artemisia, 1801	22	2	2	8	7	1	2
Rossi and Mayr	Gli Americani, 1806	23	2	2	2	8	—	9
Romanelli and Mayr	Adelasia e Aleramo, 1807	25	1	2	7	1	1	13
Rossi and Mayr	I cherusci, 1808	19	2	—	1	6	—	10
Romanelli and Mayr	Raul di Crequì, 1810	23	4	—	8	1	—	10
Romani and Mayr	Medea in Corinto, 1813	21	—	3	4	—	—	14

Where pieces brought various meters together, the meters continued to be almost always those that were used separately, *ottonario* and *settenario* principally, followed by *quinario, senario,* and *decasillabo.* It was rare to find meters smaller than a *quinario:* as established by tradition, the *novenario* was not used (although Planelli had not excluded it).[103] Equally traditional were the recognized connotations of the meters, however generic and more easily identified in extreme cases: *decasillabo* for rage, uncontainable agitation, outbursts of aggression; *quinario* where the situation required rapid delivery and intense emotions. Intermediate meters were available for every kind of emotion: if anything, the *ottonario* (and even-numbered meters in general, used much more frequently than before) was increasingly favored, and especially with the *settenario* and *quinario,* it is strongly represented in pieces based on blocks of different meters.

The search for fairly unusual combinations led to greater use of double lines (from the *trisillabo* to the *quinario*) or instead a return to split or jumbled lines,[104] while the *endecasillabo* started to appear among these as well. This happened at precisely the same time as the musical numbers were

103. See Planelli, *Dell'opera seria in musica,* 33.

104. See Daniela Goldin, "Aspetti della librettistica italiana fra 1770 e 1830," *Analecta Musicologica* 21 (1982): 128–91, esp. 182ff. (now also in the collection of her essays *La vera fenice: Librettisti e libretti tra Sette e Ottocento* [Turin: Einaudi, 1985], 3–72, esp. 56).

growing longer and being transformed into active, dynamic structures in the dramatic design, at the same time taking over the role of recitative: all these considerations tended to squeeze recitative out of the picture and reduced the space for blank verse.

From this point on, the few remaining passages of recitative, now entitled "scena," contained what remained of free, unmetered declamation, which at one time occupied such a large stretch of the libretto and which instead was now limited to a small number of dead zones—of transition, waiting, or preparation—while the omnipresent organization into rhythmic periods now also covered passages of rapid dialogue, with the determining involvement of the orchestra as well, since the characters' exchanges were inserted into its onward flow. The libretto was thus divided into scenes—often put together by the composer into extended blocks of music—generally using between one and three varieties of meter, plus, if necessary, blank verse for recitative, if any; each of these scenes contained mixed, fragmentary sequences between the various speakers or else broadened into closed strophes for the so-called cantabile sections, whether solo (aria), in dialogue, or in superimposed lines (duets, trios, and so on, up to large ensembles). It was not the case that a musical structure in multiple sections (from the simplest lento-allegro, like that of an aria and cabaletta—further accelerated in ensembles by the "stretta"— to more complex schemes in various blocks) necessarily required a change of meter, given that each sequence of stresses lent itself to more than one rhythmic pattern.[105] To stay with examples from the standard repertory, think of the first-act finale of *La sonnambula,* where the chorus, quintet, and stretta are all in *ottonari* but produce quite different musical results, or two of the duets in *L'elisir d'amore,* Nemorino and Dulcamara (1.6) and Adina and Dulcamara (2.7). Usually there are one or two stanzas (for each character in the case of the ensembles) in these "cantabiles," even where they are not balanced. More appear when required by the dramatic situation, but the delay this creates needs some justification: this is generally provided by a song, a prayer, a narration in the guise of a romantic ballad, a brindisi, or a programmatic declaration.[106] The same is the case for the number of lines included, which goes beyond eight to ten only for specific dramatic reasons, such as, for example, in Dulcamara's harangue in *L'elisir d'amore,* which is made up of several stanzas in various meters, or in Azucena's narration "Condotta ell'era in ceppi—al suo destin tremendo!").

105. See Friedrich Lippmann's pioneering "Der italienische Vers und der musikalische Rhythmus: Zum Verhältnis von Vers und Musik in der italienischen Oper des 19. Jahrhunderts, mit einem Blick auf die 2. Hälfte des 18. Jahrhunderts," *Analecta Musicologica* 12 (1973): 253–369; 14 (1973): 324–410; 15 (1975): 298–333.

106. See Rossanna Dalmonte, "La canzone nel melodramma italiano del primo Ottocento: Ricerche di metodo strutturale," *Rivista italiana di musicologia* 11 (1976), 230–313: 257 fol.

9. LINES WITH EVEN NUMBERS OF SYLLABLES IN ROMANTIC OPERA

The choice of meter, for such homogeneous sequences, in mid-nineteenth-century opera kept to those already described: *ottonari* and *settenari* in first place, followed by *decasillabi, senari,* and *quinari.* It was very rare to use any shorter lines, such as the *quadrisillabo,* which Solera used for the chorus of Evil Spirits in *Giovanna d'Arco* ("Tu sei bella": prologue, scene 5). Some meters were more frequently duplicated: double *quinari,* double *senari,* double *settenari.* The preeminence of highflown-sounding even numbers of syllables (which Bonifazio Asioli favored in his theoretical considerations, published posthumously in 1832)[107] is significant, in that their heavy accentuation is better suited to forceful depiction of strong dramatic situations. Verdi asked Piave for *ottonari* on 10 December 1846 for the sleepwalking scene in *Macbeth* and then again (22 December) for the chorus of Scottish exiles in the last act, which he felt was not "grandiose enough, because, among other things, the meter [used in the first section] is too short." It was Verdi's intention to "do a chorus as important as the one in *Nabucco*" but not one that moved along in the same way, and since he wanted to avoid *decasillabi,* he suggested using the nearest equivalent, the *ottonario.*[108] Converting the meter sketched before into pulsating *decasillabi,* the "stretta" of the second-act finale of *Rigoletto* could produce—and indeed it did produce—an "impressive, showy cabaletta."[109] For the aria for Amelia that opens the second act of *Un ballo in maschera,* Verdi asked Somma on 26 November 1857 for something stronger; this at first turned the original *quinari* into *settenari,* but Verdi asked for a further expansion: "Those two short strophes do not make the situation grander, it remains small. There's no fire, no agitation, no disorder (which should be extreme at his point)."[110] At last the solution of a line of ten syllables was arrived at ("Ma dall'arido stelo divulsa"), which Somma commented on thus: "For the form I have chosen two sestets of *decasillabi,* because this length of line can break and be broken where some impulse is needed."[111] Verdi took

---

107. See Bonifazio Asioli, *Il maestro di composizione, ossia Séguito del Trattato d'armonia* (Milan: Ricordi, 1832), 38–41. See also Renato Di Benedetto, "Lineamenti di una teoria della melodia della trattastica italiana fra il 1790 e il 1830," *Analecta Musicologica* 21 (1982): 421–43. Carlo Ritorni also deals with metrical questions in the same period—but more than anything from a theoretic and prescriptive viewpoint—in *Ammaestramenti alla composizione d'ogni poema e d'ogni opera appartenente alla musica* (Milan: Pirola, 1841), pt. 1, chaps. 29–30; pt. 2, chaps. 31–37, 59, 62–69.

108. David Rosen and Andrew Porter, eds., *Verdi's "Macbeth": A Sourcebook* (Cambridge: Cambridge University Press, 1984), 26.

109. See Franco Abbiati, *Giuseppe Verdi* (Milan: Ricordi, 1959), 1:671 and 675.

110. *Carteggi verdiani,* ed. Alessandro Luzio, 4 vols. (Rome: Reale Accademia d'Italia, 1935–47), 1:225.

111. Ibid., 231. See also Peter Ross, "Amelias Auftrittsarie im 'Maskenball': Verdis Vertonung in dramaturgisch-textlichem Zusammenhang," *Archiv für Musikwissenschaft* 40 (1983): 126–46.

care of the "disorder" himself by giving some syllables longer durations than others and hesitant, irregular stresses.

The fixed system of stresses of even-number lines was perfectly suited to modern phrasing, with a tendency to periods made up of elements homogeneous in their dimensions and rhythmic schemes, and this was encouraged by the new relationship between text and music. The inspiration was now a basically syllabic ideal that respected the literary source and was in general terms less tolerant of repetitions, vocalizations, or arbitrary manipulations. Bellini had already been widely appreciated for that "beautiful simplicity"[112] which led him to stray far from Rossinian bel canto in the direction of that "method which we know not if it may be called sung declamation or declaimed song"[113] and which allowed him to give greater clarity—and consequently more communicative force—to the textual framework and its ordering into verse.

> For a long time modern music has been accused of turning men's gullets into fifes or suchlike instruments and of having made the words, which were the mistress, into the slave of the musical ideas. It seems that Bellini wishes to free music of this accusation. His music, as far as ideas are concerned, stands out for a certain melodic smoothness and sweetness that assists rather than destroys the effect of the words and the lines.[114]
>
> Another merit of his music, the principal one which lends it its style, is the supreme expressivity and philosophy of his vocal lines and his instrumentation. He speaks with the voice and the orchestra; he makes his effects not with the majesty of sounds but with the power of music and poetry concentrated together, the source of an essential quality of his style, that of allowing the poet's ideas and verses to be enjoyed unmodified, and to this he adds with music only that which can double the impression and effect they make. In such a way he has taken away those intolerable repetitions and those miserable additions of so many repeats of "sì" and "no" which killed off any verbal effectiveness and waged war against good sense.[115]

Some of the most obvious features of the phrasing of cantabile sections in the period between 1820 and 1860, give or take a year, were its isometrical squareness (which determined above all the regular meter of the verse) and the prevalence of binary schemes, with the result that the language was simplified, completely consistent with the ideal of "popularity"—that is, immediate comprehensibility—which romanticism so longed for. One manifestation of this was in the customary use of two-part phrases (mostly "antecedent-

112. The phrase appears in an article in the *Gazzetta privilegiata di Milano* of 5 Nov. 1827 (quoted in Lippmann, *Vincenzo Bellini,* 65). See also, in connection with this question, what Ritorni has to say (in Fabbri, "Le memorie," 119).

113. From *L'eco* of 16 Feb. 1829 (quoted in Lippmann, *Vincenzo Bellini,* 99).

114. T. Locatelli, in the *Gazzetta di Venezia* of 21 Jan. 1830, quoted in Francesco Pastura, *Bellini secondo la storia* (Parma: Guanda, 1959), 233.

115. *Gazzetta di Venezia,* 17 Mar. 1830 (Pastura, *Bellini,* 238ff.).

consequent"), which could be repeated (in whole or in part) in either an unchanged or a related harmonic context. The critic Mellini reproached Verdi in 1847: "He sins in overuse of syncope; he follows the same path too often in responding to the subject by modulating."[116] The period was defined by a melodic arch generally based on four strong principal accents. Of the verse types that the composer used, only the *ottonario, decasillabo,* and some *settenari* (iambic ones, with accents on the first or second, fourth, and sixth syllables; and then the seventh syllable had to be improperly placed in a thetic position) were able to support so many stresses, while the *quinario, senario,* and *settenario* normally provided two, unless they were so compressed as to have only one (because of their exceptional rhythmic agitation, the contortions and shifts in the correct pulse were at their most extreme in the cabalettas). All this involved even numbers of lines (usually four, six, or eight) in the stanzas or the use of double lines mentioned above, which were also ideal for thinning out the monotonous recurrence of rhymes and for achieving a less concise and contracted poetic discourse. In passages of dialogue the basic type came to be the couplet.

In confirmation (and contradiction) of the pervasive need for this isometric and binary system, we can look at what Verdi wrote to Somma in the mid–nineteenth century: "In the first strophe you have made two verses, then five, then three; . . . with this sort of irregularity the musical phrase cannot help but be lame. . . . Think of the most popular cantilenas in our Italian opera and you will see how the strophes are made. . . . You never find an interruption or a break in the verse."[117] And by way of verification of the tyranny of this all-too-regular phrasing, witness the unease experienced by composers in cantabile sections using the *endecasillabo,* the verse type least adaptable to periodic schemes and the only odd-numbered one that cannot be doubled (remembering that the traditional refusal to use the *novenario* was still in force). "These lines, lacking as they do a regular cadence, are hard and impossible to set to music (that is to say, theatrical music)," wrote Verdi to Somma on 20 November 1857 in connection with tidying up details of *Un ballo in maschera,* adding shortly afterward: "It is impossible to write a melody (something which there has to be in that position) on the meter 'Qui nel cor della notte e colla sposa, etc.' The rhymes can stay, but you need to have either *decasillabi* or double *quinari* or, even better, double *senari.*"[118] Further on, other *decasillabi* for Amelia had to be changed into double *quinari.*[119] In

116. In Abbiati, *Giuseppe Verdi,* 1:494.

117. Letter of 19 Nov. 1853, quoted in Mario Rinaldi, *Verdi critico: I suoi giudizi, la sua estetica* (Rome: Ergo, 1951), 230.

118. In Abbiati, *Giuseppe Verdi,* 2:457ff., quoted in Budden, *The Operas of Verdi* (London: Cassell, 1978), 2:367.

119. See *Carteggi,* 1:226.

any case, in the past Verdi had had to be careful with that awkward meter: "As for the cabaletta, use all the verses together, if you will, but not *endecasillabi*," was his recommendation to Piave on 22 December 1846 for the tenor's aria at the end of *Macbeth*.[120]

Precisely because of its rarity in strophic forms, the *endecasillabo* could be used to give an unmistakably literary, chivalrous, or popular connotation: examples are the octave read out by the hero of Ferretti and Donizetti's *Torquato Tasso* (1.10) and Ernesto's serenade in Ruffini and Donizetti's *Don Pasquale* (3.6), where it is used both complete and in the variant of a *settenario* plus a *quinario*. On the other hand, the new romantic taste for the narrative ballad is the context for Giorgio's narration in *I puritani* by Pepoli and Bellini (2.2), written in tercets of *endecasillabi* plus a *quinario* echoed by other double *quinari* for the chorus, and for the examples in Verdi's *I masnadieri* (2.5) and *Il trovatore* (1.1). Then there was the vogue for religious choruses, for which this distinguished meter was felt to be most solemnly appropriate (*Giovanna d'Arco*, 2.2; *Attila*, prologue, 6, and 2.6; *Stiffelio/Aroldo*, 2.6; *Il trovatore*, 4.1; *La forza del destino*, 2.3).[121] Departures from the dominant isometric structure had similar characteristic goals and were perceived as Metastasian archaisms, references to the Arcadian style of Frugoni, or even timid mimicry of Chiabrera. Metastasio is conjured up in both Rodolfo's lyrical outpouring in *Luisa Miller* (2.7: "Quando le sere al placido") and Manrico's serenade in *Il trovatore*, for all that it is reminiscent of Berchet's much closer "fantasia" of the same name:

CAMMARANO and VERDI	BERCHET
Deserto sulla terra,	Va per la selva bruna
col rio destino in guerra,	solingo il trovator
è sola speme un cor	domato dal rigor
al trovator.	della fortuna.

The other writers mentioned, perhaps equally able to evoke far-off times and picturesque situations, are associated with the alternation of double and single lines, which Verdi especially uses in choral scenes: in the Spain of *Ernani* (by Piave) for the bandits' opening drinking song ("Allegri! Beviamo!—nel vino cerchiamo") and in *Il trovatore* for the gypsies' refrain ("All'opra, all'opra!—Dàgli, martella"), in the barbaric praise which greets the entry of Attila at the beginning of Solera's text (prologue, 1 and 2), and in *Giovanna d'Arco*, again by Solera (prologue, 2: "Allor che i flebili—bronzi salutano"; 3.6: "Non sembra un angelo—che a sonno placido"). And the "bacchanale" in *La traviata*

---

120. After Rosen and Porter, *Verdi's "Macbeth,"* 27.

121. See Peter Ross, *Studien zum Verhältnis con Libretto und Komposition in den Opern Verdis* (Bern: Gnägi, 1980), 57ff.

has the same sort of significance, with its refrain of *ottonari* alternating with strophes of *quinari*.

Some sequences of lines with a particular ending also have a strong connotation, especially *tronco* ones. "To have character, the witches' first strophes should be stranger," wrote Verdi to Piave on 22 September 1846 in connection with a number of scenes in *Macbeth*: "For example, if you had used many *versi tronchi*, then maybe it would have been better: in short, experiment and find a way of writing bizarre poetry. . . . Now that I think about it a little, I feel that making all the lines in the first chorus *versi tronchi* will produce a strange sound that will have character." [122] The effect was more convincing if we remember how much less common *tronco* endings had become, given the nineteenth-century preference for long clausulae, whether *piano* or *sdrucciolo;* [123] and a much more frequent use of the *sdrucciolo* lessened the well-defined and still-maintained highly charged character it traditionally expressed (see in *Macbeth* the witches' choruses "Tre volte miagola—la gatta in fregola" and "S'allontanarono . . .—n'accozzeremo," Banquo's fearful evocation "Come dal ciel precipita," and the hero's "Fuggi, regal fantasima"; in *Un ballo in maschera* Ulrica's demonic oration "Re dell'abisso, affrettati"), but which by that time had been joined by many other examples that had no particular charge.

10. ASYMMETRY AS THE NORM

It was precisely these common schemes that current use had made so threadbare and such a straitjacket that Boito thought to be the principal reason for the premature senility of Italian opera (the "rough bonds / of meter and of form," from his poem *Dualismo*). Versification alone (hopefully by a poet-musician) could provide the basis for breaking that suffocating "circle / of the old and the foolish" deplored in his famous *Ode* and could replace the prevailing stereotyped syntactical uniformity with more fluid and recherché movements, and to an irregular pattern. To see this in practice we need only leaf through *Mefistofele* (1868 and 1875): there we find miscellaneous meters, continual changes, such strange usages as *trisallabi* and *novenari* as early as the prologue (the chorus of the Cherubim), openly polymetric strophes (Mefistofele's songs and the choral ones in acts 1 and 2), and fluid dialogues in *endecasillabi* or double *settenari* (1.1, for example). Refinements for the sophisticated palate are archaic preciosities such as the opening madrigals for the Celestial Host and, even more, the "barbaric" poetry of the Walpurgis Night scene, which opens with *sdrucciolo* lines meant to stand for dactyls, the theory behind which the composer expounded in the note attached to the text:

---

122. Rosen and Porter, *Verdi's "Macbeth,"* 10.
123. See F. Lippmann, "Der italienische Vers," *Analecta Musicologica* 15 (1975): 300ff.

"I have attempted an Asclepiadean type of verse, consisting of one spondee, two choriambuses, and a last spondee foot, in this manner: Cīrcōn- / fūsă dĭ sōl / ĭl măgĭcō / vōltō." I have attempted a hexameter in this way: "Nōttē / cūpā, / trūcē, / sēnzā / fīnĕ fŭ- / nĕbrē!" A sapphic *endecasillabo* appears in the stanza for the choretids where Faust's appearance is announced." But Verdi had already shown innovative leanings in this area from the 1850s onward, and he was much less doctrinaire and deliberately disruptive. We see him trying out colloquial situations by juxtaposing fluid vocal sections in blank verse, with its irregular pulse, based on recurring orchestral periods (*Rigoletto*, 1.1, up to the Duke's ballata, and 2.3 up to the curse; *La traviata*, 1.2, conclusion, and 1.3, first part), or else letting eccentric structures appear even at moments with no picturesque context, as in Violetta's "Addio, del passato—bei sogni ridenti!" (two sestets of double *piano senari* concluded by a refrain of a simple *tronco senario*) or in "Di Provenza il mar, il suol—chi dal cor ti cancellò?" (two quatrains of a highly unusual double *tronco ottonario*, plus a *quinario*, also *tronco*). Just by playing on particular endings it was possible to give a note of novelty to familiar schemes. During the work of revision on *Macbeth*, to give the final chorus "a bit of zest" to lend it a "dry and bold feeling," Verdi had imagined it thus: "The first three lines *tronco*, and the last *sdrucciolo*." [124]

He proposed a similar trick to Ghislanzoni on 16 August 1870 for the opening couplets of act 2 of *Aida*: "And, without seeking rhythmic eccentricities, write versi settenari twice—that is, two settenari in one; and if it doesn't upset you too much, write some versi tronchi, which are sometimes very graceful in music. The melody in *Traviata* ["Di Provenza"] would be less tolerable if they were versi piani." [125] Many passages in the correspondence between Verdi and Ghislanzoni in the summer and autumn of 1870 provide a perfect illustration of the metrical and musical novelties in Verdi's new approach. The composer several times expresses his thoughts on the frequent hindrances that the habit of providing strophes for a cantabile brought with it.

> I know very well that you will ask: "And the verse, the rhyme, the strophe?" I don't know what to say. But when the action demands it, I would quickly abandon rhythm, rhyme, strophe; I would write unrhymed verse to say clearly and distinctly whatever the action requires. Unfortunately, it is sometimes necessary in the theater for poets and composers not to write poetry and music. [126]

> I myself would forget about strophic or rhythmic forms; I would not think about singing, and I would render the situation as it is, perhaps even in lines of recitative. [127]

---

124. Rosen and Porter, *Verdi's "Macbeth,"* 93 (28 Jan. 1865).

125. After Hans Busch, *Verdi's "Aida": The History of an Opera in Letters and Documents* (Minneapolis: University of Minnesota Press, 1978), 49.

126. Ibid., 50 (17 Aug. 1870).   127. Ibid., 70 (28 Sept. 1870).

Together with his occasional irritation with strophic blocks, the requests that Verdi now made to his librettists provide an opportunity to evaluate just how much the nature of operatic singing had changed. Their versifying now had to be full of lines with odd numbers of syllables (without pronounced accentuation), especially in the case of longer lines, which could then be broken into segments in various ways, and they also had to invent polymetric groupings with an emphasis on these combining long and short lines to break up the rhythmic flow: such demands would have been, not just unthinkable a few decades earlier, but completely the opposite. The act 4 duet for Amneris and Radames, for which he had imagined "a song *sui generis;* not the usual *romanza* or *cavatina,* but a declamatory song, sustained and elevated," could make use of "the double line of seven syllables, as in *Trovatore,*"[128] while Verdi frequently expresses his high opinion of the *endecasillabo.* "The backstage chorus is beautiful, but that six-syllable line seems short to me for this situation. Here I would have liked a full line, Dante's line, and even in tercets," wrote the composer on 4 November 1870.[129] Besides, "I like the long line,"[130] he confirmed shortly afterward, showing at the same time an eloquent intolerance of even-numbered lines, which before he had greatly favored, and even for the leading meter of the type, the *ottonario.* "I don't much like the rhythm of the ottonari because of those damned notes on the upbeat ♪♪. / But I'll avoid them,"[131] he declared to Boito on 10 January 1881 at the time of the revision of *Simon Boccanegra,* only to find the librettist fully in agreement: "Those damned ottonari, you're right, are the most annoying rigmaroles in our poetic metre. I have chosen them out of desperation."[132] With regard to the *decasillabo,* the composer, referring to the versification of the Judgment Scene in act 4 of *Aida,* wrote to Ghislanzoni, "Some time ago I advised you to avoid that meter because it became too bouncy in the allegri; but in this situation the three by three accent would pound like a hammer and become terrifying."[133] To point the composer in the right direction in a passage in *Otello,* Boito cautioned Verdi to note the unusual stress he had adopted: "At the beginning and at the end, and in the refrains of this chorus, I have tried a senario verse, not accented like the usual ones, but uniformly, with one strong and one weak accent; the rhythm of the verse suggests three-quarter time."[134] This different shape subverted the customary relationships, so that

128. Ibid., 85 (25? Oct. 1870).
129. Ibid., 92 (4 Nov. 1870).
130. Ibid., 197 (5 Aug. 1871).
131. After Hans Busch, *Verdi's "Otello" and "Simon Boccanegra" (Revised Version) in Letters and Documents* (Oxford: Clarendon Press, 1988), 1:58.
132. Ibid., 62–63 (14 Jan. 1881).
133. Busch, *Verdi's "Aida,"* 92 (4 Nov. 1872).
134. Busch, *Verdi's "Otello,"* 1:104 (17 June 1881).

it was now lines with odd numbers of syllables that took precedence in versification for music, precisely because the sequence of stresses was less rigid and
they could be more easily manipulated to create asymmetrical, not periodic,
phrasing. Apart from the abundance of *endecasillabi* and the related *settenari*
and *quinari,* now all frequently used in cantabiles, the double *settenario* (also
known as an Alexandrine *alla francese* or as "Martellian," in memory of Pier
Jacopo Martello, who had written on the verse type and introduced it into
Italy at the beginning of the eighteenth century) began to have some success.
In Boito's hands it was no longer an exception, as it was in the context of Azucena's narration, mentioned above, but was one possible meter for dialogue
as early as *Mefistofele* (1.1, 2.1) and *La Gioconda* (1.6), then in *Otello* (2.3,
2.5, 3.2) and even more so in *Falstaff* (1.1, 2.2), where thanks to the clever
use of a mixture of *piano, tronco,* and *sdrucciolo* endings and enjambments
(even some internal with the shifting of the caesura), it offered extra advantages for nonperiodic phrasing, as in act 2, first part:

FALSTAFF

   Io son già molto innanzi;   (non c'è ragion ch'io taccia
   con voi) fra una mezz'ora   sarà nelle mie braccia.

FORD

   Chi?

FALSTAFF

      Alice. Essa mandò   dianzi una . . . confidente
   per dirmi che quel tanghero   di suo marito è assente
   dalle due alle tre.

FORD

             Lo conoscete?

FALSTAFF

                   Il diavolo
   se lo porti all'inferno   con Menelao suo avolo!
   Vedrai! Te lo cornifico   netto! se mi frastorna
   gli sparo una girandola   di botte sulle corna!
   Quel messer Ford è un bue!   Un bue! Te lo corbello,
   vedrai! Ma è tardi. Aspettami   qua. Vado a farmi bello.

    The same need to create asymmetrical supports for the music led Boito to
attempt an off-balance variant of the Alexandrine in *Otello,* made up of an
ottonario plus a *senario* (1.1: "Lampi! Tuoni! Gorghi! Turbi—tempestosi e
fulmini!" 2.5: "Sì, pel ciel marmoreo giuro!—Per le attorte folgori!"), which
must certainly have pleased Verdi, who was himself already seeking such unusual solutions. Indeed, he had been the one to encourage Ghislanzoni in this
direction during the preparatory work on *Aida:* "If we give lyric form to the

entire [Amneris/Radames] duet, don't you think the first scene would require greater development? What if we wrote a romanza? A romanza in novenari? What the devil would come out of it? Shall we try?" [135] And later, "If you can find a slightly new form for the cabaletta, this duet will be perfect. . . . And try to write one long line and then one short one, for example

> an ottonario
> a quinario
> or an ottonario
> a senario
> or a settenario
> a quinario
> or a decasillabo
> a settenario.

We'll see what the devil comes of it." [136] His request for the final scene of the opera is even more explicit:

> The French, even in their poetry set to music, sometimes use longer or shorter lines. Why couldn't we do the same? This entire scene cannot, and must not, be anything other than a scene of singing, pure and simple. A somewhat unusual verse form for Radamès would oblige me to find a melody different from those usually set to settenari or ottonari and would also oblige me to change the tempo and meter in order to write Aida's *solo* (a kind of *half-aria*).[137]

He had drafted an outline himself ("Morire! tu, innocente! / Morire! . . . tu, sì bella? / Tu, nell'april degli anni / Lasciar la vita?"), which he commented on with the words, "You cannot imagine what a beautiful melody can be made out of so strange a form, and how much grace is given to it by the quinario after the three settenari, and how much variety is lent by the endecasillabi that follow."

Following the same pattern of breaking a series of equal syllables by suddenly moving to a small-gauge meter (such as the regular rotation of *piano endecasillabi* and *tronco settenari* in Leonora's melody in *La forza del destino*, 4.6), the composer had a suggestion for the priestly invocations at the end of the first act: "It seems that the litanies . . . should be short strophes of one long line and one quinario; or—and perhaps this would be better so that everything could be said—two ottonari and the quinario, which would be the *ora pro nobis*." [138] As it turned out, Ghislanzoni moderated Verdi's open-mindedness in favor of the more usual coupling of *settenari* and a *quinario*:

135. After Busch, *Verdi's "Aida,"* 86 (25? Oct. 1872).
136. Ibid., 95 (5 Nov.? 1870).
137. Ibid., 103 (13 Nov.? 1870).
138. Ibid., 55 (22 Aug. 1870).

"Immenso Fthà, del mondo / spirito animator, / noi t'invochiamo!" and so on for another five strophes.

Boito was best at interpreting the desires of the later Verdi: for example, in the third-act final of *Otello* he offered him the most flexible literary basis possible:

> We had agreed that the lyric part of the piece should be one meter and the dialogue part (including the chorus) another. And I have done it that way. The meter of the dialogue is an endecasillabo that can be divided as you wish and can, if it is divided, resolve itself into so many quinari from beginning to end. Therefore you can use either one of the two meters; I had to do it this way because an endecasillabo, extended in a lyrical phrase (a strict endecasillabo), might have come out too heavy, and a quinario too light. I did not want to mix the two meters openly, preferring the device that you see: besides, it seems to me that its effect is impressive.[139]

Some time later, returning to a previous scene, Boito registers a significant change of heart: "I recalled that you were not satisfied with a scene of Jago's in the second act that was in double quinari, and that you desired a more broken, less lyrical form. I suggested making a kind of evil Credo, and have tried to write it in a broken, asymmetrical meter." [140] A few pages further on, for the ensemble passage where the chorus pays homage to Desdemona (2.3), he had pictured polymetric superimpositions to get round the customary homorhythmic uniformity [141] (while in the following quartet, Desdemona and Otello's *settenari* and Jago and Emilia's *quinari* serve to make a clear distinction between different, concurrent pieces of action, just as they had for the "Miserere" at the time of *Il trovatore*.)

Versification at the end of the nineteenth and beginning of the twentieth century was highly mobile and flexible, with frequent changes of meter and stanzas of mixed meters or else blank verse of severe *endecasillabi* for tragic or pseudoarchaic declamation (as in Maffei's libretto for Mascagni's *Guglielmo Ratcliff* or later in the librettos of Pizzetti's operas). It matched a musical syntax that was not periodic and, while often leaning toward lyrical fragments, no longer culminated in grand, strophic arias.[142] As a result, more cumbersome formal elements carry the association of either folk culture (the "Siciliana" octave and stornello in *Cavalleria rusticana*) or a mannered archaicism (the sonnet in *Falstaff*, 3.2,[143] and the one in the third act of *Tosca*, "Amaro

---

139. After Busch, *Verdi's "Otello,"* 1:114 (24 Aug. 1881).

140. Ibid., 161 (after 26 Apr. 1884).

141. *Carteggi*, 56 (17 June 1881).

142. See Daniela Goldin, "Drammaturgia e linguaggio della *Bohème* di Puccini," in her *La vera fenice*, 335–74, esp. 355ff.

143. See Wolfgang Osthoff, "Il Sonetto nel *Falstaff* di Verdi," in *Il melodramma italiano dell'Ottocento: Studi e ricerche per Massimo Mila* (Turin: Einaudi, 1977), 157–83.

sol per me era il morire," shortly after one that had been left unfinished, "O dolci mani mansuete e pure"; act 2 of the same opera had seen an attempt at a "cantata" in a few short strophes, "Sale, ascende l'uman cantico," and there are also Anacreontic madrigals in *Manon Lescaut* and a *strambotto* by Panfilo Sasso introduced into D'Annunzio and Mascagni's *Parisina*).

While the metrical variety that pervades the libretto of *Manon Lescaut* can be explained by the unique encounter between Scapigliatura pretensions and an Arcadian eighteenth-century manner (but also perhaps because too many hands were involved), in *La Bohème* it produces a comic conversational style, clearly tracing descent from the model of *Falstaff*. Let us look at the opening scenes. Rodolfo and Marcello are pleasantly conversing first in blank-verse *endecasillabi* and *settenari* ("Questo Mar Rosso mi ammollisce e assidera") and then in double *settenari* ("Rodolfo, io voglio dirti—un mio pensier profondo"), then adding to these traditionally colloquial meters amphibrachic (short, long, short) *novenari* ("Eureka! / Trovasti? / Sì. Aguzza"), a verse type increasingly to be found in contemporary serious poetry, from Pascoli to D'Annunzio, Carducci to Gozzano, the last of whom uses it precisely in similarly "comic" conversational circumstances for the "delightful chats" in the salon of Nonna Speranza. The frequent changes of meter cut the action into so many juxtaposed vignettes: Colline's arrival and the first sparks in the stove ("Già dell'Apocalisse—appariscono i segni": more double *settenari*), the stove flaming up again ("Atto secondo. / Non far sussurro": double *quinari*), then going out ("Oh! Dio . . . già s'abbassa la fiamma": *novenari* again), the arrival of the "riches" ("Legna! / Sigari! / Bordò!": *ottonari*) with the entrance of Schaunard ("La Banca di Francia": *senari*), who then recounts his adventures in blank verse, and so on. Within this, the increase in rhyme (plenty of rhyming couplets and alternate rhymes, but also internal and middle rhyme) produces some cohesion in a short-breathed poetic discourse, corresponding to a generally loose-knit, "spoken" style of word setting, both in its melodic shapes and in the irregular phrasing, which occasionally broadens into a fairly brief moment of lyrical expansion: a nonchalance that can produce intentionally naturalistic results, in the last act, for instance, when Musetta breaks off from her prayer to fuss around the spirit lamp, just as Pinkerton in *Madama Butterfly* pauses in his speech on the doings of the "wandering Yankee" to offer the consul "Milk Punch, or Whiskey?"

Similar fragmentation also occurs in the tercets of *piano settenari abb* when Rodolfo introduces himself ("Chi son? Sono un poeta"), which still produces broad spans of melody: in the opening lines Puccini cuts the connection with the preceding *ottonari* (the lines "Ah! / Che gelida manina! / Se la lasci riscaldar" are in fact the logical metrical conclusion of the short scene beginning "Buio pesto! / Disgraziata!") to isolate the opening of the tenor aria, using the fact that the blank verse can be chopped up—with internal rhymes and rhyming couplets—for arioso phrases to introduce more expansive passages of song. Meter and line end up counting for little, absorbed as they are into the music. In any case, even Illica felt the same way ("I say, and am convinced, that the form of a libretto is given by the music. And that the composer for his part should set not the 'verse' but the 'idea,' the anguish of a sorrow, the impression and the instant of a situation. Verse was fine in the days of cabalettas"),[144] while Puccini, for his part, confirmed this in practice when he several times suggested metrical solutions for a poetic text that had to fit his musical idea, a preexisting one, therefore, and, to a certain extent, autonomous. For example, he wrote to Illica about *Manon Lescaut* in January 1892:

> My dear friend, I need an adjustment in the trio of the second-act finale: Des Grieux (in ensemble) "Questi tesor / ora abbandona. / Io vo' salvar / la tua persona. / Con me portar / solo il tuo cor!" Very nice, but as I have a rhythmic theme that I can't change because it works, I can't get anywhere with those *sdruccioli* [properly, *tronchi*]. What I really need is something like this: "Questi tesor / tu dei lasciar / mio immenso amor. / Ti vo' salvar / con me portar / solo il tuo cor!" Don't lengthen them or shorten them. They have to be six *tronco* lines. Absolutely, okay? Please excuse me because it's two o'clock in the morning and I'm deep in work, and I've spent a whole evening tearing my hair out trying to adapt those *sdruccioli;* and I really haven't succeeded and that's why I need what I'm asking you for. Let them work as well as the first ones, with the *piano* [properly *tronco*] accents, because that's the only brilliant, impassioned idea. . . .[145]

Puccini had himself prepared an Italian text for the "sad, sentimental, rustic folk song" for the opening of the third act of *Tosca,* a couplet of *endecasillabi* plus four *quinari,* which he sent to Alfredo Vandini to find him "a Roman poet . . . who can do something for me on the [given] meter.[146] Later he had to recognize that the stornello as he had imagined it in traditional, folklike *endecasillabi* meant that he was missing a syllable, and he took it upon himself to insert an extra one in the lines he was sent, declaring, "it will be a *dodecasillabo* line, and it will be a mess, but that's the way it has to be."[147] The official libretto arranges the lines less audaciously in alternate *quinari* and *settenari.*

Often Puccini was not content just to outline a more or less abstract metrical shape but gave an example with the aid of disjointed lines and highly amusing pieces of nonsense, which enraged his collaborators, more aware of the seriousness of their literary role. "Coccoricò, coccoricò, bistecca" (cock-

---

144. *Carteggi pucciniani,* ed. Eugenio Gara (Milan: Ricordi, 1958), 186.

145. Ibid., letter no. 60.

146. Ibid., letter no. 205, 27 Sept. 1899.

147. Ibid., letter no. 211, Oct. 1899.

a-doodle-doo, cock-a-doodle-doo, beefsteak) was the metrical pattern that Puccini suggested to Giacosa to dress with words the beginning of a *piano* berceuse that had first occurred to him in his hunting den on the lake, was later orchestrated to accompany a launch ceremony in a Genoa shipyard, and then finally was transformed into "Quando men vo soletta per la via" in *La Bohème,* giving finished sense to the composer's eccentric suggestion.[148] On 31 July 1894 Puccini sent Illica, by way of Giulio Ricordi, an outline for a section of the second act of the same opera:

> Puccini is waiting anxiously for the Latin Quarter act, but, mea culpa, I forgot to tell you that, after hearing a wonderful piece of music full of life and energy, Puccini wrote down for me on a piece of paper the meters that would suit the music: I herewith transcribe what he wrote down on the paper:
>
>> Quest'è un telegramma di molteplici parole
>>> ti posso dire il vero senza fole
>>> e chi le vuole
>>> queste popole
>> mandi telegrammi di quattordici parole.
>
>> [This is a telegram of many words
>>> I can tell you truthfully, with no fairy tales
>>> and whoever wants
>>> these people
>> let him send telegrams of fourteen words.]
>
> Martellian lines, *endecasillabi* and *quinari,* alternating as the poet so desires, possibly with these stresses.[149]

A year later (28 July 1895), there was a similar request:

> As I'm having Musetta sing a bit offstage [at the beginning of act 3], I need some lines (for a response to what Musetta sings) for the chorus carousing in the tavern. Musetta sings to the words from the second act. The short chorus needs to be in *tronco quinari.* . . . Four lines. For example: Noi non dormiam / sempre beviam / facciam l'amor / sgonfiam trattor [We don't sleep / we're always drinking / let's make love / let's depress the landlord].[150]

Apropos of Puccini's joking poetic vein, Illica himself, who well understood his literary mission and was attuned to the modern ideal of musical drama, penned the following outburst to Giulio Ricordi in January 1893:

> Puccini has confided to a friend of his that he can easily do without my librettos and that *Le nozze di Nane* is ghastly stuff and anyway *no one* can understand him

---

148. Mosco Carner, *Puccini: A Critical Biography,* 3d ed. (London: Duckworth, 1992), 370.
149. *Carteggi pucciniani,* letter no. 11.
150. Ibid., letter no. 126.

because he imagines something . . . something . . . something . . . that . . . ! You'll understand that this *something,* expressed like this, is very hard to interpret. So am I supposed to fumble about in the dark trying to find the something that Puccini is imagining, only to hear the answer, "Don't like it!" with the risk of producing a libretto to be set by Puccini according to the *Manon* scheme, with macaronic verses

primo il mio re	[first my king
col copripiè	with a foot coverlet
e il signor Giulio pagherà	and Mr. Giulio will pay
la refezion	for the refreshments
la colazion? . . .	the nourishments?]

Allow me to say that I don't feel I have the strength to go back to writing words for music—and allow me to express to you why I think this approach is so bad— now that Verdi and Boito are attempting the great artistic project of giving the music the fullest truth and effectiveness of the words, which is the hallmark of theater. . . . Unlike what Puccini thinks, I consider a libretto a collaboration. . . . Let Puccini set the words in the libretto with the emotions that these words inspire and with the characteristics that belong to the people in the libretto and not—for example—when you want to express love, write music on words like

topi – trabanti – sogliole	[mice – orderlies – sole
sego – bilance – pargoli	tallow – scales – tiny tots
son figli dell'amore!	are the children of love!] [151]

At the time of *Turandot,* the composer made some advance clarifications to Adami: "Don't be alarmed: this is how librettos are made. By rewriting them. Until we come to the definitive form necessary for the music, I shall give you no peace. Line, meter, situation, word. . . . don't look at me with that startled expression. . . . stage by stage they have to be studied and examined in the minutest detail, according to my personal desire and my personal requirements." [152] To tell the truth, even when we lack such revealing documentation as that provided by his poetic oddities, it must be said that even in the turn of his melodies and his phrasing, Puccini often gives the impression of having anticipated in the music passages that the poet has only later filled with sense and adapted to metrical traditions with greater or lesser success. To take a couple of examples, think of the awkward articulation of "Che fai? / Nei cieli bigi / guardo fumar dai mille / comignoli Parigi" at the beginning of *Bohème,* or Tosca's "Vissi d'arte," the text of which is so polymetric and lacking any sense of regularity as to recall the worst sort of whimsy of late-

151. Ibid., letter no. 80.

152. In Giuseppe Adami, *Puccini* (Milan: Treves, 1935), 67ff. (quoted in Goldin, *La vera fenice,* 362ff.).

seventeenth-century librettos. There are countless examples of indifference to correct accentuation, which, despite some metrical adjustments, is often sacrificed to the demands either of a particular rhythmic and melodic configuration or of an expressive climax to be reached by means of tightening and emphasis. The first can be seen in *Bohème* in Colline's farewell to his "vecchia zimarra" ("Pàssār nèlle tue tasche / còme_in antri tranquìlli")[153] and in *Manon Lescaut* at the end of the opening scene ("Dànze, brindisi, follìe, / ìl cortēo di vòluttā / òr s'avanza per le vìe / è la nōtte règnerā") and again in the second-act duet for Manon and Des Grieux at the words "Questa / nòn tī sèmbrà_una fèsta . . . pènsàvo / à_un avvenīr di lùce." Further on, when their duet is reaching a climax, these features are combined with intensifying devices producing musical diction that overturns the metrical system and plasters it with weighty extra accents ("īo lèggo_il mïo destīn; / tùtti_i tesor del mondo / hà_il tuo labbrō divìn! . . . Àlle mie brāmē tòrna, / deh torna ancōr! / Àlle mie_ebbrēzzē,_ai bàci / lùnghi, d'amōr," or else "dì quella tua carèzzā; / sèmpre novella_ebbrèzzā"). The same sort of thing occurs in *Bohème,* when Mimì, introducing herself, finally abandons her shy, conversational manner and launches into a passionate confession ("Mà quando vien lo sgèlō / ìl primo sole_e mïō, / ìl prīmo bàcio dell'aprìlē e mïō").

It certainly cannot be claimed that Puccini was the first to demonstrate breaches of the rules of proper word setting: we need only think of Casti's eighteenth-century satire, revealingly entitled *Prima la musica e poi le parole,* or of Felice Romani's complaints, in the following century, on the sad fate of a libretto ("It shoots into life, sketchily educated, still rough and unpolished: the composer takes control of it and sometimes subjects it to procrustean torture; he shortens it and irons it out to fit the bed on which it has to lie").[154] In this too Puccini can be seen to be carrying on a firmly rooted tradition in the professional customs of the Italian opera composer, undoubtedly effective in that it shortened the working time but also possibly injecting into the enterprise a basic lack of concern for the relationship between text and music. In any case, it was taken for granted that the task of word setting was to exalt the core emotions of the libretto, so that an obvious overenthusiasm could be forgiven. In the wake of the later Puccini operas, there soon appeared poetics that aimed to refute this—and other—fundamental principles of the theater. For example, the three *strambotti* attributed to Serafino Aquilano[155] that

153. The accents mark the syllables that fall on the strong beat of the bar, while the quantitative accents show the mensural extension of certain syllables.

154. In Emilia Branca, *Felice Romani ed i più riputati maestri di musica del suo tempo* (Turin, Florence, and Rome: Loescher, 1882), 117.

155. Barbara Bauer-Formiconi, *Die Strambotti des Serafino dall'Aquila: Studien und Texte zur italienischen Spiel- und Scherzdichtung des ausgehenden 15. Jahrhunderts* (Munich: Fink, 1967), 254 and 261, nos. 201, 202, and 223 (in combination with nos. 189 and 190, ibid., p. 250).

Malipiero used for the "Canzone del tempo" in his *Torneo notturno* (1929)[156] are almost neutered, not only by the rigidity of their relentless melodic and rhythmic shape but also by being set to music that systematically underplays the principal stresses of the *endecasillabi* by placing them on the weakest beats in the bar: despite the predominantly syllabic setting, the isometric nature of the stanzas is not respected either, because they are shortened by enjambments linked to synaloepha—where possible—and swollen by diaeresis. All that is left of this piece of literature, apart from its metaphysical reflection, is its archaic tone: the character of a piece of writing in verse has largely evaporated, as a contemporary,[157] commenting on another work by Malipiero (the Pirandello setting, *La favola del figlio cambiato*), observed in 1934.

In more recent times phonic fragmentation has entered the picture—fragmentation of the line, the word, and its smallest components. Starting from his own *Hölderlin* (1972) and looking ahead to *Per Massimiliano Robespierre* (1975), Giacomo Manzoni offered the following thoughts:

> We can already see in this piece how every word and every letter is used according to its timbral and phonetic quality. For example, if I say "parola," I can set it vertically giving one voice the letter *a*, the letter *p* is only a momentary explosion, the letter *r* can be used both voiced and unvoiced, each way separately or together, the letter *o* can obviously be used for its vocal quality; the letter *l* likewise, because it is a continuing letter that can be set on various pitches, and then the letter *a* again. ... This method, whether used vertically or horizontally, places, as I see it, each phonic value in a unique position. It is clear that comprehensibility of the text is not an issue here, but I believe that it should be grasped that the question for a composer is not how to make a text understood but how to interpret it and transform its qualities, in this case even its purely phonetic ones.[158]

The traditional metrical starting point of the textual support (whether poetically "measured" or in prose), thus violated and dispersed, is subjected to new kinds of demands by the New Music, but whatever they are they are completely alien to the world of what is known as "Italian opera."

156. See Francesco Degrada, "Strutture musicali del *Torneo notturno*," in *G. F. Malipiero e le nuove forme della musica europea*, ed. Luigi Pestalozza (Milan: Unicopli, 1984), 66–82.

157. Gastone Rossi-Doria, quoted in Gigi Livio, "I testi e le forme del teatro malipieriano: *La favola del figlio cambiato*," in *G. F. Malipiero*, 114.

158. Giacomo Manzoni, in *Poesia in pubblico: Parole per musica* (Genoa: Liguria Libri, 1981), 215; quoted in Enrioc Fubini, "Da Wagner a Stockhausen, Musica e parola: Evoluzione di un problematico incontro," *Studi musicali* 15 (1986): 147ff.

BIBLIOGRAPHIC NOTE

Before approaching the specific problems that arise from the use of verse in opera, it is worthwhile looking at the historic vision of metrics in literature provided by Mario Martelli, "Le forme poetiche italiane dal Cinquecento ai nostri giorni," in *Letteratura italiana*, vol. 1, *Le forme del testo: Teoria e poesia*, ed. Alberto Asor Rosa (Turin: Einaudi, 1984), 519–620. Also to be found in the same volume is the essay by Aldo Menichetti, "Problemi della metrica," 349–90, which looks at theoretical questions, as does Costanzo Di Girolamo in his thoughtful *Teoria e prassi della versificazione*, rev. ed. (Bologna: Il Mulino, 1983). It is always rewarding to consult such manuals as W. Theodor Elwert, *Versificazione italiana dalle origini ai nostri giorni* (Florence: Le Monnier, 1973); Mario Ramous, *La metrica* (Milan: Garzanti, 1984); and Raffaele Spongano, *Nozioni ed esempi di metrica italiana*, rev. ed. (Bologna: Patron, 1974).

Moving on to the musical aspects, which most concern us here, some theoretical sources that are useful, either in their entirety or in part, and offer a good perspective on the problems under discussion are available in modern editions. First of all, there are the two classics by Angelo Solerti, *Le origini del melodramma* (Turin: Bocca, 1903; reprint, Bologna: Forni, 1969) and *Gli albori del melodramma* (Milan, Palermo, and Naples: Sandron, 1904; reprint, Bologna: Forni, 1976); and Heinz Becker, ed., *Quellentexte zur Konzeption der europäischen Oper im 17. Jahrhundert* (Kassel: Bärenreiter, 1981). As well as these collections, see *Il corago, o vero Alcune osservazioni per metter bene in scena le composizoni drammatiche*, ed. Paolo Fabbri and Angelo Pompilio (Florence: Olschki, 1983); Paolo Fabbri, "Riflessioni teoriche sul teatro per musica nel Seicento: *La poetica toscana all'uso* di Giuseppe Gaetano Salvadori," in *Opera e libretto* (Florence: Olschki, 1990), 1:1–31; Pier Jacopo Martello, *Scritti critici e satirici*, ed. Hannibal S. Noce (Bari: Laterza, 1963); Benedetto Marcello, *Il teatro alla moda* (Venice, 1720; reprint, Milan: Rizzoli, 1959), available in a complete English translation by Reinhard G. Pauly in *Musical Quarterly* 34 (1948): 371–403, and 35 (1949): 85–105; and Antonio Planelli, *Dell'opera in musica* (1772), ed. Francesco Degrada (Fiesole: Discanto, 1981).

Putnam Aldrich, *Rhythm in Seventeenth-Century Italian Monody with an Anthology of Songs and Dances* (New York: W. W. Norton, 1966); and Erich Raschl, "Die textlichen Vorlagen zur weltlichen Monodie im italienischen Frühbarock," in *Festschrift zum zehnjährigen Bestand der Hochschule für Musik und darstellende Kunst in Graz,* ed. Otto Kolleritsch and Friedrich Körner (Vienna: UE, 1974), 185–203, are both useful for the relationship between metrics and music in the early seventeenth century. The central role played by poetry influenced by Gabriele Chiabrera is the subject of two essays by Silke Leopold, "'Quelle bazzicature poetiche, appellate ariette': Dichtungsformen in der frühen italienischen Oper (1600–1640)," *Hamburger Jahrbuch für Musikwissenschaft* 3 (1978): 101–41; and "Chiabrera und die Monodie: Die Entwicklung der Arie," *Studi musicali* 10 (1981): 75–106. For aria structures in the early and middle seventeenth century, the reader should certainly consult Nino Pirrotta, "Early Opera and Aria," in *New Looks at Italian Opera: Essays in Honor of Donald J. Grout,* ed. William W. Austin (Ithaca, N.Y.: Cornell University Press, 1968); but also Nino Pirrotta, "Falsirena e la più antica delle cavatine," in *Collectanea historiae musicae* (Florence: Olschki, 1956), 2:355–66; Thomas Walker's "Cavalli" entry in *The New Grove Dictionary of Music and Musicians,* ed. Stanley Sadie, 6th ed. (London: Macmillan, 1980), 4:24–34; Ellen Rosand, *Aria in the Early Operas of Francesco Cavalli* (Ann Arbor, Mich.: UMI, 1984), 83ff.; Ellen Rosand, "Comic Contrast and Dramatic Continuity: Observations on the Form and Function of Aria in the Operas of Francesco Cavalli," *Music Review* 37 (1976): 92–105; and Ellen Rosand, "Aria as Drama in the Early Operas of Francesco Cavalli," in *Venezia e il melodramma nel Seicento,* ed. Maria Teresa Muraro, Studi di musica veneta 5 (Florence: Olschki, 1976), 75–96. Another useful source on seventeenth-century metrics is Ulderico Rolandi, *Il libretto per musica attraverso i tempi* (Rome: Ateneo, 1951), esp. 43–46, unlike Patrick J. Smith, *The Tenth Muse: A Historical Study of the Opera Libretto* (London: Gollancz, 1971).

For the formulation of recitative between the seventeenth and eighteenth centuries, see Edward O. D. Downes, "Secco Recitative in Early Classical Opera Seria (1720–80)," *Journal of the American Musicological Society* 14 (1961): 50–69; Frederick Neumann, "The Appoggiatura in Mozart's Recitative," *Journal of the American Musicological Society* 35 (1982): 115–37; Sven H. Hansell, "The Cadence in 18th-Century Recitative," *Musical Quarterly* 54 (1968): 228–48; Winton Dean, "The Performance of Recitative in Late Baroque Opera," *Music and Letters* 58 (1977): 389–402; Jack Westrup, "The Cadence in Baroque Recitative," in *Natalicia musicologica Knud Jeppesen* (Copenhagen: Hansen, 1962), 243–52; and Dale E. Monson, "The Last Word: The Cadence in Recitativo Semplice of Italian Opera Seria," in *Studi pergolesiani,* ed. Francesco Degrada (Florence: La Nuova Italia, 1986), 1:89–105.

References or even whole sections devoted to the topic of this chapter can be found in such works as Remo Giazotto, *Poesia melodrammatica e pensiero critico nel Settecento* (Turin: Bocca, 1952); Michael F. Robinson, *Naples and Neapolitan Opera* (Oxford: Clarendon Press, 1972); and Paolo Gallarati, *Musica e maschera: Il libretto italiano del Settecento* (Turin: EDT/Musica, 1984). A substantial work of considerable importance is Reinhard Strohm, *Italienische Opernarien des frühen Settecento (1720–1730),* 2 vols. (Cologne: Arno Volk, 1976), which also contains important passages on the transformation of the text into a musical organism.

For purely literary contributions, see Gianfranco Folena, *L'italiano in Europa: Esperienze linguistiche del Settecento* (Turin: Einaudi, 1983); Gabriele Muresu, *La parola cantata: Studi sul melodramma italiano del Settecento* (Rome: Bulzoni, 1982); Anna Laura Saletta Bellina, "Personaggio e linguaggio nel libretto comico del '700," *Atti dell'Istituto Veneto di Scienze, lettere ed arti* 133 (1974–75): 331–45, and 134 (1975–76): 1–24 (as well as the eighteenth-century sections in the same writer's *L'ingegnosa congiunzione: Melos e immagine nella "favola" per musica* [Florence: Olschki, 1984]); and Franco Fido, "Le tre *Griselde*: Appunti su Goldoni librettista di Vivaldi," in *Antonio Vivaldi: Teatro musicale, cultura e società,* ed. Lorenzo Bianconi and Giovanni Morelli (Florence: Olschki, 1982), 345–63.

On Metastasio, the most important work is Bruno Brizi, "Metrica e musica verbale nella poesia teatrale di P. Metastasio," *Atti dell'Istituto Veneto di Scienze, Lettere ed Arti* 131 (1972–73): 679–740; and the review of it by Franco Gavazzeni in *Metrica* 1 (1978): 320–23. There are also useful pointers in Elvidio Surian, "Metastasio, i nuovi cantanti, il nuovo stile: verso il classicismo: Osservazioni sull'*Artaserse* (Venezia 1730) di Hasse," in *Venezia e il melodramma del Settecento,* ed. Maria Teresa Muraro (Florence: Olschki, 1978), 341–62. The examination of different settings of the same Metastasio text is the subject of such studies as Cheryl Ruth Sprague, *A Comparison of Five Musical Settings of Metastasio's "Artaserse"* (Ann Arbor, Mich.: UMI, 1979); J. Kenneth Wilson, *"L'Olimpiade": Selected Eighteenth-Century Settings of Metastasio's Libretto* (Ann Arbor, Mich.: UMI, 1982); Helga Lühning, *"Titus"-Vertonungen im 18. Jahrhundert: Untersuchungen zur Tradition der Opera Seria von Hasse bis Mozart* (Laaber: Volk-Laaber, 1983); and Reinhard Wiesend, "Le revisioni di Metastasio di alcuni suoi drammi e la situazione della musica per melodramma negli anni '50 del Settecento," in *Metastasio e il mondo musicale,* ed. Maria Teresa Muraro (Florence: Olschki, 1986), 171–97 (also found in *Archiv für Musikwissenschaft* 40 [1983]: 255–75).

Eighteenth-century metrical approaches are also examined in the following writings by Wolfgang Osthoff: "Musica e versificazione: Funzioni del verso poetico nell'opera italiana," in *La drammaturgia musicale,* ed. Lorenzo Bianconi (Bologna: Il Mulino, 1986), 125–41; "Händels 'Largo' als Musik der goldenen Zeitalters," *Archiv für Musikwissenschaft* 30 (1973): 175–89; "Mozarts Cavatinen und ihre Tradition," in *Helmuth Osthoff zu seinem siebzigsten Geburtstag,* ed. Wilhelm Stauder, Ursula Aarburg, and Peter Cahn (Tutzing: Schneider, 1969), 139–77; and "Gli endecasillabi villotistici in *Don Giovanni* e *Nozze di Figaro,*" in *Venezia e il melodramma nel Settecento,* ed. Maria Teresa Muraro (Florence: Olschki, 1981), 2:293–311. On Mozart, see also Friedrich Lippmann, "Mozart und der Vers," *Analecta Musicologica* 18 (1978): 107–37. On the structuring of act finales, see Daniel Heartz, "The Creation of the Buffo Finale in Italian Opera," *Proceedings of the Royal Musical Association* 104 (1977–78): 67–78.

For the situation at the end of the eighteenth and beginning of the nineteenth centuries, see Gianfranco Folena, *L'italiano in Europa: Esperienze linguistiche del Settecento* (Turin: Einaudi, 1983); and the early parts of Daniela Goldin, *La vera fenice: Librettisti e libretti tra Sette e Ottocento* (Turin: Einaudi, 1985); as well as Renato Di Benedetto, "Lineamenti di una teoria della melodia nella trattatistica italiana fra il 1790 e il 1830," *Analecta Musicologica* 21 (1982): 421–43; and, by the same author, the chapter "Il Settecento e l'Ottocento," in *Letteratura italiana,* vol. 6, *Teatro, musica, tradizione dei classici* (Turin: Einaudi, 1986), 365–410. The late-eighteenth-century situation is also covered in Friedrich Lippmann, "Der italienische Vers und der musikalische Rhythmus: Zum Verhältnis von Vers und Musik in der italienischen

Oper des 19. Jahrhunderts, mit einem Blick auf die 2. Hälfte des 18. Jahrhunderts," *Analecta Musicologica* 12 (1973): 253–369; 14 (1973): 324–410; 15 (1975): 298–333, which are also of fundamental importance, to say the least, as far as the nineteenth century is concerned. The same writer's equally important monograph on Bellini, *Vincenzo Bellini und die italienische Opera Seria seiner Zeit: Studien über Libretto, Arienform und Melodik* (Cologne and Vienna: Böhlau, 1969), should not be forgotten. Other useful sources are Sieghart Döhring, *Formgeschichte der Opernarie vom Ausgang des achtzehnten bis zur Mitte des neunzehnten Jahrhunderts* (diss., Marburg 1969; published, Itzehoe, 1975); Sieghart Döhring, "La forma dell'aria in Gaetano Donizetti," in *Atti del 1° convegno internazionale di studi donizettiani 22–28 settembre 1975* (Bergamo: Azienda Autonoma di Turismo, 1983), 149–78. Rossana Dalmonte deals with particular formal structures in nineteenth-century librettos in "La canzone nel melodramma italiano del primo Ottocento: Ricerche di metodo strutturale," *Rivista italiana di musicologia* 11 (1976): 230–313.

The key role of Rossini is examined in Scott L. Balthazar, "Rossini and the Development of the Mid-Century Lyric Form," *Journal of the American Musicological Society* 41 (1988): 102–25.

The following Verdian studies give some coverage of metrical problems: Mario Rinaldi, *Verdi critico: I suoi giudizi, la sua estetica* (Rome: Ergo, 1951); Philip Gossett, "Verdi, Ghislanzoni and *Aida:* The Uses of Convention," *Critical Inquiry* 1 (1974–75): 291–334; Harold S. Powers, "'La solita forma' and 'the Uses of Convention,'" in *Nuove prospettive nella ricerca verdiana* (Parma: Istituto di Studi Verdiani; Milan: Ricordi, 1987), 74–109 (also in *Acta Musicologica* 59 [1987]: 65–90); Peter Ross, *Studien zum Verhältnis von Libretto und Komposition in den Opern Verdis* (Bern: Gnägi, 1979); Peter Ross, "Amelias Auftrittsarie im *Maskenball:* Verdis Vertonung in dramaturgisch-textlichem Zusammenhang, *Archiv für Musikwissenschaft* 40 (1983): 126–46; Pierluigi Petrobelli, "Music in the Theatre (à propos of *Aida,* Act III)," in *Themes in Drama,* vol. 3, *Drama, Dance and Music* (Cambridge: Cambridge University Press, 1980), 129–42 (also available in the collected volume of his essays: *Music in the Theater: Essays on Verdi and Other Composers* [Princeton: Princeton University Press, 1994]); Wolfgang Osthoff, "Il Sonetto nel *Falstaff* di Verdi," in *Il melodramma italiano dell'Ottocento: Studi e ricerche per Massimo Mila* (Turin: Einaudi, 1977), 157–83 (as well as his "Musica e versificazione," in *La drammaturgia musicale,* ed. Lorenzo Bianconi [Bologna: Il Mulino, 1986], 125–41); James A. Hepokoski, *Giuseppe Verdi: "Falstaff"* (Cambridge: Cambridge University Press, 1983); and Daniela Goldin, *La vera fenice: Librettisti e libretti tra Sette e Ottocento* (Turin: Einaudi, 1985).

Some ideas on Verdi's contemporaries can be found in Folco Portinari, *Pari siamo! Io la lingua, egli ha il pugnale: Storia del melodramma ottocentesco attraverso i suoi libretti* (Turin: EDT/Musica, 1981); and Cesare Orselli, "Arrigo Boito: Un riesame," *Chigiana* 25 (1968): 197–214. Some of the final section of Daniela Goldin, *La vera fenice,* is devoted to this topic, while references to metrics can be found in Luigi Baldacci, "I libretti di Mascagni," *Nuova rivista musicale italiana* 19 (1985): 395–410, as well as in the volume *Teatro dell'Italia unita,* ed. Siro Ferrone (Milan: Il Saggiatore, 1980), especially in the contributions by Mario Morini and Ruggero Jacobbi, pp. 314 and 317ff.

— 4 —

Opera and Italian Literature

MARZIO PIERI

Rather than spending so much time on sonata form, something which, in theory, can be taught in half an hour, the teacher ought to be watching over the pupil's cultural awareness, both in general and in musical terms, and trying to direct him or her slowly toward the most difficult stage in an artist's life . . . that of reading for the first time, with the utmost delicacy, the book that is inside them.   LUIGI DALLAPICCOLA (1949)

Now that I have the complete libretto [of *La vera storia*] in my hands, I am struck by its somber, grim tension, the way it reflects an era when tragic news comes to us continually from all corners of the globe, and a world condemned to turn inescapably in a circle of violence and oppression. This is how it seems as mere words: in a live performance this darkness will be torn apart by the music's vital energy.   ITALO CALVINO (1982)

This account is of necessity a condensed one but, more important, one that— ideally, if not chronologically—overturns some preconceptions and is sharp in its chiaroscuros. However much the basic idea may, at the outset, seem self-

This essay was written more than fifteen years ago. With regard to the main ideas contained within it, as well as for a more up-to-date bibliography, it should be read in conjunction with my chapter "Il melodramma nel Settecento e nell'Ottocento," in the *Storia generale della letteratura italiana*, ed. N. Borsellino and W. Pedullà (Milan: Federico Motta, 1999), 9: 447–77, and with the anthology *Libretti d'opera italiani dal Cinquecento al Duemila*, part of the collection *Cento libri per mille anni* issued by the Poligrafico dello Stato, under the direction of W. Pedullà (Rome: Editalia, 2000).

The first epigraph is from Dallapiccola's *Appunti, incontri, meditazioni* (Milan: Suvini Zerboni, 1970), 129. The second is from the program booklet (p. 31) for the premiere of *La vera storia* at the Teatro alla Scala, Milan, 9 March 1982.

evident in Italy, at least on the level of great achievements such as those ex-emplified by the "shining beacon" of Wagner, the Mussorgsky "case," or the phenomenal, outdated team of Auden and Stravinsky, opera and literature have never come together.

Think of the notorious example of the failed encounter between Bellini and Leopardi[1] or the splendid original misunderstanding—a case of stating

1. The counterpart being the other, essentially rhetorical, cliché of the pairing of Verdi and Manzoni. In fact, the two men met only once: when the "Bear of Busseto" paid a visit to the "Saint of Via del Morone" in 1867, and this was the doing of two religious, intellectual women (Giuseppina Strepponi and Clarina Maffei) who intimidated Verdi. (Manzoni was in fact born seven years before Rossini and twenty-eight before Verdi. His *Osservazioni sulla morale cattolica* dates from 1819, the year of Rossini's *Ermione* and *La donna del lago,* a late and by then solidly "serio" stage in that composer's operatic career, a career that was to come to an end in Paris, with *Guillaume Tell,* two years after Manzoni's *I promessi sposi.* In both cases—Rossini and Manzoni—neuroses and a drying up of their creativity cut across a premature old age which lasted, for those two great men, more than thirty years. As for Verdi's *Messa di Requiem* for Alessandro Manzoni, it should be remembered that it was originally intended to be a collaborative work "in memory of Rossini.")

As for the connection between Vincenzo Bellini and Giacomo Leopardi, Beniamino Dal Fabbro imagines it in these terms: "Bellini's pen, in 1831, rapidly noting on the stave the arias and recitatives of first *La sonnambula* and then *Norma,* is like Leopardi's in 1824, speedily noting down his *Operette morali;* and if Leopardi, waiting for the ink to dry on a page freshly covered in his spidery writing, studies the parts of a German or English verb from a grammar lying open on his desk, within sight, we can imagine Bellini, stopping for a break and going to the window to look out on 'Armida's garden,' as the wagging tongues of Casalbuttano had it, or exchanging a few words with Armida herself, the beautiful Giuditta [Turina]" (Beniamino Dal Fabbro, "Un anno di grazia per Bellini," in his *I bidelli di Walhalla: Ottocento maggiore e minore e altri saggi* [Florence: Parenti, 1954], 107–19, quotation on 109). See also Pierluigi Petrobelli, "Bellini e Paisiello," in *Il melodramma italiano dell'Ottocento: Studi e ricerche per Massimo Mila* (Turin: Einaudi, 1977), 351–63. And the eruption, in the fourth movement of Ferruccio Busoni's piano concerto, of a grotesquely distorted version of that theme which legend continued to attribute to Bellini, *Fenesta ca lucive,* is like a grimace of horror.

Regarding Bellini's fortunes with poets see *La Norma resiada* by Carlo Angiolini (1832), which Dante Isella and Gianfranco Folena have disinterred, with results of historical significance (Milan: Allegretti, 1980), for its polemic against the opera, following the mixed reception of the Milan premiere; Ippolito Nievo, "La sinfonia della *Norma,*" in *Lucciole* (1855–57), whose ending merges into a reminiscence of Ugo Foscolo's poem (and anticipates Giosuè Carducci's celebratory style): "Mutarsi allor sembra il teatro in negra / guerra di selve, quando minacciando / vengon per l'aria quelle fiere note. / Gemono i cuori, come sartie oppresse / da vento impetuoso, il sange batte / le arterie e forse più feroce intima / l'antica furia, come in egra mente / passa più torvo il lemure notturno! / Simile a spade contrastanti, a grida / di battaglieri, di feriti, a scalpito / di cavalli, a preghiere, a moribondi / gemiti il risonante ordin si mischia / delle corde vocali; in fin che muore / a poco a poco il suon; tace l'antica / armonica battaglia; il sogno fugge; / mentre il funebre rogo incenerisce / la grandezza di Norma ed il peccato!" (Then the stage seems transformed into a black / battle of wild beasts, when those fierce notes / come threateningly on the air. / Hearts moan, like shrouds battered / by a furious wind, blood beats / in the arteries, and perhaps emulates / the more violent fury of old, when the beasts of the night / pass more grimly through an ailing mind! / Like clashing swords, like cries / of warriors, of the wounded, the galloping / horses, groans of the dying, / the sequence of resounding voices blends; until the sound / dies away, little by little; the old /

the obvious if ever there was one—of the "inventing of opera" while seeking "tragedy." (More surprising and harder to grasp is the genuinely historic balance between tragedy and extravagance which Metastasio managed to create through a perception that was by nature modern, and which the eighteenth-century critic Baretti readily recognized in his famous essay on Metastasio.)[2] Paradoxically, literary figures reached an understanding with nineteenth-century opera when it had run its course,[3] so that every new, genuine attempt to bring the genre back to life must necessarily seem a special case and need the support of strong but flexible theoretical crutches.

It is quite a different matter to be like the literary critic Giacomo Debenedetti, for example, and discover "our tragic Verdi."[4] Then one can stride forth with his Saba-like quality and his *petit maître* militancy for the twentieth-century novel (*Il romanzo del Novecento,* 1971) on what is still the principal path of the Tragic Sublime. Different again is to daydream like the poet Eugenio Montale, thinking ironically of a chaotic, domestic jungle of a Rous-

---

harmonious battle falls silent; the dream vanishes; / while the funeral pyre consumes / the greatness of Norma and her sin) (lines 84–100); Ippolito Nievo, *Tutte le opere,* vol. 1, *Poesie,* ed. Marcella Gorra (Milan: Mondadori, 1970), 399; Arturo Graf, "Casta Diva," in his *Le rime della selva* (Milan: Treves, 1906), 144ff.; and, of course, Gabriele D'Annunzio: "Ode a Bellini," in the Roman daily *La tribuna* of 30 Nov. 1901 (where his canzone "In morte di Giuseppe Verdi" had appeared on 28 Feb.). The original title of D'Annunzio's ode was "Nel primo centenario della nascita di Vincenzo Bellini" (On the centenary of Vincenzo Bellini's birth) and appears in his *Laudi del cielo, del mare, della terra e degli eroi,* vol. 2 (Milan: Treves, 1904), 88–96, with, on p. 91, the inevitable lines, endlessly recycled by the composer Ildebrando Pizzetti and his followers, "semplice nuda e sola / come nel tempio la colonna paria, / la melodia che vince ogni parola!" (simple, unadorned and alone, / like the overlooked pillar in a temple, / was the melody which conquers every word). For the alternative of a "Doric Orpheus," at the opposite end of the spectrum from Wagner, and from Verdi, for that matter, see the commentary on the ode in Gabriele D'Annunzio, *Versi d'amore e di gloria,* vol. 2, ed. Luciano Anceschi (Milan: Mondadori, 1984), 257ff. Finally, see Andrea Zanzotto, "Sonnetto di sembianti e diva" ("Deh, mostra a noi, mostra il tuo bel sembiante," no. 12 of the "Ipersonnetto") in his *Il galateo in bosco* (Milan: Mondadori, 1978), 71.

2. Giuseppe Baretti's essay "Opere dramatiche dell'abate Pietro Metastasio," which appeared in the journal *Frusta letteraria,* no. 3 (1 Nov. 1763) (included in his *Opere,* ed. Franco Fido [Milan: Rizzoli, 1967], 305–15), was written at the request of "two lively ladies of Ferrara"—models for, or sketches of, Fiordiligi and Dorabella?—"who made their request with a very courteous note written, in all honesty, with lovely spelling."

3. There is a striking contrast between Gianandrea Gavazzeni, *La morte dell'opera* (Milan: Edizioni della Meridiana, 1954) (on p. 13 we find the splendid expression, the "wonderful illegitimacy of opera") and Fedele D'Amico, "In che senso la crisi dell'opera," the opening of the special number of *Rassegna musicale* devoted to "Opera del XX secolo," 32, nos. 2–4 (1962): 111–16. See also Massimo Mila, *I costumi della "Traviata"* (Pordenone: Studio Tesi, 1984), which looks very much through twentieth-century eyes; and Jacques Lonchampt, *L'opéra aujourd'hui* (Paris: Seuil, 1980), whose empiricism stands out all the more—in a French context—against the selective classicism of Henry Barraud, *Les cinq grands opéras* (Paris: Seuil, 1972).

4. Giacomo Debenedetti, "Prefazione 1949," to his *Saggi critici,* 1st ser. (1952; Milan: Il Saggiatore, 1969), 27.

seau (Le Douanier, that is), the humble substitute for those who remain on earth.[5] Or, like the poet and music critic Giorgio Vigolo, to listen for the murmurings of history, as if it were a great rustling of branches and birdsong from paradise: the experience of opera as a function (one of many privileged ones) of an inexhaustible rite of rejuvenation, whose sumptuousness modernity seems to have ruled out of our century.[6]

All three cases—the sublime, the bohemian, and the romantic—are a rite of intellectual love: love, the missing element (because of literature's deafness to music and disdain for the "facile" phenomenology of opera), and, even more, the words to describe that love. The writer Francesco Algarotti and the composer Benedetto Marcello[7]—notorious names—and the Spanish Jesuit Stefano (properly Esteban de) Arteaga,[8] who nevertheless raised an imposing and lasting monument to the genre, were trying to clarify the secret of opera's success and where its attraction lay, but because they approached it with the intellectual equipment of the literary-minded, they became caught in a web of prejudice. Italian literary figures took too "high" a position—in terms of their theories and social awareness—for the practical, ephemeral, and commercial

5. For Eugenio Montale (1896–1981) opera and operetta are both like cuttlefish bones ("ossi di seppia"—the title of one of his collections of poetry). There is, for example, the Rimbaud-like poem "Keepsake" in *Le occasioni* (Turin: Einaudi, 1996) ("Fanfan ritorna vincitore . . ."), where (according to Montale's famous note) "reduced to a purely nominal existence, *flatus vocis,* the characters from about fifteen operettas return." Also in *Occasioni* are the "motet" entitled "La gondola che scivola" (The gliding gondola) with its reminiscence of Offenbach's "Chanson de Dapertutto" from *Les contes d'Hoffmann,* and "Il ritorno," described by Montale in a footnote as a "musical air (in the style of Valéry) in which the Mozartian snakes of hell should not themselves alone justify the infernal din." So we have operetta, the "opera" by the greatest operetta composer, and the Mozartian sublimation of singspiel: three stages in a "tragic" transubstantiation of what will always be a "humble" genre, for the literary minded. (Then we have the famous "strana pietà" from *Il trovatore* that turns up in the seventh volume of the periodical *Xenia* [1980, devoted to Montale's collection *Satura* (Milan: Mondadori, 1971)]; and the "Due prose veneziane," from *Satura:* Gesualdo, Bach, and Mozart are lined up against the "awful opera repertory" which Montale claims he loved "with a certain preference / for the inferior.")

6. Vigolo the music critic is well represented in the collection *Mille e una sera all'opera e al concerto* (Florence: Sansoni, 1971).

7. One of Marcello's admirers was Gian Francesco Malipiero. See Malipiero's *I profeti di Babilonia* (Milan: Bottega di Poesia, 1924), a magnificently tendentious anthology of writers, nonmusicians all, on eighteenth-century opera. The critic Massimo Mila reacted to the recent change in perspective, encouraged by the revival of interest in opera seria (and he mentioned Malipiero's book), praising the resurgent "idolatry of bel canto in its most obtuse form" and rejecting the accusation of "being against historical truth" for those who insist on preserving the "inflated absurdities of eighteenth-century opera seria . . . deservedly destroyed by the vivacity and realism of comic opera" (*I costumi della "Traviata,"* 45–50).

8. Esteban de Arteaga, *Le rivoluzioni del teatro musicale italiano dalla sua origine fino al presente,* 3 vols. (Bologna: Trenti, 1783–88; reprint, Bologna: Forni, 1969; 2d ed., Venice: Palese, 1785).

craft of opera; we need only think of their inadequacies in any theatrical genre, apart from written drama. Commedia dell'arte troupes had the same impact across Europe as did comic opera, and we know what that sparked off in Paris, even if only as a pretext—in fact, precisely because it was a pretext. The best librettists were adventurers or soldiers of fortune, and not just in their writing. Carlo Goldoni died in France, after all. Manzoni, in writing *Adelchi,* created his own *Cromwell,* a *Hernani* for Milan, but he lacked the courage, humility, or the supreme sense of irony to put it in the firing line. The failure to send *Adelchi* into battle illuminates the before and after of the history that I am trying to sketch:

> My very dear Sir,
> Your most warm letter, while it fills me with gratitude, also puts me in an embarrassing position, containing, as it does, a proposal worthy in itself, honorable for me, a display of what it would be a kindness to grant, and yet to which I must reply by begging you to put aside your gracious plan. The idea of a performance of my work fills me with apprehension and aversion equally insuperable; so much so that if as a result of my two poor tragedies, which you are so kind to look indulgently upon, being so contrary to general taste, I suffer the displeasure of the cries of the public raining down on me, I have consoled myself with the thought that, in part because of their very strangeness, they should never appear on stage. You see, indeed, how they proceed without any thought for the effects, conventions, or suitability for the stage: a huge dramatis personae, excessive length, speeches beyond the power of lungs, let alone ears, varied and disjointed scenes, very little of what is commonly understood as action and what there is moves slowly, obliquely, and disjointedly. In a word, everything that could possibly make a performance difficult and distasteful is brought together as if on purpose. For that reason, concerning the points on which you have asked my opinion, I must inform you candidly that I do not have, and could not propose, any ideas that might be better than that which you have proposed, for this could not ever amount to anything; for, setting out to write for readers and nothing else, I have not taken sufficient regard for the exclusion from the stage of ecclesiastical characters; and as for the choruses, I had no other aim than to express feelings, without thought for the characters to which to attribute them. That which you are pleased to imagine to that intent (possibly leaving aside Il Genio, in whose mouth you would have placed the chorus of the Carmagnola, an expedient which might, I feel, cause some difficulties, but for considerations quite unconnected with dramatic and literary logic) seems to me the best that could be imagined, but I also feel that no perfect answer could be found in this case, where the material is not capable of such form. Allow me therefore to enjoy the sweet feeling of your friendly intentions, without having to witness too hazardous a result. And I do not say it for myself alone, to whom, I admit, the sound of booing would be more bitter than a thousand hands applauding would be welcome; and, as you see, I put the case more favorably than reason would allow; I say it not for those two poor dramas, which, if they have breath enough to survive in a book, might, tested on stage, die a violent death; but I say it also on behalf of art, and for

those who practice it far better than I. An antipathy to those dramatic novelties (rather old, to tell the truth), which seems to have diminished and come to tolerate them, or at least to disguise them in dramas written to be read, reawakened and provoked by seeing them presented on stage, might turn against other works where certain rules were violated or avoided with much more skill, and with greater restraint; and so I would have the displeasure of having also ruined others' work, of being a hindrance to others with my fall.[9]

This is the unmistakable style of Alessandro Manzoni, wearing his cardinal's hat, writing from Milan on 4 January 1828 to Attilio Zuccagni Orlandini, "Royal Censor of Stage Performances in Florence." In a letter from the previous 22 December Zuccagni had asked Manzoni for permission to stage "at our Teatro Fiorentino" his *Carmagnola* and *Adelchi*. Carlo Dionisotti has famously written of the opposition between church and people in Italy (another history of the country could be traced through that of friars and cardinals), but in the superior, circumspect, and icy style of the "man inspired by the divine muse" and "highest cantor of the most sacred mysteries" (as Zuccagni addressed Manzoni in his letter), it is not only the clumsy Florentine reformer ("in the reform of the Teatro Fiorentino which I have undertaken with such vexations and with so little fruit, I have removed from the stage every minister, rite, and ceremony belonging to the Christian religion, as that was always an object of some ridicule for the baser elements in the audience") who finds himself faced with the goal of exclusion. To object that we are not dealing with opera here is beside the point: in the literary view, as I have written, fortunes of the theater are inseparable from those of the opera house. When Manzoni evokes an audience booing, the one thing he would find intolerable, like a chaste young woman hearing a dirty joke, he must have had in mind the endless booing and laughter that, not far from his door, had sunk the theatrical pretensions of Ugo Foscolo, hero and champion of the immediately preceding literary phase, with the political and literary fiasco of his *Aiace* at La Scala.[10] An enjoyable read, and an essential one for this subject, is Giuseppe Carpani's famous *Rossiniane,* which justifies its subtitle—"musico-theatrical letters"—by opening with the *Lettera prima sopra i teatri di Venezia* (8 December 1804), by which he means what we call "straight" theater—presenting tragedy and comedy—whose fortunes and, particularly, misfortunes

9. Alessandro Manzoni, *Lettere,* ed. Cesare Arieti (Milan: Mondadori, 1970), 1:472–75 (letter no. 278); information on Zuccagni Orlandini, a not insignificant figure in early-nineteenth-century Florence, is on p. 929. See also the edition of Manzoni's *Tragedie,* ed. Giulio Bollati (Turin: Einaudi, 1965); it includes Zuccagni Orlandini's invitation to Manzoni. *Adelchi* was set to music by Giuseppe Apolloni, who was the composer—fairly celebrated in Verdi's day—of *L'Ebreo* (Vicenza 1852, Venice 1857).

10. On 9 Dec. 1811. For an evaluation of Foscolo's tragedy as theater, see Walter Binni, "Lettura della *Aiace,*" in his *Carducci e altri saggi* (Turin: Einaudi, 1960; reprint, 1967), 119–46.

Carpani considered a necessary reflection of the advanced state of decline of "the musical theaters":

> [T]he erudite complaints of all the Algarottis, Arteagas, Napoli-Signorellis, Planellis, and so on, were to no avail. A frenzied desire for novelty and an aversion to studying the basic fundamentals of the art, joined together with greed for a quick return, and the rapidity with which operas are written, sometimes in the space of a week, were more powerful than models from the past or good principles.[11]

Let us wind the clock forward. At the end of the 1950s, when Vittorio Gassman and his Teatro Popolare Italiano seemed to be granting Zuccagni's wish by presenting *Adelchi* on the stage of the Teatro della Pergola in Florence, it was depressingly predictable that the incidental music was that of Verdi in full patriotic flight. Only a year before, for the 1859 centenary, Vittorio Gui, never before seen to display such assurance, awoke the notes of *La battaglia di Legnano* in that same auditorium. To the audience of that *Adelchi*, the rhetorical idea of linking Manzoni and Verdi can never have seemed so desperately wrongheaded. The sensory energy and feigned innocence (those insistent, mindless brasses) of a minor, almost insignificant opera, compared with the masterpieces of the mature Verdi, by their very presence destroyed the tempered mental vigor of one of the milestones of Italian literature. Manzoni was right to have turned Zuccagni down.

But the fact that he might also have been wrong could turn out to be the essence of this account. At its head I have contrasted the "delicate reading of the book inside" (Dallapiccola) and the raging "vital energy" of music (Cal-

---

11. Giuseppe Carpani, *Le rossiniane, ossia Lettere musico-teatrali* (Padua: Tipografia della Minerva, 1824; reprint, Bologna: Forni, 1969), 17. The "decline of opera" is an element that has reappeared obsessively almost since the beginnings of the genre. One is tempted to think that it has disappeared only to be replaced, as above, by the "death of opera." So opera either exists in a state of crisis or is dead. In Carpani's book (from p. 4) the crisis, moreover, is not in opera but in the theater as a whole, or the theater in Venice, once the "home of Goldoni and Gozzi" (letter 1, 8 Dec. 1804). However, the causes, from the baroque crisis to the first signs of romanticism, are the usual ones: "Audiences by nature always love what is new; and they are satisfied with the old only when they find in them, with their original, eternally flourishing beauty and with a high standard of performance, a compensation for not having their curiosity satisfied. . . . The scarcity of good writers, the inadequacy of the remuneration, the lack of funds to increase it, and the odd madness that afflicts almost all Italians with the idea that they are born poets have had the result that amid this flood of new works it is rare to find one that, in one way or another, might not be considered badly done and sufficient to accelerate, rather than hold back, the decline of Italian theater. These tuppence-halfpenny authors, no longer mindful of the great principle that nature is the source of beauty, and that outside nature there is only disorder and chaos, have left the breast of this mother of all praiseworthy work to wander in the realm of extravagance, in search, not of things of value, but of the unexpected, not of the truth, but of the arrresting." Carpani's polemic is aimed at those who mimic Alfieri: "obscure, bizarre, harsh, grotesque, not to mention mad." As always, it is the context that changes, not the complaint.

vino) to guide the reader to this idea: that in fact Dallapiccola sometimes managed, paradoxically, on that basis, to give new life to the violent model of Verdi.[12] But the delicate writer of what might happen on a winter's night to a traveler, who certainly knows what he is doing with words, is one of those writers who will never, ever break through.

The Reasons

I. OPERA AS A POPULAR NATIONAL GENRE

"Another important element was the rediscovery of Italian opera, after the fall of Fascism, in the light of Gramsci's and Lukács's theories, that is, in the light of Marxist criticism."[13] We should not be too surprised that Antonio Gramsci's response to opera as a "national-popular genre" was misunderstood, and continues to be so, by open-minded writers, by which I mean, in the positive sense, the integrationists and nonaligned. Was it a prisoner dreaming? By no means; moreover—almost analogously—Pier Paolo Pasolini, for example, was a free man when his historically nuanced but pitiless judgment on Giovanni Pascoli, both as a poet and as a model, seemed to authorize wild genealogies, and not so nuanced at that, on a supposed line from Pascoli to Pasolini, possibly by way of Sandro Penna or the Padani school of Bertolucci. This is what happens when rhetoric becomes involved with those who want an immediate result. Supreme essayists, both of them, Gramsci and the poet of *Le ceneri di Gramsci* (The ashes of Gramsci) had taken on board the lesson—not a "national-popular" one—of sending their words out on reconnaissance: *verba tene, sequentur res.*[14] Much was "willed" and a little happened, cleverly, to quote Pierre Boulez, "by chance."

It would however be naive to conclude that, even induced this way—as in the expression "induced abortion"—what happened later to one (or two) passages in Gramsci's *Prison Notebooks* is due solely to dubious haste or a calculation of the possible profits from a nice, historically airy piece of writing; the passage ends by imagining something that has in fact never existed in

---

12. In the essay accompanying the LP recording of Dallapiccola's opera *Il prigioniero,* in Fonit Cetra's "Italia" series (and later, slightly diluted, in his *I costumi della "Traviata,"* 283–99), Massimo Mila wrote: "Using a musical discourse that, with some freedom, obeys the rules of twelve-note composition, *Il prigioniero* reveals a sense of theater that is no less vigorous than that which we are accustomed to recognize in a *Tosca* or a *Trovatore*" (299).

13. Luciano Berio, *Verdi?* inaugural lecture of the Fourth International Congress of Verdi Studies (Chicago, 1974), now in *Studi verdiani* (Parma: Istituto di Studi Verdiani, 1982), 1:99–105, quotation on 101.

14. For Umberto Eco, in his *Reflections on "The Name of the Rose,"* trans. William Weaver (London: Minerva, 1994), 24, this "credo" was characteristic of poetry, as opposed to fiction, where "the problem is that of constructing a world," possessing the *res.*

Italy: popular literature in the modern sense. The simple reason is that in Italy, a people, in the modern sense, has not existed either. Establishing one—as seemed to be desired—meant establishing or at least postulating the other. Observers inevitably had to understand the replacement value which opera has had over the centuries, fundamental to our nation, stretching from the Counter-Reformation to Italian Unification and on to Fascism,[15] if they wished not to continue to regard the high plains of literature as castles in the air.

Opera is one of two things: either it is, in a baroque sense, a luxury, a voluptuous, nonreproductive compulsion,[16] or else it is, in a Risorgimento sense, an anticipation of action on thought, the sort of Garibaldinism described by the historian Denis Mack Smith. Once Italy had been made, did they still have to make the Italians? Perhaps the publisher Casa Ricordi, or the book *Cuore,* in all its De Amicis–like, and not always understood, dishonesty, may have contributed what they could to bring about what weavers and redshirts, *bersaglieri* and fighters, had not been able to complete, perhaps not even to foresee completely. On the level of a highly stylized collective imagination, we are close to the didactic line of the later Roberto Rossellini, in the cinema (the attempt to sketch a Risorgimento *Paisà* in his film *Viva l'Italia!* the way Stendhal and Puccini contaminate *Vanina Vanini*) or the notorious Verdi episode in the film *Casa Ricordi* featuring the rough but occasionally genuinely popular singer (and Fascist) Carmine Gallone. While the peasants are rioting, the civil forces are about to open fire on the crowd (in front of Parma city hall). Verdi arrives in his carriage (in the guise of a wickedly bearded Fosco Giachetti) and steps in between Order and Disorder; all bare their heads to sing "Va, pensiero." [17] That famous chorus, with its gilded wings, willows, and harps of gold, its fateful prophets, Zion, the Jordan, and the destiny of Jeru-

---

15. The concept of ersatz opera is also covered in Massimo Mila, *L'opera come forma popolare della communicazione artistica* (Budapest, 1967), now included in his *I costumi della "Traviata,"* 135–51. Mila refers back to Stendahl—opera "the surrogate of a life dreamt and not lived" in Italian society of the time—and also to *Cento anni* by Giuseppe Rovani (1856–65).

16. See Severo Sarduy, *Barocco: Pour une morale du gaspillage* (Paris: Seuil, 1975); a cross between Roland Barthes and Pierre Boulez.

17. See Patrizia Pistagnesi, Adriano Aprà, and Gianni Menon, eds., *Il melodramma nel cinema italiano* (Parma: Grafiche STEP, 1977); in particular, Carmine Gallone, "Il valore della musica nel film e l'evoluzione dello spettacolo lirico sullo schermo" (previously in Salvatore G. Biamonte, ed., *Musica e film* [Roma: Ateneo, 1959]), and Luigi Pestalozza, "Tramonto dei Ricordi" (previously in *Cinema nuovo* 53 [1955]). Further reading: "Follie per l'opera" in *L'avventurosa storia del cinema italiano raccontata dai suoi protagonisti, 1953–1959,* ed. Franca Faldini and Goffredo Fofi (Milan: Feltrinelli, 1979), 163–68. If the modern Italian epic (the poor man's opera, which flourished and declined amid the aura of Resistance) has Rossellini as its Verdi (in the people's trilogy *Paisà, Roma città aperta,* and, with the inclusion of Vittorio De Sica, *Ladri di biciclette*), it should not be forgotten that Gallone, again, revived (or quickly modernized) *Tosca* (to great success) in *Davanti a lui tremava tutta Roma,* "a kind of *Tosca* on the German occupation, in the very locations of the opera," with Anna Magnani, of course.

salem, is another example of that "baroque reality in the history of nineteenth-century Italian lyricism," which Carlo Emilio Gadda wrote about with reference to Manzoni's poem *Il cinque maggio*.[18]

But let us reread the passage in Gramsci, in its entirety for once, to reexamine all its subtleties and even its attempts at circumlocution; we might even appreciate that very evasiveness, partly conscious, partly circumspect, in a web of dated problems (from why Italian literature is not popular in Italy, to a polemic typical of the early-twentieth-century periodical *La voce* against internationalism or cosmopolitanism in music, to the anti-Wagnerian strain): I am convinced that it—together with Giuseppe Mazzini's *Filosofia della musica*—is one of the towering and all-too-rare examples of men of culture (and, no accident, of an entirely political culture) dealing with the phenomenon of opera without touching on any tired satirical defamation—the genre that starts with Benedetto Marcello's *Teatro alla moda* and ends with the anti-Puccinian sarcasm of a scorned D'Annunzio[19]—or ingenuously overturning that satire in eulogies of backward-looking complicity, like Stendhal or Bruno Barilli. It stands for what it is: a sometimes brilliant testimony of a lively taste, the prerequisite of poetry, leaving us unsoiled by the judgment.

Popular literature. I have remarked elsewhere how in Italy music has to a certain extent taken the place in popular culture of the artistic expression which in other countries is held by popular novels and how our musical geniuses have had the popularity which literary figures have lacked. Things to be investigated: 1) if the flourishing of opera coincides in all phases of its development (that is, not as the individual expression of unique artistic geniuses but as a fact, a historic and cultural manifestation) with the flourishing of the popular epic represented by the novel. I feel this is the case: both opera and novel were born in the 18th century [*sic*] and flourished in the first half of the 19th, so they coincide with the emergence and expansion of popular-national democratic forces across Europe. 2) If the European spread of the Anglo-French popular novel coincides with that of opera.

Why was Italian artistic "democracy" expressed in music and not in literature? Can the fact that there was no national language, but a cosmopolitan one, like that of music, be connected to the popular-national failings of Italian intellectuals? At the same point at which in every country there is a rapid nationalization of the native intellectuals, in Italy as well, although less broadly (even 18th-century Italy, especially the second half, is more "national" than cosmopolitan), Italian intellectuals continued their European function by means of music. It can be observed that operatic plots are never "national," but European, in a double sense: either because

18. From the preface "L'Editore chiede venia del recupero chiamando in causa l'Autore" to Carlo Emilio Gadda, *La cognizione del dolore*, 4th ed. (Turin: Einaudi, 1970), 33.

19. "Behold Lake Massaciuccoli: of waterfowl enough to feed the nation but miserably poor in inspiration" (from the *Libro segreto;* quotation here from Gabriele D'Annunzio, *Poesie, teatro, prose*, ed. Mario Praz and Ferdinando Gerra (Milan and Naples: Ricciardi, 1966), 1195. Cf. Mosco Carner, *Puccini: A Critical Biography*, 3d ed. (London: Duckworth, 1992), 165.

the plots are set in all the countries of Europe and more rarely in Italy, taking folk legends or popular novels as their basis; or else because the sentiments and passions of the drama reflect a particular 18th-century and romantic European sensibility—a European sensibility that does not however coincide with obvious elements of the popular sensibility in all countries, from which, in any case, the romantic current had been drawn. (This can be linked to the popularity of Shakespeare and of Greek tragedy, whose characters, in the grip of elemental passions—jealousy, paternal love, vengeance, etc.—are essentially popular in every country.) So it can be said that the relationship between Italian opera and Anglo-French popular literature is not critically unfavorable to opera, since the relationship is historical and popular, not artistic and critical. Verdi cannot be compared to, say, [Eugène] Sue as an artist, although it should be said that Verdi's popular success can only be compared to that of Sue, even if for the (Wagnerian) aesthetic aristocrats of music Verdi does indeed occupy the same position in the history of music that Sue does in the history of literature. Popular literature, in the sense of inferior (such as that by Sue and his descendants), is a political and commercial degeneration of national-popular literature, whose model is Greek tragedy and Shakespeare.

This point of view on opera can also be a criterion for understanding the popularity of Metastasio, principally as the author of librettos.[20]

This is dated 1932, and here some precise information is necessary: the young Mila's *Il melodramma di Verdi* was published the following year by Laterza at the specific request of its director, Benedetto Croce. Even today the reader will be aware of its way of recounting history—even of opera—that is first and foremost a way of making that history. The lack of emphasis in Mila's arguments belongs to a new and different type of literature, which is closer to the vital sobriety of Piero Gobetti than to the inspired, verbose, and muzzled voice of Gramsci; not in the line of D'Annunzio nor Pizzetti nor Bastianelli nor, thankfully, Bruno Barilli; and yet Gobetti is a byword for a dislike of musical extravagance.[21] Mila was aligned with the new style of the journal *La rassegna musicale,* also a product of Turin, started in 1928 by Guido M. Gatti; even in the way he wrote, his taste was antiliterary and antioperatic.[22] Opera was now part of everyday life, before coming back as farce

20. Antonio Gramsci, *Quaderni del carcere,* ed. Valentino Gerratana (Turin: Einaudi, 1975), 2:1136ff.

21. Cf. Giacomo Debenedetti, *Probabile autobiografia di una generazione* (the 1949 preface to the reprint of his *Saggi critici,* 24): "At a certain point, discovering that we had all been lost behind music, suffering from the chord of the seventh and its illusory promises, he showed us that there were tricks of the senses—he spoke, if I remember correctly, of lasciviousness—and declared that music 'was not art,' no less. It was a way of identifying to us that we were wasting our time: the selflessly harsh and intolerant apologue of one who had no more time to waste."

22. The journal was a crossroads of modern Italian culture; see *La rassegna musicale,* an anthology edited by Luigi Pestalozza (Milan: Feltrinelli, 1966); it includes articles from 1928 to 1943 and an appendix with articles from 1921 to 1926 from Guido M. Gatti's other journal, *Il pianoforte.*

and then tragedy. Here is Gramsci again (in a quotation that contradicts the previous one, as must almost naturally be the case in a tortuous thinker, fond of his own principles):

> It is not true that it is only in some inferior levels of intelligence that one finds a novelistic and not inborn sense of life. There is just as much a "novelistic" degeneration of life in working classes; and it comes not only from books but also from other means of dissemination of culture and ideas. Verdi's music, or rather the librettos and plots of the operas set by Verdi, are responsible for a whole series of "artificial" attitudes of popular life, or ways of thinking, of a "style." "Artificial" is possibly not quite the right word, because in popular examples this artificial quality takes on ingenuous and moving forms. *To many working-class people, the baroque and operatic seem a way of feeling and acting that is extraordinarily seductive, a way of avoiding things they consider low, mean, and despicable in their lives and education and of entering a higher sphere, of lofty emotions and noble passions.* Serials and below-stairs romances (the whole cloying, tearful literature) offer heroes and heroines; *but opera is the most harmful,* because when words are set to music, they are more easily remembered and become a sort of mold in which thought takes form. Look at the way many working-class people write: it falls back on a number of stock phrases.[23]

When Gramsci writes "the baroque," he probably still had fresh in his mind the Crocean battle—antibaroque as well as anti-Fascist—which culminated in Croce's celebrated 1929 compendium, *Storia dell'età barocca in Italia* (History of the baroque era in Italy). But the pairing baroque/opera, like the reference to Metastasio at the close of the passage quoted above, suggests that Gramsci's thinking was still influenced by Francesco De Sanctis's *Storia della letteratura italiana* (History of Italian literature), to which Luigi Russo had problematically and fashionably returned at precisely the same period, in his essay on Metastasio.[24] In the relationship between poetry and mu-

---

23. Gramsci, *Quaderni del carcere*, 2:969 *(Nozioni enciclopediche: La concezione melodrammatica della vita)*, my italics for the pairing of "baroque" and "operatic." See also ibid., 3:1737–40; a "Turin" Gramsci, very close to the problems and to the "style" of the intellectual music lovers of *La rassegna musicale:* "Taste is something which is 'individual' or belongs to small groups; here we are dealing with large masses, and there is no escaping culture, a phenomenon, the existence of two cultures; the individual taste is the 'restrained' one, not the other, opera is the national taste, that is, the national culture" (and yet: "one cultural goal must be the formation of a prose style that is both lively and expressive and at the same time sober and restrained") *(Letteratura popolare: Contenuto e forma,* 1739). From a similar standpoint, compare the words of a representative from the world of cinema, Sergio Amidei, one of the scriptwriters of *Roma città aperta:* "while I was writing I made it plain that I couldn't speak Italian (when I arrived in Turin as a student in 1922–23 I knew then that I would never learn to speak Italian!)." In Faldini and Fofi, *L'avventurosa storia del cinema italiano,* 92.

24. De Sanctis's evaluation of Metastasio provided Luigi Russo with the initial argument for his essay of 1915, *Metastasio* (Bari: Laterza, 1921); the question concerns the extent to which text and music succeed in creating an effective aesthetic fusion in Metastasian opera. There is a notable clarification by a follower of Croce, Andrea Della Corte ("L'estetica musicale di Pietro Metasta-

sic, the sediment of opera played the part of a fixed convention, as in the most rigid cultural line.

Now let's use just a little bit of force and bring some variety to a situation which seems to have become blocked at the very outset, either with opera against literature or against opera in the name of Art. Let us introduce a reader who is insolently typical of our day, a person of cultural refinement, suitably snobbish (and knowingly misrepresenting Gramsci's ideas), along with a sample of the sort of below-stairs fiction that flourished under the wing of opera:

> I have spent the last few months reading many Dickens novels and listening to many Verdi operas; and I seemed to recognize in the echoes left in my memory by the music and the words something that the two had in common. Sometimes, fantasizing about hybrids, I experimented with retelling *La traviata* in the style of Charles Dickens (what wonderful characters Flora and Baron Douphol became, while Germont père remained more or less unchanged) and setting to music some marvelous dramatic situations in Dickens with melodies by Verdi.[25]

The writer is Guido Almansi, the friend of irony and aesthete of the indecent, here writing a preface to one of Dickens's minor works. So much is there: the sense of a game (and the desire to play), a broad, slightly blasé cultural outlook, and the use of the god of curiosity to force one's way into opera, something that neither the scalpel of theory nor the hatchet of sociology can achieve. Naturally, one senses the slackened tension, the feeling of detachment from a battle that others have, in the meantime, won for us:

> And what was the flavor I tasted that they both had in common? Certainly not romanticism, which is of little help in understanding either Verdi or our Italian love of Verdi. And of no help at all where Dickens is concerned. What if it were, instead, vulgarity, that wonderfully exuberant vulgarity which Alberto Moravia brilliantly celebrated in an article entitled, as it happens, "La 'volgarità' di Giuseppe Verdi"? . . . There are some things that Henry James or Claude Debussy would never do or say, write, or compose; but even the most refined women[26] sometimes like to make love with lorry drivers who take them with the same grace with which they change the rear tire on a truck; and when refined men and women take a book to bed, they sometimes choose a Dickens that will seize them by the throat and make them sob

---

sio," an appendix to his *Paisiello* [Turin: Bocca, 1922]), who sees the change of direction to a "symphonic" view of music in the latter half of the eighteenth century as the reason for Metastasio's emotional deficiencies with regard to the "new spirit" in the air. Both Russo's and Della Corte's positions represent the same awkwardness in reading Metastasio in Metastasio, something of which the advent of structuralism in the 1960s made us all masters—that is, another way of avoiding the problem of the concrete style of the texts.

25. Guido Almansi, preface to Dickens's *The Mystery of Edwin Drood* (Naples: Guida, 1983), 5ff.

26. Almansi knows his Lawrence.

with pleasure. . . . if someone does not enjoy the sentimental and emotional qualities of *Great Expectations* or the "abbietta zingara" of *Trovatore,* what can we do
to save their soul but pray for a conversion?

The suggestion is clear: devil take them (and, as usual, lurking in the background is Stravinsky: "rather 'La donna è mobile' than the whole of Wagner's
Ring"). In the meantime, now that we have embarked on the path of vulgarity, even as regards Gramsci's considered words of praise on cheap literature,
we seem to have gone up a step or two, from Sue to Dickens. And what if we
really were to go below stairs? If you will kindly hold your noses, I'll read you
Antonio Ranieri's gothic novel, but that would still not make you choke
enough; the foaming anticlerical novels of Garibaldi (which Alberto Arbasino
seems to know so well) to compensate for those by Padre Bresciani, who so
troubled Gramsci; some dreadful novel by the Romagnolo Mussolini. Farther
down! This is still the illustrious stuff!

Here we have it: *La vendetta del buffone,* a "historic drama in 4 act [*sic*]
by Enrico Montazio," published together with *L'uccisore di leoni* (The lion
killer), a "comedy in one act," translated from the French. It is issue 181–82
of a *New Dramatic Repertory,* printed in Florence by the typesetter and bookseller Galletti, Romei & Co., dated 1869. Let us see what it says in the "Introduction for the Theater Management to place on the printed poster":

> Vittor [*sic*] Hugo's drama *Le Roi s'amuse* provided an Italian librettist with the
> subject of the opera *Rigoletto,* which G. Verdi imbued with sublime melodies, and
> inspired the most popular English playwright of our day, Tom Taylor, with the plot
> of a dramatic work, which, under the title *The Fool's Revenge,* was fortunate to be
> presented on some hundreds of evenings at the Sadler's Wells Theatre, under the di-
> rection of the celebrated actor Phelps.
>
>   The present historic drama, based more on the tragic death of Galeotto Man-
> fredi, lord of Faenza,[27] poisoned by his wife, than on Hugo's work, which presents
> almost insurmountable difficulties for representation onstage, is taken from the
> work by Tom Taylor, which was principally concerned with effects, the require-
> ments of the stage, and, first and foremost, moral teaching. The Italian author in-
> vented the principal characters, made the adaptation, and developed Tom Taylor's
> dramatic action with the addition of new episodes, removing all traces of his work
> in the principal scenes.

In the company of Montazio we find ourselves in the cellar of a palace that
has not yet fallen into disrepair (the play was performed in Turin, at the
Teatro Alfieri, by the Drammatic Compagnia Dante Alighieri, in 1865). At
the beginning of the first act, a stage direction reads: "when the curtain rises

27. Previously used by Vincenzo Monti as the theme of a tragedy not mentioned here (*Gale-
otto Manfredi, principe di Faenza,* 1800).

and before the characters enter, the orchestra plays the prelude to *Rigoletto*" (as far as I am aware, the last example of this sort of contamination between Hugo's Triboulet and Rigoletto is Flavio Calzavara's 1954 film *Rigoletto e la sua tragedia*).[28] Here are the opening lines:

> Messer Filippo Acciaiuoli, come here . . . and be a judge among us. . . . You Florentines are well suited to act as judges . . . since your fellow citizen Dante Alighieri descended into hell one hundred and fifty years ago, to judge the living and the dead.

When Arrigo Boito abandoned his librettist's guise of Tobia Gorrio (a younger brother of Montazio) to mark the revision of *Simon Boccanegra,* did he not present Verdi with a flamboyant reference to the "romito di Sorga" (hermit of Sorga) and "cantor della bionda Avignonese" (singer of the blonde woman of Avignon) in his newly written scene of the revived opera?[29] The fact is that we can and must descend farther. Dating from the eve of World War I, not long before Gramsci penned his thoughts, here is the "Collection of Popular Novels" by Cesare Cioffi, publisher and bookseller (via Chiaravalle 5, Milan). There are plenty of them: *Amleto di Danimarca* (Hamlet of Denmark) and *Rigoletto, Aida* and *Ernani il bandito, Gli Ugonotti, Il trovatore, Norma, L'Africana, La sonnambula, Mefistofele, Il Guarany, Roberto il diavolo;* but also a *Balilla* before *La forza del destino;* and *Cleopatra, Carmen, Lucrezia Borgia; Raffaello e la Fornarina* with *Boccaccio* and *Le cento vergini, Donna Juanita*[30]—a thrilling find for those who know their Montale—and *Il passatore, Rinaldo innamorato* and *Felice Orsini, I masnadieri*

28. Verdi's music survived partly as a "soundtrack," partly as "closed numbers," or "romanzas" in the jargon of the gallery, a remembered slice, or quotation; for example, in the scene with the courtiers, Tito Gobbi first inveighed against them in Hugo's words, then sang the "aria" from the opera ("Cortigiani, vil razza dannata"), an ingenuous duplication that sent the fans (and some unemployed intellectuals) wild but shocked the lower-middle-class audience, who saw the dogma of the unity of "verisimilitude" and "good taste" being tested to breaking point.

29. Indicative of the "high line" of a Verdian reading (premise to such operations as the highly praised "discovery" of a "political" Boccanegra on the part of Claudio Abbado and Giorgio Strehler at La Scala in the 1970s) is Dallapiccola's disdain for a current modification to Boito's text in the opera's first act: "Behold a message / from Petrarch" instead of "the solitary man of Sorga." Dallapiccola says, "we have reached a betrayal of the spirit of *melodramma.* For the very name of Petrarch, just because it is such a great name, gives us a realism in place of the surrealism that is one of the postulates of musical theatre" (see "Words and Music in Nineteenth-Century Italian Opera," a translation of a lecture that Dallapiccola gave in several places in the early 1960s and that appears in *Dallapiccola on Opera,* trans. and ed. Rudy Shackleford (London: Toccata Press, 1987), 133–63; quotation on 139.

30. See Eugenio Montale's *Donna Juanita* in his *Farfalla di Dinard* (Milan: Mondadori, 1960), 24–30 (could it be a moral and aesthetic portrait of the opera?): "Skirt and petticoat down to her calves, gloves, rope shoes, dark glasses, instead of hat a turban in a dark color; a whole armory which swelled to the surface of the water and made her, rather than a bather, an immense Medusa" (25).

and *Nino Bixio, Giordano Bruno* and *Musolino*. There are also some up-to-date titles: *Tosca* and *Fedora, Zazà* and *Adriana Lecouvreur*.[31] Hats off to the person who succeeded in condensing the finale of *Fedora* like this:

> The princess had no strength left; a piercing sob escaped her throbbing breast, while Loris, raising his clenched fists, exclaimed,
> "Dead, all dead! . . . But the vile spy will have me to deal with . . ."
> A servant entered to announce a visitor, Dr. Boroff.
> Fedora, seeing that she was irredeemably lost, opened up the talisman she wore round her neck and hurriedly swallowed down its contents.
> Then, dropping to her knees, and embracing the count's, she cried,
> "Mercy! . . . Mercy! . . ."
> "What's this? Do you dare to ask for mercy for that wicked woman? Do you know who she is?"
> "Yes . . ."
> "Ah, wretched woman, it is you . . ."
> Loris caught her by the wrists and shook her.
> "Forgive me, Loris, forgive me . . . Let death free you from my presence . . . forever . . . I love you, Loris . . . I love you!"
> Dr. Boroff appeared.
> "I know all now, my friend, help her . . . She is dying . . ."
> The doctor felt her temple.
> "Too late," he murmured.
>
> THE END

Those familiar with the writings of Giovanni Verga will be reminded of the end of *Una peccatrice* (1866): the death from opium poisoning of Narcisa, amid the tardy remorse of Pietro Brusio and the useless medical assistance of Raimondo Angiolini. But the Fedoras, Lorises, and Wandas lived on to multiply in the suburbs and small towns of Italy until a page was turned, which for us, happened in the 1950s.

2. ORPHEUS IN THE UNDERWORLD,
OR THE REBIRTH OF TRAGEDY IN THE SPIRIT OF THE VARIETY SHOW

For Bardi—the friend of Vincenzo Galilei, the adviser to Caccini and Peri, the scholar and man of taste who was to launch the humanistic reform of music—to be found still, in 1589, inspiring florid Intermedi in which bedizened gods sang the praises of a princely couple to the madrigalesque music of Marenzio and Malvezzi,

---

31. In addition to the well-known operas of Verdi, Bellini, Meyerbeer, Donizetti, Boito, Bizet, Thomas, Puccini, Giordano, Leoncavallo, and Cilea, the list includes works by Carlos Gomes *(Il Guarany)*, Pietro Raimondi *(Raffaello Sanzio da Urbino e la fornarina)*, Luigi Kyntherland *(Balilla)*, Ferdinando Bonamici *(Cleopatra)*, Franz von Suppé *(Boccaccio, Donna Juanita)*, Alexandre-Charles Lecocq *(Le cento vergini)*, Adelemo Bartolucci *(Giordano Bruno)*, and Franco Bello *(Musolino)*.—Trans.

may at first seem strange and even undignified. It was works of just this kind, so highly appreciated in courtly circles for their 'variety,' that formed the main hindrance to the emergence of any dramatic art and music based on psychology and unity.[32]

Naturally, if we were to make an anthropological study of the presence and function of opera in the "mood of the times" in Italy—and following that, through its spread among the aristocracy or the acculturation of the curious, across Europe—we might not be able to advance very far in what we actually know. Sometimes, whatever erudite and anxious questions on origins and causes are posed, the simple and truthful answer is enough—*possiedo quia possiedo:* that's the way things happened because that's the way things happened. Or, with the inspired empiricist Giuseppe Baretti, committed to lancing the chronic boil of "learned" quarrels:

Where is an Italian poet who has made a hundred wonderful, entirely different characters walk upon the stage, as Corneille has done? One who is as well known from one side of Europe to the other as Molière? What poets of the theater have half their work known by heart by the ordinary Italian people in the way those two immortal Frenchmen are known by the people of their country? Come, let us be more sincere, more dispassionate, and more upright judges of what we have, and let us not be like those who make a public display of magnificence and have empty cupboards at home. Let us declare that Italy is rich in another kind of poetry more admirable even than that of the theater: let us declare that in epic poetry we have work that in volume and variety and beauty is far greater than that of Greece and Rome; that no nation, ancient or modern, no living language can compare with Dante, Ariosto, Tasso, Pulci, Berni, Lippi, Tassoni, and our other poets; and let us leave to the French the honor of their theater, both tragic and comic, and let us laugh at their poets when they take hold of the epic trumpet, which they will never be able to play in their language; and let us not imitate their injudicious critics who come to criticize our Dante and Ariosto and to praise our Tasso and Trissino and other poets without understanding them, reproaching and praising our poetry always for the wrong reasons.[33]

32. Aby Warburg, "The Theatrical Costumes for the Intermedi of 1589," in *The Renewal of Pagan Antiquity,* trans. David Britt (Los Angeles: Getty Research Institute for the History of Arts and the Humanities, 1999), 349–401, quotation on p. 351.

33. Giuseppe Baretti, letter to Count Demetrio Mocenigo 1, in his *Opere,* 69ff. In the context of his *Prefazioni alle tragedie di Pier Cornelio* dictated by the young Baretti in 1747–48, we find this characteristic revival of an argument dear to Pietro Aretino and Giambattista Marino ("my books can be purchased . . ."): "in my opinion, Metastasio, although strictly speaking he cannot be described as a poet of tragedies, is the sole theatrical poet that I would dare to compare with Corneille, however much I may hear from others, and so it sometimes seems to me also, that he does not preserve the true characters of his heroes as they have come down to us in history. This is one of the main criticisms to be leveled at that great man; the other is that in his tragedies or dramas, or however they should be called, he has not taken heed of the precepts of Aristotle and that there are many unrealistic elements in his stories. *But what does that matter when Metasta-*

The imaginative path of "if only" is just too inviting. Let us suppose that in Florence as the sixteenth century drew to a close, it really had been possible to revive, perhaps not Greek Tragedy, a myth that only burst, like a lanced boil, with Nietzsche, but a convincing enough shadow of it, a persuasive ghost, a surrogate made out of the Phoenix of Arabia by those Idle, Erudite Minds. It would be tragedy according to Aristotle (and that was really the first battle to be lost decisively by a spirit that came to an end with the *querelle des anciens et des modernes*). Let us suppose that in the divisions of that Florentine taste, with its aspirations at once classical and modern,[34] there had been no exquisite Rinuccini nor his competitor and friend Gabriello Chiabrera, those *petits maîtres* of nicely modulated verse, but just one Busenello with his realism of dramaturgical "positions" and a "direct" taste in narrative, like the empirical realization of an ideal history:[35] opera would have begun and developed quite differently. But it was written in the stars that opera would be Italy's great invention in the art of modern times, Italy's long farewell to preeminence. It is as if Florence were trapped in a sort of gloomy mannerist magnificence, that matched the Camerata and courtly drama with music, the Uffizi and the Studiolo, the Accademia della Crusca and the villa at Pratolino. Bastiano de' Rossi, known as Inferigno, the first secretary of the Accademia, was, with Giovanni Bardi, Emilio dei Cavalieri, and Bernardo Buontalenti, speaking for the vaunted "reform of opera."

But then opera—and this should always be kept in mind—turned out to be the most successful incarnation in modern times of Festivity, for the whole of its existence.[36] Rather than an opportunity for courtly, scholarly representa-

---

sio is popular and has made so much money for the printers who have reprinted his works over and over again? Metastasio is popular read, sung, and acted; but the fact of all that money earned by the printers is, in my opinion, the greatest proof that can be offered of an author's great merits. Long live Metastasio . . ." (p. 65; my italics).

34. Precisely portrayed thus by Warburg in "Theatrical Costumes for the Intermedi of 1589": "In the Intermedi of 1589 and in *Dafne* of 1594, we have two opposite conceptions of classical sources. One tended, in the Baroque manner that sprang from the illustrious traditions of the Quattrocento, to endow the figures of antiquity with solid form and a certain outward archaeological accuracy; the other, which in a way was more classical, looked to melodrama for a new form of expression in which words and sounds would be united, as they were believed to have been united by the Greeks and Romans in the *melopoea* of tragedy" (386).

35. For material on Busenello, see Francesco Degrada, "Gian Francesco Busenello e il libretto dell' *Incoronazione di Poppea*," (1969) in his *Il palazzo incantato: Studi sulla tradizione del melodramma dal Barocco al Romantico* (Fiesole: Discanto, 1979), 1:3–26; Patrick J. Smith, *The Tenth Muse: A Historical Study of the Opera Libretto* (London: Gollancz, 1971); Bruno Brizi, "Teoria e prassi melodrammatica di G. F. Busenello e *L'incoronazione di Poppea*," in *Venezia e il melodramma del Seicento*, ed. Maria Teresa Muraro (Florence: Olschki, 1976), 51–174; Paolo Getrevi, *Labbra baroche: Il libretto d'opera da Busenello a Goldoni* (Verona: Essedue, 1987).

36. See Lorenzo Bianconi, *Music in the Seventeenth Century*, trans. David Bryant (Cambridge: Cambridge University Press, 1987), 161–70—a fundamental work.

tion (the humanist and Alexandrine premise of opera, from Angelo Poliziano onward) or "miraculous" escapism (in which the popular spirit of Carnival, the joy of [prebourgeois] civil extravagance, and casual prodigality—an almost decadent gesture—conspired together), the literary-minded were faced by another transformation of festivity. Throughout the seventeenth century the lavishness of opera and that of the tournament were easily interchangeable.[37]

To check, let us move to the source, away from any notion of how opera would turn out, and from the possible revival of Greek tragedy, to arrive in the Naples of Boccaccio *(Elegia di Madonna Fiammetta)*, in competition, not with Sophocles or Aristotle, but with Ovid brought up to date:

> Our city, more abundant in cheerful festivals than any other in Italy, not only cheers its citizens with weddings, spas, and seaside promenades but keeps its people happy with an abundance of games, now one, now the other. But among the other things in which it appears most splendid are the frequent jousting tournaments. It is a long-established custom here that after the wet winter months are past, and spring with its flowers and new grass has restored the world to its lost beauty, and youthful spirits burn brightly once more with the change in the weather and are more than usually ready to show their desires, to summon on the most solemn feast days to the balconies of knights noble ladies who gather there decked with the jewels they hold most dear. Nor do I think that the daughters-in-law of Priam, with the other ladies of Phrygia, can have appeared more noble or splendid when they came together before their father-in-law than our lady citizens in many places in our city. Seen together on their many visits to the theater, each one displaying her beauty as much as she can, I do not doubt that whatever visitor were to come upon them would not think them women of the modern age but those magnificent beings of the past come back to the world.[38]

37. For an idea of how tournaments, theatrical celebrations, theater of stage machinery, and opera were freely associated, it should be remembered that Claudio Achillini and Claudio Monteverdi—two people whom history would find it hard to bring together—collaborated on the inauguration of the Teatro Farnese in Parma in 1628. See the poet's letter to "His Most Serene Highness Odoardo Farnese, Duke of Parma," which appears as the preface to Achillini's *Rime e prose* of 1650. A pupil of Pascoli wrote a graduate thesis on the Farnese festivities: Lina Balestrieri, *Feste e spettacoli alla corte dei Farnesi* (Parma: Donati, 1909; reprint, Parma: Palatina, 1981). See also Roberto Ciancarelli, *Il progetto di una festa barocca: Alle origini del Teatro Farnese di Parma (1618–1629)* (Rome: Bulzoni, 1987). A masterpiece of baroque graphics that was devoted to the tournaments of Sicily and that absolutely has to be seen is Padre Pietro Maggio, *Le guerre festive* (Palermo: La Barbera, Rummulo, and Orlando, 1680), reprinted under the title *Le giostre reali di Palermo,* ed. Rosario La Duca (Palermo: Sellerio, 1981); it identifies the birth of opera as a predominantly worldly event—to "make Amazement itself raise its eyebrows."

38. Giovanni Boccaccio, *Opere minori in volgare,* ed. Mario Marti (Milan: Rizzoli, 1971), 3:534. But the reader should also look at the entire *Fiammetta* 5 ("Feasts in Naples"). Ovid and Boccaccio, given their Alexandrianism, are the miraculous wells from which librettists have drawn water from the origins of opera until the break ("a change of imaginative vocabulary") of romanticism.

Here is one "visitor," five hundred years later:

> The long awaited day at last: the gala opening of the new San Carlo. . . . And in those first instants, I did verily believe myself borne away into the Palace of some Emperor of the East. My eyes were dazzled, and my soul was transported. The loftiest imagination can conceive no scene more flower-like in its freshness, nor more impressive in its grandeur—two qualities which are commonly met and reconciled. *This first evening, I have surrendered utterly to pleasure;* I have not strength enough to criticize. The opening of the San Carlo was one of the main aims of my journey, and, a unique case for me, I was not disappointed.[39]

The writer is Stendhal, of course; and—let it be noted discreetly—neither on that day (12 February 1817) nor on the many subsequent ones, all filled with the same sensations of "respect and joy" ("I prefer to remain in the stalls, alone with my sensations"), do we receive the additional information of what opera was being performed.[40] For those who believe in the linking of the "national" with the "popular," however, we read:

> This mighty edifice, rebuilt in the space of 300 days, is nothing less than a coup d'état: it binds the people in fealty and homage to their sovereign far more effectively than any Constitution; . . . all Naples is drunk with patriotism. As soon as you speak about Ferdinando, they tell you, "He has reconstructed San Carlo." So simple is the art of making oneself beloved of one's people.[41]

3. "PIÙ DOLCI AFFETTI": TRAGEDY IN PASTORAL MODE

> Io, che d'alti sospir vaga e di pianti,
> spars'or di doglia, or di minacce il volto,
> fei negli ampi teatri al popol folto
> scolorir di pietà volti e sembianti,
>   non sangue sparso d'innocenti vene,
> non ciglia spente di tiranno insano,
> spettacolo infelice al guardo umano,
> canto su meste e lagrimose scene.
>   Lungi via, lungi pur da' regi tetti
> simolacri funesti, ombre d'affanni!

39. Stendhal, *Rome, Naples and Florence,* trans. Richard N. Coe (London: John Calder, 1959), 353. The italics are mine.

40. A cantata in honor of the king "in the greatest vein of sixteenth-century flattery; the text has not a redeeming feature, no more than has the music, in the courtly style of the sixteenth century: ghastly words and music" (14 Feb.; ibid., 357).

41. And he continues; "There is an adoration chord in men's hearts: I myself, when I think of the cheapness and bigotry of the republics I have seen, I find myself to be a royalist in my bones" (13 Jan.; ibid., 44).

Ecco i mesti coturni, e i foschi panni
cangio, e desto nei cor più dolci affetti.
(Tragedy, in the prologue to *Euridice,* 1600)

[I, who, eager for noble sighs and tears,
my face suffused now with grief, now with menace,
made the faces of those who crowded into the great theaters
turn pale with pity,
    no blood spilled from innocent veins,
no eyes closed by a furious tyrant,
my song if of a display unhappy to the human gaze,
on sad and tearful stages.
    Hence, far even from courtly palaces
deadly phantoms, shades of anxiety!
Behold, I change my sad tragedies and gloomy guises
and awaken in hearts sweeter emotions.]

The year is 1600. We have come in our time-machine to the Florentine court to hear Ottaviano Rinuccini's *Euridice* set to music by Jacopo Peri, then by Giulio Caccini (more like Pavarotti or the popular singer Edoardo Bennato than Handel or Rossini). The splendid occasion is the marriage by proxy between Maria de' Medici and Henry IV of France and Navarre. The poetry belongs to a tradition of restraint and is delightful. The prevailing style is that of the Tasso of *Aminta,* still poised, not yet out of control, gently made grammatical; this rare, experimental bloom has been chosen with discernment and transplanted to initiate what may turn out to be quite an intense growth. In Giovan Battista Doni's *Trattato della musica scenica* (Treatise on music for the stage),[42] concerned with the survival of the Greek dream of the Florentines (rediscovered and exceeded in modern times)[43] in the baroque era and in the Rome of the Barberini family (and so opposed to Giambattista Marino), the author gave *Aminta* as his declared model when he wrote that "true song . . . is the stuff of pastorals." This is in complete agreement with the fact that the Prologue to *Euridice,* given to a character as far from pastoral as can be imagined—Tragedy—softens the edges to exchange "sad tragedies" and "gloomy guises" for "more gentle emotions." The overwhelming

42. For the position of Doni, see Bianconi, *Music in the Seventeenth Century,* 54, and in chapter 1 of the present volume the passages on him by Renato Di Benedetto; there is a revealing shift, in the most pragmatic sense of the word, effected during the same period by *Il corago,* the treatise on staging attributed to Pierfrancesco Rinuccini (son of Ottavio), which Di Benedetto again deals with, as does Gerardo Guccini in *Opera on Stage,* vol. 5 of this *History of Italian Opera* (Chicago: University of Chicago Press, 2002), 128–29.

43. Recalling the lines spoken by Tragedy in the prologue to *Euridice:* "Vostra, Regina, fia cotanto alloro, / qual forse anco non colse Atene o Roma" (Yours, O Queen, be the laurels, / such as graced neither Athens nor Rome.)

need was to avoid the Scylla of pedantry (and Florence was already being reproached for this in the sixteenth century and throughout the seventeenth; in
Marino, Dante and Morgante rhyme with *pedante*). Equally, for all the splendor and political and worldly prestige of that wedding, there was the inescapable embarrassment of the king of "Paris vaut bien une messe," who had
more than one disavowal to his name: barely a year before he had annulled
his marriage to Margherita, the daughter of Catherine de' Medici, the true
mistress of France while the religious wars raged. The Charybdis was therefore the risk of such tragic gloom, a *Trauerspiel* that might only remind the
spectators of how much blood had been spilled; there was no point in giving
false impressions.

So, instead, there were "more gentle emotions." The keynote was not
mannerism—which belongs to Senecan tragedy—or the baroque, but that of
the Counter-Reformation, a combination of the style of the poet Luigi Tan-
sillo (*Le lagrime di san Pietro,* published anonymously in Venice, 1560, then
posthumously in Vico Equense, 1585) or of Padre Grillo (*Pietosi affetti,*
Genoa, 1595), the friend of Tasso and Marino, with that of the painter Scipione Pulzone ("Gaetano"), the divine painter of Madonnas, or of Federigo
Barocci (the "second Raphael") and the Bologna school. The neo-pagan jol-
lity of the Farnese Gallery looks like the most advanced, sensitive painting
style joined to the "delicate" atmosphere of the pastoral, but at the same time
a leap forward, as if to correct art's slowness to respond, from *Aminta* to *Il
pastor fido,* to the marvelous new image of Italy in Europe that lasted well
into the eighteenth century. It was the starting point for *Adone* (Marino
greatly admired Guarini), for Venetian and baroque opera, and for eighteenth-century opera seria itself.[44] In the pastoral, it has been written, "the
landscapes, figures, action, and events are none other than Christianity in an
Arcadian disguise"; it was a "sophistic symbolism" in which song and music
"could find their sweet, voluptuously pious resonance. The scented marriage
bed for this extrasensual eroticism was the madrigal."[45] *Adone* itself was con-
troversially defined by Tommaso Stigliani as a "poem of madrigals," while *Il
pastor fido*—the model, whatever the genre, for Marino's poem—was possibly the first example in history of the theory and practice of a magnum opus
(we are at the etymological threshold of "opera")[46] apparently constructed

44. See Michael F. Robinson, *Naples and Neapolitan Opera* (Oxford: Clarendon Press, 1972),
particularly the chapters on heroic opera. Also see Giovanni Morelli, ed., *Il tranquillo seren del
secol d'oro: Musica e spettacolo musicale a Venezia e a Vienna fra Seicento e Settecento* (Milan:
Ricordi, 1984); and Marzio Pieri, *La pazienza di Tito* (Turin: Settembre Musica, 1984).

45. The words are those of Karl Vossler, quoted by Luigi Ronga in "La nascita del melodramma dallo spirito della poesia," in *Teatro nel Seicento,* ed. Luigi Fassò (Milan and Naples: Ricciardi, 1956), xxxvii–liii, quotation on xlii.

46. As the plural of "opus"; the "monster" of "tragicomedy" (the "new species" of *Il pastor
fido*), leading to the real "monstrosity" of opera.

from precious miniatures; the "cosas sonadas y bien escritas" which Cervantes speaks of, redeemed by being sung.

Guarini's definition of Arcadian shepherds holds good as well for operatic heroes down to Metastasio: "people accustomed not to converse, not to think, never to do anything other than sing with the utmost dignity and declaim the prettiest poetry."[47] But let us not forget, to quote from a sensitive twentieth-century scholar:

> To speak, as did De Sanctis . . . in connection with *Il pastor fido*, of a literature that has left the passions of life behind—when the book of the Renaissance is *The Courtier;* when history, in the hands of Tasso, was transformed in the way it was; when the ideas of *Aminta* largely undermined its heroic and religious structure— we are placed in the position of no longer being able to understand the reasons for this art and no longer to be able to grasp its forms.[48]

So in "grasping the forms" all we need to do is not forget to understand the reasons, which are certainly not merely formal: the art that concerns us sprang into life fully developed and filled with artifice, more a Corisca than a Silvia or any other innocent sylvan nymph. The justifications of the composers and of the poets, the appeal of the singers, and the thoughtful determination of the theorists are elements that one must never fail to think of together and yet keep separate. When, by the time of Metastasio, the two competitors—music and poetry—although still combinable and almost infinitely recyclable, become more clearly distinguishable (a Metastasio text can be read in two ways: functionally, as a libretto for music, and as a musical drama in its own right, to be read or declaimed without music), it comes at a price.[49] The price is what we might call the suspension of Orpheus's spell: that of the

47. Battista Guarini, "Compendio della poesia tragicomica" (1601), in the edition of his *Il pastor fido e il compendio della poesia tragicomica,* ed. Gioachino Brognoligo (Bari: Laterza, 1914), 219–88, quotation on 254.

48. Domenico Petrini, "Note sul barocco," in his *Dal Barocco al Decadentismo: Studi di letteratura italiana,* ed. Vittorio Santoli (Florence: Le Monnier, 1957), 1:1–56, quotation on 39 (the essay originally appeared, in part, in *Solaria* as a review of Croce's *Storia dell'età barocca in Italia*); see also Cesare De Lollis, quoted by Petrini on p. 11: "the passage from Humanism to the overblown 17th-century style can be measured quantitatively, not qualitatively."

49. "Metastasio once blurred the distinction between a libretto and a spoken drama by writing: 'I know by daily experience, that my own dramas are much more certain of success in Italy, when declaimed by comedians, than when sung by musicians.' Burney . . . declared that, when he went to Italy in 1770, he heard of no successful dramatic representation of a Metastasio drama without music" (M. F. Robinson, *Naples and Neapolitan Opera* [Oxford: Clarendon Press, 1972], 49 n. 26). Burney is referring to a letter by Metastasio (16 July 1765, at Chastellux) to be found in Bruno Brunelli, ed., *Tutte le opere,* 5 vols. (Milan: Mondadori, 1943–54), 4:397–99. On the other hand, such extramusical fortunes of the poet seem to be backed up by the unequaled favor his works met with in print: more than forty editions during the author's life and countless more in the anti-Metastasian nineteenth century.

infinite mystery of the voice. His commanding position reconfirmed, the literary man will be once again able to gird himself in the historic armor of Cicero, Quintilian, Horace, Virgil, and Plutarch: Ovid moralized. But a purely literary reading of those works reveals them today, for the most part, to have undergone the fate of too much that was written in Italy once the Arcadian reform had taken place. Arteaga (one of a thousand examples) described seventeenth-century literature as "unfortunate": for its "corrupt manner of style," for that "eccentric manner" (speaking of opera) which Giacinto Andrea Cicognini, a sort of minor, "operatic" Marino, transferred from imperfect "dramatic poems" into opera. There was a widely felt, comforting sensation of a culture rediscovered—looking at the material of the texts—because of the pleasingly interchangeable uniformity of eighteenth-century poetry (such as it was generously represented as late as Leopardi's *Crestomazia* of 1828). This is the background against which not only Metasasio and Calzabigi, Gluck and Pergolesi, moved, but also Lorenzo Da Ponte and Domenico Cimarosa; the last two with greater restlessness as the century became more restless and strange, during the convulsions in France. And, as it so often happens, in between the lines dwells a confession that tends to control itself and to become at the same time more rigid. Here is a text—a possible terminus post quem—from *Le rivoluzioni del teatro musicale italiano* (1783–85), by a powerful supporter of Metastasio, the Jesuit Arteaga:

> To show the different progress in public morals at that time [that is, in the Middle Ages] and in our own, we need only glance at the moral literature of our time. I speak not of the novels of Chiari, which for their insipidity can do neither good nor ill; nor yet of that flood of French novels, the fruit of dissoluteness and wickedness, which shame both those who read and those who write them; I speak only of the two most celebrated works modern Europe possesses, *Clarice* [Richardson's *Clarissa*] and *La nouvelle Eloïse* [of Rousseau]. One cannot deny that the author of the first has great genius coupled with a profound knowledge of the human heart, but with regard to morals, what fruit did he extract? Richardson, wishing to make a true portrait of men, as frequently to be found in society today, depicted in Clarissa's lover a monster of treachery all the more dangerous, as one supposes him filled with great acuteness of spirit and other dazzling qualities that almost make one forget his despicable villainy. Cleverness is always on the side of the seducer, and misfortune on that of the innocent woman. The entire novel is nothing more than a textbook to educate men in the most studied and sophisticated arts with which to deceive well-brought-up young women. I have thus encountered not a few readers who envy Lovelace his talent and acuteness, but few who take a lively interest in Clarissa's virtue. What is the reason for this? That today cunning is preferred to honesty, and that a woman's virtue is considered foolishness or savagery. Rousseau, wishing to avoid this defect, has introduced no wicked characters into *La nouvelle Eloïse*. But what is the outcome? That his characters, as unique as their author, philosophizing while raving, full of loftiness and madness, of eloquence and

extravagance, have no originals nor models among men. It appears that, in writing his novel, he was thinking more of Plato's world than of our own.[50]

A man of spirit, Arteaga had got the point;[51] the world of Plato was that of the pastoral and Metastasio. Richardson is the precursor of *Don Giovanni* and romantic opera.

4. FORBIDDEN PLEASURES

Pur che porti la gonnella,
voi sapete quel che fa. (Leporello)

The picture we have is incomplete and is taking shape only by fits and starts, but some constant elements are starting to emerge.

(*a*) The more the literary man takes a declared interest in opera, the more it approaches, and attempts to identify itself with, tragedy, the myth of tragedy, as a status symbol. In this case, of course, the more accurate term is "music drama," the very term whose mythical and mystical path from ancient Greece to Wagner was traced by the continuously inspired Édouard Schuré in a once valuable book. A passionate Wagnerite, Schuré had some very clear ideas on the subject:

> As for opera, it would be difficult to assign a precise character to it, since one finds in it the intrusion of all genres, a confusion of all styles and an absolute lack of a specific direction. . . . It is only at rare moments, amid privileged groups and under the breath of genius, that this pandemonium of humanity's good and bad spirits becomes the sacred temple of the Ideal.

50. Arteaga, *Le rivoluzioni del teatro musicale*, 1:286–288 n (in the Venetian edition). But the entire chapter, "Riflessioni sul maraviglioso: Origine storica e propagazione di esso in Europa: Cause del suo accoppiamento colla musica e la poesia nel melodrama," is worth reading: "Among the phenomena that present themselves to whoever wishes to observe the revolutions in the Italian theater, not the least in my opinion is that abundance of marvels which, joined to opera from its very beginnings, kept pace with it for the whole of the last century and part of the present one, not only in Italy but abroad as well, wherever the form took root. This could hardly not attract the attention of Italian writers: there is not a single one of them who, having undertaken to write a history of literature, has not spoken of stage machines, decorations, mythology, and fables as the principal characteristics of opera in that century" (ibid., 267–68). But the problem is 'whether the affliction came from the poetry or from the music or whether everything arises from the circumstances of the day.'"

51. Current interest in light fiction has returned Pietro Chiari to favor: a key moment was the Venice convention of March 1985, marking the bicentenary of the death of Goldoni's great rival (see Carmelo Alberti, ed., *Pietro Chiari e il teatro europeo del Settecento*, [Venice: Pozza, 1986]). His posthumous, short, satirical poem "Il teatro moderno di Calicut" (Venice, 1787) has considerable bearing on things musical-theatrical. It is in the line of descent from *Il teatro alla moda,* although not quite so stern, or rather from the once-famous intermezzos in Metastasio's *Didone.*

On the contrary:

> By the term *drame musical,* I have intended something completely different from, and much more than, opera: the most elevated and complete dramatic form that human art has been able to create. This form, which appeared for the first time with a purity, an incomparable majesty, in Greek tragedy. Why is it that today this kind of tragedy gives a hazy or cold impression? It is because we consider it no more than a literary monument rather than seeing in it the highest kind of living art, complete and truly human; it is because we view it with the lackluster eyes of the modern man.[52]

According to Schuré, Greek tragedy is the meeting point of the three great original Muses—pantomime, poetry, and music—and "reveals constantly to us what we have too much forgotten, that the separate arts are only fragments of a great All which one could call the universal human art."

Certainly this sort of emphasis, always effectively in force, today discourages more than it entices whoever has organized a seating plan for the banquet with the greats. However it is not a case of having to give up exercise and patience, to learn to distinguish between empty rhetoric and what might be the launchpad (even in an age patently "uninspired," such as the eighteenth-century Enlightenment in some of its areas or lasting pockets), renouncing perhaps the feared, equivocal love of opera of artists or worthy thinkers. Thinking of literary figures—apart from D'Annunzio, who, we might say, serves as the honored, splendid original aberration—we might consider the Wagnerism of the symbolist poet Arturo Onofri, pathetically late by the time the twentieth century was under way; for composers, an example would be the theater and ideas of Ildebrando Pizzetti. (Incidentally, food for thought: Onofri links Wagner more to Pascoli than D'Annunzio, while Pizzetti values in D'Annunzio a modern Greek quality, which is not found in such a pure and familiar form in Wagner.) And as far as a union between composers and writers is concerned, we can think of the lifelong relationship between Pizzetti and Giuseppe De Robertis: emblematic, in its haughty manner, of the age-old division—Boito's sovereign dedication to Verdi remaining a case apart—between writers, convinced that they are working in a kind of eternity, and the festive atmosphere of opera. "We, the temporary, must seek for eternity."[53]

52. Édouard Schuré, *Le drame musical,* 2 vols. (Paris: Sandoz and Fischbacher, 1875), 1:2 and 4 (my italics). On the title page (it reached its 12th ed. in 1920) we read: "Danse, Musique et Poésie / forment la Ronde de l'Art vivant." (The tireless author's writings include the famous *Les grands initiés,* which ran to nineteen editions, again in the 1920s, the three series of *Le théâtre de l'âme,* and *Histoire du Lied.*)

53. This is a principle and a formula typical of De Robertis, in his period as director of the periodical *La voce,* of "knowing how to read" and "collaborating with poetry," which was so influential on the literati, artists, and musicians between the wars; we find it quoted by Pizzetti, in the

(*b*) The other way round: the more that opera displays the features of the Equivocal, the Ephemeral, Capricious, Carnival, the Humoral, Meteorological, Irregular, and Fantastic (and even the newly fashionable "Phantom of the Opera"), the more it will be rooted in Usage and Pleasure—on two levels: pleasure to be taken by the spectator, pleasure to be given by the composer, librettist, impresario, theater manager, set designer, costume designer, dancer, and so on—and the more the literary man will feel at peace with himself only when he has pronounced a condemnatory "get thee behind me." The "disorder" (in the censorious sense customarily used by religious moralists in the phrase "a disordered life") has the same negative value in the theater as in politics, which we shall avoid. The "intellectual" becomes important again—having discovered his "commitment" as the guns fall silent—only when he thinks he has the right, on the basis of one or two famous passages in Gramsci, to "discover opera," just as he was "discovering" the novel in the same period. (One should not be misled by the success, not in any case particularly great outside the schoolroom, of *I promessi sposi*, which was criticized as "degenerate art" when it came out, and when it triumphed, it was celebrated more willingly, however improbably, as an "epic poem.") In the same way—just as it was disappearing as a popular form of entertainment, to be replaced by television—cinema was, with a great display of passion, "discovered."

All the same, it was a step forward.

For Francesco Milizia at the threshold of the neoclassical period opera was a "magnificent folly," "prepared with great thought, and even more outlay" (disorder, waste, foolishness, ugliness). And he was amazed that from something "so excellent in itself, Tragedy"—"put together with so many spices, each one exquisite in itself"—"instead of turning out a perfect whole, produces an utterly mindless dummy of no use whatsoever."[54] Giuseppe Mazzini—cleverly opportunistic, like the quasi priest he was, in seeing the propaganda possibilities in such a popular and richly emotional form of entertainment—had, no less, similar theoretical resistance to the lack of unity in the mixture, however successful and passionately admired:

---

dedication to De Robertis of his *La musica italiana dell'Ottocento* (Turin: Edizioni Palatine, 1947), 9; and in Vittorio Gui, *Battute d'aspetto: Meditazioni di un musicista militante* (Florence: Monsalvato, 1944). It is a counterpoint of Jacobi and Schopenhauer, Christ and Buddha, Rebora and Rilke, with *Pelléas* and *Ariane et Barbe-Bleue* mixed in. Compare it with the Steiner approach of Bruno Walter and, possibly, in our own day with the plain declaration by the "mystical" Carlo Maria Giulini: "We performers are only luggage in transit."

54. The passage (Francesco Milizia, *Del teatro* [Venice: Pasquali, 1772], chap. 5, "Dell'opera in musica") was taken up by Malipiero in his *I profeti di Babilonia*, 409–12. The prescription is typical: "Look at the Opera in detail, bit by bit, that is, the Subject of the Drama, the Music, the Actors, the Dances, the Decor, and the Theater itself: when the location and the level of what is wrong in all these sections has been discovered, one can apply suitable remedies."

An opera cannot be defined save by enumerating its parts—a series of cavatinas, choruses, duets, trios and finales—interrupted, not connected, by nondescript recitative that is not listened to: a mosaic, a gallery, a jumble, more often a conflict of different ideas, independent and unconnected, which wander like spirits in a tight magic circle: a tumult, a whirlwind of musical motives, phrases, and little ideas, which remind the listener of Dante's lines on the souls of the dead, on the words of grief, the sounds of anger, the voices loud and weak, and the clapping of hands heard in our theaters as at the gates of the Inferno. You might think it a witches' sabbath. You might think it a journey of fantasy, across different lands and fields, as described in a ballad by Bürger, and the horse of hell that carries Leonora and a corpse—the music and the audience—furiously from shore to shore to the sound of that monotonous cadence, *I morti camminan veloci.* Hurrah! Hurrah! Where are we going? What is this music about? Where is it leading? Where is the unity? [55]

It would be idle to invite a comparison with the calm, precise, and dignified prose of Arteaga, or with the similar style of Milizia, with its sudden flashes of bile—*nomen omen*—"the Don Quixote of idealized beauty" as Carlo Calcaterra describes him in *Il Parnaso in rivolta.*[56] Idle, too, to suggest a connection with the contemporary "new prose" of Manzoni. But Mazzini's gutsy, jolting, fists-on-the-table style, with its groans, fury, and hurrahs, is the one on which the new style of romantic opera fed. Apart from the Donizettian references of this ideologue in the land of unbelievers, who weeps with Anna Bolena and exults with Marin Faliero, it seems clear that Verdi was programmed, invented in fact, by Mazzini—probably the only prophecy he got right.

But when, with the twentieth century, literary figures—before Gramsci—returned "to opera" in small groups at first, Giacomo Debenedetti revived the formula of "our tragic Verdi," convinced that he would be redeemed. Toscanini had passed the same way, and we know how "tragedy" (including the romantic legacy of Shakespeare) had been strengthened by "epic poetry" (Wagner). Siegfried had met Manrico, who was thus delivered—for the twentieth century—from his most likely and realistic mood. Emilio Cecchi, in his notebooks, recalls the elderly Cesare Pascarella (the eminent voice of "united Italy") remembering the Bologna premiere of *Falstaff,* a Verdi opera "without tragedy": "as he was coming out, Carducci said, 'I can't understand it at all.'"[57] Carducci—as we know from a faithful pupil, Adolfo Albertazzi—

55. Giuseppe Mazzini, *Filosofia della musica* (1836). The quotation here is drawn from his *Opere,* ed. Luigi Salvatorelli (Milan: Rizzoli, 1967), 2:285.

56. Carlo Calcaterra, *Il Parnaso in rivolta* (1940), ed. Ezio Raimondi (Bologna: Il Mulino, 1961), 255–58.

57. Emilio Cecchi, *Taccuini,* ed. Niccolò Gallo and Pietro Citati (Milan: Mondadori, 1976), 441 (note of 23 Aug. 1927). But read the note of 12 Apr. 1925 (ibid., 410ff.) on *Parsifal:* "I had a memory of a heavy, tangled machine, with a fearful strain of means and expedients; instead I found

used the same formula in connection with spoken theater. It was an honest admission, and a pretense, on the part of a poet deaf to music, who had invented new metrical systems. With the gangplank of tragedy removed, there was no alternative but to barricade oneself in with the aim of exclusion, while our little story performs a "da capo."

The Effects

c'est à travers des connotations, des
impressions, un angle de vue, un détail que
le rapport au concept sera établi.[58]

5. *ADONE*, OR OPERA BEFORE OPERA

At a certain point in his *Recherche,* Wagner's executor, Marcel Proust, names that *partie commune* which sometimes exists "entre deux oeuvres, entre deux sensations." In *The Birth of Tragedy* Nietzsche announces that he is going to speak about the Greeks and in fact interprets, reconstructs, and deconstructs *Tristan.* This is to say that the "birth of opera"—having referred to the useful textbook example of Romain Rolland's "opera before opera"—was, and in part remains, after so much erudition and philology, an *opus oratorium maxime.* Ever since the appearance of the first volume (but fourth in number) of the series to which the present study belongs, it has chosen to tackle materials: production techniques, actual forms of development and dissemination, the specific solutions offered from time to time to concrete problems. It is a way of escaping the two sides, the Scylla and Charybdis of deprecation and celebration of the literary attitude to opera. Our job here is quite the opposite: to face up to it, to pass between Scylla and Charybdis with open sails toward what might be possible (even in Aristotelian terms). And it will be carried out in that cheerful, "allegro" mood that the prince of musicologists, Nino Pirrotta,[59] has exemplified. It is as if a haunted wing of the house, left in disorder and darkness since time immemorial, were undergoing restoration.

---

it, while still a machine, a light, airy one. Nietzsche was right to see a perfect operetta situation in *Parsifal.* Aristophanes. Amfortas is a king suffering from venereal disease, Klingsor is a senile old man, who wants to use Kundry to seduce the clean-living Parsifal. The atmosphere is one of a bourgeois theosophical meeting, with old prostitutes and aristos. . . . And as for those boys who serve and march in the church of the Grail, you can tell that they're in a homosexual relationship with the knights." And he wasn't even an opera producer.

58. Jean Nouvel, *Images et imaginaires d'architecture,* exhibition catalogue (Paris: Pompidou Centre, March–May 1984), 141.

59. See Nino Pirrotta, *Music and Theater from Poliziano to Monteverdi,* trans. Karen Eales (Cambridge: Cambridge University Press, 1982), with a critical essay on stage design by Elena Povoledo; and see also his *Scelte poetiche di musicisti: Teatro, poesie e musica da Willaert a Malipiero*

We can trust Pirrotta's studies to tell us everything that we really need to know about *Orfeo,* indeed the two *Orfeos,* by Poliziano: the "opera before opera" of 1480 Mantua. In the birth of Florentine opera, the dramatic example of Poliziano probably counted for less than the faux-early melodic style of sturdy Florentine dialectic given to ideal figures of tenderness and fearfulness in his *Stanze della giostra.* Cultivated readers have always praised the polyphony of Poliziano's *ottava rima:*[60] the quality of the inspiration matched to the diligence of the act of writing, thereby redeeming what is clearly a minor work. It is the tradition of the vulgar Petrarch—*Rerum vulgarium fragmenta . . .*—in contrast with the humanists' greatest effort. Poliziano staging an *Orfeo* for a "festa teatrale" or polishing the fake folk *ottava rima* of the *Stanze* is rather like Sartre writing screenplays or Voltaire producing allegorical librettos, but it goes without saying that he was much better.[61]

With the advent of mannerism, Poliziano the humanist seems to have been shelved, and only the lyric poet was still used: ideas and poetry were separated, in the typical schizophrenia of Italian literature.[62] Poliziano's stanzas flow into *Adone,* through the complex strategy of Marino, who includes Ambrogini among the "philosophers and humanists" of the *Galeria,* rather than among "the vulgar poets." Thus, the critics who would want to look for your sources are deceived (Marino did it before Montale used the word and the practice); in this way Marino, almost casually, restores a culture to those who have forgotten it. Poliziano was one of the beacons of this culture, which had been removed by the combination of the spirit of Cardinal Bembo and the Counter-Reformation (and linked to those Medici from whom descended "the woman who has taken the name of the sea," Maria de' Medici, Marino's protectress at the French court and already the target, as we know, of the birth of Florentine opera in the year of grace 1600).

(Venice: Marsilio, 1987). These two books are also absolutely fundamental for their treatment of the relationship between music and poetry, considered and reassessed by a musicologist who is also a beautiful writer.

60. See Giuseppe De Robertis, "Le *Stanze* o dell'ottava concertante" and "Le *Stanze* o del chiasmo," in his *Studi* (Florence: Le Monnier, 1944), 62–75; also "L'arte del Poliziano," in his *Saggi* (Florence: Le Monnier, 1959), 9–33. In the wake of this, in his preface to Poliziano's *Poesie italiane* (Milan: BUR, Rizzoli, 1976), 7, Mario Luzi has written: "The mixture of mannerism and spontaneity, exquisite references to Latin and the *stile novo,* and the freshness of the rustic idiom produce an amalgam that it would be difficult to tease out, and the border between artifice and spirit is continually moving, almost to the point where it is lost." This is a clear anticipation of what in the coming century would be the Rinuccinian "birth of tragedy."

61. Sartre is known to have written a screenplay, *Freud,* for John Huston, which was never filmed. Voltaire wrote *Le temple de la Gloire* for music by Rameau (1745), after a proposed *Samson* for the same composer was blocked by the censor.

62. See Rodolfo Quadrelli, *Il linguaggio della poesia* (Florence: Vallecchi, 1969).

Part of Marino's design was to refuse openly to take on the humble role of the courtier-versifier for parties, librettos, or tournaments. The ancient fables which the Caccinis or Monteverdis set to music produce reams of musical writing in *Sampogna, Galeria,* and *Adone.* The immensely learned Claudio Achillini, a man of vast experience capable of rivaling Marino's primacy (no coincidence that in Manzoni, Achillini's verse is taken as an example of baroque monstrosity), did not—on honorable, glittering occasions, like the opening of the Teatro Farnese in Parma—eschew such humble, practical roles. The lawyer Busenello, whose career runs from a critical letter on *Adone* to his libretto for *L'incoronazione di Poppea,* seems quite at ease moving between Marino—from 1625 on the Index of forbidden books—the libertinism of the *Incogniti,* and the latest, newly invented form of theater.[63] Recent interpreters of Marino's work have limited themselves to assessing an imposing stylistic catalogue and have paid no attention to his proud abstention. While the "modernists" of the early seventeenth century busied themselves with an advantageous venture, the leader of the most innovative group denied himself any possible theatrical experimentation, whether pastoral or in Florentine tragedy (poetry in *stile rappresentativo* sung on stage) or any other form of that "Musica rappresentativa" which set the scene for opera. It might seem surprising to turn down this specific request, this increasing popularity since— in the case of his greatest poem—it was precisely market success ("L'*Adone* can be purchased . . .") that had provided Marino with his poetic liberation from the canon. Between the "Book" of the Renaissance and the "Theater" of the baroque, Marino trusted the book, an elevated idea and, given his cynicism, almost a superstitious one, of literature. This idea was troubled by a sort of Michelangelism (which he certainly got from Vasari's "book") and was freshened up by the senses of the Carracci family of painters; by analogy, this idea imagines a writing space as a microcosm, a *Wunderkammer,* a Sistine Chapel, or a gallery of what can be turned into poetry, the Ovidian, metamorphic Bible, or the Library of Babel. Having lived as a soldier of fortune, with a pedigree similar to that of the comedians of the music for acrobats and of painters who are not yet "professors" (but would become such in that very period), Marino aspired to lasting recognition, the objective consecration of his own adventure. And it was resplendently resolved in the creation of one book: the Paris *Adone,* a folio edition financed by the king of France, like a missal or cradle-book: the Ultimate Book.

There was a nasty side to this ambition that, once recognized, assures the poet the perpetual homage of those who love the energetic illusions and laby-

63. See Marzio Pieri, "Di puntillismo in meraviglia," in *La Salmace e altri idilli barocchi,* ed. Girolamo Preti, Giovanni Argoli, and Gian Francesco Busenello (Verona: Fiorini, 1987), 19–37.

rinths of historical excess. But—on the real plane of the invention of open, new structures for which the age was yearning—Marino, together with his huge, cumbersome poem, was sidelined.

6. FROM THE ONE-SIDED POEM
TO THE SEGMENTED UNIVERSE, OR OPERA IN PURGATORY

Perhaps some might think that I have overplayed the role of *Adone* in this summary. All the more since with the collection of received ideas comes the suspicion that the bearing Marino has on the age is less than that which at one time one loved to imagine. It would seem incredible if, having no influence on the writers of idylls, madrigals, and lyrical sonnets and on constructors of poems in *ottava rima,* the poet of the discredited "marvel" should reappear to decide the fate of the—thought to be uncontaminated—garden of Opera Nuova. (Remember the Idealist position: *no* to the baroque of Cavalier Marino, *yes* to the baroque of Claudio Monteverdi.)

And yet I refute the objection: *Adone* is at the same time the cause and the effect of a changed model of perception; Marino plays his card while the received "genres" are in abeyance and the process of their replacement is already under way. The "poema heroico" which Marino equates with a "poema grande," easier to identify than to define, in terms of quantity rather than quality (thinking again of the plural etymology of the term "opera"), is the starting point of a move from the deductive organic qualities of a static and hierarchical poetic style to the inductive mechanism of metonymic practice anchored to the principle of progressive or developing shifts of "pleasure." From a (Renaissance and mannerist) "theory of form" to a (baroque and modern) way of "formulating": here is the leap of genres—from the poem to the opera.

The familiarity of the young Busenello's enthusiastic letter on *Adone* should not detract from its importance:

> Your Lordship continues to reveal in the happiest vein some delights of language that fill the heart of those who read them with joy; nor is there a stanza in the entire poem that, wonderfully alluring, does not draw unto itself the spirit of whosoever reads it. And as sometimes when gazing at the stars it is not possible to fix one's eye clearly on one, without the twinkling of the others diverting our vision, so great is the frequency and number of those shining objects, so it is not possible to reflect on one of the aforementioned stanzas without the others dispersing one's thoughts, interrupting speculation. It is certainly true that such interruptions do not diminish the enjoyment of the reader and do not detract from the glory of what is being read, and one must turn to Nature to supply our senses with better organs so as not to betray at the same time the book and the mind of the person looking at it with the incapacity of the equipment. . . . I admire in particular the uniformity of the style, which, always bold and lively, never weak and thin, mirroring itself, gleams in the

constant parity of all its parts. . . . The milk of the verses, the manna of the phrases, the nectar of the words, and the ambrosia of the invention prepare such a sumptuous banquet that Adonis himself rather than Ganymede is its choice cupbearer. The rhymes have an agility that, recited, do not touch the tongue; heard, they do not tire the ears; read, they seduce the eyes; sung, they bless the music; and the soul would wish to be entirely memory to rob them from the page.[64]

The open-minded invention of a learned, imaginative style, what we might call the march of victory toward argument by analogy (the poetic universe of the figurative poem reflects, however much of a cliché it may now sound, a heaven resoundingly rent asunder and an infinite, but no longer Ptolemaic universe), finds only one possible equivalent. It is still in the same Venetian area, in the visual freedom and the critical impressionism that Marco Boschini applied to painters (and in fact: "Concepts are scattered so profusely and with such richness throughout the poem that, as I read them in every line as well as every stanza, I imagine I see a canvas where the brush of Titian has drawn those *ignudi* who, much as the rising Dawn, flood the air with the most scented and pretty flowers").[65] We recognize here the characteristics of disdain, partly sociological, and of antiestablishment shrewdness which gave rise, there in Venice in 1637, to the fateful venture of San Cassiano, the first opera house— "*Adone* can be purchased . . ."—open to a paying audience. One more historical leap: to consider the part played in the venture (even more so after the controversy with Pope Paul V in 1606) by a libertine Venetian aristocracy, one need only think, by comparison and contrast, of the role played by the educated Neapolitan aristocracy—between the end of the seventeenth century and the birth of the next—in the invention of opera buffa. In the case of the San Cassiano, what is striking is the fact that opera took over a theater that up until that time had been given over to commedia dell'arte, while Neapolitan opera enjoyed a glorious period of dialect work by Giambattista Basile, Giulio Cesare Cortese, and Gabriele Fasano, the translator into Neapolitan of *Gerusalemme liberata*. The Venetian undertaking involved, as well as a mercantile entrepreneurial element, a calculation on culture and novelty based on investment and return (always risky, as things turn out, if not completely ruinous). An aristocracy with mercantile forebears that, instead of setting sail for Cathay or the New Indies, excluded from them by a "world" exchange of power and influence, opens theaters, must take some insidious pleasure in dissolution. Standing at the center of the Venetian baroque was

64. Busenello's letter is reproduced in Giambattista Marino, *Epistolario, seguito da lettere di altri scrittori del Seicento*, ed. Angelo Borzelli and Fausto Nicolini, 2 vols. (Bari: Laterza, 1912), 2:100–104, quotation on 100ff.
65. Ibid., 101.

the Accademia degli Incogniti, whose leader, Gian Francesco Loredano (the author of a *Life of Marino*), seems to mask that pleasure in tempered libertinism—the city has a history of genuine rebels, from Giordano Bruno to Ferrante Pallavicino, betrayed by their confidence in the security of Saint Mark's —and in a voracious tendency to publishing ventures, which were, in the short term, highly successful. It is no contradiction of Loredano's "Marinism" that his area of experimentation is the open one of prose: in short stories and novels (the century's "new genre," together with opera, whose destiny of rejection by outraged theorists and shocked moralists it shares) roles and levels are contaminated to the point where a famous collection of letters can turn into one of the least "narrated" and most lively novels (albeit of a stylized life, segmented under rubrics) of the seventeenth century.[66]

Connected with the explosion of opera around the middle of the seventeenth century was a reappraisal of the role of literary figures as a rigid, efficient craft; now they were required to elaborate, or rather complicate to the *n*th degree, various basic narrative schemes, traceable back to the old, inexhaustible Ovid, to the Boccaccio of *Filocolo*, rather than to short stories or the metrical novel (or novel in Alexandrines) as disseminated and transformed in the Middle Ages. (Ellen Rosand has pointed out the amazing achievement of Aurelio Aureli's *Orfeo*, set to music by Sartorio, as an example of Ovid transformed.)[67] Or else they were used as metricians, carrying on from the work of Chiabrera or Rinuccini, who had contributed fine literary scores in the first stirrings of opera; they also provide a link to the mid-seventeenth-century literary taste, eager to sink into the delights of Arcady.

Alessandro Guidi's "double practice" is a perfect example of this. For a short time he seemed to be a sort of cleansed Marino of literary revival. The "prima pratica" was that of the Farnese court, courtly ballets and hair-raising operatic medleys: either *La Parma, Le navi d'Enea, Il Giove d'Elide fulminato,* or *Amalasonta in Italia* (1681); besides, Guidi's contemporaries preferred to praise his "genius" rather than his "taste."[68] Thus did the opposition to Arcadian reform, at risk of becoming merely an alternative, come into being, and Guidi was its protagonist, in his "seconda pratica." The goal was to lop off excrescences and focus on a clearly lit, well-defined area, under the banner of a new professionalism. In opera this era saw the triumphs of Carlo Fran-

66. See Giovanni Francesco Loredano, *Delle lettere . . . divise in cinquantadue capi, e raccolte da Henrico Giblet Cavalier,* pt. 1 (Venice: Tivani, 1693) (this is the 11th ed.; the original was published in Venice in 1650).

67. Aurelio Aureli and Antonio Sartorio, *L'Orfeo,* ed. Ellen Rosand (Milan: Ricordi, 1983), part of the series Drammaturgia musicale veneta promoted by the Fondazione Cini and the University of Venice, another fundamental location for the interaction of musicology and literature.

68. See Alessandro Guidi, *Poesie approvate,* ed. Bruno Maier (Ravenna: Longo, 1981); the introduction is important.

cesco Pollarolo and Alessandro Scarlatti, but the novelty of Guidi can be better understood today if we compare him with another musician of the same generation, absent from the operatic stage, Arcangelo Corelli. For Corelli, too, the artistically influential baroque fervor that greeted his debut gave way to a need to rethink his individual artistic formulas. The poem as universe, the *Adone* syndrome, if you like, now enticed only the "rabble of the semi-educated," against which—undoubtedly remembering Petrarch's "endless hosts of fools"—Gravina inveighed in his open letter to Scipione Maffei.[69] We are in the middle of Arcady, where the search for "order" certainly does not belong to polemics against the supporters of Marino, or operatic pasticcios. Gravina, again, in *Della divisione d'Arcadia,* quoting Jacques Cujas, writes, "forsan captiosa nimis, et scrupolosa, sed meo judicio tolerabilior, quam actionum confusio, agendi temeritas, et nullus ordo, qualis est hodie."

The traditional condemnation of theater folk lands on the "virtuosos." As the eighteenth century progressed there was an upsurge in thoughtful, high-minded treatises on opera. There were also satires, like the one that, to be honest, too much is made of still today, to the point of banality, in fact: Benedetto Marcello's *Il teatro alla moda* (1720).[70] In any case, the first signs had appeared in the middle of the baroque century: Daniello Bartoli had started to correct, in order to defend, "the man of letters" in 1645. The Jesuit writer Emanuele Tesauro had skillfully brought Aristotle into his sights in 1654 with his *Cannocchiale.* Naturally, in Tesauro's "man of letters" we would seek in vain even a trace of the new Siren. Amid the foliage of an antique and modern culture, almost suffocating in its dazzling luxuriance of riches, literary and otherwise; a lapidary, symbolic art, full of heroic sayings and emblems; in the separate rooms of his ideal gallery where Aristotle and Cicero, Solomon, Pope Leo I, or Saint Gregory of Nyssa but Galileo as well sit side by side, there is no place for the gurglings of virtuosos or for the comedy of errors of Venetian opera. Perhaps a reference or two for the "gratiani" of the commedia dell'arte. Certainly, in Tesauro, a lapsed Jesuit, as much as in Bartoli, a faithful Jesuit, there is a powerful ambiguity (the title itself, "Aristotelian spyglass" is a clever oxymoron); the enthusiasm of the writing increases the caution of his judgments. We have not yet arrived at the perfect image of the well-to-do scholar, as in this portrait of Guidi by the other Supreme Arcadian, Giovanni Crescimbeni:

> [H]e was affable and likable and generous; and he spiced his conversation with no little grace and amusement. Although he was not profoundly lettered (that is, cul-

---

69. This is Gravina's famous letter "Della divisione d'Arcadia" (1712), often reprinted in connection with Guidi's poetry.

70. A history and defense of Marcello's work can be found in Mila's *I costumi della "Traviata,"* 45–50, included in an attractive new edition (Alpignano: Tallone, 1983).

tivated), nevertheless he spoke appropriately on every subject: and he was also well informed on the affairs of the world. In caution and in advice he was unquestionably singular, so that while at the same time the great lords would take delight in the harmony of his verse, they admired the acuteness of his advice; nor was there anyone, among the many he served, who recognized him more as a poet than a politician and did not make use of him to handle important matters and to produce noble compositions. Likewise, for the sound moral sense with which he was much endowed, he had few superiors; and above all he was highly honored in every action he took . . . nor did he ever make less than honest use of his gifts, as he was very much aware of every type of poetry and might often have had occasion to write satires rather than songs.

Whatever high opinion he might have had of his style, nevertheless he was of the gentlest nature, and was happy to listen to others' opinions and be corrected.

Ill-advised singers, with their train of monstrous mothers and hungry, shrewd impresarios, seem in the end to have nothing to do with perfect good manners. While it might seem off-target, one reservation is enough to rouse us: "Just as his intellect was so quick, and spirited, so was he sometimes lacking in feeling and in ways of expressing it; and so often the same things are repeated in his verse with the same words." [71] A hit, if only an indirect one, against Arcady, and Reform Opera; and against Metastasian opera itself, which, in its way, was full of feeling and expressive formulas.

7. DON GIOVANNI

Mozart gave the age its big jolt. As we know, in him genius and sociology came together, and Amadeus was destroyed as a result. That kick in the backside which set the son of Leopold Mozart on the path—bourgeois and then instantly romantic—of free individual enterprise makes for an extraordinary allegory. He was a mixture of physical shortness, exaggerated outspokenness, and nobility of spirit, a combination of "poverty and nobility" that is hard to swallow, even today, when one realizes that one has forgotten (see the chronologies that are now available for all the great and not-so-great theaters) that it has taken more than a century, and not only in humble Italy, for Mozart the opera composer to acquire or reacquire his place in the repertory. Besides, Mozart the piano composer spent a long time being smuggled in under the guise of a "graceful" style, between lingering traces of the rococo and the establishment of the classical style. (Glenn Gould's first recordings of the sonatas provoked a storm of protest from tender souls and for some time, ever since Gould's postmortem canonization got under way, have been al-

---

71. Giovanni Maria Crescimbeni, "Vita dell'abate Alessandro Guidi," in *Poesie,* by Alessandro Guidi (Verona: Tumermani, 1726), vii–xl, quotation on xxxvi–xxxvii.

lowed to circulate under the sort of watchful eye reserved for the mad or the underdeveloped.)[72]

Let us carry on spying through the peephole of piano music. Between the end of the baroque century and the decades preceding the French Revolution, opera sailed along the channels of Extravagance (at a sublime, courtly level) or of Festivity (the Carnival in Venice, etc., the piazza, luxury, gambling, immediately turning bourgeois), until the arrival of Napoleon. The descendants of those sensitive, refined intellectuals who, a hundred, a hundred and fifty years before, had invented opera for the "happy few" at court, saw the invention blow up in their faces and turn into something public and commercial, an attack on the court economy, which is all about prestige and co-opting; long before the romantic era those intellectuals who were highly sensitive to "poetry" invented something technical and technological. They invented the piano.

Once again they began to think about a "machine." Opera, too, had been conceived as a "machine" in the Renaissance sense. This time, to avoid a revolt by the human mechanism (the slaves being the librettists, the composers, the singers, the dancers, the designers), they planned a Machine at the height of perfection, that is, one that can almost do without human intervention, except for the single one (the Single One) who operates it. Yet at the center lies a powerful contradiction (it's really only things that have a contradiction at their center that interest us); the machine does not threaten "emotions" or the "heart": it is, instead, the conclusion—perfect, verifiable, syllogistic—of a century during which the best philosophers have tenaciously pondered the passions of the soul. The year is 1700; at the Medici court they are not discussing opera-tragedy anymore but instead Bartolomeo Cristofori's newly invented Arpicembalo, "which plays soft and loud" in such a way that it can "render on instruments the voice of the heart, now with the delicate touch of an angel, now with a violent outburst of passions."[73]

For all that, when Mozart set off on his third visit to Paris in a year of cabalistic significance like 1777 (and in Paris the following year, his mother, who was accompanying him, was to die of typhus),[74] the journey was one, we have read, "of freedom and hope, in which one of the greatest spirits known to humanity came to maturity;" he took with him, in theory, a piano that was no more than an accessory: "a work instrument, which he made use of but which did not embody his aspirations." In that period only Muzio Cle-

72. For Gould's "break" with tradition, see Piero Rattalino, *Da Clementi a Pollini: Duecento anni con i grandi pianisti* (Milan: Ricordi; Florence: Giunti Martello, 1983), 369–74.

73. Piero Rattalino, *Storia del pianoforte: Lo strumento, la musica, gli interpreti* (Milan: Il Saggiatore, 1982), 15ff.

74. In 1778 Rousseau and Voltaire both died; and La Scala was inaugurated.

menti fulfilled—for the first time—"the credentials of performer-composer-teacher-theorist-publisher-builder-dealer,"[75] closely bound up with the new instrument, which, more efficiently than the invective of any moralist or theorist, would begin to dismantle opera. It is a paradox, but the nineteenth-century glories of opera are, on close examination, the genre's seductive, splendid funeral song; rather like the twentieth-century glories—and we know which ones and how many—of the novel.

If then Mozart's individual experience induces even historians opposed to such an idea to shift the stress on to almost Rolland- or Mann-like "great spirits," it should be said that, on the other hand, the history of eighteenth-century opera seems to bank on no future, like a sort of historical heart attack; no less if we look at it from the viewpoint of the literary figures, journalists, or the philosophes themselves, in whose case (thinking of the famous *querelle* over *La serva padrona,* a mere trifle, after all) there is a strong suspicion that the "eggheads" are using it as a pretext. This indicates a mass effect: history stands still, or seems to be blocked; in simple dialectic terms, it could be said that if the structure was fixed, "revolutions" in the superstructure could be no more than apparent. Things had to move on, as has happened, in research and revivals, in an age closer to our own; for the eighteenth century is once again familiar, not so much because of the frequent "Amadeus effects" as the various "Rossini Renaissances" or the "*Pulcinella* effect," the main line—despite Adorno's attacks—of twentieth-century neoclassicism. So we have histories rather than History; "schools," geographical views, and detailed studies of brief periods.[76] The young Goldoni, as he himself relates in his *Memoirs,* is asked by a well-established and brazen Vivaldi to retouch and adapt a work by Apostolo Zeno.[77] Contrary to Goldoni's intention in telling

75. Rattalino, *Da Clementi a Pollini,* 13ff.

76. See Giovanni Morelli, "Storia e geografia di un'idea musicale settecentesca," the introduction to the Italian translation of Michael F. Robinson's *Naples and Neapolitan Opera* (Venice: Marsilio, 1984), 7–16.

77. See Carlo Goldoni, *Mémoires,* pt. 1, chap. 37, in the edition of Goldoni's *Tutte le opere,* ed. Giuseppe Ortolani, 14 vols. (Milan: Mondadori, 1935), 1:164–66. The encounter is treated at greater length and more comically in the Italian version (ibid., 721–23). For Goldoni's relationship with opera (apart from the consideration of his melodrammi giocosi and drammi per musica, his tragicomedies and various theater pieces, for which see vols. 10, 11, 9, and 12 respectively of the Ortolani edition, which are powerful evidence of something alternating and dialectic in his approach to "inventing" for music, as well as his inspired "reform" of playwriting) there is a passage that gives his judgment on the relationship between Zeno and Metastasio (ibid., 188): "If I dared to make comparisons, I would propose that Metastasio imitated Racine in his style, and that Zeno imitated Corneille in his forcefulness. Their dispositions were related to their own natures. Metastasio was gentle, polite, and charming in society. Zeno was serious, profound, and professional." This is an insight into the complexity of relationships—Goldoni, no lover of Vivaldi, has reservations about Metastasio which to some extent match his reservations on the "Prete Rosso"—

us this, we have learned not to be hypocritically scandalized—a point to us. The poet was being asked, not to be a poet, but to be a theater poet, something closer—as already indicated—to the idea we have of the screenwriter. It is no coincidence that it has only been very recently that attention has moved—after the boom in librettists—to this realistic, mercurial craft.

The eighteenth century was the age of the grand tour. Italy was being visited by those in search of the Sublime Past, the landscape of the poets of antiquity and the "romantic" painters of the seventeenth century: Virgil and Poussin. Outside Italy the search was for the Active Present, the traffic of goods and ideas, "natural" philosophy, profit, or the fever to achieve it. Italy still had the best schools and long-established, worthy traditions. Almost imperceptibly, it was something different and opposing that was sought: immersion in what was vital, savage, and primitive, that is, Wilhelm Heinse's *Ardinghello* as opposed to the neomannerism of Henry Fuseli—the approach of Stendhal, whose pro-Rossini stance will always have to be measured against this longing for things in their raw state.

Outside Italy, a literary figure who risked stepping across the Alps was immediately an adventurer. For him it was a way of approaching those musicians, those actors, those strolling players he had long been accustomed to despising. This was an initiation shorn of ritual. It may seem rather rhetorical to say so, but it was not exactly rhetorical to find oneself occupied, every day that God sent, in obtaining one's daily bread and a bed for the night, and perhaps something to go with the bread and a partner for bed. It was Farewell to the Court.

Almost like a confirmation of an encounter between history and myth, we find Giacomo Casanova in Prague, hunched over Da Ponte's libretto for *Don Giovanni*. He may have little comment to make, but the importance of this connection remains. From the London of Handel it is possible to grasp, better than in Italy, the historical importance—in anti-utopian terms—Metastasio had for Baretti. This is operative sociology (the word slipped out already with Mozart). It may be—as some Baretti scholars believe—that the ideas in his famous essay were not so new; what was new and, I would say, radical was the way he dealt with them. One by one the ideas of Aristarco Scannabue (Baretti's Arcadian pseudonym) turn up in the Arcadian repertory, although he himself does not. Baroque criticism was divided between the concision of the "letter" (Busenello) and monumental treatises (Tesauro). Baretti's *Metastasio* marks the meeting between a structurally bourgeois critic, interested in life, and an instrumentally aristocratic writer heavily bent on language, the last

which correspond to the huge, if unresolved, vitality of the age, as soon as we pass beyond history's crystallizing effect on ideology.

gasp of the courtly world. There is a correspondence between the mental articulation of Aristarco (minimum unit: the energy of a phrase that is instantly quotable and recyclable out of context) and the poetic articulation of Metastasio (minimum unit: the sentence as a type of gracious perfection, seemingly untranslatable, being locked into a brief play of syllables and rhymes but in fact essentially exportable and almost portable).[78]

More serious historians generally prefer to focus on the historic break produced by the encounter between Ranieri de' Calzabigi—a sensitive writer, and not a particularly inspired one—and an inspired and not always uptight[79] composer, Christoph Willibald Gluck. Judging more by abstract ideas than by concrete examination, there is a strong case for seeing anticipations of Wagner in Calzabigi's work; but then, one can find pre-Wagnerian tendencies in Arteaga and other theorists.[80] Sooner or later all the travelers on the path of tragic seriousness meet up at the turn of the century. Gluck seemed the single serious consequence of Monteverdi—an abstract Monteverdi, robbed of his more appropriate "aura," reorchestrated and repainted. Then came a sort of interregnum, before the eventual restoration: Antonio Sacchini (with

---

78. Baretti, in his 1763 essay on Metastasio, referred to here in n. 2, writes: "for all that a multitude of people have made enormous efforts to achieve the manner of Metastasio, not one has managed to come within a thousand miles of it; it can thus truly be said that he is the one, unmatched original of our poets, and the only one who merits to the letter the rare description of inimitable. How many operas do we hear sung nowadays that were clearly written with the intention of sounding like Metastasio? And yet where can we find even ten lines of recitative or a single aria which for simplicity, charm, animation, tenderness, loftiness, and the proper union of idea and expression has even the least in common with the most obscure recitative or the least carefully wrought aria by Metastasio?" It is well known that Baretti's criticism takes up strange positions and often the polemics of conformism, but it is clear that here we have open support for Metastasio on the part of a polemicist who did not spare either the dominant Arcadian mood or Goldoni's "reform." In this light, it is worth taking note of his insistence on Metastasio's inimitable quality, since the essence of the Arcadian reform was the fact that its products could be passed on (Zeno is a case in point) and were easily imitated and interchangeable. Baretti's signaling of Metastasio's utter originality is to be understood in contrast to the verbal and conceptual poverty of the model of Guidi: "Metastasio did not and could not use more than around a seventh part of our language . . . no style is so overwhelmingly tied to such a limited choice of words than that of our operas; and so any other style offers more verbal combinations, that is, the possibility of more phrases, than can be formed with the small number which Metastasio was able to use. And yet with the help of barely seven thousand words Metastasio found the art to say so many new, beautiful things, things that are so hard to express even in prose." It is as if Baretti, starting from Metastasio's "French" characteristics of "clarity and precision," were approaching an "English," empirical, and realistic judgment. (For the passages quoted, see the critical edition of his complete works, *Opere*, 307 and 314ff.)

79. In the sense of Adorno's "uptight" listener.

80. For all these see Nino Borsellino's entry on Arteaga in the *Dizionario biografico degli italiani* (Rome: Istituto dell'Enciclopedia Italiana, 1960–), 4 (1962): 352–55.

Edippo a Colono, and Parini's famous ode),[81] Luigi Cherubini, Gaspare Spontini, the noble, tragic side of Bellini; a more or less explicit and conscious opposition to Giovanni Paisiello and Cimarosa and Rossini himself; on to Meyerbeer, Berlioz even, who, in other respects, has more in common with the first name on the list. And finally, Wagner.

And yet it would not be mere eccentricity to point out the contradictions in Wagner with respect to this great barrier of that which is heard over and over. If we compare the finale of Metastasio's *Didone* with that of *Götterdämmerung* we see a "baroque" reality that has been archived, ready for unexpected rebirth, in the historic memory of opera. Wagner may be the stuff of Sistine Chapels and the Pyramids, but he does like to please.

As for Calzabigi and Gluck, it is entirely appropriate that, in the famous *Lettre sur la musique* of 1775, which Calzabigi's supporters are so fond of quoting, Gluck did his utmost to award the credit for the "reform"—*Orfeo, Alceste*—"à M. De Calsabigi." [82] When things go well, well-mannered people always know they must share their credit—which no one denies them—with their collaborators. Gluck recognized that Calzabigi had induced him to "develop the resources of my art." These resources must have been considerable and—as in the case of Wagner—happily contradictory, if the composer had no difficulty, subsequently, in exceeding them. The French versions of the Calzabigi tragedies show one thing above all: that for Gluck the "reform" was only an episode. But one could, and should, look beyond it. This was the secret of opera as an *opus musicorum maxime,* a secret that only the literary continued to struggle to see.

It was a stroke of genius to refer to the Parisian "philosophers" who, in an intentional and ultimately disastrous disproportion between cause and effect, had found the future (and the real past) of opera in *light music.* With typical and enchanting eighteenth-century empiricism, Utopia came down from the clouds of the world of Ideas to be worked into something far from a slavish imitation (Rousseau and *Le devin du village,* compared with *La serva padrona*).

This was the path Mozart was to take: utopia as an invention of other genres. From *Entführung* to *Zauberflöte* he creates "light music" that is German and modern (Goethe took the same path, from puppet shows to *Faust* I and II,

81. The ode *In morte del maestro Sacchini* (1786) appeared in Andrea Rubbi's *Giornale poetico* in 1789 and can be found in Giuseppe Parini, *Opere,* ed. Gianna Maria Zuradelli, 2 vols. (Turin: UTET, 1961), 1:442–46.

82. See Paolo Gallarati, "L'estetica musicale di Ranieri de' Calzabigi: *La Lulliade,*" *Nuova rivista musicale italiana* 13 (1979): 531–63, in reference to Gabriele Muresu's 1977 edition of the poem. See also Gallarati's *Musica e maschera: Il libretto italiano del Settecento* (Turin: EDT/Musica, 1984); Muresu's *La parola cantata: Studi sul melodramma italiano del Settecento* (Rome: Bulzoni, 1982); as well as Francesco Degrada's three essays on Gluck in his *Il palazzo incantato.*

the "invention of romantic poetry"). From *La finta giardiniera* to *Don Giovanni* Italian opera (in its baroque guise, that of Cesti, the limit of eighteenth-century storytelling) moves toward romantic opera and the young Verdi. The two other key trends of the eighteenth century were Metastasio and Goldoni, that is, opera seria and comedy (Handel and Piccinni, if you will); Mozart isolates them in vitro to give birth to two different, fertile strains: from *Le nozze di Figaro* (on one side the comic Rossini, on the other the farcical or bourgeois Donizetti) comes that twentieth-century glance backward of Hofmannstahl and Strauss; from *La clemenza di Tito* (Metastasio as summarized by Baretti, an "essay opera") comes the neoclassicism of Auden and Stravinsky.

That leaves *Così fan tutte*, which is a message from Mozart to himself: the absolute Utopia, revealed only to those of us who are used to encountering Mozart "outside the opera house."

8. *ROSINA*

In the eighteenth century an intellectual wrote letters. The growth of opera, when there is an opera to grow, is mirrored by ever more correspondence, in which interests and relationships, the social and cultural means and end of an existence, are articulated and the core of Arcady has almost disappeared. While Metastasio's extensive correspondence confirms the expected image of an artist in a comfortable balance between transparent formal furnishings and polite passion, it also adds something more ethical and, in the final analysis, realistic.[83] If in Metastasian drama—a drama to be understood as real or potential, almost a reversal of the relationship described above of opera to piano in Mozart—the Metastasio formula acts to marginalize life completely, with characters and dramas derived from Theophrastus-like psychodramatic mechanisms, the poet's letters reveal a life pursued calmly and sensibly, shown by the sincere pleasure he takes in exchanges and in existence. Metastasio rarely left his home: he spent his time in what we would now call a tiny flat— a nest in the court—allotted to the poet laureate. But he was happy to receive visitors and he learned to extract much from half hours spent at the window, a window, it should not be forgotten, on to a part of Europe that was on the point of being overwhelmed.

Was it because he had an inkling of this twilight that Metastasio denied himself humor? The sort of humor that can be scatalogically "too human" in the occasionally repugnant and violently lively letters of the "divine" Mozart? "The word 'humour,'" as the novelist Hildesheimer has written,[84] "is much

83. Franco Gavazzeni gives an example of the connections between Metastasio's poetry and the culture that is broadly and almost placidly revealed in his correspondence in his introductory essay to the poet's *Opere scelte* (Turin: UTET, 1968).

84. The caustic definition is Massimo Mila's; however, see Wolfgang Hildesheimer, *Mozart* (1977; English trans., London: Dent, 1982, 1985), 116.

abused." "Among the supremely gifted . . . a humorous bent does not spring from the wish to contribute to merry-making or to see the world happy. On the contrary, it comes from the urge to emphasize the weight of daily living, the 'business of life.'" (And, through "the fear of revealing oneself by being serious," it becomes "a handy means of self-protection . . . it serves as a cloak to make the wearer unrecognizable.")

And yet, as Hildesheimer continues, "it is rare to find humour in those whose genius is not verbal: from Beethoven to Gustav Mahler there extends an exemplary line of great men who seem never to have laughed; their minds were allied exclusively with poetic minds of similar bent." It is, by happy contrast, a good introduction to the letters of Donizetti.[85]

Donizetti is the first Italian musician to have left in his correspondence a legacy that is not only worthy of his best work but actually preserves a more lofty, sensitive, refined, and perhaps darker image of the composer and his music. Although he may have happily fished in the past and, when he traveled across Europe, like the musicians of the preceding centuries, did not ignore the recent past or near-present (there are frequent obvious quotations of Beethoven, Schubert, and other Viennese composers), Donizetti was the first Italian to be wholly romantic. Mazzini—who occupied the same place in politics—instinctively recognized their common aim and, in the tradition of the philosopher, at once loaded it with meanings that in part went beyond the immediate objective.

But it has to be said that the path of modern Italian opera, from the moonrise of romanticism to the rather embarrassing twilight of the long twentieth-century farewell, is marked by two great bodies of correspondence that are more than simple witnesses to their eras, signed by two leading figures of the operatic world, Donizetti and Puccini.[86] Between these two monuments, and only indirectly linked to music, is the almost indecently vigorous and vast correspondence between Arrigo Boito and Eleanora Duse.[87] However, and let it

---

85. The fundamental text remains Guido Zavadini's *Donizetti: Vita, musiche, epistolario* (Bergamo: Istituto Italiano d'Arti Grafiche, 1948); see also the *Atti del 1° convegno internazionale di studi donizettiani* (Proceedings of the First International Convention of Donizetti Studies), 22–28 Sept. 1975 (Bergamo: Azienda Autonoma di Turismo, 1983).

86. One of the products of Puccini's centenary was the publication of his correspondence in *Carteggi pucciniani*, ed. Eugenio Gara (with the correspondence between Illica, Puccini, and Ricordi edited by Mario Morini) (Milan: Ricordi, 1958). Additional material is available in Giuseppe Pintorno, *Puccini: 276 lettere inedite* (Milan: Nuove Edizioni, 1974); Giacomo Puccini, *Lettere a Riccardo Schnabl*, ed. Simonetta Puccini (Milan: Il Formichiere, 1981); "Lettere a Luigi de' Servi," ed. Simonetta Puccini, *Quaderni pucciniani*, 1982, 17–45. A number of Puccini's letters can be read in English in *Letters of Giacomo Puccini*, ed. Giuseppe Adami, trans. Ena Makin (1931), ed. Mosco Carner (London: Harrap, 1974).

87. See Eleonora Duse and Arrigo Boito, *Lettere d'amore*, ed. Raul Radice (Milan: Il Saggiatore, 1979). Although, as far as Boito is concerned, it is less surprising than his correspondence

be said without any prejudice against Boito, given the author's exhausted arsenal of polemic, this depends mostly on the actress's flagrant, carnal contribution. It is Boito's destiny to see life (the "warm life" of the new poets), approach it, and then, when difficulties arise, retire, puzzled. He was a great, fastidious poet.

In the bold extravagance of Boito's first two efforts, from *Re orso* to *Mefistofele* (a legendary fiasco at La Scala on 5 March 1868), he was not actually aiming at the street or the theater but at a sort of noble, melancholy monastery cell, where he could dully pass the time with a few venerable, enigmatic books. Since he lacked public support, he found within himself a different, ideal strength: the "Boito era" lasted exactly half a century. It closed, posthumously, with the much trumpeted premiere, almost neurotically played (by Toscanini and Milanese officialdom) against the age, of *Nerone* at La Scala on 1 May 1924. Puccini died that same year, and we can understand why Croce—rarely so openly pro-Italian—described Boito as the only true Italian romantic.

Staying with correspondence, we find Manzoni and Verdi, two powerful monuments, collectively unlovable and, in the final analysis, elusive. Rossini is more genial, but it could not be said that his letters shed any great light on a composer whose splendors are on the surface, and underneath lies only laconic mystery.[88] Bellini's letters[89] show his fundamental inability to express himself in words (is it unpatriotic to say so?). He takes us back to an earlier age in Italian art, when the pen and the brush, the chisel and the lyre, were quite separate. And this is the composer who, more than any other nineteenth-century Italian musician, inspired floods of admiration from writers—"the melody that conquers every word"—himself the least literary of men.

---

with the great Duse, another essential volume is the *Carteggio Verdi-Boito,* ed. Mario Medici and Marcello Conati (Parma: Istituto di Studi Verdiani, 1978), trans. William Weaver as *The Verdi-Boito Correspondence* (Chicago: University of Chicago Press, 1994).

88. See *Lettere inedite e rare di G. Rossini,* ed. Giuseppe Mazzatinti (Imola: Galeati, 1892); *Lettere di G. Rossini,* ed. Giuseppe Mazzatinti, F. Manis, and G. Manis (Florence: Barberà, 1902). Luigi Rognoni expresses a sound viewpoint: "Even when he was famous and his immortality saluted by the whole world, Rossini wrote like any mortal who takes up his pen to hurry on practical matters. Nevertheless, on the few occasions when Rossini, simply and without a thought to posterity, replied to someone by jotting down opinions, judgments, considerations, and ideas on music, art, and the society of his day, he did so with spirit and vivacity, often with an acute and prophetic awareness" (Luigi Rognoni, *Gioacchino Rossini* [1956; reprint, Turin: ERI, 1968], 87). A new, multivolume critical edition of Rossini's correspondence is now under way: Gioachino Rossini, *Lettere e documenti,* ed. Bruno Cagli and Sergio Ragni (Pesaro: Fondazione Rossini, 1992–).

89. Vincenzo Bellini, *Epistolario,* ed. Luisa Cambi (Milan: Mondadori, 1943). The editor writes: "The letters, especially these particular letters, so full of life and overlooked, so candid, vigorous, and good-natured, require some particular comment . . . and it will be seen that there are not two Bellinis" but a single Bellini, "as he seems to have been, without attempting to make him any more human." Possibly she was being somewhat disingenuous.

Nor was Duse particularly literate, and for this she makes a striking contrast with the great, elegant Boito. She does not tolerate the act of writing but attacks the paper, ripping off like chunks of bleeding flesh—long before futurism—every new scheme for the neat use of paper: graphic elements, alternate crammed and empty spaces, sudden gradations of the letter shapes, and impassioned, over-the-top use of punctuation.[90]

Returning to the age of Rossini, if everything there seems, generally, less passionately exposed, it is again a woman of the theater who provides us with "live" knowledge of changes in taste that we would seek in vain from those for whom writing is a profession. No point in setting the serious, petulant, boring Giuseppe Carpani against Stendhal. It takes only the letter on Rossini by Geltrude Righetti Giorgi (the first Rosina and Cenerentola) to draw us away from that ordinary enthusiast's overstretched abstractions. Our singer is a fairly animated woman, who writes good sense; she is quite at ease on paper, and the picture she draws is one of an Italy ambling toward romanticism and, without universal enthusiasm, the Risorgimento. The land of flowers, sounds, and poetry would sooner or later—this is certain—become the land of arms, but in the meantime it was easy to bend once more toward a gentle civilization, sensual intelligence, and languid culture *(nonum prematur in annum)*. This was the land of the neoclassical poet Vincenzo Monti, the tragedian Ippolito Pindemonte, the Viganòs (the choreographer Salvatore and his wife, Maria Medina), the sculptor Antonio Canova of *The Three Graces;* of the young Manzoni and the Leopardi not in permanent utter despair of the *Lettera ai signori compilatori della "Biblioteca italiana."* In the twentieth century this spirit was revived in Antonio Baldini, the famous father of the best Verdian writer and critic on the literary side, Gabriele. But the thing that is most enjoyable is that Righetti Giorgi—taking up arms against the "English journalist" who had given a preview in the *Paris Monthly Review* of a sketch for *La vie de Rossini*—unknowingly encountered Stendhal. And where Stendhal hoists his mast with open-minded dandyism, his egotistical bad side, the singer is earnestly concerned with emotional aesthetics:

> [A]s a woman and as a singer I often read Metastasio. So entranced am I by him that I read not only his librettos but also his *Canzoni*, his letters, his translations. See how Metastasio translates Horace in his book of *Ars poetica:*
>
> > L'uso e il dispor delle parole esige
> > gentilezza e cautela. Allor sarai
> > egregio parlator, quando le voci

90. In the words of the editor, Radice, "Duse's letters are characterized . . . by sentences, words, sometimes just letters that are underlined once, twice, three, five times, and they give a very clear indication of their sound and meaning (in Duse and Boito, *Lettere d'amore*, viii).

note ad ognun, mercé la cura industre
che in collocarle avrai, nuove parranno.

[The use and placing of words demands
delicacy and discretion. You will be
a speaker of distinction when the words
that all know, thanks to the diligent care
that you take in placing them, will seem new.]

There is a trace here of the Rosina which Righetti Giorgi brought so beautifully to life onstage; she seems almost to be winking at the reader remembering how, in *The Barber of Seville,* Bartolo replaces the name Giannina with that of Rosina in a song:

I have applied the concept to *maestri di cappella* and to Rossini, to make this version:

L'uso e il disporre delle note esige
gentilezza e cautela. Allor sarai
bravo compositor, quando le note
che molti sanno, colla cura industre
che in collocarle avrai, nuove parranno.

[The use and the placing of notes demands
delicacy and discretion. You will be
a fine composer when the notes
known to many, thanks to the diligent care
that you take in placing them, will seem new.]

Behold all that needs to be known on modern music.[91]

This is going, consciously, or rather, naturally, to the heart of a culture that trusted translation to make a sensitive and discreet adaptation of a legacy that was neither austere nor a museum piece. The rupture between Monti and Foscolo over the version of Homer anticipates that between Giovita Scalvini and Boito as translators of *Faust.* For nineteenth-century Italy *Faust* was like the ghost of the Commendatore in *Don Giovanni.* It is no coincidence that Righetti Giorgi's letter closes with an attack on those who support the "German" Mozart against her Rossini:

And since, by continually referring to Mozart's *Don Giovanni,* foreigners would like to cast a shadow over that little glory which comes from our Italian music, I call on the crowd of music lovers or amateurs to take my side.
    This *Don Giovanni* by Mozart, which made such an effect in Milan and Flor-

91. Geltrude Righetti Giorgi, *Cenni di una donna già cantante sopra il maestro Rossini* (Bologna, 1823), in Rognoni, *Gioacchino Rossini,* 366 and 370ff.

ence,[92] in the theater of Santa Maria, went on to be received coldly in the other Italian opera houses. . . . The general coloring of this, as of other operas by Mozart, does not seem to me to be carried through, much less that of the various characters and their emotions. The peasant sometimes sings in a heroic manner, and the most serious character sings in a popular style. The scene in hell in *Don Giovanni* is frightening and majestic. Those who idolize Mozart and those who spout hypocritically about his music declare that they found it blood-curdling. Things went rather differently at the Teatro di Corso in Bologna.[93] No Catholic litany was said, but the audience had no difficulty in making out the *Quantus tremor* or *Tuba mirum* of the most severe purists of the last century. It is not my intention to instill contempt for Mozart: on the contrary, homage should be paid to a German soul that dared to occupy itself with Italian verses [that is, Da Ponte's librettos] and adorned them with beautiful, contrived accompaniments in such a way as to give even the most antiquated things the appearance of newness.

But I demand Italian taste and call for sweet song that you can feel in your heart; this is absolutely sovereign in music and must be obeyed. Originality is found in song, in that song which comes from the depths of the heart. This part of feeling, which will last forever, is the only one that should be appreciated in music for the theater.

In the same year in which Righetti Giorgi was writing these words, Rossini was exploiting *Don Giovanni* in his *Semiramide,* where the ghost of Nino corresponds to the specter of the Commendatore. A few years before, the young Leopardi (in 1816, the year of Rossini's *Barber* and *Otello*) had, vainly, from a cultural solitude which he already found distressing, tried to make his voice heard by the romantic intellectuals of Milan, with arguments that Rossini's friend would have recognized as her own:

Let us open all the channels of foreign literature, let all the waters of the north gush into our fields, and in an instant Italy will be flooded, and all its little poets will throng to drink, to paddle in it, and be filled up to their throats. . . . This may not displease Madame [de Staël], but many Italians who very frequently find in those [northern] writers exaggerations and outsize images, and very rarely true, most pure, holy, and graceful nature, would feel great displeasure.[94]

For real Rossinians, true, most pure, holy, and graceful nature is to be found in song. It is eternal because it is natural. It is not inaccurate to bring together Leopardi's future polemic against "harsh nature" and his aversion for "new

92. Clearly in this context as well, the two "romantic" capitals of early-nineteenth-century Italy.

93. The stronghold of Rossini's support, of course.

94. Giacomo Leopardi, *Lettera ai signori compilatori della "Biblioteca Italiana" in risposta a quella di Madama la baronessa di Staël Holstein ai medesimi* (Recanati, 18 July 1816), in his *Opere*, ed. Giovanni Getto (Milan: Mursia, 1966), 594–96.

believers," affectations of the romantics (as Righetti Giorgi has it, "those who spout hypocritically about" Mozart). It does seem that Righetti Giorgi failed to see how Rossini's extraordinary orchestral sensitivity (not the facile symphonic qualities of his famous overtures) was the most bold and genuinely novel aspect of Rossinian opera in the way it supported and counterpointed the voices. Rossini is no Metastasio. (In the same way, Leopardi seemed to be unaware of how much his own palette owed to transalpine influences, for example, what he had gleaned from "the great Cesarotti's"[95] rough but productive version of *Ossian,* or from *Werther,* decanted into soft, evocative Italian verses by the supreme Vincenzo Monti of the *Pensieri d'amore.*)

It was not chance, nor adventure, that led Rossini to set his sights on Paris. Between *La gazza ladra* at La Scala in 1817 (and the story of the poor servant girl unjustly accused and persecuted is perhaps not unconnected with the beginnings of *I promessi sposi*) and *Semiramide,* a veritable monument to voluptuous, neoclassical bel canto (Rossini's *Così fan tutte?*), the composer had looked at Tasso's legacy *(Armida),* Trojan and French tragedy *(Ermione,* inspired by Racine's *Andromaque),* the biblical epic oratorio in *Mosè in Egitto,* and the romantic landscapes of Walter Scott in *La donna del lago,* with something of a mellowed Cesarotti in there, too. It therefore comes as no surprise to read, in the rapidly changing climate, after 1830, a reliable observer such as Niccolò Tommaseo noting in his *Diario intimo,* with reference to Rossini, "the immense variety of that genius moves me to envy."

And what prompted this? *La Cenerentola.*[96]

9. IL DUCA D'ATENE

On the penultimate day of Carnival 1833, around evening time, Niccolò Tommaseo of Sebenico was at a window in via Fiesolana in Florence.[97] He, Mazzini, and Donizetti; later on came Verdi and also meteoric Ippolito Nievo:

95. Leopardi's famous letter to his brother Carlo is undoubtedly informed by the emotion of having heard Rossini's "Fingal" (Rome, 5 Feb. 1823): "At the Argentina they're playing *La donna del lago,* the music of which, sung by astounding voices, is something stupendous, and I myself might cry, if the gift of tears had not been taken from me temporarily, inasmuch as I realize that I have not lost it completely. And yet the performance is intolerably, mortally long: it lasts six hours and here the custom is not to leave one's box." In Giacomo Leopardi, *Lettere,* ed. Francesco Flora (Milan: Mondadori, 1949), letter 248. As far as tears are concerned, Leopardi might have been writing about the impression made by Malcolm's cabaletta. On the general subject of "Fingalism" in opera, see Gianfranco Folena, *L'italiano in Europa: Esperienze linguistiche del Settecento* (Turin: Einaudi, 1983), 325–55.

96. Niccolò Tommaseo, *Opere,* ed. Aldo Borlenghi (Milan and Naples: Ricciardi, 1958), 586. "I go to the Giglio to see *Cenerentola.* The music seems fresher than usual: and the immense variety of that genius moves me to envy. I ate eggs for breakfast, lunched on soup with pasta, trotters, casserole, salad, and an egg; for supper eggs, salad, casserole" (do these relate to the opera?).

97. The title of this section derives from *Il duca d'Atene* (The duke of Athens), a "narration" by Niccolò Tommaseo, first published in 1858; also the title of a "pantomime" by the librettist Felice Romani.—Trans.

there weren't many more real Italian romantics. A couple of tenors, perhaps: Duprez (he of the high C as a chest note) and Mario de Candia. A page in his *Diario intimo* records this evening at the window among those that Tommaseo calls "the pleasures of my life."

> As the sun was going down, contemplating the sky of mixed light and clouds, I said the Act of Contrition. . . . I was watching a little girl of six, with her hair plaited into a ring, smiling to hear the more lively passages of the overture to *William Tell,* accompanied by her hands and head, and . . . with her eyes sparkling. The trio for Duprez, Matteo, and Porto was repeated twice, . . . and Duprez's fourth-act aria.[98]

The Italian premiere of *Guglielmo Tell* had taken place two years previously, in Lucca, in the summer of 1831 (a year of unsettled political transition as well); the impresario was the same Antonio Lanari who, in 1847, commissioned Verdi to write *Macbeth* for the Teatro alla Pergola in Florence. The Lucca cast of *Tell* moved to the Pergola: Gilbert-Louis Duprez (his reputation dates from that time, when his ringing sound recalled the bombardments of Napoleon's hussars during the revolts), Domenico Cosselli, Santina Ferlotti, and Matteo Porto. The trio ("il padre, ohimè, / mi malediva / ed io la patria / ognor tradiva") became a craze. When the opera returned to Paris in 1837, it was as the romantic piece associated with Duprez, which so irritated Rossini ("leave your top C on the hat-stand"). It should also be said that today's "authentic" outlook asks tenors to sing the role of Arnold in the style of Nourrit, even though this tenor had already had to start omitting the fourth-act aria and cabaletta from the opera's second performance in 1829 onward. Opera had always been, for Rossini no less than any other composer, a compromise, an invention based on the available technical resources, including those of the "virtuosos"; and it is well to remember that Rossini, up until then an infallible judge of voices, might have made a mistake in placing his bets on Nourrit.[99]

So Tommaseo was at the window saying a prayer, thinking about and enjoying one of the successes of the day. As for that little girl: perhaps she was being spied upon with the impure eyes of a father of Alice.

For Tommaseo opera is like the air, part of life, of habit. For an intellec-

---

98. Tommaseo, *Opere,* 581.

99. William Weaver, *Rossini and "William Tell,"* pp. 25ff. of the booklet accompanying the CD release of the Decca recording of *Guglielmo Tell* first issued on LP in 1980. Conducted by Riccardo Chailly, it uses Calisto Bassi's historic Italian translation. A conference dedicated to *Tell* at the University of Cagliari in 1987 culminated in a complete performance of the opera, which immediately passed into legend for the involvement of one exceptional North American tenor, Chris Merritt, who could combine the bel canto sound of Adolphe Nourrit with the ringing "romantic-bourgeois" tones of Duprez. When Nourrit turned to Donizetti, with *Poliuto* in prospect, to adopt the new, revolutionary style of singing, he succeeded only in losing the "old" and dealt with this in his own way by throwing himself out of a window in Naples.

tual this is a new attitude. Everything has a part to play. In his *Diario* we can follow frequent, and generally acute, observations on various nights at the opera: from Bellini to Donizetti and on to Verdi *(Nabucco, Rigoletto)*. But there is nothing to be gained by reading them in isolation: his admiration for *Tell,* for *Norma,* which had caused such a sensation in Milan, going from dust to the altar, again in 1831, and his commitment to ideology (almost worthy of Mazzini for all that Tommaseo disliked him, calling him ironically "our liberator"), which comes across from the pleasure he takes in the everyday realities of the theater ("I go to the Pergola to hear *La straniera:* music utterly of its day, that is, rather characterless but with a vague feeling of melancholy, ineffectual . . . "),[100] must be sensitively and systematically viewed against the backdrop of such comments as these:

> A young wife accompanies me from the Scoti silk mill to the piazza. She is a woman who knows shame.

> I dreamed of Barbieri in a high boat. We were sailing together along the pleasant waters of some river. I said, with emotion, "and one day, when I am far from you. . . . But no, I cannot think of it. O pleasant banks, O gentle waters, etc." It was a beautiful exclamation, really poetic.

> I ate soup, beans, *baccalà,* a herring, apples.[101]

In the dramatic days when the liberal writer Giovan Pietro Vieusseux was finishing his *Anthology,* we find, from a phrase let slip by Tommaseo and from his resolution to take the path to exile in France, life flourishing again: days that were "hardworking and productive," "full of life," Tommaseo himself notes down in his *Diario.* Whom he met, what he read, what he dreamt, whom he loved, his illnesses, his eating, again what he read, avidly, and what

---

100. Tommaseo, *Opere,* 595. "I heard *La straniera* at the Pergola and I still enjoyed it. The choruses are coarse, the melodies lack delicacy, but the melancholy tone is beauty enough. This is an opera which depicts our day. There is something deep and ineffable below the commonplace forms" (591). From another point of view, this amounts to posing the same question as the "C as a chest-note" (see 597), a singer "with a silvery voice of the utmost delicacy" but nevertheless "with no energy or emotion to her delivery" ("she has breath but no spirit: a chest but no heart: she can be heard but she makes us feel nothing and does not feel.").

101. Ibid., 582, 584 (and see 583: "I dreamed that I was in court for having slandered Gregory XVI as a prince and for having insulted an innocent young girl. It was the latter accusation that tortured me. When I awoke, how sweet it was to remember that I went to communion only yesterday. As I was getting up I happened to touch the little picture which hangs above my bed, *La Madonna della tenda.* This touch roused a gentle feeling in my spirit. . . . I go to hear the second performance of *Tell.*"). See also 587 passim, but with a hallucinatory stubbornness, like a latter-day Pontormo, on parks and meals, with every mouthful superstitiously counted. In the same period Tommaseo wrote one of his greatest poems, the canzone *Una voce in cuor mi suona* (a distortion of Rossini's "Una voce poco fa / qui nel cuor mi risuonò").

he saw at the theater, all are diligently noted down and commented upon. A life of forcefulness. His *Dizionario dei sinonimi* was appearing, and by mixing Byron and Scott, Manzoni ("the beauties of that sovereign book"), and Leopardi ("a petty, false genius"), Dante and the fourteenth-century chroniclers, Obermann and Fieramosca, and above everyone and everything the Bible, Tommaseo was arriving at the blistering style of *Il duca d'Atene.* Here we must pause for a digression: not so long ago literary Italians, it has frequently been said, steered clear of opera, preferring *Fede e bellezza* to *La traviata.* When the wind changed, one would not have expected them to memorize, from recordings, the trio from *Ernani,* formerly food for the nonliterary,[102] or Mina's aria from Verdi's *Aroldo,* but they would be found mixing up the Tommaseo of *Il sacco di Lucca, L'assedio di Tortona,* or *Il duca d'Atene* with historical romances ("written for the age, not for the ages," to use a favorite distinction of Tommaseo's)[103] by d'Azeglio and his once popular colleagues. These belong to the sort of lyrical culture of the tender, dated imagination of a painter like Hayez[104] or in the indeterminate poetic arsenal of Tommaso Grossi, whose *I Lombardi alla prima crociata* contains Hayez-like images, known to the young Verdi. They share nothing with the lyrical wizardry of Tommaseo: "I wrote, I'm not sure if by mistake, a *Duke of Athens,* not a novel but a picture with dialogue, . . . visible speech—new to us—in the style of *Il sacco di Lucca*" (Tommaseo is writing to Capponi). On *Il sacco:* "a poetic painting freed from meter."[105]

This would be the right key to understanding Verdi were it not for the fact that their encounter—much more decisive than that with Manzoni—never took place. The encounters are only of interest to those who beat the drum for the winners.

10. RE ORSO

The La Scala seasons from 1954 to 1958 constitute a kind of postwar "golden age," the point, in terms of musical taste, when the drive toward the bel canto revival, not yet touched by academe, got under way (the "Callas era"); in effect, peering down with the literary figures who were taking new pleasure in opera, it was the time of Montale, as the "chronicler of La Scala," at his

---

102. See Giovanni Verga, *Una peccatrice* (1866; Milan: Mondadori, 1985), chap. 4: "then some random sounds from the piano, as if fingers were searching for the notes of some fantastical melody, which they then grew tired of playing and continued with the final trio from *Ernani;* after a short while this was also interrupted, with the same whimsical inconstancy, in favor of a fashionable waltz of the day, Arditi's *Il Bacio*" (77).

103. Tommaseo, *Opere,* 590.

104. See Fernando Mazzocca, *Pittura e melodramma: 1828–1850,* in the catalogue of the Hayez exhibition, Milan, 1983–84 (Milan: Electa, 1984), 144–59.

105. Niccolò Tommaseo, *Memorie poetiche,* in his *Opere,* ed. Mario Puppo (Florence: Sansoni, 1968), 2:332.

best.[106] The literati can face opera without complexes, now that the art is once again wooing the emblematic works of Mozart, the neoclassics, and the early romantics, and thus facilitating a connection—long seen as impossible—to the sphere of traditional literary values gladly shared. After all, this is in the Parini-Foscolo-Manzoni-Leopardi line (updated in the Lombard arena through a daring connection with the writer Carlo Emilio Gadda, and then with the Gadda of Alberto Arbasino); and it was also in the line of Felice Romani, given the infamy he generously scattered on the exercise of libretto writing, save at most for his name and for a few memorable lines.[107] Not surprisingly, the dismissal of "verismo" went hand in hand with that of Boito, which could now be shouted aloud: verismo opera "lost its temper only at the beginning of the twentieth century, that is, when composers took up the invitation from singers to place their bets on the sobbing shout at the upper limit of the middle register, exactly where, in tenors, sopranos, and baritones, the voice, moving across the passaggio, tends to break. And break it did." [108]

Such a diagnosis from a reliable critic like Fedele D'Amico seemed all the more persuasive for its technical clarifications, for which readers hungered as the 1960s drew nearer. And the way was opened for another conviction, a dislike of Boito. His *Mefistofele,* which had maintained its reputation for the whole of the Toscanini era, up until the middle of the twentieth century, was

106. "Callas clearly would require a whole separate discussion. Polemics on her *Medea* went as far as essays by literary figures and historians, something that has not happened for nearly a century (Praz dedicated two columns to her, Paratore four: all six very persuasive in defending her from a music critic's censure)." The critic in question was the poet and refined translator Beniamino Dal Fabbro, historian of the twilight of the piano (Fedele D'Amico, *I casi della musica* [Milan: Il Saggiatore, 1962], 83); and see Eugenio Montale, "Dal teatro alla vita," one of his *Sei prime alla Scala* (Milan: Mondadori, 1981), 49–54. This is a reprint of an article of 21 May 1969, written for the publication of a short volume on Callas by Camilla Cederna.

107. Once again, it is Montale who clarifies, one might say definitively, something that the literati have taken centuries to understand (with the famous exceptions, although it is not saying much, of Proust's "bad music" and Auden's "translating opera librettos"): "'M'hanno detto che Beppe va soldato / e che vi han visto pianger di nascosto. / Far pianger sì begli occhi è gran peccato: / Beppe non partirà: prendo il suo posto'" (They told me that Joe was going for a soldier / and they saw him cry in secret. / It's a terrible thing to make such lovely eyes cry: / Joe won't be going: I'll take his place). A composer in the late nineteenth century took these words and wrote a song that touched our parents' hearts. This was possible because the obscure composer, Augusto Rotoli [1847–1904] grasped not the poetry, since there is none, but the situation [a Verdian term] that the awful lines expressed. Historically one can try to distinguish between composers of *recitar cantando,* those who take care with the words . . . and those who are content with the situation the words express (almost all opera composers, including Verdi); the truth is that true poetry already contains its own music and will not accept another; it is only words that are only slightly poetic, or hardly at all, that can have another poetry hung on them" (from Montale's "Parole e musica," in *Prime alla Scala,* 23–25).

108. D'Amico "L'*Andrea Chénier* e l'opera verista," in his *Casi della musica,* 229.

for D'Amico (and for his father, a distinguished theater critic) the musical equivalent of the Victor Emmanuel monument in Rome:

> If for certain European musicians of his time an attachment to *Mefistofele* was simply a generic act of solidarity which the avant-garde instinctively declares for every other avant-garde, the public at large found that *Mefistofele* was an opera whose effective musical basis was a modest meeting of salon song and operatic aria, with a bit of La Scala "ballet," but all put together by an amateur.[109]

Even in D'Amico's writings[110] the preparation for Puccini's assumption to the Olympus of the Classics was already under way: it was favored by fortunate circumstances such as the concurrence of the centenary of the composer's birth, Puccini's "internationalism" promoted in a successful book by an Anglo-Viennese critic,[111] and a wonderful recording of *Tosca,* of all Puccini's operas the most defamed by critics up until that time. The recording was made at La Scala by a great Wagner and Strauss conductor—one who was, nevertheless, an enthusiast for Giordano's ultraverismo operas as well—Victor De Sabata, the decadent rival to Toscanini, and by a singer whose qualities were beyond suspicion, Maria Callas: it was almost an antiverismo manifesto displayed on verismo territory.

Montale was at the beginning of his stint as music critic for the *Corriere d'informazione;* he did not miss the opportunity to contribute to the change in taste in his much-heeded, epigrammatic desire to clarify and systematize, but at the same time he did not attempt to speed it up. On Wagner: "the present-day (Italian) listener to Wagner understands neither the words nor the action and his or her enjoyment is in direct proportion to the absurdity of the situation in which he finds himself immersed"; on Bellini: "*La sonnambula* could be performed in a palace or a shed"; on Rossini (*Il turco in Italia,* rediscovered by Gavazzeni, Callas, and Zeffirelli and on its way to becoming a cult opera

109. D'Amico "Il segreto del *Mefistofele,*" in ibid., 279–80.

110. See "Naturalismo e decadentismo in Puccini" and "Le ragioni di *Manon Lescaut,*" in ibid., 284–97, 281–83.

111. Mosco Carner, *Puccini: A Critical Biography,* rev. ed. (London: Duckworth, 1992). Essential reading for Puccini's fortunes in Italy includes Fausto Torrefranca, *Giacomo Puccini e l'opera internazionale* (Turin: Bocca, 1912), although this great musicologist's prejudiced views should be compared with those expressed in his *La vita musicale dello spirito* (Turin: Bocca, 1910), and *Le origini italiani del romanticismo musicale* (Turin: Bocca, 1930); Bruno Barilli, "Omaggio a Puccini," in his *Il paese del melodramma* (Lanciano: Carabba, 1930), 179–214; Giacomo Debenedetti, "Puccini e la melodia stanca," in his *Il personaggio uomo* (Milan: Il Saggiatore, 1970), 105–15. Other, literary commentary can be found in Cesare Garboli (1969), Luigi Baldacci (1974), Alberto Arbasino, and Enzo Siciliano (1976). See also the Puccinian qualities of Sylvano Bussotti's (productively theatrical) work, midway between poetry and music. A "Tuscan," resentfully antiliterary viewpoint can be read in Leonardo Pinzauti, *Puccini* (Florence: Vallecchi, 1974).

for "anonymous Lombard" followers of Alberto Arbasino—and the Spoleto Festival was at the door, looking for novelties where they could be found):

> [Rossini] was not a scrupulous man or an aesthete. And it is curious that today he is falling into the hands of aesthetes who find in him daring harmonies that critics, to a man, conventionally denied him. [Verdi said of the *Barber*:] "It is not melody, it is not harmony, yet it is music." Modern composers, who detest melody, with reason, because they are incapable of creating it, have accepted Verdi's judgment, altering it, however, as far as regards the harmonic part. It is recognized today that Rossini's harmony is not dialectic, is not interior, but is rhythmic, vital, and always musical. Rossini's effects, big, coarse effects, are structural, not filler, and if you tried to take them out, you would distort his operas completely.[112]

For those who are familiar with Montale's career as a poet it is immediately apparent that here, at a distance, he is preparing the final, otherwise unforeseeable, phase in his poetry, its strange technical fireworks, its game of cat and mouse with the malicious and the banal: not poetry, not thought, but still music, "in the form of a pear," we might say. As for Rossini, so also, at the beginning of the twentieth century, for the Verdi revival. The death of the great patriarch of Italian music had provided the literary world with nothing more than an opportunity to show its inadequacy. To accept that Verdi wept and loved for all, according to D'Annunzio's overused phrase, is to show that one has grasped nothing from *Falstaff*, a work that gained few ready, intelligent listeners, and none at all from the literary world.[113]

112. Montale, *Prime alla Scala*, 157, 159, and 161. For the literary vogue for *Il turco in Italia,* see Alberto Arbasino, *Anonimo lombardo* (Milan: Feltrinelli, 1959) and Alberto Arbasino, *Fratelli d'Italia,* both in its first edition for Feltrinelli (1963) and in the "rewritten" version published by Einaudi (1976). But for the Arbasino effect on Italian literary taste between the 1960s and 1970s, its omnivorous mixture of writing, theater, and opera, see Alberto Arbasino's *Grazie per le magnifiche rose* (Milan: Feltrinelli, 1965), "La Belle Époque per le scuole," in his *Certi romanzi* (Milan: Feltrinelli, 1964), and *Fantasmi italiani* (Rome: Cooperativa Scrittori, 1977), titles that are presented, lest anyone think of avoiding them, in the revival of opera (as a legend and museum) in Italian "postmodernism." One should not avoid either the analogous, but "modern" affiliation of theater, literature, and music found in the essays of Giovanni Macchia; for the relationship between new approaches in literature and music, Giorgio Petrocchi seems to have struck a good balance in *Cultura letteraria e musica nel primo trentennio del secolo* (Naples: Guida, 1981), recalling a "harsh judgment" by Montale (in order to refute it): "it does not seem that words chewed up by a meat grinder can give rise to new, profound music." It might be true for Montale and his associates, "but certainly not for Sanguineti or Giuliani, Porta or Manganelli, whose experiments have started a literary genre that is obviously linked to electronic music but cannot be directly associated with what is known as electronic poetry," even if, for the moment, "it would be impossible to draw up a plan of debit and credit between the new avant-garde and visual poetry and the music of Cage or Bussotti." New forms of "musical space" are coming into being, forms that have nothing in common with traditional opera, apart from perhaps their intellectual and experimental origins.

113. An exceptional exception is Giovanni Vailati's *Epistolario (1891–1909)* (Turin: Einaudi, 1971), 22.

Then, as if to clarify any possible misunderstanding, came the scandalous breakdown between Toscanini and the Ricordi company in 1902, when this new conducting star—a Wagnerian, a symphonist (and therefore presumably "anti-Italian"), a futurist, and intellectual, although no man of letters—decided to revive at La Scala that piece of old rubbish known as *Il trovatore*. Bruno Barilli's fledgling eagles had yet to take wing for this opera, nor had George Santayana yet compared it to the poetry of Leopardi.[114] These were years of agitation, and not only in opera. Fiasco followed fiasco, but in an unpredictable, schizophrenic way; Mascagni's *Le maschere* failed because it was "too different" from the vainly hoped-for "second *Cavalleria*"; *Butterfly* failed because it was "too similar" to the successful (but not universally accepted) Puccini of *La Bohème*. *Der Rosenkavalier* failed in Italy because it was "German" and not futurist. . . . All the acclaim was ultimately for *Fedra*: an "aura" of endless words by D'Annunzio smothered in an endless veneer of tremulous notes by Pizzetti. It was first heard at La Scala in 1915, and then the war came to try to put everything right; the result, as always, was that absolutely nothing was put right.[115]

114. See Santayana's foreword to the first edition (1935) of Iris Origo, *Leopardi: A Study in Solitude* (London: Hamish Hamilton, 1935): how to express the purely Orphic character of Leopardi's poetry? "Suppose you were held up in some minor Italian town where by chance an itinerant company was to perform *Il trovatore* . . . suddenly you heard, coming from behind the wings, an unexampled heavenly voice, a voice as pure as moonlight, rich as sorrow, firm as truth, singing *Solo in terra*." A commonplace, after all, for an author to misquote the text when referring to an opera; Saba recounted that one of his favorite lines was that of the "partisan" Ernani—"Udite or tutti del mio cor gli affanni"—"in the introduction of the cabaletta [!] 'Aragonese vergine [!!]'" (*Scorciatoie e raccontini* [Milan: Mondadori, 1963], 84).

115. A quick rundown of events—great and small—and fiascos, however full of "history": (1) just before the premiere, given in six theaters simultaneously, of *Le maschere* (Mascagni's provocative and ill-fated bid for the leading position in the opera world at the dawn of the new century), Roberto Bracco, one of the leading dramatists of the day, who, five years earlier, had written his own play of the same name, gave a lively commentary, first in the periodical *Il marzocco* of 20 Jan. 1901, then reprinted in his *Tra le arti e gli artisti* (Naples: Giannini, 1918). In this piece, entitled "Che cos'è Mascagni?" ("What is Mascagni?"—note the "what is," not "who is"), Bracco portrays the composer as a "jester," the super-Tuscan "artful child" of legend: but his words reveal an avant-garde poet ahead of his time, to the amazement and disorientation of his contemporaries, in search of a more normal, domestic type of performer. (2) Pascoli's short poem (". . . the little butterfly will take wing . . .") to console Puccini for the disastrous first performance of *Butterfly* at La Scala in 1904; and apart from any imagined organized protest, a sign of an aesthetic, modern desire to rob Puccini of his preeminence (see Puccini's complete failure to reach an agreement with D'Annunzio, the librettist). (3) The failure of *Der Rosenkavalier* at La Scala (1911), recalled by Marinetti as the "First Artistic Punitive Raid" ("Prima spedizione punitiva artistica," to be found in his *Teoria e invenzione futurista*, ed. Luciano De Maria [Milan: Mondadori, 1968], 513–14, dedicated to "the dear, great Benito Mussolini"): "During the first performance of Strauss's *Der Rosenkavalier,* we flooded La Scala with thousands of manifestos bearing this declaration: 'We futurists demand that La Scala cease to be the Pompei of Italian Theater or the noisy

Harvey Sachs, Toscanini's reliable biographer, has written:

> I think that more than anything else, Toscanini was undecided in his approach to
> these works [that is, Verdi's "popular" operas]. He had grown up hearing them per-
> formed in the "traditional" way—with interpolated notes and cadential passages,
> illogical transpositions, and tempo fluctuations which went far beyond the bounds
> of inflection or *rubato* into the realm of gross distortion. . . . It took years for
> Toscanini to decide that the investigative method he applied to other music, the
> method of trying to find and play what was in the score instead of trying to adapt
> the score to his own or others' needs and preferences, was an equally just and log-
> ical process when applied to the more thickly encrusted Verdi works.[116]

There was much more to it than simply cutting out the high C at the end of
"Di quella pira," as it has seemed to historically minded conductors of the recent, ignorant generation. Toscanini won the battle of *Trovatore* (just like
Napoleon III at Solferino, according to D'Ormeville, a critic who was also a
librettist and a businessman involved in the colorful world of the theater in
various ways) and "that production initiated the 'Verdi Renaissance'—which
might be better termed the 'Verdi Restoration'—in a double sense: the re-
conditioning-restoration of a work of art, and the restoration of Verdi to his
rightful position." [117] Of course, Toscanini's recorded legacy does not include
Il trovatore, and we have to make an effort to guess how it might have
sounded, transferring what we know of a chunk of *Rigoletto* (the third act,
which Dallapiccola was fond of), the late, emphatic *Traviata,* attacked by Toscanini's opponents, and a turbulent, almost crystallized *Ballo in maschera,* in
which all the singers are castigated. Perhaps it might be easier to understand
that scandalous *Trovatore,* pruned of customs and partisan diversions, by a

---

shop window for the great publishing huses, and in every season experiment with at least three
works by Italian composers who are young, boldly innovative, and as yet unknown.'" (4) The similar uproar by the young Turks of *La voce* in 1915, in favor of *Fedra* by the modern and "D'Annun-
zian" Pizzetti ("a hope for something new that will come to break up once and for all the bourgeois
drivel we have been laboring under since Verdi, that genius of Italian musical idiocy"). (5) Appropriately enough, with all the shouting going on both in and out of the theater, no one lent an ear
to the fragile voice of *Pelléas et Mélisande,* except to boo at it (see Vittorio Gui, *Battute d'aspetto,*
213–17). Gui, five years younger than Pizzetti, had led the successful performance of that composer's incidental music to D'Annunzio's *La nave* the year before. Their relationship was to break
down—as did that between Pizzetti and Malipiero over their completely opposing views of Stravinsky's *Rite of Spring*—in the wake of the sophisticated account of the history of European music theater, from Mozart to Mussorgsky, given by the cultivated and highly literate Gui.

116. Harvey Sachs, *Toscanini* (London: Weidenfeld and Nicolson, 1978), 79–80. But it is
worth reading the entire chapter (60–120) on Toscanini's relationship with the culturally dominant class in Milan, as reflected in the repertory and customs of La Scala.

117. Ibid., 82.

comparison—made possible by the recording—with *La Bohème,* which, in any case, Toscanini was the first to conduct, in Turin in 1896. Stripped of any sentimental languor, of tenor indulgences, and of the impressionist touches that audiences and performers normally delight in, Puccini's opera seems closer to the Murger model, to the bourgeois realism of the *Scènes de la vie de bohème.* At the same time, the opera is played with symphonic, almost Beethovenian clarity. The important point is that the practice introduced by Toscanini at the beginning of the century, to restore Italy's musical legacy, was not matched by anything in literature, whether current or emergent. We need only compare Toscanini's Wagner with that of D'Annunzio: in the former it is the intellectual synthesis that dominates; in the latter, the oratory and voluptuousness. Some think of the Alps in terms of peaks to be climbed, and some as "heavenly" locations for a chalet.

In the literary world (in Italy the musical nineteenth century ended in 1945, with the death of Mascagni, the literary one, depending on how you look at it either fifteen years before or twenty years later) the chalet ideal was still somewhat dominant. There is some nice talk, a sensuality of the mind changes, without limit, into self-satisfied morality, unverified by liberal thought. There was Mascagni and D'Annunzio, Zandonai and D'Annunzio, Pizzetti and D'Annunzio, Malipiero and D'Annunzio, Casella and D'Annunzio, Dallapiccola and D'Annunzio. Then, when the ghost had been laid to rest, everyone, without realizing, became followers of D'Annunzio again and will always remain so. Just as happened to the writings of Benedetto Croce, the single arbiter of taste and thought in Italy who was his equal during in those crucial years, no one buys Toscanini's recordings any more.

For all that, it should also be said that the feeling remains that in the Verdi restoration, Toscanini lost sight of something essential to the composer. And possibly this derived from the fact that Toscanini never had any doubts about the artistic position—and even the taste—of Arrigo Boito. Biographers continue to dig up the story of the discourtesy shown by Toscanini toward Puccini when he prevented him from attending the rehearsals of Boito's *Nerone.* Certainly there were too many cooks in the kitchen, and feelings were running high. *Nerone* was fundamentally an anti-Puccini, and equally an anti-modern, project. Like Croce, who, faced with the choice of Pascoli or Boito, had resolutely chosen Boito or Carducci, so too Toscanini made his choice between Boito—the upper-middle-class nineteenth century, Verdi's aristocratic side—and the petit bourgeois *larmoyant,* Puccini. Floods of ink have been poured out over the "librettist for hire" of D'Annunzio and the *"vorrei e non vorrei,* in fact, we can't" of Puccini. But Puccini and D'Annunzio had some features in common: sensuality, lyricism, outsize theatricality, hysteria. Anyone can understand why Duse went from Boito to D'Annunzio.

We return to the significance of what Boito had done, to himself and the cultural environment of which he was long to be the admired lord, with the bizarre curiosity of his fable *Re orso*.[118] It is striking that neither Arrigo nor his talented brother Camillo, for whom, in the period of this poem, the black beast was Verdi, the composer of *Lombardi* and the recent *Ballo in maschera* (*Re orso* is from 1865), grasped that this open-minded reflection on what was ugly in art had to imply, for Italy, Verdi. Certainly, not even Verdi wasted a single word on defending the inspired awfulness of *Alzira*. It has a surreal reality, like *Re orso,* of Lombard and Italian romanticism. From the Scapigliatura period onward, Italy was making ready to reconstruct itself, again, with the beautiful as its foundation.

11. ULISSE

A bad libretto begins with the problem of—or with the senses exposed to—the bad libretto.[119] That is to say, with the Scapigliatura movement.

It is typical of the Italian situation that praise for the very formality of opera librettos is thought legitimate comment. The decisive battle was fought in the same year as *Falstaff,* or rather in the years immediately preceding, by the many hands involved within the "collective" of Puccini librettists in completing—goaded by the fact that the young composer was so extremely hard to please—the libretto for *Manon Lescaut.* The result ended up being anonymous, or, significantly, unsigned (those involved were Domenico Oliva, Marco Praga, Giuseppe Giacosa and Luigi Illica, Leoncavallo, Giulio Ricordi, and Puccini himself). This marked the farewell to the bankrupt stock of Scapigliatura ideas, the historically orientated fixation with death and the fantastic that had tried to take control of Puccini.

In *Falstaff*—whose libretto is a masterpiece in its own right—literary virtuosity grows and grows and grows, then bursts, when, like the far-off baroque model, it pushes the self-destruct button. Verdi was aware of the fact, and the opera has the merry, gallows atmosphere of the *Satyricon:* like the suicide of an ancient Roman, Seneca's, for example, to the accompaniment of cheerful music and erudite conversation on the man's death. Seneca had returned to the opera stage: it is possibly no coincidence that shortly after *Falstaff, L'incoronazione di Poppea,* lost or forgotten but certainly of no interest to anyone for centuries, was rediscovered. Malipiero rediscovered it and then spent his entire life pursuing it without ever managing to lay hold of it: too many years had passed on the waters of the Venetian lagoon since the lawyer Busenello had dramatized the story of ancient Rome for a realistic, pleasure-seeking audience. Malipiero—pleasure-seeking but in no way realistic—had no audience for his art.

118. *Il re orso* (The bear king) is a fable *(fiaba)* by Boito, first published in 1865.—Trans.
119. *Ulisse* (Ulysses) is an opera by Dallapiccola, first performed in 1968.—Trans.

Manon Lescaut offered a middle- to-upper-middle-class alternative to the sublime suicide of Boito in the very idiom used. Illica and Giacosa continued the model successfully—*Bohème, Tosca,* and *Butterfly* are three little monuments to the librettist's art—but nothing is to be gained from glossing over the tensions and uncertainties which that "pact of three," which fell apart after the failure of the third opera and, two years later, with the death of Giacosa, engendered. Giacosa was a solid and occasionally inspired leader of middle-class drama, today too neglected by changed taste. Illica was—for better or worse—the greatest librettist of the period, the most daring and adventurous, the last in the line of Busenello, Cammarano, and Piave. It is worth taking a lengthy look at a document that shows his extraordinary professional and sociological awareness; it saves us further work, for it is also a piece of "behind the scenes" history:

Dear Puccini, Giacosa's contribution to the famous question between myself, Oliva, and Praga for *Manon* made a pleasant start to our collaboration; so pleasant that I had no hesitation in repeating it with *Tosca*, a collaboration that only death could break, and has done. This episode—and my associated attack of nerves—which you refer to, can and must show you how much my viewpoint has always been contrary to the rare situations that only chance can occasionally and happily offer but that— desired or sought—do not create or abort operas that are still only in gestation.

To be honest, I doubt very much if I feel like tackling another collaboration.

Recently—after *Germania*—Franchetti asked me for Fontana's *Antigone;* I said no and he then chose *La figlia di Jorio.* Giordano aspired to do a Puccini and proposed my friend Stecchetti, and my answer to Giordano was to suggest one of Spatz's chefs [that is, the owner of the Hôtel Milan, Giordano's father-in-law] or a porter at Casa Sonzogno. . . .

It is true that toward every libretto which is "by only me" (and possibly because I have no circle of friends and do not belong to any secret literary group, any little mafia, any theatrical, dramatic, journalistic, and political Masonic lodge and am not worth a brass farthing to the Society of Authors) a croaking chorus erupts against the syllables, the feet, and rhythm and everything else to do with so-called form, which, if nothing else, serves as a good pretext.

. . . The success or—if you prefer—the fortunes of the operas or—if it suits you better—of those few operas which have my name on them have only aroused a phalanx of critics, most of them failed librettists or playwrights. And I read their fine prose but was always repaid with interest every time I saw their perfect, precious poetry cut the most dismal figure when such geniuses went so far as to try to expose their facile theories to the footlights.

. . . For this reason in my librettos I shall continue to concentrate solely on how to draw the characters and the shape of the scenes and the realism of the dialogue, for its natural qualities, and of the emotions and the situations. . . .

. . . In the past—ever since the days when Metastasio was writing librettos—a libretto would be headed: "words by so-and-so." This contained a profound truth.

Verse in librettos is no more than a widespread habit, a fashion that has become established, like that of calling librettists "poets." What has real value in a libretto are the words. For the words correspond to the truth of the moment (the situation) and of the emotions (the character)! They contain everything; all the rest is rubbish.

However, nowadays the Decadent movement and D'Annunzio's style, by spoiling the simplicity and naturalness of the language, have (in the theater) come to threaten truth and logic (the two guardian angels at your shoulders when you write music), especially where the Decadent movement and D'Annunzio distort the words, trying to put their gambles onstage.[120]

And in a postscript to Ricordi:

Whether he wanted to or not, when we collaborated Giacosa always brought the so-called "Truce of God" between me and the usual croaking chorus against me, since Giacosa was one of them. And this is something I never hid from Puccini. Now Giacosa has gone, and a replacement can't be created.

"Truth" and "logic," the guardian angels of the opera composer, were about to shift their protection to the film director, who also had to be defended from undeserved literary ennoblement. In a few decades, during which the cinema was a living thing—and, as in opera, technique caught up before ideology—it produced dreadful things only when, laboring under an inferiority complex, it consigned its vague aspirations toward improvement to critics, ideologues, or literary circles. Running parallel with the twilight of opera in the twentieth century and the high tide of cinema were Chaplin, Lubitsch, Ford, Keaton, Hitchcock, Wilder, and Wyler, all jumbled together and, at their best, able to rival Cimarosa, Rossini, Auber, Donizetti, Puccini, Bizet, Massenet, and Offenbach (but where were the Mozarts, the Verdis, and Wagners?); meanwhile, opera entrusted its fate to composers the equivalent of Bergman, Fellini, Antonioni, Zanussi, Resnais, and the Death of Cinema. As for Puccini, with his indecision, and his egotism, he was able to see beyond his Illica, who—with his "natural" sensibility—remained trapped on the far side of the crises and the demands of the new century.

Perhaps Berio is right that there is "something shortsighted in the unconscious" when we look to Puccini as a "precursor"

because a "precursor" is judged by what comes afterward. In his case this means Menotti, Rota, and company. Composers who are useful in confirming, if anything, the real position of the verismo school: the last branch of the 19th century which came to maturity on the eve of the birth of a new epoch which saw society's and art's solid values crumble in favor of new values which have still to be confirmed.[121]

120. *Carteggi pucciniani,* 357–59, Oct. 1907.
121. Rubens Tedeschi, *Addio, fiorito asil: Il melodramma italiano da Boito al verismo* (Milan: Feltrinelli, 1978), 167.

And also—let it patiently be said—in favor of respectful chitchat. It does not help us to consider Puccini the precursor of nothing; better to see in him one of the most sensitive leading figures of a time, genuinely of the twentieth century, of a change in the nature of fiction. Puccini probably lacked the capacity, and the conviction, to theorize on what he was discovering and doing and what, at the same time, he was excluding and washing out of imaginative and sentimental convention. Not even Italo Svevo—to mention another leading figure of that transition—was much interested in generalizations, away from the life of his work. (We should keep in mind the possibly accurate description of him by someone who knew him well and admired him, Bobi Bazlen, as "an idiot of genius.") [122] And yet, Puccini was clear-sighted: his search for an international audience—going as far as his American adventure with *La fanciulla del West*—was only part of a strategic retreat from the impassioned taking up of positions and schizophrenic taste and expectations of Italy. If audiences were more easily overcome, critics remain skeptical. The music critic of the *New York Times*, Richard Aldrich, gave a judgment on *Fanciulla* that stands out partly because of the contrast it makes with the Italy of Torrefranca in those days, and tells us much more about verismo formulas than that which fifty years later would seem so convincing to Fedele D'Amico:

> The place of music in such a drama as rapidly moving, of sharply focussed realistic situations, of a few tensely theatrical climaxes, in which the emotional and psychological elements rise only rarely to influential or commanding place, is not easy to find. In setting this drama to music, Mr. Puccini undertook a task that not so many years ago would have been deemed impossible, almost a contradiction in terms of all conceptions of what the lyric drama could or should be. But the Italian composers, of whom he stands indisputably at the head, have evolved a technique, a treatment to which this drama and others like it can be subjected. . . . This treatment involves a more or less detached and formless paragraphic, sometimes a rapid and staccato vocal utterance, projected against an equally expeditious and hastily sketched orchestral background, to which is given the task of accentuating, emphasizing and intensifying—if it can—the significance of the dialogue with points or broad stretches of color, thematic fragments, quickly shifting, kaleidoscopic harmonies. There is no broad weaving of a broad tapestry of the thematic development in the orchestral fabric; the music has no time to wait for that—it must hurry along after the action and try to keep pace with the spoken word. This is interrupted now and again, however, by pages in a broader style—lyric movements of psychologizing, when the music is given more opportunity to rise to its true task of expressing emotion or passion or sentiment. Here the voices may likewise sing in a broad

---

122. In his famous letter of 25 Sept. 1928 to Montale, given in Roberto Bazlen, *Scritti* (Milan: Adelphi, 1984), 380: "[Svevo] had only genius: nothing else. Otherwise, he was stupid, egotistical, opportunistic, gauche, calculating, and tactless. He had only genius, and this is what makes my memory of him so fascinating."

arioso, in phrases that at least have melodic outlines and shapeliness. The music of *La fanciulla del West* in its style is broader and more convincing than that of some of the operas just mentioned [that is, *Tosca*, *Fedora*, and *Adriana Lecouvreur*], but it is a characteristic exemplar of this evolution of the modern Italian style.[123]

It is noticeable that in Italy the modern novel came into being when opera was no longer there to absorb certain expressive urges, in the same way as poetry can make a clean sweep of the space—setting, situation—and accumulated expression, as content slowly became an independent element, similar to the move in European painting toward pure abstraction. Some paradoxes arose as a result. The novel's defense against lyrical stylization, intended to overcome Italy's provincial barriers, involves a return to opera, in terms of culture and passion, for the most entertaining of literary critics, and a return to Puccini, opera's brightest and best modern Epiphany, without the conditions imposed by Italian musicians and musicologists, more attracted by the false nobility of D'Annunzio. We think immediately of Giacomo Debenedetti and the "character-man" in Puccini, and the connection made almost naturally by that prince among critics between his love for Umberto Saba and his passion for Verdi. Debenedetti is the sort of critic, however, who does not simply take up a position in terms of taste and hold to it: for instance, in the case of the pro-Saba and pro-Verdi novelist Quarantotti Gambini, a fellow countryman of Dallapiccola, Debenedetti was not slow to admit his disappointment with Gambini's *La calda vita:*

> You don't donate your time to books. You lend it with every right of imposing loanshark's rates. [Quarantotti Gambini] takes our time for his personal and probably arbitrary use; he makes use of it as if it were his own, for his own personal pleasure, maybe for a long act of self-castigation, but carried out licentiously, voluptuously, sometimes even lasciviously.[124]

The same objections could be raised against the narcissism, the decadent mannerism, of the "generazione dell'Ottanta." Puccini—and Illica—understood. The search for a libretto was the search, not for a libretto "che forse in cielo ha norma," but for the one in which the time taken to tell the story, and the narrator's time, intersect with everyone's time. This is not a decadent

---

123. *New York Times*, Sunday, 11 Dec. 1910. Aldrich's criticism is given in full in his *Concert Life in New York (1902–1923)* (New York: G. Putnam, 1941), 300–307. With rather more firmness than would have been likely in Italy after such a short time, he also looks at Puccini's debt to Debussy: "Hence Mr. Puccini has but taken rightfully what is his to take, if it suits him to take and use it. But he has used it in his own way and filled it with the contents of his own ideas. There is plenty of the personal note in what he has written, and nobody would suspect it of being Debussy's. Yet it may be doubted whether any who knew the composer only through *La Bohème* would recognize him in this, so far has he traveled in thirteen years" (ibid., 304).

124. Giacomo Debenedetti, *Intermezzo* (Milan: Il Saggiatore, 1963), 265.

solipsism, nor a surrender to populism. It was not Fascism, for example, but populism that undermined the last verismo operas. Let us examine the incredible *Caracciolo* by the mediocre Venetian playwright Arturo Rossato—Riccardo Zandonai's Piave or Illica[125]—and the not completely useless composer from Pavia, Franco Vittadini, performed at the Teatro Reale dell'Opera in Rome, during the season of Year XVI (1937–38), rehearsed and conducted by Tullio Serafin. It had everything in it: maskers or clowns dying of hunger in the street (the setting is Capri, 1787), Marinella thrown out of her house:

> Son Marinella,
> ho rubato a mio zio
> per far la carità a un poveretto,
> ed egli, adesso, m'ha cacciata via,
> alzando anche il bastone.
> Ladra, m'ha detto . . .

> [My name is Marinella,
> I stole from my uncle
> to give alms to someone down on his luck,
> and now he has chased me away,
> threatening me with his stick.
> Thief, he called me . . .]

There are serenades to roses, to life:

> Amo tanto le rose.
> Come son belle, calde, profumate!
> . . . .
> Ma mi piace di più
> la vita! Ah! Tanto! Questa vita bella
> che va, ritorna, cade, balza e vola,
> oggi nell'ombra, ma domani su . . .

125. For Zandonai, Rossato wrote the librettos of *Giulietta e Romeo* (1922), *I cavalieri di Ekebù* (1925), and *Giuliano* (1928); for Igino Robbiani, *Romanticismo* (from the more popular Rovetta) and *Guido del popolo;* and for Riccardo Pick-Mangiagalli, *Notturno romantico* (1936). In 1924 Robbiani produced *Anna Karenina*, evidence of the success the Russians had in verismo opera, Franco Alfano's *Risurrezione* (libretto by Cesare Hanau) of 1904, and Arrigo Pedrollo's *Crime and Punishment* of 1926 (on a libretto by Giovacchino Forzano, who yet "aimed" at Puccini). Another Robbiani piece, *Roma dei Cesari,* had a solemn broadcast performance in 1941. Vittadini's output of operas, ballets, and oratorios includes *Anima allegra, Nazareth, La Sagredo, Vecchia Milano* (all on librettos by Puccini's Adami), *Fiammetta e l'avaro, Il Natale di Gesù, Fiordisole, Il mare di Tiberiade,* and *Sirenetta*. A merciless but sophisticated judgment (as opposed to Tedeschi's arrogant one) can be read in Gianandrea Gavazzeni's "Il costume operistico," in his *La morte dell'opera,* 11–105. And theater (not only opera), the early cinema, and graphics during the verismo and postverismo period are evocatively brought together in Roberto Curci and Gianni Gori's valuable book *La dolcissima effigi: Manifesti italiani dell'opera lirica* (Trieste: LINT, 1983).

[I love roses so much.
How beautiful, warm and scented they are!

. . . .

But much more I love
life! Ah! So much! This wonderful life
which goes, returns, falls, springs up, and flies aloft
today in the shadows but tomorrow in the light . . .]

There is the song of the sailor: "Amo il mio mare / . . . / Ma io credo anche in
Dio / . . . / penso alla terra, al focolare mio" (I love this sea of mine / . . . / But
I believe in God, too / . . . / I think of land, and my hearth). There is a deluxe
brothel ("a little temple to Venus") where Marinella is presented nude, somewhere between Illica and Mascagni's Iris (à la Yoshiwara) and the Neapolitan
evergreen *Pelle*. We have a street song, a cross between Sem Benelli and Fellini
("Se sapessi che cosa è la strada / per una creatura ignara che vi cada" [If you
knew what the street meant / for a simple girl ending up there]), a wild tarantella, a piece of folklore ignobly grafted on to the Bacchic finale of *Elektra*, a
King Ferdinand who sings in Neapolitan, and a Caracciolo in the guise of Andrea Chénier: "Soldato, / son pronto anch'io a morire; / ma per la vostra e per
la mia bandiera" (A soldier / I, too, am ready to die / but for the flag which is
yours and mine). And we have Fabrizio di Carafa, who, when the riot breaks
out in Naples, also plays *citoyen* Gérard ("His Highness, Revolution"), ending
with the martyrdom of Caracciolo, by an English hand (may God curse him),
and glorification ("a funeral march for a hero with no glory," a cortège of "all
the distant fallen") with a cry from a little girl ("Daddy! . . . Daddy! . . .). It's
not over yet, because there is even a sort of cabaletta, a "warlike, impetuous"
tutti: "Meglio vivere un giorno da leone / che languire da pecore mill'anni"
(Better to live one day as a lion / than languish like sheep for a thousand years).

   You don't say. Here the ideology is really "in your face," and it is this be-
having like a fishmonger that is really offensive, more than the ideology itself.
Puccini had grasped the point, like the sensitive neurotic he was: he could no
longer count on an audience as a given but each time had defiantly to reinvent one. It is likely that *La fanciulla del West,* a masterpiece of "writing,"
sinking act by act, *La rondine,* unresolved at the end, and the incomplete *Turandot* have to remain, even for those who are best disposed to them, splendid but stunted operas. A composer less attentive to the moods of history
would not have found it hard to finish them off, trusting in ability alone. This
is not the case with *Il trittico,* Puccini's twentieth-century masterpiece, after
Butterfly. Verismo, colorful strokes of the pen, pathos, and doting mothers
(and even a caricature of Sem Benelli) are all thrown liberally into the pot.
The only thing is that the game has moved on. Was Barilli right when, mis-

understood by almost everyone, he wrote on Puccini's death, "one of the last who have seen the Sphinx up close"? [126]

Puccini had decided to aim at Allegory. When Giorgetta, in *Il tabarro* (a piece of Grand Guignol?), sings the lines

. . . il fiammifero acceso! . . .	[. . . the lighted match! . . .
Come tremava sul braccio mio teso	How it flickered against my tense arm,
la piccola fiammella!	that little flame!
Mi pareva d'accendere una stella . . .	I thought I was lighting a star . . .]

(note Puccini's variation, with the accent on the fourth and seventh syllables, compared with the libretto, which reads "sul mio braccio teso"), we are immediately aware that that match is not merely a match of wood and sulfur. Impressionism has given way to symbolism, *Pelléas* too stylized an opera for Puccini to be completely convinced, but full of new Debussyan harmony. Puccini dodges round allegory: what is transient in his stories is appearance, as we understand it in the Bible or Dante; the single, immobile, eternal, "true" mortal story of humankind. In this Pascoli has a twofold significance: whether in the aspect of Pascoli illuminated by a critic such as Edoardo Sanguineti ("and yet he knew how to teach our petit bourgeoisie, cynically urbanized and utterly ashamed of their own rural roots, capable only of the cult of the white collar, its only possibly human trait: a truly chthonic mercy for the dead, as superstitious and pathological as can be, and profoundly exiled within the tentacles of the city but at least generating powerful hallucinations and terrible raving") [127] or in the aspect of Pascoli valued by a scholar like Maurizio

126. As expressed in his "Omaggio a Puccini" (in his *Il paese del melodramma*). One case, one Sphinx, stands apart: the endless dramatic output of Malipiero. From his youthful attempts (*Elen e Fuldano*, libretto by Silvio Benco, a follower of Smareglia and Svevo; and *Sogno d'un tramonto d'autunno*, libretto by D'Annunzio) to the tireless composer's great works: *L'Orfeide, Torneo notturno, I capricci di Callot, Mondi celesti e infernali, Il figliuol prodigo;* and his controversial encounter with Pirandello, *La favola del figlio cambiato* (1934). There is also the "mystery" *San Francesco d'Assisi*, the *Tre commedie goldoniane*—a million miles away from the "Venetian" cordiality of Wolf-Ferrari—*Filomela e l'infatuato*, and *Merlino mastro d'organi*, the trilogy *Il mistero di Venezia, I trionfi d'Amore, La bella e il mostro* (after Perrault, *Beauty and the Beast*), *Il festino* (after Gian Gherardo De Rossi), *Giulio Cesare* and *Antonio e Cleopatra* (after Shakespeare), *Ecuba* (after Euripides), and *La vita è sogno* (after Calderón). And he kept busy in old age: *Donna Urraca* (after Mérimée, but also *Tosca* and *Trovatore*), *Il capitan Spavento, Venere prigioniera* (a beautiful baroque libretto), Aretino's *Il marescalco*, Pushkin's *Don Giovanni* and *Le metamorfosi di Bonaventura*. He finished, in Siena in 1971, with the double bill of *L'Iscariota* and *Uno dei Dieci*. To collect this immense literary output in a single volume would involve flying over a manneristically mortuary country to which the practical provocation of theater seems fundamentally alien.

127. In *Poesia italiana del Novecento*, ed. Edoardo Sanguineti (Turin: Einaudi, 1970), x. Apart from Sanguineti's various collaborations with Berio and Luca Ronconi, see his "Teatro con mu-

Perugi: [128] no page is turned in Pascoli without Dante wishing it. A hunger for allegory.

So that orchestral tapestry of brief details, of sensitive splashes and touches, that rapid, staccato vocal utterance to which Aldrich referred, take on a haunted role of "another" discourse. We could read all fifty of Malipiero's librettos and find them imaginative, delightful, cultivated, simple. They refer only to themselves. They have no respect for "our" time.[129] Dallapiccola, the most ideological of the leading figures in the next generation, knew everything about music and literature. He has authority when he illuminates, with plenty of scholarly diagrams, the "Birth of an Opera Libretto." [130] But when that opera, his life's dream, is born, we have, once again, beautiful music without a libretto. Nice verses (there's the example of Giuseppe Ungaretti, who, by digging around, found Monti but thought it was Manzoni) and noble thoughts. What is there of Pascoli? Only the symbolist Pascoli of the *Poemi conviviali*, which nourished Pizzetti. In a successful opera the music is not superior to the libretto; it can be superior to the poetry, which is the poet's department. But not to the libretto, because it cannot not be the stuff and the story of everyone.

---

sica, senza musica" (1984), which appeared in his *La missione del critico* (Genoa: Marietti, 1987), 189–201.

128. Maurizio Perugi, introduction to Giovanni Pascoli, *Opere*, 2 vols. (Milan and Naples: Ricciardi, 1980), 1:xiv–xviii.

129. As indicated above, n. 120.

130. This 1968 essay, "Nascita di un libretto d'opera," can be found on pp. 171–87 of Dallapiccola, *Appunti, incontri, meditazioni.* The discourse really ends with Dallapiccola's *Ulisse* of 1968. (But see Massimo Venuti, *Il teatro di Dallapiccola* [Milan: Suvini Zerboni, 1985].) There have been alternatives to this manner of high tragedy in Calvino's libretto for Liberovici *(La panchina),* Bacchelli's for Nino Rota *(La notte di un nevrastenico),* and Buzzati's for Chailly *(Ferrovia sopraelevata),* often connected in mood to the work of the Teatro della Novità in Bergamo (1937–73), which in the Italian context was quite remarkable. Openness to new music theater, in which we are all implicated, of course, not just music lovers, implies a tabula rasa that could put everything back into discussion. Including the Death of Opera.

— 5 —

The Dissemination and Popularization of Opera

ROBERTO LEYDI

The Myth of Popularity

I. PRELIMINARY OBSERVATIONS

Any attempt to seek out and follow the various paths taken by Italian opera when it left behind the environment for which it was created and moved out even into the countryside to touch the sensibilities and consciousness of those who would now be described as "the masses," excluded from direct contact with opera in "bourgeois" theaters for geographical, economical, or social reasons, is fraught with difficulties, if not a hopeless undertaking.

Nothing in the countless pages devoted to celebrating, chronicling, and offering critical commentary on Italian opera provides any sort of support. Their goals are other kinds of knowledge, and they are generally most wide of the mark precisely when they try to tackle one theme which refuses to go away, that of the "popularity" of opera. There is a total lack of serious research on the "dissemination" of the music of Italy's nineteenth-century masters that is free from preconceptions and is based on written or oral evidence. By that I do not mean extensive research on the whole complex, fragmented phenomenon, or even observations on particular aspects of what is certainly a wide field, one whose limits, it must be agreed, are very hard to establish.

Even folk and ethnomusicological research has so far cast not so much as a sidelong glance at this aspect of the "people's" musical awareness and knowledge. Research has placed it in the margins, as it were, because of its hybrid implications, or perhaps because it is felt to be alien, if not contrary to the "tradition," with its debatable terms of reference, to a (fundamentally abstract) agricultural, pastoral, and "age-old" reality. It is only in the past few years that the discipline devoted to "folk" music has started to turn its gaze toward those areas of musical communication that have unmistakably recent, bastard origins and to compile a musical scenario that encompasses not only memories of the "tradition" but also the profound changes wrought by the industrial revolution and the consequent restructuring of social classes.

Ethnomusicology has thus started to examine the musical products that, despite their frequently hybrid nature, are strongly defined—not only in formal terms but also because of their socially representative character—and have come into being and developed over the last 150 years wherever new modes of production have effected a transformation and made their results felt indirectly. It is only very recently indeed that Italian ethnomusicology has also opened its ears to this area and fostered a new concern for phenomena that, in the past, were habitually neglected, if not rejected or condemned out of hand. The old idea of the "folk" and "tradition" was happy to accept a two-dimensional view of the agricultural and pastoral world without criticism. For some time it has been clear that even things that today seem "authentically" traditional are the fruit of an "innovation" introduced at a particular (if often not identifiable) time in history, in the wake of both alterations in working-class living conditions and, coincidentally, the personal acquisition of the means of expression and communication of the ruling class of the time, and of different times. We have also become aware that these phenomena—which give working-class culture a historical context, not an ageless, unspoiled one—have continued to the present day, although in different ways and at an increasingly rapid rate, and have produced results that might appear destructive, especially with the arrival of mass communications and the consumer culture.

In this light, the great phenomenon of what is known as *ballo liscio,* or ballroom dancing, would start to attract scholarly attention. *Ballo liscio* has had a profound effect on the state of Italian folk dance, and even in peasant cultures and in marginal geographical, economic, and social areas, the great "middle-class" novelties of the waltz, the polka, the mazurka, and then the one-step and the tango have supplanted the old "traditional" dances. Current research into *ballo liscio* is proving revelatory, not only in understanding the truth of the modern relationship of dance to the folk world, but also in obliging us to view the old dances that we consider "traditional" in a new light. Neapolitan song, too, in its various manifestations, might finally merit some attention for more than its celebratory or evocative content, as a complex manifestation of urban musical "production" in the social, cultural, and economic context of Neapolitan life over the years, ending with the "nationalization" (and "internationalization") of the repertory and style.

It goes without saying that observations of this kind require the boundaries of ethnomusicology as a discipline to be widened beyond their conventional horizons of the "folk world." If the industrial revolution altered class relationships profoundly and, indeed, generated new social structures that not only involved the industrial proletariat but also affected the entire system, creating the complex structure of the middle class (or, rather, the middle classes), the new modes of production introduced examples of musical communication that could no longer be described as belonging specifically to one social group: they cross class boundaries and no longer necessarily have connotations of various types of usage, whether they are linked to particular social, economic, and cultural situations or to a multinational system of musical distribution.

The presence of opera, whatever term is used *(opera lirica, melodramma),* in the fabric of the awareness and sensibilities of the vast "masses" in Italy in the nineteenth century and the early decades of the twentieth is a revealing example of how influential processes of innovation can be in the capitalist age and of how permeable the social, cultural, and economic areas can be in relation to a phenomenon that seems resoundingly to involve different, and often opposing, strata of society. This is the area of my study. It covers both the peasant world (excluded for geographical and economic reasons from the direct production of opera) and, at the opposite extreme, large areas of the more prosperous, those who, again for geographical reasons, were not adequately served by the theater but who "enjoyed" the music of Bellini or Verdi through a combination of means.

To map the roads and paths which opera has traveled as it has expanded beyond the areas served by the opera houses entails, first of all, identifying what this combination of means is: it is my belief that it is principally responsible for having made opera a cultural symbol of the Italian nation, in such a way that it permeated a large section of middle-class society and small-tradesmen and also filtered out into peasant and working life to a considerable degree. Such an undertaking, however, requires documentation which can place in a historical context that sum of notions, vast but unconnected, something of a shared inheritance, which each one of us can infer from our everyday experience, and which reveals its social depth in the little that has emerged from investigation of the cultures of the "folk world" so far—fragments that have been overlooked, often as a result of superficial research. Apart from some rare exceptions, we cannot depend on any such documentation and so must proceed by way of examples and observations in an attempt to reconstruct the overall shape of the phenomenon, employing, if not imagination, certainly intuition to extend and link the scarce, unconnected material provided by the sources, against a background that shows not much more than the sheer immensity of the phenomenon.

2. THE PHANTOM OF THE OPERA

Before entering the labyrinth of "opera for all," before, that is, we discover or rediscover some examples of the grand cultural process that allowed opera to spread across the different levels of Italian society, it is useful to examine some of the myths or legends that surround the problem and not only complicate understanding the process of diffusion and dissemination of opera but place "ideological" liabilities on the very way we view the primary phenomenon, that is, opera as a "genre" and, especially, as a representation of a period and a society. In other words, we have to understand that a ghost has been walking the corridors of historical accounts of Italian opera, and to some extent still is, that a cliché, and a resilient one, is still lurking between the lines of historical and critical views of our nineteenth-century "masters," with Giuseppe Verdi at their head. This ghost, this cliché, goes back to the historical representation of the Risorgimento and offers a model image of a happy "critical" union: but when we look at it closely, it turns out to be based much more on ideological interests than on documentary evidence and comparison of the cultural and social facts. According to this cliché, nineteenth-century Italian opera, from Rossini to Verdi, is a sign and symbol of popularity; more than that, it is the best, most complete synthesis of the "spirit" and "emotions" of "our people," miraculously balancing the credits and debits of Italian "popular culture." And this "popular" character is one of the supporting players in the story of Italian opera; it is able not only to express the "spirit of the age" but, even more, to encapsulate the image of national edification based on the values of "the people"; in a word, the realization, in the arts, of a sort of synthesis of the unitary and "popular" spirit of the Nation, beyond the obvious inequalities apparent in Italy in the long unfolding of historical events from the age of Napoleon to that of Prime Minister Giovanni Giolitti at the beginning of the twentieth century.

If in using the word "popular" it is meant that Italian opera had, in the nineteenth century—and especially in the last decades—broad, widespread success that involved, in various ways, on different levels, and by routes that have not all been recognized, different strata of Italian society, widening its appeal to reach even the citizens whom we can consider "the people," in a growing diffusion "downward," then this "popularity" can reasonably be ascribed to opera. But if by "popular" it is meant, instead—as a great deal of propaganda seems ambiguously to suggest, directly or indirectly, and as openly declared by not a few writers—that the music of Rossini, Bellini, Donizetti, and Verdi was the music of the people, that this music drew more or less directly on the inheritance of traditional music, that it became widely established in oral repertories and was clearly superimposed on the preexisting traditional legacy, then a whole series of checks and verifications is necessary, and the entire phenomenon requires historical and critical examination, in terms of both what can be documented musicologically and what is socially and economically credible.

It is true that serious, discerning historical scholarship has almost never risked taking this route, as attractive as it is full of pitfalls, and has left the myth of the "popularity" of Italian composers at the level of the most facile propaganda.[1] However, it is worth drawing attention to some approaches found in works on a different level of scholarship and with a different cultural basis, in which, naturally, things are done more subtly, and "the people" and "the Nation" are drawn together. For example, there is a passage that, on the one hand, rejects the cliché that folk music was "elevated" into nineteenth-century Italian opera but, on the other, refers to Verdi's "sharing" the signs and values of an undefined "nation," leading to a representation of the society that, like Croce, not only makes no distinction between bourgeoisie and peasants, rich and poor, rulers and ruled, literate and illiterate, but offers a concept of "nationhood" derived from Risorgimento ideology:

> Italy and Verdi: in other words, a father-son relationship between the nation and the artist, so different, in fact the exact opposite, from what came about in the nineteenth century in other countries that were also rising up to claim or reclaim national unity and independence. In Poland, Bohemia, and Hungary, generally speaking in those nations that were shaking off Habsburg domination, artists heard the simple voice of their land and re-created it in art. . . .
>
> In Italy, miraculously, the opposite was the case. The relationship of son to father was that of the artist to the nation, and concerned more the spirit than the senses.[2]

From today's perspective it is not difficult to understand the basis and the reasons for positions that, in the end, are expressed in a general way that matches the tendencies of the dominant ideology of Italian Risorgimento culture; however differentiated, these tendencies exhibit a common preoccupation, which was to guarantee that the many contradictions raised by the gulf between decisions, events, and consequences of the bourgeois-liberal hegemony and the attitudes, behavior, and even open statements of dissent by the working classes were patched over. Nowadays we are well aware that the working classes took up a wide variety of positions with regard to the process of national unification, and not just because of geographical, historical, or economic differ-

1. See, for example, Giannotto Bastianelli, *Pietro Mascagni* (Naples: Ricciardi, 1910); Pietro Mascagni, "L'evoluzione della musica nel sec. XIX," *Rivista d'Italia* 3, no. 1 (1900): 407–31.
2. Massimo Mila, "Verdi come il padre" (1951), in *L'arte di Verdi* (Turin: Einaudi, 1980), 287–304, quotation on 290.

ences, and that the whole picture was a blend of suspicion, disinterest, disappointment, and even open (and armed) hostility.

However, it would be simplistic and inaccurate to attribute responsibility for this critical manipulation solely to political and economic interests. Much of the mystification in history and criticism, at that time and in that context, has at its roots the undying concept of the "people" that was born during the French Revolution and passed triumphantly into romantic ideology. The beginnings of this lie far back in Bürger's original identification of "popular poetry" with "national poetry." National values are thus a projection of "popular" values, in the plan of a new Europe arising from the collapse of the *ancien régime* and seeking the basis of society in the "people." This is the source of those undeniably successful, effective, and enduring slogans, which the advertising industry of today might envy, and which filled our no-longer-nineteenth-century schooldays and are possibly still to be found in textbooks: "When the people arise, God is at their head" or "Voice of the people, voice of God."

This eagerly pursued "discovery" of the "people," and its elevation to the high altar of cultural generation and political regeneration of the Nation, have been—it goes without saying—perfectly in tune with the requirements of the nationalist and bourgeois-liberal hegemony, to ensure for the new regime the legitimacy which the monarchs of the *ancien régime* drew from God. The People and the Nation together signify a single social (and ethical) entity, composed of women and men who must sacrifice those parts of their cultural and economic identity that might be sources of conflict and "disunity": having become an undifferentiated mass, they gather round a banner that is no longer decorated with the coat of arms of a king but with the (symbolic) colors of the fatherland. There is no need here to retrace the steps taken by Italian folklorists, from the time of Tommaseo onward: we need only recall how, throughout the nineteenth century, a large part of the work of collecting and publishing folk songs (not only in Italy) was not directed toward discovering the uniqueness, diversity, and otherness expressed by the people—even when they used the simplest words in their dialect—but was driven by an anxiety to reveal to the nascent nation its "poetic" roots, the source of its self-expression in terms of "national" culture.

Against the background of this cultural and political representation, it is no surprise that opera, too, with its capacity to manifest "sentiments" that spoke to levels of the population which up until then had been almost self-contained, was adopted as a symbol of the building of a nation, outside its specific context of artistic activity and its specific value as creative display, reaching even into the areas of social and political awareness. But if opera is truly "national," that is, the voice of the fatherland under construction, it cannot, in consequence, fail to be "of the people." And this is how—simplifying a little—Rossini, Bellini, Donizetti, and Verdi became, in the projection of a myth consciously or unconsciously fed by enthusiasms and interests, not only a tool to "make Italy" and so to "make the Italian people" but also an instance of synthesis of every virtue, every inheritance, every legacy of "the people."

An ideal approach seems to me to be that taken by someone of such great intellectual discernment and vast knowledge as Francesco De Sanctis, when he undertakes to place the phenomenon of opera in the context of the story of Italian literature. De Sanctis is probably right when, quoting Tasso, Guarini, and Marino, he sees in the establishment of opera the end point of a literary, as well as musical, process that had long promoted the emergence of "singing, musical" qualities in Italian poetry; I also concur with his apparently contradictory affirmation that, with the arrival of opera, "literature died and music was born." But I cannot accept his subsequent, critically unfounded comment that opera "is the people's genre par excellence." One can still come across assertions that nineteenth-century opera provided a miraculous point of contact among all social classes in Italy just before or immediately after unification.[3] But after John Rosselli's illuminating study,[4] we have no need to waste any more words, with the accounts of the "opera industry" to hand, on demonstrating the fundamental, effective alienation of the people—in their true, cultural, social, and economic connotation—from the life of the opera house. The costs and the rigidly hierarchical structure of the opera house did not allow the masses to take any direct part in the development of opera; it was accessible only to very marginal fringes of nonprivileged classes, fringes that were in some way connected, in a dependent relationship, to a privileged class that had, in any case, conceived and constructed (and therefore administered) those theaters in their image. As Rosselli rightly has it, "contemporary statements that 'the people' or 'the lowest class' were to be found in the gallery suggest, more than anything else, the restrictive definition of 'the people' common in the early nineteenth century. Labourers, peasants, beggars were not 'the people.'"[5] In that representation of society, the people consisted of artisans, small traders, and employees and servants of bourgeois and aristocratic families, a significant extension of the hierarchical division of society of two centuries before, which considered the "people" to be a category that

3. A glaring example of the persistence of this myth can be found in the passages which Alberto Asor Rosa dedicates to opera as a "point of cultural contact" between "the popular audience" and the "intellectual audience" in his "La cultura," in *Storia d'Italia*, 6 vols. (Turin: Einaudi, 1975–77), vol. 4, pt. 2:962–65.

4. John Rosselli, *The Opera Industry in Italy from Cimarosa to Verdi: The Role of the Impresario* (Cambridge: Cambridge University Press, 1984); see also his essay in *The History of Italian Opera*, vol. 4, *Opera Production and Its Resources*, ed. Lorenzo Bianconi and Giorgio Pestelli (Chicago: University of Chicago Press, 1998), 81–164.

5. Rosselli, *Opera Industry in Italy*, 45.

"for reasons of birth does not correspond to the Nobility, and by virtue and riches is very far from the Plebeians, but constitutes a third species, which is called the People particularly by itself."[6] To be more precise, "the people" were defined as being made up of traders, public employees, artisans of a certain rank (typographers, goldsmiths, doctors, painters, architects, and so on); all the rest, the lower ranks, were in the category of "plebeians" or "rabble." It is true that the concept of "the people" did not remain so restricted throughout the course of the nineteenth century: in the latter decades there was a different idea of social divisions, as the post-Unification transformations which affected the country opened up new opportunities for cultural communication between classes. Once again John Rosselli correctly highlights the changes that took place in the latter part of the nineteenth century, but he also confirms that the transformations did not substantially modify the people's relationship with opera: "Opera in the first two-thirds of the century, the period when *Il barbiere* and *Lucia* and *Rigoletto* were first performed, can scarcely be called a popular art within the opera house, a building most of which was taken up by the well-off [*benestanti*], with perhaps a gallery occupied by artisans. . . . How far was it a popular art outside through the kind of diffusion" represented by performances given by bands, choirs, the church organ, or by mechanical pianos pushed through the streets?[7]

The question of the "popularity" of Italian opera during the nineteenth century therefore stands between two fairly clearly defined areas, which can be contained in two schematic models. One is the model of "ascent" (or the presumed elevation to the sphere of artistic development held to be "superior") of musical materials, models, or perhaps only of the "feelings" (a category which I feel is difficult to define) of the Italian folk tradition, a contributory or fundamental factor in, or at least characteristic of, operatic music. The other is the model of the "descent" of operatic music (its passage from the site of its artistic appearance on a "superior" level and in its proper home) not only into broad popular use but also, more subtly (and much more difficult to document), into popular "awareness," producing results that are partly extramusical—that is, ethical, ideological, and possibly political.

In the way the story of Italian opera is conventionally represented, this second process appears, more or less explicitly, as the direct, inevitable consequence of the intrinsic "popularity" of the music by the "masters," itself full of signs and values derived from the people and thus "restored" to the people sublimated as art.

6. Camillo Tutini, *Dell'origine e fundazion de' seggi di Napoli* (Naples: Beltrano, 1644), quoted in Keith A. Larson, "Condizione sociale dei musicisti e del loro committenti nella Napoli del Cinque e Seicento," in *Musica e cultura a Napoli dal XV al XIX secolo*, ed. Lorenzo Bianconi and Renato Bossa (Florence: Olschki, 1983), 61–77, quotation on 62.

7. Rosselli, *Opera Industry in Italy*, 164.

Then there is a third level, which is much easier to verify and which in my opinion constitutes the first requirement for any research into the "popularity" of opera that hopes to leave behind ambiguous theories and ideologically driven descriptions. This is the level that touches on the periods and modes of the diffusion of opera outside the opera house, the processes by which it was disseminated throughout Italian society. It is of course true that opera did indeed leave the confines of its temples to spread through Italian society, even if—as has already been mentioned several times—we still do not have any reliable assessment of either the magnitude or quality of this phenomenon. Instead, we pick it up or sense its many traces in our personal, daily experience.

So in the following pages of examples and observations, I shall attempt above all to give data and observations relating to this third level while also touching on the problem posed by the theory of a model of "descent."

3. BELLINI'S SPINNERS AND VERDI'S CROCKERY SELLER (OR BAKED-PEAR SELLER)

Not a single one of the hagiographers, chroniclers, or even historians who have contributed to disseminating the legend that folk music elements are directly mirrored in Italian opera (melodic content, singing style, and so on) has ever attempted to produce an example of his assertion, sometimes implicit but often explicit, that can be reliably tested.

In biographies of our opera composers, it is not rare to find references to the composers' tendency to listen to "the voice of the people," possibly noting down "in the field" the melodies they find most attractive, or anyway worthwhile storing for possible reuse. Michele Scherillo tells us that Bellini used to keep a notebook in which he wrote down Sicilian folksongs,[8] and Felice Romani's widow writes that when Bellini was in Moltrasio, before composing *La sonnambula,* he listened closely to the songs of the spinners around Como, while they sailed across the lake:

> On Sunday he took pleasure in following the peasant girls when they were all together in the boat, going home from the spinning mills, singing songs that were now tender, now cheerful, and was no less won over by the beauty of the singers than by the desire to study their songs. The Maestro had already noticed the simple manners and sincere sentiments of those peasant girls; and the enchanting setting, full of poetry and harmony, woke within his exalted mind the sweetest musical ideas, veritable idylls, which he then noted down in his book. Thus, little by little, he made a precious collection of rustic themes, embellished and decorated by his wonderful imagination and softened by the exquisite sensitivity of his heart.[9]

8. Michele Scherillo, "Bellini e la musica popolare," in his *Belliniana* (Milan: Ricordi, 1884), 53–56.

9. Emilia Branca, *Felice Romani ed i più riputati maestri di musica del suo tempo* (Turin, Florence, and Rome: Loescher, 1882), 161ff.

It is quite possible that Bellini really did note down folk melodies, first in Sicily and later in Moltrasio, but this would certainly be easier to establish more convincingly if something of that material (however "embellished" and "softened") had entered the music of his operas, leaving some identifiable trace. It could easily be the case that Bellini was interested in the folk melodies he happened to hear, but his approach to composition revealed in what he wrote conforms to a sensibility very far from that of the folk music tradition, whether Sicilian or Lombard. Already that implicit need to "embellish" and "soften" the folk songs heard in the mouths of the people reveals the distance that Bellini the musician—or his devoted biographer—placed between his world as a composer and man, and the harsh, aggressive "other" world of folk song. Those composers who made a conscious choice and approached folk repertories with different levels of direct involvement—Bartók, of course, but also Mussorgsky, De Falla, and even Bizet—"extracted" from the folk experience precisely those elements which more than anything seemed to denote its "otherness."

The idea of "popularity" derived and drawn directly—or almost—from the people really gains substance with Verdi, of course, in the effort to document Verdi's "debt" to the national melos. This hypothetical debt is felt to be, not a sign of poverty of inspiration, but proof of a "natural" link between Verdi's creativity and the "spirit of the people," but it is symptomatic that no scrap used to construct the myth of Verdi as the "voice of the people" makes any reference to the one thing that could confirm the thesis objectively—the music—but remains instead in the sphere of anecdote and hagiography.

The eagerness to "certify" the direct line of descent of Verdi's music from the folk tradition is also to be found, deep down, in some Verdi scholars who actually have some knowledge of Italian folk music: this results in some critical commentary studded with subtle contradictions. The name of Marcello Conati springs to mind: he is the first commentator (and, I believe, the only one at the time of writing) to have tackled the question of the "popular" in Verdi. Conati openly acknowledges that "the relationship between Verdi's music and the character of folk culture still awaits detailed investigation, not only in a strictly musical context, since even a comparison of the narrative technique of folk ballads and that of many librettos of Verdi operas could turn out to be of fundamental importance." [10]

Attempting to begin documenting the myth of the presence of elements derived from the folk tradition in Verdi's music, Conati looks at some dances and links them with Verdi documents that are certainly of interest. He quotes passages in letters from Verdi to his Neapolitan friend Cesarino De Sanctis,

---

10. Marcello Conati, "Ballabili nei *Vespri:* Con alcune osservazioni su Verdi e la musica popolare," *Studi verdiani* 1 (1982): 21–46, quotation on 44.

in which the composer asks for information on the feast of Santa Rosalia in Palermo, and if, during that feast, "it has anything peculiar to it, a dance or something of the sort"; and more specifically, "if the Tarantella is always in the minor and in 6/8 rhythm. If there's an example of one in the major and in a different rhythm please send it to me. . . . I'd also like to know whether there is a local folk dance other than the tarantella." [11] And he asks for relevant material. Verdi was working on *Les vêpres siciliennes* at the time, which explains his interest in Sicily. De Sanctis had no better idea than to contact the publisher Cottrau, who then sent Verdi some "dance music." Conati is right to note that Cottrau must have sent Verdi some music that was already highly stylized and quite far from the folk model of the tarantella, at least to judge by the result, the tarantella in *Les vêpres*, which has nothing in common with the character of the folk dance. Conati makes the same observation in connection with the tarantella in *La forza del destino*. Verdi turned to De Sanctis once more to ask for details and examples of the siciliana (again for *Les vêpres*):

> I have need of a favour from you, but I should like it as quickly as possible. I would like you to send me a Sicilian song or air or whatever. But I want a real Siciliana, that's to say a folksong and not a song manufactured by your composers: in fact, the finest, the most characteristic that there is. Have it copied on to a piece of paper with a simple bass accompaniment and send it to me with a letter by the quickest means possible.[12]

When Verdi received the "little piece of paper" not only had he already completed *Les vêpres*, but he could find nothing relevant in what was sent to him.

Now of course these requests indicate not only a certain interest on Verdi's part in the use of folk forms or themes but also his awareness of the existence of "real" folk music, different from what he could find in the publications of the day, although still defined as "popular." Quite rightly, Conati observes that Verdi's correspondents were probably not the most suitable people to provide him with the "real" material he asked for, and that in any case the absence of serious, specific attention to folk music meant that it was not possible to uncover any authentic traditional music.

In this light, it might be thought that on other occasions, when Verdi was able to find something "popular" close or familiar to him, it could be possible

---

11. Letters of 4 Dec. 1853 and 18 Jan. 1854 (ibid., 22). The letters are quoted in English in Julian Budden, *The Operas of Verdi*, 3 vols. (London: Cassell, 1973–81), 2:178 (rev. ed. [Oxford and New York: Clarendon Press, 1992], 2:178).

12. Letter of 10 Apr. 1855 (Conati, "Ballabili," 39), quoted in Budden, *Operas of Verdi*, 2:183. The request to have the melody harmonized seems, at least to me and in the context of the request, both curious and revealing.

to verify its "true" nature; but the music of *Rigoletto,* an opera that has the Po Valley in its bones, provides no comforting points of reference.[13] It could even be thought that the decision to search for "local" models in the case of Sicily and *Les vêpres* was prompted by a felt need for exoticism.

Having established that there is no detailed research into the "folk" element in Verdi, Marcello Conati nevertheless accepts the picture of Verdi affected by folk culture:

> Verdi's music has roots which penetrate deeply into the fabric of folk culture. How could it be otherwise for a composer who, as a boy, was irresistibly attracted by the music of a traveling player? Those first musical impressions must have remained fixed, on an unconscious level, in the composer's sensibility, just like the first songs he would have heard from the women of his village, the first music he heard played by folk musicians.[14]

In support of this memory of music heard as a child in his village and which then took root in his unconscious, Conati refers to some evidence that is again useful to quote.

The reference to the traveling musician dates from a visit to the composer by a German journalist in the spring of 1883: "Verdi also told us of an eccentric wandering musician, named Bagasset, whose violin playing had given him his first idea of music, and to whom he had listened raptly when still a child." [15] The episode, Conati adds, is confirmed in a biography of Verdi by a native of Busseto, Hercules Cavalli, who might have heard the anecdote directly from Verdi's mother:

> The child was by nature fairly good, docile, and obedient; but he was very introverted and loved to be alone. It was rare for his mother to have to go in search of him, but when barrel organs or traveling musicians came by, it was impossible to keep him back, and force had to be used to get him to come home. His poor mother used to say to her friends, "This child could not be better, but if he hears a barrel organ, he gives me no peace." [16]

13. Not even the Perigordino in *Rigoletto* (act 1, scene 3), which recalls the *bigurdén* of the Parma Apennines (and the *perigurdìn* of the entire Apennine range, from Parma to the maritime Alps, and therefore the French dance of the same name, the *périgourdin*), provides a point of reference even if it could be established that Verdi had remembered it.

14. Conati, "Ballabili," 44.

15. A. von Winterfeld, "Unterhaltungen in Verdis Tuskulum," *Deutsche Revue* 12 (1887): 327–32 (reproduced in Marcello Conati, *Interviste e incontri con Verdi* [Milan: Il Formichiere, 1980], 141–51, quotation on 147). In English it appears in *Encounters with Verdi,* trans. Richard Stokes, edited, introduced, and annotated by Marcello Conati (Ithaca, N.Y.: Cornell University Press, 1984), 146–56.

16. Hercules Cavalli, *Biografías artísticas contemporáneas des los célebres José Verdi, maestro de música y Antonio Canova escultor* (Madrid: Ducazcal, 1867), 8 (cited in Conati, *Interviste,* 150).

Verdian hagiography, keen to collect every possible early sign of the composer's musical genius, and of his roots in folk music in general (and that of Parma in particular), does not halt even when faced with the complex problem of the child's learning process, or, if you will, the symbolic value of biography. In one of the first biographies of Verdi, which appeared in installments in the journal *Il fuggilozio* in 1857, an anonymous piece of work but probably written by Carlo Viviani (who must have had access to the *Cenni biografici* compiled by Giuseppe Demaldè, a native of Busseto), we read that "an old man from the village of Le Roncole used to relate, as if to indicate how a sort of premonition came true, that the young child's godfather wanted cheerful fanfares played by a brigade of traveling musicians to accompany the baby at the font, as a sign of joy." [17]

But if we look for more concrete references to folk "quotations" in Verdi's music, they are pretty thin on the ground, and vague, at that. Conati refers to the review of *Les vêpres* by Salomone Fiorentino in the *Constituionnel*,[18] in which Fiorentino declares that the barcarolle in the second-act finale bears the traces of a Neapolitan *pont-neuf*, and Conati refers to another review, of *Un ballo in maschera* by the Roman critic Nicola Cecchi,[19] who points out "a certain similarity" between Riccardo's ballata "Di' tu se fedele" and "songs of the sailors of Bari." Leaving aside the barcarolle's presumed debt to a Neapolitan melody, one can only question the idea of a resemblance between Riccardo's ballad and the songs of the sailors of Bari (of course, we don't know what they sang in Verdi's time, but we do have a fairly good idea of the structure and style of folk song in Puglia today).

Another case, which is better known because Bruno Barilli reports it, is that of the priestesses' invocation "Soccorri a noi" at the beginning of act 3 of *Aida*. The fact that it lends itself to supporting the myth of Verdi's concern to catch the voice of the people is demonstrated by the way this anecdote has become fictionalized as it has passed from pen to pen, mouth to mouth.

Stefano Sivelli, who played the ophicleide in the first Cairo performance of *Aida,* relates that, one autumn afternoon when he found himself in Verdi's company in a square in Parma, the composer was so struck by the call of a vendor of baked pears that he at once noted it down in a notebook. And it was the same melody which Sivelli was amazed to hear during the rehearsals for *Aida*. Bruno Barilli retranscribes the anecdote in these words:

One day an old mentor, a well-known person who was Parma's Methuselah, touched us on the shoulder. We were under the porticos of the Governor's palace. Thirty-two degrees in the shade. In that trancelike, dog-day atmosphere I heard the

17. "Giuseppe Verdi," *Il fuggilozio* (Milan) 2 Jan. 1857 (cited in Conati, *Interviste,* 151).

18. Reproduced in part in the *Gazzetta musicale di Milano* 13, no. 26 (1 July 1855): 206 (quoted in Conati, "Ballabili," 44).

19. In the *Filodrammatico* (Rome), no. 36 (10 Mar. 1859) (quoted in Conati, "Ballabili," 45).

querulous song of a crockery salesman rising into the sky. "My boy," said our authoritative friend, pointing to one of the arcades that open out on to the light of the main square, "it was just there that I saw Verdi approaching, leaning on Teresa Stolz's arm. In the heavy stillness of the heat these two visitors suddenly came out in front of me. The same tiresome, lonely cry that you hear now was ringing round the arches then, too. Verdi seemed struck by it. He left his partner's grasp, took out a little book and wrote down those four vague notes. The song of the traveling merchant went on to become embedded in his imagination. Iron attracts, my son. The human brain is like a magnet when it's working. Sometimes something switches the machine on, and a result comes out like ripe fruit falling to the ground. Do you see how creativity picks up on surprise elements and indications? Could you not imagine perhaps that in a dull, sleepy afternoon like this Eve came forth from Adam's rib and fell asleep by his side? Anyway, if you want to know, that lazy cry just now found its place in *Aida*. Twenty years ago, when I heard the opera, I recognized in the ritual evocation of the priests hidden in the temple, during the Nile Scene, the song of our crockery vendor, who has been dragging his complaint and his wares round the streets of Parma." [20]

The story was repeated by others,[21] and even Massimo Mila took it into consideration.[22]

I think it is obvious that here we have entered the realm of Parma anecdote or café gossip, in that it is difficult to make out in the fragment from *Aida* any

---

20. Bruno Barilli, *Il paese del melodramma* (Lanciano: Carabba, 1930), 53. Now also in the critical edition by Luisa Viola and Luisa Avellini (Turin: Einaudi, 1985), 3–76, quotation on 28. For the "original" version of the anecdote of the baked-pear vendor, dating from 1869, see Stefano Sivelli, "L'origine d'un motivo dell'*Aida*," *L'Italia* (Milan), 14 Jan. 1941), reproduced in Conati, *Interviste e incontri,* 79–87, and *Encounters with Verdi,* 83–91.

21. By Giovanni Cenzato, *Itinerari verdiani,* 2d ed. (Milan: Ceschina, 1955), 153; and by Virginio Marchi, "Un'invocazione dell'*Aida*," *Aurea Parma* 34 (Apr.–June 1960): 101. Marchi places Verdi's use of the Parma baked-pear vendor's cry (which he does not doubt) in relationship "with an observation by Proust on the connections between the cries of street vendors of Paris, and the chant of the Catholic Church" (Conati, "Ballabili," 45 n. 28). Proust is a genius of quite another order, and no praise is high enough for him, but for different reasons, certainly not for this observation. If I may, I'd like to recount something that happened to a musician from Bologna who was traveling through West Africa a few years ago. Sailing down a river, possibly the Senegal, but it's not an important point, he was accompanied by a "savage" who rowed a canoe. It was an exciting moment in the elaborate dance of exotic tourism. At a certain point, the "savage" began to sing something which helped him with the rhythm of the paddle, and that aroused the interest of the musician, who wanted to let his oarsman know that the song reminded him of a type of singing that was very old, belonging to the Catholic church. But the "savage" immediately interrupted him to tell him that Gregorian chant and his African music had nothing in common, because—and there followed a precise musicological explanation. This was how the Italian musician discovered that his "savage" was a music teacher who had studied in Paris and worked as a "savage" for tourists during the holidays.

22. Massimo Mila, *Il melodramma di Verdi* (Bari: Laterza, 1933), 96ff., and again in his *L'arte di Verdi,* 53ff.

reference other than a generic one to an "invocatory" style that might or might not reveal a family connection with hundreds of popular forms (not forgetting the more or less "Egyptian" and more or less "liturgical" elementary exoticism of the phrase). Nevertheless, it is interesting to read what Conati writes when he accepts Sivelli's identification: "The really surprising thing about this episode, and an indication of what an incredibly fine ear Verdi had, is how he used the song he heard in Parma, as if he had obeyed an ancestral call and restored its character of sacred song."[23]

The theme of "ancestral" values (whose only drawback is that they cannot be checked) weaves its way through page after page of operatic literature. In one of his last works, a heartfelt profile of Amilcare Ponchielli, Gaetano Cesari claims to hear a relationship between the "naturalness of the accents and inflections," the "cadential stylization and expressive richness" of Ponchielli's music, and "the characteristic sound of my dialect speech"—that of Cremona—renewed and "idealized" in the music. What emerges is an imaginary musical-popular map:

> The particular characteristics, Ponchiellian and Lombard, of the music I heard made an impression on my personal sensibility as a Cremonese musician. And they allowed me, from then on, to distinguish Ponchielli's compositions from others. While the latter may sometimes reveal the broad, rhythmic span of the Emilian working-song ennobled by Verdi, the fiery sensuality of the Mediterranean Neapolitan composers in the wake of Mercadante, the colorful Tuscan balladry of the masters from Lucca, or the eclectic and superficial flow of little themes by Petrella, Pedrotti, Gomes, or Marchetti, I recognized the voice of our Maestro in the sweep and drive of his dances, in the lamenting funereal rhythm of marches as they die away at sunset along the road sacred to the memory of our dear departed ones, in the descriptive music vulgarized by the Banda, and in the mournful mastery of the elegiac mood with which his most inspired operatic music is shot through.[24]

There are "voices" on the Lombard plain to which the direct descendants of the Lombard writer Carlo Cattaneo show themselves to be particularly sensitive. For example, Gianandrea Gavazzeni writes:

> Lombard song tends to assimilate the melodic styles of composed songs, and of opera from the last century as well. This is absolutely symptomatic and it shows how ethnophony, in this case, is transformed according to popular preferences, the innate capacity of certain types of operatic music to be assimilated by peasant and working people, artisans and petit-bourgeois. It is also why ancient Lombard songs have not remained in current use. Equally, it can also be established that composers such as Donizetti and Verdi were influenced, in some turns of phrase, some broad

---

23. Conati, "Ballabili," 45.

24. Gaetano Cesari, *Amilcare Ponchielli nell'arte del suo tempo* (Cremona: Cremona Nuova, 1934), 6.

rhythms, by Lombard and Emilian folk song. The melodies of the young Verdi, from *Nabucco* to *I Lombardi,* and even later, up to his folklike "Rataplan" in *La forza del destino,* undoubtedly bear the imprint of these places, of what these places express in their landscape, voices, calls, and songs. The Donizetti of *L'elisir d'amore* must be taken as a model of folk gestures and vocal style and felt as an image of a village of Lombardy, of Bergamo, in fact, through sublime ethnic transformations brought to a height of artistic perfection. Let us not forget that Bellini wrote his *La sonnambula* in Lombardy, and the physical features of Amina and Elvino seem to recall—as we imagine them—the features of Manzoni's betrothed. This is how many folk tunes that flourished during the last century in Milan, on the shores of Lake Como, in gentle Brianza, came to take on the structure, the tone, the emotional manner of operatic melodies. It is something that simply did not happen in other regions, apart from the two-way traffic between Neapolitan songs and Neapolitan opera in the eighteenth century.[25]

Apart from the fact that the Neapolitans laid claim to various passages in Bellini and Donizetti as "theirs" in lineage and descent, it is clear that the process Gavazzeni describes allows for any kind of hint of a connection, especially if it is filtered through "sublime ethnic transformations brought to a height of artistic perfection": in other words, realized in a sphere where any sort of objective comparison is impossible or at least arbitrary.

Gavazzeni tells us that the folk songs which flourished in Milan, on the shores of Lake Como, and in "gentle Brianza" were indebted, in structure, tone, and emotional manner to operatic melodies and that the people of Lombardy and Emilia are, in any case, more inclined than others to forget the old songs and adopt new, composed ones (operatic in manner); but, as he himself informs us, his sources in the field of Lombard "ethnophony" are the *Canti milanesi* and *Canti comaschi* which Giulio Ricordi published in 1857, and which were even listed by the publisher as his own compositions (or, at least, largely reworked melodies). He gave the Milanese collection an opus number of 46, and the Como collection that of 56; it is no surprise, then, that Giulio Ricordi's songs of Milan, Como, and Brianza have such a strong operatic flavor, or give so much the odor of music in a cultivated, or subcultivated, or bourgeois or composed style. Even the perceptible, profound alterations in folk music repertories during the nineteenth century are quite generalized: if they seem most apparent in Lombardy, the reason lies, not so much in a "magical" identification of place/opera/people, as in the fact that Lombardy was much more affected by the industrial revolution, with all its economic, social, and therefore cultural consequences, than other parts of Italy (although other regions were affected, not only in the north).

25. Gianandrea Gavazzeni, "Canto popolare e paesaggio in Lombardia" (1942), in his *Le feste musicali* (Milan: Gentile, 1944), 167–75, quotation on 172–74.

It can be shown how the continual modification of style, repertory, and function, which has always been the case in historical processes, shifted up a gear in folk music over the course of the nineteenth century, leading to a crisis in oral and traditional communication. For example, the nineteenth century saw a move from a modal sensibility to a diatonic one, with all that such a process implies, in different parts of our country. It has to be recognized that the crisis in modality took place rather later in folk cultures than in the dominant "cultivated" areas, and the main reason for this phenomenon—although it did not by any means cancel the "melodic" sensibility of the modal system in favor of the "harmonic" one inherent in the establishment of diatonic tonality[26]—was the growing circulation in the working-class environment of musical products that stemmed, not from tradition, but from an urban and subcultivated musical craftsmanship. The nineteenth century saw not only a vast growth in the circulation of cultural products—or, at least, of some of those products—but also a mobilized population within the economic areas opened up by new means of production. Elementary education, military service, growing internal mobility, emigration, new groupings at work (the factory), and the formation of the modern proletariat all contributed to accelerating the otherwise "natural" process of matching the instruments of folk communication to the conditions of life, requirements, opportunities, and "taste."

I need only refer to the spread of new folk instruments in the nineteenth century, such as the barrel organ, accordion, and mouth organ, replacing such earlier instruments as the bagpipes and hurdy-gurdy, which had drones (and so were predisposed to modal structures). And these new instruments,

26. Proof of the resistance of modal "melodic sensibility" while a "harmonic sensibility" closely linked to the development of diatonic tonality became widespread can be seen in models of vocal polyphony in northern Italy, which might seem, from a cursory listen, to belong to the tonal model. Vocal polyphony in thirds has certainly prevailed over other types which we might consider of an earlier date, because of its compatibility with harmonic and tonal sensibility, but in fact it has not absorbed completely modern, tonal rules of harmonic organization. The two or three parts in the great majority of polyvocal songs in thirds in northern Italy—both on the plains, where the process of "moving toward" tonal structures has been strongest, and in the mountains (despite the devastation wreaked by what are known as "Alpine Choirs" or, as they are termed nowadays, "folk-inspired" choirs, on a late romantic model)—preserve apparently older polyvocal practices and always display their "autonomy," in that each line can exist separately as a possible vocal melody. Every researcher has had the experience of encountering folk singers who, listened to in isolation, sing, not the principal melody, but the line a third below (more rarely a third above), not "feeling" it as a part of the whole, part of a musical item displayed in an incomplete state, with something missing, and not completely recognizable. Then there are cases when the singer gives the same text with two melodies which he or she considers different but which are only two parts of a polyvocal structure in thirds. All this serves to demonstrate that, despite the partial coincidence of vocal polyphony in thirds with a modern, tonal harmonic model, folk "sensibility" has preserved the reference to a modal melodic model.

conceived and built according to the principles of equal temperament and intended for diatonic harmony, undeniably contributed to that process of "modernization" of a fairly large part of Italy's folk repertory. The spread of choral singing also certainly had some effect on folk song, and the brass band culture undoubtedly helped the push toward a tonal and harmonic "sensibility." In addition, this helped to circulate a new repertory.

We also have to ask ourselves what part opera played and where, in this complex, underresearched process. It would be a mistake to declare that the "past" was canceled, marginalized, or submerged everywhere. Large stretches of Italy, especially—but not exclusively—in the south, remained (until recently) almost untouched by new models,[27] and where social and economic conditions favored the distribution of the "new," the resistance of traditional ways was demonstrated in unexpected forms and with unexpected strength. It is not the case, for example (as Gavazzeni seems to think), that in an area such as Bergamo, Brianza, or Como, the "old" repertory was swept away by nineteenth-century operatic styles (directly or indirectly). Up until at least the immediate postwar period, authentic traditional customs and repertories were still strongly rooted in Lombardy, despite its being affected and transformed by the industrial revolution and its many consequences. Still today, although repertories are in a state of real crisis, research has shown how they are not being "replaced" by nineteenth-century composed music, but that in fact folk music practice, indeed all musical practice, is becoming extinct. It could even be claimed that opera seems to have touched folk music practice only superficially and has not altered its nature; folk music has been influenced much more by popular songs and dances distributed by the mass media (radio and record before World War II and later sound film and finally television).

When faced by the declarations of those who hear in the music written by the "great Italian masters" an echo of folk musicality, we have also to consider the fact that it is genuinely difficult to recognize any kind of fundamental unifying characteristics in the music of the Italian oral tradition; and yet this would have to be a precondition to ensure that there was something recognizable to represent the entire nation in the "sublimation" of operatic music.

There is no question now of being able speak of a single Italian folk tradition. The differences in repertories and musical models of broad stretches of this country—reflecting the ethnic and historical experience of those areas

27. However, in these cases it has been the models of light music that have brought about modifications. It is indeed true that the "melodic" (or "Italianate") style of light music in Italy owes a debt to the operatic tradition (only the entry of Afro-American models, from the time of World War I onward, brought in elements that are alien to the operatic tradition and passed them through operetta, the romanza, and the first "bourgeois" songs in mass-circulation consumer music, not only in Italy), but in such modifications any reference to operatic music was merely indirect.

which today form the administrative territory of the Republic of Italy—are so large and so evident as to place Italian ethnic music within the many stylistic spheres connecting the regions of the country to larger musical areas extending across the Mediterranean, on the one hand, and continental Europe, on the other. In fact, the musical tradition of Piedmont, for example, is much closer to that of France, part of Spain, the British Isles, Germany, and even Scandinavia than to that of Calabria or Sicily, which, in turn, belong to the wider area of Hispano-Arabic and Mediterranean music.

Leaving aside other aspects of Italian ethnic music and focusing our attention on "ways of singing," it is certainly not difficult to make out some reference to an operatic style in this or that different vocal tradition in our country. Nor is it difficult to recognize a preference for "melody" that in some ways can be linked to what is renowned as the "typically Italian" melodic vocal style of our operas. But if one returns for a moment to the picture of Bellini busily noting down the songs of his native Sicily or of the Como spinning girls, anyone familiar with the singing style of Sicily and Lombardy would be genuinely puzzled by the idea that one could find a trace of it in Bellini's vocal style—and not only Bellini's, of course—when it is in fact the opposite to traditional vocal styles whether in Mediterranean Italy or in the Italy which, in ethnomusicological terms, is linked to continental Europe.

Nevertheless, there is an area in which the cultivated models of nineteenth-century music have had a profound effect: the so-called folkloristic and characteristic music. It is my belief that the widespread conviction that operatic music had a determining effect on the style of our folk music arises from having confused folk music with the many products of the folklore business, as expressed by choirs, folk groups, and folk-style singers. There is no doubt that Rossini's so-called tarantella (*La danza*: "Già la luna è in mezzo al mare"), which bears absolutely no relation to the folk tarantella, has become *the* tarantella, an inevitable part of any evocation of Naples, even in television variety shows; and it is equally clear that the harmonizations used by folk choirs and vocal groups are related, not to those of traditional vocal polyphony, but instead to romantic and late-romantic structures. Even the singing style of folkloristic singers tends to the operatic model and ignores the "different" styles of folk song.

There are two reasons for the way this process has developed: one is the "commercial" drive to make the expressions of a culture that is by nature "different," "aggressive," and, by bourgeois standards, "unpleasant" acceptable to the general public; the other is the conviction that the "voices of the people," while full of "poetry," need to be improved, embellished, elevated, separated from their "simplicity," "spontaneity," and, especially, "uncultivated nature," and transferred to the "high levels" (or rather middle) by "agents" who are expert in the art of what is "beautiful." Certainly, anyone who heard these products and assumed them to be evidence of folk culture would have no difficulty in recognizing in them the influence of cultivated and bourgeois models, directly or indirectly linked to the tradition of operatic music.

4. DONIZETTI (OR BELLINI) AT ALL COSTS

There are some points in the history of the Neapolitan song that throw welcome light on the attitude of large areas of Italian culture (however different and separate) toward opera and opera composers. The "modern" Neapolitan song is a typical example of an urban musical craft that has turned into an industry; that is, it exemplifies a new musical "genre" produced by the profound social changes wrought by the industrial revolution, and the way it developed during the nineteenth century illustrates how a product that, putting all discussion of terminology to one side, we can define as "light music" came into being.

While the Neapolitan song of the first half of the nineteenth century shows characteristics of a folk craft in the way it was produced and distributed, in the latter part of the century its production and distribution are almost industrial, with a "market" that extends far beyond the boundaries of the city, region, or even country. The limits of this investigation suggest that we should leave aside the question of the relationship between opera buffa and "popular" song in eighteenth-century Naples. As we know, the question is still open, and perhaps the time has come to abandon Michele Scherillo's not infallible studies, which have fed so much propaganda in Naples and beyond, and move in the direction of a more serious analysis of the musical and literary material. In this regard, it is worth recalling the doubts expressed by Michael F. Robinson on the evidence of the "popular songs" that Scherillo gleaned from the librettos of Neapolitan comic operas:[28] "Scherillo rarely states a concordance proving that the operatic stanzas he quotes stem from popular or traditional songs"[29] and instead offers musical references that are absolutely generic with respect to any knowledge of southern Italian folk music.

It is more worthwhile to look at some specific examples of nineteenth-century Neapolitan song, which can reveal both the strength of the attraction of the great nineteenth-century opera composers and at the same time the inferiority complex of those Neapolitan commentators involved in discussing their song culture.

There is no doubt that even in the first half of the nineteenth century, the Neapolitan song reflects the "bourgeois" musical taste of the day and shows musical characteristics that can be traced back to generic operatic models.

28. See Michele Scherillo, *L'opera buffa napoletana durante il Settecento* (1883), 2d ed. (Palermo: Sandron, 1917), 461–85.

29. Michael F. Robinson, *Naples and Neapolitan Opera* (Oxford: Clarendon Press, 1972), 209.

La Compagnia Marionettistica **LUCIANO ZANE** esporrà:

AIDA

Grandiosa Pantomima decorata di sorprendenti scenari e ricco vestiario, tratta dall' opera del Cav. Maestro VERDI, con Musica espressamente scritta.

N.B. — L' ultimo quadro finale sarà variato da quello dell' Opera.

PERSONAGGI

FARAONE Re degli Egizi	AMONASRO Re d' Etiopia
AMNERIS sua figlia	AIDA sua figlia
RADAMES Capitano delle Guardie	Un Messaggiere
RAMFIS Gran Sacerdote	Custode del Tempio d' Iside

Guerrieri — Ministri — Sacerdoti — Sacerdotesse — Donzelle
Soldati. — Schiavi — Popolo Egizio — Prigionieri Etiopi — Un Barcaiuolo.

L'azione ha luogo a MENFI e a TEBE ai tempi dei Faraoni.

·Le scene sono dipinte dal rinomato scenografo sig. PIETRO FAGIANI di· Torino.
Il vestiario ricco e sfarzoso eseguito sotto la direzione della signora ZANE.
La Musica è scritta appositamente.

36. As the poster states, the "grand pantomime" for marionettes is indeed of *Aida,* but "the music is specially written." This must have been a subterfuge to avoid paying the performance royalties to the Ricordi publishing company; however, it is hard to believe that nothing of Verdi's score, not even the grand march, was used in the Zane show.

LA COMPAGNIA MARIONETTISTICA

DIRETTA DALL' ARTISTA

ATTILIO SALICI

darà un breve corso di Rappresentazioni con scelto repertorio

═══════════════ **B A L L I** ═══════════════

Excelsior - Amor - Mefistofele - Dea dei Mari - Orfeo all' inferno - Gli assassini
puniti - Incendio di Cartagine - Braama - Misolongi - Disastro di Messina:

═══════════ **P R O D U Z I O N I** ═══════════

Africana - Gioconda - Aida - Roberto il Diavolo - Guerra d'Africa - Guerra Russo
Giapponese - Forza del destino - Giuseppe Musolino ecc.

TUTTE LE MASCHERE DEL TEATRO ITALIANO

Primeggiando : Arlecchino - Facanappa - Fasolino - Rogantino - Sandrone - Meneghino

La prima recita avra luogo SABATO *26 Luglio* alle ore 21,30
col grandioso spettacolo in 3 atti

ELISABETTA

la figlia dell' esiliato in Siberia

OVVERO

37

37. According to this poster from 1909, the "choice repertoire" of the Salici marionette company sought the spectacular at any price: the earthquake at Messina or the war in the Sea of Japan were worth a ballet by Manzotti or a grand opéra by Meyerbeer. The "grandioso spettacolo" scheduled was based on the subject *Otto mesi in due ore* (Eight months in two hours), which had come to Donizetti from Pixérecourt by way of the Italian version by the actor Luigi Marchionni.

38–39. Toscanini's tough, bald pate and Donizetti's fetching, romantic coiffure: in the years immediately after World War I, "artistic characters" made their way into the puppet theater.

38

39

A mon élève **THÉRÈSE FERRERO**

Quando le sere al placido.

ROMANCE
de l'Opéra

LUISA MILLER
DE
VERDI

Variée pour Piano
per

Polibio Fumagalli

Op.118

Prop. dell'Editore
35389

All'estero deposto
Fr. 2

MILANO
R. Stabilimento Nazionale di
TITO di G. RICORDI

Firenze, Ricordi e Jouhaud. Mendrisio, Pozzoli e Bossi.   Napoli, Ricordi e Clausetti. Torino, Giudici e Strada.

40

ALLA SUA ALLIEVA

La Sig.ra

Olimpia Politelli

SECONDA
FANTASIA
PER
Pianoforte
SULL'OPERA
NORMA
del Maestro
VINCENZO BELLINI

DI
V. DE MEGLIO
Op. 15.

Dep. al Conserv. Naz. Proprietà dell' Editore N.º 38270. Fran. 3.

NAPOLI
MILANO — FIRENZE
TITO DI GIOVANNI RICORDI

40–41. Chosen almost at random, these two title pages of nineteenth-century operatic paraphrases demonstrate, on the one hand, the search for "dignified" graphic elegance and, on the other, the explicitly amateur market for which these products were intended, especially young women pianists of the upper middle class.

42

42–44. In the new century, the "talking machine" rapidly replaced many other forms of domestic diffusion of operatic music. The catalogues exemplified here are ordered both by singer (plate 43) and by title of opera (plate 44). In the first case, the names of the composers do not even appear. Undoubtedly, they are too well known to need to be given, but perhaps they are also considered secondary to what is really important in the new means of reproduction: the miraculous physical presence of the voice.

Dischi doppi CELEBRITA firmati, della:
SOCIETA' ITALIANA DI FONOTIPIA
Diametro dei Dischi cent. 27

Ogni disco essendo inciso dalle 2 parti, porta 2 differenti pezzi di musica
sono perciò i dischi Celebrità più convenienti di tutti.

NB. — Nelle ordinazioni dei dischi doppi è sufficiente indicare solo il numero stampato per primo e non tutti e due

Teresa Arkel

39380 Il Trovatore	— D amor sull'ali rosee	L.	8,50
39381 I pescatori di perle	— Siccome un di		
39386 Mefistofele	— Nenia di Margherita	»	8,50
39467 La Wally	— Ebben ne andrò		

Péricle Aramis

39140 Hymne d'amour	in francese	L.	15,—
39361 Hymne à la Muse	in greco		
39141 Nenna mia	in francese	»	15,—
39155 Sérénade triste	in greco		
80143 L'âme des fleurs	in francese	»	15,—
39151 Pendant cinq année que je te cerche	in greco		
39144 T'amo ancora	in italiano	»	15,—
39154 Chanson d'amour	in greco		
39145 La Bergère aux yeux noirs	— Chanson Montaguarde grecque	»	15,—
39972 Hymne de Pindare	— in greco		
39146 Un petit oiseau	in greco	»	15,—
39148 Dernier vœu	in franc		
39147 Lyngos	in greco	»	15,—
39288 Lyngos	in francese		
39150 Le champ des Pavots	in francese	»	15,—
39864 Ma jolie petite Irène	in greco		
39152 Eperdument	in greco	»	15,—
39453 Eperdument	in francese		

Amedeo Bassi

39643 Siberia	— Orride steppe	L.	15,—
39644 »	— T'incontrai per via		
39661 Tosca	— Questa notte ho fatto un sogno	»	15,—
39662 »	— Il sogno è la coscienza		
39796 Canzone guerresca in si bemolle		»	18,
39797 Fedora	— Amor ti vieta		

Ramon Blanchart

39380 A Granada	— Canpion espanola	L.	8,50
39396 Pensament de Nit	— Canpion catalana		
39365 Adios a Mariquina	— Romanza gallega	»	8,50
39308 Cansaros	— Alvares		
39382 L'Africana	— Figlia di regi	»	8,50
39383 L'Africana	— Averla tanto amata		

Maria Barrientos

39010 I puritani	— « Son Vergin vezzosa »	L.	15,—
39026 Le nozze di figaro	— « Deh! vieni non tardar »		
39011 La Sonnambula	— « Ah! non giunge »	»	15,—
39013 Lakme	— «Aria delle campanelle»		
39012 Voci di primavera	— « Valzer di Strauss »	»	15,—
39084 I puritani	— A te o cara (tenore A. Bonci)		
39457 La Sonnambula	— Co me per me sereno	»	15,—
39458 »	— Sovra il sen la man mi posa		
39459 Barbiere di Siviglia	— Una voce poco fa	»	15,—
39460 »	— Io sono docile		
39461 Mignon	— Io son Titania	»	15,—
39462 Canzone del Solvej			
39463 Chàteau-Margaux	— No sé que siento	»	15,—
39464 Las Hijas del Zebedeo	— Al pensar en el dueño		
	Artistas en miniatura - Tiene fama Sevilla		
39465 Lascia ch'io pianga	— Aria	»	15,—
39480 El cabo primero	— Zarzuela		
39503 Dinorah	— I. parte. Ombra leggera	»	15,—
39504 »	— II. » » »		
39535 Fra Diavolo	— Or son sola	»	15,—
39534 »	— Gia per la danza		
39542 Rigoletto	— Caro nome	»	15,—
39543 »	— Tutte le feste al tempio		
40002 Dinorah	— « Ombra leggera» (disco da 35 cm.)	»	25,—

Alessandro Bonci

39079 Mignon	— «Addio, Mignon, fa core»	L.	15,—
39111 La Favorita	— «Una vergine un angiol di Dio»		
39080 Mefistofele	— «Giunto sul passo estremo»	»	15,—
39084 I puritani	— «A te, o caro»		
39061 Rigoletto	— «La donna è mobile»	»	15,—
39082 Tosca	— «Recondita armonia»		
39083 L'Elisir d'amore	— «Una furtiva lagrima»	»	15,—
39120 Caro mio ben (Giordani)	- Romanza		
39127 Elena e Paride	— «Spiagge amate»	»	15,—
39149 Il Flauto Magico	— «Ah, cara immagine»		
39229 Rigoletto	— Questa o quella	»	15,—
39241 O del mio dolce ardor	— Romanza di Gluk		
39240 Carmen	— Il fior che avevi a me tu dato	»	15,—
39242 La Violetta	— Ro nanza di Mozart		
39215 I' l sing thee songs of Araby	— Romanza in inglese	»	15,—
39816 Tre giorni son che Nina	- Romanza di Pergolesi		

NB. — Tutti i dischi doppi celebrità firmati dalla Società Italiana di Fonotipia ad eccezione dei pochi doppi da
cent. 30 e semplici da cent. 35, sono del diametro di cent. 27.

— B —

ELENCO
dei Cilindri Artistici di pasta dura per Fonografo

Piccoli, misura usuale L. 1,25 cad. — Grandi, detti Inter, L. 2.— cadauno

Nelle ordinazioni indicare chiaramente oltre ai numeri dei cilindri la qualità che si desidera; e cioè
se i cilindri piccoli o cilindri Inter; non indicandolo la Ditta spedirà sempre i cilindri da L. 1,25

PREMESSA Ordinando i cilindri pregasi segnarne un numero maggiore per sostituire quelli che
al momento mancassero, altrimenti saranno sostituiti d'ufficio.

OPERE

ADRIANA LECOUVREUR (Cilea)
416 Monologo di Michonet. br.
892 La dolcissima effige. t.
893 L'anima ho stanca. t.
894 Racconto della battaglia. t.
895 No, più nobil sei. t.

AFRICANA (Meyerbeer)
35 O paradiso. t.
129 Adamastor. br.
130 Averla tanto amata. br.
170 Addio terra natia. s.
183 All'erta marinar. br.
302 Ho veduto, o signori. t.
303 Figlio del sol. s.
400 O Selika io t'adoro (duetto). s. t.

AIDA (Verdi)
12 Ritorna vincitor. s.
27 Morir si pura e bella. t.
28 Celeste Aida. t.
78 Rivedrai le foreste. br.
79 Quest'assisa ch'io vesto. br.
288 O cieli azzurri. s.
453 Nume, custode. t. b. e coro.
863 O terra addio (duetto). s. t.
1000 Rivedrai le foreste (duetto) s. br.
1044 Terzetto (atto I). s. ms. t.
1065 Su del Nilo. coro.
1084 Possente Età s. e coro.

AMICO FRITZ (L') (Mascagni)
247 Son pochi fiori. s.
248 O amore. t.
249 Tutto tace. t.
401 Tutto tace (duetto). s. t.

ANDREA CHENIER (Giordano)
111 Nemico della patria. br.
304 Un dì all'azzurro spazio. t.
188 Son sessant'anni. br.
305 Su dalla terra. t.
306 Come un bel dì. t.
307 La mamma morta. s.
481 Io non ho amato ancor. t.
482 Sì..., fui soldato. t.

BALLO IN MASCHERA (Un) (Verdi)
99 Eri tu che macchiavi. br.
100 Alla vita che t'arride. br.
193 Morrò, ma prima in grazia. s.
194 Ma dall'arido stelo. s.
195 ./ scherzo od è follia. s.
293 Re dell'abisso. ms.
294 La rivedrò nell'estasi. t.
295 Di tu se fedele. t.
856 Saper vorreste. s.
1002 T'amo, si t'amo (duetto). s. t.
1045 Consentimi Signore (terz.) s. ms. t.
1085 Posa in pace. b. e coro.
1087 Ve' se di notte. b. e coro.

BARBIERE DI SIVIGLIA (Rossini)
115 Largo al factotum. br.
116 La calunnia è un venticello. b.
191 Se il mio nome. t.

192 Una voce poco fa. s.
289 Ecco ridente in cielo. t.
454 Manca un foglio. b.
486 Il vecchietto cerca moglie. ms.
488 All'idea di quel metallo (duet.) t.br.
489 Numero quindici (duetto). t. br.
864 Dunque io son (duetto). s. br.
1046 Zitti.... zitti.... (terzetto). s. t. br.
2196 Mille grazie. coro.

BOHÈME (G. Puccini)
69 Che gelida manina. t.
70 Presentazione di Mimì. t.
140 Vecchia zimarra. b.
173 Mimì è una civetta. t.
197 Mi chiamano Mimì. s.
198 Valzer di Musetta. s.
296 Mimì e tanto malata. t.
483 Addio di Mimì. s.
1003 O Mimì tu più non torni (duet.) t.br
1004 Ci lascerem alla stazion (duet.) s.t.
1005 Sono andati (duetto). s. t.
1057 Quartetto. s. s. t. br.

BOHÈME (Leoncavallo)
199 Io non ho che una povera. t.
200 Chi batte alla porta? br.
297 Presentazione di Schaunard. br.
497 Mimì Pinson. s.

CABRERA (Dupont)
274 Ah illuso cure uman. t.

CARMEN (Bizet)
11. Là sul bastion. ms.
47. Romanza del fiore. t.
119 Canzone del toreador. br.
201. Io dico, non son paurosa. s.
202. Alto là, chi va la ! t.
208. Amor misterioso augello. ms.
308. Finale atto III. t.
1007 Mia madre vedo ancor (duet.) s. t.
1008 Lassù lassù (duetto). ms. t.

CAVALLERIA RUSTICANA (Mascagni)
1 Voi lo sapete o mamma. s.
33 Siciliana. t.
34 Brindisi. t.
203 Addio alla madre. t.
204 Fior di giaggiolo. ms.
309 Lo so che il torto è mio. t.
402 Ad essi non perdono (duetto). s. br.
1009 Bada Santuzza (duetto). s. t.
1010 A te la mala Pasqua (duetto). s. t.
1055 A casa, a casa. coro.
1088 Brindisi. t. e coro.
2181 Gli aranci olezzano. coro.
2188 Preghiera. coro.

CENERENTOLA (Rossini)
455 Miei rampolli femminini. b.

CONTESSA D'AMALFI (La) (Petrella)
634 Tra i rami fulgida. t.
635 Povera Tilde. br.

CRISPINO E LA COMARE (F.lli Ricci)
310 Bella siccome un venticello. br.
311 Io sono un po' filosofo. br.

CRISTOFORO COLOMBO (Franchetti)
67. Dunque ho sognato. br.
90. Per la conca d'argento. br

DINORAH (Meyerbeer)
128 Sei vendicata assai. br.
206 Ombra leggera. s.

DON CARLO (Verdi)
113 Dormirò col. b.
205 Per me giunto. br.
313 Io morro, ma lieto in cor. br.
1011 Dio che nell'alma (duetto). t. br.

DON GIOVANNI (Mozart)
314 Serenata. br.
456 Madamina, il catalogo è questo. b
457 Notte e giorno. b.
608 Là ci darem la mano (duetto) s. br.

DON PASQUALE (Donizetti)
41 Serenata. t.
126 Bella siccome un angelo. br.
300 Cerchero lontana terra. t.

DON SEBASTIANO (Donizetti)
127 O Lisbona. br.
315 Terra adorata. ms.

DUE FOSCARI (Verdi)
97 Questa è dunque. br.
98 O vecchio cor che batti. br.
233 Non maledirmi, o prole. t.
874 Questa dunque. br. e coro.

EBREA (L') (Halevy)
50 Rachele allor che Iddio. t.
316 O mia figlia diletta. s.
458 Se oppressi ognor. b.

EBREO (Apolloni)
137 Fu Dio che disse. b.

EDUCANDE DI SORRENTO (Usiglio)
1026 Un bacio rendimi (duetto). ms.br.

ELISIR D'AMORE (Donizetti)
121 Udite, udite o rustici. b.
291 Una furtiva lagrima. t.

ERNANI (Verdi)
64 Come rugiada al cespite. t.
83 Infelice e tuo credevi. b.
84 O de' verd'anni miei. br.
85 Lo vedremo o veglio audace. br.
86 Da quel di che t'ho veduta. br.
87 Vieni meco, sol di rose. br.
142 O sommo Carlo. br.
208 Ernani, Ernani involami. s.
317 Solingo, errante, misero. t.
1012 Da quel di che t'ho veduta
(duetto). s. br
1049 Terzetto finale. s. t. b.
1067 Coro d'introduzione. coro.
1068 Si ridesti il leon di Castiglia. coro
1096 O sommo Carlo. br. e coro.

FALSTAFF (Verdi)
124 Quand'ero paggio. br.
225 Dal labbro il canto. t.

NB. — In un pacco di Kg. 3 si possono spedire fino a 12 Cilindri piccoli oppure 8 Inter
» » » » 5 » » » 20 » » » 12 »

44

45

45. In a country like Italy where the practice of chamber music has never taken root on a wide scale, this "Scuola Quartetto" in Taranto is adorned with the name of the true father of Italian music. Mr. De Fazio, the teacher, holds up for the photograph, not Haydn's op. 33 nor Beethoven's op. 18, but the score of *Aida*.

46

46. In Italian cinema, allusions to the world of opera are often made to evoke the deepest and longest-lasting web of shared material which, beyond class conflicts, knits different levels of Italian society together. In Bernardo Bertolucci's 1976 film *Novecento* (1900), a drunk Rigoletto appears from the shrubbery and yells in dialect, "Giuseppe Verdi is dead," and then drops to the ground, vomiting; meanwhile, above the "curse" chords in the opera, the piercing cries of a mother in labor are heard. The date (1901), the location (the Parma lowlands), and the atmosphere (poverty and social struggles in the countryside) are sketched in a single gesture. In the following sequences, the cripple dressed as Rigoletto is the only one, however, of all the villagers dependent on the powerful Alfredo Berlinghieri to join his master in a toast to his heir.

47. The third act of *Il trovatore* is reaching its climax, as Verdi's "L'onda de' suoni mistici" soars among the velvet hangings of the hall of Castellor, in a scene shot from above. Then, when his men arrive, Manrico draws his sword and, leaning out over the proscenium, launches into the furious cabaletta ("Di quella pira"), while the camera looks over his shoulder to show the packed auditorium of the Teatro La Fenice. It is like a challenge, an accusation hurled against the Austrian officers decked out in their dress uniforms in the front rows and the dress circle; and the Venetian audience takes that challenge literally. Robert Krasker's wonderful cinematography also plays a part as the excitement of Verdi's music is turned, through a narrative device, into an exciting political allegory: this is the first sequence of *Senso*, Luchino Visconti's 1954 film version of Camillo Boito's short story. This episode, which triggers the love story and political plot, is, however, an invention of the filmmaker and his screenwriters, one with no basis in reality. In the spring of 1866, when the film is set, there was no opera season at the Fenice, and even if there had been, there would have been no interval between the third and fourth acts, with those conversations in the boxes and foyers that set the emotional intrigue in motion, but a ballet. It is a clever invention, all the same, one that exploits the unfailing effectiveness of a piece of operatic music that has long been stamped on the collective Italian memory and in the image of Italian opera abroad.

48

48. The worldwide fame of the "Mozartkugeln" chocolates has been countered in Italy with some sporadic attempts to link the cult of Verdi to Parma gastronomy, such as the Spongata Muggia of Busseto ("a delicate sweet for dessert") decorated with pictures of the house where the composer was born in Le Roncole and of the villa of Sant'Agata, or the Falstaff anchovies produced by Rizzoli in Parma. Italian opera, by its very structure of closed forms and memorable dramatic effects, in any case inclines toward representation in series, which is useful for selling small consumer items. Among the less well known examples of this in Italy are the matchboxes that show the key scenes, in numerical order, of an opera like *Norma* or that caricature the "unrealistic" plots of librettos like *La traviata*.

There are certain, proven cases of opera composers who wrote songs—real songs, not romances or chamber pieces—that entered popular circulation: Saverio Mercadante and his song "La rosa" for one. But then there is much discussion of attributions and of various "derivations," which continue to be quoted to the present day, passed uncritically, from writer to writer, with no attempt to check the facts. Many of these attributions and derivations seem to be the product of pure fantasy even on a cursory listening, in that the points of contact, when there are any, are so generic that, according to those criteria, they can suggest derivations from almost anything.

An example of this widespread tendency to "find" operatic quotations or reminiscences in a great many Neapolitan songs is given in the following passage by Sebastiano Di Massa:

> It was under this influence [of operatic music] that, I believe, *Fenesta che lucive* was created, a song which blends phrases from Bellini's *La sonnambula* with Rossini's *Mosè.* . . . ; the same influence gave life to *Palummella zompa e vola*, which derives from Brunetta's aria in *La molinarella* (by Piccinni), "Ma vattenne a lo saputo"; *Santa notte 'on Salvatore*, which is reminiscent of the aria "A te vengo, o mia Lucia" from Rossini's *La gazza ladra; Voca, voca, tira 'n terra*, which echoes Arsace's cavatina in *Semiramide*, again by Rossini; *Santa Lucia*, which contains echoes of a phrase in Donizetti's *Lucrezia Borgia*, "Com'è bello, quale incanto"; *Scetate, scè*, in which there is a memory of a motif in *La favorita;* and *Carulina*, the melody of which is taken from the introduction to *I Capuleti e i Montecchi;* and *Te voglio bene assaie*, whose melody is taken from "Vi ravviso, o luoghi ameni," in *La sonnambula*. An air for harp by Godefroy, *The Waltz of Garde*, gave rise to *O matarazzo 'e stoppa* and Tosti's paraphrase, *Vorrei morire!* It also seems that *La scarpetta* was put together from the melody in the great finale to *Ernani*, and that the tune in the scene of Rodrigo's death in *Don Carlos* was adapted to make the cheerful song *'A pacchianella è fora*, and that *La Sorrentina* derives from Rossini's lovely duet *La remigata veneziana*, and *'A ricciolella* is a variation on his *Carnevale di Venezia*. The comic song *'A mano d' 'a gnora* is none other than the ballad in *I vespri siciliani* and also the barcarolle in Donizetti's *Marin Faliero*. Lastly, the famous *Maria, Marì*, by Di Capua, is very reminiscent of the aria "Nume, custode e vindice," in Verdi's *Aida*.[30]

It is not within the remit of this study to check these concordances, which, significantly, are all put forward with great caution ("echoes," "is reminiscent of," and so on).[31] What is important is to emphasize the zeal of the commen-

30. Sebastiano Di Massa, *La canzone napoletana e suoi rapporti col canto popolare* (Naples: Rispoli, 1939), 142.

31. It is interesting to point out the "corrections" to this passage that Di Massa introduced in a subsequent edition (*Storia della canzone napoletana dal '400 al '900* [Naples: Fiorentino, 1962], 243ff.). Di Massa realized the flimsiness and inconsistency of his attributions, partly because some serious study had upset a number of historical certainties (the attribution of *Fenesta che lucive*, for example). In the new version, *Fenesta che lucive* no longer "blends phrases" from *La sonnambula*

tators, who seem more concerned to show the debts of their city's songs to operatic music than their independence or (relative) originality.

It can be taken as read—until such time as we have the necessary concrete evidence, as examining magistrates are wont to say—that the composers of the songs that circulated in nineteenth-century Naples were influenced by operatic music, to a greater or lesser extent. The musical "craftsmen" who fed the blossoming trade of "light" music publishing were probably in a position to have contact, even direct contact, with the music that was performed in our opera houses, and in any case, although they were concerned to serve the taste of a "popular" audience, they must have harbored some ambitions. It may seem that Francesco De Sanctis became rather carried away when he declared that in Naples "the announcement of *Norma* or *Barbiere* excited the entire city," [32] but it can reasonably be stated that a certain level of "craftsmen" connected with the production of "popular" music had access to the opera houses and direct opportunities to encounter the music of Bellini and Donizetti. It has been proven that this music spread through the city along various channels, even in purely working-class environments. This is why "echoes" are possible, apart from the tendency to make songs conform to musical models that were in some way connected to the operatic models of the day; and it also accounts for the possibility of "disguising" melodies from one opera or another, that is, their adoption, partial or possibly total, with a new text, either a song one or in dialect.

Some Neapolitan songs—not those that have become classics but those pieces that are associated with performers and particular personalities—effectively adopt a "parody" technique by borrowing a piece of music, even a nonlocal one, for a new text. Away from the operatic world, there is the example of an extremely successful French song from the end of the century, "La valse brune" by Villard and Krier, which provided the musical content for one of Raffaele Viviani's most intense, harsh songs ("So' bammennella," 1915) as well as for an associated song from the same period, "Bambeniello," by Pietro Mazzone, a strolling musician of the end of the nineteenth and beginning of the twentieth centuries.

It cannot be stated unequivocally that no opera composer, even a leading one, wrote—anonymously or under another name—the music of certain Neapolitan songs, but there is so far no convincing evidence to confirm that any composer did in fact do so. In the Tafuri collection in Naples there is a

---

but "seems to," etc. Many of the songs previously mentioned are now missing from the list, together with their operatic forebears.

32. Francesco De Sanctis, *La letteratura italiana nel secolo XIX* (1897) (Naples: Morano, 1910), 188 (my italics). English translation by Joan Redfern, *History of Italian Literature* (New York: Barnes and Noble, 1968).

receipt dated 5 October 1838 made out to Gaetano Donizetti, for 370 ducats paid in respect of unspecified musical work commissioned by Guglielmo Cottrau. And in Donizetti's correspondence there are references to the work of "songs" to be written on commission (for example, on 12 September 1837: "I'm supposed to write twelve songs, as usual, to earn twenty ducats apiece, something which I used to be able to do while the rice was cooking.").[33] But one needs to be cautious in accepting the terms "canzone" and "canzonetta" in the Donizetti documents as synonyms for "popular song," loose-leaf, street music.

I have remarked on the odd obsession found in Naples to attribute to Bellini and Donizetti—the two names that come up most often—the paternity, direct or indirect, of many songs, including famous ones. Neither Bellini nor Donizetti was Neapolitan, and the need to enlist them seems to contradict local self-conceit, for want of a better term, but also any justifiable pride in a musical legacy of some worth; the list of Neapolitan songs is studded with little masterpieces which have had widespread "success" (financial as well), and they are normally seen, as a whole, to be the "profound expression" of a people and a city. Faced with the names of two famous opera composers, Neapolitan self-promotion puts its feelings and pride to one side to assign to a native of Catania, and even one of Bergamo, some of the songs that have been most successful and are most symbolic of the Bay of Naples.

While the attraction of a prestigious attribution may have its part to play in this, the behavior of music historians who fall in line with Neapolitan commentators in assigning this or that song to Bellini or Donizetti shows that once again the "myth" of the popularity of our great composers and their music is at work. To confirm blandly that "Fenesta ca lucive" is by Bellini (or "derives" from Bellini) and that "Te voglio bene assaie" is by Donizetti not only confirms the popularity of the two composers but adds another stone to the comforting monument of Italian opera in popular guise.

I do not think it necessary here to follow the entire complicated story of the unwarranted attribution of "Te voglio bene assaie" to Donizetti, with a possible digression on its parallel attribution to Bellini:[34] we need only look at the key points in the story. The text of "Te voglio bene assaie" is without doubt the work of the Neapolitan optician Raffaele Sacco and presumably dates from 1835 (or shortly after). The composer remained unknown for a long time. *Coppielle,* or loose-leaf sheets on which songs were distributed, provide various editions of the piece, but none of them with the composer's

33. See Guido Zavadini, *Donizetti: Vita, musiche, epistolario* (Bergamo: Istituto Italiano d'Arti Grafiche, 1948), 445.

34. According to Scherillo, "Te voglio bene assaie" derives from the aria "Vi ravviso, o luoghi ameni," in Bellini's *La sonnambula* (see his "Bellini e la musica popolare," 55); see also the quotation from Di Massa at n. 30, above.

name.[35] Luigi Settembrini mentions it in his *Ricordanze* as a melody that was in vogue in 1839 (he had heard it sung by the gaoler's daughter).[36] Cesare Cantù refers to it and describes it as "popular."[37] In the first known edition, published by Girard (1840), no composer's name is given for the music, and it remains anonymous in the subsequent reprintings by Guglielmo Cottrau.[38] Martorana makes no mention of Donizetti in his biographical note on Raffaele Sacco ("He was the author of the song whose refrain is 'Te voglio bene assaje, e tu non pienze a me'; a song that was so popular that it inspired many who considered themselves to be poets to infect us with songs that were more or less good"),[39] and not even Regaldi, who between 1840 and 1848 collected interesting information at firsthand on the Neapolitan song, shows that he has heard mention of Donizetti as the composer of "Te voglio bene assaie."[40]

35. A loose-leaf copy of the song held in the Museo della Canzone Napoletana in Naples bears the name of a certain M. Battista as the composer of the music.

36. See Luigi Settembrini, *Ricordanze della mia vita*, 2d ed. (Naples: Morano, 1859), 1:159ff.

37. See Cesare Cantù, *Della letteratura delle nazioni: Saggi raccolti . . . in relazione alla storia universale* (1889–1890), 2 vols. (Turin: UTET, 1914), 2:361. Cantù's reference, previously unknown in the vast collection of writings on "Te voglio bene assaie," was first brought to attention by Marcello Sorce-Keller, "Io ti voglio bene assaje," *Nuova rivista musicale italiana* 19 (1985): 642–53, esp. 646. Sorce-Keller's essay covers all the stages of the "critical" commentary on the song and concludes by denying the existence of any reliable evidence for the attribution to Donizetti.

38. Bernardo Girard went into business with Guglielmo Cottrau (a Frenchman who had come to Naples with his father, following Murat), and by 1824 he had started to publish songs, arias, and romanzas in installments, according to the fashion of the day. These were called *Passatempi musicali, o Raccolta di ariette e duettini per camera, inediti, romanze francesi nuove, canzoncine napoletane e siciliane, variazioni pel canto, piccoli divertimenti per pianoforte, walz, balli diversi.* There is a publication of "Te voglio bene assaie" headed "new song of 1840"; but Sorce-Keller, in the article referred to in n. 37, gives the date of first publication as not later than 1835. The *Passatempi* saw various later editions under Guglielmo Cottrau, who had taken over the directorship of the publishing house after the death of his partner. As for the "popular" songs which appear in the *Passatempi,* it should be remembered that Cottrau was careful to indicate that they were anonymous and that he did no more than arrange the melodies. From 1841 onward, the follow-up to the *Passatempi* appeared: *25 Nuove canzoncine nazionali napoletani formanti seguito alla raccolta intitolata "Passatempi musicali."* After the death of Guglielmo Cottrau in 1847, his son Teodoro carried on the publishing business, reprinting the old material with various "novelties" and some of his own compositions. (The most famous is undoubtedly "Santa Lucia," which curiously was to have greater success with the Italian text by the Dalmatian-born but Neapolitan-by-adoption Enrico Cossovich than with the original Neapolitan text: "Come se fricceca / la luna chiena! / Lo mare ride / l'aria è serena / vuje che facite / mmiez' a la via? / Santa Lucia! / Santa Lucia!")

39. Pietro Martorana, *Notizie biografiche e bibliografiche degli scrittori in dialetto napoletano* (Naples: Chiurazzi, 1874; reprint, Bologna: Forni, 1972), 363.

40. Giuseppe Regaldi, "I canti del popolo di Napoli," *Poliorama pittoresco* 12 (June 1848). The article by Regaldi (an intriguing, cultivated figure, a native of Varallo, near Vercelli, who was a successful improviser, not an improviser of folk melodies, who went on to be a university professor in Bologna and Cagliari) stands out as one of the few examples of close observation of how

The first attribution pops up in 1865, when Teodoro Cottrau made a new edition of *Passatempi musicali;* eighteen years after the death of his father, partly out of filial devotion and partly for commercial interest, he attributes the song in question to his father (which Guglielmo, as mentioned above, had published anonymously). Guglielmo Cottrau's name appears again in the collection *L'eco del Vesuvio,* published by Teodoro a little after 1870, but "Te voglio bene assaie" is once again anonymous seven years later in the Ricordi collection, edited by Vincenzo De Meglio, *L'eco di Napoli.*

A reference to Donizetti emerges in highly ambiguous terms in one of the first biographies of the composer, by Cicconetti:

> But the flower of elegance, of simplicity and grace, is the one which is commonly known by the words "Io te vojo bene assaje, e tu non piense a me." Improvised on a poem by Sacco, it sparked a malicious desire in a number of people to vaunt their authorship, since Gaetano had decided not to put his name to the piece, and every time he heard those arrogant lies, far from treating them with contempt, he would laugh about them with his friend Ghezzi, who knew to whom the work should rightly be attributed.[41]

However, it was only with Salvatore Di Giacomo that the attribution became "certain" and took its place both in the history of the Neapolitan song and in Donizetti's biography. In 1909, in *Napoli: Figure e paesi,* Di Giacomo published a letter supposed to have been written by an elderly Neapolitan to a friend, in which we read: "Incidentally, I forgot to tell you that *Te voglio bene assaie* was set to music by Donizetti: you can swear on it, and if I'm still alive, I can provide you with the evidence." But this evidence did not appear, and Di Giacomo himself, five years later,[42] returns to the subject, supporting the attribution to Donizetti with evidence from a grandson of Sacco ("an optician in Naples in Sacco's old workshop on the old via Quercia, who remembered clearly what his grandfather told him"), Riccardo Carelli. On Di Giacomo's authority,[43] the attribution to Donizetti became "certain"; he was supported

---

popular culture is disseminated. Regaldi gives a highly reliable account of the situation of song "production" in Naples between 1840 and 1848, mentioning typesetters and even giving details of the print runs of the most successful songs. For "Te voglio bene assaie," he cites a print run of 180,000 copies ("La Luisella," 45,000, "Don Cicillo alla fanfarra," 100,000, "Alla finestra affacciati," 12,000, "La palommella," 30,000).

41. Filippo Cicconetti, *Vita di Gaetano Donizetti* (Rome: Tipografia Tiberina, 1864), 120.

42. Salvatore Di Giacomo, *Napoli: Figure e paesi* (1909) and *Luci ed ombre napoletane* (1914) in his *Opere,* ed. Francesco Flora and Mario Vinciguerra, 2 vols., 10th ed. (Milan: Mondadori, 1979), 2:430–576, quotation on 465; 577–796, quotation on 730.

43. A fine poet and stylish writer but a rather casual historian: we need only remember the famously falsified "coppiella" of "Michelemmà." Wishing to prove at all costs that this song was by

by Costagliola, who declared that he had learned from a barber that the composer of "Te voglio bene assaie" was Donizetti himself.[44] After this, any doubts were set aside, not only by chroniclers of Neapolitan song but also by Donizetti's biographers. Donati-Pettèni calmly accepted the attribution,[45] and it is strange that when doubts had already emerged,[46] Guglielmo Barblan confirmed Donizetti's authorship: "So it was that in '35, to words by Raffaele Sacco, the Bergamo-born Donizetti set down the melody of *Te voglio bene assaie,* which, in achieving immediate universal fame, showed that the new popular song of the nineteenth century had been discovered."[47] Barblan continues to give the song as one of Donizetti's works in his subsequent writings,[48] and it is attributed to him without reservations in the catalogue of the Donizetti Museum in Bergamo[49] and in countless other publications.[50]

What is important is not so much to reconstruct the history of the song and check its tortured "critical" history as to note the persistence of an attribution that confirms convictions that are more ideological than critical: an attribution that suits the people of Bergamo and of Naples, the chroniclers of

---

Salvator Rosa, and finding no proof, Di Giacomo, a skilled calligrapher, himself "created" the song sheet. This false version, which appeased the aspirations to age and nobility of lovers of Neapolitan song, received wide currency; even today, one frequently reads that "Michelemmà" is the work of Salvator Rosa.

44. Aniello Costagliola, *Napoli che se ne va: Il teatro e la canzone* (Naples: Giannini, 1918), 307.

45. Giuliano Donati-Pettèni, *Donizetti,* 2d ed. (Milan: Garzanti, 1945), 202.

46. Maria Ballanti (a pseudonym for a writer who, it seems, has never been unmasked), in 1907 (*La canzone napoletana* [Naples: Melfi e Joele, 1907]), already doubts the attribution to Donizetti, believing that the song has a folk flavor, and writes: "According to Scalinger ("La lega del bene," 2, no. 38, 1887), it might be said that *Te voglio bene assaie* is also entirely a folk tune." And contradicting Cicconeti, she suggests that it is a matter of opinion. Massimiliano Vajro, in *La canzone napoletana dalle origini all'Ottocento* (Naples: Vajro, 1957), defines the supposed document published by Di Giacomo as "letter of fantasy." Ettore De Mura, in *Enciclopedia della canzone napoletana,* 3 vols. (Naples: Il Torchio, 1968–69), vol. 1, opposes the attribution to Donizetti (on the basis of a doubtful shift in the date of the song's composition, which would render Donizetti's involvement impossible) but suggests one of his own, Filippo Campanella.

47. Guglielmo Barblan, *L'opera di Donizetti nell'età romantica* (Bergamo: Banca Popolare di Bergamo, 1948), 236.

48. The entry "Donizetti" in *Enciclopedia storica,* pt. 1, *La musica* (Turin: UTET, 1966), 2:259–83, quotation on 280. Guglielmo Barblan and Bruno Zanolini, *Gaetano Donizetti: Vita e opere di un musicista romantico* (Bergamo: Bolis, 1983), 477.

49. Valeriano Sacchiero, ed., *Il museo donizettiano a Bergamo* (Bergamo: Centro Studi Donizettiani, 1970), 152.

50. On the other hand, the unreliability of the attribution is revealed by William Ashbrook in the Donizetti entry in the *New Grove Dictionary of Music and Musicians,* ed. Stanley Sadie, 6th ed. (London: Macmillan, 1980), 5:568, where "Te voglio bene assaie" is listed with the qualification "often attrib. Donizetti."

song and of opera, so that only positive testimony comes to the surface, and doubts are submerged.

Opera and Folk Culture

5. CIMAROSA ON YOUR SHOULDERS AS YOU WANDER THE WORLD

Raising doubts about the widespread presence of a more than superficial knowledge of opera in working-class life over the course of the nineteenth century does not mean ignoring some specific cases in which material derived from the opera repertory entered folk use, admittedly in urban areas. As far as we know—but further research is required—Naples seems to have been the city where the "people" were most involved in opera.

Enrico Cossovich, painting a picture of the life and pastimes of a Neapolitan *guagliune,* or urchin, in the middle of the nineteenth century, describes their typical orchestra, which consisted of a *siscariello* (a small reed flute), *scetavajasse* (scraper), *tricchebballacche* (clapper), *tromba degli zingari* (mouth-harp), and *puti-puti* (friction drum):

> He [the *siscariello* player] is the one who might be described as the conductor of the orchestra, inasmuch as the concerts emerge principally from him: he always plays the principal melody, and the other instruments act as an accompaniment. The place where these *siscarielli* are made is none other than at the entrance to the Teatro di Fondo. Pan himself would have given his pipe for one of these magic flutes. In fact, the *guagliune* does not limit himself to playing on that little reed pipe the popular melodies of "Luisella," "D. Ciccillo," "Marinella," "Te voglio bene assaie," and "Guarracino" but can also give a fine rendition of "Ah! perché non posso odiarti" from *La sonnambula,* "Dunque andiam" from *Bellisario,* and on to "Qui ribelle ognun ti chiama," a dramatic piece that usually serves as the orchestra's finale.

Cossovich again, in a note, writes:

> These heroic melodies originate from the theater lamplighters' boys, who, climbing up the wings, listen up there to the singers, and from the extras (or mute performers), or those who are asked to fly, appear in the background, or cover roles, who then offer the arias, cavatinas, and choruses they have learned, in their own fashion, at cheerful gatherings, at weddings, and most of all when Bacchus fires and swells the imagination.[51]

51. Enrico Cossovich, "I guagliune," in *Usi e costumi di Napoli e contorni,* ed. Francesco De Bourcard, 2 vols. (Naples: Nobile, 1853–66; reprint, Naples: Reprints Editoriali, 1976), 1:289–322, quotation on 307ff.

Operatic extracts were also found in the repertory of the "Viggianesi," traveling musicians who were originally from Viggiano in Basilicata. Throughout the entire nineteenth century, the Viggianesi could be heard not only in Naples but across the whole of Europe, in Turkey, North America, and even in Chile. The Viggianesi's main instrument was the harp: a Renaissance-type portative harp up until 1820, then a small, diatonic, positive harp (but easily transportable, carried on a strap). The Viggianesi group was completed by a viola player (later, toward the end of the century, a violinist), sometimes a transverse flute or a clarinet, and always by a boy playing a triangle, who also had to collect the money (in a hat).

This is not the appropriate place to cover the whole question and documentation of the harp tradition in Viggiano (which disappeared around the time of World War I), and I refer the reader to an article of mine that deals specifically with the subject.[52] In this context I want only to refer to the repertory of these players, as it is documented in various sources. Like the little orchestras of the Neapolitan boys, the Viggianesi played not only traditional melodies, Christmas novenas, and Neapolitan songs in vogue ("Te voglio bene assaie," "Lo cardillo," the songs of Totonno Tasso)[53] but also operatic items. An informant from the middle of the nineteenth century reports that his "grandfather played the songs of Cimarosa and Jomelli" and his father "those of Rossini and Mercadante;"[54] others confirm that Rossini and Mercadante formed part of a repertory which had developed to include famous pieces by Bellini (like "the aria from *Il pirata*" and "Ah, non giunge uman pensiero" from *La sonnambula*).

There is more evidence of popular, improvised performances of music from the opera repertory around the middle of the century, again in Naples. Cossovich writes:

> It would be a mistake. . . . not to mention our hunchback Pascariello. . . . Pascariello was the first to take heroic singing boldly out into the open air and tragedy out onto the street; he has had many followers, but none who have attained his fame.
>
> This ringing tenor voice, a true *absolute* tenor, because he possessed absolutely nothing other than his voice, still resounds through our streets and our squares. Few readers will have remained unaware of his fame, which was such as to merit biographies and portraits in engravings and lithographs. He who compensated powerfully for his natural defects with a precious art has left a memory at once pleasant and unhappy, and while not even his music was immune from the terrible

52. See Roberto Leydi and Febo Giuzzi, "Alcune schede in margine alla mostra degli strumenti della musica popolare in Italia," *Culture musicali* 2, no. 4 (July–December 1983): 97–306, esp. 100–153.

53. Ibid., 141.

54. Giuseppe Regaldi, "I viggianesi," *Poliorama pittoresco* 12 (June 1848); reprinted in *Usi e costumi,* ed. De Bourcard, 1:123–28.

persecution of an occasional "raspberry," he allowed the finest pieces from *Il pirata, Roberto, Bellisario,* and many others to be *relished,* and I say *relished,* because if he shouted sometimes, it was well to consider that he had to catch the attention not only of those standing around him but also those who lived on the top floors. In fact, his singing was mostly crowned with success, and visitors would open the windows of their inns and shower him with alms, sometimes with overwhelming generosity.[55]

So opera, in the streets of Naples, around the middle of the century, could be heard played by extremely popular boys' small orchestras, by the strolling Viggianesi on harp and viola, or else sung lustily and unaccompanied by these tenors. And opera was also heard in other Italian cities, across Europe, and in America, played again by the Viggianesi.

The available sources give us some indication of what these "popularizers" chose from the opera repertory on offer in the Neapolitan theaters of the day, but all (or almost all) record that the street musicians' repertory, including its operatic content, was much wider than the examples they quote. However, on the basis of concurring evidence, it can be stated that certain composers and certain operas were performed more than others, evidence, itself, of popular taste. The predictable names of Bellini (confirming his Neapolitan "fortune"), Donizetti, Rossini, Mercadante, and Meyerbeer predominate; Meyerbeer's far greater success in his own day than in ours extends even into the context of Neapolitan street music.

Perhaps this "passage" into the street was more intensive in Naples than in other Italian cities; but the absence of information for other locations (partly because of the scant attention generally paid to these small local sources) does not give us authority to suppose that a similar phenomenon was not generally found, albeit with different approaches to the organization of street music.

6. OPERA BECOMES A BIG STEW

Recent research into folk music in Italy now allows us to verify, at least in outline, many aspects of the "presence" of nineteenth-century Italian opera in working-class culture. It has already been pointed out how, although it was not the only active ingredient, operatic music contributed to speeding up the transformation of Italian folk music as it moved in the direction of modes and forms more or less in line with the models introduced by the establishment of tonality, of harmonic sensibility, and of equal temperament, a general drift toward the typical forms of making and listening to music in the nineteenth century. One thing is certain, however, which is that it was not common practice to perform operatic pieces in the peasant environment, not even in places where operatic activity was fairly close and strong. Certainly, operatic arias

55. Cossovich, "I guagliune," 309ff.

were known almost everywhere, especially in the Po Valley, but they were performed by "specialists," that is, singers who rarely took part in true folk singing, but who stood out as opera lovers and who tried to replicate in their singing the performance styles of tenors, baritones, and basses.

It is more interesting to observe how common it is for material derived from opera to be "reused" in profoundly different communicative contexts. I am referring to the interesting genre of the *incatenatura,* or chain, which, in the present-day *osteria,* or pub, seems to resemble the older model known as a *minestrùn* (minestrone) or *risott* (risotto) in Lombardy, and a Ligurian *remescellu* (mixture), to make the point of its being a blend or a mixture. While this vocal genre does not always include operatic quotations, it nevertheless follows their outline to create a sequence of fragments from songs with different meters, melodies, and subjects, to comic, or joking, effect.

Opera often has a part to play in such compositions, which belong to the world of the *osteria* and to male "society," and the fragments selected to create an apparently jumbled sequence with other fragments of different origin merit closer attention. I shall restrict myself to quoting a pair of such sequences, or *incatenature,* collected in various parts of Lombardy, to indicate the widespread success of the genre.

1. Vico di Capovalle (Brescia), 31 October 1971 (recorded by Paola Ghidoli, Glauco Sanga, and Italo Sordi): Tullio Lombardi (landlord), with his son, his daughter, and a group of customers (accompanied by guitar and accordion).[56]

Redemès discòlpati	[*Radamès discòlpati*
Redemès discòlpati	*Radamès discòlpati*
è Redemès l'e chì l'e sà l'e là	and Radames is here and there
l'e sót el pónt de Calvisà	he's under the bridge of Calvisano
co le bràghe 'n mà	with his breeches in his hand
che l'e drì a cà——	and he's sh——.
dísìga ch'el végna	Tell him to come,
dísìga ch'el végna	tell him to come.
Redemès l'e chì l'e sà l'e là	Radames is here and there
l'e sót el pónt de Calvisà	he's under the bridge of Calvisano
co le bràghe 'n mà	with his breeches in his hand
che l'e drì a cà——	and he's sh——.
dísìga ch'el végna	Tell him to come,
faré l'amor	and make love.
celèste Aìda	*Celèste Aida*
formà divìna	*formà divina*

56. Recording published on Albatros VPA 8223 RL, text and musical transcription in Roberto Leydi and Bruno Pianta, eds., *Brescia e il suo territorio* (Milan: Silvana, 1976), 326–28.

mandéme i basì	send me your kisses.
batìma sui ciàp	Let's slap buttocks.
celèste Aìda	*Celèste Aida*
formà divìna	*formà divina*
mandéme i basì	send me your kisses.
batìma sui ciàp	Let's slap buttocks.
ài nostri mònti	*ài nostri mònti*
rìtornerémo	*ritornerémo*
làntica pàce	*l'antica pace*
a che pace pace non voglio dare	What about peace? I don't want peace.
sóno ostinàto	I'm stubborn.
se non mi dici prima chi t'à	If you don't tell me first who
e sínf e sùnf e séla	and sinf and sunf and sela
chì t'a r'ota la pa. . . .	who broke your steeple
la và sul càmpo la s'éra sognàta	Go to the field, she dreamed
ch'erà 'l so Gingìn	that her Gingin was there.
uè Gingìn tòchem chì tòchem lì	Hey, Gingin, touch me here, touch me there,
e g'ò un dolór che mi fà morì	and I've a pain that is killing me.]

2. Milan.[57]

Radamès!	[Radamès,
Parobon, parobon, parobon!	*parobon, parobon, parobon,*
Radamès!	Radamès,
Parobon, parobon, parobon!	*parobon, parobon, parobon,*
Fiol d'un can d'un Radamès	what a son of a bitch,
dove te se' mai scondù?	where are you hiding?
L'è chi, l'è scià, l'è là,	He's here, he's there,
l'è sott el pont de san Damian	he's under the bridge of San Damiano
che'l fa la legna. . . .	gathering firewood. . . .
Disigh che' vegna	Tell him to come
a fare l'amor.	and make love.
Celeste Aida,	*Celeste Aida,*
forma divina,	*forma divina,*
battemegh i man,	let's clap
cia-ciach, cia-ciach	cha-chak, cha-chak,
battemegh i man.	let's clap.
Menelich	Menelich
clic-clic, clic-clic.	click-click, click-click.

57. Text and music in Attilio Frescura and Giovanni Re, *Canzoni popolari milanesi* (Milan: Ceschina, 1939), 293–96.

La regina Taitù,   Queen Taitù,
Taitù, Taitù,   Taitù, Taitù,
l'è la rovina,   she's the ruin,
l'è la rovina   she's the ruin
della nostra gioventù.   of our youth.

Ma fu troppo breve, ahimè,   But alas, how brief
la dolcezza di quel ben. . . .   was the sweetness of that love. . . .
Svanì. . . .   She vanished. . . .
clic-clic, clic-clic. . . .   click-click, click-click. . . .
La regina Taitù,   Queen Taitù,
Taitù, Taitù,   Taitù, Taitù,
l'è la rovina,   she's the ruin,
l'è la rovina. . . .   she's the ruin. . . .

Menelich. . . .   Menelich. . . .
Una rondine non fa primavera   One swallow doesn't make a spring
e di sera, Salomè,   and in the evening, Salome,
tutti i gatti son bigi, lo sai,   all cats are dark, don't you know.
chissà mai, se un po'   What if a bit . . .
clic-clic. . . .   click-click, click-click. . . .

La regina Taitù,   Queen Taitù,
Taitù, Taitù,   Taitù, Taitù,
l'è la rovina,   she's the ruin,
l'è la rovina. . . .   she's the ruin. . . .
Menelich   Menelich
clic-clic, clic-clic. . . .   click-click, click-click. . . .]

A similar type of *osteria* composition, making use of operatic quotations, is also documented for other northern Italian regions, such as Liguria.

3. Ceriana (Imperia), 10 December 1962 (recorded by Roberto Leydi and Luciano Berio): male group.[58]

Dai cieli bigi   [*Dai cieli bigi*
vedo fumar quei mille   *vedo fumar quei mille*
comignoli di Parigi   *comignoli di Parigi*
Parigi oi cara   *Parigi oi cara*
noi lassieremo   *noi lassieremo*
la vita unita   *la vita unita*
trascorreremo   *trascorreremo*
dai dolci afanni   *dai dolci afanni*
compenso avrai   *compenso avrai*
la tua salute   *la tua salute*
rifiorirà   *rifiorirà*

58. Unpublished.

la tua salute
rifiorirà

la tua salute
rifiorirà

fior di giaggiuolo
gli angioli belli stanno in paradiso
e belli come me ce n'è uno solo
fior di pianura
io mi son data a te fidente e pura
ed ora gli uocchi tuoi mi fa paura
fiorin di canna
chi vuol la canna vadi alla maremma
chi vuol la figlia inammori la mamma

fior di giaggiuolo
gli angioli belli stanno in paradiso
but there's only one as lovely as me,
flower of the plain.
I gave myself to you faithful and pure
and now your eyes fill me with fear.
Little flower of the reed,
if you want reeds, go to the fens.
If you want the daughter, make the
    mum fall in love with you,

pa para pa pa pa pa para. . . .

pa para pa pa pa pa para. . . .

ai sergenti ghe fa ma i denti
ai furieri ghe fa ma i pe

The sergeants' teeth ache,
the quartermasters' feet ache,

. . . .

. . . .

ai sergenti ghe fa ma i denti
ai furieri ghe fa ma i pe

the sergeants' teeth ache,
the quartermasters' feet ache.

castagne seche
castagne seche

Dried chestnuts,
Dried chestnuts.

e da quando l'amica mia se n'andò via
sentii na stretta al cuor ma non fiatai

And ever since my girlfriend left me,
I've felt a pain in my heart, but I didn't
    breathe.

prese la roba sua lasciò la mia
come se non l'avessi amata mai
quando l'amica mia se n'andò via
il giorno apresso
ebbi un espresso
dalla mia bella ingrata
era pentita
della sua vita
poi s'era avvelenata
ma il giorno apresso
n'ebbi un espresso
dalla mia bella ingrata
si era pentita
della sua vita
poi s'era avvelenata

She took her own stuff but left mine
as if I'd never loved her.
When my girlfriend left me,
the next day
I had a telegram
from my thankless love.
She regretted
her life,
then she took poison,
but the next day
I had a telegram
from my thankless love.
She regretted
her life
then she took poison.

e la mia mamma è morta
m'a fatta testamento
e mi a lasciato la chitarra
mi a lasciato la chitarra
e la mia mamma è morta

e la mia mamma è morta.
And she made out her will to me
and she's left me her guitar.
She's left me her guitar
e la mia mamma è morta.

mi a fatta testamento	And she made out her will to me
mi a lasciato la chitarra	She's left me her guitar
pel mio divertimento	for me to play
e l'o prestata a tanti	and I've lent it to lots of people.
nesun me l'a mai rotta	No one's ever broken it
e l'o prestata al parroco	and I lent it to the priest
e l'o prestata al parroco	and I lent it to the priest
e l'o prestata a tanti	and I've lent to lots of people.
nessun me l'a mai rotta	No one's ever broken it
e l'o prestata al parroco	and I lent it to the priest
e me l'a tutta rovinà	and he wrecked it completely.

e daghela ricciola	Give it to the girl with the curly hair,
e daghela bionda	give it to the blonde,
e daghela bionda	give it to the blonde,
bionda bionda sul sofà	the blonde on the sofa,
e daghela ricciola	give it to the girl with the curly hair,
e daghela bionda	give it to the blonde,
e daghela bionda	give it to the blonde,
bionda bionda sul sofà	the blonde on the sofa.

il marito	The husband
e la moglie sola in ca	and the wife alone at home
e col piede sulla culla	with her foot on the cradle
a cantare la ninna na	singing a lullaby
a chi manca le scarpete	and some don't have shoes
a chi manca gli scarpon	and some don't have boots.
chi a una figlia da maritare	Some have a daughter to marry off
e una grande soddisfazion	and it's a great satisfaction.]

7. HOW VERDI SAVED THE ANARCHIST FROM THE GALLEY

Political hymns have been a notable vehicle for transmitting musical models and instruments of musical enculturation across fairly broad stretches of the Italian proletariat. Although their melodies are not in any way folk tunes, they have become such by virtue of their textual content and in declaring and confirming their function as collective social song. If we take a close look at the rich legacy of anarchist, socialist, and republican hymns which spread through Italy in the nineteenth century and the first years of the twentieth, we can see that the practice of "parody" or "disguise" was widespread. Social song thus also adopted the old expedient of using familiar melodies to convey new content, ensuring that the songs were more easily circulated and more quickly and directly learned. The Catholic church had itself used the same method, which was found to be efficient in the heat of political struggle and social conflict.

The melody of the "Marseillaise" already had an obvious symbolic significance;[59] it seems that the use of the melody of "Funiculì, funiculà" is more instrumental, and part of a practice that is fairly close to the folk procedure of
"disguising" folk airs.[60] However, one striking feature is the completely marginal position of operatic material, which one might think particularly well
suited because of the hymnlike tone of many pieces and the presumed familiarity of the proletariat with the most famous choruses and arias.

In fact, I have found only one, extremely famous Verdi chorus, with a new
text written by the anarchist lawyer Pietro Gori, that has attained broad popularity, enough to be published in all the many anarchist and socialist "song-
books,"[61] and, more important, is still quoted, remembered, and sung by elderly militants, whom I have encountered in the course of research on social
song undertaken since the end of the 1950s. The chorus is "Va, pensiero, sul-
l'ali dorate," and the new song that derives from it is entitled "Canto di maggio" or "Il Primo maggio." The text is as follows:

Vieni, o Maggio, t'aspettan le genti,	[Come, May, the people are waiting for you,
ti salutano i liberi cuori;	free hearts greet you;
dolce Pasqua dei Lavoratori,	sweet Easter of workers,
vieni e splendi alla gloria del sol.	come and shine with the glory of the sun.
Squilli un inno di alate speranze	Let a hymn of winged hopes ring out,
al gran verde che il frutto matura,	on the green expanse which ripens the fruit,
alla vasta ideal fioritura	on the immense, blossoming ideal
in cui freme il lucente avvenir.	glimmering in the shining future.

59. Besides the many Jacobin translations of the original French text into Italian and the many
adaptations, including those with texts that are at some remove from the original, produced in
Italy during the revolution, the strongly symbolic melody of the "Marseillaise" found an effective
application in one of the very first international Italian hymns. This is the "Inno dell'Internazionale," written by Stanislao Alberici Giannini, which can be dated to 1874 or 1875 (see Gianni Bosio, "I canti della Prima Internazionale in Italia: Prime ricerche e chiarimenti sulle fonti scritte: Lettera aperta a Roberto Leydi," in *Movimento operaio e socialista* 11, nos. 1–2 [Jan.–June 1965]:
5–40, esp. 31ff.). The hymn, which opens with the words "Su leviam alta fronte / o curvati dal do-
lor" (Let's raise our heads / O men bowed down by work) is interesting partly because it includes
the image—traceable to Garibaldi—of the "sun of the future," which was to return in Turati's familiar hymn. Another hymn in the anarchist tradition, written by Carlo Monticelli, does not use
the French melody but borrows its title as "The Marseillaise of Work"; first published in 1896, it
has received widespread circulation up to the present day.

60. Camillo Prampolini's "Inno della libertà" uses the melody of this most famous of Neapolitan songs, dating from 1880, with words by Peppino Turco and music by Luigi Denza.

61. Pietro Gori's text is an encouragement to workers to celebrate the First of May, decreed
by the Second International in 1890 in memory of the "Chicago martyrs." Banned throughout Europe and America, the holiday, judged to be "subversive," was for many years—even during the
Fascist period—celebrated in Italy in open defiance of the police or in secret. The singing of Gori's
hymn was also prohibited: this was the cause of the incident referred to below. The text appears

Disertate, o falangi di schiavi,	Ranks of slaves, leave
dai cantieri, da l'arse officine;	your building sites, your burning
	workshops;
via dai campi, su dalle marine,	away from the fields, up from the harbor,
tregua, tregua all'eterno sudor!	respite, respite from endless toil.
Innalziamo le mani incallite,	Let's raise our callused hands,
e sian fascio di forze fecondo,	to make a productive band of strength,
noi vogliamo redimere il mondo	we wish to redeem the world
dai tiranni de l'ozio e de l'or.	from the tyranny of idleness and money.
Giovinezze, dolori, ideali,	Youth, pain, ideals,
primavere dal fascino arcano,	the springtime of secret beauty,
verde maggio del genere umano,	the green May of the human race,
date ai petti il coraggio e la fé.	put courage and faith in our hearts.
Date fiori ai ribelli caduti	Offer flowers to the fallen rebels
collo sguardo rivolto all'aurora,	with your eyes turned toward the dawn,
al gagliardo che lotta e lavora,	to the brave man who struggles and works,
al veggente poeta che muor.	to the prophet poet as he dies.]

It may be more than an anecdotal digression to remember at this point a story told by an elderly anarchist from Pisa:[62]

LEYDI

So, the "Primo Maggio" is based on the tune from *Nabucco,* and before you were telling me about a strange misunderstanding that happened . . . or how a group of you caused a misunderstanding . . .

CIUTI

No . . . there were a few of us young lads, we were about fifteen years old and were singing "Il Primo Maggio," and then the *carabinieri* arrived, grabbed hold of us, and took us to the police station.

LEYDI

What year was this?

CIUTI

I was fifteen, so that makes it sixty years . . . I can work it out, you know, . . . it was 1906 . . . 1907, that's it. So then, when I was inside the police station, they asked me why I was singing these songs, and I said, "Look, I wasn't singing any-

---

in the works of the Rosignano lawyer, one of the leading figures in Italian anarchism and the writer of some of the most successful social songs, from "Addio a Lugano" to "Stornelli d'esilio," which are still remembered, if not sung, today; see Pietro Gori, *Opere,* vol. 2, *Battagli: Versi,* 3d ed. (Milan: Editrice Moderna, 1947), 2:80.

62. Interview with Foresto Ciuti (originally from Pisa, but who had long since emigrated to France), conducted in July 1962 by Roberto Leydi and Gianni Bosio. Ciuti was seventy years old at the time.

thing bad," and the *carabiniere* said, "They were singing subversive songs," and the brigadier said, "What were you singing?" "I was singing that opera *Nabucco*," and he said, "What bit?" and so I sang the chorus from *Nabucco* . . .

LEYDI

To the words . . .

CIUTI

To the words "Vai pensiero sull'ali dorate" because actually "Il primo Maggio" begins "Vieni, o Maggio." Then the *carabiniere* said, "Yes, yes, that's what he was singing." Right? So then the brigadier said, "So why did you arrest him then? He was singing a Verdi opera, not a subversive hymn." So that's how they let us go . . .

What can be deduced from this small, marginal appearance of operatic music in the repertory of socialist and anarchist hymnody? It would be going too far to claim that such minimal usage of operatic choruses and arias in political hymnody, even though largely made up of disguised and parodied material, is a sign of its limited popularity in proletarian circles at the end of the nineteenth and beginning of the twentieth centuries. Nevertheless, while recognizing that many of the melodies in socialist and anarchist hymnody not in the folk strain and not "spontaneous," show marked traces of operatic models, their limited presence remains an unsolved problem.

8. LONG LIVE THE BAND

There is no doubt that band culture played an important, if not essential, part in making operatic music widely known, at least up until the interwar period (and particularly up to the time of World War I).

Only very recently has research in this field got under way in Italy, but almost all of it has dealt with reconstructing the histories of individual bands, with attention, in the best work, more on the social aspect of the bands' involvement in collective life than on specifically musical questions (changing repertory, sources of material, stylistic modifications and alterations in the makeup of the band, the relationship to musical life in general, and so on).

However, in very general terms, we can establish that the development of the "municipal" band in Italy from the middle of the nineteenth century onward involved a highly complex process of interaction between changing habits and taste and social organization. In Italy the band has a predominantly civic connotation and was more or less directly and openly associated with a lay, liberal, and republican position in the early days, and a socialist one later on. Growing out of the military bands and the municipal guards, the civilian bands gradually expanded their function beyond the duties of ritual and celebration. It was probably the growing requirement for music that led to the bands' transformation into genuine "people's orchestras," with a repertory increasingly open to orchestral and operatic music. This transformation did not take place only where audiences had no other or different opportunities to hear music, especially operatic music. The band thus came to assume an important position not only as the provider of music (and of information on music) to groups excluded from direct experience but also as the conveyor of music that was already familiar and was to be heard in the opera house.

The opera repertory thus moved from the opera house to the street, in adaptations and arrangements that tended largely to replicate the original in an instrumental version but also included virtuoso solo instrumental pieces based on operatic material. Indeed, "concertos" for a solo instrument are frequently found (principally for various clarinets in various keys, particularly E-flat and B-flat, but also for trumpet and other brass instruments), which have operatic material as their starting point. In this way the band attempted to establish its distinctive nature, and it achieved this through the formation of a partly original repertory of "symphonic marches," a halfway house between marches for marching and marches to be listened to. Of course, bands did not serve up only marches, symphonic marches, and operatic extracts in different arrangements for their audience; they also offered a vast selection of "characteristic" pieces, which were selections from the great ballets of the day, dance pieces that were for the most part dressed up in concert hall and symphonic guise. As for disseminating operatic music, we can assume that the central position of the operatic repertory became established in the second half of the nineteenth century, while not forgetting that the historical chronology of band music has still to be constructed.

The importance of the band and of band music, which now encompassed all or almost all musical output (indeed, genuine orchestral compositions now entered the repertory), is not a phenomenon limited to Italy but can be seen across Europe in the second half of the nineteenth century. Evidence is to be found in the strong showing of band music in the gramophone and phonograph catalogues from the last decade of the nineteenth and first decade of the twentieth centuries. Sousa's band has an impressive position in the American Victor catalogue; and, by way of example, when in 1907 the Argentine record dealers Gath and Chaves thought of producing the first recordings of tangos, they turned to a French band (there were no recording studios in Argentina), the world-famous band of the Republican Guard. So the first tango to be documented on record was played by a band.[63]

There is no general inventory available today of the repertory of Italian bands in the nineteenth and early twentieth centuries; in any case, systematic research is made enormously difficult but the extremely incomplete and dis-

63. "El Sargento Cabral," by Manuel Oscar Campoamor. Gath y Chaves disk no. 219, recorded in Paris in 1907.

ordered nature of the surviving band archives. It should not be forgotten that scores and parts have always been practical material for bands, to be looked after as long as they were in use and usable but certainly not thought of as documents to be preserved for the purposes of future historians: they shared the common fate, after all, of so many other musical archives.

In my opinion, the most careful reconstruction of a band's repertory was carried out by Nino Albarosa (working from the research done by Alida Zanardelli, Giovanna Amighini, and Ermanna Barbaglio) on the municipal bands in Piacenza and Cremona during the period when they were directed by Amilcare Ponchielli, between 1861 and 1874.[64] It cannot be denied that the research shows the position of a band in two cities of a certain size, both having opera houses, and this is a "limitation" that should be kept in mind, as it should equally be kept in mind that the bandmaster of both was Ponchielli, a musician who was still young but who had strong tastes and ambitions (the "reductions" were mostly done by him). No doubt the situation was different in smaller centers or in villages where the band was, if not the only, then at least the principal expression of musical activity, with fewer economic and organizational means at their disposal and with a lower level of musical skill on the part of the players and bandmaster. Nevertheless, the material from Piacenza and Cremona, even for the period to which it refers, provides striking documentation and gives us an eloquent idea of the presence of opera in the band repertory of the second half of the nineteenth century.

Adam	*Si j'étais roi!* (1852)	Overture
Auber	*La muette de Portici* (1828)	Overture
Bellini	*Beatrice di Tenda* (1833)	Concerto for piccolo clarinet
		Fantasia for E-flat clarinet
		Duet
	Norma (1831)	Duet
	Il pirata (1827)	Overture
		Chorus and duet
	I puritani (1835)	Concerto for clarinet
	La sonnambula (1831)	Concert duet for E-flat piccolo clarinet and B-flat clarinet
Cagnoni	*Michele Perrin* (1864)	Overture
	La tombola (1868)	Overture
Campiani	*Bernabò Visconti* (1855)	Overture
De Ferrari	*Pipelè* (1855)	Aria
Donizetti	*Betly* (1836)	Overture
	Dom Sébastien (1843)	Souvenirs
	L'elisir d'amore (1832)	Concerto for clarinet

64. Nino Albarosa, "Amilcare Ponchielli, 'capomusica' a Piacenza e Cremona (1861–1874)," in *Amilcare Ponchielli, 1834–1886: Saggi e ricerche nel 150° anniversario della nascita* (Casalmorano: Cassa Rurale ed Artigiana, 1984), 93–124.

	La favorita (1840)	Ensemble piece
		Potpourri
		Aria and chorus
		Souvenirs
		Final duet
		Act 2 finale
		Act 3 finale
	Gemma di Vergy (1834)	Potpourri
		Final aria
	Linda di Chamounix (1842)	Duet and trio, act 2 finale
		Scena and final duet
	Lucia di Lammermoor (1835)	Concerto for clarinet
		Divertimento
		Cavatina
		Aria
	Lucrezia Borgia (1833)	Cavatina for B-flat clarinet
		Scena, duet, and trio, act 2 finale
	Maria di Rohan (1843)	Cavatina
		Reminiscences
		Aria
	Roberto Devereux (1837)	Cavatina
		Aria
Flotow	*Alessandro Stradella* (1844)	Overture
	Martha (1847)	Medley
		March
Foroni	*I gladiatori* (1851)	Aria
	Margherita (1848)	Duet
Gounod	*Faust* (1859)	Potpourri
		Kermesse chorus
		Chorus, introduction to act 2
		Serenade, trio, and act 4 finale
		Waltz
		Ballad and Jewel Song
		Grand duet and act 3 finale
		Duet
Hérold	*Le pré-aux-clercs* (1832)	Overture
	Zampa (1831)	Overture
Lamberti	*Malek Adel* (1851)	Overture
Manna	*Preziosa* (1845)	Overture
Marchetti	*Ruy Blas* (1869)	Duet
		Duet, trio, and finale
Mercadante	*Il bravo* (1839)	Aria
	Il giuramento (1837)	Recollections
		Prelude and aria
		Prelude, chorus, and aria
		Duet and chorus
	Gli Orazi e i Curiazi (1846)	March and chorus
		Chorus and oath
		March, chorus, and oath
		Chorus and trio
	La vestale (1840)	Overture

		Act 2 finale
		Aria
Meyerbeer	*Dinorah* (1859)	Potpourri
		Trio and act 2 finale
	Les Huguenots (1836)	Oath and blessing of weapons
	Robert le diable (1831)	Potpourri
		Final trio
Pacini	*Saffo* (1840)	Cavatina
		Duet
		Aria
		Act 2 finale
		Chorus and act 2 finale
Pedrotti	*Fiorina* (1851)	Potpourri
		Overture
		Souvenirs
	Isabella d'Aragona (1859)	March
	Tutti in maschera (1856)	Overture
		Duet
Petrella	*L'assedio di Leida* (1856)	Cavatina
	Il carnevale di Venezia (1851)	Buffo quartet
		"Bivacco"
	La contessa d'Amalfi (1864)	Scena and duet
	Jone (1858)	Scena, duet, and act 2 finale
		Duet and act 2 finale
	Marco Visconti (1854)	Romanza and march
		Prelude, romanza, and march
Ponchielli	*La savoiarda* (1861)	Souvenirs
		Overture
Federico Ricci	*Una follia a Roma* (1869)	March
Luigi Ricci	*Il birraio di Preston* (1847)	March
L. and F. Ricci	*Crispino e la comare* (1850)	Reminiscences
Rossi	*Gli artisti alla fiera* (1868)	Overture
Rossini	*Il barbiere di Siviglia*	Rosina's aria
		Cavatina
	La cenerentola (1817)	Overture
	Guillaume Tell (1829)	Duet
		Trio
		Chorus and pas de six
		Act 2 duet
		Overture
	L'italiana in Algeri (1813)	Overture
	Mosè in Egitto (1818)	Prelude and introduction
	Semiramide (1823)	Chorus and cavatina "Bel raggio lusinghier"
		Duet
		Aria
		Potpourri
Sanelli	*Il fornaretto* (1851)	Recollections
		Duet and final aria
Usiglio	*Le educande di Sorrento* (1868)	First potpourri
		Second potpourri
Verdi	*Aida* (1871)	March and act 2 finale

Aroldo (1857)	Overture
	Scena and aria
	Act 2 prelude and aria
	Duet
Un ballo in maschera (1859)	Reminiscences
	Potpourri
	Fragments from the introduction
	Ballata and act 1 finale
	Romanza and act 3 quintet
	Act 3 introduction and quintet stretta
	Act 2 introduction, romanza, and final duet
	Act 3 introduction, oath, and quintet
Il corsaro (1848)	Aria
	Gulnara's aria
Don Carlos (1867)	Duet
	Philippe's aria, Song of the Veil, and the queen's romanza
	Festive chorus and march of the cortège
	Act 3 festive chorus, funeral march, and grand ensemble
	Act 3 march and grand finale
I due Foscari (1844)	Medley
	Fantasia
	Souvenirs
	Aria
	Final scene
	Grand potpourri
Ernani (1844)	Aria
	Scena and cavatina
La forza del destino (1862)	Overture
	Prelude, romanza, and rataplan
	Act 2 finale
	Prelude and romanza
Giovanna d'Arco (1845)	Overture
I Lombardi (1843)	Aria
Luisa Miller (1849)	Selected highlights
	Souvenirs
	Potpourri
	Aria
Macbeth (1847)	Aria
	Brindisi and act 2 finale
	Prelude and introductory chorus
	Romanza and act 3 finale
Nabucco (1842)	Overture
Rigoletto (1851)	Grand capriccio
	Souvenirs
	Concerto for clarinet
	Scene and duet
	Duet
La traviata (1853)	Concerto for flugelhorn

	Duet
	Concerto for cornet
	Concerto for clarinet
	Prelude, introduction, brindisi, and duet
	Concerto for trumpet
	Prelude, introduction, waltz, and duet
Il trovatore (1853)	Duet, trio, and act 4 finale
	Duet
	Grand potpourri
	Souvenirs
I vespri siciliani (1855)	Duet and act I finale
	Overture
	Duet
	Scena and duet

The influence of opera on band music, by an apparently indirect route, can be seen in the fortunes of a unique band from the Po Valley, now more than a century old, which has always operated in a village and peasant environment, playing exclusively for dances. This is the Concerto Cantoni, which was formed in the 1860s by a peasant from Mezzani, a village between Reggio Emilia and Parma. Giovanni Cantoni played the flugelhorn in the band in Brescello and had the idea of making use of his musical ability outside his band duties; so he put together a small group of players to provide dance music in Mezzani and the surrounding villages. It was at this time that the "modern" dances—the waltz, polka, and mazurka—burst into working-class life; these dances entered popular use from an "elevated" milieu and were superimposed on the traditional dances. Such was the success of the first Concerto Cantoni—"concerto" being the name given to dance bands in the duchies of Emilia—that Giovanni Cantoni made all his thirteen children, including the girls, learn an instrument and formed a musical group that was almost entirely made up of family members. The group is still going, although no longer as a family concern, and is led by one of Giovanni's great-grandsons, Serino Cantoni. (The Concerto Cantoni make a memorable appearance in Bertolucci's 1970 film *The Spider's Stratagem.*)

The Concerto Cantoni put together its own repertory, entirely made up of original compositions. Its uninterrupted tradition means that it is possible to pick out important details of the Cantoni style and to isolate the different musical levels that have taken root in their repertory. As I have said, the Concerto Cantoni now, as in the past, performs only dance music, but the style, remarkably rich in musical terms, has high aspirations: indeed, it is easy to make out its operatic nature in the sophisticated taste for "bel canto" forms. In many pieces the E-flat clarinet tackles long, demanding phrases in imitation of the acrobatics of bel canto opera. These pieces have their roots far more in Bellini, Rossini, Donizetti, and early Verdi than in late-nineteenth-century composers;

many passages and closing sections are operatic in style, as indeed can be the case for the entire tone of a composition. Opera is joined by operetta and other more "modern" sources in an extraordinary mixture that inevitably reminds one of the formative period of early jazz, with its synthesis of black tradition with many elements from white culture, including opera, which a leading opera house, that of New Orleans, contributed to the new musical style.

Some research into bands has now begun, and there has been an awakening of interest, not merely as local history, in the story, function, and social and cultural position of this important musical institution. However, there is still a lack of interest in two other agents of the dissemination of music in working-class environments (and elsewhere): choral singing and mandolin groups. And yet choral and mandolin groups have been a constant presence in musical life in the past and have been important in shaping taste and in making certain repertories widely known.

A last example comes to mind, to broaden out this colorful but still mysterious landscape populated by the instruments and voices that have passed operatic music on to an audience excluded from the opera house: the panpipe bands, which have become remarkably widespread (despite their irritating "folksy" quality) in the provinces of Como and Bergamo, with offshoots in those of Varese and Milan.

These are genuine all-panpipe bands (whose dialect names are *firlinfö, siful*, or *gratamüsun*). Some have quite a few players, on different-sized instruments, from sopranino to bass, and they perform a fairly mixed repertory: as well as arrangements of Lombard popular and folk songs, composed songs (canzonets), operetta numbers, marches, and "characteristic" pieces mostly devoted to celebrating the beauties of the village (and its women), there is room for operatic pieces. The *firlinfö* could already be found in Lombardy in the first half of the nineteenth century, played either as a solo instrument or in groups of two or three, but in the beginning of the twentieth century, ever larger, ordered groups, organized along band lines, started to appear. And in the villages that had these panpipe bands, they were viewed as a surrogate for or alternative to the more usual municipal band. We can therefore surmise that the *firlinfö* took over the operatic repertory of the band, marginal though these pieces may have been, especially nowadays, when the stress is on the folkloristic function of the groups and the presentation of "local culture" at fairs, tourist festivals, and the like. From the limited data available at the present moment,[65] it seems nevertheless that in the past, when the *firlinfö* carried

---

65. Until recently there was only local journalism on the *firlinfö*, which lacked historical depth and was written in a chauvinistic, provincial tone. Giorgio Foti's research, under my guidance ("Il flauto di Pan in Lombardia" [graduate thesis, Bologna University, 1985–86]), began to open new perspectives on a phenomenon that, behind the rather irritating image of facile folklore, conceals folk roots and causes.

out a local musical role, operatic music had a stronger presence. Even today, for example, a potpourri from *Rigoletto* is in the repertory, and the performance is, for good or ill, unforgettable.

9. THE VILLAGE MUSIC LOVER AND VIOLETTA IN CHURCH

I'm sure that many readers will remember men from their town who entertained themselves and their friends in the *osteria* by singing operatic arias. And I imagine that these people were peasants, carpenters, or postmen, or in any case men "of the people."

I am perfectly aware that in the past there were many such "village music lovers," and that they still exist (although I doubt if any is younger than fifty): such people are undoubtedly evidence of the circulation achieved by operatic music in places far from cities, great or small, with an opera house and an opera season, but at the same time they testify to the "nonpopularity" of opera. In fact, they are eccentrics and represent something "abnormal" with their sincere passion and their fairly extensive knowledge of the operatic repertory (not always the most typical), and although they bring opera into lives that might even be prepared to welcome it, they are nevertheless not able to implant a musical tradition that, in spite of everything, remains "alien" to the world of the peasant and village culture. Their attitude toward music and singing is the opposite of the community one of folk practice, and they turn their listeners into an audience. In this connection I can cite two experiences of my own. In a village in the Mantua area, beside the Po, there was (and possibly there still is, although he must be quite an age by now) a porter at the station who had an almost extreme passion for opera and a repertory that was as unusual as it was interesting. In the *osteria,* as soon as conversation faltered or died, and when the other patrons stopped singing, he would burst into a loud "operatic" voice and sing arias from *Marino Faliero, Poliuto, Les Huguenots* (to him *Gli ugonotti*), and *Rigoletto*. His friends would listen to him for a minute or two, then one of them would make a gesture of turning a button on his chest, as if switching the radio off. And the singing would stop instantly. It seems to me that that humorous gesture indicated an attitude of alienation from operatic music, music that arrived in the *osteria* by way the radio. "Proper" songs would then start up again, sung by everyone who was there, no longer spectators but actors.

I had another interesting (but very different) experience more than thirty years ago in an *osteria* on the outskirts of Milan. The *osteria* is no longer there, nor are the house and delightful summer arbor. On Sunday afternoons, the men whose local this was (workers, some craftsmen, a taxi driver, retired men) would organize an extraordinary kind of *café-chantant*, a show that almost everyone took part in, alternately actors, singers, and spectators. These performances were an incredible anthology of the history of theater: the satirical singer (and it was here I first heard the surreal story of the "Balilla," long before it became a Milan cabaret number), the ventriloquist, the reciter, the comedian, the singer of Neapolitan songs (in a beautiful Milanese accent), the impressionist, someone who performed the comedian Ettore Petrolini's most successful routines, and also an operatic singer accompanied by accordion. The atmosphere in that bar was quite different from that in the one beside the Po: an urban, modern concept of the "show" had entered their consciousness, even if such a show was expressed in a continual change of roles, which ensured simultaneously the popular function of participating and the bourgeois taste for "attending." Despite being restored to the urban context (but still "popular" in nature) of a "variety show," the operatic quotation sounded alien and different from the other numbers, which popular opinion deemed far less dignified and, in a number of cases, were downright lewd.

As I see it, in popular culture the presence of opera can be found in circumstances that, within the prevailing context, place the operatic idiom in a space that is entirely or relatively "alien." Of course, anyone who has undertaken research will have found folk singers who include some operatic quotations in a repertory of traditional or popular songs. But these have been infrequent cases in my experience; and each time I have had to take account of how the operatic piece is modified and, especially, adapted—changes that may not make it less immediately recognizable but nevertheless express the (incomplete) tendency to align the music with the manners of the folk tradition. The melodic line and the text stayed relatively intact, but all the modulations—a procedure which is unknown in folk song—had been eliminated, just as all the stylistic signs of operatic singing had been lost. It is precisely in the extreme difficulty of reproducing operatic music beyond the melodic surface (itself largely reduced) that the alien nature of this music to the folk context is displayed.

Another area of musical activity that has undoubtedly taken on elements directly and indirectly from the operatic tradition is that of church singing; it is an area that has long been ignored, though it has represented something important in the life of the people, and only now has it started to be considered. An enormous body of songs has been divided into repertories that are extremely varied and thus able to coexist. Indeed, musical styles that are undoubtedly archaic, oral, and popular in nature and have mostly been applied to liturgical texts in Latin have long been present. But we come up against an equally vast repertory of nineteenth-century compositions, many of which are clearly operatic in style. Furthermore, there are examples of particular operatic melodies being adapted to sacred texts, also in Latin. I shall give two examples.

In Sessa Aurunca, in the province of Caserta, during the Lenten liturgy, a "Miserere" of very problematic origins is sung by three male voices, using a polyvocal style (as well as a way of producing the sound) that suggests that it is an archaic piece.[66] But in the course of the same liturgy, one of the singers of the "Miserere" performs nineteenth-century songs of clear operatic derivation, including the Lamentations of Jeremiah (in Latin, naturally) on a particularly lovely Donizettian tune. The Sessa Aurunca example demonstrates how the "new" can coexist with the "old" without influencing it: the two levels are felt and experienced independently.

In the Ossola valleys, Carlo Oltolina, the only Italian researcher to have made a systematic study of liturgical music in the oral tradition, has revealed the wide use of the Verdi aria "Di Provenza il mar, il suol," to intone litanies. As Oltolina observes:

> The writer has experienced this directly [i.e., litanies sung to the Verdi aria] and can in all sincerity declare that there was nothing disturbing about this melody for the litany, in the context of the ceremony; in fact, it had a certain weight, an intrinsic appeal which left no one untouched, to the extent that it itself electrified the place, drawing everyone in to a collective and enthusiastic involvement, and transforming the encounter with evening prayer into something festive.[67]

10. RADAMES, A.K.A. BARATIERI

Remo Melloni's research[68] has revealed to us the existence of an extremely interesting tradition of folk theater in the Po Valley, which has aroused considerable curiosity. I'm referring to what is known as "stable theater," which was a living tradition across the Reggio plain until World War II.

The stable, as we know, has always had an important function in folk culture. During the winter, this location, kept mild by the presence of livestock, was a meeting place for peasant families. Usually, the larger, more comfortable stables would accommodate several families, and whoever was not a family member, that is, a guest, would make a contribution by bringing some oil for the lantern. In northern Italian stables, whether in the mountains or on the plain, the placing of participants in the evening was rigorous and functional. In the center, under the lantern, would sit, when present, the "reader," who entertained by reading popular novels (like the hugely successful *Guerrin Meschino,* for example) or even frankly "difficult" and demanding texts, such as the Book of Wisdom. Next to him were the women, sewing or embroidering, and round about, the babies and young children. Farther off were the men, who, doing nothing, had no need of light. In the stables, people would listen to the reading, tell stories, converse, and begin love affairs; young men

---

66. See Pierluigi Gallo, "Il 'Miserere' polivocale in Sessa Aurunca," in *Musica e liturgia nella cultura mediterranea,* ed. Piero G. Arcangeli (Florence: Olschki, 1988), 69–94.

67. Carlo Oltolina, *I salmi di tradizione orale delle Valli Ossolane* (Milan: Ricordi, 1984), 81.

68. See Remo Melloni, "Aida e Radames appesi a un filo," *Gazzetta del Museo Teatrale alla Scala,* no. 1 (winter 1985–86): 51–55.

would go from stable to stable to look for marriageable girls. In this way, the stable represented the location and the opportunity for encounters, under the universal gaze, permitted by fairly rigid laws—at least formally—of peasant society.

In the Canavese Mountains, at Locana, in the province of Turin, Amerigo Vigliermo has collected a song that exemplifies the function of the stable:[69]

E sa nan sun i fijöi dël Gile	[It's the young men of Gile (place-name)
ca van a fè l'amur 'l Tet	going to make love in Tet (place-name).
van a ca de l'Angilinota	They go to the house of Angilinota,
ca l'è la pì bela del temp	who is the loveliest at the moment.
Giuaninot entra ant la stala	Giuaninot goes into the stable
e cun al sò capel burdà	with his cap with the hem.
buna seira l'Angilinota	"Good evening, Angilinota,
e pöi tuta la stala	and to all in the stable."
Sua mare i prunta la banca	Her mother (Angilinota's) gets him a seat.
Giuaninot venive stè	"Giuaninot, come and sit down
si dacant a l'Angilinota	beside Angilinota,
a venila a cunsulè	and come and comfort her."
A sun bütase ciancé discure	They started to chat and talk
ciancé e discure dell'amur	chat and talk of love
o sentì 'n po' l'Angilinota	"Listen Angilinota,
cuma 'l va si bel discurs	how this lovely talking goes.
E l'ureta l'è già 'n po' tarda	Now it's a little late
e'l me camion l'è 'n poc luntan	and I've a long way to go.
buna seira l'Angilinota	"Good night, Angilinota.
o tucheme 'n poc la man	Oh, touch my hand."
E mi la man la tucheria	"And I would touch your hand
mac si füsu mac nui dui	if it were just us two alone,
pöi mi sun d'üna povra fia	and I'm a poor girl,
Giuaninot fas pa per vui	Giuaninot, I'm not for you."
Ma si seve na povra fia	"But if you're a poor girl,
e tüt lulì völ pa dì nen	none of this means a thing.
ma si veni en casa mia	If you come home with me,
là au mancrà pöi pa pì nen	you'll want for nothing.
Dizime an pò Angilinota	Tell me, Angilinota,
ëd chi nan sun cui bei bö	whose are these fine oxen?"
a nan sun del mio padre	"They're my father's.
l'à vendüne dui ancöi	He sold two of them today."

69. The LP record *Canti popolari del Piemonte*, vol. 1, *Il Canavese*, ed. Roberto Leydi and Amerigo Vigliermo, Albatros VPA 8416.

Dizime ancura Angilinota	"And tell me this, Angilinota.
'd chi nan sun cui bei crin	"Whose are these fine boars?"
a nan sun della mia mamma	"Oh, they're my mother's,
o che Dio av daga del bin	may God bless you."]

The stable, the winter "arts center" of the peasant world, was also the location for "theatrical" performances. In essence, the rite of admission of young men visiting the stable was already a piece of theater: from outside a group of boys would sing a verse by way of request, and those inside would reply by posing questions, and those outside would, still in song, have to give the correct answers. The game consisted of leaving the "visitors" out in the cold as long as possible. Then permission to enter would be given, after the young men had paid due homage to the head of the family: one "trick" would be to change the tune of the questions (the song would have at least two different tunes), and if the answers were not given in the new form, then the whole thing would have to begin again. But more complex forms were also presented in the stable: at Christmas, across Piedmont, the pastoral drama of Gelindo[70] would be played, and during Carnival ballads would be acted out, not a difficult feat, since the dialogue structure makes it easy to adapt them to a dramatic form.

This digression on the activities in the stable forms a backdrop for the remarkable phenomenon of "stable theater," which, according to the research data available, came into being in the middle of the nineteenth century in a part of the Reggio plain bordering the (mountain) home of what is known as the dramatic *maggio*. The Reggio stable theater thus seems to correspond, on the plain, to the epic *maggio*, in more modern forms and to a certain extent influenced by "bourgeois" theater.

Among the many scripts which Remo Melloni has identified, one is particularly important with regard to the discussion of the dissemination of opera. This is the incredible—and amazingly inspired—reinterpretation of Verdi's *Aida* that was found in manuscript form in Bibbiano and was performed during Carnival in 1897. The script of this stable version of *Aida* is taken from the enormously successful reelaboration of the libretto of Verdi's opera by Valerio Busnelli, published in 1887 (*Aida, o I Faraoni,* drama in four acts and two scenes), with the probable insertion, during the course of the performance, of some sections sung to Verdi's music. The author of the script, Anselmo Alvisi, also added some comic interludes between each act and in the middle of the fourth: the characters in the interludes are "buffo" ones, comic characters called Tibicinci, Scanapolastri, Caganespole, Portacagnett a pissèr, and two "blacks," who do not speak but, according to a stage direction, "make African gestures." The buffo characters represent those soldiers under

70. See Rodolfo Renier, *Il Gelindo, dramma sacro piemontese della Natività di Cristo* (Turin: Clausen, 1896).

Radames who in the libretto of the opera, as in Busnelli's reelaboration, do not speak and appear only as extras; but, at the same time, they are also the Italian soldiers who, in that very period, were being sent on the orders of General Baratieri to fight the Abyssinians. And Anselmo Alvisi noticed this "coincidence," making the point that the four interludes are "intelligently in harmony with the drama and at the same time touch on and correspond with the present day."

It is hard to believe that the eighteenth-century tradition of the intermezzo reached the stable theater and survived there until the beginning of our century; it is more likely that this theatrical form was "invented" by the stable theater. Normally, there were two genres in stable theater: *rime* and *farse*. *Rime* were texts on serious subjects, proper plays or dramas, in Italian for the noble characters and in dialect for the comic ones; *farse*, however, were entirely in dialect. The style of the *Aida* is a fusion of the two genres.

In the intermezzos, the buffo characters transfer the action of *Aida* to contemporary life: whereas in the part derived from the Verdi original, the Egyptian army wages war on the king of Ethiopia, in the intermezzos, the Reggio peasants relive the same situation as desperate soldiers of the royal army, who, under the orders of General Baratieri, who has taken the place of Radames, are being sent to fight in Abyssinia. The shift of the remote "Egyptian" action to the Italy of 1896 logically involves a "critical" reading of the libretto of the Verdi: for example, the Italian soldiers (played by the buffo characters in the intermezzos) will personally encounter the "humanity" of the Ethiopians, who are not the savages described in propaganda but "Christian folk" who eat bread the same way the Emilian peasants do. However, the stroke of genius is the interpretation of the fate of Radames as equally the enemy (like Baratieri) of the peasant-soldiers and the Ethiopians; but when, for love, he is condemned to a terrible death, he reveals himself to be what he is in reality, nothing more than an instrument in the hand of those who really hold the reins of power, that is, the Egyptian religious leaders, or, in the folk reading, "priests."

This stable version of *Aida* is certainly evidence of the popularity of Verdi's opera, but the way in which it is represented suggests a few considerations. The Reggio peasants' *Aida*, I am well aware, throws the merest chink of light on the topic: after all, it belongs to an area where opera was present and widespread, where opera had greater circulation, even in genuinely "popular" and peasant areas, than elsewhere; furthermore, this part of the country, as early as the end of the nineteenth century, was very sensitive to political life and was where new socialist, antimilitary, and anticlerical ideas were broadly in evidence. As Melloni rightly observed:

> Such a piece of work [that is, the Bibbiano *Aida*] [is] a decidedly avant-garde one for the period, but, as always, profoundly functional for the world of the people; it

allowed a community to articulate its attitude not only to a war it considered unjust and absurd, but also toward a power which administered a justice with which the people did not always agree. It should not be forgotten that in Bibbiano a mutual aid association had developed several years before, and that various cooperatives had come into being. In addition, there was a lively opposition between political power and the Church, and so it was not difficult to identify the Church with the priests who condemn Radames to death.[71]

Nonetheless, even considering the text as something special or exceptional, one cannot avoid the feeling that, broadly throughout the world of the people, opera and its echoes were received quite differently from the bourgeois audiences in the theater; opera was measured against an experience of life and culture that was not that of the well-off or of urban tradesmen, and it was compared with the material conditions of a class that was still paying, with their efforts and their hunger, for the beginnings of capitalism.

11. THE WOODEN-HEADED PRIMA DONNA

It is well known that marionettes have been involved in opera since the seventeenth century, lending their shapes of wood and cloth, capable of incredible verisimilitude and at the same time of acrobatic flights, to the music of some famous composers. It is not my intention to discuss the singspiels that Haydn wrote for the puppet theater at Eszterháza (their music has been almost entirely lost), but it is perhaps worthwhile to consider briefly some Italian examples to try to understand the revolution that the nineteenth century wrought in this area as well.

While nowadays we are accustomed to linking the puppet theater with a rather generic idea of "folk" theater, this is at odds with the position in the seventeenth and eighteenth centuries, when marionettes were primarily an aristocratic theatrical form. The Venetian marionette opera seasons to which historians have referred admiringly were given in noble, sophisticated surroundings. In Venice in the seventeenth and eighteenth centuries—as in most Italian cities—puppet shows were often given in the squares, for the entertainment of an urban audience of predominantly the common people; in them a large part was played by improvisation, and references to everyday life added an essential spice. While puppets played in the public squares, marionettes appeared in grand houses and theaters with another repertory, other intentions, and another audience: and above all they were performed with music.

Reporting to his master, the resident minister of Tuscany, Matteo Del Teglia, noted on 14 October 1679 that among the "remarkable" things in Venice, "at the Teatro di San Moisè there will be an opera with some newly invented figurines."[72] In the summer of that very year, musical performances

---

71. Melloni, "Aida e Radames," 55.
72. See Nicola Mangini, *I teatri di Venezia* (Milan: Mursia, 1974), 47.

with marionettes had been seen in a private Venetian home: according to Giovanni Carlo Bonlini's theater chronology, *Il Leandro,* text by Camillo Badovero and music by Francesco Antonio Pistocchi, was "performed with wooden figures, with singers behind the scenes, in a house on the bank, or Fondamenta, known as Le Zattare, toward the Ogni Santi church."[73] In the Carnival seasons of 1680–82, when the San Moisè was not presenting a regular opera season and was "entirely dilapidated inside," it "was made to serve for the playing of figures, sometimes of wood, sometimes of wax, with which operas were performed."[74] In 1680, *Damira placata,* a remake of Aureli's *Fortune di Rodope e Damira* (1657), was given, with the music completely rewritten by Marc'Antonio Ziani. The sort of interest the undertaking aroused is indicated by the poetic dedication in the libretto "to the curious," signed by "Fine humor," who boasts of "the most hidden secrets / of art and of nature," the "effort of human ingenuity" which has come to "bring to life a piece of wood with silent gestures." It must have been quite a success, as the following year the same successful theater gave *L'Ulisse in Feacia* (an anonymous libretto—attributed, without much foundation, to Filippo Acciaiuoli—set to music by the Neapolitan cavalier Antonio Del Gaudio), but this time with improved actors (if they can be described as such): figures of wax rather than wood. The libretto announces: "if eyes were formerly delighted by the sight of human attitudes well expressed by a piece of wood, now with wax figures they will experience greater amazement than did Daedalus, for they will not expect to fall headlong." *L'Ulisse in Feacia* was revived in Naples in January of the following year, 1682, "in the home of the duke of Atri." It is entirely possible that when the composer set out from Venice to Naples with his score, the wax figures traveled with him. Nonetheless, operas with marionettes continued to be given at the San Moisè: in the 1682 Carnival season, *Gl'amori fatali* was nothing more than a revival, under a different name, of the private *Leandro* from the summer of 1679 (possibly with the same puppets), while with *Il Girello* we definitely encounter, if only as the author of the libretto, the poet Filippo Acciaiuoli, an impresario and adventurer who had had a trade in marionettes—and opera—in both Florence and Rome.[75]

73. Giovanni Carlo Bonlini, *Le glorie della poesia e della musica contenute dell'esatta notizia de' teatri della città di Venezia* (Venice: Bonarigo, 1730), 90. The time of year is given by Cristoforo Ivanovich in "Memorie teatrali di Venezia," in his *Minerva al tavolino* (1681), 2d ed. (Venice: Pezzana, 1688), 361–452, quotation on 442.

74. Bonlini, *Le glorie della poesia,* 22.

75. Alessandro Ademollo refers to Acciaiuoli, his puppet theater, and his staging of operas with marionettes (without, however, discriminating between verifiable and fictitious information) in his *I teatri di Roma nel secolo decimosettimo* (Rome: Pasqualucci, 1888; reprint, Bologna: Forni, 1969), 123–28, 256 (where the name "Cav. Ricciardi," who is supposed to have staged a *Giasone* in 1678 "with his puppets in the home of the signora principessa di Sonnino," should be read as "Acciaiuoli"; see Filippo Clementi, *Il carnevale romano nelle cronache contemporanee dalle origini al sec. XVII,* 2 vols. [Città del Castello: R.O.R.E.-NIRVF, 1939], 1:603).

In Venice, puppet shows with music continued to flourish throughout the eighteenth century. The ones given in Ca' Grimani at Santa Maria dei Servi in a little theater "for opera performed by marionettes in which ladies and knights sang" (1720)[76] and at Ca' Contarini at San Barnaba, and at Ca' Loredan at San Vio have all remained famous. And the fashion took hold on dry land as well, as can be seen in the marionette performances promoted by the Ravegnani counts in Verona. Here we need only focus on what was probably the eighteenth-century high point in Venetian puppet opera: the performances in the private puppet theater that Abbé Antonio Labia had built in his palace in Cannaregio, in the San Girolamo quarter, which was active during Carnival between 1746 and 1748. This was a scale model of the then famous Teatro San Giovanni Grisostomo:

> The stage, the boxes, and all the other decorations were equally a precise imitation of it, and even the machines and the internal wheels operated in exactly the same way. The whole building was comfortably contained in an average-sized room in the house. And the performers were represented by figurines of wax or wood, who walked, gestured, and made all the other necessary movements with such ingenious artifice that it was as difficult to grasp as it was entertaining to see. The costumes and lighting also corresponded; in the orchestra the players were represented by a host of other figurines, in the boxes were the masked members of the audience, and in the *piazza* [that is, the stalls] were the other spectators. A company of fine singers, men and women, behind the stage, brought the performers to life and sang the opera, with the customary accompaniment of numerous instruments, in such a way that nothing was left to be desired.[77]

The performance was open to local and visiting nobility—the duchess of Modena also attended—on invitation from the master of the house, the "generous, not to mention splendid, gentleman," who "generously served the listeners with excellent and copious refreshments." The librettos of the operas given also appeared in miniature form, printed in 24mo. The operas shown were, in 1746, *Il Cajetto* (by Antonio Gori and Ferdinando Bertoni), *Lo starnuto d'Ercole* (a reworking of an old libretto by Pier Jacopo Martello, with arias by Hasse), *Eurimedonte e Timocleone ovvero I rivali delusi* (seemingly by Girolamo Zanetti, again with arias by Hasse); in 1747, Metastasio's *Didone abbandonata* in a setting by Andrea Adolfati; in 1748, the same libretto but set by Ferdinando Bertoni, as well as *Gianguir* by Zeno with music by Geminiano Giacomelli.[78]

76. See Mangini, *I teatri di Venezia*, 181. The Grimani theater is preserved in the Ca' Rezzonico Museum in Venice.

77. Antonio Groppo, *Notizia generale de' teatri della città di Venezia* (Venice: Savioni, 1776), 13ff., 178.

78. The repertory information is taken from Taddeo Wiel, *I teatri musicali veneziani del Settecento* (Venice: Visentini, 1897 *ad annos;* reprint, Bologna: Forni, 1978). Antonella Zaggia has

Mention could be made here of other examples of opera performed with marionettes—and often written especially for this type of "toy theater"—found throughout the entire length of Italy in the seventeenth and eighteenth centuries, with a great deal of information on Rome, Florence, and Bologna in particular. The Venetian examples are sufficient, however, to make the alterations which came in with the nineteenth century stand out all the more clearly. I have already mentioned how the essential difference between puppet theater and theater with marionettes lies, apart from the different techniques of construction and operation, in the type of audience, at least up until the middle of the nineteenth century, and in part afterward as well. Because they were able to imitate "human" performers, marionettes generally followed and supplemented the "leading" dramatic genres in their work: this explains why they had basically the same repertoire as "superior" theater, and why they had basically the same audience: an audience that was originally an aristocratic one, then an urban, middle-class one. When, with the upheaval caused by the French Revolution and Napoleon's bayonets, court and family theaters lost their raison d'être and function, and more public theaters opened their doors, marionettes persevered in offering audiences astounding spectacles of fantasy and acrobatics. But the reference was always to that level of performance, spoken or sung, that constituted the "superior" theater of the day.

It should not be forgotten that, to take only one example, for the entire first half of the nineteenth century and for a number of years afterward, the Teatro Fiando in Milan, also known as the Gerolamo, was the place to be seen not only for the best Milanese society, headed by the viceroy, but also for every visiting traveler who was the least bit alert and discerning, but when marionette theater as a "high art" example of urban theatrical life reached a crisis point, it became plebeian and itinerant, reaching the provinces and even villages, with a different audience, which was largely made up of the common people.

The repertory was renovated but did not, however, become independent. It no longer referred to what was seen in the great, principal theaters where the middle class celebrated its status as an empowered class. Instead it became a "folk" theater, in which, despite the rhetorical and sentimental nature of the performances, the audience was hoping to see onstage the fears, anxieties, and even the problems of their day, however much disguised in a confused and jumbled style that was feeling its way toward literary naturalism. It is in this way that the "material" of nineteenth-century opera penetrated marionette theater. And it penetrated, for the most part, not by repeating the successes of the leading opera houses, but by suggesting lively "stories," "facts,"

given a detailed historical account of this subject in "'La fiera delle bagatalle': Il teatro musicale per marionette di San Girolamo (Venezia 1746–1748)," *Rassegna veneta di studi musicali* 2–3 (1986–87): 133–71.

and "events" which could be read, possibly obliquely, in the light of current events. Undoubtedly the fame of the most successful operas played a part in the choice of what was transferred to the marionette theater; it is symptomatic, however, that not only were the great operas presented and rewritten for marionette theater, but other dramas not sanctified by operatic setting made their way into the repertory. Victorien Sardou dominated this area, and often it was his original texts, rather than their transformation into librettos, that provided the puppet-masters with the material for their scripts. I use the term "original text," but perhaps it would be better to say popular version, already rewritten and possibly transferred from the original script into story form, circulated in the nineteenth century and into the early twentieth by popular publishers. So one has to approach a *Tosca* in the marionette repertory with caution: while one would instinctively think that this was a transposition of the libretto of Puccini's opera, a closer observation of the text can often reveal that the marionette version does not derive from the libretto but rather from Sardou's play or from a popular reduction of it.

This is an important point in the discussion of the diffusion of opera, even beyond its reuse in marionette and puppet theaters. As Remo Melloni has rightly observed, the "plots" of the operas became largely independent of the music. If it is then taken into consideration that the music of the operas was encountered in versions for instruments alone (principally performances by bands), then we must seriously reconsider the value and meaning of this "dissociated" circulation of Italian opera outside the theater before the advent of records and, later, radio. Returning to marionette-players and puppeteers, Remo Melloni makes the following observations:

> The textual reductions that marionette-players and puppeteers made were almost exclusively related to the plot. Very often the music was absent. In some cases they inserted masked characters who served as a conduit between the drama and the audience. So in the reduction of *Attila,* the masked characters of Sandrone and Sgorghiguelo appear among the Roman soldiers led by Ezio.
>
> In some marionette companies, especially those that worked in permanent theaters, a small group played the dances, songs, and a reduction of the prelude to the opera being performed. This was partly because a dance repertory was circulated before the operatic one, which obviously required a small band, usually five or six players, with piano, violin, double bass, and clarinet.
>
> The puppeteers often used mechanical organs, and when the "piazza" allowed, they also enlisted members of the band of the village where they were performing. Only Giulio and Guglielmo Preti, both puppeteers from Modena, who were active for a large part of the year (from four to six months) in a permanent theater, had a small band mostly made up of wind instruments.[79]

79. Melloni, "Aida e Radames," 53.

Through the puppet shows, the "stories" of the operas reached the audience in this way, without music, or almost. And generally they reached the audience not, as has been noted, directly from the libretto (in verses that were hard to understand) but by way of popular reworking. To quote again from Melloni:

> There was a huge amount of activity in publishing popular stories at the end of the nineteenth and beginning of the twentieth centuries: these were booklets of around 130 pages, all taken from librettos, which related the stories of *Aida, Trovatore, Traviata,* and *Roberto il diavolo* in simple language. These texts, which were also sold from market stalls, were intended exclusively for a popular readership and were read in the stables during the winter by the peasants of Emilia. It was these very texts which inspired the performances given at Carnival time in the stables. The texts included *Aida, I due Foscari, La forza del destino, Roberto il diavolo, Giuditta e Oloferne,* and *Otello.*

It should be noted that the majority of these popular reelaborations of opera librettos introduced profound and quite decisive alterations to the original text. Tragic endings, for example, were almost always transformed into happy ones, a reversal to serve the audience the booklets were intended for that counters the very sense of the dramaturgy of the opera. Valerio Busnelli's *Aida, o I faraoni,* ends thus:

> Scene Two [of act 4].
> The houris' paradise, splendidly lit by Bengal fires. A large number of virgins will form a tableau, and two of these will crown Aida and Radames. The music at this point will swell to full orchestra.
> End of the drama.

Clearly, the audience for whom Busnelli was writing his adaptation of *Aida* would not have gone home happy with a lingering dark image of the dead lovers in the terrible tomb. This, too, asks us to think about the way in which our operas were received by the popular audience: in a sort of reversal of their sense, which raises many questions on the "connections" between opera and people.

Also striking is that it was not only the most "popular" operas which reached wooden performers but also operas which we might judge to be sophisticated for the time. It may be no surprise that the company of Luciano Zane (one of the leading ones) staged *Aida.* The company announced on the poster the work's descent "from the opera of Cavaliere Maestro Verdi" but transformed it into a "grandiose pantomime adorned with astounding sets and lavish costumes" and accompanied, not by the original score, but by music that was "specially written" (the Ricordi publishing house's determined defense of copyright must have played a part in this rewriting). It is more surprising to find in the repertory of the Rame Family (a popular traveling marionette company that never had anything to do with the leading marionette theaters, and whose audience was strictly a provincial, village one) no less an opera than *Lohengrin:* that is, of all Wagner's operas, the only one that was successfully and lastingly transplanted into Italian operatic repertory of the day. In this case, the "material" used to put together the script was undoubtedly that of the opera. The cover actually has stuck on it the frontispiece of the libretto, in the classic Ricordi edition with its correct description: "Grand Romantic Opera in 3 Acts." [80] The Rame version is thus based on the Italian translation by Salvatore Marchesi De Castrone, but very little remains of the original versification, and the opera becomes a play (still "grand and romantic") in prose. It is worth quoting a few passages of this reduction, which give a fine example of "original" utilization of operatic material, taken over for its theatrical, evocative values, not strictly connected to the music or its level of "popularity." (It should not be forgotten that in the first edition of a book that was fundamental to Italian culture, *Il novissimo Melzi,* in 1901, Wagner is described thus: "German opera composer. Many find his music intolerable."

In the marionette version, the opera is divided into four acts (plain on the banks of the river Scheldt, with the river forming the back of the setting; garden with a castle to be lit, then Elsa's room, then square with the exterior of the church; grand square, then lavish hall, then wedding chamber; scene as in act 1). The props required are, naturally, the necessary ones: swan pulling a boat; prop swords for Friedrich and Lohengrin (sound of bells); flowers for the maidens; dove for the boat; swan that plunges into the water, and out comes Gottfried. Reading the script we find that Wagner's music was present in a few passages made possible by gramophone and records (the text dates from the early years of the twentieth century). This is how the play opens:

HERALD

Nobles of Brabant! I, the first herald of our magnanimous King Henry of Saxony, speak, first making known to you that our supreme sovereign recently left the royal dwelling and brought together here the valiant dukes of Brabant for the honor and greatness of our homeland, and his wise will is to be followed.

FREDERICK

With joy we hear the royal words. Welcome to our beloved king.

ALL

Welcome to our beloved king.

KING

Hail to you, valiant dukes and knights of Brabant. It is true, I left the royal palaces and wished the leading commanders of the Saxon army to assemble on the

80. The script is in my personal collection.

banks of the shining river Scheldt. Grave reasons of state brought me here. Listen. A grave danger in the East continues to threaten. The bold Hungarians still attempt to devastate our land with sword and fire. I, the head of the realm, shall put an end to such boldness. They were conquered by me once before, and for nine years I have assured peace for the people. I built cities and towers, and I drilled the troops for the trial of war. The hour of war has sounded. The honor of the kingdom must be saved. All Germany will take up arms and none shall insult her anymore. I depend on you, people of Brabant: death to the Hungarians and swear to die for the honor of your country.

FREDERICK
We shall die for the honor of our country.

ALL
We shall die for the honor of our country.

Then, moving on, this is how the swan, to an Italian the *cigno gentil,* appears:

ALL
What a marvel, a swan leading a boat.

KING
A knight, the splendor of whose arms and attire dazzles our eyes. He approaches. But what a wonder.

ELSA
Thank you, thank you, my lord.

A direction in the script at this point tells us that the music starts, using the recent marvelous discovery of the gramophone. We read:

GRAMOPHONE
Mercé, mercé. *He sings as he steps onto land; the swan exits. L[ohengrin] steps forward.*

LOHENGRIN
I thank you, gentle swan [*Mercé, mercé, cigno gentil*]. I have crossed the wide ocean. Now return to your sacred refuge, into which no human eye may look. You have carried out your duty honorably: farewell, farewell, singing swan.

The gramophone makes a reappearance in act 2, scene 1, to introduce Ortrud ("a malevolent lady") with Elsa's "Euch Lüften" ("Aurette di cui spesso"):

ORTRUD
Follow me. Listen to Elsa's singing: she rejoices in her love.

FREDERICK
Oh, my rage!

In this choice of music, of course, there has to be a place for the Bridal Hymn at the beginning of scene 3 of act 3; however, it seems not to be given to the gramophone but rather to the puppeteers, in that the direction reads: "Ad lib. Sing the Bridal Hymn." The gramophone reappears, in act 4, for "In fernem Land" ("Da voi lontan") and "Mein lieber Schwan" ("Cigno fedel"); after this, there seems to be no more music.

All the marionette companies had in their repertory plays derived from operas, but we cannot know—lacking the evidence of scripts and having only posters, advertisements, and lists—how faithful they may have been to the librettos and how "musical" (from the beginning of the new century on, with the providential aid of the gramophone). By way of example, a publication by the "Compagnia marionettistica diretta dall'artista Attilio Salici" gives the following list of "productions" in the repertory: *Africana, Gioconda, Aida, Roberto il diavolo, Guerra d'Africa, Guerra Russo-Giapponese, Forza del destino, Giuseppe Musolino,* and so on. The material of the Rame Family, for whom we have good information, is illuminating in this respect: scripts reveal that their version of *Aida, la schiava etiope* (but, I believe, not only theirs), does not derive from the libretto of Verdi's opera but from the edition in novel form based on the material of the opera by Valerio Busnelli and published in booklet form. *L'africana* is given, in the Rame lists, as "from Scribe," *Ernani* from Victor Hugo, *Fedora* from Sardou, *Linda di Chamonay* (!) (or *La perla di Savoia*) from d'Ennery, *Norma* from Alexandre Soumet, *Otello* from Shakespeare, *Sonnambula* again from Scribe, *Rigoletto* again from Hugo, *Tosca* again from Sardou, *Trovatore* from García Gutiérrez, and so on. Still in the lists of the Rame repertory, we find other operatic titles, for which, however, we have no indication of the source: *Favorita, Forza del destino, Lucia di Lammermoor, Roberto il diavolo,* and *Un ballo in maschera.* For these scripts, the absence of an indication of the author might lead us to imagine that they were drawn from the opera libretto, because fear of Casa Ricordi—or of any other music publisher, more likely than the general publishers close to the marionette companies to claim copyright—would have led them to suppress the origin of the text, trusting to the huge appeal of the title. But as no scripts are to hand to check this, it is risky to guess at their origins. To take one example: there is a *Gioconda* in the Rame repertory, but it is not Ponchielli's but a completely different play, attributed to a certain Pellico (not Silvio).

While marionettes touched on opera, even if at a tangent, and exploited its popularity, puppet shows also sometimes became involved with opera. Their presentations were neither directly nor indirectly inspired by famous operas but made use of the fame of opera stars. Various puppeteers, for example, used to end their shows with an announcement of a recital by a famous singer, most often Tamagno; and while onstage a puppet would impersonate the great tenor (with appropriate gestures), from behind the booth would come the voice of Tamagno, on a gramophone playing the earliest recordings.

Another "idea" dreamed up by traveling artists to exploit the success of opera should not be forgotten, one with which they themselves helped to circulate opera. I have a copy of an advertisement for the Politeama Ariosto in Reggio Emilia, which in October 1904 announced "only three extraordinary performances" by the "Famous Lilliputian Company" led by Professor Ernesto Guerra. This Famous Lilliputian Company was made up of child actors and singers brought together by Guerra, a theater manager from Reggio, at the end of the nineteenth century, and it remained in operation until around 1912, presenting operas. The repertory included *Pipelè* by De Ferrari and Donizetti's *L'elisir d'amore,* and the evening would end with a competition between three children (clearly, the best in the company: seven-year-old Pasqualino Tammaro, nine-year-old Edoardo Ghirotti, and ten-year-old Carlo Massarolo), all singing "Di quella pira." It is hard for us, even those accustomed to the shame of the *Zecchino d'oro,*[81] to imagine these performances, which all the same must have had an audience; they were even presented at court, before Umberto I and Queen Margherita, who, we know, were no great musical experts, but nevertheless, if only for reasons of prestige, they must have had some standards.

The last appearance of opera in marionette theater, before the recent cases of deliberate revival, seem to have been in the performances by the "Piccoli" of Podrecca: as late as the 1950s, just before it disbanded, this famous company presented in South America musical scenes inspired by various "classics" of our opera tradition, such as Boito's *Mefistofele* ("Visão do Inferno") and *Cavalleria rusticana* ("Adieu à la mère").

Opera outside the Opera House

12. READING OPERA, AT HOME AND IN PUBLIC

However superficial, any study of the spread of opera cannot restrict itself to "popular" contexts, even if they are of primary interest for the social and cultural history of opera. Even in the "middle-class" context, the remarkably consistent ways and means by which opera was disseminated are evidence of its success, to the point where it reached even an audience for whom access to the "natural" setting of opera, that is, the opera house, was not necessarily to be taken for granted and was neither frequent nor regular.

We must consider the years before the huge development of mass communications, which for some decades have profoundly altered the panorama of musical "consumption." The first evidence to be taken into consideration consists of the countless transcriptions for piano and for the most varied and, on occasion, unlikely instruments (solo flute!) of whole operas, fantasias, para-

---

81. A hugely popular television talent show that is organized by monks, is relayed from Bologna, and has children as young as five or six singing pop songs written specially for them.—Trans.

phrases, and separate numbers. Music publishing in the nineteenth and early twentieth centuries presented this multiform material to a public which, if able to use an instrument like the piano or to attend concert halls, was certainly not, a priori, excluded from the opera house. Of course, such transcriptions also operated as primary carriers of information, as a vehicle for music that was not always heard directly in performance onstage. But it is fair to assume that, directly or indirectly, piano transcriptions, fantasias, and derivatives usually operated in a fairly close relationship with live performance.

To gain an idea of the remarkable range of this practice of transcription, we will have to raise our sights beyond the few that are now familiar. Everyone knows that the great (and less great) pianists of the nineteenth century included in their concert programs operatic fantasias and paraphrases; and it is well known that, in several cases, these pieces acquired some autonomy in the hands of gifted pianists, to the point where they took on the form of "independent" compositions. As Beniamino Dal Fabbro has wisely observed:

> The practice of transcription, not unknown to musicians of the classical period, became persistent, dominant in Liszt, whether he turned to Bach's organ music or took Beethoven's symphonies as his object. An insatiable pianist, interested in all new music, obliged on his concert tours to change his programs on a regular basis and to find new things to feed to his piano, Liszt inaugurated a kind of interpretive journalism, with his transcriptions of Berlioz's *Symphonie fantastique,* Schubert's *Soirées de Vienne,* Rossini's *Soirées musicales* and the overture to *Guillaume Tell,* with fantasias and concert paraphrases of Verdi's, Donizetti's, and later Wagner's operas. In other words, Liszt devoted himself to "public readings" of all the music that interested him; and who knows in how many European cities the singing lines of Verdi were heard for the first time from Liszt's piano, in a phantasmagoria of brilliant decorative figuration, through which Liszt was able to make it appeal to his listeners. . . . It must also be added that Liszt's popularizing transcriptions, an artistic hybrid but a useful practice, degenerated into something parasitic when other, contemporary virtuosos imitated his example. Thalberg, Rubinstein, Tausig, and countless other pianists, with their concert paraphrases, did no more than help existing successes, by marketing to the public "favorite" operatic music which audiences already knew well, not new music as in the day of Liszt's "preaching." In this way the piano became a surrogate for the opera house, with its summaries of arias and orchestral moments, and altogether a pretext for the most disgusting and vulgar virtuosity.[82]

While the virtuoso practice of transcription is, at least in broad outline, well known—partly through having been recently reassessed in concert custom—less consideration has been given to the flood of publishing which built on the success of opera, and to the resulting wide public demand, which of-

82. Beniamino Dal Fabbro, *Crepuscolo del pianoforte* (Turin: Einaudi, 1951), 86ff.

fered to the amateur musician an operatic repertory in, especially, piano reduction. What is striking—or, at least, has struck me—is the huge number
of "complete operas for piano solo" found in the old catalogues of music publishers alongside the classic vocal scores: while the use of the latter—still predominant today in the professional environment as well as at home—is obvious, reductions for piano solo must have responded to an eminently private
need. It is interesting to look at the repertory of "complete operas" for piano
solo offered to the public by Ricordi at the end of the nineteenth century. The
list gives us an idea of how widespread the exquisitely amateur use of this musical "genre" must have been and also what were the most successful operas
of the day. Indeed, it must be presumed that Ricordi—like other publishers,
of course—prepared these reductions, under the highly significant listing of
Library of Popular Music, in the light of sales expectations based on the large
number of commercial indicators at the company's disposal.

Auber	*Fra Diavolo, La muette de Portici*
Beethoven	*Fidelio*
Bellini	*Adelson e Salvini, Beatrice di Tenda, Bianca e Fernando, I Capuleti e i Montecchi, Norma, Il pirata, I puritani, La sonnambula, La straniera*
Bizet	*Carmen*
Boito	*Mefistofele*
Catalani	*La Wally*
Cimarosa	*Giannina e Bernardone, Il matrimonio segreto*
De Giosa	*Napoli di carnevale*
Donizetti	*Alina, regina di Golconda, Anna Bolena, Don Pasquale, Dom Sébastien, L'elisir d'amore, La favorita, La fille du régiment, Gemma di Vergy, Linda di Chamounix, Lucia di Lammermoor, Lucrezia Borgia, Maria di Rohan, Poliuto*
Flotow	*Martha*
Gluck	*Alceste, Armida, Orfeo ed Euridice*
Gomes	*Il guarany*
Gounod	*Faust*
Halévy	*La Juive*
Hérold	*Zampa*
Marchetti	*Ruy Blas*
Mercadante	*Il giuramento*
Meyerbeer	*L'Africaine, Dinorah, L'étoile du nord, Les Huguenots, Le Prophète, Robert le diable*
Mozart	*Don Giovanni*
Pacini	*Saffo*
Petrella	*Jone, I promessi sposi*
Ponchielli	*Il figliuol prodigo, La Gioconda, I Lituani, Marion Delorme, I promessi sposi*
Luigi and Federico Ricci	*Crispino e la comare*
Rossini	*Il barbiere di Siviglia, La cenerentola, Le Comte Ory, La gazza ladra, Guillaume Tell, Mosè in Egitto, Otello, Semiramide*

Spontini	*La vestale*
Thomas	*Mignon*
Verdi	*Aida, Alzira, Aroldo, Attila, Un ballo in maschera, La battaglia di Legnano, Il corsaro, Don Carlos* (four acts), *Don Carlos* (five acts, without the ballet), *I due Foscari, Ernani, Il finto Stanislao, La forza del destino, Giovanni d'Arco, I Lombardi alla prima crociata, Luisa Miller, Macbeth, I masnadieri, Nabucco, Oberto, conte di San Bonifacio, Rigoletto, Simon Boccanegra, La traviata, Il trovatore, Les vêpres siciliennes*
Wagner	*Der fliegende Holländer, Lohengrin, Die Meistersinger von Nürnberg, Parsifal, Der Ring des Nibelungen, Rienzi, der Letzte der Tribunen, Tannhäuser, Tristan und Isolde*
Weber	*Der Freischütz*

It would be hopeless to try to sketch a picture of the collections, small and large, of operatic extracts reduced for piano in "varied" form or "freely transcribed" for the Italian musical public of the nineteenth century. Choosing from the mountain of arias, ariettas, canzones, romanzas, characteristic pieces, and dances, which a possibly unhealthy vocation for the most minor and the frankly dreadful has led me to accumulate, I shall quote, by way of example, the titles of some of these collections:

An hour of comfort / Six Short Pieces / Brilliant, Easy, and Progressive / for Piano / Forte / composed / on favorite melodies from the opera / and dedicated / to his pupils / of the Boarding School of the Very Reverend Franciscan Fathers in Monza / by Davide Antonietti / Milan, by Gio. Canti.

The collection consists of six pieces inspired, respectively, by *Norma* (Bellini), *Amleto* (Buzzolla), *Poliuto* (Donizetti), *Columella* (Fioravanti), *La favorita* (Donizetti), and *Un ballo in maschera* (Verdi).

Agreeable evenings / Collection of favorite Melodies from the operas / by famous composers / freely transcribed / for / piano and accordion / by / Domenico Caldi / Milan, G. Ricordi & Co. (nos. 81224–81241).

The first collection consists of "Miserere" (*Il trovatore*, Verdi), "Melody" (*Poliuto*, Donizetti), "Barcarolle" (*Marino Faliero*, Donizetti), Quartet (*I puritani*, Bellini), "Final aria" (*La sonnambula*, Bellini), "La Carità" (Rossini). The second collection consists of "Final aria" (*Norma*, Bellini), Finale II (*Poliuto*, Donizetti), "Duet" (*Martha*, Flotow), "Romanza" (*Faust*, Gounod), "Duet" (*Giulietta e Romeo*, Vaccai), "Romanza" (*Luisa Miller*, Verdi). The third collection consists of "Prayer" (*Mosè*, Rossini), "Country ballad" (Caldi), "Fantasia" (*Linda di Chamounix*, Donizetti), "Fantasia" (*Un ballo in maschera*, Verdi), "Fantasia" (*Les Huguenots*, Meyerbeer), "Fantasia" (*Faust*, Gounod).

Musical / Photograph / Collection of the most pleasing Operatic Melodies / Freely Transcribed / For / Pianoforte / in easy style / by A. Giamboni / Florence / O. Morandi.

The collection consists of thirty-six pieces, taken from *Martha* (Flotow), *La tra-*

viata (Verdi), *Beatrice di Tenda* (Bellini), *L'elisir d'amore* (Donizetti), *Rigoletto* (Verdi), *Il trovatore* (Verdi), *Un ballo in maschera* (Verdi), *La sonnambula* (Bellini), *Lucrezia Borgia* (Donizetti), *Lucia di Lammermoor* (Donizetti), *Gemma di Vergy* (Donizetti), and *Don Giovanni* (Mozart), two pieces from each opera; *Faust* (Gounod), *Ernani* (Verdi), *Saffo* (Pacini), *I Lombardi* (Verdi), *Il barbiere di Siviglia* (Rossini), *Anna Bolena* (Donizetti), *I puritani* (Bellini), *Norma* (Bellini), *I due Foscari* (Verdi), *Nabucco* (Verdi), *Macbeth* (Verdi), and *Poliuto* (Donizetti), one piece from each.

These are no more than drops in an ocean of sheet music, all of modest musical worth (although something intelligent and well done can always be found), almost all more attractive for their covers, often nicely lithographed, than for their musical content, but nevertheless revealing of the taste of their day and of the operatic approval of a middle-class society profoundly impregnated with opera.

13. OPERA IN BOXES, SMALL AND LARGE

Around the mid-1950s, a Milanese antiquarian, one of the first to consider Pianolas, musical boxes, and old gramophones worthy of consideration, "retrieved" from an inn not far from the city an "Ariosa" made by the Ehrlich Company of Leipzig, datable to the very first years of the twentieth century. An Ariosa was a music box with perforated, ring-shaped cardboard disks, whose mechanism was operated by a handle and whose sound apparatus consisted of tubes with reeds.

Long before, the Ariosa had been taken out of service and consigned to the loft, but for many years it had amused visitors to the inn, giving them a vast and varied musical repertory with the changeable disks. Indeed, together with the player, the cardboard disks had been preserved, and there was a bit of everything in them, something for every taste: dances, characteristic pieces, Neapolitan songs, even Italian folk dances, anthems, marches, and a small operatic selection, as follows:

> *Miserere der Troubadour,* von Verdi
> *Carmen-Polka (Oh toreador),* von Bizet
> *Marcia trionfale aus der Opera Aida,* von Verdi
> *Faust-Waltzer,* von Gounod
> *O wie so trügerisch (La donna è mobile) aus der Oper Rigoletto,* von Verdi

I have retained the original titles to indicate the German origin of the disks (like the player, for that matter). Other disks, however, had Italian titles, for compositions of more limited, specifically Italian horizons: for example, the *Marcia reale d'ordinanza* by Giuseppe Gabetti, or *La Marianna la va in campagna.* One in fact had a title in Lombard dialect, *Se ti Rachella te moueret,* and it is clear that these latter disks were produced for the Italian, and particularly Lombard, market only. Then there are some disks with Italian titles, but German indications (for example, "*Santa Lucia,* Neapolitanisches Volkslied"). It is clear that the software for these musical boxes had international circulation for one part of the repertory, but another part was produced for national and local markets. And the Ariosa was not a special case: this was a manufacturing procedure common to all mechanical instruments.

While we can be sure that the Ariosa we have been discussing had an effective popular use, offering operatic extracts to a village audience in an inn, no generalizations can be made for all the countless music boxes, Pianolas, player pianos, and the like that, from the beginning of the nineteenth century until the interwar years, were produced and distributed internationally. Indeed, this enormous and hugely diversified output also includes instruments that by reason of their cost and characteristics could not have found a popular use but were on the contrary intended for well-to-do customers.

It is not my intention to cover the history of mechanical instruments, which in any case has largely been reconstructed and has engendered a considerable bibliography. In the second decade of the nineteenth century, the invention of the rotating brass cylinder, with teeth that set steel prongs vibrating, opened the way for the success and development of music boxes, which became increasingly popular and had a massive circulation. The first boxes with a rotating drum were small and naturally could not offer very complex or lengthy "performances"; for the most part they played tiny, brief quotations of melodies, continually repeated, and this, the result of the limited dimensions of the drum and the number of prongs, continued to be the case for the majority of instruments produced until the end of the history of the music box. By way of example, I can quote the durations of some operatic music boxes:

> music box made in Geneva, manufacturer unknown (1810–20): Rossini, "Languir per una bella" (*L'italiana in Algeri*); duration, 40 seconds
> music box by Jules Cuendet (1895): Gounod, Soldiers' March (*Faust*); duration, 45 seconds
> music box by Jaccard-Dugrand (ca. 1910): Donizetti, duet (*Lucrezia Borgia*); duration, 53 seconds
> music box by Barnett H. Abraham (c1910): Bizet, Toreador's Song (*Carmen*), duration, 48 seconds

These pieces were very short and allowed for a simple quotation of the basic melodic elements. In those (not exactly rare) cases where the music box played a "selection" from an opera, the durations were even shorter. To give only one example, a Heller box (with a singing bird) offered 47 seconds of a "Selection from *Rigoletto*"!

While the production of small music boxes continued and expanded, to-

ward the middle of the nineteenth century the inventiveness of Swiss craftsmen resulted in boxes of increased dimensions, able to hold cylinders of much
greater length and diameter, and so containing hundreds of teeth and a far
larger number of corresponding vibrating prongs. At the same time, we can
see the appearance of more and more technical innovations, which gave the
boxes greater variety of sound, especially in the form of "effects": for example, of a mandolin, a harp, a bell, and various other percussion effects.
These large music boxes were meant to sit on a shelf, but the even larger models were nothing less than automata, with legs and all.

The large music boxes could offer long, complete performances: an entire
opera overture, a whole piece from an opera, and so on for other musical genres. If the piece—an overture, for example—were very long, it would be divided between two cylinders or sometimes given in an abbreviated form on
one. Among the machines of this type, some of the most complex and precise
are those from the Geneva workshops of the Nicôle Brothers and Lecoultre
Brothers between 1850 and 1870: the cylinders reached a length of 50 centimeters, with a diameter of 15; they could be removed and replaced, so the
customer could acquire a sort of "cylinder collection" of favorite pieces.

To date, there has been no census of cylinders preserved in museums and
private collections, and so it is not possible to form a complete enough picture of the repertory offered to customers. Among the opera overtures, those
that occur with greatest frequency are *The Magic Flute, Norma, The Barber
of Seville, The Thieving Magpie, William Tell, Semiramide, Robert le diable,
Fra Diavolo, Belisario, Parisina,* and *Il matrimonio segreto.* As far as vocal
extracts are concerned (actually less numerous than overtures), again the operas named above are those with the greatest circulation. It can be said with
some certainty that operatic music constituted the basis of the repertory of
large music boxes: the pieces chosen were given in remarkably complete form,
and the resulting sound, while a long way from the original, was extremely
sophisticated and appealing. With an immense number of teeth and a comb
with a wide range of vibrating prongs, it was possible to realize a score in all
its essential parts, chosen, often, with rare sensitivity: the boxes did not merely
reproduce the melodic line alone or the melodic line with a simple accompaniment: in fact, many instrumental lines were joined together to superb musical effect. These were very expensive, luxury products and, naturally, were
intended for a limited market, so one cannot speak of them in the context of
popular diffusion. Nevertheless, the large music boxes had a significant role
in circulating operatic music in given social and cultural contexts; rather than
a primary source of information, they supplemented musical knowledge that
had already been acquired directly.

From 1870 onward, in addition, music boxes began to be manufactured
in relatively economical models. In 1880, for example, there were already at

least thirty firms operating in Switzerland with a workforce of hundreds. This "mass production" (as it were) even after 1880 based its repertory principally on operatic music.

> During the period that may be called the heyday of the popularity of the cylinder musical box (1850–1880), it is safe to say that 75 per cent of the music reproduced was operatic in character. There were, of course, various reasons for this; the good quality musical boxes then produced were expensive and, on the English market at any rate, were purchased by the upper and middle classes who generally appreciated the music of such composers as Donizetti, Rossini, Mozart, Weber, Verdi and the like. A further point is that many of the arias from these composers' operas were found to be particularly suitable for reproduction on the combs made at this period and they were also of a suitable length or duration. For the most part only the "gems" of an opera were selected by the transposers for reproduction on a musical box cylinder. These selections were usually the pieces most popular with the music loving public but there were, of course, exceptions and thus it is that some musical box programmes include little-known arias from operas that were not very successful. On the other hand there are some well-known arias that for some reason are rarely heard on the cylinder type of musical box. One such is *Forever Goodbye* from *La Traviata*, a charming piece of music and, at one time, a favorite solo at concerts both amateur and professional. Only once have I found this piece set up on a musical box—a two-comb piccolo box by Dawkins, made about 1890.[83]

On the basis of the very incomplete data available, it can be added that Verdi does not seem to have been the composer most represented in musical boxes; instead, the names which constantly reappear are Bellini, Donizetti, Rossini, Meyerbeer, Auber, and Bizet; and in the last thirty years of the nineteenth century, when Verdi's international fame was at a peak, the operatic repertory of music boxes was more or less consistently reduced and replaced by other, "lighter" genres.

Here again, music boxes offer a faithful reflection of the rapid and decisive shift in taste caused by the appearance of more modest social strata in the potential market for music. It is certainly no coincidence that the last two decades of the nineteenth century saw the establishment, led by the taste of the lower-middle-class and urban craftsmen, of that new type of music which, for convenience, has become known as "light"; nor is it a coincidence that the end of the century saw the development of mechanical instruments that were very different from the "classic" one of a rotating cylinder and vibrating prongs. Dominance in the new instruments passed from Switzerland to Germany, and there was an incredible flourishing of types and models. I am referring here to music boxes with free reeds set in motion by a small bellows and operated by

---

83. John E. T. Clark, *Musical Boxes*, 3d ed. (London: George Allen & Unwin, 1951), 22ff.

a handle. These were much less sophisticated machines, in the sound they produced, than the old comb music boxes; their sound is penetrating, slightly vulgar, with a fairly pronounced popular character, not very different from that of the accordion (an instrument that, in those very years, all over the world, was conquering vast stretches of folk music production).[84]

Our Ariosa, the instrument mentioned above that ended up in a Lombard inn is one of these. This type of instrument shows no lack of complicated, sophisticated, and expensive mechanisms. But what we are interested in are the cheaper models, which could have reached a more popular audience, although not as a domestic acquisition but through the sort of collective use offered by an inn and other locations of social interaction.

Hardly anyone knows what the repertory of these instruments was. It is highly likely that operatic music—as seen in the case of the Ariosa—was always a feature, even if it did not constitute the basis of the repertory, which probably consisted of "light" genres. Among the disks provided with a music box similar to and contemporary with the Ariosa, a Swiss-produced "Stella," we find a substantial collection of operatic pieces:

Gounod, *Faust:* Choeur des Soldats
Rossini, *Il barbiere di Siviglia:* "Rien ne peut changer mon âme"
Rossini, *Guglielmo Tell:* Prière
Thomas, *Mignon:* Polonaise
Meyerbeer, *Le pardon de Ploërmel:* "Ombre légère"
Wagner, *Lohengrin:* Choeur des fiançailles
Verdi, *Rigoletto:* Quatuor

As far as the playing time is concerned, these music boxes do not generally offer anything longer than the small and medium boxes with vibrating teeth do. For example, the perforated disks of the Ariosa, produced in two diameters, had durations of 30 seconds and 1 minute; and it should be kept in mind that the speed of rotation of the disk in music boxes operated by hand could vary considerably according to the taste of the operator, who could speed it up or slow it down in an ad lib tempo.

Before touching on the questions of player pianos and street and fair organs, this is a good opportunity to take a step backward. A much trumpeted musical event was the public presentation, in London in 1817, of the "Apollonicon," a large mechanical organ built by Flight and Robson. Ten years later, this was the instrument's repertory:

84. In fact, reeded mechanical instruments were already present when this instrument first began to be developed. German craftsmen applied the system and developed it in the context of music boxes, using a perforated disk rather than other means: for example, the wooden cylinder with teeth—to stay with popular instruments—of the *serinette* and the barrel organ.

Mozart, *La clemenza di Tito, Die Zauberflöte, Le nozze di Figaro, Idomeneo:* overtures
Cherubini, *Anacréon:* overture
Beethoven, *Prometheus:* overture
Weber, *Oberon, Der Freischütz:* overtures
Handel, *Dettingen Te Deum:* introduction
Haydn, Twelth Symphony: Grand Military Movement
Paër, *Sophonisba:* overture

The Apollonicon continued to be exhibited, drawing large crowds of amazed Londoners for many years to the Apollonicon Rooms at 101 St. Martin's Lane. The repertory always included a large amount of operatic music, but very little by Italian composers: in 1835 Rossini's duet "All'idea di quell'metallo" and Zingarelli's aria "Ombra adorata" were performed; and in a program of sixteen or seventeen years later, we find Rossini again, in selections from *Semiramide* and *Guglielmo Tell*. The recurring names are those of Handel, Haydn, Mozart, Weber, Auber, and Boïeldieu, alongside various English composers of the day. The position of Italian opera in Great Britain in the first fifty years of the century thus appears to be peripheral, to judge from the information provided by the Apollonicon. But, in fact, Great Britain soon became, together with the United States, "privileged territory" for the cult of Italian opera.

Street pianos and organs, which worked by way of a drum with teeth, similar to that of the music boxes, also had a limited playing time; these were mechanical instruments of strictly popular use, intended for people walking by and public spaces, and until around twenty years ago, they were still to be seen in our streets. Today they have disappeared and have been replaced by "mock-up" pianos, that is, containers that conceal a cassette recorder that plays recorded piano music through a loudspeaker.

Even if there are no statistical data in support, we can say that these were very successful instruments, both those taken round the streets and those set up in social centers (associations, societies, and other groups). The catalogue—by no means complete—of the builders and distributors contains over sixty names of companies and craftsmen for Italy alone, spread throughout the country but concentrated principally in Piedmont and Lombardy. The following table shows the distribution and geographical density of the producers and distributors of mechanical pianos with cylinders (the figures indicate the number of single craftsmen or companies that constructed or distributed such machines):

Piedmont	24	Alessandria, 2; Casale Monferrato, 6; Cigliano, 2; Cuneo, 1; Ivrea, 1; Novara, 3; Pinerolo, 4; Turin, 2; Vercelli, 3
Liguria	2	Genoa, 1; Vezzano Ligure, 1
Lombardy	12	Como, 2; Cremona, 1; Milan, 7; Treviglio, 1; Varese, 1

Veneto	2	Venice, 2
Emilia	2	Bologna, 2
Umbria	1	Gualdo Tadino, 1
Abruzzo	1	Chieti, 1
Lazio	7	Rome, 7
Campania	3	Benevento, 1; Naples, 1; San Angelo dei Lombardi, 1
Puglia	2	Bari, 1; Bitonto, 1
Sicily	5	Caltanisetta, 1; Catania, 1; Messina, 1; Ragusa, 2

The concentration of production and distribution in northern Italy should not give the impression that these instruments did not have wide circulation; because of the more advanced technological, "industrial," and economic level of the north, factories and workshops sprang up there, but their customers were found throughout the country. Undoubtedly, mechanical pianos on wheels played a considerable part in disseminating music: they were, by a wide margin, the main vehicle for the diffusion of new music, new fashions, and new musical sensibilities in spaces where other influences were excluded.

It is extremely difficult nowadays to reconstruct, even partially, the repertory of these instruments, because the majority of surviving examples have been "reprogrammed." Indeed, specialist craftsmen brought the repertory up to date continually, with new cylinders of fashionable music: in all probability, opera was present, but the instruments I am familiar with have exclusively hit songs from the 1930s and 1940s. However, there is plenty of documentation to tell us of the presence of operatic pieces in the street musicians' repertory. Arthur W. J. G. Ord-Hume reprints an article published in 1888 in *Musical Opinion,* from which we learn about the decision of the Paris police to introduce stricter laws against street musicians, who were accused of disturbing the peace:

> These perambulating cacophonists will no longer be allowed to murder the compositions of their illustrious countrymen—Rossini, Verdi and Donizetti—in the streets of the sprightly capital. If found grinding out the "Miserere," the "Tempest of the Heart," or any other operatic air, the grinders are to be, in the words of the police order, *dirigés sur le depôt,* or "relegated to the lock up," and their instruments are to be sent to a kind of pound, which contains all the *flotsam* and *jetsam* collected by the representatives of the law on their diurnal beats.[85]

These were, apparently, Italian street musicians, who were scattered across the whole of Europe and traveled half the world. Italian documentation also tells us that the operatic repertory played a substantial part in the activities of these mechanical instruments, especially in the second half of the nineteenth

85. Arthur W. J. G. Ord-Hume, *Barrel Organ* (London: Allen and Unwin, 1978), 245.

century and the first half of the twentieth: a government provision of the autumn of 1904 confirms a total ban on mechanical reproduction of parts of Verdi's last operas, with direct reference to *Otello* and *Falstaff*, because they were protected by copyright; and the builders of mechanical instruments and the craftsmen who "programmed" them had to make an agreement with Verdi's heirs and pay any royalties due. The demand for operatic music was thus considerable, and the pressure of the needs of customers and audiences meant that the producers of the instruments could not do without even protected works.

A separate question is that of the automatic, or mechanical, piano operated by rolls of perforated paper. These instruments constitute a decisive turning point in the history of mechanical instruments, in that they could offer, not an "imitation" of a piece of music, but a more or less real performance of it, on a "real" instrument. Automatic pianos thus belong to the old mechanical organ tradition, like the Apollonicon mentioned above, realizing piano music on a piano.

A decisive move toward perfecting the mechanical piano started in the mid-1880s. This can be confirmed by quoting the numbers of patents—related to entire mechanisms or their parts—filed between 1883 and 1904 (the years when the instrument was developed):

	Patents		Patents
1883	25	1894	9
1884	14	1895	13
1885	27	1896	25
1886	28	1897	27
1887	32	1898	23
1888	14	1899	13
1889	12	1900	20
1890	9	1901	42
1891	5	1902	41
1892	6	1903	79
1893	6	1904	72

It is interesting to note how zeal for innovation and the drive to perfection were particularly strong in the very years, at the turn of the century, when the phonograph and gramophone (that is, the wax cylinder and disk) were developed and began to be established. In battling against the new means of sound reproduction, the Pianola tried to stand up to the competition, which had now taken the lead by becoming more and more "faithful."

In Italy there was no production of mechanisms for pianolas, but a large number of firms produced (upright) pianos adapted to take imported mechanisms: Racca (Turin), Anelli (Cremona), F.I.P. (Fabbrica Italiana Pianoforte,

Turin), I.N.A.P. (Industria Nazionale Autopiani e Pianoforti, Turin). Instruments also began to be imported: by Ricordi Finzi (Aeolian, Bechstein, Steinway), Natale Gallini (Irmel and Grotrian-Steinweg), Tedeschi and Raphael, Umberto Gorli (Hupfeld), Umberto Strinasacchi, Borsari all Sarti, all of them companies in the north, based between Milan, Como, Verona, and Bologna.

A clear distinction, which also covers a social function, must be drawn between the "player piano" and the "reproducing player piano." The player piano produced music from ribbons of mechanically perforated paper; the music, that is, was transferred onto the paper ribbons by craftsmen working from the written notation. Consequently, when it was played, it did not reproduce a specific performance by a pianist, and often, to enrich the tone and make the rendition more complex, holes were added which resulted in a perfectly impossible virtuoso display: some rolls give a performance on the player piano which would require three hands. Player pianos of this kind certainly cost more, but were within the grasp of a not especially restricted clientele.

The situation was different with reproducing player pianos, which, in contrast, recorded on a roll of paper a specific performance made by a pianist. The machines produced by the Welte (Welte Mignon) Company and installed on splendid, top-quality grand pianos were able to simulate to perfection an actual performance (and the thing that counted was that it was one specific performance).[86] These were fantastically expensive instruments, within the grasp of only a few: before World War II, a Steinway with a Welte Mignon mechanism cost more than 30,000 lire, and it is interesting to note that already in the 1920s, there were companies that, by subscription, loaned piano rolls to their customers, much like video stores do today.

So there is an extremely significant difference between the player piano and the reproducing variety, not only one of musical quality—all the great pianists of the day played for reproducing player pianos—but also of (partly)

86. "On February 3, 1920, the American Piano Co. put on a large demonstration at Carnegie Hall, New York, before a numerous invited audience. Five eminent pianists—Artur Rubenstein, Leopold Godowsky, Benno Moiseiwitsch, Leo Ornstein, and Mischa Levitzki—each played one or two pieces, interspersed with renditions by the Ampico. For the final number, the program merely announced that Levitzki was to play Liszt's *Hungarian* Rhapsody No. 6. The pianist began it vigorously, arrived at the hold that ends the first section, and extended his hands expectantly over the keys before the beginning of the following slower episode. The music came forth gently— but Levitzki removed his hands and the sounds went on without him. The Ampico had taken up where the artist stopped, and just as skillfully! That would have seemed the proper moment for the audience to make some demonstration of admiration; however, the people remained silent and attentive. The rhapsody proceeded; at the top of its fast final furiousness, Levitzki jumped back into it and played the close in person. It was at his plunge that the audience became electrified, breaking into the music with a salvo of applause"; Arthur Loesser, *Men, Women and Pianos* (New York: Simon and Schuster, 1954), 585.

different social function. Only a few thousand reproducing instruments were imported into Italy, whereas player pianos were much more numerous in Italian homes.

There were also differences in repertory. The reproducing player piano offered nothing other than piano music, and in fact, the instrument was a real piano, which could be played. The ordinary player piano, in contrast, had a wider repertory, with adaptations for piano of all sorts of music. Certainly, opera also featured in the repertory of the reproducing player piano, but in the guise of the operatic paraphrases that formed part of a pianist's repertory; the player piano repertory was more open to opera, offering actual transcriptions of arias, duets, overtures, and so on. However, even for the player piano (considering the era when it was popular, in the early twentieth century), operatic music did not form the basis of the repertory: an analysis of the piano rolls offered in the Aurora catalogue (an 88-note player piano) distributed by the Perrone Company in Milan (corso Roma 17) in 1934—the last years of the instrument's life—shows the following percentages of various genres of music:

Light music	60%
Operatic music	15%
Classical music	10%
Operetta	10%
Various	5%

It was not just the change in taste and the specific "pianistic" quality of the player piano that determined the shrinking of the operatic repertory;[87] it should also be remembered that although the instrument offered a mediocre-to-excellent reproduction of piano music, the record, which was rapidly improving, especially after electrical recording, had become the basic, if not inevitable, vehicle for reproducing vocal music.

14. SIGNOR GALBIATI TAKES OPERA HOME WITH HIM

It is impossible to cover the discography of opera in a few pages. What *is* possible, though, is to offer a few examples from the early years of the life of the record, to set in motion some observations not so much on the part played by record production in the dissemination of opera—certainly a very large part, if not exactly the principal one during our century—as on the value of the music recorded on disks as evidence of taste in the first decades of the twentieth century.

87. Indeed, the period when there is a strong operatic content in the piano repertory comes to a close around 1880.

Let us imagine that on one weekday in 1908 a well-to-do Milanese gentleman—for convenience let's call him signor Galbiati—goes to Vittorio Bonomi's shop at no. 32 via Vincenzo Monti. Signor Bonomi's is one of the best-stocked shops in Milan for talking machines, of both the cylinder (phonograph) and disk (gramophone) variety, and offers his highly select clientele a wide repertory of cylinders and disks "of the finest makes." Signor Galbiati, for his part, is a well-to-do citizen who, attracted by the advertising and encouraged by the happy experiences of his friends, wishes to possess that extraordinary novelty of the moment, a "talking machine." It is Vittorio himself who greets him and guides him in his choice, showing him the many models which the company (winner of the Gold Medal at the 1906 International Exhibition in Milan) offers its clientele. Depending on the model, the phonographs (with clockwork movement) cost from 7.75 lire (the Principe model, which, according to the catalogue, "Sings powerfully and naturally, without grating. Voices do not sound nasal") to 65 lire (the Fonografo-Grafofono VB model, which allows the listener not only to hear prerecorded cylinders with "clear, loud sound" but also to make cylinder recordings at home, offering the satisfaction of "preserving the voices of loved ones" and of enjoying the pleasure of "reproducing songs, sounds, poetry, monologues, etc. of one's own and of one's friends").

Signor Galbiati is inclined toward a model priced in the middle range, and his attention has been taken by the Loreley (20 lire, plus 1 lira for packaging), partly because he is attracted by its varnished and bronzed cast-metal base, which represents, in a genuine piece of sculpture, "the Loreley seated on a rock" with her lyre in her hand. But then he is persuaded by signor Bonomi to turn his attention to the gramophones, which seem to offer a few more advantages than the phonographs, and which constitute, if not a novelty, a more recent solution to recording speech and music. While the phonograph (invented, or at least exploited industrially, by Edison) has now been around for more than twenty years, the gramophone, the outcome of Emile Berliner's inspired idea of replacing the cylinder with a disk, is ten years younger and—even if the battle has a few more years to run—seems to be the solution of the future.

And so our friend decides to acquire one of the best gramophone models that the Bonomi shop has on its premises: the Sultan Senior, which costs 150 lire (with 200 steel needles included in the price). It is presented in the catalogue with these words: "Cased in the richest and most solid manner in hand-carved polished walnut, measuring 42 centimeters. Two-spring silent movement, 5-disk carrier, loadable even during operation. Acoustic arm. 30-centimeter turntable. Large lily-shaped enameled trumpet with gold inlay, or 70 centimeter brass conical trumpet." It's a real piece of furniture, therefore, something to command the attention, and unlikely to be overlooked even in the crammed decorative style of houses of the time.

Having acquired the Sultan Senior, signor Galbiati naturally requires some disks. And the Bonomi shop has the best selection available in Milan. Signor Galbiati is an opera lover, and signor Bonomi submits everything he has in the store for inspection. There are Odeon disks (double, that is, two-sided, a new feature introduced that very year) and Fonotipias, also double-sided. We do not know what signor Galbiati will acquire to grace his new gramophone, but a glance at the Bonomi catalogue will help us identify the tastes and the trends in the area of operatic music in those first years of the twentieth century.

It is reasonable to assume, in fact, that the record companies (which at that very time were at the beginning of their long industrial history) put on the market those operas and those operatic extracts that they felt were most requested, closest to the taste of the public;[88] a public, let's not forget, that was certainly not "popular" but was in fact predominantly made up of the wealthy. The cost of disks was fairly high and stayed that way at least until after World War II; indeed, double-sided Odeon disks cost 7 lire each in the C series, in which "classical" repertories, mostly of operatic music, were collected, and 3.50 lire for the P series, of variety music, comic scenes, café concert items, and the like. More expensive still were the Fonotipia (of decidedly superior quality, possibly the best of their day): from 8.50 lire to 20 lire and more. Each side of the disk could guarantee 3 minutes of music or slightly more (today an LP can contain up to 30 minutes of music per side) and that the 20 lire of then is something like today's 60,000. They were products for the few, in a word, even if records managed to have a certain "popular" presence all the same, since a number of public premises (including inns) installed a gramophone, like modern-day jukeboxes.

But to return to the catalogues at Vittorio Bonomi's, let us follow signor Galbiati as he comes to grips with the far from easy choice of choosing his recordings. Let us look at a summary (combining disks and cylinders) by opera title.[89]

---

88. Remember that up until World War II a recording constituted the confirmation, both for performers and for the compositions, light or "classical," of an existing success. Records were made by players, orchestras, and singers who had already had success in "live" performance, and the same was true of compositions. The recorded repertories of that period, therefore, are an excellent point of reference in establishing the taste of the "real" public. Nowadays, in contrast, it is often the disk (and not only for so-called music for consumption) that sets the taste. Sometimes live appearances are only promotional events for an existing disk.

89. The table is laid out as a kind of hit parade, putting together the recordings of single pieces from each opera included in the catalogue of cylinders and records distributed by the Bonomi Company. Naturally, in many cases, the same piece may have been recorded two, three, or four

Ranking	Title of Opera	Total Number of Recordings of Separate Pieces
1	Rigoletto (Verdi)	60
2	Faust (Gounod)	50
3	Il trovatore (Verdi)	49
4	La Gioconda (Ponchielli)	48
5	La traviata (Verdi)	42
6	Il barbiere di Siviglia (Rossini)	37
	La favorita (Donizetti)	37
7	La forza del destino (Verdi)	35
	Lucia di Lammermoor (Donizetti)	35
8	Ernani (Verdi)	33
	Un ballo in maschera (Verdi)	33
9	La bohème (Puccini)	32
	Mefistofele (Boito)	32
10	Mignon (Thomas)	26
11	Tosca (Puccini)	25
12	Cavalleria rusticana (Mascagni)	24
13	Andrea Chénier (Giordano)	23
	Norma (Bellini)	23
	Les Huguenots (Meyerbeer)	23
14	Carmen (Bizet)	22
	Pagliacci (Leoncavallo)	22
	L'Africaine (Meyerbeer)	22
15	Fra Diavolo (Auber)	21
	Otello (Verdi)	21
16	Siberia (Giordano)	20
17	Lohengrin (Wagner)	19
	Adriana Lecouvreur (Cilea)	19
18	Fedora (Giordano)	18
	La sonnambula (Bellini)	18
19	Zazà (Leoncavallo)	17
	Germania (Franchetti)	17
	Manon Lescaut (Puccini)	17
	I puritani (Bellini)	17
20	Tannhäuser (Wagner)	15
	Guillaume Tell (Rossini)	15
21	Lucrezia Borgia (Donizetti)	13
	Ruy Blas (Marchetti)	13
	Don Giovanni (Mozart)	13
	Manon (Massenet)	13
22	Samson et Dalila (Saint-Saëns)	12
	Evgeny Onegin (Tchaikovsky)	12
	Les pêcheurs de perles (Bizet)	12
	Don Pasquale (Donizetti)	12

---

times. In determining the "success" of the various operas, as certified by the record industry, the number of individual pieces recorded from an opera is not as important as the total number of recordings made of pieces from that opera.

Ranking	Title of Opera	Total Number of Recordings of Separate Pieces
23	Die Walküre (Wagner)	11
	Der Freischütz (Weber)	11
24	Il Guarany (Gomes)	10
	Iris (Mascagni)	10
	La Juive (Halévy)	10
	La bohème (Leoncavallo)	10
25	L'elisir d'amore (Donizetti)	9
	Le nozze di Figaro (Mozart)	9
26	Robert le diable (Meyerbeer)	8
	Dinorah (Meyerbeer)	8
27	Luisa Miller (Verdi)	7
	L'amico Fritz (Mascagni)	7
	Nabucco (Verdi)	7
	Crispino e la comare (Ricci)	7
	I Lombardi alla prima crociata (Verdi)	7
28	Jone (Petrella)	6
	Don Carlo (Verdi)	6
	Madama Butterfly (Puccini)	6
	Le maschere (Mascagni)	6
	Martha (Flotow)	6
	Chopin (Orefice)	6
	La damnation de Faust (Berlioz)	6
29	Poliuto (Donizetti)	5
	Falstaff (Verdi)	5
	Dom Sébastien (Donizetti)	5
	Salvator Rosa (Gomes)	5
	Le educande di Sorrento (Usiglio)	5
	Amica (Mascagni)	5
	Sigurd (Reyer)	5
30	L'arlesiana (Cilea)	4
	The Queen of Spades (Tchaikovsky)	4
	Werther (Massenet)	4
	Linda di Chamounix (Donizetti)	4
	Cristoforo Colombo (Franchetti)	4
31	Die Meistersinger von Nürnberg (Wagner)	3
	The Demon (Rubinstein)	3
	Saffo (Pacini)	3
	Die Zauberflöte (Mozart)	3
	Mireille (Gounod)	3
	Le prophète (Meyerbeer)	3
32	Maria di Rohan (Donizetti)	2
	Parsifal (Wagner)	2
	La contessa d'Amalfi (Petrella)	2
	Papà Martin (Cagnoni)	2
	Semiramide (Rossini)	2
	Pipelè (De Ferrari)	2
	La figlia di Jorio (Franchetti)	2
	Le roi de Lahore (Massenet)	2

Ranking	Title of Opera	Total Number of Recordings of Separate Pieces
	Il Rolando (Leoncavallo)	2
	Lakmé (Delibes)	2
33	I vespri siciliani (Verdi)	1
	La gazza ladra (Rossini)	1
	L'italiana in Algeri (Rossini)	1
	La muette de Portici (Auber)	1
	La Cenerentola (Rossini)	1
	Silvano (Mascagni)	1
	Chatterton (Leoncavallo)	1
	I Medici (Leoncavallo)	1
	Tristan und Isolde (Wagner)	1
	Manuel Menendez (Filiasi)	1
	La cabrera (Dupont)	1
	L'ebreo (Apolloni)	1
	Hérodiade (Massenet)	1
	Elena e Paride (Gluck)	1
	Thaïs (Massenet)	1
	Hamlet (Thomas)	1
	Guglielmo Ratcliff (Mascagni)	1
	Simon Boccanegra (Verdi)	1
	Macbeth (Verdi)	1
	Le Cid (Massenet)	1
	Vita brettone (Mugnone)	1

As for the composers who are most represented in the catalogues of cylinders and of disks in 1908—again according to the repertory offered to the people of Milan by the Bonomi Company—we have, in the leading places (with at least ten pieces):

Ranking	Composer	Number of Operas	Total Number of Recordings of Separate Items
1	Verdi	16	340
2	Donizetti	9	122
3	Puccini	4	80
4	Meyerbeer	5	64
5	Giordano	3	61
6	Bellini	3	58
7	Rossini	6	57
8	Mascagni	7	54
9	Gounod	2	53
	Leoncavallo	6	53
10	Wagner	6	51
11	Ponchielli	1	48
12	Bizet	2	34
13	Boito	1	32
14	Thomas	2	27
15	Mozart	3	25

Ranking	Composer	Number of Operas	Total Number of Recordings of Separate Items
16	Cilea	2	23
17	Auber	2	22
	Massenet	6	22
18	Tchaikovsky	2	16
19	Gomes	2	15
20	Marchetti	1	13
21	Saint-Saëns	1	12
22	Weber	1	11
23	Halévy	1	10

It is interesting to see how some composers have taken leading places just by being represented by a single opera, or two; such is the case, to focus on the principal positions, with Ponchielli (with only *La Gioconda*), Boito (only *Mefistofele*), Cilea (with *Adriana*, and much further down, *L'arlesiana*), Auber (*Fra Diavolo* far outstripping *La muette de Portici*), and Gounod (with *Faust*, which takes the lion's share, with fifty items out of a total of fifty-three, and *Mireille*). The picture matches exactly the "state" of operatic consumption of the time, just as the presence of operas and composers who are today almost forgotten but then enjoyed great fame is evidence of the taste of the day (Franchetti, Gomes, Petrella, Orefice, Usiglio, Cagnoni, and so on).

This is not the place to follow the recording history of the great singers of the beginning of the century (headed by Caruso), which is already widely known. The thing to remember is how the operatic repertory played a very substantial part in record production up until the period between the two world wars: up until the time, that is, when light music came unstoppably to the fore, as, to a lesser but not minor extent, did orchestral and chamber music. From the time of its appearance, the disk made broad use of operatic items to fill out the catalogues—and opera with closed numbers in the Franco-Italian tradition naturally lent itself more easily than Wagnerian opera to the dismemberment imposed by the short duration of a 78 rpm. But very soon there was an attempt to assemble "complete operas" (the *Pagliacci* recorded in 1907 under Leoncavallo's supervision was one of the earliest examples). It was only toward the end of the 1920s, however, that recording companies scheduled production of complete operas on a large scale. This was the beginning of a new period in the recording life of opera. The separate pieces continued to appear up until the end of the 78 era, replaced by long-playing records at the beginning of the 1950s, but taste rapidly shifted toward complete versions, or large selections, and with long-playing records this tendency became dominant, if not exclusive.[90]

90. An exhaustive picture of the early days of recording, taken from the various contemporary national catalogues, is provided by John Reginald Bennett, Eric Hughes, Michael Smith, Wilhelm

Our signor Galbiati, acquiring his Sultan Senior, was looking forward to hearing short "great" pieces of opera at home, not complete operas. And certainly he did not find anything strange in the fact that, of his favorite operas, he would hear and hear again always and only the most famous, most tearjerking, most electrifying pieces, those classic scenes which he knew by heart at home and frantically applauded (or booed) on the few occasions when he heard them in their "natural" habitat, in the theater: for this was the dominant way of "feeling" and hearing Italian opera in the Italy of the late nineteenth and early twentieth centuries.

15. THE HAMMY BARITONE, MAESTRO MUDDLE,
DINETTA, AND MARGHERITA, WHO IS NOT WHO SHE WAS

A clear sign of the presence of opera in everyday life, for the whole of the nineteenth century and for at least thirty years of the twentieth, is the continuous use which satire, comedy, and humor made of those grotesque, absurd, and "abnormal" elements which were (and are) an essential ingredient of opera and its characters. The stars of the high noon of opera were thus caricatured on countless occasions, and it was not only the famous *prime donne,* with their adorable weaknesses, and the hoarse, desperate, and conceited tenors who sparked irony and satire, but opera itself, in its incongruous essence, in its sophisticated conventions permanently verging on the ridiculous, which provided the material for some illuminating, often hilarious reflections.

It would not be going too far to view this satirical impulse against the background of age-old discussions and arguments on the "unreality" of music theater, with all the time-honored trimmings of the "whims," loose behavior, arrogance, and eccentricity of *prime donne* and their male counterparts. This "critical" output belongs to the minor genres of "light" theater, songs, comic characters, common literature for entertainment, caricature, and cartoons; and from the eighteenth century onward it not only was based on opera but had a place within opera as well.

In illustrating this picturesque area of operatic caricatures, I feel it is important to remember the example of two satirical comic characters created by one of the greatest actor-authors of the second half of the nineteenth century; he was by culture and nature a Milanese, a native of a city deeply involved in

---

Wimmer, Ian Cosens, and Frank Andrews, *Voices of the Past,* 11 vols. (Lingfield: Oakwood, 1955–77), which can usefully be supplemented by the now fundamental book by Riccardo Bauer, *The New Catalogue of Historical Records, 1898–1908/1909* (London: Sidgwick and Jackson, 1947). Carlo Marinelli provides an annotated investigation of the phono- and discography of famous operas, with exhaustive documentation, in *Opera in disco da Monteverdi a Berg* (Fiesole: Discanto, 1982). Alan Blyth has a similar aim, although the individual essays are more succinct, in *Opera on Record,* 3 vols. (London: Hutchinson, 1979–84).

things operatic. I am referring, of course, to Edoardo Ferravilla (1846–1916), who had personal connections with the world of opera (his mother, Maria Luisa Ferravilla, was a singer).He studied music a bit, loved opera, and was one of the few who applauded the opening night of *Mefistofele.*

In the parade of characters and caricatures that Ferravilla created and brought to life in his hugely successful acting career, cleverly drawn from easily recognizable models, we find both the opera composer (a third-rate one, however) and singer, as hammy as he is voiceless: Maestro Pastizza (muddler) and Gigione (ham) were by no means minor characters in Ferravilla's imaginative world. Gigione was "created" for a production assembled—the only word for Ferravilla's texts—with Edoardo Giraud in the highly productive period between 1872 and 1880 and was eloquently entitled *Minestron.* This "minestrone" was a jumble of four scenes: the celebration, the parody play, *la traviata,* and the parody ballet. It was thus a satire on four basic aspects of the theater of the day. However, the best part was the third scene, which depended entirely on Ferravilla's presence and inventiveness and was devoted to opera. In the first version, the scene had *La traviata* in its sights, and Ferravilla, dressed as a woman, sang Violetta's most famous arias; but then *Il trovatore* took the place of *Traviata* because Ferravilla—at least according to the explanation in his memoirs—was afraid that someone might fall in love with him in drag. The real reasons, of course, were the difficulties the performance involved, and the audience reaction, and so he decided to transform the caricature from a soprano to a baritone. For the scene from *Trovatore,* as Ferravilla points out, again in his memoirs, permission was actually obtained from the Ricordi publishing house, which is very revealing of the power of Tito Ricordi, bearing in mind how Ferravilla (and others) casually appropriated other artists' material for adaptation without asking permission.

Ferravilla explains the birth of Gigione thus:

> It is then that I thought up the character of Gigione, that is, the character of many singers who have lovely voices as long as they are in the Galleria in Milan telling their circle of courteous friends of their amazing achievements but, as soon as they get an engagement, find the air in the theater fatal for them, their voices fail, and the audience boos. I probably had the idea from seeing an absolutely typical example of those great artists walking through the Galleria. But rather than this or that person it was my natural instinct for observation that certainly made me take advantage of the characteristics common to all living Gigioni.[91]

Like all Ferravilla's creations, a mere reading of his script for this scene just does not stand up today, but we do have a "live" description by Cletto Arrighi:

91. *Edoardo Ferravilla parla della sua vita, della sua arte, del suo teatro,* 2d ed. (Milan: Società Editoriale Italiana, n.d.), 48ff.

Anyone who has seen Gigione in the role of the Conte di Luna and has heard him, with his thin but perfectly modulated baritone voice, sing the famous solo in the prison has no need for me to explain it to them. Whoever has not seen it may imagine everything that is most subtle and inspired in a parody of a terrible, cracked-voice singer and that might win applause. The thread of a voice, the interruptions when the orchestra plays a little louder, the little walks up and down to add tragic significance and to conceal the lack of a voice are all the funniest things imaginable. A bell rings. He turns round in terror. He stands for a moment, lost in thought, then throws the edge of his white cape across his sword and says:

   Better it were to flee!

And on armored tiptoe he creeps offstage. The famous trio with the chorus then follows. The prima donna shrieks as she embraces Giraud as the troubadour:

   Sei tu dal ciel disceso

   o in ciel son io con te?

Ferravilla wants to attack the troubadour but is continually held back by his faithful followers. Then all his repressed rage is channeled into a wordless double-bass-type accompaniment:

   ro, to, trom; trom, trom;

   ro, to, trom; trom, trom

which produces an incredible effect. And the act ends as he disappears astride one of his followers.[92]

It is easy to imagine, from this description, how the scene not only provided the "dreadful sight" of a "terrible, cracked-voiced" baritone but also evoked, overall, the irrational, grotesque, and naturally comic side of operatic convention to an educated audience able to grasp the allusion.

Maestro Pastizza also had an operatic context; he, too, like Gigione, burns with ambition, a third-rate composer, an amateur desperate to measure himself against the "master." But here, too, in the *Opera del Maester Pastizza*, laughter and the sense of satire are created not only by the "characters" (or caricatures, depending on how you view Ferravilla's creations) with their excesses but also by the whole context in which they operate, or wish to operate. This explains the function of the more extended presence of arias and choruses in Pastizza's opera, which certainly, in the minds of the audience, went beyond a satire on an incompetent, bungling amateur to cover the whole world of opera. References, quotations, evocations, and hints are readily identifiable. The soprano, signora Gallettini (Little Chicks), sings:

Io son la prima donna	[I am the prima donna
che note ho nel garguzzolo	and the notes in my throat
simile ad un violin.	are like a violin's.
Udrete un gran portento,	What a wonder you will hear,

92. Cletto Arrighi [Carlo Righetti], *Ferravilla: Studio critico biografico* (Milan, Aliprandi, 1888), 70–74.

o mio signor garbato,
udrete il mio zin zin!

O my kind sir,
you'll hear my zin zin!]

And the tenor, Tapponi (Podgy):

Io son più di Rubini,
ho note così flebili
che fan rabbrividir.
Udrete un gran portento,
o mio signor garbato,
che vi farà stupir.

[I am greater than Rubini,
I have such plaintive notes
they make people shiver.
What a wonder you'll hear,
O my kind sir,
that will amaze you.]

And the bass, Bergamasco:

Un basso io son profondo
che note ho sì terribili
che sembrano un cannon.
Udrete un gran portento,
o mio signor garbato,
udrete il mio pimm pomm!

[I am a deep bass
with such terrifying notes
they sound like a cannon.
What a wonder you'll hear,
O my kind sir,
you'll hear my pimm pomm!]

And lastly the chorus:

Noi siamo tai coristi
con voci sì diaboliche
senz'altro paragon.
Udrete un gran portento,
o mio signor garbato,
udrete un gran pimm pomm!

[We are choristers
with such diabolical voices
beyond compare.
What a wonder you'll hear,
O my kind sir,
you'll hear a great pimm pomm!]

And the aria that Maester Pastizza himself sings against those who wish to prevent him from staging his opera becomes, playing cleverly with a scheme of an aria within an aria, an irresistible all-encompassing parody of Italian opera; but it should not overlooked that there is genuine "affection" for opera there as well: opera was so ingrained in the consciousness of the day that it allowed total freedom to whoever chose to make fun of it in comic scenes in a vaudeville act:

Ah! lei chiama pazzie
dell'arte il sacro amor?
Di tai parole rie
non sente in cor orror?
Si scosti, io lo ripudio,
indegno egli è di me,

[Ah! so you call the sacred love
of art a madness?
Do you not feel horror
in your heart at such wicked words?
Away, I reject you,
you are unworthy of me,

vanne dai cieli *ad inferos,*	go from the heavens to the infernal regions
fra noi distanza v'è.	we are poles apart.
Ah! dove siete, o martiri	Ah! Where are you, O martyrs
dell'arte musicale?	to the art of music?
Venite qui, schiacciatemi	Come hither, and crush
quel misero mortale.	this miserable mortal.
Oh! Donizetti, oh! Porpora,	Oh! Donizetti, oh! Porpora,
Pedrotti, Paganini,	Pedrotti, Paganini,
oh! Mercadante, oh! Coppola,	oh! Mercadante, oh! Coppola,
Beethoven, Boccherini,	Beethoven, Boccherini,
Coccia, Mozart, Vaccai,	Coccia, Mozart, Vaccai,
Mendelssohn, Bottesini,	Mendelssohn, Bottesini,
Gobatti, Pergolesi,	Gobatti, Pergolesi,
Meyerbeer, Rossini,	Meyerbeer, Rossini,
Ponchielli, Cimarosa,	Ponchielli, Cimarosa,
Auber, Petrella, Peri,	Auber, Petrella, Peri,
Wagner, Asioli, Nini,	Wagner, Asioli, Nini,
Rossini, Aidin, Pacini,	Rossini, Aidin, Pacini,
oh! Glinka, Majer, Weber,	oh! Glinka, Majer, Weber,
Paisiello, Cherubini,	Paisiello, Cherubini,
oh! Generali, oh! Manna,	oh! Generali, oh! Manna,
ah! angelico Bellini!	ah! angelico Bellini!
E Verdi? Oh! sommo aiutami,	And Verdi? Oh! Come to my aid, Most High,
tu pur invoco, inspirami	I invoke you as well, inspire in me
tal melodia terribile	such a terrifying melody
da farlo tramortir!	that will knock him unconscious!
Di tal bestemmia	Still I hear
l'orrido accento	the awful sound
ancor io sento	of such a curse
per l'aer suonar.	ringing in the air.
Deh! vanne, scostati,	Ah! go, leave
dal guardo mio,	my sight,
o giuro a Dio	or I swear to God
l'avrai a pagar.	you'll regret it.]

These are words of satire, parody, and excess put into the mouth of a chaotic maestro, but apart from the inspired litany of the "martyrs to the art of music," can we hear the style, the vocabulary, the rhetoric, and the meter as anything other than those of the librettos of the day? I think not. Edoardo Ferravilla's audience certainly had a very broad social base; his admirers were people of some standing in all the Milanese social strata: the aristocracy, the middle-class, and the artisans. A fair number of Ferravilla's lines left the Teatro Milanese and became everyday expressions for the populace (*Me foo a ciapal se 'l sta minga fermo?* "I could get him if he would just stand still"; from the *Duell del Sur Pànera*), and Ferravilla was undoubtedly a "popular" actor, in the sense that many of his characters were "of the people" and his theatrical presentations had no intellectual ambitions. But Ferravilla's audience was still an urban one, and it would be a mistake to imagine that Maestro Pastizza's grotesque arias could really be greeted by knowing, involved laughter by the majority of Italians of his day, still largely isolated in cultures that were archaic or at the very least behind the times.

I have already mentioned how the genre of satire of opera, of its characters, of its world thick with ambition and exhibitionism, did not spring into life with Edoardo Ferravilla; nor did it end with him. In fact, it continued for quite some time, only to die with the decline of the active presence of opera in the consciousness of society; looking for an approximate date, I would put it at around the 1930s.

During this twilight period, the world of opera nevertheless managed to continue to inspire intelligent and acute observations from talented comedians. I wish to recall three of these here, all of whom were active between the 1920s and the end of the 1930s: Ettore Petrolini (1886–1936), Rodolfo De Angelis (1893–1964), and Dina Galli (1875–1951). Among Ettore Petrolini's less well known but in no way "minor" pieces is a sketch entitled "Lirica," which certainly loses much in being simply read, without hearing his cleverly grotesque, sophisticated musical rendition of the commonplaces and most blatant idiocies of bel canto. Petrolini catches the repetitive nature of operatic poetry to perfection and constructs his "aria" on the words "O Margherita, non sei più tu" (Margherita, you are not who you were), words that he makes a point of declaring (and repeating) to be his own, all the better to expose, through his pride in authorship, their very insignificance:[93]

"Lirica": the words are my own.

O Margherita!
O Margherita!
You are not who you were!
You are not who you were!
You are not, you are not, you are not . . . no, when I said not, I meant not, oh!
O-o-oa-ohhha-ohhha-oa-ou-bu-bu-bo-bo-bo-bo-bo-bobò . . .
bop-bop-bop-bop . . .
I've never understood a word of this . . .
You are not who you were!

Margherita!
You are not who you were!
You are not, not you, not you, not my Margherita!

93. Ettore Petrolini, *Lirica,* spoken by Ettore Petrolini, matrix number BM 1050-1 (251074), La voce del padrone HN 534.

Ohhhhhhh Margherita
(the words are still my own),
   you are not who you were!
   Aa-aaa-aa-aaaa-a-aa . . .
   Ee-eee-aa-eeee-e-ee . . .
(god, you're subtle!)
   E-ee-eeee-ee-e-eeee-ee-e . . .
   I-ii-iii-i-i-iiii-ii-i . . .
(damn it!)
   I-ii-iiii-aa-aaaa-aaaa-aa . . .
(I must ask you to accompany me to the police station.)
   Oh Margherita,
   you are not who you were
      you are not who you were, not who you were, are you, my Margherita?
   Oh Margherita!
   You are not who you were!
   Do not be angry,
   life is short.
   You are not who you were, my Margherita,
   you are not who you were,
   you are not who you were,
   YOU ARE NOT WHO YOU WERE!

The character of the opera singer could not escape the acerbic eye of Rodolfo De Angelis, a minor genius who only now, in a rather fashion-led spirit of revival, is beginning to be rediscovered. De Angelis was an actor and café concert singer but also a delightful painter, a stylish writer, and a not-always-successful impresario; it was also his fate to be involved in the uproar of futurism, and he was marked by this experience. As a Neapolitan transplanted to Milan, he was able to grasp the lesson of the great line of Milanese culture, which extends from Carlo Porta to Carlo Emilio Gadda, by way of Carlo Dossi, the Scapigliati, and the futurists; possibly De Angelis was not just the only person able to make practical use of the spirit of futurism but also the most inspired interpreter of Marinetti's teaching, with its celebration of music hall, in opposition to opera.

In one of Rodolfo De Angelis's songs from the period following his futurist involvement (1933, to be precise), the hero is a great, famous, trumpeting tenor: we see him singing a jumbled serenade to his adored, who, despite the hero's successes in South America, in Russia, and in Paris, no longer loves him:[94]

94. Rodolfo De Angelis, *Romanza di un tenore innamorato,* sung by Rodolfo De Angelis, matrix number 100-2802 (OW 2267), Grammofono HN 435.

A romanza I must sing,
a romanza I must sing,
for my beloved, who loves me no more
for my beloved, who lo-o-o-o-o-o-o-o-o-o-ves me no more!
    When I sang in South America
    I was so successful
    that I was in the papers
    and you love me no more.
When in Russia the horses lifted me from the troika,
when in Paris the ladies threw me kisses and flowers,
ah, what emotion, a-a-a-a
what fantastic success
and what millions, a-a-a-a
and what millions!
and you love me no more, alas!
    For you have no love
    for your famous teno-o-o-o-o-r.
    for you have no love
    for your famous teno-o-o-o-o-r.
Ah, who can sing "Lucia" better than I?
[woman's voice:] (windbag, windbag)
Ah, where can you find a great tenor like me?
[woman's voice:] (windbag, windbag)
And you don't love me, why?
    But if you don't love me
    there are others who do.
    Why don't you love me?
    Why don't you love me?
    And the public acclaims me,
    it wants me,
    it calls for me,
    still to the footlights,
    still to the footlights,
    and you love me no more,
    and you love me no more,
    no mo-o-o-o-o-o-o-o-o-o-o-o-re!

In this case, too, the text on its own gives only part of the satire at work continuously between the words and the music; the representation of operatic styles is far from hackneyed, and approaches vulgarity, certainly, but is no less indicative of their "abnormality."

Lastly, let us hear Dina Galli in two delightful sketches on record, also from the 1930s. The texts are by Ermete Liberati and were recorded for the Gramophone Company, which was soon to become His Master's Voice (La voce del padrone) in Italy as well. This Milanese seamstress, explaining operas to a girl, the youngest worker in the shop, can easily be heard as an anticipation of Franca Valeri; equally, it is not difficult to pick up the delight (not particularly refined but certainly entertaining) in double entendre (to be honest, thinking of Milanese dialect, not very double).

Dinetta (the seamstress) explains two operas to the young girl. To start with, here is a hilarious account of the plot of *Lohengrin*:

> "Never, as thou dost love me . . . aught shall to question move me . . ." Ah, *Lohengrin,* what an opera! Not the music, but the show, it's absolutely wonderful. When the curtain goes up, there's the king in the square, waiting to pass judgment on Elsa, who's accused of killing her brother. She's full of remorse and contrite, and she says, "Your Majesty, you have to believe me, I'm innocent, because I had this dream that a bird will come out of the water." (That's going to be the swan.) And in fact, after a minute, they all go, "The swan! The swan!" (That's the bird in the water.) And in the middle, just like an Easter egg, out jumps Loingrìn. "Your Holy Majesty," he says, "I can tell you that this girl is innocent, and I'm going to marry her without even putting up the banns." Then the king says, "Well, if that's the case, I've nothing else to say." But Loingrìn takes Elsa to one side and says to her, "Remember that you're never to ask me my name. It's absolutely none of your business." So Elsa says, "No, I couldn't care less; you're going to marry me and so I'll take everything blind." "All right?" "All right!" So off they go and get married, all happy, but then one of Elsa's best friends arrives, and she's jealous because she'd like to take her place, and she says to her, "Hang on a minute, you're a right one . . . are you really going to marry a man when you don't know what his name is? He might be a criminal, he might be the devil." "No, no, don't you come putting ideas in my head. He's so good, he's so kind . . ." Oh well, now she's gone and put a suspicion in her heart. Know what I mean? When they're in the wedding chamber, Elsa says to Loingrìn, "Excuse me, it's quite something not being able to say your lovely name." "Just forget it," he says, "feel the lovely breeze, look at the lovely flowers . . ." "Forget the flowers," she says. "It's my garden, I know what they look like. Do you understand that sometimes I'd like to be able to call ou Francesco, Ambrogio, whatever you're called? Come on, what am I supposed to do? What if I called you Archimede by accident, think how silly I'd look . . ." Then he gets into a rage, gathers the whole council before the poor king, who's still sitting in the square, and drags up Elsa, who's a bit embarrassed. And he says, "Your Majesty, I'm sorry to have to say this, but because of this woman's inquisitiveness I'm going to have to leave, because we're not permitted to give out our address to anyone." And in fact as soon as he says, "My name is Loingrìn," you hear them saying again, "The swan! The gentle swan!" and once again the water bird turns up, with Elsa's brother on board, the one who was dead but is alive, and then Loingrìn says, "To prove your innocence, here's your brother, but remember, and I'm not just saying this, but you'll never find another young man like me." In fact, off he goes, with his lovely swan, and she's left high and dry. She doesn't know what to do then, so she dies. Poor girl, I got such a fright that now when anyone wants to make love to me, I always get terribly wor-

ried about swapping names ... of course ... I'm afraid that he'll go off with his lovely water bird,[95] too, know what I mean?[96]

And this is the summary of *La traviata:*

"*Sempre libbera degg'io trasvolar di gioia in gioia* ..." Eh? What did you say? Song? Oh you idiot, this is an opera ... a thing where everyone talks by singing, know what I mean? For example, if you go to take a dress to a customer, you knock gently on the door and go, "Excuse me!" But in an opera, first there's a big bang on the bass drum and then you come in and when you're right in you sing, "*Si può? Io sono il prologo,*" that's all ... is that clear? If a woman loves her boyfriend, she shrieks right into his face, "*Amami Alfredo, amami com'io t'a* ..." Got it? It's because she's thinking to herself, "Maybe if I say it in music, he'll pay more attention ..." And so that thing I was singing before that was the *Traviata* by Giuseppe Verdi. That's a conversation they have in the first act. There's the lady Violetta, who cools herself down with her fan—because in that opera the prima donna is always cooling herself down—and while she's having a chat with another man, all of a sudden along comes the tenor, who's Alfredo. As soon as she sees him, she says, "God, what a handsome young man!" And as it happens, when he sees her, he says "Blimey, what a lovely girl!" Then they're introduced. He says, "Pleased to meet you," and she says, "Oh no, please, the pleasure's all mine," and Alfredo says back to her, "Oh no, it's really mine, because ... I'm a bit shy ... but there's something I'd like to say ..." "Say it, then, don't be shy." "Well, you know, I, I wanted to say that the minute I saw you I thought you looked nice and if you think the same way ... well, maybe we could get together ..." Well, she stands there for a moment, hesitating and a bit worried, and then she says, "Yes, I wanted to tell you, too, I like you, I think you're nice, but you know ... I can't give you an answer just like that. Wait till two or three days have passed and then I'll tell you for definite." Then they do all the polite things and afterward he goes away. Then she's on her own. And while she's cooling herself down—because she's always cooling herself down—she's thinking, "Oh, what shall I do? What shall I not do? He's a nice young man, I'm not denying it, I like him, but what about later on? What if he dumps me? That's all I'd need. No, no, no, it's much better if I hang on to two or three, because at least if he leaves, then I've always got another one ready." And then, d'you see, she sings, "*Sempre libbera degg'io* ..." Got it? It's a shame because after she's found love, she gets a terrible cold and has to call the doctor, who tells her, "*La tisi non le acorda che poche ore.*" And in fact, she dies while she's saying goodbye to the past. Oh, my dear, let me tell you, opera's a wonderful thing![97]

95. *Ucello* (*uccello* in standard Italian) also means "prick."

96. Ermete Liberati, *Dinetta al "Lohengrin,"* spoken by Dina Galli, matrix number OBA 542-1, Grammofono GW 1100.

97. Ibid. The reader might like to supplement this eminently Milanese documentation of operatic parody and caricature for the music hall with the very early Neapolitan documentation in Roberto De Simone, "Il mito del San Carlo nel costume napoletano," in *Il teatro di San Carlo*

After that, the world of so-called light entertainment found no more reason to quote from opera. At most, as the war was starting, Italian opera provided a rather casual and careless reference to the serenade of a penguin in love:

> Guarda guarda guarda il bel pinguino innamorato
> col colletto duro e con il petto inamidato
> va passeggiano sopra il pack
> con un'aria molto chic
> dondolando mollemente il frac.
> Sotto il chiar di luna va a cantar la serenata
> dove fa la nanna la pinguina innamorata:
> "O bella figlia dell'amor
> schiavo son dei vezzi tuoi"

> [Look, look, look at the lovely penguin in love
> with his stiff collar and his starched breast
> as he walks across the pack ice
> with an air that's very chic
> swinging his tailcoat gently.
> By the light of the moon he goes to sing a serenade
> where the lady penguin in love is sleeping:
> *"O bella figlia dell'amor*
> *schiavo son dei vezzi tuoi"*][98]

(Naples: Guida, 1987), 1:413–41, who gives selected passages from the comedies written for the Teatro San Carlino by Pasquale Altavilla (1806–72) and the Punchinello Antonio Petitto (1822–76). Altavilla's comedy *Na famiglia ntusiasmata per la bella museca de lo Trovatore* (1860) is memorable for its hopeless attempt at a summary of the "tough plot" and the events before the curtain rises on Verdi's opera. The narrator gets himself out of this fix by declaring, "Anyway, as I see it, the libretto isn't that important. The thing that gives you an electric shock is hearing those tunes and especially the tenor's top note, because you would need a steam train to hold on to it that long!" (He picks up his guitar and sings "Di quella pira"; at the end everyone applauds.)

98. Casiroli and Consiglio, *Il pinguino innamorato*, sung by Silvana Fioresi with the Trio Lescano (1939), Cetra record GP 93133.

— 6 —

Opera in Italian National Culture

GIOVANNI MORELLI

I. THE QUESTION OF POPULARITY

"At the opera the other evening the head of the claque must have fallen asleep." With these words Eugenio Montale begins his short piece *Il successo* (1950),[1] a witty story with a curious kind of charm that seems to go to the root of the problem of defining the relationship between Italian opera and Italian culture.

"The opera," writes Montale, "was lovely, *but not popular,* and encouraged sleep." This is why the head of the claque, suddenly wakened by some dream or other, begins to applaud at an inappropriate and ineffectual point in the bass's aria. So when, shortly afterward, the bass actually does decide to drop down to his low note, no one in the auditorium is any longer convinced by the renewed applause of the claque, emanating from the "suspect" location. The story continues:

> We ought to show considerable indulgence toward those who belong to the claque. I doubt if they earn very much, and on occasions when the audience displays unjustified coolness toward the champions of the *lyric art,* they fulfill a perfectly understandable function. An opera with no applause warms no one's heart, it doesn't even amount to a performance. If we were to miss out on seeing Radames and Ramfis appear before the curtain after their simultaneous bellowing of "Immenso

1. It first appeared as a feature on the literary page of *Corriere della sera* on 17 May 1950 and was published in its definitive form in Montale's *Farfalla di Dinard* (Milan: Mondadori, 1960), 61–65. In the subsequent quotations, the italics are mine, apart from the reference to "failed artists."

Ftà," and forego the chance to inspect their bathrobes and turbans at close quarters, then we would lose half the pleasure *Aida* can give. If we don't grunt some approval of Sparafucile's gargling note as he leaves Rigoletto after suggesting his hideous bargain, then at the very least we show a lack of charity, of solidarity with our fellow human beings. That modest scraping noise is not a difficult sound to produce, but it is not simply a sound, it symbolizes a whole life underground. If you have lived in rented rooms, or fourth-rate hotels and pensions, then you will have heard thousands of these, non-Dostoyevskian "voices of the underworld."

More than one idea comes out of this little incident: after defending the members of the claque, Montale sets off on a series of lighthearted reminiscences. He recalls how he himself once joined a claque, in the pay of a barber from Liguria, for the premiere of an opera by a local avant-garde composer, José Rebillo, and how he rebelled and betrayed his orders when he joined in the disgraceful chorus of condemnation shouting "Death to Rebillo!" The composer in question was the sort of artist who believed in the purity of art, and he lived in a Gothic revival tower on the seafront, where he punched holes in "picturesque" patterns onto piano rolls to create the most unusual combinations of sounds. Montale also recalls how the unfortunate Rebillo was associated with a local poet, Armando Riccò. Aloof, dandified, and sporting a monocle (although not, as one might expect, a follower of D'Annunzio), Riccò was proud of his verses chock-full of diaereses and enraptured by the sound of musico-poetic declamation, which echoed round the tower in its splendid isolation by the sea. Now they are no more. The little castle has tumbled down, Riccò's papers have been lost, and who knows where the piano rolls have ended up. That little flash of memory prompted by the sound of the incident of the claque leads the writer to formulate a truth which he believes to be too little known: "art," Montale has discovered, "bestows its consolations *on failed artists most of all.*"

Montale's haphazard sequence of parables is more than a series of literary doodles or caricatures, however. Consider each element: the member of the claque; his sense of timing; the whole idea—buried in autobiographical details (down to the hellish sounds of life in cheap hotels)—that opera is there to be received, from Ramfis's bellowing turbans to Sparafucile's guttural realism; the isolation of poets and intellectual purists (all failures); and popularity (in Italy, it seems, not always aligned with the *beauty* of the operas, and liable to be undermined by the mistakes of the claque-receiver-guide). Each is far from being marginal to the history of Italian national culture. Quite the reverse.

The story is in fact an allegory. Its real subject, not touched by design, is the opposition of the two poles characterizing Italian culture as it came into being together with the Italian people themselves, from the time of Napoleon to the present day. On the one hand, clearly delineated, stand those writers consoled by their art, the artist-philosophers and the great lyric poets, acclaimed and eternally unpopular. Perhaps Montale is even humorously intending to portray some of the greatest names as "failures": either because in their obstinate love of things eternal they fell from the heights of public art to the abyss of private poetizing, or because they grasped at theories they could bend to prove that they, the writers, existed as cultural icons even before the Italian nation did, or else because of their attachment to past experiences of a unique work of art. On the other hand, Montale lets us see the unrestrained, shared, and exuberant popularity, both official and unofficial, of the "lyric art" in its strict sense of opera, and Verdian opera in particular. This is a popularity that is easy to make out and is deep-rooted—from the original texts down to texts on its reception and history—according to mixed systems of performance practice and assumptions of varying durability (whether thematic, textual, or figurative) and to still other combinations of variables and the enduring parallels between the character and function of the audience. These characters are as much interpreted in the texts as expected and can even be seen as completely typical of Italian behavior and sensibility—so typical, in fact, that we can perceive them in the pit and in the gallery, alive and accountable, just like the claque. The member of the claque is indeed one of the few reliable witnesses for the existence of an Italian cultural character: we find him in the very act of awarding "success" at every lyrical moment designed to please in the most complex tangle ever seen of public and private art, of "sentimental" and "naive" philosophy, of the old and the new.

Such hybrids of good and bad romanticism—one the cult of liberty, the other a crisis of the will—may be loved by the people and disapproved of by such a stern critic as Benedetto Croce, but they seem to feed entirely on something subcultural. Their success has frequently been castigated as a kind of original sin in that national lack of culture to which Italy the nation is only too ready to confess.

An interesting feature of Montale's piece is that he is happy to accept, possibly for the first time in a literary text, the expropriation of the term "lirica."[2] Through denial of its principal meaning, which (for the classicists, romantics, and in ancient times) referred to the highest form of literature, this term had come to refer solely to Italian opera (from Verdi on and, perhaps, retrospectively, from Verdi back a little). Montale happily accepts the fact that the new term is, so to speak, twice consecrated, not only by the people but by

---

2. Salvatore Battaglia's *Grande dizionario della lingua italiana* gives another arguably "literary" use of the term "lirica" in Stuparich's *Simone* (1953): "the sentimental aria from an *opera lirica*"; clearly, "lirica" is used to indicate, with veiled indifference, more a genre than an Italian "art form." [*La lirica* and the adjective *lirico* are generally used to mean "opera" and "operatic" in modern Italian—Trans.]

the government as well: the concept has become law with the establishment and management of the Enti lirici,[3] the administrative term for Italy's eleven leading opera houses.

Nowadays Montale's distinction amid the "consolations" of Italian art (both of the Risorgimento and after Unification)—between hearing an opera *with* and *without* the presence of a claque—is probably taken for granted by the cultural world and found to be of little interest: that is, with and without widespread popularity of pieces whether fixed or variable, with and without acknowledging, in creating works of art, the essential importance of the public's response to a performance (that is, allowing for a "Bravo!" at the correct point).

On the *with* side, opera is the perfect manifestation of the function of popular art. To its immense ambiguity we owe the equally immense swelling of the empirical audience, from which, for Italians, the "assembly" of a people's "character" (created, tended, and ever under a watchful eye) seems to derive. (From now on, "people" will be taken to mean a vast national middle class, possibly the one to which the poet and patriot Giovanni Berchet looked forward as a new class, which would dissolve that perverse division of the Italian people into refined "Parisians" and coarse "Hottentots," as they had been in the early years of the move toward nationhood, at the time of *Il conciliatore*,[4] the periodical he helped found.)

2. THE UNOBTAINABLE CULTURAL CHARACTER OF THE NEW NATION

Never has the birth (spurred on by political faits accomplis more than anything) of a new culture been attended by so much disgust and pessimism as in the period, starting at the very end of the eighteenth century, that paved the way for the construction of the nation of Italy during the Risorgimento: the period that stretches from the very last events of the eighteenth century to the crucible of Unification, which immediately made a holocaust of unwitting generations with the entry into World War I.

At the outset, in the period of protective governments, of states small and large, in the "Italic"[5] period par excellence, there was much scrambling after

---

3. See the very title of the royal decree of 3 Feb. 1936, XIV, n. 438: *Disciplina degli Enti lirici e delle stagioni liriche gestiti dai Comuni e dagli Enti autonomi* ("Vittorio Emanuele III, by the grace of God, etc.").

4. The figure of the "Hottentot" comes from Berchet's *Lettera semiseria* (the reference is to the individual in the crowd who becomes dangerous when he is multiplied within that crowd, as in the riot in *I promessi sposi*). For the democrat Berchet, the true "people" are quite different, a great middle class, culturally salvageable.

5. The first flurry of activity in the search for definitions of "Italic" and "Italian" came in the wake of the earliest commentaries on the revolutions at the beginning of the nineteenth century; in particular, see the work of the economist Melchiorre Cuoco, writing in Milan after the Neapolitan revolution (both in the context of the anthropological myth of his *Plato in Italy* and in his commentaries on current events in the *Giornale d'Italia*, where, interestingly, he frequently makes

a character model: the Latin, Catholic, Jacobin, Samnite, Etruscan, the long-forgotten indigenous Italic people from the dark ages, or the ranks of the Roman army—Legionary, Conscript, and Rustic.

Then came the malaise of pessimism. Commentators turned to self-criticism or took up extreme positions, and groups were formed to campaign alternatively in favor of theoretical representations and moods—all interpreted in different forms but sharing similarities in outward appearance and intensity of expression. It is worth noting down some points on expressive phases of the phenomenon. We can see this attitude growing from Manzoni's "So why write verses?" of 1804 to his description "filthy century" (at times "dreadful") whose "fetid slime" he was ready to "stir up" a year later, on the death of his mother's companion, Carlo Imbonati. (The young Manzoni, the influential godparent of Italy's foremost literature, is possibly playing here with the double meaning of "secolo," referring both to the century and to the secular world, and gently leading the reader to perceive all history in the term. Perhaps he means all secular, political history, either because it can never be understood or because it is the foundation for those absurd, false types of scholarship that claim to study earlier generations in order to provide a model for later ones. Manzoni thus favors any and every kind of "sacred" interpretation of humanity's age-old ills. He then assigns these interpretations to a historical, sacred function, that of Providence. If Providence can never create any kind of reality on its own, in achieving and providing reparation for injustice, then it can easily be introduced as a kind of highly sophisticated deus ex machina in a novel of "philosophical" observations.)[6]

Different but related commentaries would follow Manzoni's disgusted appraisal: among the last of them, Carducci's "cowardly little Christianizing century" or Leopardi's "great haze of tedium"; and the never-ending irritations of all "classical" pedants (the perfect—and prophetic—example being that of Giordani[7] inveighing against a nation "rich only in trifles"). Particu-

---

comparisons with the supposedly "national" politics of the thirteenth-century Holy Roman emperor Frederick II.

6. With reference to *I promessi sposi*, it should not be forgotten how, in the twenty-five details of the first twenty-five readings of the Lombard intellectual club—as in the story itself—Manzoni creates a value system to support the validity of "economic" thought in the progressive movement of eighteenth-century Lombardy. This system stands in opposition to the rhetorical and metaphorical thinking typical of Italian culture in medieval and ancient times (many acts of Providence recurring in the novel arise from cues in Gioia's 1802 book on the commerce of foodstuffs and "provisions"). Manzoni's hidden (and realistic) modernity lies behind many of the narrative approaches that most jeopardized the "popularity" of his book.

7. Pietro Giordani (1774–1848), the leading figure among left-leaning classicists and progressive pedants and a model for those who strenuously yet unsuccessfully pursued Enlightenment philosophies, was the person most keenly aware of the bitter war of the "mass of thoughts" threatening the style of writing that found least fulfillment in what he called the "age of trifles." He did not hesitate to strike mortal blows at "classicism for its own sake," which he branded "the prin-

larly because of its relevance to many of the arguments in this essay, it is worth recalling Carlo Tenca's criticism of his "century" [8]—that it was sick with an endemic sickness in which Italians think only of "old ideas in new forms or new ideas in old forms." (Decades of conflict between these two obtuse tendencies created a paralyzed culture in an immobile country where two enemy hearts beat, and light skirmishes would break out between the classical and romantic corners.)

That paralysis and immobility went on to be highly productive, in terms of ideas and forms, both fixed and fluid, and the explanation does not lie in the lack of "reconciliation" between the various cultural standpoints. I have spoken of two hearts, but the two souls were fraying at the edges: the internal contradictions of so-called romanticism were revealed by all romantics to bring out both a propensity for the old (even a reactionary gaze back to the Middle Ages) and a need for the new, allowing for certain compromises between modern, eighteenth-century materialistic culture and a newly spiritual nineteenth century. The model was a certain ideological sensibility that was almost always in awe of intellectual religiosity but led toward hybrid democratic visions, ever ready to reflect while waiting for action.[9]

As the two sides became frayed, the opposition of classical and romantic began to break down. Thus, the patriot (and pro-reconciliation) Piero Maroncelli coined the monstrous distinction between a classical "scuola profilare" and a romantic "scuola cormentale." [10] De Sanctis suggested that

---

ciple of the current age" and as one showing "a *helpless* desire to reinvent itself as the Italian culture; see his *Scritti,* vol. 5, in his *Opere,* ed. Antonio Gussalli, 14 vols. (Milan: Borroni, Scotti, and Sanvito, 1854–62), 12:140.

8. See also the similar application of a concept close to Tenca's in the (not always consistently applied) formulation of Francesco De Sanctis: in his *History of Italian Literature,* trans. anonymous (New York: Harcourt Brace, 1931), he alludes to romantic rationalists and freethinkers in literature who are "loyal" traditionalists in matters of religion, as well as to other romantics, who are unbelievers in religion but "superstitious" in art. Then there is the ultratraditionalist Cesare della Valle, duke of Ventignano, who, in the same Naples that was home to the purist Basilio Puoti, mixed everything together: progress, philosophy, science, harsh rhythms, "demonic eruptions from music's impure lips," echoes of wailing, and so on. With critical shrewdness, he accused all manifestations of modernity of being "old rags in new forms."

9. Manzoni's *Observations* of 1819 (on Catholicism and its moral outlook), all evidence of the author's precocious maturity, continue to refer persistently and often irritatingly to the single theme of the improbability, instability, and indefinability (with a touch of all smoke and no fire) of the "philosophical" promises of a practical transformation of the world: man in general—but, it seems, the Italian more than ever and more than others—is unable to establish a "public morality" (thus the assumption that "public morality" is pure nonsense).

10. Piero Maroncelli, in his "Additions" to *My Prisons: Memoirs of Silvio Pellico: Addizioni alle "Mie prigioni"* (Lugano: Ruggia, 1833), 46–48. English edition: *My Prisons: Memoirs of Silvio Pellico,* 2 vols. (Cambridge, Mass: C. Folsom, 1836); vol.2 has "Additions to My Prisons: Memoirs of Silvio Pellico." [The "cormentale" style was understood to indicate an aesthetic viewpoint aimed at matching emotional expression to its rational control, and it was shared by many

his own distinction between a "democratic school" and a "liberal school" should be used with great care; his aim was also to defend the potential for unification, which he himself foresees, at the end of his examination of history, will be won both on the battlefield and in the historians' achievement of power—political, academic, and ministerial.[11]

Labels aside, the facts alone suggest that plenty of hybrids were taking shape: some writers (such as the Tuscans Capponi, Vieusseux, and others) pursued them in order to create a national culture of the happy medium, prejudicially vague in its relationship to the precarious existing powers,[12] and so avoid the naiveté of the Milanese, Piedmontese, and Neapolitans, who accepted and paid the price for false promises; others pursued them in a frenzied exercise in style; still others accepted and voiced them in their collected works (and only a complete analysis of their writings, read in strict critical order, can reveal the phenomenon). As the desire to form a group of intellectuals was increasingly frustrated, these last turned into writers with highly individual voices (almost classics, like the two greatest, Manzoni and Leopardi).

Quite another resolution, with quite a different recipe, was that propounded by actual Risorgimento politics: "state policy" was a combination of various blends of nondemocratic moderate politics, completely unconnected to culture. The mood was fairly secular but by no means free of the influence of the clerical party (especially where the worlds of popular culture and domesticity were concerned, and children, women, the old, almshouses, nurseries, minor literature, rustic backdrops at the theater, puppet shows, etc., were all affected).[13] If the politicians agreed on a resolution, it was to cre-

---

late-eighteenth-century poets. In Maroncelli's critical definition of the mid-1840s, a "profilare" style was, in contrast, one that was both superficial and formally poised. By way of example, he defined biblical literature as "cormentale" and much of Roman and late Greek literature as "profilare."—Trans.]

11. See De Sanctis's *La letteratura italiana nel secolo XIX: Scuola liberale—scuola democratica; lezioni raccolte da Francesco Torraca, e pubblicate con prefazione e note da Benedetto Croce* (Naples: A. Morano, 1897; reprint, Manziana [Rome]: Vecchiarelli, 1996). Selections from four courses of lectures delivered at the University of Naples, 1872–76. Originally published from summaries and shorthand reports made by Torraca and revised by De Sanctis in the periodicals *La libertà* and *Il pungolo,* 1872.—Trans.

12. See Sebastiano Timpanaro's masterly critical observations "Sui moderati toscani e su certo neo-moderatismo," in his *Antileopardiani e neomoderati nella sinistra italiana* (Pisa: ETS, 1982), 49–96.

13. Although minor, ephemeral, and popular literature is, apart from the familiar promotion of the "noble poor" and the "devout wretch," not entirely lacking in progressive, scientific, semisecular, and edifying elements, it is always sugarcoated in the most cloying sermonizing style. See, for instance, the journal *Educatore del popolo* of the Mazzinian Enrico Mayer and the translation-parody-paraphrase of the great American prototype *Poor Richard's Almanack* by Benjamin Franklin. See also the Italian imitations of the latter, plainly written introductions whose aim was the education of a class of small savers and the collection of capital by the savings banks in more

ate many instances of nonagreement between political and cultural procedures. Out of this came a sense of unease and of unspoken opposition (especially to foreigners, such as the French, who had always been felt, simplistically, to be the principal "enemies") and the long-lasting malaise of the founding fathers of the new nation's culture, who viewed with suspicion the reconciled, middle-class Italian audience, which had no background in the hard-won paper skirmishes of an exclusively cultural nature. With this in mind, it is useful to look at the simplest, most innocuous of the analyses considered thus far, to try to throw some light on the question of how the old and the new intersected in terms of form and content, whose mixed parentage Tenca had already discovered.

3. HYBRIDS OF OLD AND NEW

This kind of analysis, which does not preclude helpful hints for cultural renewal, however illogical, led Carlo Tenca (a driving force in modern Milanese cultural life, associated with Verdi, by way of Clarina Maffei) to develop a genuine theory, which he published in pamphlet form and was consequently fairly widely read. In his neoromantic view, abuses such as harsh Schilleresque 'sentimental' aspirations, and obeisance to the cold mysticism of Manzoni, eaten away by ironic English or Byronesque doubts and by other raids on what was culturally possible, were to be superseded. Tenca's opinion (expressed in "Delle condizioni dell'odierna letteratura in Italia")[14] was that these "pastimes for the idle" and "riots of ideas" had held back Italy's cultural life, which seemed destined to proliferate desires for modernity that disappeared even before they had been hypothetically enjoyed. Italian culture, writes Tenca, "would like to take a leap into the future, but the concept of humanity, contested by many, and undecided for all, has not yet come into view. . . . No sooner has it won some brief acclaim and the sympathy of a small circle of readers . . . than it is lost behind a thousand other concepts." This problem touches on the chronic Italian tendency to continue to wait for political modernization to be translated into cultural experiences; so while waiting for the fruits of what the economist Jean-Charles-Léonard Sismonde de Sismondi called the "seedbed of the nation" to appear, after the hymns and patriotic songs, people turned to a depressed kind of poetry, witness for the prosecu-

---

or less rural areas. Given that none of the recently published, excellent studies on intellectual and literary life in Milan refer to it, it is also worth noting that *Buonuomo Riccardo* went through 100 editions in three years (1814–17) in Milan alone, on Silvestri's presses. For information on minor literature and its vast sales, the reader should glance at Dina Bertoni Jovine, *I periodici popolari del Risorgimento* (Milan: Feltrinelli, 1959).

14. See the "literary" pages of Tenca's journal *Il crepuscolo: Rivista di scienze, lettere, arti, industria e commercio* (1852), collected by Gianluigi Berardi in Carlo Tenca, *Saggi critici* (Florence: Sansoni, 1969), parts of which will be quoted from below.

tion against "boredom." But it would be unfair to focus on this tendency at the expense of political plans and schemes which did indeed come into being. Almost all were intended (by the right, the center, and the left) either to deny the mess already made by the French Revolution or to hold back rapid social changes that might be dangerously similar to those of the Revolution or else to step back in horror bfore the "true nature" of the Revolution's "materialism." [15]

Only strong feelings of expectancy and regression had a cultural identity. For example, there were the activities of movements for preserving medieval customs, which were actually put into practice. This tendency can be attributed to neomoderate intellectuals, who, to give the single clearest example, began to champion that historical and cultural monstrosity, the invention of sharecropping (later they were all to become ministers and leaders).[16] There was antihistorical propaganda in favor of the beneficial effects of misfortune, which persuaded a group of rather more than Manzoni's "25 readers" to a show of patriotism—dangerously close to Pascal's "wager"—when they stood against absolutely every form of "action" because as laity they did not know what woes Providence would bring to repay pragmatism. There was the classicist experience, unfortunately praised to the skies, which pessimistically retreated from the legacy of Enlightenment materialism (the "other philosophy" that "was seen to reign" and on whose appearance "brave, alert" modernity stepped back, cast down by its "bitter, sad" substance). To find some candid information on the question of how such backwardness can largely be attributed to the woeful lack of readers, both cursory and more searching, of writings on Italian poetry and art, we should look at women's literature, at the two ends of a period whose very length is eloquent (and remembering that stimuli were few and that there was little awareness that backwardness was something to be overcome and little sense of cultural service).

Let us begin in 1820, when the writer Silvio Pellico, chief editor of *La conciliazione,* sent a copy of Manzoni's "divine" verse tragedy *Il conte di Carmagnola,* which had just appeared, by express post to his brother Luigi, secretary to the governor of Genoa. Pellico first relates the rather hasty judgment of Vincenzo Monti, who has something of his own to say on the "negligent and prosaic" style (clearly the discussion here actually concerns something else: to be precise, the first signs of conscious importation of the Shakespearean mixture that later, in opera, would help to capture larger crowds of

15. "Thus you were displeased with the truth / of the bitter fate and sad home / which nature gave us. So, like a *coward,* / you turned your back to the light." (Is this a bitter confession or a violent expression of the panic at the cultural scope of the century and the nation?)

16. For information on the "reforming" attempts of Cosimo Ridolfi and Vincenzo Salvagnoli and on Tuscan moderate politics as well as the establishment of sharecropping in the "failed agrarian reform" of the highly feudal nineteenth century, see the essay of Timpanaro, cited above.

middle-class listeners, both cultivated and not, and women in particular). He
then conveys his appreciation of Manzoni's language, "free of idioms and
terms unrelated to prose"[17] precisely because this is what will endear it, and
make it tolerable, to the uneducated, particularly women. He goes on: "Most
women, for example, find it an effort to read Italian poetry (with the exception of Metastasio). Why is this? Because Italian poetry uses a language which
they do not know. Give them a language they already know and poetry will
gain many women readers and many more men." In 1855, thirty-five years
later, it seems that the problem of the "popularity" of Italian literature or
even of the very "written history" of Italy and of Italian culture as a whole
had not moved on. In that year, Ruggero Bonghi, one of the last anti-Bourbon
exiles from Naples living in the north, where he advocated modern cultural
organization (Carducci described him as "professor of everything at every
university," and he was the founder of that most forceful journal of opinion
La perseveranza), published sixteen long letters in the Florence *Spettatore:
Why Italian Literature Is Not Popular in Italy.*[18]

4. HOW AND WHY ITALIAN
LITERATURE DID NOT BECOME POPULAR IN ITALY

Bonghi's focus was not so much on the why as on the how, a question he lingered over: "books, I feel, of whatever genre, serious or light, are read less"
here than in the other European countries. Foreign authors, the preference of
those few existing Italian readers, "deal with our history in general and in detail," and we

17. The assimilation of and return to prose is an area of inquiry which, if it were not so fear-
fully kept in check (see the reticence of the double negative), ought to touch on the embryonic
question of the "national" recovery of the most "direct" style of writing, such as that in dialect.
Giordani decided to attack it, even if, anticipating Croce, he defended his position by maintaining
the nonaesthetic nature of his argumentation ("true poetry" could "never exist" in dialect) and
chose to fight against dialect in order to honor the (progressive) idea and the (democratic) dictate
"not to perpetuate the people's coarseness." In this sense, Giordani was refuting both literature inspired by dialect folklore as well as that concerned with perpetuating Latin. The fundamental
range of the national language is thus well outlined by Giordani (see *Scritti*, vol. 2, in his *Opere*,
9:379–83). There is no sign, however, of any interest (in debating the question) in the critical
problem of the single, unified language: not dialect, not coarse and distinguished by class, a language already unified and active—that of opera. Access was thus lost—and thereafter remained
forever barred—to a consideration of the problems of the mixed "success" of opera, both cultivated and folkloric.

18. Reprinted as *Lettere critiche*, with the subtitle *Perché la letteratura italiana non sia popolare in Italia* added by the publishers of the *Spettatore* (Milan: Colombo-Perelli, 1856). It went
through various editions under its more informative title (3d ed., Milan and Padua: Valentinier
and Mues, 1873; 4th ed., Naples: Morano, 1884). The passages quoted below are on pp. 1ff. (my
italics) and 191.

seem to feel more at home with a French or English book than with one of our own. At least, this is the feeling of the majority of readers, and especially of the women among them. In fact, for women . . . an Italian book either never falls into their hands or falls out again immediately, and one cannot prudently suggest something for them to read, since they will hand the book back before finishing it or, if they are on close terms with you, will tell you that you have caused them to be bored. Now, if modern literature is alien to women, it means that it is not alive. . . . A woman must be involved in literature more from above than from within; with her shrewd, accurate discernment, her delicate ability to feel, her tendency to observe the ways of the heart, her capacity to point out what is ridiculous, her grasp of the world, her need for truth, her living in the present, her natural inclination to be content only with ideas that have specific application or a boundless emotion, and her ability to express and support her own judgment with a smile and grace, she has a powerful, useful influence on the literature of a modern people. In addition, with her position in the family and in society, she is the most dependable and best-suited instrument for the dissemination of that culture. . . . We have had, *alas*, literary women, . . . but in our literature women have not exercised that role to which I have referred. . . . So our books, lacking [that is, in comparison with competing literature, like that of France, urbane, acute, vital, alert, and containing what is needed and enough to satisfy a female readership] the majority of readers, almost remain limited to those who make a profession of letters, who read to write, with the goal of being read by others like themselves.

Bonghi's observation is rather more acute than it might seem on first sight. In focusing on the reading habits of Italian women, who were all wearied beyond words by both classical pedantry and romantic chaos, as well as by the "reconciliation" of the two, he raises the issue of the general indifference to defining the type of national readership that should be created as the primary motive for conception and writing. Further on in one of his *Letters,* Bonghi points an accusing finger at those men of letters who aspire to imitate the supposed Italian classics and the untranslatable foreigners, who are likewise suffocated by the ostentation of their respective belles lettres. It also seems clear that in these early years of Unification, there is a powerful contradiction between two languages—one of common usage (irregular and local) and one of the stylistic norm: one lost to culture, the other considered unbearable by readers.

All those who have learned their language from their mothers think themselves unsuited to writing: and those who learn it from a teacher neither wish to know nor are taught their own language, but instead a "fine" language. In this fine language there are few things one is able to say, and none of them of any interest. Now, the timidity of those who have real language and the limited vocabulary of those who have fine language contrive to create a single truth: that the nonliterary do not write, or if they do write, they think that they don't, and hence so many intimate emotions, so many illustrations from life, for which the literary have no time, remain outside literature, turning it into a falsehood.

This description seems to fly in the face of theories for establishing cultural guidelines for the new nation. There was a flood of fine language (classical, romantic, Greco-Latin, Parisian), memoirs aplenty (catastrophes of both social conscience and of weak will), disdain for the problems of communication, and no interest in the emotions experienced in collective intimacy, while the same themes were rehashed in the eternal academic fine style. The Dalmatian-born writer and patriot Niccolò Tommaseo[19] was quick to propose (in *Della letteratura considerata come professione sociale*, 1832) a new profession, that of the intellectual; this would be a fundamental role with adequate remuneration and would no longer necessarily be the product of spare time and a private income. Tommaseo inveighs against the vacuities of "mythological fantasies," the orgies of generic declamation against tyranny and the "mannered lamenting of personal unhappiness, often exaggerated from weakness of invention"—simply put, against the excesses of "amateurism." But when faced by the question of "material reward," he is unable to propose anything better than the (sordid) goal of a "new aristocracy," that is, the establishment of a state nobility for the intellectuals. The whole matter is considered from the point of view of giving new weight to the activity of writing (governmental? ministerial?) as a means to the end of realizing Tommaseo's own ultimate dream: the destruction of freethinking, of spiritual revival, and of science, followed by the agitated reassertion of nostalgic populism in a neomedieval sideshow—all in his imagination—with the basic premise of turning back the clock on the French Revolution. In order to start curing readers of their attachment to "fiction" and the other maladies, general thinking seemed to tend toward a therapy based on doses of the language of everyday, domestic life (the thoughts and emotions either of the home or of the parish in a kind of linguistic maternity ward for the alleged "spoken language."

There were various instances of growing centralization, no less fictitious than Tommaseo's demand for a nobility; some of them, from outside the Christian establishment, were fanciful schemes of easy compromises between liberals and democrats. There were flights of fancy on the native, spoken language (but which one?) and fantasies that unification would come through the "central" collection of supposedly existing materials. (But which ones? Perhaps the popular almanacs of Sesto Cajo Baccelli, for example, or the

19. In the journal *Antologia* of July 1852, in an appendix to Tommaseo's own review of Giuseppe Manno's essay "Della politica e delle lettere."

more modern, scientific-literary ones of the *Nephew of Sesto Cajo Baccelli?* Orations? Books for newlyweds? Folk songs, set to music more or less from scratch, or not set to music at all, by Luigi Gordigiani and Pietro Paolo Parzanese? Reactionary folklike ballads against the workers' unions? Little imitations of Jacobin hymns? Extemporized drinking songs and other aspects of lower-middle-class culture?)[20] The search was on for themes that were "vivid and true," neglected, alive but disregarded, suitable for the people, who were said to have invented them, and who would like them back, restored by "art." If indeed there was anything answering this description, something of the "native," oral tradition, it was to be found only in the few shards and other small leavings abandoned by "Mother" Church (but the secular-liberal-democratic culture would certainly not be satisfied with these). Furthermore, the pointlessness of this interest was confirmed in the writings of the real scientific linguists of the time—Graziadio Ascoli, to choose one at random—who alerted their contemporaries as to how any sort of quandary in dealing with "imaginary" (or "thematically" formed) language ought to be avoided in the honorable drive to create "a common movement of minds"[21] in founding the new nation.

This was too complex a creative commitment. Certainly, for naive authors, it was easier to call up a phantom audience, one that was culturally undemanding and inclined toward a pleasant flow of "received ideas," and was just sensitive enough to the comforts of social and patriotic reassurance. Such, however, was the slippery slope of the nineteenth-century's collective stupidity, the one most feared (almost to the point of obsession) by genuine authors, who aspired more and more to certain forms of unpopularity (or

20. The easy reply to this sort of question corresponds to the widespread phenomenon that De Sanctis concisely labels as "examples of various classical and romantic idylls," and that should at least be considered a kind of middling folklike repertory. These were replacing other, true repertories of folk poetry and were put forward as edifying, consoling, and educational works that, as time passed, became ever more tainted with a reactionary tone. See, for example, the way the democrat Tenca changed his spots once he had become a liberal member of Parliament, in his brilliantly catchy anti-union rhymes. As for Parzanese, even a cursory reading of his *Poesie edite ed inedite* (Naples: Stamperia dell'Iride, 1857) provides a good overview of his hypocritical "project" to create a neo-pseudo-folk national repertory. The significance of Giordani's creating "Tuscan" folklore in fine language from scratch in his *Canti popolari toscani* (popularized by Ricordi and enjoyed by Verdi) has not yet received detailed investigation.

21. Ascoli was attacking the tendency to inertia in the movement to "popularize" the Tuscan dialect, or make it into the vernacular, against the precarious ideals of both "classical terseness" and "popular terseness" and other contemporary "idolatries." It is worth quoting the form of rejection Ascoli employs in urging avoidance of "the appearance of maintaining the purity of the national character . . . by way of those poetic and terse elements which only the long immobility of centuries can [appear] to give us;" see Antonio Cesari, *Elogi latini e latini editi ed inediti*, ed. Giuseppe Guidetti (Reggio Emilia: Artigianelli, 1898), xlvii–l.

failure), which would guarantee salvation, rather than security, from such "downfalls." [22]

Even Carlo Tenca, for all his credentials as a progressive and a democrat, fell into a fine quandary in 1852 when writing "Shadow and Light in the Romantic Movement" (Ombre e luci nel moto romantico) in the pages of his own journal *Il crepuscolo;* [23] after attacking the "imprudent resurrection" of the Middle Ages effected by the prophets of the neoclerical party, he praised the educational merits of that very medievalism. A democratic critic could in fact accept that those "embellishments" of Catholic mysticism, even the most generically backward-looking, were the "necessary evil" that would reveal some kind of practical continuity ("immutably, from generation to generation") to guide the people to a taste for the knowledge of beauty. Slightly conscious of the contradiction, Tenca writes:

> Feudal and knightly traditions had always been popular, even when literature, reborn in the spirit of ancient Latin thought, continued their development. . . . There were, it is true, ineffective, parasitical traditions, revealed as foreign intrusions, which lacked the splendor and grandeur of our national heritage. And art, as we have seen, rejected them and condemned them to molder in the imaginations of that multitude which had not yet come into legitimate possession of culture. But when the new school decided to find the living, eternal source of Italian thought and a fertile beginning for literary regeneration for those traditions, it had, of necessity, to approach that class in which this treasure of inspiration seemed to lie unnoticed.

The quandary that Tenca thereby agreed to tolerate consisted of a conception of the Risorgimento that did not compensate for the humiliations suffered by the Italian people. Instead, sidestepping the ideas championed by the classicizing advocates of the traditional school—described as "esoteric rhetoric," "partial narratives," and abstract "glorifications" of the hated "age-old" conditions—he promulgated a type of "cult of truth" which a priori denied "classical betterment" (both for the individual and as an ideal) and brought together subcultural memories (of feudal times, for example) of the previous underclass. This collecting activity provided ready yet interesting images of Christian, "domestic" virtues, along with an infinite variety of re-

---

22. They did so both by returning to "antibourgeois" themes and by refusing to accept any prebourgeois ideology developed in places where the first "democratic" and "enlightened" powers had soon shown their true faces, as well as by analyzing the paralysis caused by the entanglement of the old stylistic rhetoric with the new rhetoric of content and sentiment. Nothing had so poisonous an effect on the national intellect as quoting from anthologies and the complacency toward copying of the most perturbing aristocratic models. Not least among the many contemporary descriptions of the "sickening" average intellectual state during the (nineteenth) century is the common conviction of its hypocritical and oppressive stupidity, its beggarly state, and its repeated denseness (a stupidity that nevertheless had the merit of rousing alarm and starting an uprising).

23. See Tenca, *Saggi critici,* 310.

lated incidents covering the gamut of interpersonal feelings, such as—to take an example that Tenca himself uses—the vicissitudes of an entirely homespun version of the sacrament of marriage, with all it brings to mind for the average person. Tenca was proposing a cult of truth that may seem to correspond to the historical, compromise-laden rapprochement between high culture and the common people, but it continued to exclude, in the manner of Manzoni, any treatment of the progressive virtues of commerce. It was the idea of wait and see, a cult that was intended to bypass natural philosophies and gently repress reliance on experience and pragmatism (neither Plato nor Brutus would remain honored saints in this cult). Society's believer (in Croce's terms, the person whose religion is freedom), Brutus, was caught by Manzoni (in *Dialogo dell'invenzione,* 1850) at the most critical point in his career, at Philippi, when the vanity of that name, the very symbol of the virtue of tyrannicide, is unmasked in this monologue:

> Certainly, if virtue [the cult of freedom, that is, good romanticism] has as a condition divining all the possible effects of human actions, then it is a word as worthless as the cabala. Certainly, that virtue is worthless which, when deliberating whether it is good to attack a man while pretending to be a friend, with petitions in one hand and daggers concealed under one's toga, to send him from this world, does not listen to the eternal "no" . . . spoken by its conscience . . . ; but decides instead that not only is that action permissible, but it is sacred, because it is the means for restoring the real consuls . . . , and a true senate. And indeed they got them! Certainly, virtue is a vain word, if its truth depends on the outcome of the Battle of Philippi.[24]

If we are dealing here with a cult of truth, then this truth was a "no": it was an incitement to poetic skepticism, to patience and self-pity (never a "truth" constructed from action). The real "truth" seems to be rather the series of dire consequences intended (as at Philippi) for anyone who acted without knowing how many "weaknesses of the will" lay in wait for him upon the failure of his actions. Through the fancies that it was called upon to bring to life, this cult of truth also seemed to be the one that awakened picturesque or domestic situations, functioning in the realistic and efficacious guise of a lesson in transcendental philosophy. It was an old lesson to be transformed into modern language (by using all sorts of devices—faked documents, false historical manuscripts with which to invent a story), in such a way as never to permit any decisive deductions of a pragmatic or political nature. Thus, one could avoid thinking about real transformations of the mentality of the underclass, "dragged down by the coattails" toward a culture common to all classes, once it has been shown that the tastes of the underclass had been pre-

24. Alessandro Manzoni, *Tutte le opere,* ed. Mario Martelli (Florence: Sansoni, 1973), 1599ff.

served, in good old-fashioned traditional style. In other words, one could put aside the Brutus-like image of the occasionally rebellious people—the danger of Manzoni's "essay" on rebellion in *I promessi sposi* is primarily resolved in a kind of operatic "storm interlude"—without having to deal with the real peril of those subcultural habits such as superstition and irrationality which remained fixed in the popular mind. (And this was an error, for the state would have to work hard to contain those remaining reactionaries, ruffians, and bigots, the legacy of backward states in the distant regions of Italy, one of the geopolitical situations least suited to unification in the whole of Europe.)

Notwithstanding Tenca, who openly referred to the model of *I promessi sposi* to prove his theory of "rapprochement" (a necessary evil, etc.), many of the most clear-cut sections in Manzoni's novel seem instead to invite dismissal of any fusion between the "well-dressed and badly dressed multitudes," in terms of both education and economic standing. For example: "Here everyone agreed . . . ; but the uproar was perhaps greater than if there had been just a difference of opinion . . . ; some said: 'It's the hoarders. . . .' 'And the bakers,' said another. 'String them up.'" And elsewhere: "From the ideas of the common people, educated people took what they could accommodate to their own ideas; from the ideas of the educated people, the common people took what they could understand, and as they were able; and from it all came a vast, confused mass of public folly." Hardly gems for inspiration! And what terrible implications, how many thousands of possibilities for the worst consequences in putting into practice such a theory of "rapprochement"! Enough to try the patience of Providence!

The most forward-looking approaches to "realism," forerunners of today's tabloids, had not been encouraged. The fate of Antonio Ranieri and his *Ginevra, o L'orfana della Nunziata*,[25] for instance, was forty-five days in prison, destruction of the printing equipment, a lapse of twenty-three years between the appearance of the first edition and the second, and censorship of its essentially revolutionary approach toward institutions by historians of De Sanctis's stamp (with a summary order that it be cast into the dustbin of the history of Italian literature). Written in a classical, almost purist style, interspersed with sketches of depravity, angels of virtue, oppressors beaten about the head, and figures of sad, deformed rustics, Ranieri's book was an isolated attempt to focus on the chasm between the words and the deeds of revolution; denouncing "the authorities," it was entirely up to date on the degenerate conditions of Italian institutions. Ranieri's work shows a belief in a kind of rapprochement, with little of Tenca's depth (and without recourse to popular Gothic, chivalrous settings), and a superficiality along the lines of the re-

---

25. Capolago: Tipografia Elvetica, 1839; 2d ed., Milan: Guigoni, 1862; modern edition edited by Riccardo Reim (Rome: Lucarini, 1986). See also Francesco Chicco, *Antonio Ranieri: Saggio biografico* (Bari: Cannone, 1864).

lationship to a mass readership that had already developed in London and Paris. Indeed, Ranieri, through his volume of memoirs of Leopardi,[26] had become known principally as a disloyal detractor of his friend (who was rapidly acquiring an unwelcome, legendary reputation as the Great Man of the Risorgimento mixed bag). The antipathy Ranieri soon attracted, and possibly also his odd mixture of working-class language and overtly "European" politics (such as his criticism of the industrial economy and his adherence to Filippo Buonarroti's utopian socialism or Saint-Simon), did not help his attempt at a horizontal solution to rapprochement. (Not only because of Manzoni's overwhelming influence, but also on the basis of Risorgimento good sense: a proposed reconciliation of social classes based on the demonization and humiliation of unmasked institutions could not hope to capture anyone's enthusiasm.)

From such "lowly" interventions, little critical or expressive satisfaction was to be drawn, either by the few authors interested in cultivating this kind of popular fusion (those whom De Sanctis, in a few testy notes on a supposed Neapolitan romantic school, defines as à la Hugo) or by the historians who crossed those writers out of their history. It seems that there was, in effect, a "short-lived" Neapolitan school of disciples of Cesare Malpica,[27] a renegade follower of Basilio Puoti, who wrote the *Elementary Rules of the Italian Language* (1833). Such a group might be thought to anticipate the Scapigliati movement of the 1860s, in the way they deliberately sought out "ugliness." Perhaps they might have established a sort of Arcadia of horrors, alternating descriptions of the Ideal and the Actual, along the well-oiled tracks of Metastasian meter and prosody, with deliberately "banal" embellishments (something similar to the style of opera librettos). However, as all their texts have disappeared from the Italian national libraries, it is difficult now to recover the sense and significance of their intentions. Those few books to have survived drip with similarities in their manner of expression to the paraliterary manner of librettos for operas in the "serious" genre. It is strange that De Sanctis did not refer to librettos when he came across an isolated baroque element which he defines as a "seventeenth-century mannerism dictated by the situation" in the slim volume of verses *Mea culpa! e qualche altra cosa* (Brussels, 1840) or in *La corona di chiodi* (Brussels, 1842) by the poet Antonio Valentini, born in Lecce but living in exile. In the first of Valentini's books, De Sanctis notes the frenzied search for a poetic style that will satisfy the "aesthetic dictatorship" of the reader. Take, for example, his hymn to Maria Malibran,

26. Antonio Ranieri, *Sette anni di sodalizio con Giacomo Leopardi* (1880), ed. Giulio Cattaneo (Milan: Garzanti, 1979). For information on the relationship between Leopardi and Ranieri, see Luigi Antonio Villari, *Leopardi e Ranieri* (Naples: Pesole, 1898).

27. Malpica's works cannot be found even in the Italian national libraries, and the contents of his *Hours of Melancholy* (1836), *Thoughts at Sunset* (1839), *The Last of the Savelli* (1839), and *A Widow and a Mystery* (1846) are left only to the imagination.

which describes the thrilling feeling of oneness with the artist aroused by the diva's singing:

Odi, al tuo pianto piangesi,	[Listen, at your tears they weep,
al tuo voler si cede,	to your will they yield,
al riso un riso, al palpito	a smile by a smile, a heartbeat
un palpito succede.	followed by a heartbeat.]

We can also consider certain theoretical proposals that Valentini high-lighted in a kind of compendium of commonplace aesthetics (a few elements in the three short pages at the end of a pamphlet in 16mo). One of these is the urgent need for an "eclectic set of rules" for poetry that can be written "even while asleep" in response to the exhortation: "Weep, tremble [poets and/or readers] and we [readers and/or poets] will weep and tremble!" Leafing through the booklet in search of evidence of those shaky eclectic rules, we find pieces that amount to arias and cabalettas and one or two "scenas and arias" on the theme of the "weakness of the will." A short poem entitled "Nullità" (Emptiness) resonates with a mixture of a fiercely idyllic quality, common pessimism, folly, and bohemianism. Following the dedication "To the true friend, so to no one," following the images of the "deceitful lover" who kisses and betrays, following the simile of a bundle of wheat harvested from the bed of an empty grave (etc.), it concludes in a manner as facile as it is irritating:

Mie speranze son oche invischiate,	[My hopes are lamenting geese,
lamentose, spiranti nel fango,	lured to die in the mud,
le mie voglie son bisce affamate,	my wishes are famished snakes,
avventatesi quelle a sbranar.	pouncing to destroy them [my hopes].]

Valentini's volume may be small, but it is full of examples inverting the content of Manzoni's hymns: cryptoblasphemies along the lines of "God does not always pay when evening falls," the refrain in "Idealismo della miseria," and other awkward instances both supporting and threatening faith ("Re-deem the redeemed/ and the gospel will survive!"; the opposite is also true, as in an ode to Christmas filled with questions as to why the Lord wishes trouble on man); likewise, there are profoundly depressed passages that in-vert the formalities of the traditionally optimistic Metastasian manner. It would not be fair to leave Valentini's *Mea culpa!* without at least pointing out how strange it is that such a "seventeenth-century mannerism dictated by the situation" managed to produce a narrative lied like "Requiem!!!" Eight years before Dumas's Marguerite Gautier and twelve years before Verdi's Violetta, it tells the story of a certain Marianna, a kept woman, in a tragic "forest" of highly melodramatic scenes (with phrases such as "fallen angel / on her deathbed" and the return of her lover to "redouble" vainly "her sighs") and concludes with the familiar, touching, neomoralistic sanctification of the fallen woman:

E morì, ma l'alma eletta	[And she died, but her noble soul
non fu offesa dal peccato.	was not stained by sin.
Dal Signore benedetta	Blessed by the Lord
al Signore ritornò.	to the Lord she returned.
Il soggiorno riscattato	God did not create redemption
Dio pe' santi non creò.	for the saints.]

Examples such as these prompt the suspicion that there existed a semi-oral tradition of spontaneous lyric poetry that was at once facile, perturbing, a little baroque, and somewhat in the bizarre manner of the seventeenth century. In both its active and passive gestures toward the reader-listener, it might be confused a bit with a style of mediocre poetry—in the Italian mode—to be created and heard "almost in sleep."

Be that as it may, the historic irrelevance of such extremely modest attempts at a humbler mode of communication and forced stimulation of direct popular contact as those cited here confirms that no one representing Italian high culture actually desired to realize such a contemptible "Hottentot" literary style. And this corresponds to the known facts: there were absolutely no "requests from below" either to be educated in the "new" folk legacy or to be given back the "old" one (which to a large extent was already on loan to high culture to experiment with).

Everything seems to confirm that basic image of the Italian masses as harmless, patient, and somnolent, which the eighteenth-century critic Giuseppe Baretti had already suggested in his comparison with the London slums—in other words, the dormancy of the popular character.[28] The search to identify the nature of this character, however, was limited to stories of the authors' own personal development. In all biographies of such artists, whether major or minor figures, we always find an early period when the writer was prone to voice an immediate, unpremeditated, sometimes even repetitive style of social expression (such as in Manzoni's sermons and Leopardi's *Canzoni*). However, the motivations for these similar beginnings were likely to be rather different. A large part stemmed from the international Italophile spirit of youth promoted by Byron ("It is a grand object—the very *poetry* of politics. Only to think—a free Italy!!! Why, there has been nothing like it since the days of Augustus").[29] Then came the tendency to the slow, ritualistic gestures of a

28. See chapter 1 of Baretti's book, *An Account of the Manners and Customs of Italy*, 2d ed. (London: Davies, 1769), published later in Italy as *Gl'Italiani, o sia Relazione degli usi e costumi d'Italia* (Milan: Pirotta, 1818).

29. See the extensive descriptions of this intriguing phenomenon collected by Piero Treves in *L'idea di Roma e la cultura italiana del secolo XIX* (Milan and Naples: Ricciardi, 1962).

generally imaginary intellectual overview, observing from a variety of "look-outs" (an aristocratic library, a foreign vantage point, a café, a reading room). All these positions were useful in protecting ideas that had no continuity, whether deep-rooted, projected, or idealized: here we might think of the continuing Arcadian academicism in Rome, the mixture of local Etruscan folk-lore and ethnology in Florence, classical philology in Recanati and elsewhere, and the passion for modern journalism in Milan, where an Italian equivalent was sought for every novelty from Paris (or elsewhere, but in any case directed toward a new Italian identity).[30] Much effort was exhausted in variations on the cyclical theme of criticizing the century, soon to become one of the most fertile fields for those with spare time to explore. This kind of writing did not so much serve to increase the numbers of women readers (who wanted up-to-date, fashionable material) as to justify the recurring collapse of an intellectual profession exhausted by the frustrations of literary and civil work. That collapse gave rise to much writing in the expressive field of the so-called crisis of the will: there were monuments to solitude, hymns on the disconsolate recognition of nature's incoherence, comments on the incompatibility of poetry and humanity, poetry and government, poetry and events, poetry and the people. Here lie the roots of those "great consolations" that Montale in his fable attributed to the two artists eager to create who knows what in their little Gothic revival castle on the seafront: a vast eclectic area.

This development, viewed objectively, seemed to be a fatal one in the careers of artists in the new Italy, as they moved from a sense of crisis and collective defeat to contact with the resurgent nation (not only in the refutation of the "proud, foolish century" but also, more specifically, in the real distaste for "progress" as conveyed in "gazettes" concerning various "vapors, consumption, and cholera" or the closing choral lament of "Ermengarda / the most fortunate of all" in Manzoni's verse-tragedy *Adelchi*). For, ultimately, they were ready to be the objectives, means, or goal of an artistic launching that retreated from engagement to disengagement (or to another philosophy, endlessly pondered, of waiting for modernization).

Both Manzoni's novel *I promessi sposi* and Leopardi's later *Canti*—for the sake of argument, those coming after the song "Il Risorgimento"—have been understood by wave upon wave of subsequent readers (down to ourselves, aware of evolving history, and equipped to effect the political transformation of Italy) as illustrious achievements in clarifying the function of the Italian author. The two works have always been presented together, but never in relation to any kind of theory explaining how they relate to the development over

30. See ibid. and Piero Treves's edition of *Lo studio dell'antichità classica nell'Ottocento* (Milan and Naples: Ricciardi, 1962). For information on the different "cultural" behaviors of the Italian intellectual, see the enlightening "Postilla su Maffei e Muratori," in Sebastiano Timpanaro, *Classicismo e illuminismo dell'Ottocento italiano* (Pisa: Nistri and Lischi, 1965), 359–70.

time of the function itself. In this sense, while they are unique, rare works, they are not necessarily dissimilar structurally from many, many others in the line of development, in fact, from all the others.

I promessi sposi could be read as a kind of hugely extended account of a philosophical journey, intended to cover the changing Italian situation, both in literary and in biographical terms. Granted, it is a model narrative of model stories "low" and high, interspersed with idyllic snapshots "from life" (all, it will be remembered, with footnotes, in logical contradiction, to explain the philosophical point of the story). Yet it is practically impossible to state with confidence whether there is or is not a real model for contemporary reader-ship functioning as a constant element in the text. All the members of the claque whom we know—not only those of the past, who applaud the novel's "naivetés"—have learned to shout "Bravo!" at such and such a point, for during the course of long cultural contact with the text, through generation after generation, they have mastered all the potential variants inserted there in a more or less innocent manner. Let us imagine, however, that Manzoni did not at all have in mind the active presence of any "implicit readers," and that his text came into being all on its own, as if through a miraculous resur-rection of the *roman philosophique,* reproducing its messages in varied form (as if it were a singular, independent variant without any intended recipient— something that can be proved by referring to the novel's roots in Diderot).[31] Let us imagine that it is a text that attempts exclusively through reciprocal re-lationships within the novel to reformulate a single problem (without, how-ever, going back to any magical-literary anachronism and, even less, advanc-ing toward the communication of states of scientific awareness).

The problem is on a national level (in terms of content); what needs to be done, immediately and as many times as it takes, is to

- depict the countless incarnations of an age-old but unknown people, before sum-marizing them;
- find, isolate, and concentrate interest on the point of interruption in historical continuity (in the succession of so many Italic peoples); a moment of nonhistory from which to project the new nation and which, at the time of writing and read-ing, has to be a fixed point (if possible some time before the French Revolution).

31. On the figures of Manzoni's nun of Monza and Diderot's *réligieuse,* see Alessandro Luzio, *Manzoni e Diderot: La monaca di Monza e la "religieuse"* (Milan: Dumolard, 1884); and Man-lio Duilio Busnelli, "Per la genesi della Signora di Monza," *Atti del Reale Istituto Veneto di Scienze, Lettere ed Arti* 92 (1932): 1–26. On the fatalistic pessimism of late Diderot and his "ide-ological" wheel spinning toward loss of awareness of what that practice is worth, see Paolo Ala-tri's introduction to the Italian edition of Diderot's *Le paradoxe sur le comédien: Il paradosso del-l'attore* (Rome: Editori Riuniti, 1972). Also, on Diderot's contribution to Manzoni's "European" education, see Luigi Russo, "Manzoni poeta e Diderot oratore," in his *Ritratti e disegni storici: Da Machiavelli a Carducci* (Bari: Laterza, 1937), 242–59.

To represent the idea of this point of nonhistory, the author leaves a kind of placeholder for the public which must be awaited, the identification which must be postponed. All the following by turns keep watch over the vacant post of the public, keeping out the twenty-sixth reader,[32] like scarecrows formed of intractable questions: the universal groundlessness of praxis; the unlimited danger of "action"; the irreparable absence of worldly justice; the uncertainties of language; the incomprehensibility of history; empirical experience subordinated to what comes afterward (possibly only until what comes after the novel); the incurable and progressive isolation of the individual; the denial of expectations of Providence's righting of wrongs; the obtuseness of the actions of the masses; the vanity of learned culture; the discrediting of natural and materialistic systems; and so on, and so on.

The unknown nature of the readership of the novel (in that muddle of thematic intrigues that make its intentional "failure" a triumph and its "negativity" a success) can be quickly described. Indeed, we can go from Tommaseo praising its great, divine, bigoted, catechistical power to Giordani, who "saves it for the Left" by cleverly anticipating the imminent consequences of its reception ("Oh, let it be praised; the impostors and oppressors will come [but late] to understand what a profound [subversive] mind and a powerful summons (to action) belong to the man who has taken such care to appear simple, almost stupid: but stupid to whom? To the impostors and oppressors, who were and always will be the most stupid. Oh, why does Italy not have twenty such books!"), and on to Padre Salvatore Betti, who, complaining of Manzoni's having given his best in a novel, a bastard genre, pontificates on the low state a literature must be in when it cannot "offer anything better than novels." [33]

Thinking back to some of the emphasis in Manzoni's juvenilia, the impression we get is that from the very beginning, he was deliberately writing with no audience in mind, seeking a sort of intersection between modern art and stasis. "De le umane cose / tanto sperimentar quanto basti / per non curarle (Experiment as much as you will / in the things of the world / to become indifferent to them)," he had written many years before, although in the context of a poem of 1805 heavy with "moral" implications and only just before

---

32. In *I promessi sposi,* Manzoni addresses his "twenty-five readers."—Trans.

33. Giordani, *Scritti,* vol. 4, in his *Opere,* 11:132–34 *(Pensieri per uno scritto sui "Promessi sposi" di Alessandro Manzoni).* See also his *Epistolario,* vol. 6, in *Opere,* 6:15, as well as his view of the neocatechistical function that Giordani attributes to the novel. For example, he writes to Bianchetti in 1827, "As a book of the people, a catechism in dramatic terms, it seems marvelous to me," and then closes with a robust, "I wish [the novel] could be preached from every pulpit and in every tavern in Italy." See Pietro Giordani, *Pagine scelte,* ed. Giovanni Forlini (Piacenza: Comitato per la Promozione di Studi Piacentini, 1984), 298.

pretending to waken from a didactic dream (when the poet is about to find himself alone, his hand held out, while a warm tear clouds his vision).

His was not a rare attitude. The entire Italian middle class, on every different embryonic level, together with all the Italian landowners, had been even more unwilling to follow a Jacobin leader than the French, however temporarily. Even more than the French, the Italian middle class had done away with the "new ideas," chasing them off with half-baked, partly new repairs to feudal systems of production (such as the sharecropping system referred to above). And then, chiding themselves for the irritation of that "lack of action," the middle class had gone on to cultivate all obstacles to national unity which inoculated against revolutionary fever, as well as all the melancholy consequence of such indecision and solitude (and therefore nonassociation). The proposed aristocracy of the intelligentsia, in other words, the condition for the intellectuals to be co-opted into government, imposed on them like a uniform that "crisis of the will" in the form of melic voices spreading awareness of the historic defeat of materialist Jacobinism, even before any Italian battles had been fought. Such a voice opposed the hardly artistic one of stupidly activist, liberal religious pragmatism that puts its faith in a

Dio che talora a stranie posse,	[God who at times betrays the valor
certo in pena, il valor d'un popol trade;	of a suffering people to foreign powers;
... l'inique spade	... he breaks
frange una volta, e gli oppressor confonde;	the unjust sword, and routs the oppressors;
e all'uom che pugna per le sue contrade	and inspires the man who battles for his
l'ira e la gioia de' perigli infonde.[34]	homeland with the rage and joy of danger.]

The "Lord of Italy's Fortunes" had not harvested the "scattered rods" nor "bundled" them in his hand—all the most prominent Milanese romantics had drained the chalice of these lay and "worldly" frustrations of faith in a political and just Providence, passing from the aesthetic cult of cardboard lutes (as it has been described) to the real iron bars and chains, the medieval truth of the Spilberk prison.

Manzoni's poetic itinerary was a *via crucis* of this type: although it is lacking in actions and consequences and woes, he had already traveled the path to its end in his series of Sermons and Hymns. The work of discovering Providence's oversights in protecting the nation's just political progress had become almost systematic:

34. Alessandro Manzoni, *Il proclama di Rimini* (1815), lines 43–48.

- In *April 1814,* echoing the uprising against the Italian Napoleonic kingdom, he had promised the "bereaved mothers" a new, peaceful Kingdom of Italy, the product of providential action, to punish the guilty (the French).
- Also in 1814, Providence had turned French again and in *Il proclama di Rimini,* he defends Murat as if he were a Moses figure, a "leader" and savior (as long as he stays close to his people).
- Action once again, while encouraged, loses the favor of Providence and is even more frustrated after *March 1821.*

Three notable contradictions of the crumbling positive idea of Providence: his civic poems had become too hard to understand (two opposing Providences, pitted against each other but united in putting off the moment of rewarding the just). Manzoni took refuge in two "negative" solutions, making himself the recipient of his own messages, in the stable point of his art:

- On the one hand, the hymn for Pentecost: the mothers of *April 1814,* no longer sad to be fertile and to be announcing the miserable birth of some child, now rejoice in the news of the promised elevation of the unhappy to the kingdom of justice in the next world.
- On the other, the revenge in the novel: Providence, in the author's possession as a narrative scheme, serves to give a perfect negative description, not so much of God's actions in the world, as of the semiserious or tragic consequences of the faith men and women place in God's actions in the world.

The ambivalence of this is as essential as it is unreadable; it decants from the text only the work of art, as a single historic moment in the artistic career of the individual author. It is a genuine one-off (far from the "twenty such books" which Giordani invoked!). Providence no longer lets us say, "At last!" when "scoundrels" are finally cast down; instead, there is an author who says to those who allow themselves a pathetic "at last," when a provident solution to so many unjust woes arrives: "Certainly a man overwhelmed by grief no longer knows what is being said." Or else he mumbles an ironic: "Just see how that blessed instinct of referring . . . everything to ourselves alone sometimes makes us speak," when the same character dares to name, using the circumlocution of "such a fine occasion" to mean Providence, that plague which is truly, or at least in point of fact, the single providential mechanism included either in history or in the narrative mechanism.

The author is so "alone," so unidentified with any of the characters as an internal recipient, that he actually manages (only in *Fermo e Lucia*) to assume a critical distance even from the character of the monk, who, even if only because of his calling, has to preach positive faith in Providence. When the character of Cristoforo says he believes that Rodrigo's pride and villainy have risen "to those heights where Providence will stop them," Manzoni replies, offstage, as it were, that such reckonings "are ofttimes mistaken, and injustice in this world continually rises," even when we think that "at its height it can only fall."

There is a systematic contradiction at work here and it is revealed in two ways.

1. One way is in the acceptance of Diderot's philosophe poetic of a narrator who demonstrates how history, psychology, and empirical experience lead toward systematic truths (in this case, a "theology of how one is in the world," no less) only through contradiction and in their presentation through "writing" (Diderot's Jacques contradicted himself all the time, "like you and me").[35] This is also a possibly Sternean assumption of the private game of the "reader who writes" without arranging solutions for all the contradictory themes that arise;

2. The other is the decision, having thus loaded all the functions of the text onto that of the author, and having left the reader's position vacant, to dedicate that position to the non-Italian who is there in the empty place of the Italian: the ghost of the most unretrievable of historic models of the Italian (the silent victim of the dark ages of Longobard domination; to retrieve such a person is no mean feat; the text is waiting).

The solution (having reconsidered the empty descriptions of the Longobard victim,[36] and having reduced the picture of the future Italian to that of the author in the act of writing) lies in a pronouncement of the suspension of the historic relationship of art and nation during the time of the suspension of the knowability of history. And there are many such pronouncements: pronouncements on the ugliness of political relations that "punch out" forms of people, on the incalculable nature of the effects of political acts, and on the mixture of greatness and baseness in political systems. In the *Osservazioni sulla morale cattolica,* he writes:

> The power to act on humanity independently of political relationships seems to me one of the greatest features of religion. . . .
>   . . . Political systems are all complicated [incomprehensible], and sustaining them and attacking them are enterprises that, too easily, involve honest and evil means, and the results are a mixture of the good and bad, impossible to calculate for the most part.

35. In *Jacques le Fataliste,* Diderot describes Jacques as being "comme vous et comme moi."—Trans.

36. "The chroniclers of the Middle Ages mostly recount only principal or exceptional events . . . of the conquerors alone. . . . They almost never speak . . . of their relationship with the conquered. . . . Among all the accounts of the Middle Ages, the most laconic, in lack of information on everything that concerns the conquered population, are possibly those which have come down to us on the Longobard rule in Italy." From the *Discorso sopra alcuni punti della storia longobardica in Italia* (chap. 2) in Manzoni, *Tutte le opere,* 1987.

Or, in the words of the faithful Mauri:[37] "The history of the most illustrious nations is like the life of the purest man, a mixture of the grand and the abject, the magnanimous and the cowardly." These are not exactly traditional religious positions; they seem more like clever pretexts, directed at holding the destination of their own thoughts suspended, or preventing them from becoming vulgarized—a limited battle between author and nation on "exploitation," or possibly a command to teach the nation not to trust either the religion of liberty or crises of will. The champions of the former are always struck down, rather like the baroque punishments meted out to atheist freethinkers (the eternal tragic consequence of blind action). The second is found, in ironic terms, in semi-Brutus-like characters or other believers in the nonexistence of original sin and in the "natural" goodness of humanity, dumbfounded and surprised, destroyed at the sight of evil (human and natural, spiritual and material), struck too late by profound "truths."

At this point the author takes on the responsibility of being the Perfect Censor, of identifying the readership of an immature national culture; he becomes the critic of believers in the political miracle of cultural relations that, by themselves, can make a people.

Since it is well known, and requires little in the way of new interpretation, we can quickly survey Giacomo Leopardi's career as an artist in this context of what was expected from the organic relationship between Italian culture and the Italian nation. There is, however, one point that, mistakenly perhaps, critics have not always considered central but that is in fact highly characteristic of the establishment of a new awareness of the Italian intellectual when waiting for his function to be specified.

Having first embodied the most intensely classicist version of patriotic preaching on the coming of the nation (or for the regeneration of the world), without enjoying the success of his *Canzoni,* possibly because of a misunderstanding, Leopardi approached the assignment that a "national" publisher, Antonio Fortunato Stella, had given him with great seriousness: this was to put together a *Crestomazia della prosa italiana* (Anthology of Italian prose), to be published in 1827, the same year as *I promessi sposi.*

This undertaking fits into a program of civic liberation, through the assembling of a new stylistic-rhetorical "common" prose repertory parallel with the philosophical affirmation that history of the nation was knowable. Its subject matter was prose, and its goal was to create a new rhetorical and stylistic "shared" repertory as reflected in the linguistic choices and readings

37. Achille Mauri (1806–83), Manzoni's philosophical alter ego, was a teacher and literary scholar. His career in the church already under way, he was secretary of the provisional government of Milan in March 1848 when he launched the Manifesto of European Nations in the city. He took Manzoni's place as deputy for Arona when the writer stepped down. Mauri was later a senator and died in Rome.—Trans.

scientifically put forward for new generations to make their critical decisions about.

Leopardi had already made his position clear in a letter of 1819 to Giuseppe Montani (he of the *Antologia*), later the lukewarm reviewer of the *Crestomazia*. In the unanimous chorus of utter rejection of Leopardi's work (for such was its "national" reception), Montani was actually the most cordial gravedigger, generous out of friendship and so even more offensive. Having first spoken of the wall that had grown up between the literary world and the people, from the fifteenth century onward, and having argued that the classic authors had "written for their times," Leopardi's aim in his letter was to establish that there would be poets in Italy only when there were citizens who had an "eloquence" of their own. In 1821, he had written to Giordani that an Italian nation would be viable only when its modern literature had acquired a "philosophical language" ("suited to the times"). And in 1826, referring to a young lady in Bologna, a certain signorina Franceschi, an aspiring author, he had asked his friend to advise the young lady not to write verses (and not in accordance with Bonghi's ideal of the woman as reader and "internal audience" and if possible absolutely never a writer—so as not to have to say more "unfortunatelys"), adding: "This is what I force myself to preach in this blessed Bologna; where it seems that literary person and poet . . . are synonyms. . . . By going back to verses and frivolities (I'm speaking in general terms here), we do a service to our oppressors." Clearly (and with an almost Jacobin enthusiasm), he is agitating here against lyric or idle poetizing, into which he felt the proper role of literature, "regeneration of the homeland," [38] had too long been disappearing.

The public experiment of inventing an active readership for Italian literature was, for Leopardi at this time, his work on the *Crestomazia*. The book was, and is, a model of intentions. It contained

> *a*. Italian texts chosen "in chronological order" (to give the impression that there was a continuous itinerary of linguistic stages that could be followed);
> *b*. everything required to reveal to an Italian—or to a "foreigner"—what "the Italians are capable of in their writing";
> *c*. the maintenance of references to the rhetorical tradition in terms of ordering of genres (the anthology is divided into sections of Allegories, Descriptions and Images, Definitions and Distinctions, Parallels, Philology, and so on) without indulging in ideological arrangement according to theme, something that Tommaseo seized on at once in his immediate response to the *Crestomazia* in his *Letture italiane* (with *The Good, The Correct, The True and Beautiful*, etc.);[39]

38. Letter to Puccinotti of 5 June 1826.
39. Niccolò Tommaseo, *Letture italiane* (1841). This anthology was later expanded with the addition of several prefaces in the form of a grand essay (Milan: Reina, 1854); it is in this version

d. a clear-cut opposition to modernization according to the sort of moderate-Catholic-Jesuit catechistical teaching later exemplified by Tommaseo and his associates, with a remarkable new structuralist modernization of the oldest orders of education in eloquence and effectiveness of language;

e. startlingly impulsive choices of what to include and exclude, to give a traumatic impulse to creating Italian literary history;

f. a suggestion of disconnected readings as the point of departure for contemporary variations on repressed and forgotten aspects of national cultural continuity. (With total self-conviction, the poet returned to this point after the bitter defeat of his *Crestomazia,* and for the rest of his life he devoted himself to treating in poetry messages derived from prose and philosophy that he had already included in his repertory of national eloquence but that had been rejected by national culture, whether official or not.)

Yes, indeed. The rejection was total, from both romantics and classicists, those on the Right and the Left, moderates and radicals. However, the *Crestomazia* was misunderstood. For some, it lacked fourteenth-century fine writing and grand style. For others, it dripped honeyed satisfaction for all possible academic vices (secular and, even worse, eighteenth century). Others produced persuasive arguments for its "uselessness," while still others criticized each of the selections, one by one. Others again accused it of deepening the ivory-tower tendencies of "schools of humanities" (putting intellects off the "true," the close observation of things); and on it went.[40]

The message from that anthology, treated as undisciplined, incompetent and useless, was something Leopardi's contemporaries could just not accept. Since it was a cultural contribution (and not a literary work whose unpopularity could even be tolerated, if not extolled, as proof of some rare quality), its resounding lack of success could also be interpreted as proof of the failure of a human existence. And that was how it was.

His reaction was private and did not correspond to what, instead, he had proposed a few months earlier during a public reading—before the cardinal legate, the members of the Bologna Academy, and the dedicatee—of the letter to Carlo Pepoli (Easter Monday, 1826) in which the sweet artifice of lyric poetry is prescribed for those forced into idleness and excluded from action as a sham remedy for boredom (precisely in virtue of his faith in the "useful" work of compiling the *Crestomazia*). On that occasion he added solemnly:

---

that the radical contradiction of the *Crestomazia* is systematically laid out: "not by rhetorical genres . . . but by subjects."

40. Treacherously and shrewdly, Tommaseo accuses the "schools of humanities" of putting young minds off the "observation of things" (set at a distance as if they were "base") and defines them as factories for producing inept and inane armchair constructors of worlds, cut off from society. (This is the beginning of the great campaign of denigration of "intellectualism" and of the

E se del vero	[And if thinking then
ragionando talor, fieno alle genti	of the truth, my words are
o mal grati i miei detti o non intesi,	unwelcome or misunderstood by the people
non mi dorrò.	I shall not complain.]

But complain he did. First, by letter, in the strongest possible terms:[41]

> Even if I could continue with congenial studies, given the quality of this world's judgment, I would not have the heart to wear myself out doing things that pleased me. . . .
>
> Study and work are things I have forgotten, and every day they grow more distant to me. With the type of judgment and criticism found in Italy today, whoever takes the trouble to think and write is a fool.

The world's criticism, endured with mortification, of his failed encounter with national modernity could no longer take the form of "sentimental" poetry. It could no longer take the form of an artificial identification of the author with an imaginary Italian, burning with plans and desires. It was a private letter, barely translated into verse at all. A monologue on paper. It was an opportunity to "write no more," a fundamental return to expressing an intimate awareness of the abyss of the void beneath the will in crisis ("I need only desire something for the opposite to happen, I know not what I am doing in this world") which had previously been consigned to the most private letters to his family. At the very moment when the Right was calling upon the intelligentsia to supply known, manageable materials to channel toward expressions of humiliating nationalism, we know that that "writing no more," that protest of one who had dared to give of his best by proposing a total reworking—stylistic and linguistic—of Italian culture, shaken up in its knowable history of styles and languages, transformed itself into an answer to his question (in *Ad Angelo Mai*) "Why so many rebirths?" with the poetic revival of the vigor of Leopardi's poetic inspiration.

So the "return to song" got under way, ironically, with the title once more of "Risorgimento" (a return to Metastasian and operatic forms and meters—such as the quotation of Cimarosa's famous "pupille tenere"[42] and the refer-

---

difficulties of developed thought which would serve, equally before, during, and, alas, after Fascism, the censorial needs of the enemies of "culture.")

41. The letters of 5 May 1828 to Giordani and 25 Feb. 1828 to Papadopoli.

42. The reference is to "Quelle pupille tenere / che brillano d'amore" (those tender eyes / which shine with love) in *Gli Orazi e i Curiazi* by Sografi and Cimarosa. The cavatina for Curiazio (an alto castrato in the early years of the opera's popularity, then a trouser role for a female contralto) was widely known between 1796 and 1830 and afterward. It serves as a first text of the

ence to the castrato Crescentini—which stood as the symbolic cancellation
of everything to do with creating a broad, civic objective national readership,
cherished and immediately broken). The solitary song of the author (his *Canto
solitario di un pastore errante*) retreated, almost too singable, with its *sdrucciolo* endings, to a kind of endless super-cavatina of confession of nullification
(of himself, of the present). A *larmoyant* complaint:

Che ignora il tristo secolo	[For the wretched age
gl'ingegni e le virtudi;	recognizes no genius and virtue;
che manca ai degni studi	and worthy study still
l'ignuda gloria ancor.	lacks unadorned glory.]

Leopardi's systematic search to deny expressive contact on every level confirms increasingly how his work (ever more demanding, conceptually and linguistically, up to the Vesuvian masterpieces) was an illustration of the solitary
fate of the Italian writer. On the one hand, he tragically and ironically denied
"the idyll within an idyll"; on the other, as a reader, he refused even to read
himself (Count Giacomo Leopardi being less and less himself in his texts, and
more and more Art alone before the Void).

Could this be the "poetry to be created," which Leopardi had written ex-
citedly about to Giordani, drawing attention among the secret complaints of
the letter quoted above ("I know not what I am doing in this world") to "a
classical and ancient style which appears modern and is both easy to understand and pleasant, equally to the people and the learned"? No.

A deliberate turning aside from "popularity"—an important factor in both
Manzoni's and Leopardi's careers—embraces a certain feeling of the lack of
and a vague anticipation of the coming of a national "prophet" (the word
used at the time was *vate*, a literary term for both prophet and poet). This expectation was subsequently expressed politically by the landowning classes
and various leading figures. It was the expectation that the boundaries of socioeconomic hegemony would be defined.

But until this happened, the Italian cultural audience could not yet be
defined anthropologically. At the same time, a loose pantheon of a small number of authors was created, along with a series of legends of what was to come
(the coming marriage between authors and people and the arrival of new
prophets, the ministering priests of that lyric union).

This last is a theme that we can touch on only briefly here. We might refer,
for its symbolic content, to the "fantasy" elaborated around the figure of an

---

new tragic sensibility in musical theater in the transition between the eighteenth and nineteenth
centuries: the style is a confusion of the cantabile and the pathetic, vaguely tragic in the feeling of
foreboding of sacrifice, the first signs of the neo-operatic commonplace of the expressive lyrical
qualities of the "defeated" and the "victim."

"Italian poet" lost in an act of patriotism and thus missing an "encounter" with an unknown Italian readership (unknown to us, to him, and to the readership itself). Luigi La Vista[43] won a place in the panorama of Italian literary history despite having died before writing very much of anything: a martyr to a blood-soaked repression of the religion of liberty, embraced by literary history in honor of the idea that an early death is "the greatest poetry."

A brief mention should also be made, perhaps, of Alessandro Poerio,[44] another poet and soldier, a quasi martyr who perished in an episode in the 1848 uprising, in a halo of civic idealism. As an author he was practically unpublished (less than Antonio Valentini: a single slim volume of ninety pages, published in Paris); his endless "suspended lyrics" were almost always dedicated to hymning the expected Risorgimento:

Sorgiamo; e la stretta	[Let us rise up; and let
concordia dell'ire	unanimous anger
sia l'italo Amor.	be Italian love.]

A poet, still young, Poerio was already penning hundreds of lines of appeal to future poets:

Forse poeti splendidi	[Perhaps splendid poets
succederanno al pianto	will come after these tears have been shed.
. . . .	. . . .
Sente l'affetto surgere,	He feels his emotions swell,
ma un gelo antico affrena	but an ancient chill checks
l'onda sepolta e correre	their hidden flow
non lascia la sua piena.	and they cannot surge freely.
. . . .	. . . .

43. He fell during the '48 uprising at the age of twenty-two. The image of the young, lost genius, sacrificed on the altar of civic religion, is even projected on to the figure of the late lamented Leopardi, whom De Sanctis seems to want to fuse with that of the beloved disciple, the genius not allowed to flower ("If destiny had prolonged his life until '48 you would have found him by your side to comfort and battle for you"). La Vista in turn had cultivated, in the few writings he left, Leopardi's equally confused image of Tasso in the idea of a poet who "speaks for those afflicted by misfortune." And it is no coincidence that De Sanctis returns to the inspiration of poetry on the deaths of poets, in the chapter of his *Letteratura italiana nel secolo XIX* devoted to the "degeneration of literature in Naples" (after himself and after La Vista), when he holds up to public shame De Lauzières, who survived unborn Neapolitan romanticism (and went on to be an important librettist). For De Sanctis, De Lauzières's reference to the ashes of Tasso—made to rhyme with *sasso,*" "stone" ("Calpesta il piede un rozzo ignoto sasso: / leggete: è il cener di Torquato Tasso" [He bumps his foot on a rough, unknown stone: / read: these are the ashes of Torquato Tasso])—is an indication of how "it could not be possible to represent something so capable of furnishing inspiration in a more vulgar and empty manner."

44. The complete edition of Poerio's works appeared only in 1970, edited by Nunzio Coppola, as part of the Laterza series of "Scrittori d'Italia" *(Poesie).*

e d'alto infaticabili	and tirelessly looking down
veggenti i sacri vati	from on high, the sacred prophets
su curveran com'angeli	will bend low like angels
con occhi innamorati,	with eyes full of love,
versando in ampj giri	generously pouring out
un'Armonia che spiri . . .	a floating Harmony . . .]

Amid the rather affected prophetic expectation, amid the indecision that stemmed from an inability to stand up to the constraints of heroic poetry of liberty and those of the poetry of "abandonment to grief," a poetry that was aggressive, patriotic, national, classical, and romantic, and so on but completely unread, Poerio was hardly convinced himself that he was the "future poet" of whom he sang; following the lead of the "sacred prophets" already taken up to heaven, he urged national poetry to describe a national event, a musical metaphor.

5. A MISSION FOR OPERA

In April 1858, just as Verdi was leaving Naples with Giuseppina Strepponi, they received from the Lucanian poet Nicola Sole[45] (one of the most expansive of the thriving school of glowing, hyperbolic improvisers in Naples, who wrote "odes" to every conceivable thing) poetic proof that the mission Verdi had accomplished on the path to the advent of the figure of the national poet, which we have just been discussing, was being sincerely recognized. In his poem of Naples's farewell to Verdi—a Verdi who, having staged a *Batilde di Turenna* (a disrespectfully censored version of *I vespri siciliani*), had lingered fruitlessly in Naples, hoping to produce *Un ballo in maschera* and who, in actual fact, was leaving the city in a bad mood (he was soon to get over it)—Nicola Sole offered his wishes for his return trip to his "fields," those fields where he is accustomed "to live / in isolation for art and love," to him who has made so many Italian hearts beat faster (at the "touch of the hand which wrote / Manrico's lament," and so on). He sends him back to "the tranquil, playful shadows of Agata" with an order to continue the artistic work which Verdi seems to have already honored to the point of making it a national tradition:

> Addio! La mente con più forte amore
> guarda le cose che sparir. Siccome
> più bello appar quanto men presso il miri
> pennel fiammingo, le rimote gioie,
> le ricordi o le speri, assai più vaghe

45. The most extensive edition of Sole's work is, and will remain, that of his *Canti*, ed. Bonaventura Zumbini (Florence: Le Monnier, 1896). The hymns and the prayer quoted later are on pp. 90–98 and 238.

ridono a l'alma. Un crepuscol rosato,
una nebula d'or confonde e vela
quanto v'ha di caduco, e a la speranza
la memoria somiglia. . . .

[Farewell! Our minds look on things that have gone
with greater love. Just as
the Flemish brushstroke looks more beautiful the less close
you observe it, so distant joys,
whether remembered or hoped for, light up our souls
the more. A rosy twilight,
a golden cloud now obscures and veils
all that is transient, and hopes
resemble memories. . . .]

In his poem's double dimension (back and forth between Sole and Verdi, Naples and Busseto), the poet sends a "remembrance" together with the hope that all will "leap up" on "wings of fire" at the "first new notes" of Verdi's future operatic works. A modest poet, almost a failed one, he identifies himself with the average Italian listener to Verdi's work (and not as one of the other Italian poets, who, as he will say, were gripped by vain expressive aspirations), ready to respond to what the new opera, whose passive interpreter he will be, will urge him to do and be:

. . . Ad una meta
moviamo insieme, e per diverse vie:
tu glorïoso e grande, io di sì breve
luce precinto; tu felice e lieto
d'assolte promesse, io d'impotente
speme agitato! . . .

[. . . We go together
toward a single goal, along different paths:
you, great and glorious, I bathed in
such a short-lived light; you happy
at promises fulfilled, I troubled
by ineffective hope! . . .]

And now, now that "[Italian] humanity travels / to distant shores," Sole adds:

Oh, tu che il puoi
(la gloria no, ma questa
possa t'invidio) sul cammin la desta!

[Oh, you who can
(not your glory, but this power
that I envy in you) waken it and send it on
        its way!]

And, Sole continues, this power of harmony, which "the changing times bestow," is such that the language "set to music" sets all free and shows all the sweetness of native expression of their homeland, which has long been only the experience of exiles on foreign soil on hearing their native language (even dialects). That same sensation of homeland is then immediately evoked and disseminated throughout the natural geography by those operas where, "certainly, one note on different shores / moves all people."

Such is the miracle: that the century (no longer filthy and abject but "wise" and "civil") seems to "recognize itself" in an operatic nation that "strikes its palms," that is, applauds, "and weeps." It seems to be that, if not actually an entire people, a visible quintessence of that people, in other words, a tangible "popularity," has been discovered in that applause which is compared, by ideological assimilation, to the most promising aspect of progress, "the electrical spark," the "bearer of thought, which it resembles." The "scattered humanity" of Italy finds in operatic music the principle that presides over its embrace, the thing that provokes communion, the lowest common denominator of a state of mind, the stimulus for brief but frequent and intensely felt great moments of unity, so that "there, whence Opera breathes / man turns his enamored eyes!"

Before the final farewell (with mention of a great silence, to which—after the opera—"all return, singing, in their thoughts"), we have two crystal-clear historical and critical definitions of the state of Italian culture with regard to opera.

1. on operatic music's capacity to "stir the depths," to move that ardent something "that darts between grief and hope," wandering "far, far" amid other regions of "sickness" and "disquiet" but not allowing the listeners' souls to breach the confines of what is in the notes (in other words, a certain decorous popularity, all the stronger for being circumscribed by its texts and so not entirely transferable);

2. on the capacity of this established "popular" work of art to create a school ("other melodies will follow," even if everything is dust and everything changes "below the clouds"), so that all the "ineffable tears" shed will have ushered in a new cultural tradition, easy to remember and disseminate (reproducible).

A good improviser is never happy saying something just once; he is gripped by the temptation to go back to his first thoughts, and compelled to give them a new form, possibly a better one. So after Sole has finished his first farewell, he immediately begins a second one, offering Giuseppina ("To G.S.V., happy, courteous teacher of nightingales") a symbolic pair of orphaned nightingales, captured among the Camaldolensian roses. They go to the domestic, first recipient of Italian opera, to the woman who "seated at the altar of Genius / nourishes his divine inspirations / and, an envied and beloved / priestess of his ardent notes, / is the first to receive the sovereign numbers / that will make theaters tremble tomorrow." She is the person who indirectly alleviates the sadness of the eternal "exile in the Italians' homeland" (those who, in going to the opera, have the experience of the native tongue of their lost homeland restored to them, like exiles in foreign lands at the sound of their native tongue). The two little orphaned birds (themselves a miniature symbol of a couple who will create generations to come) will owe their education in their native voice (which she knows through her daily access to the source of Italian music) and in the lost/lost-no-longer voice of the most ancient of natural and indigenous languages to the woman who is the living symbol of the communion between artist and people (founded on her conjugal proximity to the "powerful nightingale").

Finally and inevitably comes a repetition of Sole's farewell, a third homage by the extemporizing muse to the maestro: a *Prayer*. In the end we see a Verdi—and we know how quick he was to rid himself of bores—not in the least irritated by this impertinent poetizing on his own poetry and on the happy effects of his powerful "lyric art." All the artists in Naples seem to have joined him at the Hotel Roma: some paint his portrait; others follow him around more quietly. The "people" try to imprint the physical features of the great man on their memories or else listen for the music drifting out of his hotel window into the clear sky, stopping under his balcony when the maestro is at work, or seems to be at work, at the piano.

Before the farewell, there were nights of talking and singing. In a letter of 1896, the painter Domenico Morelli reminded Verdi of those nighttime strolls, when Nicola Sole extemporized and Verdi immediately set his light verses to music as they walked down the street, singing them on the spot. One of these ephemeral hymns has survived, and the written tradition preserves it as it was. It is the *Preghiera del poeta* (ex. 1) to which I have been referring, a poem that pretends to inspire a new type of poetry, supported and consecrated by the test of "success" (observe the reference in line 4: "not fail in its generous purpose"): a poetry possibly "safe" (or saved) from "doubt" and from "craven oblivion," confident, fortunate, or rather affirmative, unforgettable and even less forgetful of the duty of social contact and communication.

If we want to draw some benefit from the survival—thanks to Sole's boundless love and certainly not intended by Verdi—of this stray, occasional, and possibly slightly tipsy "sacred piece,"[46] we shall have to roll up our sleeves and rummage through it until we find something symptomatic. We might ask who is the "celestial" person, the fiery God addressed in the *Prayer*. It takes no great leap of the imagination to realize that that God is none other than the broad audience of so-called Italian popularity: "the dispersed humanity," sought on many "shores," forced into an echoing musical embrace in response to the "serious anxieties of the age." In other words, the empirical listener, who, by direct linear descent from the person who first receives the music, Verdi's companion Giuseppina, down to the excited devotees in all the theaters up and down the peninsula, miraculously corresponds with that imaginary listener, the Italian (but only, and this is important, when hearing the

---

46. The version reproduced here is the one found in Paolo De Grazia, "Una musica di Giuseppe Verdi," *Rivista musicale italiana* 45 (1945): 230–32, quotation on 231.

Ex. 1.   "The Poet's Prayer."

operas revived, not at their first appearance), who is always being invented and whose existence is assumed with every note and every *parola scenica* in the "promises fulfilled" of each new opera. Let us not forget that the song of supplication to this Italo-Lombard God (an increasingly unitary deity) on behalf of a city that had declined to partake of the great adventure of *Un ballo in maschera* is asking him to "waken them"—as in the *scetare* of so many street songs, and just as the nation awakes in Goffredo Mameli's national anthem, in putting on a Roman helmet—on the path of the poet. The goal is to give him the success he deserves, seeing in the shared aim of applause the outcome of popular self-knowledge.

However foolish they may seem (and indeed are), Sole's hymns mark the precise point *(in vino veritas)* of the critical rapport between Italian opera and literature and culture in crucial years for the nation. That eloquent gesture of the old art ("troubled by impotent hope"; "I write badly," Manzoni had previously written in a postscript to *Fermo e Lucia,* "and in spite of myself")[47] abdicating in favor of the new, musical "lyric art" corresponds to something far less futile than yet more confirmation of the southern love of praise and displays of friendliness.

Opera (Verdian opera, let's say by way of simplification) gained other authorizations to add to this one, gained on the field, of participatory lyricism impressively proved by collective thrills, permitting it to continue with the creation of a new set of cultural principles of shared excitement. These were in the form of "contact" identification with the empirical, effective audience for national art. Having cleverly cultivated its cultural backwardness, Italy did not give up its pre-nation characteristics of unchanging, proud conservatism. This was particularly evident, and note the paradox, in the context of ideologically progressive culture. The country was generally hostile to "easy" reading, such as that of novels (and in this the "pedants" on the Left stood shoulder to shoulder with such reactionaries as Betti, mentioned above, and even avant-garde novelists such as Manzoni, who, in proscribing the genre of the novel, eventually praised the nation's "glory" that it could boast so few, indeed, only one: his own). In a country that, forced to become a nation, did so anyway in its economic and social structures, and was sufficiently "modern" for tension to arise between the old and the new (confusing the content and, even more so, the forms of both), in a scale of measurement of "how" and "how much" in terms of popularity, that backwardness continued to survive. We have seen how, around the 1820s, Silvio Pellico took up the question of "women's literature"; his position, with all its quotations from Metastasio, as seen in his letter to his brother, was not just taken in private, as the article

---

47. "and if I knew how to write better, I could certainly not neglect to do so." The quotation appears in Manzoni's *Seconda introduzione redatta da ultimo* to his *Tutte le opere,* 245.

in the *Conciliatore* on the *Lettere di Giulia Willet*[48] confirms. The question
leads on to the problem of identifying the general readership as implicitly the
primary basic element, reason, and style of a good literature dealing with the
"growth" of bourgeois conscience (confirmed by the success of literature that
is read, such as English literature)—in other words, literature intended for an
unlimited readership, possibly one undergoing rapid expansion, such as the
Italian middle and lower-middle classes. (It is interesting to find Metastasio
again quoted by the romantic poet Giovanni Prati in a *poemetto* on his personal modernization as an artist—"Al mio futuro biografo"[49]—when he recounts how, reading under his desk something faintly "feminine," there came
to the intellectual boy "tired and weary / of barbarous Latin, / the song / of
Metastasio and Tasso," making him dream of "fair heroes" and impelling
him to write *scapigliato* verses.)

The key to this success, which comes from identifying the readership, is,
as the context requires, twofold: we need to multiply the satisfaction of the
need for realism (*a*) by identifying morality with choices and feelings experienced in domestic circumstances and by (*b*) satisfying expectations that run
counter to these, of vivid depictions of customs too soon considered "obsolete" by the new society and its social classes (which have not yet crystallized
into recognizable ranks and to a certain extent lack genuine ethical and linguistic characteristics). The (*b*) type of expectations represent a love of resid-
ual, half-forgotten visions which both the classically and the romantically inclined have been too hasty in considering old-fashioned, the former by their
selectivity, the latter because of their infatuation with the unfamiliar foreign
images that have been imported, sometimes shockingly couched in an Italian
atmosphere that is so un-Italian that it can represent neither the "true" present nor the "true" past, let alone the anticipated confusion and multiplication
of the two.

An interesting comparison was made, with useful implications for a History of Opera, between the loathed excesses of the seventeenth-century style,
the "obsolete" ancient origin of Italian "follies" (starting with opera), and the
current, foolish modernity of the romantics. Giordani initiated this comparison ably when he replied to Mme de Staël in the *Bibilioteca italiana*, speaking of a change "for the worse" in the love of folly of the current century, compared with that of the style—possibly "popular" in its day—of the mad

48. *Il conciliatore,* 7 Jan. 1819.

49. Prati's poem of 1884 opens the short collection entitled *Poesie* (Rome: Perino, 1885), edited by his disciple Giacinto Savelli, who, significantly, ends his brief preface by self-consciously
quoting Carducci ("[Prati] was truly and richly the only poet of the second generation"), and his
judgment also refers to the way his verses lend themselves to be anthologized in the *Libro d'oro*
because they are perfect examples of easy, lyrical, and fragrant work.

writing of the seventeenth century.[50] He adds that, in his opinion, writers of the seventeenth century "at least" had an art, which may have been mad, but it was original and "Italian" (while that of the present he considers completely "deformed" by mimicry). More than the beauty or otherwise of witless, European and intercultural borrowings, what Giordani rejects is not so much the mixture itself as the nonspecific national quality of the new "follies."

It is not the case that, having frequently expressed their discomfort, Leopardi and Giordani on one side, Manzoni on the other—to name only the most promising intellectuals—ever abdicated in favor of opera (as did poor Sole, later on), whether in all seriousness or in a moment of inattention. Nor did they sing its glories, nor recognize—even polemically—how much of a mélange it was,[51] not an intellectual or unspecified one, but "popular" in other words, just as it was, representing a particular area of practice where the functions of the writer and the Italian audience intersected.

The fortunes of opera, its "successes" in the context of the historic, episodic, and rapid enforced nationalization of the country (successes possibly more irresistible than any political, military, diplomatic, and ideological ones, and their immediate reflections in official culture), can strike one, all things considered, as scandalous but not mad. The cultural backwardness and skepticism which we have already examined a little was showing itself to be not a defect of the Risorgimento but rather a valid, even primary and productive, identity of the Risorgimento. Those barricades of values, feelings, and philosophical reflection erected in radical opposition to the foolish age and the dynamic relativism proposed both by secular liberals and by religious conservatives, barricades erected by the "thunderstruck" or by the "moderates" or the Catholic liberal "pessimists" (and so on and so forth), that permanent inclination toward voicing doubts on the credibility of the very idea of the nation

---

50. "[T]he art of writing, which in the seventeenth century was distorted by very many through the simple folly of novelty, has genuinely changed in our century, but possibly for the worse; in that it has strayed not only from the old but from the national." The words are those of Pietro Giordani in his *Lettera di un italiano ai compilatori della "Biblioteca italiana"* (1816), in reply to Mme de Staël's essay "De l'esprit des traductions." They appeared in the first number of the *Biblioteca* in Giordani's own version (under the title "Sulla maniera e l'utilità delle traduzioni"): see his *Scritti*, in *Opere*, 10:345.

51. The correspondence between appreciation of a mixture of elements and modern politics (an implacable, discordant confusion of social classes and, in parallel, of ideas, passions, needs, habits, customs, and aspirations in a highly confused "set of images" of existence), with certain neo-Christian connotations (the religion that worships a God who came down to earth amid the misery and contradictions of the world to create a model of unbalanced and grief-stricken sublimity), goes back to Guizot's *Shakespeare* and Guizot's *Cours* of dramaturgy; amid the problems of a return to Shakespeare, the discussion of the importance of the relationships between author and audience prevailed over the stylistic questions of the relationships between one author and another.

("O patria! O patria . . . quanto mi costi!"), were far from being obstacles, on the one hand, and invitations, on the other, to artistic disobedience; instead, they seem to be—for opera—salutary ferment for its popularity.

Nothing from that direction seems to be able to discredit the power of opera to make contact:

- not the absurd idea of "backwardness," considered equally something to be overcome and preserved, for obvious political reasons;
- not the slow and despairing analysis of the "unmoving chaos of the possible": prose "sang" of how no public morality could ever prevail over the private, based in religion (in Manzoni), while poetry "recited" conversational monologues on the philosophical panic of materialism astounded by the power of nature (for Leopardians);
- not the dull, irrevocable sleep of the Italian cultural audience under the age-old blanket of disaster and irrevocable errors it has suffered (thinking of the country's historic familiarity with marauding foreigners, tyrants, large landowners, and so on) or desired (such as the new spirit in business, politics, finance, and commerce which had sprung up between the cracks of countless preserved sanctuaries of uninterrupted feudalism).

6. A CULTURAL IMPASSE BECOMES AN ARTISTIC STANCE

Opera seemed to be able to turn these aspects of low-level culture, "poverty," "backwardness," or habitual "hesitation" around and reveal poetic (or a semblance of poetic) representations that made those very conditions of cultural impasse its subject and to invent a bazaar of its many examples of catharsis.

So opera performed a service for the nation, producing success after success in creating a credible picture of cultural unity; the nation was now ready to confirm that there is indeed an Italian "used language," which made the most of the "functional," elastic properties of a lyric art that had been preserved through the long period before the nation came into being. There were two ways in which these properties and opportunities could be adapted to the neonational situation of the Risorgimento.

1. A prejudicially "easy" one was based on the almost unlimited opportunities offered, docilely, by the genre for adaptation and variation (in a way that is almost folkloric, especially through powerful creative intermediaries— true art directors of their day—first the singers, then the impresarios, and finally, in our time, the producers). The texts of opera supported this to the point of legitimizing variants that were effectively incompatible with the most sacrosanct claims to the "unchanging nature" of great texts (but without giving rise to any particular problems).

2. A casually "free" one offered up in a good light images of the cultural residue that the nation was not using in the scientific, political, literary, an-

thropological, and spiritual levels, particularly those things that remained stuck like glue to everyday life (a mixed bag, selected from the unexhausted scenarios of the pre-nation: the "Roman," evolving from tribalism to the great, imperial dream; the "Druid" and other Gallic barbarisms; the "Nordic" barbarian; the wild "rural-rustic"; the baroque epic or magical-sentimental medievalism; the disturbing, witchlike "pagan"; Middle Eastern psalmodic-contemplative "enchantment"; and so on). There could be a bit of everything, an inextricable and necessary mixture of forms of content and content of forms, so that the accusation of "old content" and "new forms" (and vice versa) could not be raised.

It was impossible to tell one from the other because both met easy approval from broad groups of listeners ready to award regular success to each new lyrical appearance of recognized interrelationships of the new ("quasi-new") with what had gone before. The "quasi-new" was enjoyed simultaneously with scenes that were pleasingly "old" or "quasi-old."

The first of these established properties, or good opportunities (the "easy" variant), is the more specific one in the order of formal codification and evolution of the "language" of Italian opera. It also governs the structure of finance and production of the genre, and its evolution over time has been amply dealt with in the course of the many chapters of this *History of Italian Opera*.

The second property, the one which carries more information on the subculture and on change and "discarding," is actually the theme of the unformed, as-yet-unwritten chapter, which will bring together the individual problems of how to define the points of contact (already turning aside from the paradox of a popularity that precedes and is not consequent to the discovery of the artistic quality of the texts) between Opera and national culture.

7. SUBLIMATIONS OF THE SUBCULTURE

Before we move on to a provisional inventory of these problematic features, it is possible to recognize already that they correspond in large measure to an answer to the enigma of Montale's "success" (my starting point) and its points of intersection between the function of the transmitter and the function of the recipient (the role played with the greatest expertise by the member of the claque) as revealed in their details. The success, lyrical nature, and popularity of Italian opera are seen in the market for these "details," in the bargain-basement sell-off of leftovers from the pre-nation, or rather represent a kind of great political episode of selling off incomplete Italian identifications of what was Italian, defeated and compromised in the nation's prehistory. In searching for an end to all that remained from incomplete histories of the country, and exploiting its attachment to cultural backwardness and the expressive inhibition of modernity that, lacking a true foundation, was for the most part on loan from the "classics" or "foreigners," Italian opera became the model of the first, original nationalization of the real "land" that was most "lived," not to mention "lived together," both quantitatively and qualitatively. When it became a nation, Italy was the last of the European countries to attempt to create a single political and military center and superimpose a dubious macromodel of the "people" on the resistant micromodel of dialects and ethnic groups and so on.

This is not to say that we are dealing with a monolithic monument, but neither are its constituent elements so scattered that they can only be listed one by one. Its basic character is, above all, the essential immediacy of its "contact" (this is what makes opera rather different from other instances of the nation's greater search for a political, literary, and scientific culture greater than itself). It is an immediacy which guarantees popularity and frees the texts of opera, as nothing else can, from the fetters of preparation, precognition, and instruction, which condition all readings (whether poetic, philosophical, or scientific) of nonoperatic Italian culture. And yet it should not be forgotten how the instantly involving nature of opera's lyrical messages (that is, its instantaneous "comprehension") is by no means the reason for the speed of the contact: the manifest messages, the very developments of the subjects of opera, are or seem to have to be terribly confused and almost always at least a little hermetic. In a sense, the fortunes of opera seem to exemplify how little profit can be gained from investing in mediation (information, preparation, and ideological predisposition) in attempts to program the cultural awakening of a group, a class, a city, or a nation; it almost suggests general models for the coming conventional immediacies of electrical and electronic mass media.

Still outside the terrain of opera, alien to its popularity and outside the frame of its logic, is a quality that other European nations, in the process of formation, have required from music: that is, the prediction, or presentiment, not to mention the first appearance, of a new "tonality" for humanity, revealed by the new nation, in a new people either revived or rid of false awareness (think of the interpretations along these lines applied or revealed in Beethoven, in Wagner, even in the Haydn of *The Creation,* by the proponents of the German nation, both on the Right and the Left).[52]

The fortune and considerable cultural importance of opera in the dynamic of the formation of the average intellectual life of Italy (from the Risorgimento to the genuinely "unifying" holocaust of the Great War) make an odd and rather overburdened mixture: there are (Italian) linguistic problems, wa-

52. Both in the sense of works of "critical" value (on the historic and political dehumanization of humanity) and of works prophetic of new "tonalities" in the existence of the liberated species (in a system of relationships and passages across the bridges in the sky connecting the peaks of ideology).

vering between "usage" and "good style," an Italian historical self-awareness (some rather daring interpretations of its own unutterable history, just like *I promessi sposi*), a moral urge to shake up the codes of conduct, a continual preoccupation with how Italy is reflected in the eyes of foreigners, boundless nostalgia for the natural beauty and ready Italian expressivity which provided Europe with the species "song," one of the primary absolute aesthetic experiences (during the eighteenth century, and principally from opera); there are resonances of the sacred, mystical playing to the Catholic gallery, partly a compromise, partly an example of business acumen (and Leopardi's important evocation to which I have already referred stands as a noble model of the desire for "a classical style . . . which seems [!] modern, and easy to understand and pleasure giving, to the people and the scholarly alike").

More than anything, the poetic that, casually, dominates the culture of the Italian nation is neither a true ideological critique of the false awarenesses that have hindered it politically nor the dawn of true self-awareness in a great people, but for the most part is that of a great "education through pastime." This pastime, let it be understood, is of enormous structural tension, positively embracing Leopardi's prophecy: a *seeming* (or appearing) having the same value as *being*, in place and time, as the as-yet-unborn cultural identity of an "artificial" nation (largely "destined" by the European powers; the product of north-south self-colonization, violent at times, and to a large extent undesired).

8. SEMBLANCES OF UNITY

Moving on swiftly to some "theses," all still requiring elaboration on the reasons and descriptions of what I have labeled an "education through pastime (or of the exploitation of 'backwardness')," in its success, in its popularity, both active and passive, its capacity to create imaginary representations of the nation through the "lyric quality" of its details, such as Montale's "gargling" and the "un-Dostoyevskian voices of the underworld," I must now honestly confess that here my aim is to attribute a fixed-term historic role, actively and passively sustained, to the Italian nature of opera as a whole. This role was sustained without explicit compromises by its creators through involvement in a political strategy (and because of their immediate empirical identification by some—but not many—generations of listeners), by the fact that its very historical assumption was due to or could be ascribed to one of the few uncontaminated, fairly progressive, reformed, and reformable linguistic "continuities" in Italian cultural history. This continuity, well known abroad, is fairly old, but younger than other possible ones known abroad, connected with the socioeconomic structure of its milieux, less than pure but not filthy, usefully tenacious, and endemically exciting: a continuity of Italian opera that has made it possible to begin this history of Italian opera—rightly and without undue patriotism—not at the period when the country became a nation but at the very birth of opera (not coincidentally in a Venice which in politics and art seems—to the very end—no less than a state of compromises, backwardness, and mixtures, all inspired by the paradox of an oligarchic, demo-aristocratic monarchy, which might easily stand as a prophecy of the modern Italian state).

Briefly, this promised, preliminary notion could be represented in terms of the unity of success, the induction from the popularity of opera to the existence of the people, which has the significance of a functional semblance. It is not an anticipation of a dawning unity (of another imperial *grande Nation,* another great, underinhabited agricultural and financial realm, or great commercial and piratical state, and definitely not a "Great Proletariat"). By realizing and practicing an amalgam of various forms of backwardness and modernity (the latter essentially European, but by free choice, not through invasion), and an amalgam of tradition and revolution, of conservation and innovation (ethically, of the "passion" of the subjects and, linguistically, as a series of "unitary" lexical and phraseological references), opera actually fulfills the intent of *Il conciliatore* without second thoughts (à la Leopardi) and without major delaying adjustments (à la Manzoni). It had been assumed that this was going to be laborious and, in other forms and hands, it became easy, an ease not shared, however, by the leading culture (as we have seen, either hesitating or rotting away in chains in the Spilberk). Opera won a type of success that—confounding suspicions—confirmed the possibility that the character who had become necessary actually existed: the Italian sui generis (the producers of opera casually not troubling to analyze his character, whether "Parisian *or* Hottentot," "*neither* Parisian *nor* Hottentot," "Parisian *and* Hottentot"). A character whom those who had "thought" of the nation had always endured as a problem to be solved, either temporarily or purely symbolically. (And in this light certain aspects look rather different: we can think differently about Carlo Cattaneo's preoccupation that "it might be a crust of wax to be stamped," and Vincenzo Cuoco's preclassical fantasy on the unburied and innate preclassical and Sanite virtues of the inhabitants of the peninsula; then there is Paolo Greppi's glance across the Alps at the Jacobin conscript-soldier, dreaming of importing the armed patriotism of the peasant defender arm in arm with the landowner in common interest, or the Utopianism of Giuseppe Pecchio, still picturing in *Il conciliatore* the figure of the docile Italian apprentice of liberal-philanthropic or scientific autodidactic systems.[53] And this refers to the time, not long before, when the question of the sublime passivity and docility of the vague figure of the near-invisible Ital-

---

53. See Carlo Cattaneo, *Alcuni scritti,* 3 vols. (Milan: Borroni and Scotti, 1846), 1:75; Vincenzo Cuoco, *Platone in Italia* (1806), ed. Fausto Nicolini (Bari: Laterza, 1916–24); [Paolo

ian was never raised by those—whether essayists, moralists, or tourists—
who in the eighteenth century, semianthropologically, had collected descriptions and been satisfied much more with the distribution of different types of
local color than by allowing themselves to be drawn toward the question of
discovering a visible, single, or least general Italian character.[54]

Opera achieved both the amalgam and the epiphany of the "character" to
identify and most of all to "make identifiable"—this being identical to Leopardi's "seeming modern"—thanks to the multiplication, referred to above,
detail by detail, of operatic images of everyday life (domestic life, increasingly
that of the petite bourgeoisie, the greater lying within the lesser) and of dis-
carded bits and pieces of inconclusive lives (vaguely historic but still known,
perceived as an uneasy background or enfeebled state of mind, and inadmis-
sible because barely known, and inherited, just as they were, by the invisible
antecedents of the Italian). For ease, it is useful here to think of a Verdi (accompanied by the applause of the acolytes at the mirror of his national art)
pursuing his plan, whether through conviction or to "take up time," to make
many "other Carmagnolas." And let "other Carmagnolas" be taken as a slo-
gan, not to call to mind the fact—which I shall come to in a moment—of the
assumption of the model of a linguistic idea "free from modes of speech and
words not similar to prose," that is, a non-lyrical-cultural language, not fine
language, therefore not customary language that can catch readers, men and
women, or the illiterate, or those attached to their little native (non-Tuscan)
tongue, or loyal to Metastasio on the wings of song; instead, its use should
show how in that recurring and highly important search for the "subject" of
his new operas, Verdi, imitating Manzoni, demolished the vision of Italy of
Sismondi, author of the *History of the Italian Republics in the Middle Ages*,
all the while describing it more than ever and exploiting the charm of what it
portrays.[55] Sismondi's imagery, which brings together the ardor and vividness, psychological as much as anything else, of the Italian character, ancient
or premodern, of the communes and lordly societies, in individual strength of
purpose and the energy of the struggles, is taken up both to rain off countless
details of exciting reevocations of Italian prehistory, confusedly repressed or
repressively confused, and also to represent the negative judgment on the violent, anti-unitarian anarchy of those political annals, which is tragically re-

Greppi], *La Rivoluzione francese nel carteggio di un osservatore italiano*, ed. Giuseppe Greppi, 3
vols. (Milan: Hoepli, 1900–1904), 1:220 passim; [Giuseppe Pecchio], "Des systèmes actuels d'é-
ducation," *Il conciliatore*, 16 May 1819.

54. From Calepio (1727) to Denina (1796), no Italians other than scholars or artists seem to
exist, or at the most survive as comic caricatures, recognizable only in tourist snapshots.

55. From *De la littérature du Midi de l'Europe* (1813) to the *Histoire des républiques itali-
ennes du Moyen Âge*, which appeared in translation in Italy in 1844 and was widely read and
made a profound effect.

flected both in lyrical moments and in more integral plots (and *Simon Bocca-negra* is possibly the ambitious prototype of this, paradoxically coming after its "imitations").[56] This was articulated in ambivalent images of courage versus ferocity, pride versus mindless arrogance, the (Italian and Machiavellian) art of politics versus moral loathing, knightly valor versus fratricide, and so on.

Manzoni's impracticable, abstruse, and ambitious solution was set aside. In fact, Verdi, in the "positive" nature of what he puts onstage, did not follow the man he called his saint. He did not glorify invisible images of "true" victims, sacrificed and disfigured in their nonhistory of silent Christian suffering (the new Italian is being offered a mute progenitor, with a face covered with dry tears, powerless, patiently aware of the illusory, tragic nature of the nonprovidential, beneficial consequences of any act). It is true that Verdi looks for victims, but he does not deduce their unsung existence in the background of history so much as artificially imbue Sismondi's own figures with moral qualities, a yearning for justice and other great, positive, identifying sentiments. With a pile of "details" filling the blank spaces and through the technique of interior, or at least domestic, conflict, he adds on some emotional psychology and makes them into x-rays of true history revealing shadow after shadow of Italian victims, martyrs to be redeemed. Aside from the primary ambiguity of operatic bel canto, the purely "musical" conventions that are always to the fore, he places everything in a sea of episodic and representative ambiguities, distributed or, rather, astutely anchored in non-Italian settings (apart from *Messa da Requiem,* only *Oberto, La battaglia di Legnano, I Lombardi, Simon Boccanegra,* and *I due Foscari,* with *I vespri,* that is, only seven pieces out of twenty-seven, never shifted their weapons and narrative and ideological baggage somewhere else).[57]

In this form, national-romantic serious opera could be an ex-Sismondian representation (prudently set elsewhere) of a great Italy of people *and* nobles (of the communes and the Renaissance), dominated by energetic figures, first as a group then by the super-individual Great Italians, energetic and even too ambitious, or an ex-Manzonian critique of the portrayal of those (ex-Sismondian) annals themselves, both coming together as a pretext for interior dramas or contained moral conflicts (with a tragic finale). As such it went on to "personalize" (make psychologically "readable" and arouse empirical identifications in its audience), not so much the political and moral themes of that cultural divide, as the cultural divide itself (two images of Italy) removed from present-day criticism and transferred to characters who acted out the "sub-

56. One basic contribution of Verdian dramaturgy is the theme of an existential failing, in history, where morality is "identified" in a character who dies, conquered, as he or she conquers his or her own personality as a "victim": the victim of the power of the family, of political intrigue and ignobility, amid the splendor of a grand setting and fleeting intimacy.

57. Not counting *Rigoletto,* which has the censor to thank for its Italian location.

ject." Almost all the Italian national operatic texts deal with this: representing the dilemma of the identity of Italian culture turned into a story within the limitations of musical time (real and tyrannical, measured, unstoppable), to be taken for what it is. Almost always, as we have seen, it represented itself in terms of an interior or generational conflict (on the male, paternal side, of course) concerning the definition of the true Italian character and the identification of a "victim." In its revelation is the revelation of the "truth," because the truth is what arises again and again from the historic darkness in the form of an expressive desire for redemption: if the character succumbs in this aspiration, if he or she dies for it, then that victim will appear all the more, ultimately knowable and modern, the true voice of the undefined character, the desired object of the entire nation's intellectual curiosity.

Something else increased the burden on this superform and colored its features: on it was superimposed a plot-driven, generalized idea of eroticism (of the absolute minimum sexual or symbolically sexual content) plus all sorts of sound bites from the common memory of "life in Italy," whether modern, remote, or archaic. This memory, in order to draw off the related anxieties (given the immeasurable ignorance of the causes and the structures of fear,[58] of pleasure,[59] of death,[60] of cruelty,[61] of seduction,[62] in Italy), was associated only with aspects of a continuum of feelings, given to and taken from the people of what Italy had always meant to the Great People of the Earth—a battlefield and a place to prove one's power).

We can see here, purely by a process of deduction, now that the "documents," the immediate protocols, have been destroyed by more than a century

58. The ignorance of causes and the privileged representations of details, which are fairly constant features of Italian folkloric entertainment, might possibly be a genuine example of cultural continuity. As an example of the theme of "fearful" entertainment, think of the story of the collapse of the bridge over the Arno, which, as described accurately by Villani, is even more shocking than the folk imagery of the real death of so many people.

59. A scorn exhibited (with, in, and on hunger) in the many examples of mocking a gift of food at a feast (such as those found in Verona, Bologna, and other places where foodstuffs, imaginary and real, are publicly wasted).

60. The imagery of a good and a bad death forms a circle, with the latter at the point of utter despair (echoing "Eli! Eli! the critical moment of Christ's despair touches on the bad death of the unbeliever). Despair is the greatest test and mortal—and extraordinary—temptation of the sickly and the conquered (see the command in Francesco da Mozzanica's *In nomine Iesu*: "The sin of despair is the only one that cannot be healed . . . and even if one were sure to be counted among the damned, nonetheless one should not despair on this account").

61. Public executions, as celebration—as Beccaria reminds us—were intended more for the spectators than for the condemned.

62. "Sinister" sexual typologies were injected into new Italian folklore when superstition and witchcraft flourished again, post-Counter-Reformation, as pure and simple, "seductive" reintroductions of what had historically been "repressed": pagan memories, country practices that followed the dissolution of the structure of the rural world, and so on.

of wear and tear, the first point of opera's convention (in the sense of "pact")
stipulated, in separate but corresponding contracts, both with the empirical
recipient (the audience of the entire, single country) and with contemporary
molders of ideology and critico-cultural commentary (and other artists), as
well as the political weavers of the Risorgimento compromise. By this point,
facing all three—the audience, the cultural world, the politicians—stood the
honorable promise to test the country's ability to be portrayed in the light,
transient form of a "pastime." For the audience, it was a "stopgap," before
the definition of still prohibited class or rank consciousness; for the cultural
world, it preceded a true or positive decision on ideological or philosophical
alignment (whether in favor of Enlightenment materialism, idealism, or a
new, religious, and Catholic exegesis, responding to the calls of liberalism and
socialism); and for the politicians, it preceded the formation of a structure of
government alliances (whether with financial capital or old landowners, with
proposals for division into small, private, light-industrial investments or distant trusts and supranational monopolies).[63]

This is a promise to assume responsibility for efficiency, in a context of unconditional trust, to be maintained exclusively on the level of what was
termed above "the capacity for portrayal" of a national character, understood as a single one, but shared by breaking up its current imagery as bequeathed by all the traditions which, if interrupted, are still dimly remembered, here giving a face to new, unresolved figures, and there using nuances
or absurdity to make the most pressing problems or actual identification of
vital interests less urgent. It is therefore clear that that laborious choice of subjects which so seems to have preoccupied the composers of opera—at times
Verdi's autobiographical comments seem no more than obsessive stories of
searching for the "right" story—is used as a pretext.[64] In fact, this first point
of the convention established with the "people," the "others" of the culture
world, and with the national government, current or to come, turns wholly
on representational formalization of the right details to be inserted into the
unchanging story of conflicts between the new and the old, the just and the
unjust, redemption and humiliation, and so on. Out of these disputes and
conflicts comes the great "lyric" character of one or more victims explained
as the tragic determination of a generic Destiny *ex machina*. These were appealing victims, poets as characters, poetic shades whose nature was entirely
passed on from the great Italian "lyric" tradition of the days so dear to Sis-

---

63. For a brief outline of the critical situation of the political and economic dimensions of
post-Unification Italy, see chapter 4 of Alexander Gerschenkron, *Economic Backwardness in Historical Perspective* (1962; Cambridge, Mass.: Belknap Press of Harvard University, 1966).

64. It is not rare to find Verdi happily taking potluck with subjects, which he can then work
on, altering them by freely adding or subtracting elements (and moving the location or condensing elements).

mondi in the form of the supreme privilege of being able to give voice and swan song to grief and agony, that is, to the moment in which "other," non-lyric peoples, not inclined to song, seem to have been allowed by nature patient or panic-stricken silence as the only possible form of expression.[65] (This privilege had recently been acknowledged, in Europe, in the last chivalric epic, *Gerusalemme liberata*, which was already exploited for its lyricism by opera: see Goethe's play on Tasso.)

More than the choice of subject, then, the prevailing poetic decision in opera was to include in the representation of these "victims" all the detailed expression of cultural or subcultural residue that has been discussed above (still surviving, but at the bottom of the uncertain social and cultural life of the reborn country).

A culture of "victimhood" (excluding any facile or colloquial connotations in the use of the term) can be honored on three levels, the ones considered above as the conditions in the convention.

1. It gives the old Italian folk the chance to relive, in the lyrical development of the story, the nostalgic theme of sacrificial identification with the Passion of Christ, as translated into modern terms. One example is the theme of Christ-Pulcinella,[66] famously practiced in the town squares of the south. Subsequently, as opera evolved through time, the distance between the divine sacrificial victim and the human masked characters lessened on both sides: from the great and powerful man who is also human down to the last feminine versions. Such characters were dragged willy-nilly from one setting to another (the Latin Quarter, a teahouse, the walls of the Violet City, Rome without the pope, and so on), producing a sequence of up-to-the-minute, petit-bourgeois characters, of seamstresses, geishas, Tartar slave girls, and so on.

2. Opera provided the deceptive expedient of a wholly melodramatic "convention" of tragic fatalism that suppresses and sacrifices good and bad by illustrating, through the punishment meted out to any misguided faith in individual rational action, a philosophical victimhood, that of the true, absolute power of Manzoni's "Dio che atterra e fulmina." Such an antibourgeois cri-

---

65. See act 5, scene 2, of Goethe's *Torquato Tasso*, where there is the unexpected "heroic" image of the silkworm: "Try to / Forbid the silkworm to continue spinning / Though it is spinning on to its own death. / It will evolve its precious weft from deep / Within its inner self and will not cease / Till it has cased itself in its own coffin" (*Goethe's Plays*, translated by Charles E. Passage [London: Ernest Benn, 1980], 581).

66. In the letters of the traveler Samuel Sharp (*Letters from Italy* [London: Cave, 1766], 183ff.), then in Croce's *Teatri di Napoli* (Naples: Pierro, 1891), 143ff., and in Jacques Lacan's *Écrits* (Paris: Seuil, 1966), 764, we find the story of the preacher who waves a crucifix, shouting, "This is the real Pulcinella!" This serves as a measure of the communicative power of the gestures of rapid, spectacular, violent, and indisputable "alteration" of "meanings": a model of the historical existence of the functional relationship of a concept seen to be identified by a single figure (or of the power of an unrealistic scene: the "lyric quality").

tique of the creative will, entrepreneurial and utilitarian, does not so much illustrate openly Manzoni's ideas as represent, at the end of the "lyric" digression, the gestural nature (something expected on the folklore side as well, after all) of the art of dying. (Performers who have become famous on this account, such as Moriani,[67] whose historical reputation is as the "tenor of the beautiful death," stand as confirmation of this.)

3. It goes without saying that opera, through its seductive fictions, provided support for the theme of political sacrifice to a government founded on a litany of martyrs.

Naturally, there were other subsidiary aspects lent by opera in establishing the three patterns of the creation of the character of the Italian (even if on all three levels, the folkloric, the critico-cultural, and the political, they inevitably come with an aesthetic element).

The balance of prenational cultural-thematic leftovers and clutter was considerable. It gave the people, in representative form, so limited to identification and really with the character of a "release," different, interrupted, folklike satisfactions. Let us not forget that the same techniques of dividing into small pieces[68] and dramatizing texts, with "appropriate music" ("on compunction" and the "grief of sin"), had been employed in ejaculatory prayers or mixtures of prayers and other texts (such as the eighteenth-century lullabies of the type "Verbum caro fantinello / circonciso col coltello" [the word made flesh little boy / circumcised with a knife]);[69] think, too, of the amorous, lascivious hymns to beautiful Madonnas[70] or such grandiose, gruesome ges-

---

67. The great opera singer Napoleone Moriani (1808–78) was associated with the enormous popularity of such operas as *Pia de' Tolomei, Lucrezia Borgia,* and *Luigi Rolla,* which held the stage until he retired in the middle of the nineteenth century. His great skill lay in being able to portray dying when overwhelmed by destiny, rendered, according to eloquent commentators of the day, as if he were "a narcissus, broken and bowed, in whose breast the fleeting echo wept in lament," sighing, falling and falling again, like one who is about to "fly to happier skies," holding "his head in his hands, in anguish," clutching the heroine's neck, and expressing in "the tone of his singing" the terrible reality of "life being extinguished," and so on.

68. The church's intensive but gentle penetration of the countryside was effected through these little sermons, as the great Jesuit and Dominican sermons were progressively replaced by miniature, everyday addresses, brief anecdotes, and little proverbs of the poor man's devotions. Proof that they were part of a cultural plan can be found in the many pastoral Instructions printed and distributed among parish priests in the eighteenth century. There was a watchword current at the time: "Break the truth of Faith up into small pieces for the people," to bring ideas and dogma to the miniaturized level of everyday, domestic life.

69. Texts of a repertory of sacred anecdotes of the most simple, singable kind, on sheets of paper and in little volumes, circulated an ephemeral tradition almost as a gentle literacy campaign; these pamphlets, from the early seventeenth century, alternate and superimpose grim, sinister subjects with sugary expressions of lyrical abandon to Our Lady or the baby Jesus.

70. The Marian hymn traces its liturgical descent from antiphons and vespers texts, eventually becoming a little song of sacred love and part of the unlearned folk repertory.

tures with cries "like bolts from heaven" and other "vehement squawking" coming unexpectedly (shock effects, in a word)—practiced by the Jesuits when they took their missionary zeal to colonize and nationalize the south of Italy (the so-called Indies down south).[71] But it is worth remembering, as well, how opera absorbed many folk ideas that have been appeased or repressed, such as the belief in or terror of witches,[72] the world turned upside down, and an evaluation of one other great prenational cultural fragmentation: the popular fortunes of "pamphlets," little books, sung proverbs, almanacs, which the dominant culture expelled too quickly and were quietly picked up, by assimilation (actually, substitution) in opera, in the transformation of the old arioso style. As "closed" texts were parceled up into operatic "lyric verses," their survival in abbreviated form (think of how many ex-arias, redone in cantilena style, in the manner of almanacs or proverbs in ten or twenty bars are found in Verdi at his best!)[73] is much more a case of folk identification than respect for formal tradition (much more the fulfillment of the new "convention" between opera and people than displaying its own "convention" internal to the history of opera).

In taking on all this, sweeping up the inexhaustible micromodels of different patriotic sensibilities bequeathed by history (in order to use them up), the half-forgotten but unsatisfied themes of expectation, even the unworthy odds and ends—especially unworthy of "Catholic" reflection now matured and forward looking—of the *novi miraculi* accompanied by all sorts of indiscriminate festive mingling with pagan leftovers, opera is providing a great service to the dominant culture; it is helping it to overcome its indecision (whether or not to begin examining the small, genuine folk legacy without recourse to bookish medievalism, whether "cardboard" or imported). The significance of this is confirmed by Ermes Visconti's correspondence with Manzoni on this very question of the character of contemporary poetry ("What can be the character of poetry in our day?"). When Visconti[74] wonders what would happen should poetry drop all convention (and by "convention" he clearly means the slavish imitation of both the classical tradition and the romantic, or else

71. It is worth reading the superb descriptions collected by Friar Scipione Paolucci in his *Missioni dei Padri della Compagnia di Gesù nel Regno di Napoli* (Naples: Roncagliolo, 1651).

72. Miscellaneous repertories exist, impossible to date and full of ejaculations and vows closely linked to the style of the wording of black ritual and superstitious exorcisms; such increasingly mixed and confused material is found together with the hermetic ingenuity of a sacred phonic and vocal configuration.

73. Verdi's proverbial "brevity" is directed toward finding more opportunities for lyrical expansion in a given scene (for example, how to insert a tiny cantabile even in the *tempo di mezzo* sections) and shows a predisposition to lyrical touches in the widest variety of locations (erratic, secondary, interrupted, shortened, recurring).

74. From Paris in 1819 to Manzoni, in the *Carteggio di Alessandro Manzoni,* ed. Giovanni Sforza and Giuseppe Gallavresi (Milan: Hoepli, 1912), 442–44.

the sublime Nordic or the grotesque French strain), and how it might be possible to create poetry using elements which "still" truly live in "our minds," he at once tries to describe an art capable of giving the illusion of indiscriminate mixing of both classes (the people and the educated). But which art? Just as the question had been, Which language?—a language that might "still" be intelligible to all.

There is an aspect that, apart from those already mentioned, in opera solves some problems for the well-meaning "educated" class by satisfying the "people," and at the same time in part resolving some intrinsic problems of the genre. This is the dual undertaking that Italian lyric opera fulfilled in importing from the French musical stage the majesty and pomp of the monumental spectacle of French grand opéra, not *in toto*, but by fragments and functional quotations, and from the spoken theater—as well as from its narrative antecedents and followers—the fragments and quotations of Charles Nodier's and Victor Hugo's shocking style and black, grotesque manner.[75] These were the grandiosity, cheap effects, big choruses, and stomach-churning shocks, lavish backdrops and terrible lapses of taste, and after the need to reinforce Italian romantic opera by alternating its lyric, cantabile qualities with sudden, grandiose effects or disturbing images had been fulfilled (in simple terms, a mixture of contrasts within a basic lyrical style), and after Verdi had perfected the style for all time through an ingenious two-way traffic between bel canto, grand opéra, and the theater of the boulevards (twelve trips to Paris!),[76] this vocabulary fulfilled another function. It served to confirm as a backdrop, however criticized, the pomp and power—grandiose, spendthrift, and monumental—of the Sismondi vision of Italy, against which were projected the sinister figures glimpsed in northern European literary romanticism, but always feared as unpopular and abstract follies (remember Giordani's severe judgment). But also, in the same dimension described above, they served to satisfy instances of folkloric revival of the recent prehistory of the nation and so, despite Giordani, to satisfy tastes that were "foolish" *but* popular, or *still* popular. Both the "grandiose" and the shocking, "sinister" elements served this need and, if we are honest, were "imported" specifically to make a European blend of the single original wine, the Rossinian tradition—and once again evoke something of the popular images of the Italian *festa*. In the era following the penal reforms of Cesare Beccaria, the end of terrible punishments (the gallows, traitors turned on the spit, burning at the stake, driving

75. In Paris such a mixture of effects formed part of the armory of the so-called *grand spectacle* and arose from the closely and conventionally reciprocal conditioning of invention and reception; its conventional nature was paradoxical in that it was determined almost exclusively by the character of surprise.

76. Verdi's many regular trips to Paris were undoubtedly taken to discover and compare the city's new theatrical trends.

out of whores, bullfights of cuckolds, thieves tortured with pincers) marked the end, too, of the popular feast where Horror and the Power of rulers were simultaneously displayed.[77] The simultaneous appearance of elements of both, here and there, in the mixture, which is charged with a sense of expectation and with comparison with the other emotions involved in the contact with opera, makes for great consolation, constituting those lost recurring cult practices taken imperiously from the people with no communicated explanation of the progress which their passing signaled. And it can be added that the recurrent positioning of religious ritual in the background, typical of the quotation from the grandiose style—from the offstage prayers in Verdi, even on the banks of the Nile, to the mass celebrated during the orchestral intermezzo in *Cavalleria rusticana,* in other words, with the whole offstage stage—could not help but please a lay government that aspires to a painless, nonviolent relegation of the church to the background of life in the new nation.

The descriptive picture of the relationship between opera and national culture—as we have seen, a "service" relationship, in which the good offices of the former are resolved in a progressive affirmation of its popularity established during the time of delays in the building of the latter—also covers some solutions to questions of pinning down exactly what the "national character" is when it comes to language. When Pellico hailed in Manzoni's *Conte di Carmagnola* its language, "which avoids expressions and words not similar to prose," using "not" both to say that the language of *Il conte di Carmagnola* was shaking off the "unpopular" connotations of academic poetry and also to announce enthusiastically the start of the an era of linguistic conquest of Italian reading, he had been overoptimistic. At the beginning of this essay, we took stock of the persistence, at the height of the Risorgimento, of the problem that a section of the readership rejected the fine style of the literary scene, and this is not the place to reexamine the torments inflicted by Manzoni both on his own text and on the *Vocabolario* of the Accademia della Crusca—in search of a nonexistent Italian tongue as true as the vernaculars, genuinely in common use, "still" alive in the flow of tradition, and so on. Here more than ever what national intellectuals needed was to take a long time and to hold on to many opportunities to experiment without having to reply immediately to the nation on the problematic absence of a modern language. For a long time, the language of librettos had maintained the role of unifying the Italian

77. Civil reform, or rather the end of the "nation's war on the citizen," and the abolition of torture, in other words, the victory of Beccaria's proposals, together mark the end of the state's penal infamy. At the same time, however, they mark the end of popular "festivals." Cruelty would no longer be a real spectacle, experienced in the times and places of the festival. It could only be, and was only, a real event (unforeseeable, unknown, or shrewdly anticipated) or else a real fiction (the art of illusion, well served by lyrical decoration and phantasmagorical settings stemming from the dissolution of the archaic world).

language, favored by the former, universally shared pleasure—of women, too—in reading Metastasio. It had disseminated enrichments to the lexicon and exploited in a form of blackmail the interest paid to opera: all those who wished to act out the events narrated by opera, or just sing the words, had memorized all their abstruseness and delicacy, their brutality and tenderness, their verbal expression of passion, or rage, of the art of dying, of prayer, or of "the comic side." Opera had a unique linguistic blend, an open and at times highly poetic fusion of the educated and the commonplace, a mix of the elevated (sometimes too much so) with the low and prosaic, but, for all that, set as lyric verse with exciting rhythms driven on by the urgent tempo of the cabalettas (possibly the points of the greatest linguistic excess). This had communicated to its Italian audience an equally open-minded faith in the existence, or, if not exactly the existence, at least the promise of its imminent arrival, of a language that crossed regions and classes, to be marked with the reassuring and shared effect of lyric perceptions. (The final seal on this faith can be seen in the strange case of a realistic, peasant, ideologically dialect opera, such as Mascagni's triumphant *Cavalleria,* where the original dialect of the Siciliana is used by way of an abstract, we might say "orchestral," introduction with the curtain down, before the beginning of the rustic action, in which, to take only one example, Alfio, a carter, uses the literary verb *ire* to tell the women to go to mass and talks to his horse about his thudding hooves using a sophisticated optative subjunctive.)

Another element that should be mentioned on the level of semifolkloric communication is the incomprehensibility, the deliberate oddity, of certain words and phrases: examples are Norma's "sacri bronzi," Violetta's "egre soglie," the sarcastic Samuel and Tom's "raggio lunar del miele," Azucena's "perigliarti ancor languente," the Hebrew slaves' "ove olezzano tepide e molli," Lady Macbeth's "rimondar sì piccol mano," and Aida's "fuggiam gli ardori inospiti." These frankly indecipherable expressions give the common listener the same intoxicating feeling, translated into "modern" sounds, of the indecipherable phrases that mark the blessed sense of the sacred, in liturgical hymns, vespers, litanies, and the masses sung on the feast of a patron saint everywhere, since time immemorial. And so, once again, they provide indirect linguistic links between popularity and national communion, on the broadest scale.

9. OPERA GOES OUT OF CHARACTER

A new structural element creeps in at this point in our reconstruction of the network of relations between "lyric art" and Italian culture, an element that is no longer an expression of mediation between the old and the new or of the suspension of expectations of identifying an Italian character in the real and popular consumption of an experience which is in its way cultural and unifying. Something different that initially occurs (bringing with it the first signs of semi-unpopularity: such as Verdi's famous "partial fiascos") on the level of cultural contribution made by a genre that still seems to be "serving," if no longer a "stopgap." There are certain operas that aspired to hurriedly anticipate a more Europeanized middle-class culture (common to all levels of the bourgeoisie) or, surrendering both the Italian language and popularity, to reinforce texts that Italy, not having found them within itself—whether in the original or in translation—sought out in foreign literature; these are no longer "other Carmagnolas." The prototype of this deviation (even if Verdi had already made a few effortful experiments along these lines) is *La traviata.* Here is an opera that does not fail duly to portray sacrifice or to refer to operatic "conventions" new and old, both in the preservation of bel canto, the space allotted to grand choreographed scenes, and in the mixture of high and low linguistic styles. But it does show worrying signs of deviation. First of all, the background no longer touches on sacred perceptions and suggestions, and it peppers the narrative invisibly (lost in the endless perspective of bourgeois tedium) with other representations of the main story of illicit love affairs and the *beau monde.* Furthermore, the choice of the subject clearly does several things: it expresses an aspiration to engage the attention of those who read foreign literature (remember, women mostly), and it attempts—or measures— the emotional ability to take on foreign sensibilities (the fallen woman's redemption rather than her naked run between the whiplashes of the popular Renaissance festival), and it calls on the "lyric art" to express individual experience—no longer having to compensate for the backwardness of the national culture—instantly modernized by using sources of material more typical of the truly international nineteenth century. These aspects can be seen in the genre of the moralizing novel, in ideology, in the "psychological" interpretation of the individual, and in the symbolistic value placed on language.

It is from this area of experience, from opera composers' increasing unwillingness to provide a stopgap in maintaining cultural backwardness cultivated for political purposes and never overcome, through the deliberate creative indecision of the "great artists," that we find a certain tendency within the "lyric art" itself to put its own popularity at risk. To put it on trial. To betray it.

Once again, a mixed pattern is at work: while, on the one hand, the whole thing seems to echo, almost like a parody, the creative aura of Wagnerian opera, mixed with other European examples of symbolism, and can be summed up in the will to create operas that are sui generis and not further numbers in a series, on the other hand there is a sense of a "return." This is a "return" to order, in terms of aspiring to an ideal Italian cultural continuity.

It is a continuity rediscovered in many places, almost as if it were a native treasure, vulgarly betrayed and buried by pure Verdian opera, by its mixtures, by its delaying compromises.

Some decisions are connected with these last aspects, which have to be tackled first because historically they had the greatest impact and did probably appear first—even if late, in that they were closely linked to interventionist and post–World War I veterans propaganda, as well as the preparation for Fascism.

The first is that of the "end of backwardness": particularly in the light of an explicit belief that an answer to the problem of identifying the people and their character had been found; a belief rocked in the cradle by newspaper lullabies during the "Great War" and by the paternal and high-sounding clamor of artistic manifestos. A character that had finally been revealed. Where? To give an example: in the combination of forms that had become "historic unity"; a historic unity that had transcended action, making the Italian people itself a "transcendental unity" or no less than a harmonious "idea" (the real people) for its own renewal. It is easy to sketch this first aspect without resorting to the joking of more ridiculous propaganda, by quoting the words of the painter Carlo Carrà, who directed his friends and colleagues thirsty for "consolation" toward "metaphysics,"[78] and one can easily align with it the other, aesthetic decision of the idealized return, the reconstructed continuity (transcendental and metaphysical) of an innately Italian, antimodernist character: a pastoral, Arcadian character, *but* in the tradition of Piero della Francesca, *but* fairly Umbrian, *but* blessed with the deserted aura of an authentic and silent countryside, and the countryside had indeed become deserted and silent after the massacre of peasant men in the trenches.

On the level of these aspects, opera was attacked, almost violently, by the criticism and rejection of the "educated."[79] This attack had the rapid effect of destroying the peculiar nature of Italian opera. To save itself and stay on its feet, the "lyric art" would have to purge itself of everything it was, invent a nonexistent "continuity" of a deep-rooted and uncontaminated tradition (which it did not possess), and find its own archaism in that nonexistent tradition—since the much discussed problem of resolving the "antitraditionalist" needs, which throughout the entire nineteenth century it had embraced

78. Carlo Carrà, *La pittura metafisica*, in his *Pittura metafisica* (1919), 2d ed. (Florence: Vallecchi, 1945), 72ff. In connection with artistic activity in the light of the new, post-Risorgimento national conscience, he writes: "We know that the present moment does not lend itself to homilies on taste, but we affirm that there are some works which in themselves declare that their creators have done everything possible to bring back to life the plastic virtues of our race" (Carlo Carrà, *Tutti gli scritti*, ed. Massimo Carrà [Milan: Feltrinelli, 1978], 142).

79. Either they had crossed over to Wagner or genuinely returned to the past but without making much progress (cataloguing and publishing early music).

on behalf of the culture of the new nation, had gone stale. Plenty of false trails appeared: the acrobatics of *Pagliacci,* which managed to combine the archaicism of the Strapaese literary movement and commedia dell'arte with "reality" smuggled in as a pretext for a tragic scene of return to "transcendental" Italian images (a triple somersault, which has preserved the work's popularity); Puccini's incomplete *Turandot,* which remained immortal, like an unfinished cathedral, erected to the memory of the compliance of the genius who both gave in to the aesthetic tyranny of the "breach" of "operatic" convention (Gozzi and the fable vouch for this) and at the same time once more popularized in opera small-scale psychology, that of weak, feminine, or petit-bourgeois characters, to an unrealistic extent in the double (historical and geographical) alienation of the setting; Malipiero's "musicological" reveries with the "launch" of Monteverdi and the use of Monteverdi himself for endless variations on the theme of the twentieth-century "return to the roots" of lyric opera from the exact point of its historical beginning (possibly a bit before).

Among the opera composers who passed, victorious, through the metaphysical experience, not one managed to betray his or her own defining aesthetic as Giorgio Morandi was able to do, reinforcing in that betrayal the moral content of the lyric "pastime" in a quite different lyric art.[80]

I have carefully delayed describing the first stage in the trial, challenge, and overcoming of its own national-cultural role by Italian opera, before the great assault effected by the new generation of futurists, Strapacsists, the metaphysicists, Fascists, neo-Gothics, neobaroques, neoclassicists, who bombarded their monuments from the fortresses of the Italianness proclaimed by the Great War. I wanted to leave open the interpretation of that challenge (a self-directed challenge) because the reasons for it continue to develop today. I have spoken of a kind of revolt against the role of endless mediation, borne by the "lyric art" in a spirit of service, patriotic, but also wearing, in endlessly producing a series of variations on a single theme, and all the more inspired as the more subtle and persuasive (and wearing because of the squandering of inspiration, sacrificed to cultural "service"). The models of revolt seem to be first and foremost other areas of experience, quasi-Wagnerian ones, of access to individual and identifiable works unsuited to popularity or to the national characterization of the product consecrated by Italian opera, in other words, numbers in a series.

This search for the "unique" work, standing outside the series and outside

80. Very quickly, having finished with his museum experience and inventions from memory, objectively revived, Morandi was almost alone in tackling the only possible continuity of national figurative art: the problem of the artistic oppression of truth without the disappearance of any of its semblance. See the lucid diagnosis by Francesco Arcangeli in *Giorgio Morandi pittore* (1964) (Turin: Einaudi, 1981).

convention, opened with the spectacular, grand fiasco of Boito's *Mefistofele* at La Scala in 1868. Unpopularity, programmed in, even in the tiniest performance details, in the design, and so on,[81] was already implicit in the choice of a subject that was philosophical, foreign, derived from a foreign classic in translation, and crammed with elements that in no way fulfilled the customary need to satisfy the expectations of the return of the half-buried repertoire of Italian imagery. A text poorly endowed with bel canto, Beethovenian and not Bellinian or Rossinian in its lyric approach, and where the grandiosity of the stage spectacle, the dance scenes, and the lighting were abstruse and symbolical.

A little later on, Verdi, in his *Requiem,* used an entire Catholic ritual entirely for his own individual and unique creation and brought it straight into the theater, to show to those who had not yet understood that it was indeed an opera, but one outside any "pact." And then Boito got down to working with frantic diligence on *Nerone,* whose intended audience, day by day over the thirty years and more of work, became more and more tiny, tragically inexpressible. Of course, he did not manage to finish the work, and it was staged at La Scala, posthumously, at the behest of Toscanini, only in 1924.[82] But in the meantime, Verdi and Boito had got together and thrust on Ricordi a piece of operatic nonsense, abstrusely formalized, from the sonata-form opening scene to the fugal finale, and inspired—female victims, bel canto, shocks, and the pathos of grandeur having by now all fallen by the wayside— by a joke that was neither lewd nor communal nor Renaissance, in no way reevocative but self-propelling and philosophically autocombustive in the triumph of "Tutti gabbati" (everyone's been taken in).[83]

What with comic skepticism, lack of cultural service, the collapse of interest in the national character, a change to extreme intimacy of expression (Verdi's late *Te Deum* stands as an example of this most public of public rit-

---

81. In *Il secolo* of 7 Mar. 1868, Parravicini wrote, "The structure of the opera has another grave defect, that of the unusual difficulty of the intrigues, the arrangements, the tempos, the distribution and grouping of the parts, so that even with a thousand rehearsals, it would still be mere chance if there were a perfect performance of the whole, as much as of the details."

82. "This is possibly what gave rise to the awareness, to the very end, of not knowing how to achieve his goal. Aware of what a miracle of art needs to be, and equally aware of the distance separating him from achieving that miracle, on the day before he died Boito told one of his young friends that, as soon as he was better, he intended to go to Lake Como and devote himself again to *Nerone.* . . . Carlo Gatti, too, who had gone to visit the invalid in via Filangeri, had heard him say, 'As soon as I'm home, I'll do two hours a day of work, and the piece will be ready in two months.'" In Piero Nardi, *Vita di Arrigo Boito* (Milan: Mondadori, 1942), 727.

83. *Falstaff,* act 3, scene 2: "Tutto nel mondo è burla. / L'uom è nato burlone, / . . . / Tutti gabbàti! Irride / l'un l'altro ogni mortal. / Ma ride ben chi ride / la risata final" (All the world's a joke. / Man is born a joker. / Everyone's been taken in! / We can all laugh at one another. / But he who laughs last / laughs best).

uals given an intensely private expression), and the systematic search for the incomplete and the work prevented from being produced (much as was the case between 1984 and 1986 with Nono's *Prometeo,* in a state of continuous, Hölderlin-like "reconstruction," as fragments were offered to the listener, always for the last time, calling up once again the operatic ghost of *Nerone*), Italian opera ceased to be an instance of national cultural life. Instead, it changed into a universal art form, one of many which resist the death of art.

Let us ask ourselves where Montale's "unpopular" heroes Rebillo and Riccò stand: are they among the "taken in" or among the intense deserters of national cultural service? Are they among those exonerated from this service by the Metaphysical painters? Are they Italians?

On the other side, there is the unaltered "success"—now achieved without a claque—of Italian opera as it has been from the time of Italian cultural backwardness. This is a success possibly connected to continual imaginative re-creation—probably still a "pastime" but certainly still bound up with the structure of civic life in the country. This is a lyric "pastime" that in the law of the Italian state has been on the point of having its income linked with the public games of chance: the "national" lotteries.[84] Those lotteries, it is said, were invented by Calzabigi, the father, as he is called, of the so-called reform of Italian opera itself—before the national Italian opera was even born.

84. The allusion is to a solution that has been floated a number of times and was suggested and discussed during the preparatory work in drawing up the law later presented to the Italian Parliament on 30 Oct. 1984 (no. 2222). Its appearance and disappearance have come to represent a kind of almost legendary index of the multiplicity of fantasies on the development of the eternal embryo of a precarious sociocultural structure. See the initial laws (no. 43 of 17 Feb. 1982 and no. 182 of 10 May 1983), the provisional laws (nos. 311 and 312 of 13 July 1984), and the consequent law of 30 Apr. 1985 (no. 163) to set up a Single National Fund, still undefined and communicating nothing on when and how the economic guarantees for Italian opera, as always the premise for perpetuating the form's necessary existence in a state of imminent dissolution, will be arranged. The *Relazione sull'utilizzo del Fondo Unico dello Spettacolo,* presented as law no. 163 by the minister Lelio Lagorio and communicated to the prime minister on 31 Jan. 1986, states: "The widespread malaise that, with connotations of varying levels, covers artistic activity is fundamentally rooted in the planning vacuum of the undertaking, in regard to which public financial intervention has for too long been hasty, inadequate, and, above all, uncertain."

Index